Michael Obrist
Antonietta Putzu
(eds.)

Contemporary phenomena and strategies of living in Italy

THE LAST GRAND TOUR

PARK BOOKS

Reflections about the Grand Tour 14
Transformation through 138
technology and politics
Il bello, il brutto, il cattivo 322
Migration 408

100 km

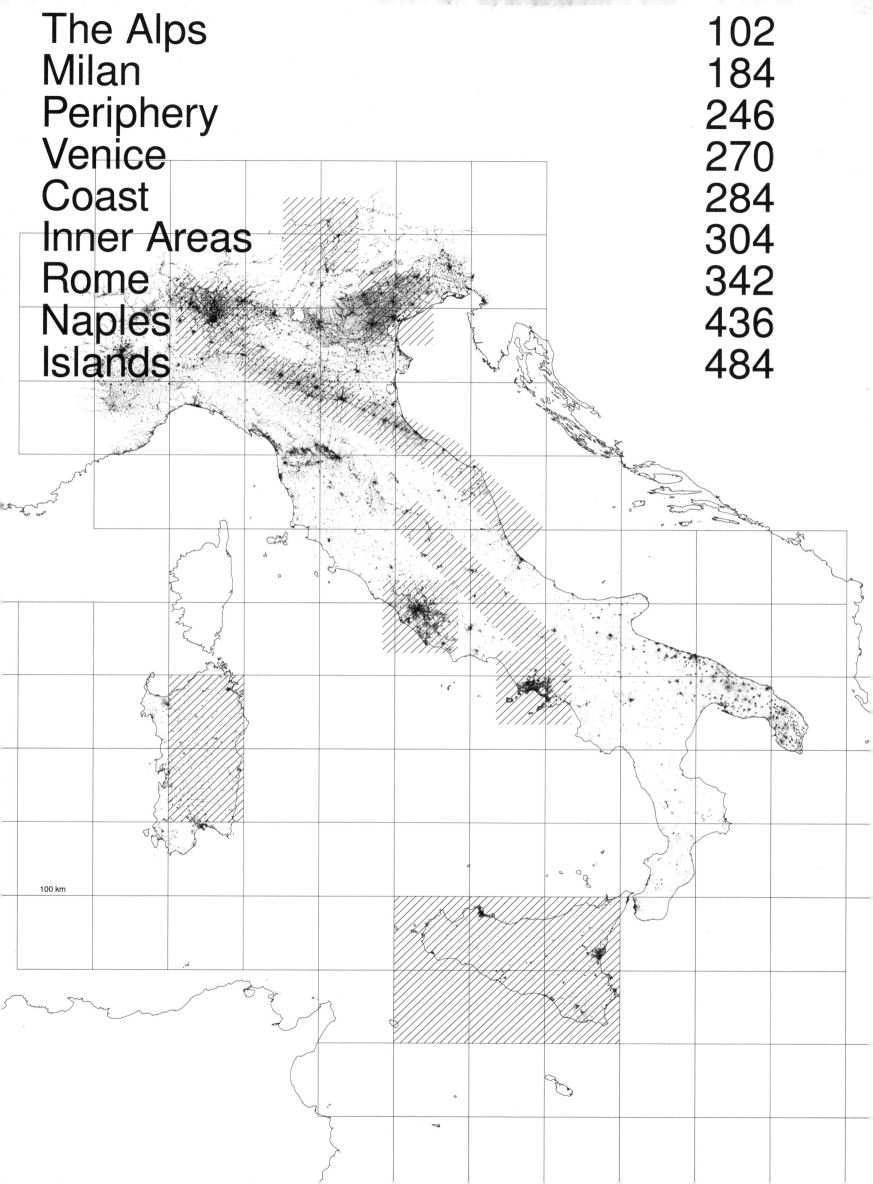

The Alps	102
Milan	184
Periphery	246
Venice	270
Coast	284
Inner Areas	304
Rome	342
Naples	436
Islands	484

Contents

Introduction

	The Last Grand Tour Michael Obrist, Antonietta Putzu	12

Reflections about the Grand Tour

	Beyond the eyes of gods Michael Obrist	17
	Return to the Sun of Nothing Carolina Sartori	18
	Reflections on contemporality Michael Obrist and Antonietta Putzu in conversation with Pippo Ciorra	32
	The anti-city and us Michael Obrist in conversation with Stefano Boeri	40
	Italy: Love it, or Leave it Michael Obrist and Antonietta Putzu in conversation with Luca Ragazzi and Gustav Hofer	43
	A diagonal overview on beauty, places and change in Italy Michael Obrist in conversation with Massimo Bricocoli	46
	On the road Michael Obrist and Antonietta Putzu in conversation with Gianni Pettena	56
	On the radical normality of emancipatory alienation Michael Obrist in conversation with Wilfried Kuehn	65
	On geography, politics and form Michael Obrist in conversation with Pier Paolo Tamburelli	69
	Detours to Italomodern Martin Feiersinger, Werner Feiersinger	74
	The importance of being Ernesto Shumi Bose, Roberta Marcaccio	89
	Deceitful Habits in a Human's Soul Michael Meier, Christoph Franz	93
	Tourism in the cracks of the Italian economy Sarah Gainsforth	95
	Regenerating Rome and Europe through the practice of hospitality Lorenzo Romito	99

The Alps

	Through the Alps: A photographic account of the changes in the Alpine landscape Viviana Rubbo, Alessandro Guida, Davide Curatola Soprana, Isabella Sassi Farìas	104
	Landscapes Ursula Aichner	124
	Reading the Alps Alberto Winterle	128
	Reusing the historical architectural heritage inside UNESCO's Dolomites Gianluca D'Incà Levis	134

Transformation through technology and politics

A Grand Tour through (post-)operaist criticism Michael Klein	140
Reproductive work, the body and the politics of the commons Michael Obrist in conversation with Silvia Federici	145
The hut as an image of the future present Leonardo Caffo	150
Placemaking through mobility Michael Obrist in conversation with Lowie Vermeersch	153
Share screen architecture Luigi Savio	158
Riders not heroes Ippolito Pestellini Laparelli	162
Reconnecting civitas and urbs: Making tourists and remote workers temporary urban citizens Daniele Belleri, Michael Baick, Carlo Ratti	168
Journeys in Italy Armin Linke	174

Milan

Inhabiting the urban realm: Metamorphoses and migrations of contemporary housing types Cino Zucchi	186
Housestories: Waiting for the city	194
Transmedia urbanism: Berlusconi and the birth of targeted difference Andrés Jaque	197
Environments of Resistance for Social Individuals Fosbury Architecture	205
Backgrounds and sequences (or what is missing in contemporary Milan) Angelo Lunati	208
Reclaiming care: Bottom-up feminist spaces in Milan Florencia Andreola, Azzurra Muzzonigro	213
Someone's-land Paul Sebesta	218
Ideal gatherings Beniamino Saibene (Esterni)	230
Experimental Laboratory Milan Emanuele Braga	236
I am here to learn Sophie Schaffer, Alexandra Torggler	242

Periphery

	Laboratories of the transition Michael Obrist in conversation with Paola Viganò	248
	The spaceships of the Po Valley: The rise and fall of northern Italy's suburbia and of its architectural masterpieces Alessandro Benetti, Martina Motta	251
	Villeggiatura: The contemporary retreat Isabel Köhler	258
	Housestories: #casasperimentale	262
	Sabaudia Lotte Schreiber	264
	Periphery and freedom Lorenza Baroncelli	267

Venice

	The Venice Syndrome Andreas Pichler	272
	Venetian impressions: Lines of flight from the terrace-city Marco Baravalle	280

Coast

	The Adriatic: An ancient door to a new world order Manuel Orazi, Marco Vanucci	286
	Nightswimming: Discotheques from the 1960s to the present Giovanna Silva, Chiara Carpenter	298

Inner Areas

	Community and welfare houses: Experiences and projects in Italy starting from the margin Antonio De Rossi, Laura Mascino	306
	Letter on paesologia Franco Arminio	313
	Searching for the 'Italian code' Lukas Spreitzer	314
	Towards a critical rurality Iain Chambers	316
	The Million Donkey Hotel feld72	317
	The grammar of reconstruction Julian Graf, Isabel Köhler	320

Il bello, il brutto, il cattivo

	The aesthetics of beauty Caroline Faber, Roswitha Goy, Julia Maretzki, Theresa Reiter	324
	Una casa all'Italiana: The emergence of the vernacular Antonietta Putzu	336
	Elements of the Italian city Andrea Di Tommaso, Fit Phuong	339

Rome

Roman bigness: Large-scale architecture as a design tool in Rome Diego Martínez	344
As above, so below: A large-scale solution for conflictive conditions Diego Martínez, Marek Nowicki	350
Rome: Does Pasolini still live here? Amongst shanties, tower blocks, Roma camps and squats Francesco Careri	356
Housestories: Good idea, wrong site?	367
An elsewhere to discover otherness Giorgio de Finis	368
Hypothesis Rome Giulia Fiocca, Lorenzo Romito	372
Spin Time Lab Zara Pfeifer	380
Borgate Lotte Schreiber	392
Roman notes: The free life of elements of architecture Simone Capra	396
Inhabiting Rome Lorenzo Romito	401

Migration

4 Stelle Hotel: From non-place to self-organised plug-in city Carina Sacher in conversation with Irene Di Noto, Valerio Muscella and Leroy S.P.Q.R'DAM	410
Social regeneration versus urban rent Irene Di Noto	416
Privatised push-back of the Nivin Charles Heller	419
Life on the edge: Migrants in Italy Alessandro Penso	422
The Riace model and the Domenico Lucano case: Is another world possible? Alice Lomonaco	427
Planning Riace: Urban regeneration and reception Giorgio Sokoll	428
Built on Sand feld72	430

Naples

Naples, hybrid city: The Quartieri Spagnoli Giovanni Laino	438
In 'city making', there is the city Umberto Napolitano, LAN Architecture, Cyrille Weiner	445
Naples: A porous modernity Iain Chambers	450
Vele Tobias Zielony	468
The porous quarter: An experiment in combination Marlene Lötsch	475
Strategies of prevention Katrin Kirschner	480

Islands

Housestories: Power	486
The Incompiuto manifesto Alterazioni Video, Fosbury Architecture	488
Incompiuto: Nostalgia or harbinger? Marc Augé	493
Unfettering reveries: The Incompiuto Siciliano Robert Storr	494
Housestories: Passion	497
Towards an entity of decolonisation Sandi Hilal, Emilio Distretti, Alessandro Petti	500
La Maddalena: Atlas of an occupation Eterotopia	502
Contributors	511
Imprint	520

The Last Grand Tour

Michael Obrist
Antonietta Putzu

For centuries, and still today, we have found in Italy a frame of reference for central themes of architecture and culture, which have developed there in an exemplary and often universal way. Following the tradition, and in part the itinerary, of the classical Grand Tour, this publication takes a differentiated look at the territory of Italy, with the aim of presenting alternative narratives and positions on contemporary issues that may also be relevant beyond the context under study. Which national phenomena can provide answers to questions of a global dimension?

The overarching theme is the question of housing, a barometer of economic, political and social conditions. Housing is examined as a complex construct affected by diverse interests and needs, but also by historical legacies. The spatial aspect of housing is a crucial building block of these reflections, which can have massive implications for both land resources and the landscape. In the spirit of 'learning from …', proposals and strategies are opened up for discussion.

On the concept of the Grand Tour

From around the time of the Renaissance, the Grand Tour was the name given to the journey through Central Europe, Spain, but above all Italy, that was undertaken by young aristocratic men (and later also members of the bourgeoisie) as the last part, the culmination, of their education. The visits to a succession of cities and landscapes were intended to inculcate a knowledge of history (especially of antiquity, the Middle Ages and the Renaissance) and to provide an insight into other cultures. They were at once a means of intellectual, social and political education, and a rite of passage from adolescence to adulthood. The Grand Tour found rich expression in the arts and literature, especially in the eighteenth century; one of the most famous texts is Johann Wolfgang von Goethe's *Italian Journey*. If educational travels such as the Grand Tour were the preserve of a privileged elite, travel would later come to form an essential basis for artistic exploration for others as well.

The Grand Tour was also of exceptional importance for architecture and planning, sowing the seeds that spread classicism throughout Europe; the work of Karl Friedrich Schinkel in Berlin, for example, would have been inconceivable without his trips to Italy. The influence of sojourns in Italy would prove enduring. For a long time, the Prix de Rome, a scholarship allowing for a stay of several years in Rome, was the most sought-after prize for French architects and artists. Bernard Rudofsky's thinking was significantly influenced by his impressions of Italy in the interwar years. More recently, we can see in Peter Eisenman's architecture the influence of his stays in Italy and his studies of Terragni. Likewise, a knowledge of the impact on Robert Venturi or Louis Kahn of their stays in Rome is essential for understanding their work as a whole.

In the Research Unit of Housing and Design at TU Wien, the method of the Grand Tour has been used from the start of Michael Obrist's professorship to locate recent developments in concrete places in Italy that might be seen as expressing the great themes of our time. These phenomena, negotiating the different forces at play, are gathered in this book as possible contemporary sources of inspiration. Together with the work of architects, theorists, philosophers, activists and artists, a small but highly diverse selection of student projects presents a holistic 'body of knowledge' as a new departure point for action and reflection.

The Grand Tour was always also a rite of initiation, a moment when the young person came of age and grasped the complexity and contradictions of the real world, when they lost the childhood innocence that shaped the world according to their own wishful thinking. A Grand Tour is always a reality check.

The journey leads to different places and themes. While it may unfold in a linear manner in this book, in reality readers will choose their own direction of travel, depending on their particular interests or urge to explore, each time confronting the conditions of the places and social spaces anew. Every explorer will put together their own itinerary.

The book offers a suggestion.

This Grand Tour is a search for the most current (housing) phenomena in Italy, for developments that manifest in spatial form some of the major social issues facing the country. By definition subjective and far from comprehensive, it shows a series of fragments — each of which, however, points to something bigger than itself and tells us something universal about us as a society.

The old form of the Grand Tour, with its canon of the unequivocally good, beautiful and true, no longer exists. Nor, thankfully, does the quasi-colonial attitude of the wealthy upper classes from the north who journeyed to the south in their quest for knowledge. Nevertheless, exploring the spaces of society and their manifestation in architecture and urban form seems more relevant than ever today, to gain a better understanding of the complexity and challenges of our living environments.

The book begins with reflections and conversations with actors from across Europe and across different generations who have engaged closely with Italy and current developments in its territory.

The chapter on the Alps leads us to specific questions and places in the Alpine region – a space characterised on the one hand by similar geographic conditions, but on the other by a rich juxtaposition of the most diverse cultural and historical and socioeconomic contexts. It is a space undergoing major processes of transformation at varying speeds, where everyday life and the means of livelihood are often expressed in completely different ways from one valley to the next, either through an interconnection with the outside world, or a remoteness from it.

The effects of technologies and spatial productions on ways of life are considered in the following chapter, which discusses the impact and potential of digitalisation as well as the struggle for social participation and justice – for an emancipated, inclusive, equal society. The transformation of mobility and its impact on spatial production are key to understanding the changes that are now taking place within the territory.

In Milan, we encounter the commodification of housing as well as the resistance it provokes, a profound reflection on the morphology of the city and the resilience of its buildings as well as the enmeshing of real-estate investment, politics and the power of the media.

In the periphery and on the way to the *Zwischenstadt*, we find the unexpected. Though the 'in-between city' was never a consciously planned meta-project, but the result of a variety of territorial, mostly economic, conditions, this space nevertheless manifests itself as a multitude of 'laboratories of the transition', in Paola Viganò's description.

Transitions of a very different kind can be found in Venice, where overtourism and the money to be made from those in search of an exclusive, romantic place to stay for just a few days has reduced the availability of affordable housing for locals and fundamentally changed everyday life in the Serenissima.

Along the Adriatic coast, where lively summer resorts and tourist destinations overlap with major centres of production, we find another form of diffuse city, where millions of people live in territorially dispersed habitats shaped by the hilly coastal topography and a rich history – a space defined by the specific phenomenon of the absence of a dense metropolis.

'Il bello, il brutto, il cattivo' (the good, the bad, the ugly) lead us to consider elements of the architectural landscape that are firmly anchored in the collective imagery of the Italian peninsula. In its critical reflection it attempts to crack the Italian code of spatial production and its aesthetic.

But all roads lead to Rome. Here, the commodification of housing, overtourism and the issue of migration coincide with questions of how to build among and inhabit the 'eternal' yet constantly changing ruins. Rome is a city that has seen it all. In the history of the Eternal City we find practically every theme of architecture and urban development: tabula rasa, rapid growth, reuse, contextual additions, radical ruptures, hybrids of architecture and landscape, shrinkage. Today, Rome appears ungovernable, a city constantly beset by infrastructural problems, where living space has become increasingly commodified, a plaything of the most diverse interests and powers. Global tourism and new migrations create, and require, their own space. For an ever-increasing portion of the inhabitants, housing is becoming an existential question. Resisting this condition, new activists within civil society have found and invented alternative ways of living together that are economically affordable, which provide for basic needs but also give spatial form to people's desires and new ways of life.

Italy's geographical location and geopolitical situation mean that the issue of migration also finds quite a particular spatial expression here. The engagement of civil society, along with new strategies for addressing this important challenge of our time, are pointing to new possibilities and spaces.

The Inner Areas, structurally weak interior zones of great beauty, have been profoundly marked by emigration. Nevertheless, a new beginning is possible here, too, as the journey to specific places shows.

In Naples, facets of the relationship between urban space and social space manifest themselves in a 'porous modernity', as described by Iain Chambers. Here, an oscillation between order and chaos, between archaic spaces and hypermodern phenomena, gives rise to a specific spatio-social way of life that becomes an art of living.

Last, but not least, the islands: Italy's spaces of longing par excellence. Here, too, we find particularities and places that merit our attention, since they speak to – and to some extent renegotiate – fundamental themes of society.

'Last'

The old 'Grand Tour' for the well-heeled few with a large budget and endless free time no longer exists. The societies we live in are structured differently and in this era of mass tourism we have to contend with short holiday periods, overcrowded cities and means of transport that help to fuel the climate crisis. As travellers, we are also part of the problem of local housing shortages. What would alternative ways to travel and explore look like? Several essays in the book open up possible answers to this question.

The research trips for this Grand Tour began before the pandemic. Italy would be the first country in Europe to go into lockdown. With huge restrictions placed on free movement, it became impossible to travel. Our former lengthy explorations of these territories began to seem like a distant memory, and the journey itself like the 'Last Grand Tour', a remnant of another time and world. The end of the pandemic, however, has opened up new horizons, with the push for digitalisation (for example, smart working), the longing for encounters with real places and people, and an emphasis on climate-friendly travel.

Each Grand Tour becomes a specific Grand Tour when a canon is questioned. Each is unique, yet has the potential to be infinitely expandable, allowing for all manner of combinations, directions and cross-connections. It functions like a rhizome in the sense of Deleuze and Guattari. The phenomena repeat themselves, but find their own specific expression in the places and the most varied social spaces. *The* Grand Tour no longer exists. Perhaps there was once a last tour of its kind, but it has been carried to the grave.

However, our desire to understand places and spatial productions endures and, with it, the need to travel and explore. As the complexity of territories grows, new paths continually open up, leading to new flashpoints that overlap with the existing hotspots to form a multilayered network of possibilities. The Grand Tour ends with a homecoming. With an understanding of its uniqueness – for the travellers and explorers themselves – and an awareness of the completion of the journey, the most recent Grand Tour invariably becomes the 'Last Grand Tour', waiting to be overwritten by the next one.

Reflections about the Grand Tour

Beyond the eyes of gods

Michael Obrist

1   Michel de Certeau, *The Practice of Everyday Life* (Berkley: University of California Press, 1984), 92.

2   Jean Baudrillard, *America* (New York/London: Verso, 1989), 54.

3   Vilém Flusser, 'Planning the Unplannable', in Anke K. Finger, ed., *The Freedom of the Migrant: Objections to Nationalism* (Chicago: University of Illinois Press, 2003), 28. See also: Michael Obrist, 'Von göttlichen Augen und menschlichem Irren. Raumphänomene in Zeiten von Google Earth', in Elsa Prochazka, ed., *food&grid: raum&designstrategien* (2009), 37–42; Michael Obrist, 'Trojan Horses and Other Social Animals', in Lukas Feireiss, ed., *Space Matters Chronicles* (Wien/New York: Springer, 2013), 1067.

It was not a small step from the 'Why haven't we seen a photograph of the whole Earth yet?' campaign, launched by Stewart Brand in 1965, to the invention of Google Earth, though both were searching for an instrument and strategy to comprehend the complexity and unity of the world. Whilst the first images of the Earth caused an immediate impact, and the interconnectedness of the whole world suddenly dawned on people, with Google Earth we observe the reverse phenomenon. The small image of the globe on our screens obscures the outrageousness of the program's ability to show a large part of the complexity and variety behind unity at any scale.

The following words are said to have been engraved above the entrance of Plato's Academy: '*Medeis ageometretos eisito*' (those who are ignorant of geometry may not enter this place). With the knowledge of geometry in the Platonic sense, we can try to decipher the pattern we recognise from above. But the illusion of objectivity the view from above of satellites and planners confers is an elitist and deceptive one: it was the perspective of the gods and goddesses.

Michel de Certeau writes about the viewpoint of the observer from the top of the former Twin Towers of New York: 'His elevation transfigures him into a voyeur. It puts him at a distance. It transforms the bewitching world by which one was "possessed" into a text that lies before one's eyes. It allows one to read it, to be a solar Eye, looking down like a god. The exaltation of a scopic and gnostic drive: the fiction of knowledge is related to this lust to be a viewpoint and nothing more.'¹

Our urban agglomerations, which could once easily be called the 'city' (whereas today we have to invent new words), are still the most socially, culturally and technologically complex artefacts mankind has invented. Today, the development of our built environment and new technologies of zenithal perception has brought us an epistemological dilemma. The more we observe from above, the less we seem to understand. In the manifestation of the chaos of late-twentieth-century urbanism, as in the Rorschach inkblot test, we are convinced we recognise certain shapes, when in fact this tells us more about ourselves and our starting points of perception. Territories of amnesia, schizophrenic landscapes, hysterical cities, all searching for a definition of their new identity.

In this past century of the most rapid acceleration in the history of mankind, the world has changed, even where its form seems to have remained the same. From the rapid transformations of China and Dubai to the global success of gated communities and the unstoppable spread of slums within huge agglomerations in parts of South America, Africa and Asia – apparently nothing escapes the satellite's gaze. From above, we can see the 'cementation' of power and authority, the substantial manifestations of production relationships, the inscribed cultural manifestations and constructions of landscape, but often what is most essential escapes our view: life within forms.

To understand the transformation of software in our built hardware, we have to dig deeper, amplifying our methods, trying to understand 'context' in the broadest possible sense. We have to immerge in the labyrinth of daily (urban) life without allowing ourselves to be deluded by the tricks of Daedalus, as Michel de Certeau reminds us in *The Practice of Everyday Life*. Space is not a neutral box. Space is the result of social relations and cultural techniques. Without knowing the different codes and rituals of the different societies we are operating with(in), we will be always 'lost in translation'.

Jean Baudrillard understood that the key for understanding the society of the United States was (the abundance of) space, and the cognitive tool to realise this was the car: 'the point is not to write the sociology or psychology of the car, the point is to drive. That way you can learn more about this society than all academia could ever tell you.'²

In the book *The Freedom of the Migrant: Objections to Nationalism*, Vilém Flusser writes in his essay 'Planning the Unplannable' that 'tourism is travel for travel's sake' and suggests that, at present, tourism plays a role that is more or less analogous to the one played by theory in antiquity: 'Theory is a little like sightseeing (being a spectator of the sight-worthy), and classical theory differs from its modern counterpart in that it is pure – it was never its purpose to be applied. Modern tourism and classical theory have in common a gratuitous purposelessness as catharsis.'³

Towards new territories in understanding and practising architecture

The study of the established body of knowledge of various disciplines is combined with a 'theory through praxis' in which the experiment seems to be the only possible response to the new conditions of contemporary space, because there are no users' manuals around to follow. A new discourse is formed on the margins of the disciplines, the emergence of a new practice, which is grounded not only in the broad tradition of knowledge of classical architecture schools, but amplified by the experience of different cultural strategies and tactics. In the understanding of reality through travelling and real-site experience, in the overlapping of architecture and new strategies and tactics, we leave traces in the material world, which the 'eyes of the gods' can see, but cannot understand. Because the key to the understanding of our privilege as human beings may lie in a reinterpretation of the old Latin proverb: '*errare humanum est*' (to err/wandering around is human).

Parts of this essay were originally published in Antonia Dika and Bernadette Krejs, eds., *Mapping the Croatian Coast: A Road Trip to Architectural Legacies of Cold War and Tourism Boom* (Berlin: JOVIS Verlag, 2020), 10–13.

Text by Mattia Chinellato

■ Carolina Sartori's *Echoe*s series encapsulates, through its simple presence and curious ambiguity, almost everything we could ever say about shades. 'Return to the Sun of Nothing' is a project born of the legacy of more than one year of confinement, a visual transposition of the void and its spatial consequences. The infinite reflection of a sound, as well as the repetition of apparently always the same days, leaves behind an absolute silence that these places seem to enclose. The series abandons the statements of 'decisive moments', the analysis of language in and of itself, the concept of an all-consuming idea, the emotion of the poet, the erudite quotation, the search for a new aesthetic creed, the use of a style.

The duty is to see with clarity, leaving any attempt of appropriation. A focus on the unassuming fragments of contemporary conditions real and represented in our cities towards the definition of urbanity and its opposite. The boundaries of the visible are pushed to reveal an alternative panorama, questioning our role in the inhabited world. In this emptiness, through the gaze, we can find our understanding of space.

A field of grass, a sequence of modernist towers, a cave, a hole – every picture appears without content, maybe too wistful if not too gloomy; but what remains is this floating sense of stillness: space. It is without content, but surely not without intentions. Still, what Carolina Sartori wants to say is never about photography, but rather about the relationship we have with elements, objects, architecture and (micro)landscapes. It is not so much another comment on the world we inhabit, but rather the development of a toolbox to deal with the world as a whole.

The main tools she introduces are distance and familiarity. She uses distance to neutralise the subjective gesture of framing, leaving to the observer the articulated task of interpretation: the series is a visual stimulation for our own experience – we see what we are and we are what we see.

The photographer does not document but collects elements, and lists a set of possible members of a family of things: one picture can refer to another one. This power of association is a direct translation of the way in which any tool, any element of cultural production, is always rooted, both in the culture of the world and in the world itself. Distance and association make a completely coherent world where each element refers to the next. Nothing is a discovery, but a materialisation of something already latently there. Far from seeking a sense of nostalgia, these photographs are a claim of emptiness as full, filled by the imagination of a different future: a common shade.

Return to the Sun of Nothing

Carolina Sartori

Reflections about the Grand Tour

Michael Obrist and Antonietta Putzu in conversation with Pippo Ciorra (architect, teacher and Senior Curator at MAXXI Architettura, Rome)

Reflections on contemporality

Porto Recanati, 2015. Credit: Olivo Barbieri

OBRIST Our starting point on our Grand Tour is an attempt to understand something of this current 'Italian' software whose development has actually taken centuries. We find ourselves in a context in which design, architecture, urban planning, fashion and space, but also the term 'beauty', hardly ever used in other countries, have become fundamental to understanding the roots of a culture. We will also be talking about urban sprawl, as in the Covid pandemic we have been made to grasp and deal with new realities in parallel to the classic compact city. We'll go on a journey together, a little alternative Grand Tour of contemporary Italy.

I think you, a curator, writer and teacher, can act as a vigil and guide us through today's Italy, as someone able to grasp contemporary phenomena and help us to reflect on them.

CIORRA By a strange coincidence, just this morning I was at the German Academy in Villa Massimo to discuss with its director Julia Draganović and some of the fellows the meaning of Ursula von der Leyen's strange proposal to merge the forces of architects, designers and artists around a project called the New European Bauhaus, and how it should be tackled. The idea is to revive the concept of beauty, a very difficult word for me, as a necessary counterpart to the slogans about technological innovation, ecology and social inclusion that are already widely bandied about. For me it's interesting to compare this European project with the work we've been doing for twenty-five years on an 'ugly' but fairly 'happy' urbanised space, the town/countryside/coastline that extends for over 300 kilometres along the Adriatic Sea from Ravenna to Vasto. The impression we have gained over these years is that it is in reality an experimental urban laboratory of the future, a *rururban* phenomenon that long before Rem Koolhaas's *Countryside* exhibition has made us realise that we have to reset many of our ideas about the town, the countryside and the landscape.

PUTZU Beauty in Italy is an almost natural given, omnipresent in the urban fabric and in the landscape. It is a familiar backdrop to our everyday activities. At the same time, we know that since the Second World War much more has been built and at a much faster rate than in previous periods. Evidently, these buildings rarely achieve the characteristics and architectural quality of the buildings and public spaces of earlier centuries. Due to a series of unfortunate intersections between laws, administrative procedures, habits and cost-cutting, Italy has become a country constructed chiefly by professionals with not much of an architectural education, above all '*geometri*' [Note: The word loosely translates as 'surveyor'. Unlike in other countries, the Italian surveyor, or *geometra*, is able to design buildings on a modest scale, and of often equally modest quality, without the aid of an architect.] and, in the best case, engineers. What happens in a society and a territory in which beauty is rarely produced as an expression of complexity and contextual interconnection? And here I'd also like to bring in the factor of the disorder that has been produced in contrast to this beauty, which is however very resilient.

CIORRA It's a wide-ranging and difficult question. One that certainly involves the role and the responsibility that architects have had in the transformations of our territory in the last few decades – decades in which order and urban quality have often given way to chaos and very poor quality. To start with, it should be said that the prime responsibility of architects in determining the status quo should be sought in their involvement in urban planning processes and in the scanty effort they have put into including the theme of quality in instruments of planning (or at least the poor results of that effort).

In recent times a difficult word like 'beauty' has come back into frequent use. Architects resort to it when seeking a persuasive language, but it is also used by European Union leaders when proposing programmes like the New European Bauhaus. In reality, for several decades at the end of the century my generation preferred to give a more disruptive sense to the concept of beauty (or rather *appeal*). We explored the potentialities of junk, of chaos, of landmarks that had little to with traditional monuments: filling stations, motorway restaurants, airports, shopping malls, buildings in various degrees of neglect. In short, something halfway between Luigi Ghirri and punk. All this was connected both with the progressive crisis in modernism (and postmodernism) and with the ferment over a phase in which a historical alliance between architecture and politics was coming to an end. Architecture was emerging from the age of welfare to enter that of leisure, when not that of architectural lasciviousness.

In the 1960s and '70s the relationship between the profession and society was mediated entirely by politics. It was not mayors who chose the designers of their public buildings and the drafters of their plans, but the parties to which those mayors belonged and the 'critics' affiliated to those parties. On the one hand this doctored the judgement on quality (and thus on 'beauty'), but on the other it kept to some extent alive the relationship between architects and the social fabric of what were then called 'users', in a society that at the time was still divided in an orderly fashion into social classes, political alliances in permanent opposition, different generations and so on. All this was undermined with the evolution of political and social geography in the last decades of the century. The army of urban blue-collar workers was transformed into a much more complex mix, made up of the self-employed, micro-entrepreneurs and neo-farmers, much less tied to the traditional 'modern' relationship with urban space. The rejection of the choice between bourgeoisie and proletariat in architecture and urban planning was matched by the rejection of the city and modernist housing models, and with them of the architects who proposed those models. 'I'm going to build my own house', thought many Italians, 'how I want and where I want (or at least where I can)', at a certain distance from others and, if possible, with a bit of garden. The consequences of this evolution on the territory are evident (Italy has been transformed into a jigsaw puzzle of 'sprawling' urban mega-systems), but so are the consequences for architectural culture, which in any case cannot help but be a mirror of its time and of reality, and which in fact has devoted itself to finding a way to insert expressiveness and up-to-date landmarks into the new (post)-urban system.

Naturally the phenomenon has had fairly significant cultural and political repercussions. The metropolitan and 'progressive' version of this affair corresponds to the work of regularisation (amnesty) of almost half the city (the illegal part) carried out by councils of the centre-left. The 'amnesty' given to the working-class suburbs brought with it the legitimation of the small house known as a *villetta* in the politically correct conception of urban planning. The northern Italian, and certainly less illegal, version of this passage was the subject of the studies first of the Lombardy–Veneto area undertaken by Bernardo Secchi and his students and then of the metropolis of the Adriatic coast by various groups of researchers from the architecture schools of Pescara and Ascoli Piceno.

One of the consequences of all this has been another blow to the professional authority of the architect, since the scale and mode of construction of the new houses (the *villette*) seemed to have been studied expressly for them to be designed by professional categories who are 'underqualified' with respect to the full range of capacities of the graduate in architecture: *geometri* and engineers of all kinds. All this took place while the authority and credibility of the political parties with regard to the social fabric were also fading away. And with the parties, all those professional categories that were, more or less rightly, protected by the parties. With just (or almost) one well-known exception, Renzo Piano, who for some time had decided to speak directly to users and adopt a language that instead of political engagement drew on social empathy. So, the first problem relating to the general quality of architecture and the diffusion of its disciplinary status in the real fabric of our cities lies in this intricate tangle of political, economic and professional factors.

Then there is a problem of a less concrete nature, linked to changes in taste and in the culture of the discipline. Not everything that looks ugly to us today will seem so tomorrow. The historical sedimentation of what surrounds us is important, so to say that Bramante's Cloister is beautiful is fairly easy for everyone; but, for example, the attitude towards the piers of large viaducts, or the pylons of major works of engineering, varies over time and with the evolution of social sensibility. They can seem very beautiful or very ugly depending on the context in which we are going to make this evaluation. The principal response to the question is the scanty part that architects have played in the development of the territory in Italy. As if this abstention had spilled over into a sort of paralysis of taste.

Probably architects did not have the social, political and cultural means to curb the unbridled land take that has been going on in Italy since the 1950s. But when they did realise what was happening, they had to make way for the defence of the threatened heritage, obliged to live with the sense of guilt – this is still a Catholic country – of those who insisted on getting historical fabrics to coexist with modern architecture. The result has been the creation of a system of opposing camps: on the one hand the more sophisticated architectural culture (developing around Rogers' *Casabella*), on the other an ample and composite majority of people who simply think that old is beautiful and new is ugly.

So, millions of newspaper articles, books, essays and conferences have gone on telling us that modernity corrupts, modernity ruins, modernity is the city outskirts. Modernity is an enemy of beauty. All this has made it very difficult, for someone with a profession like yours and mine, to educate people or in some way work with them on deciding what is beautiful and what is ugly (or at least what is the right thing to do) in the new world. Seeing that you've introduced a parameter like that of beauty – having continually to contend with this initial prejudice against the 'contemporary' (all too slippery an adjective) culture of design has made it very difficult to establish the aesthetic and disciplinary parameters needed to tell what is good from what is bad in today's production. So, for an insufficiently Benjaminian 'man in the street', Zaha Hadid's museum, in as much as it is 'modern', is as ugly as the building designed by a *geometri*. The same *flâneur* will be nonplussed for a while in front of a design by Aldo Rossi: at the beginning he will think it is an attempt to gratify his need for something reminiscent of the past, but then he'll find it too bare, plain, lacking in decoration. Since the 1950s, from the time when Italian architecture went in a slightly different direction to that of modernist orthodoxy, it has been difficult to defend the arguments of the modern and the new. This made it hard to understand what was right and what was wrong in terms of new interventions.

OBRIST The first question referred to the classic Grand Tour as a journey of enlightenment to new lands where different forms of beauty from those of the travellers' home countries could be found. Beauty as a word and, in its most banal sense, one that has never been questioned, we find in every advert for Italy, while in the world of architecture notwithstanding, or precisely because of the complexity of its meaning, it has almost become a four-letter word. Now, in this Grand Tour, we are interested in something else in order to comprehend the contemporary landscape and context.

For decades we have had to deal with a mass culture that has an attitude of unbridled consumption with regard to land, to the production of housing, and even a nobler approach to the design or construction of one's own house has been subject to these mechanisms.

'Let no-one ignorant of geometry enter here' is said to have been the motto inscribed above the entrance to Plato's academy, and by this first 'spatial turn' in philosophy 2,400 years ago was certainly not meant the *geometri* who have transformed the Italian territory. The solipsism of seeing only the individual house, and the total lack of any reflection on and relationship with the setting, turns the house into an object, and with the mass production of houses, and a great social fluidity, into a consumer item as well.

In the last decade especially the commodification of housing and the speculation in land and building have turned houses into assets in a property investor's portfolio, things that have little to do with the proclaimed right to housing.

How do you view these phenomena?

CIORRA The phenomena to which you are referring are very interesting and very complex, and fairly contradictory as well. Up until the 1970s and '80s it was possible to talk about the right to housing. People fought to obtain the right for sections of the population that did not have a high enough income to be helped to obtain a home. The politicians took this on board and made it part of the planning process, intervening with a level of quality that has diminished over time. In the sense that, in the immediate postwar period, at the height of reconstruction and urban migration, the whole country was involved in the process of building new housing estates, into which almost all the best architects in the nation put their ideas and design skills. The fifteen-odd years that followed the passing of the law that established the INA-Casa (a government agency for the construction of 'subsidised' housing) produced an avalanche of fine housing projects. They were interventions of great quality that reflected some interesting aspects of society, sometimes utilising them in a polemical manner, as in the case of Quaroni and Ridolfi's Tiburtino estate. Giving everyone a home also meant giving everyone a job, with all that this represented in political and social terms. The mechanism worked well until the 1960s

– that is to say, for as long as the social alliance of all classes for the reconstruction of the country held. The atmosphere changed between the 1960s and '70s, when the radicalisation of political conflict was reflected in the world of architecture by a sort of ideological overload. At that point the public housing projects of the big names turned for the most part into political manifestos of architecture, not particularly concerned with the fate of those who would have to live in them. I recall a passage from Tafuri's *Storia dell'architettura italiana 1944–84* which said that the four most important urban projects of the period were the Gallaratese in Milan (Aymonino and Rossi), the Corviale in Rome (Mario Fiorentino), the Zen in Palermo (Gregotti) and the Villaggio Matteotti in Terni (De Carlo). At bottom I agree with Tafuri but I also think that if a referendum were to be held to pick the four least popular housing estates in their respective cities, the names, perhaps with the exception of Terni, would be the same.

The excess of ideological tension has made the dialogue between the people (the 'users') and those who were providing them with a benefit (the home) that was considered part of welfare more difficult. If we think that from the 1980s onwards the public actors (municipalities, regions, various institutions) progressively lost their spending power, it can be said that the idea of the architect as a builder of collective housing of quality vanished in the final part of the twentieth century under the double burden of an ideological change and the lack of funds.

From the realm of public finance, housing has shifted into another (micro)economic area. The family builds its own home, with the help of a minor technician, and perhaps associates with the house some basic production facilities: a floor with a flat to be rented out, a vegetable garden, a space in which to work, another to sell things. In short, a sort of at once molecular and primitive economy that is connected to a diffuse system of production and a certain freedom in the consumption of land and the landscape. What's more, in the third millennium it is difficult to imagine linking the destiny of architecture of quality to public housing, especially in a country where almost everything that could be built has been built and where there are hundreds of thousands of empty housing units. At the time of the *Re-cycle* exhibition our position was fairly favourable to a public commitment to providing subsidies for low-income users to help them rent empty flats in our cities. All this has occurred in resonance with a certain crisis in architectural thinking and the theory of architecture. The fact that it is no longer possible to see housing as an architectural project of welfare directly produced by the discipline has had a major influence on architectural thinking and teaching. Over the course of twenty years I don't think I've ever given my students a housing collective as a design theme. We've worked on everything – museums, infrastructural spaces, motorway toll booths, supermarkets to be recycled – on the assumption that housing had by now been removed from the field of action of architects. The theme has reappeared only in recent times, but in very different versions, in part under the influence of new modes of living (co-housing and other forms) and in part out of a need to challenge society on what seems to be its own ground: the low-cost detached house.

Otherwise, the house today is a real-estate commodity. As such it answers solely to the logic of speculation. In which all references to the environment, inclusion and accessibility are in general ploys of marketing. If we wanted to come up with a different logic from that of real estate, I don't believe it would be possible today to go back to the idea of the mass collective housing project that held sway in the last century. I think what we need instead is a strategy of reuse and recycling, bringing the millions of empty flats in historic centres and the suburbs back into circulation. Moreover, it seems to me that the distinction between historic centre and city outskirts, between urban and non-urban, no longer makes much sense. Residential projects were used by our predecessors to assert their idea of the city and architecture. Today the priorities are different.

OBRIST Perhaps this brings us directly to the question about resilience. In this time of pandemic there is a lot of talk about the dichotomy between city and rural areas and of a possible renascence of villages. But we have produced a territory that is a blend of classical cities, new areas, ancient towns and villages, and a lot more that we could call urban sprawl. Maybe it is a territory that reflects the multiplicity of our customs, lifestyles and ways of thinking, living and working. Do you think it is also a resilient territory in the face of change?

CIORRA In Italy now there is a lot published in the press on the question of the *borghi*, the 'villages'. Perhaps too much, especially if we think that many of those who are calling for people to move to the villages live in luxury apartments in the city centre. I really do live in a village, although one that is rather privileged by its proximity to the sea, and so I can give a first-hand account.

I believe it is a mistake to isolate the question of the 'inland areas' as if it were a theme of planning in its own right. If I think of the region in which I live and teach as a great conurbation that stretches from Ravenna to the south of Abruzzo, I cannot help but conclude that the solution to the problems of the villages scattered amongst the hills and foothills of the Apennines is closely bound up with the smooth running of the whole system (economic, infrastructural, social). It's in and around the villages that we find two of the main systems of production in Italy: agriculture and tourism. Agriculture and tourism function if they are well integrated and if the relationship between the coast and the hinterland works well. To upgrade the villages of the 'Adriatic city', for instance, it would be much more useful to upgrade the system of railway lines that used to connect the coast with Urbino and Fermo, with Ascoli and Macerata, which were splendid small works of infrastructure that limited use of the car by providing an alternative. For the only real problem with people living in the villages and countryside is obviously excessive use of the automobile.

So, as at bottom you were saying, it is necessary to work more on the relations between these different modes of dwelling than on their specific form. And then we also need to recognise the qualities of the ugly, in the sense of the metropolitan urban area. Always bearing in mind that one of our main aims is to bring spatial and social quality precisely where there is none, to the most confused territories of urban sprawl, among tourist complexes that turn into slums, filling stations and abandoned factories.

In the end we are all working on the definition of new concepts of city. What you call resilience. Or what Koolhaas has tried to capture in his concept of the 'countryside'. We also need to go beyond the idea of a multiform and all-embracing metropolis. In the case with which I'm most familiar, that of the Adriatic, the glue of the 'urban' territory is the landscape, a lot of landscape. A landscape made up of infrastructures, historical fragments scattered amongst the hills, small and medium-sized towns, uninterrupted coastal urbanisation, and then sheds and warehouses, sheds and warehouses. In this context the single/double/triple-family house, as we were saying earlier, is an incredible system, one to which left-wing architects have paid no attention.

All this will be speeded up even more by the pandemic. People have grown accustomed to working from home, while what moves to reach you is merchandise. Besides, it doesn't take much to adapt to the new post-pandemic lifestyle. The house – a rented one – in which I live is in a medieval village a few hundred metres from the sea. The city is about ten kilometres away. The walls are more or less the same as when they were built in the thirteenth century. With respect to then, what is 'new' in the house is running water, electricity, a bathroom, a modern kitchen and wi-fi. Nonetheless it took me only a few minutes to adapt it to the necessities of contemporary life. If I were to be given the job of regenerating this village, I would think about its relations with the world outside and not its typological deficiencies.

Given all these conditions and its high degree of diversity, the experience of these years spent studying obsessively the 'Adriatic city', a sort of metropolitan sprawl stretching from Ravenna to Vasto, seems useful today in tackling urban and post-urban questions from a more or less global perspective. We are going to have to work everywhere on mobility, on the relationship between work, residence and infrastructure, on a system of spaces and public services that can be adapted to different and unaccustomed densities, extreme in some places, very low in others.

OBRIST   I agree. A lot of us are the product of an area of urban sprawl ('*Zwischenstadt*') that has undergone enormous changes over the last few decades, changes that were unimaginable before. The huge revolution that is coming with mobility will make it much more sustainable. But in the biography of every Italian of the north born prior to the 1980s, a part has been played by the phenomenon of the super discotheques on the Adriatic. The famous long weekends in those discotheques that have gone down in history, the rise in drug taking, the ritual of driving across the country from Milan to Rimini, with the tragedy of the many deaths in road accidents at night, news of which was published like war despatches in the national press on Mondays: these are part of the collective memory of an entire generation – memories of things experienced at first hand or merely as a spectator. Phenomena like this seem to have disappeared.

CIORRA   Yes, I don't see any significant persistence of those phenomena. It's true that if you drive along the Adriatic autostrada on a Friday afternoon or evening in the direction of the places symbolic of the old 'district of pleasure' (which is what Aldo Bonomi called it) you'll encounter heavy traffic and risk getting stuck in a jam for a few hours. But I'd say it's a phenomenon that involves everyone, families, tourists and commuters on their way home, and not just the *flâneurs* of the Adriatic night. However, the culture of the old discotheques of Rimini is an interesting one. The late lamented Paolo Fabbri, a philosopher and semiologist from Rimini who belonged to Eco's group and who died a short time ago, had observed the first hybridisations between clubs, artists, digital media and communication from close up and often spoke about it.

My own is a rather strange 'academic' biography. In 1987 I enrolled in the PhD programme of Architectural Composition at the IUAV, with a faculty of teachers that included Aldo Rossi, Giorgio Grassi, Francesco Tentori, Gianugo Polesello, Guido Canella and so on. The same year I started to teach as a visiting professor at the school of architecture of Ohio State University, in a period in which Peter Eisenman, Daniel Libeskind, Jeff Kipnis and many of their followers were teaching at the school. Moreover it was a phase in which, with a certain naivety, we believed that Eisenman and Rossi's positions were truly opposed. In any case I think this 'double life' (Columbus from September to December and Venice/Rome from December to September) allowed me to observe both the American and the Italian situation from a detached perspective, or at least with a dual vision, one in three dimensions. Gradually this has helped me to understand many things – for example, the similarities and differences between the two different conceptions of 'autonomy'. At the same time, though, it has accustomed me to never feeling completely 'part of' a situation, a group, a tendency. At bottom all this served to bolster the little that had sunk into me of the teaching of Ludovico Quaroni, past master of doubt. This hasn't made me very popular and for a while I was seen as someone who had departed from the architectural straight and narrow of 'Italian identity'. A situation that strangely resurfaced with the emergence of a generation (or at least a group within a generation that is now around forty-five or fifty years old) that thought it was its duty to resuscitate certain of the modes of design and above all representation used by the 'masters' and that considered me a minor obstacle (although not a particularly influential one) to their hegemony. In reality, I have always taught Aldo Rossi to my students, but trying to place him clearly among their history books and not among the references to 'copy' when working on a project. In short, I thought that to make headway Italian architecture needed to stop mourning the fabled 1960s and '70s and make a break with the past. This is true for Rossi and Aldorossism (if such a thing exists), but it is also for those who seemed to be opposed to Rossi. It is no accident that in the last few years we have held exhibitions at the museum on Aldo Rossi, on Superstudio and on Bruno Zevi. They are three fine pieces of the history of Italian architecture, but it is no longer the time to side with one or the other. Instead, we have to view them from a less factious (ideological?) and more complex perspective of our architectural history.

Apart from this, or along with this, there was also the attempt to understand what was happening to the European city and what means could be used to try to adapt the culture of architects to the changes under way. In a way (I'm referring to myself and to some of the people with whom I carried out initiatives or collaborated in the 1990s) we forged a tactical link between the metropolitan chaos that so surprised and fascinated us and the 'organised' chaos in the projects of the 'deconstructivists'. This was the means we adopted in order to free ourselves of a disciplinary (typomorphological) framework that was unable to function in the new context (or in the context of reality). Obviously we were drawn to 'disruptive' attitudes and needed examples like Koolhaas, Eisenman and Tschumi, even if we interpreted them in our own way, to free us from the old discipline of 'composition'.

In my generation there was a tendency to combine two potentially subversive impulses, the architectural hedonism we had absorbed in the 1980s and the instinct for troublemaking we had imbibed in the years of the most intense political struggles (1960s and '70s). Many of our ideas and our architectural actions in the period at the turn of the millennium were the fruit of this intellectual condition. Now it seems to me that much of this *rebellious* (and in some cases self-destructive) attitude has vanished. The new generations are more mature. They retain a measured dose of hedonism, and when they go into battle they do it in a more targeted and conscious manner, even if they have less 'political instinct' than their parents.

The efforts of the millennials (and those who have come after them) seem oriented towards combining quality of life and sustainability, obviously within the discipline of space. In short, they are more New European Bauhaus than Bauhaus, without getting here into a discussion of Ursula von der Leyen's 'synaesthetic' project.

OBRIST We already talked about resilience, which is found in certain territorial structures, such as cities or villages. There are meta-themes of our time that have a strong influence on the practice of architecture, sustainability for instance, but digitisation too, and which are changing fundamentally the way we are organising ourselves – living, working, moving around, taking care of things, etc. – as a society. The theme of the resilience of architecture is growing more and more important, and with the question of modes of spatial typology or organisation that are resilient in the face of change, perhaps after decades the theories of Aldo Rossi and others are coming back in play but are viewed in a completely different light. And the theme of artificial intelligence, which in the future could increasingly become a partner in the process of development of suitable and resilient forms for certain architectural and urbanistic questions. In the latest issue of *ARCH+* on Vienna, for which the Housing and Design research department at TU Wien under my guidance has acted as guest editor, we posed ourselves the question of 'The end of housing (as a typology)', precisely in order to take account of the research into houses that are fundamental elements of the city with a possibility of wide-ranging planning that goes beyond the function of dwelling, giving space to work, commerce, production and leisure as well through a resilience of the form itself.

CIORRA The exhibition we devoted to Aldo Rossi (curated by Alberto Ferlenga) tended to stay away from the idea of an architect so strongly tied to the desire to found the project on the orthodox application of concepts like typology and morphology. Perhaps this is an identikit more reminiscent of Giorgio Grassi. For Rossi they were above all ways of interpreting the historical city. His projects are more like inspired urban visions, and not so interested in what went on inside the houses. I agree with what you're saying. I think that housing is indeed very pliable material that is therefore fairly easily adapted to perform functions of a different kind. Naturally, the pandemic has greatly strengthened this conviction, with rooms quickly turned into bedrooms/offices/gyms/dining rooms/digital lounges. The house has great resilience. So, I believe that the work which needs to be done is not on the typology but on the internal and external infrastructure that makes the house adaptable to different uses. Personally, I have no liking for home automation. The words artificial intelligence put me immediately on the alert. But I'm conscious of the important role that new infrastructures will play in the use of spaces in the near future. It suffices to think of their implications for the world of health care, or what has happened with distance learning (which I still don't like).

This doesn't mean that the legacy of the great Italian architectural culture is not necessary or useful to the mental gymnastics which are now required from us as architects. And it was from Aldo Rossi that we learned that the identity and role of a building depend little on its function (beautiful architecture is in itself 'generic') and that the nature of a building depends greatly on how it relates to what it has around it. All notions essential to an understanding of the contemporary city (where by 'city' we mean a very wide range of modes of settlement) and to imagining how we can work within it. Provided that we don't think we can use yesterday's answers for the questions posed by today's inhabited space. The result of that is hardly ever satisfying. This holds for all the forms of 'fuzzy' nostalgia that have pervaded the community of 'cool' architects of recent years, from *La Tendenza* to the radicals to organicism to postmodernism. It's more interesting, in my view, to learn from their research and then come up with independent and updated responses, capable above all of combining an awareness of the need for creative and intelligent reuse and the ability to connect 'old' buildings with the new needs of infrastructure and communication.

PUTZU What would you say about the disconnect between the ideas of architects and the built environment as its manifestation and the people who ultimately inhabit them? The mainstream method of regulation and decision-making though a top-down system often causes estrangement. How can architectural space be reclaimed as a source of empowerment by the inhabitants?

CIORRA This is a question we have asked ourselves many times. As you are all well aware, Italy is a country with many layers of bureaucracy. All in all, postwar Italy managed its growth fairly well. But it was heavily conditioned by the polarisation of the two alignments, Catholic-conservative on the one hand and Marxist-socialist on the other. Two fronts that were clearly separated but also willing to make many compromises (some evident, others tacit, culminating in what was referred to directly as the 'historic compromise' in 1978), and above all allied against any possibility of the emergence of a secular and progressive culture in the vast political space between them (it suffices to think of the story of Olivetti). This strange diarchy, in terms of land use and exploitation of the territory, resulted in an anomalous but simple system in which the rules were very strict, but there were no 'penalties' for not following them. A sort of mix of revolutionary anarchy and the Catholic propensity for offering pardon that we saw work politically at the highest level up until the times of the kidnapping and murder of Aldo Moro. As far as the management of the territory is concerned, the scheme functioned without major upsets (although with a grave increase in corruption in the final phase) until the end of the First Republic (brought down by the scandal known as Tangentopoli). Or rather up until the Prodi government took office in 1996. In this sense the bureaucratic structure made corruption easier. Essentially in Italy there were (and still are) so many layers of bureaucracy you have to pass through between the letter of the law and its application to a specific project that the effect on quality, on time and on the straightforwardness of the procedure could only be negative. Obviously, the programme of harmonisation with EU rules has resulted in some improvements, but there is still a long way to go. So, the effect has been not so much the arrogance of a top-down process as an extremely extensive and complicated system of governance and decision-making, which in the end means that you even lose sight of where the procedure has got bogged down or has been badly handled. The combination of hyper-trophied governance and inefficient bureaucracy also results in a great weakness of the publicly funded project in the face of economic and speculative forces, which find it easy to worm their way through the loopholes in the system.

Clearly it is not just a problem of laws and rules. There is a grave deficit of general culture with regard to architecture and the quality of spaces. A deficit that at various times and on various sides it has been suggested could be overcome with another law (along the lines of the French one for the promotion of architecture) – but in my opinion another layer of regulation is the last thing we need. It's much more a problem of education and aesthetic updating. Among the enemies of architecture there are often actors who ought to be its allies. There are the defenders of the heritage, who fail to grasp that the contemporary project is the prime agent of good preservation. There are the passionate environmentalists, or 'technoecologists', who think that to make a city beautiful it's enough to make a city (apparently) environmentally 'friendly'. Making at bottom the same mistake as the functionalists of a century earlier. The cultural gap is more harmful today than at any time in the past because the economic framework of the relationship between architecture and society has also changed. Up until twenty, thirty years ago, the architect's client was very often a public actor, the state, the region, the municipality, the hospital or school administration. Today this, for obvious reasons, is increasingly rare, with the result that we now have to ask private clients for good architecture. Who, philanthropists apart, can only be driven by two motives: the economic one provided by aesthetic surplus value (a well-established process in industrial design), and that of falling into line with a context of cultural quality. We can draw two conclusions from this. The first factor can only bind architecture closer and closer to the market. The second is that the only lever we can use to react is that of culture. And that the best way to convey political and socially sustainable messages today is through cultural and educational action.

To be sure, the EU recovery fund will have a counter-cyclical impact on all this, pouring billions into the coffers of public actors and institutions (with the hope that they will be well spent), but in the long run the impression is that in the future the relationship between architecture and welfare will have to go down increasingly imaginative roads. And that our mission as disseminators of architectural quality will be all the more likely to succeed the more we are able to talk to people, rather than to the mayor or the minister.

OBRIST Speaking of power and image, if you recall, we already saw in 'An Italian Story', the biography that Berlusconi sent to 'all Italian families' (as he put it) during his first electoral campaign, the promotion of his ideas on housing and the city that had found expression in Milano 2 and its ilk. Through his media empire, not only did new customs make their way into Italian households, but the TV studios of Mediaset with their specific kitsch became an extension of Italian living rooms, kitchens and piazzas.

CIORRA It's true, yet Milano 2 was nothing but the long and belated tail end to the Italian infatuation with gated communities of the 1960s and '70s – years in which people were fleeing from historic centres. It's just that – as you say – in the 1980s it became a cult by way of the illusion of a direct relationship with the dominant media empire.

OBRIST In Milan we have recently seen huge transformations of former industrial areas with an investment of large amounts of private capital, often from international investment funds. In parallel for decades there has been talk of privatisation and the sale of state-owned properties to pay off the public debt.

Most Italians live in a house or flat they own. But for the new generations who do not inherit one the prospect of acquiring a home of their own is going to be very difficult, if not impossible.

If we look at the developments of these decades, some very simple questions (which clearly have very complex answers) arise: Who do our cities belong to? Who does Italy belong to in this moment?

CIORRA Challenging questions. First of all, I'd say that today who rules Italy is one thing, who owns it another. A lot of people own Italy but only a few are in command. In a country in which most people live in houses they own, in which there are no longer any large, landed estates and in which major industrial concentrations struggle to survive, it is not easy to identify a class of oligarchs. Rather, there is a fairly extensive and ramified ruling class that has a lot of power. But in a country that remains essentially anarchic. It is hard today to think of hegemonic ambitions like those of the plots to stage a coup in the 1960s or the freemasonry of the 1980s and '90s. Prior to recent events (economic crisis, pandemic, war) and the advent of Draghi it could have been said that there were very strong and interconnected networks of power, but not a clear and established elite. The crises have probably greatly diminished the power of the big real-estate groups (for a long time the true oligarchs, alongside the worst of the bankers), while the role of the energy giants seems ever more central; giants to whom we look with apprehension, owing to the rise in prices, but also with hope in the expectation that they will invest all (or most) of their profits in non-fossil fuels. Until a short time ago this question would have made me think of Turkey. A country that presents itself as a 'new Lebanon' for non-Western finance, but whose state of economic health is still measured by the number of cranes that can be seen in Istanbul and the other main cities. In short, while we wait for digital capitalism to consolidate its hierarchies of transnational power, the rich and powerful of many countries can still be found by following the money invested in real estate. And this is certainly not a good moment for them.

It should also be said that it is now fairly evident that local (national) authorities have a somewhat reduced range of action, limited by geopolitics (for us the EU), the excessive power of the media tycoons and international finance. I don't know whether it is more important right now to investigate the structures of local power or to try to deconstruct the structures of transnational and immaterial power. Unless we want to end up waging our political struggles in the metaverse.

You refer to the phenomenon of Milan. Certainly, Milan is a city where in recent decades there has continued to be a great deal of construction, often with the involvement of good and/or famous architects. Then there was the Expo 2015, with a very positive impact and an attempt at sustainable recycling that is still too early to judge. All this on the one hand has resulted in a good quality of life for residents, on the other in a rapid increase in prices that hints at the start of a new 'housing crisis'. I don't know if the problem lies in the quantity and use of public property. In Italy the amount of publicly owned building is immense and it is often left to its own devices, owing to the excessive resources that would be required to keep it in good condition. So, a private owner is welcome if he makes good use of it. For me the main cause – and consequently the solution – of the housing problem is the enormous number of empty flats, accommodation that its owners prefer not to rent out and that has an impact on the property market, on the quality of urban planning and on city life. Instead of going back to taking more land and constructing new public housing developments, I think we ought to be working on this phenomenon, by taxing heavily those who keep empty housing off the market and subsidising those who want to rent it; in short, by recycling the existing stock rather than adding to it.

OBRIST In a sense, in your 'Letter to a young architect' we also see a moment on your journey. You speak of Gibellina, of Burri's *Cretto*, of Francesco Venezia's museum. You speak of your meeting with Maria Giuseppina Grasso Cannizzo. Let's take a similar tour with you, a virtual one. If you were to go on a journey and invite people to see new phenomena or even some old ones in Italy, what would you show us?

CIORRA This is an interesting question. But where the old is concerned I'd take all my foreign friends to see Mario Fiorentino's monument at the Fosse Ardeatine – the most beautiful contemporary work of architecture in Rome that no one knows. A complex that could have been designed the other day. The second stop would be a strange building located between the Adriatic autostrada and the sea. It's called Hotel House and used to be a tourist complex but has now become a metropolitan slum in the middle of the countryside. It is a cruciform building, a Cartesian, vaguely Le Corbusierian, and fairly low (seventeen storeys) skyscraper that perfectly embodies the transformation from holiday home to urban periphery; an urban periphery inhabited almost entirely by immigrants. The architecture is very interesting; the social and urbanistic problems enormous. For me it represents the ideal theme for the Italian (or even foreign) architect who wants to tackle the hot topic of the relationship between architecture and society.

If I wanted to give a positive example I'd say Maria Giuseppina Grasso Cannizzo, because she works almost exclusively on houses, often with very limited budgets. She works above all on the dialogue between herself and her client. In a way, Maria Giuseppina is a metaphor for many of the interesting themes of this century: reuse, the importance of domestic space, individuality, the nature of the author, the attention to what is going on far away from the big cities, the artistry of the design and the materials and much besides. Perhaps she also helps us to understand the difference in the relationship between the individual and the masses in the twenty-first century with respect to the twentieth.

In the twenty-first century individuals want to be considered individuals, not single elements of a mass. This puts them on a sort of psychological drug that makes them feel very powerful, since they think they can speak to the whole world, as if they were leaders, through the social networks. Obviously, it's an illusion, an illusion that in the end leaves the individual even more alone and defenceless than before, a single atom versus the mass of global forces. We don't like this individualism, but it's there and we have to deal with it somehow, take it on board in our work in order to reintroduce it, if possible, into the dynamics of democratic life. Grasso Cannizzo's work is for me a good metaphor for this process: it is individual, but deconstructs individualism through architectural quality, a minor miracle.

Going back to the Hotel House I'd like to add that, for me, it represents the fact that we can no longer identify the problem of marginality with the traditional city outskirts of Milan, Rome and Naples, or Palermo. In Italy there are beautiful and ugly suburbs. Some work and others don't. There are historic centres that have problems typical of the outskirts (Naples, Palermo and Bari up until ten years ago) and there are spruced-up historic centres. The old spatial hierarchy of the bourgeois city has been broken down and spread out into the hinterland, overthrowing relations of value and urbanistic convictions. So, the old concept of good or bad applied to the city has to be reexamined almost case by case, renouncing pre-established systems. The lessons of the past, recent and remote, should help us to develop the means to act in this new context, but are of no use in finding directly applicable solutions, lest we end up with more of the disasters and ruins with which the country is filled.

Transcript of a conversation that took place in June 2021.

Michael Obrist in conversation with Stefano Boeri (architect and full professor of urban planning at the Politecnico di Milano)

The anti-city and us

Vertical Forest. By Boeri Studio. Credit: Dimitar Harizanov

Polo del Gusto in Amatrice. By Boeri Studio. Credit: Giovanni Nardi

OBRIST Let's start with something you once said: 'We need to recognise the forms of the anti-city, to understand where and how they operate, what rules they follow and who promotes them, because, whether we like it or not, we are in the anti-city in the majority of today's spaces.'

Looking at your work as intellectual and architect, as urbanist and publisher, what emerges is a strong sense of social empathy, a closeness to things in which there is no sign of that cynical distance we see in others who look at the territory while asking themselves 'who are we and where are we?' After the crisis of the pandemic, we are dealing today with an energy crisis generated by a war in the east of Europe, but that is perhaps just a foretaste of the crises that will be caused by climate change – and that are raising fundamental questions about the kind of city dwellers that we are and that we will be. And in all this, the cities remain. In the light of these recent crises and of the questions that they bring with them, how do you see the current state of the city?

BOERI The statement you have quoted alludes to the coexistence of two impulses that are almost always present in the practices of inhabiting: on the one hand, a genuine reflection on the modes of collective living, on the sharing of our lives and on the forms of meeting, relationship and vicinity that inhabiting offers; on the other, a tendency towards an accentuated individualism, towards a form of spatial egoism that leads to a self-representation of one's own identity. The story that stems from the constant balance or loss of balance between these two forces could be called 'the history of the practices of living in the city'.

OBRIST What do you understand by city?

BOERI A fundamentally European phenomenon, one that arose in a period stretching from the Sixties to the mid-Nineties. A period in which a new form of individualism emerged out of what could be called an 'economic democracy'; that is to say, the possibility for individuals, families, enterprises and small businesses to obtain the capital needed to modify their living space without having or wishing to submit to common rules, whether they were those of planning, those of building regulation or those of public policies in general. This attitude has allowed the mushrooming of a multitude of buildings both solitary and crowded together that has in fact transfigured much of the territory, at least in southern Europe.

However, similar developments have also taken place around the urban centres of central Europe and northern Europe, although in a very different way from how they have occurred in other parts of the world. In a sense this 'economic-democratic' phenomenon has also been an act of liberation: the possibility of moulding space to suit one's own needs has been a way of coming up with a response – individualistic and in some ways dramatic – to the inadequacies of urban and infrastructural policies in some parts of Europe, especially Italy.

The state's response to the major conflicts of the Sixties and Seventies was not an effective intervention of social infrastructuring, but a distribution of capital to families, which operated thanks to a form of paradoxical laissez-faire in defence of the territory. Notwithstanding a huge mass of laws, standards and building regulations, in reality there was almost total freedom of movement: in the snarl of institutional rules, spaces in which to act could always be found. The result was a surge in unauthorised building and short-sighted town plans that, when all is said and done, made no effort to look beyond their own little patch: this chaotic multitude transfigured whole areas, since individual town councils only exercised control over what lay within the bounds of their municipality, allowing a Wild West expansion outside the limits of their geographical jurisdiction. Moreover, they didn't look at what was happening in the municipality next door where exactly the same thing was going on. As a result of these attitudes the nebula of the city of deregulation expanded like wildfire. That's who we are.

OBRIST Do you think this 'we' can have some form of resolution?

BOERI This impulse cannot be resolved simply by repression or a form of moral condemnation or a hypocritical public pillorying. That would be too facile, since we have all been complicit in this transfiguration. I am saying this in contrast to those who thought, especially in those years, that these forms of uncontrolled urban expansion, of unrestrained disregard of the law, ought to be judged and condemned without any pity, without any concern. I believe, on the contrary, that, all things considered, there were within this sort of movement aspirations that had to do with a profound change in customs, in the culture of the regions and even in daily life.

The work I did with Gabriele Basilico, for example, was aimed at showing that the mythology of the single-family home of clearly American inspiration had already been completely revamped by Berlusconian ideology as a counterpart to the various social stamping grounds – for instance the shopping mall or the large multipurpose meeting room. In the Italian version of the detached house we find the familiar petit bourgeois identity; the TV set was the focus of the spatial dynamics that were articulated through the private television channels. The private television that took on the role of the hearth was a very powerful element of legitimisation as well as support, giving a boost to this individualistic mode of transformation of space that we all accepted. We were unable to put up an effective opposition to a phenomenon that was – like it or not – the expression of something common to all of us.

This is why I'm always very sceptical when I hear someone demonise this phenomenon: hampering that impulse, obstructing it, also meant imposing its dismissal. Instead, I always think back to figures like Bernardo Secchi or André Corboz who, in the 1980s, when at schools of architecture, they were studying historic centres and urban matters, pointed out that outside the city a new and unfamiliar urban attitude was emerging. The great merit of these and other scholars lies precisely in their having been able to shift the focus of attention from historical and academic discourses to realities that were coming to the surface in that moment.

In that sense, we tried to identify the rules, or at least the constants, that were hidden behind this apparently chaotic form of urbanisation in order to reveal the most interesting part: that search for a balance between individualism and sharing I was talking about before. So that, on the one hand, we tried to understand the ways in which the various family networks were structured into clusters within the residential expansion that was occurring in those areas; on the other, we adopted a purely typological and stylistic perspective, pointing out the elements that were repeated more or less everywhere: the fence around the edge of the private property, service spaces like the cellar or the recreation room or artisanal workspaces linked to the garage. A sort of genealogy of the detached house of the 1970s, 1980s and 1990s. A very limited vocabulary but one that displayed a great range of superficial variations.

These last thirty or forty years have brought about a radical change in the historical city through the fragmentation of the building and the urban block, the reuse of attics, changes in the use of courtyards, but also – and above all – through a multitude of events that have taken place in a larger area, and one outside the city itself. At the urban level, a momentous change in contrast to all the ideas and developments in the Haussmannian mould that at the end of the nineteenth century and the beginning of the twentieth century had shaped the historical cities of a medieval and Romanesque character, imposing the modern city on them.

OBRIST This 'more extensive territory' has recently displayed an unexpected resilience and generosity: during the pandemic, in a specific moment in history when it was not possible to leave the home, people living in a suburban detached house rediscovered the value of having a little private garden and more room inside. While this type of housing cannot return to being the future, it has reacted better than the flats which, during the pandemic, had to change and adapt to the concentration of many different needs. What is the pandemic's legacy in this sense?

BOERI The reaction to the pandemic is interesting because, on the one hand, it has in a way confirmed the close historical link between hygiene and town planning. We know, for example, that it was cholera which gave birth to the urban policies with regard to the primary infrastructures and sewage systems that still structure the city today. On the other, the health crisis has simply emphasised – not caused – a problem that the lockdown has made evident. The extraordinary and dramatic experience of coercive distancing we have undergone has shown that, for me, this is the real battlefield of the city today, the fact of having lost the perception of bodies, the cognisance of the proximity of bodies. This is something that implicates complex reflections about the contemporary way of life even before the pandemic. It certainly raises questions of urban order, but also, and above all, it means we need to think in sociological terms, about the very concept of neighbourhood unit and the way we live together today.

Recently, there has been much talk of the 'fifteen-minute' city that, while not new, remains an interesting proposal since it focuses on urban time rather than space, and in this sense, I repeat, it is more a sociological question than one of urban planning. Jane Jacobs was already thinking along these lines and the legacy of her ideas ought to be brought to bear on the relationship between city dwellers and services within the dimension of historic European districts. In this way the question would be plausible and could add to the vision of how we live together today.

The great challenge of the city is no longer so much that of proximity, but that of coexistence, of variety, of making room for diversity, of the combination of people who are not all the same and have very different stories. The problem does not lie in being close or far, but in staying close while being far away. For me, this is the real question of our day: the variety that lives nearby. I truly believe that what makes a city interesting, both as a place in which to live and as an object of study, is in fact the combination of the density of its spaces and the diversity of the cultures that inhabit those spaces, which creates a multiform intensity that, at times, truly becomes a city in the strict sense of the word. I often find myself thinking about this theme, but I don't know if I have any answers. I've tried to bring some fresh air to it …

OBRIST This reminds me of my conversation with Silvia Federici in which she talked about what was the political and social significance of what architecture 'injects' into neighbourhoods through the choices that architects make in the design of people's flats. Questions that, I think, you too asked yourself when you were a councillor, but now as president of the Triennale as well. This system is based, in reality, almost exclusively on inherited property: the population is divided between those who inherit and those who do not inherit. Both find themselves in a situation where the growth in income no longer keeps pace with the rapid rise in the market prices and rents of flats. Those who inherit are OK, while an ever-larger number of people can no longer afford to live in the city. In parallel the great influx of investment capital into the real-estate market has turned the 'home' into a financial asset, creating an ever-wider gulf between individuals: cities are becoming part of a 'portfolio', flats are more economically attractive if no one lives in them, but are placed instead in the short-term rental market, especially in the big cities, or – in an even more extreme case – they are left empty and simply become the objects of financial transactions. And yet attempts are being made to imagine a different city – and I'm thinking of the case of Spin Time in Rome – applying models driven by a desire for something different. For them to last, they need stable foundations and policies that give them support. How do you relate to models of this kind and what do you think is the potential of such phenomena?

BOERI The variables that would need to be taken into account are multiple. In any case I think that, to some extent, we have to go back to what we were talking about at the beginning – that is, to that individualistic impulse which predominates. It's not so much the case of Airbnb or the form taken by the gentrification of urban centres, but rather the question of the uniformity that prevails, of the uprooting of the different, which allows the owners of small amounts of property to earn a fixed income through the investment of family capital. The real problem with these phenomena is not that they depopulate cities, but that they fill them with a totally uniform population that is similar in its lack of care for the area in which they live. An intense, greedy, abstract and indifferent form of habitation.

And it is for these reasons, too, that I stress the theme of diversity as a cornerstone of thinking about the city of today. Diversity and density. I know that in this I am in disagreement with Paola [Viganò, editor's note], who is still in favour today of a model of low-density inhabitation – we have discussed it many times – but I'm convinced that low density is no longer appropriate for today's way of life and for the transformations of the territory it would now require. I'm of the view that there is no longer enough room for low density; I consider it a choice that is not able any longer to 'reckon' with contemporary ways of life and needs.

Transcript of a conversation that took place in January 2023.

Michael Obrist and Antonietta Putzu in conversation with Luca Ragazzi and Gustav Hofer – journalists and authors of various documentaries on contemporary Italy, including the 2011 documentary

Italy: Love it, or Leave it

PUTZU — The starting point of your respective films often takes the form of a conversation you're having in your flat. The domestic interior becomes a place for political debate and reflection. To what extent is this choice a way of drawing attention to the effects of politics on private life?

HOFER — For us the private is political. The media are present in the home, for instance when you listen to the radio while you're eating a meal. In Italy, especially, the table is a place not just for conviviality but also for political debate. This set-up has become a mark of our work, so we always start with this scene of the two of us sitting at table.

OBRIST — In the urban fabric and landscape of Italy, beauty forms a backdrop to daily activities. At the same time, things built since the Second World War rarely attain the characteristics and qualities of the buildings and public spaces of previous centuries and disrupt the harmony of that urban structure. Italy has become the land of *geometri*. [Note: The word loosely translates as 'surveyor'. Unlike in other countries, the Italian surveyor, or *geometra*, is able to design buildings on a modest scale, and of often equally modest quality, without the aid of an architect.] What happens in a society and a country in which beauty is rarely produced as an expression of contextual complexity and interconnection?

HOFER — It is true that great value is assigned to beauty in Italy, but in my view it is often used for propagandistic motives. The historic centres are marvellous, and yet at the same time their outskirts are excluded from aesthetic consideration. In the same way, politics forgets all about the peripheral areas, which are a reality of life for many people. The rhetoric of the beautiful negates the existence of the architectural eyesores that have disfigured Italy since the Second World War.

RAGAZZI — In my opinion it was the unfortunate conjuncture of the postwar period between the Christian Democrats, the party that was in power in Italy for

Film stills from *Dicktatorship*, 2019.

Film still from *What is Left*, 2014.

	almost fifty years, and the so-called *palazzinari* that smoothed the way for the reconstruction of the country without any respect for beauty, on the pretext of the so-called 'economic boom', invented in theory as a way of kick-starting the economy. Did you know that Gustav and I found a lamp from the 1960s in the rubbish that we then discovered was the Pistillo designed by Castiglioni? This is a metaphor for the sloppiness of this country, which does not even seem to be aware of its value.
HOFER	It irritates me to hear this ode to beauty because it ignores the huge gap between the reality of the country and the system of politics and the media. These two worlds do not speak to each other; no longer are there the interlocutors of the past who were taken seriously. For example, the unions, which had an important role, which had the power to facilitate so-called 'social mobility' for the working class. These intermediate bodies no longer exist, or if they do, they have lost their credibility. Our generation is cursed by job insecurity and, for the first time since the war, children are poorer than their parents.
OBRIST	In your film *Italy: Love It, or Leave It* you challenge the romanticised image of Italy and show us a disenchanted reality. What does it feel like to live in a country characterised by strong political, cultural and social contrasts?
HOFER	Italy is indeed a country full of contrasts, and so lends itself to our documentaries and to an exploration of its problems. Especially, when in Italy you have these spaces and monuments of great beauty and cultural value that are also the protagonists of our films like *Diktatorship* and obviously *Italy: Love It, or Leave It*. These artistic and urban riches work for external financiers, many of them foreign TV channels. They fund us because they know that our documentaries in a way provide an opportunity to discover Italy, much loved by people all over the world. When shooting the scenes, we didn't realise that abroad they were going to notice the architecture, the piazzas, the monuments. For us it is an urban landscape to which we are accustomed, I would even say inured.
PUTZU	Italy is known for its objects of design, some of which are accessible for mass consumption. The Bialetti Moka Express is an excellent example. In your film *Italy: Love It, or Leave It* you show how its production has been completely detached from Italian territory and the repercussions this has had on workers. What do you think of the 'Made in Italy' brand?
HOFER	Globalisation imposes production at low cost, which is inevitably in China, in India or in other such places. In the end, it's the idea of the product that makes it Italian.
RAGAZZI	But there is something I have to say in all fairness: on the question of Bialetti, we went to the factory in Omegna and talked with the workers, and they explained to us that to all intents and purposes it is true that production has been relocated. That the Bialetti Moka is now made in Romania. But a minimal part of the process of production is still carried out in Italy so that the 'Made in Italy' label can be put on it. So, there are ways of getting round things and I imagine that many firms do this in order to stay competitive in a globalised market.
HOFER	If you ask me, 'Made in Italy' is always a question of promotion. Above all it serves the process of education, of finding the funds to allow young researchers to develop their idea. In Italy this is so difficult that they are usually obliged to emigrate. It is only when this idea has become a success that it is appropriated again with the 'Made in Italy' label. It is used for propaganda by politicians.
OBRIST	I'd like to raise the question of regions that are places of innovation and the home of specific products that have become symbols. It's always amazed me that, in the former DDR, which had proclaimed itself a workers' and peasants' state (negating with this myth the historical reality of the sole real power in the state being in the hands of the SED, the East German Communist Party), the expression of innovation in the transport sector was the Trabbi, while in the towns and villages of Emilia Romagna the peasants not only invented tractors, but products with a worldwide reputation for excellence like Ferrari and Lamborghini. Or, if we look at the birth of Arduino, the open-source platform for hardware and software, in the specific context of Ivrea.
HOFER	I think this is still the case and very much so in those regions where the Ferrari is made, and where today there is a whole series of entrepreneurs, both men and women, who are doing innovative work, especially in the electronic field. There is this engineer Livia Cevolini, the female CEO of Energica, which for some years now has been producing electric motorbikes with great success. These areas of innovation and experimentation continue to exist, not thanks to state aid but due to a bottom-up approach and with international shareholders.
OBRIST	Your film *Italy: Love It, or Leave It* falls within the tradition of the Grand Tour as an educational journey. In your case an alternative Grand Tour that visits and analyses problematic questions and themes of contemporary Italy which contrast with the often-idealised perception of the country from the outside. What would you add to an educational itinerary to adapt it to the realities of contemporary Italy?
HOFER	I'd go to a residents' meeting in a block of flats in Rome. I think that there you would get a great insight into the dynamics of Italian society. In every block of flats all the various political forces of this country are mirrored. Someone wants to install a lift, someone else puts themselves forward for the common good, yet another has not paid the service

Film still from *Italy: Love it, or Leave it*, 2011.

Film stills from *Suddenly, Last Winter*, 2008.

charges for years, and then there's the fascist who starts shouting at everybody and frightening them …

PUTZU What influence has Berlusconi's media and real-estate empire had and still does have in Italy?

RAGAZZI In my view he is responsible for the creation of imagery that has wrecked this country. Today people often talk about the two decades during which Berlusconi was repeatedly prime minister, but we forget that he has been a public figure for over forty years now. In 1978 he started to propose with his TV channels a role model for women in particular. He succeeded in dismantling the battle-hardened feminism that had been a very important phenomenon in the 1970s. By proposing aberrant models of conduct, lifestyles borrowed from America and based on consumerism.

OBRIST What relationship or contrast do you see between the historical literary salons of the bourgeoisie as a place of discussion and political influence and the demonstration of political will or representation in public space?

RAGAZZI I'm afraid that the literary salons of the nineteenth century no longer exist. The contemporary salons of the upper middle class are certainly places where the establishment exercises its power and decisions are taken. But the physical spaces in which this occurs are not necessarily drawing rooms but may even be on the beach. Gustav and I once went to the seaside at Capalbio (in Tuscany, a place that has always been regarded as the preserve of the left-wing intelligentsia) to see a friend. By chance the man under the beach umbrella next to ours was the chairman of RAI, a friend of my friend's mother. Our friend introduced us. After chatting with him he told us: 'This is my number. Call me as tomorrow I'm going back to Rome …' We had been trying for months to get an appointment with this gentleman, but in vain. And then, just because we happened to be under the umbrella next to his on the beach at Capalbio, we were able to make contact.

On the other hand, I find mass demonstrations scary. The street is the place where the political debate that is conducted has become impoverished and debased in recent decades. In my opinion, the entry of populism onto the scene has resulted in the street losing its value as a place of protest. The politicians say nothing of substance, making empty promises they will never be able to keep. So today we are living in a time of general disenchantment and total lack of trust in the institutions. The Five Star Movement, for example, wanted to turn this fairy-tale of changing things from the bottom up into a reality. And then when they entered the corridors of power it took them a quarter of an hour to acquire the same attitudes and the same reputation for sleaze that had taken other governments fifty years. And perhaps by now people are disillusioned. They are resigned to the fact that things are unlikely to change.

OBRIST The theme of resilience: What are the opportunities and potentialities following the crisis in Italy and where can they be located (socially/spatially)? Where would you go to investigate the themes of the future?

HOFER For me the question of gender equality is central. If this country wants to change it is really going to have to deal with the white, heterosexual male. In my view this is the point where this country can change most profoundly. Because if the conception of power changes and it is no longer in the hands of a privileged minority, I'm convinced that some very interesting and fruitful roads will be opened up. There is a great deal of talent that is crushed by this system of power. And when those people who have never been able to make their voice heard and put across their own version of history finally and belatedly find their place in Italian society, I'm sure that really important things are going to happen.

Transcript of a conversation that took place in February 2021.

Michael Obrist in conversation with <u>Massimo Bricocoli</u> (full professor in Urban Planning and Policies and Policy Design and Head of the Department of Architecture and Urban Studies (DASTU) at the Politecnico di Milano)

A diagonal overview on beauty, places and change in Italy

OBRIST — In Italy beauty can be found everywhere in the fabric of our cities and in the landscape; it forms the usual backdrop to the activities of everyday life. At the same time, more has been built since the Second World War than in all previous eras. These structures rarely attain the characteristics and quality of the buildings and public places of previous centuries. Italy has become a land of '*geometri*'. [Note: The word loosely translates as 'surveyor'. Unlike in other countries, the Italian surveyor, or *geometra*, is able to design buildings on a modest scale, and of often equally modest quality, without the aid of an architect.] What happens in a society and a country in which beauty is rarely produced as an expression of complexity and contextual interconnection?

BRICOCOLI — The association of beauty with Italy is undoubtedly an image that carries great weight. Beauty is a dimension that has left its mark on the life of the Italian people from many points of view: whereas in other countries the use of the adjective 'beautiful' in daily life is almost perceived as being politically incorrect, in Italy it is widely utilised.

I understand your concerns but I think that beauty and aesthetic quality are still being produced. From my position, which is one very attentive to social phenomena and the way cities are changing, I continue to be optimistic. I find that beauty is still there, even where according to some canons apparently there is none; and, in any case, it seems to me that there are signs of evolution in Italian cities whose significance I recognise. I think there is a different beauty. A beauty that also corresponds to a profound change. Perhaps it is no longer the beauty that was represented in the Italy of the prewar period, of films, of that sort of imagery. A certain kind of beauty of the past, and one that is linked as well to a certain structure of Italian society, made up of places of outstanding quality and reserved for the elite, but also a minute beauty of the landscape, of urban spaces. From the viewpoint of the architecture of the 1950s, '60s and '70s, there is an important legacy of constructions, the housing of the economic boom, which has great qualities.

Your question prompts me to think about which are the places that I define as beautiful.

The theme of beauty calls to mind Trieste, a city of which we have an image that is very focused on the past. The Trieste of the Habsburgs, the Trieste of the Austrians, of the early twentieth century ... It's a very poetic vision. In reality it is a city on which postwar development has had a very strong impact. There are public housing estates in Trieste of a size and character that you won't find in other Italian cities. Rozzol Melara, among others. Enormous, and in very difficult environmental conditions. Or Valmaura, the estate next to the ironworks that separates it from the sea, right up against the elevated Via Valmaura. But Trieste is also the city of deinstitutionalisation, of the process of profound reform of psychiatry in Italy that after Gorizia found its centre of action and reference in Trieste with Franco Basaglia and that led to the closure of the psychiatric hospital. A very beautiful asylum it was, though, from the early twentieth century, and one that even in its location greatly resembles the Otto-Wagner-Spital in Steinhof, Vienna. The former psychiatric hospital of San Giovanni stands on a hill, a series of beautiful pavilions set amidst greenery. Following the closure of the asylum, 'mental health centres' were opened in several parts of the city, often in very ugly places and truly difficult districts. In the mental health centres in Trieste a lot of work was also done on beauty. They worked on an aesthetic treatment that could go hand in hand with a new approach to mental health, considering that if there was going to be social and medical innovation, it had to be visible, too. A motto of those years was 'more aesthetics less ethics', in the sense that in respect to some very profound reflections on mental health, at a certain point people said to themselves that it was necessary for this reform to be expressed in terms of a new aesthetic for these places as well. The work on beauty at these mental health centres was done with great care, in particular by a designer – Antonio Villas – together with the psychiatric staff. There are health services there of a kind I have never seen in other Italian cities or even in other countries.

Piazza Cordusio, Milan, April 2020 – from *The Missing Piece*. Credit: Giovanni Hänninen

Porta Vittoria, Milan, 2011, from *MilanoUP*. Credit: Giovanni Hänninnen

OBRIST I find this reflection on antipsychiatry very interesting …

BRICOCOLI I wouldn't call it antipsychiatry … The key is the concept of mental health, of a different psychiatry, oriented towards the promotion of mental health. A different kind of psychiatry, but still psychiatry.

OBRIST The question about beauty was intended as a bit of a provocation, given that we're also fans of 'dirty realism' and like to look at things differently. This notion you've brought up interests me greatly and has made me think of Gregory Bateson. His thinking has had a deep influence not only on anthropology, biology and ecology, but also on semiotics, linguistics, cybernetics and of course psychiatry. He was interested in the 'pattern that connects', and in 'beauty' in a more profound sense, going beyond the superficial way the term is used in our daily lives.

In Italian culture (which is an interweaving of many cultures) the term beauty is used a great deal. I was born in South Tyrol, where three cultural worlds overlap, and it is very interesting to look at these different paradigms in relation to the world of objects, too, and therefore of architecture, design, fashion and so on.

In the expression of the universal geniuses of each culture we also see traces of each paradigm: if we compare Leibniz in Germany with Leonardo da Vinci, and with Galileo Galilei too, we see the differences at once: artistic expression remains part of the thinking. Goethe became the bridge between these different ways of approaching reality, and Jacob Burckhardt defined Leon Battista Alberti as the model of the 'universal man' to follow. In the southern spectacle of life, objects are part of the celebration of life itself, and we are dealing with a culture in which devoting yourself to objects and their surface does not automatically lead to superficiality.

At times, as Hugo von Hofmannsthal wrote, profundity itself needs to be hidden – on the surface. Italian culture seems to be made up of fractals – we find this search for these creative expressions everywhere – in every sphere and every tradition. They become an expression of individual and collective approaches and codes of taste, and of power, too. We find it in the way food is prepared, in fashion, in the design of objects of everyday use, in people's homes, in cities. For Gio Ponti the starting point of design for the masses was the demand for a reproducibility of the sort of high quality that before could only be found in the well-crafted object. Clearly today we are faced with new and interesting phenomena of a mass culture with strong global influences, and visiting Italy on a new, alternative Grand Tour we would find other sources of inspiration. But the question of how to relate to the world and its objects as those who invent them or who use them remains.

BRICOCOLI The people you cite are coming together in my mind and taking shape … Because first you mention Galileo Galilei and then Gio Ponti. My thoughts turn to Padua, to Palazzo Bo. You mentioned Galileo Galilei who taught for eighteen years at the University of Padua, which is one of the oldest universities in the world. In Palazzo Bo there is Galileo's chair, a sort of wooden platform, and it is located in the rooms designed by Gio Ponti in the 1930s. They are absolutely extraordinary spaces. I've spent time there recently because I was a member of a qualifying committee of the Ministry of Research that met for three years in the offices of the rectorate. Every time you enter, stay and set to work in those spaces, it allows you to immerse yourself in great beauty and to enjoy it. Talking about these things tempts me to go out and explore. Even here in Milan. Modern Milanese architecture has earned itself a great and widespread reputation in recent years. Milan has rediscovered its beauty, in part thanks to a growing appreciation of its twentieth-century architecture. Architecture and urban context, in an indissoluble relationship. There are other places, too, where a lot of work has been done on beauty, taking it as the principle of organisation of a project. For example, a place that I visited recently after a gap of many years, is the Parco delle Cave. The *cave* are the quarries where the big building contractors, the major property developers of Milan in the 1950s, '60s and '70s, extracted sand, gravel and the like for construction. Then these quarries, which are located to the west of Milan, filled up with water because the level of the table rose. The place gradually fell into decay. Between the 1980s and '90s the situation came to a head: at one time this area was one of the main locations for drug dealing. Terrible degradation: rubbish and cars dumped in the quarries in a rural setting and at the same time close to Baggio, a densely populated area. The project of the park was developed incrementally by the municipality, following a plan drawn up and managed by the Italia Nostra association, which is very active and effective in Milan. An extraordinary effort was made and the park has become a great resource for the city. Today it is a place that has an absolutely incredible aesthetic quality. I went there a year ago because there are several weeks each year when it's full of fireflies. It's a really magical place, the lakes have all been cleaned up, the habitat is extraordinary and this has brought back the fireflies, which put on a spectacle at night. Going back there after years, I reflected on the sort of work they've done. It's not simply a matter of rewilding. As in Trieste, beauty has become an incentive for the project and for the policies. You need to consider the context: in an area like Baggio, densely populated and very distant from the centre, it's as if beauty were due recompense. A better world to recompense that part of the city. The park offers beauty and variety, tells stories and speaks of stratifications. Its forms and the people who frequent it are a reflection of a city in which highly varied processes of development are at work. It's not a nature reserve. It's a park that also has a strong element of artificiality. The attention paid to aesthetics is not usual and is very palpable.

Thinking it over, another situation with which you're undoubtedly familiar is the Metro in Naples. In a city like Naples, going into the stations of the Metro is like entering another dimension, one of wonder and even dream. A very powerful impact, I believe. A source of pride for the Neapolitans. It's incredible the way they talk about it, the way they describe it to you. They tell you how beautiful it is, not how well it functions. They talk about how beautiful the stations are.

OBRIST It's an interesting and ambiguous strategy. Strangely these places of art have so far produced a sense of collective respect. Clearly there are other interventions in Naples that are socially much more important for the city, but it remains an interesting question whether respect for beauty or collective pride or continual surveillance or some other factor is the cause of this behaviour.

In other districts, too, we see many very interesting projects with a lot more participation that all make strong reference to the words 'beauty' and 'poetry', as well as that of 'liberation'; projects where bottom-up strategies are mixed with top-down institutional approaches.

This also brings us to an idea that had been put forward by Simone Weil, the French philosopher, essayist and activist of the last century, who wrote after years of battle and a tough experience with factory workers in the 1930s that it's not just bread the poor need. Beauty, dignity and a life that could also be a poem for them were fundamental:

> 'Workers need poetry more than bread. They need their life to be a poem. They need some light from eternity.'
> [Simone Weil, *Gravity and Grace* (Oxfordshire: Routledge, 2023), 180.]

This reappropriation of people's own history on the one hand and telling the story of peripheral places through the media on the other are things we find in many other contexts, if we think of the places that feature in films and TV series: from the ruins of Calatrava's Città dello Sport at Tor Vergata to the outskirts of Ostia, which become places of myth in *Suburra*, from the Villaggio Coppola in Matteo Garrone's *Dogman* to the suburbs of Scampia and Secondigliano in *Gomorrah*. Obviously, these different narrations get mixed up, and cinematic reality becomes the template for imagery that produces itself, becoming the reality of life and vice versa.

BRICOCOLI In Milan now you have to watch the trap music videos made by musicians who are having a lot of success. Their videos are fairly extraordinary, and are all set in the more troubled working-class neighbourhoods of Milan. It's a phenomenon that's taking on more and more substance. They are having a very great impact through their success.

OBRIST There the real place and life and the contemporary are mixed with ancient tales, with the myth of the 'hero with a thousand faces' described by Joseph Campbell.

BRICOCOLI I could respond by saying that a fair number of these singers are gender fluid. They're not all tough guys, like American rappers. And this, too, is very interesting …

The most famous to arrive on the scene has been Mahmood, with an Italian mother and Egyptian father. His suave and very soft style has made him a hit even at the European level. But then there are Ghali and Sfera Ebbasta too … Between trap, hip hop and pop. They're not tough guys, they can be very gentle, with the outlying neighbourhoods from which they come in the background. Then, of course, there is also a rougher and more violent scene, like the one that surfaced recently among the rappers of San Siro.

OBRIST Do you see in this an overlap of various global models of male stereotypes in a certain kind of music with different images of the male pluriverse of Italian culture?

BRICOCOLI Absolutely, in fact, if you look at them … It's certainly not the image of the tough guy from the suburbs. The effect is that they mobilise a different imagery in these more difficult, more peripheral districts of Milan. They set some very interesting processes in motion.

OBRIST What's your view of what's happening in these districts of Milan, seeing that you've studied them? How do you see their potentialities above and beyond the problematic aspects? If you compare them with various foreign contexts, where do you see specifically Milanese things and where do you see the possibility of real change?

BRICOCOLI Milan is a relatively small city located in a very large urban area. It's not like that in Rome. Rome is a city with a gigantic perimeter. When we talk about the issues faced by Milan's districts, we are referring above all to the housing estates, where the problems include questions of social justice, and the need to work on the preservation of certain contexts of public housing. Public housing in Milan is very limited and personally I believe very strongly that it should be safeguarded. It is absolutely fundamental for there to be housing available at subsidised prices in the city. The question in Milan is that when you go outside the administrative bounds you find entire towns that are like suburbs: they don't have a particularly strong identity and function as dormitories for people who work or have businesses in Milan. The level of commuting is very high. As soon as you leave the city bounds, property values drop considerably. As do costs, but the quality of life also declines and around Milan there are difficult contexts that face some very significant problems. Milan remains a monocentric city and one that in these years has seen soaring property values. The effect on the context has been to reduce its attractiveness in proportion, and those who can't afford to live in Milan move to the surrounding towns. These are in fact the suburbs of the city, large urban centres but which are much less attractive and suffer from being peripheral. So, they are places that are not attractive beyond the local level ... Notwithstanding the attempt to imagine them as part of an urban region.

OBRIST What have we learnt in this pandemic and in these times of rapid digitising and new models of mobility? Is there post-Covid housing, and what in your view are models of sustainable cities?

BRICOCOLI I'm very cautious: what I think you can observe is the impact of the pandemic on cities. What is going to be the lasting effect, how our lives are going to change, I find it very hard to imagine. We are accustomed to things moving fast, but some transformations take place on a longer timescale. I don't think it's possible to make any particular predictions. We are seeing a withdrawal from community life, a retreat into the dimension of the family. An increase in long-distance commuting is evident: the high-speed railway is allowing many people to live in two places. The effect is a multi-local mode of residence, in places that can be quite far apart. In a country where there is strong imbalance between north and south this can have major effects. Because while the imbalance is typically economic, it exists on the environmental plane as well: the south can offer an extraordinarily high quality of life with respect to the north. Many people are taking advantage of this situation, in which they are able to keep working in the north while spending much of their life in the south. We are starting to notice it on a smaller scale, too: for example, along the line joining Milan and Bologna. In this period, I've come across a lot of people who are based in Emilia Romagna and in reality spend five days a week there and two in Milan. Before they didn't do that, before they stayed in Milan all the time. And this has been made possible in part by networks of infrastructure that to some extent work. It's a very important change and I'm wondering what effect it is going to have, not only on cities like Milan or Turin but on other contexts, too, on smaller cities and towns. If we look instead at a more local dimension, I see home working as a big trap. Remaining trapped in our homes, even if some of them are beautiful and pleasant, is a sign of withdrawal from contact with the world outside. And this is undoubtedly much more of a problem for people who live in ugly and cramped homes in which living conditions can be difficult. The result is growing isolation and a decline in the public dimension. The possibility of meeting people whom you haven't decided to meet is lost.

OBRIST During the pandemic we have seen what happens to us if everything has to be done in our houses and our flats: living, working, taking care of children and ourselves, education, sport, recreation, private and intimate activities. Everything has to find room in flats whose size we were already trying to reduce because of their environmental footprint. It becomes a solipsistic concept of society. A set of flats connected only through the digital network and flows of goods that arrive from elsewhere. Perhaps the flat is not the answer, and perhaps not even housing with common spaces like we see in Vienna. Maybe you need a whole district for it to become a society. We have tried to analyse this specific moment in history at several design studios and in a number of research programmes. We have reflected with Lorenza Baroncelli on the 'Post-pandemic city and countryside', and we have carried out other research with experts from the digital world aimed at understanding the possibilities the new digital media offer the countryside, whether villages really might have a different future or how life is going to change in the dispersed city. At a summer school on post-pandemic housing we thought a great deal about the housing estate, and how by introducing 'in-between' entities of support for work and education and the community, from co-working facilities to elements scattered around the district as communal spaces or social hubs, it would really be possible to create an 'emancipated' district of short distances.

And we realised that we must build spatial structures so resilient that they are able to change over time and that are no longer called offices or homes, but can be both at once.

BRICOCOLI What I find interesting in what you're saying is the thing about not taking the housing estate too seriously. Not imagining making it a closed unit. I'm somewhat resistant to this vision in which the estate is equated with the image of a community. On the other hand, I think there's a need for these exchanges, for something that is outside the housing and is at an intermediate level. It's already happening. When you get yourself ready to move physically to hold a meeting and then discover that five minutes later you have to be online and you don't have time either to go home or to go to the office. If you're in Vienna the café is still a possibility. Here in Milan, there are situations where sometimes all you need is a wi-fi connection and you can even do it in a garden. This is also a use of public spaces that is very different from the past.

OBRIST Do you see these potentialities for work, for a different future in the districts you were talking about before?

BRICOCOLI This is very difficult. I struggle to do so in some contexts. What I do see, however, is that there is always a gap between a segment of the population that gains the maximum advantage and that lives in the so called 'city of short distances' and a segment of the population that lives on a very different plane. The problem in some areas is the access to a whole series of services that by now can be handled very rapidly online and that you can only access online. Such as the PCR test for Covid. There are people who are totally incapable of utilising this online service and so in my view it's of great importance to set up service centres. In which those who are not familiar with this mode of access, which is so easy for us, can receive help. This gap is a really big one and the situation has been greatly exacerbated this year. So there is a problem of inequality in access to the web, a digital divide, but it is also a question of different occupations. If there is work to be found, it is often in the form of jobs that cannot be 'transmitted' online: they are jobs in the services, which require the movement of bodies and physical presence. It is a dimension of practical work.

OBRIST   The theme of resilience: What are the opportunities and the potentialities after the crisis in Italy and where can they be located socially and spatially? What are the places and the phenomena that have potential for the future?

BRICOCOLI   There are places that are becoming relevant again. For instance, a very important theme in Italy is that of the middle-sized cities, not the small centres which may have extraordinary environmental qualities, but the middle-sized ones that are faced with a lot of difficulties, because they have lost out from the perspective of production, culture, even tourism. So, many middle-sized cities that have been rather overshadowed are now evidently gaining new possibilities, because they are settings of some interest and so it is possible to imagine that they will attract more energy, assuming that people can make somewhat different life choices.

OBRIST   The last time we met you talked to me about Puglia, about the new phenomena that you see emerging there. What are they, how would you define them? In what way are they different from other places?

BRICOCOLI   Puglia by now is a clear example of a region that on the one hand has been able to manage its great exposure to the impact of foreign immigration across the Mediterranean and has then gone through a phase of considerable growth. The turning point can be traced back to the regional government of Nichi Vendola, which marked an important change with regard to the image of Puglia as well. Now it is a clear case of success and a motive of pride for a region that has greatly enhanced the assets of a territory which is rich on both the cultural and the environmental level, with a strong potential for the promotion of tourism. Following the experience of the pandemic the people of Puglia are showing a growing tendency to stay in their own region while working elsewhere, and many of them have bought houses and invested in property there. Many Milanese have been attracted to this region and have houses there. Puglia has in a way overturned the all-embracing image of the south of Italy as a uniform place. It has shown how, above and beyond a policy for the south, a different and innovative local government has been able to bring about a change of perspective. But it's an interesting case because of the contrast: the conditions in other regions of the south are more difficult. The most critical situation, undoubtedly, is in Calabria.

OBRIST   How do you see the role of digital technology in this development? Italy was one of the first countries in Europe to have its own version of *WIRED*, the bible of Silicon Valley. With the use of digital technology, we have seen a revival in jobs in more remote locations, where the cost of living is considerably lower than in the big cities, ranging from company call centres to programmers scattered around the country and only connected through the web. This is also resulting in the creation of small and invisible economies, which even organised crime finds it hard to detect, and this may allow them to stay below the radar where certain forms of oppression are concerned.

With digital technology it becomes possible to get different models of life in the south to fit with other models of life and above all with new economies, and to create situations of coexistence. Are these important developments?

BRICOCOLI   Yes, for sure, and not just in the south. Online purchases have accelerated processes that were already clearly under way. From the small-scale producer of olive oil to wine and so on, but craft products as well, very specific products that have now found it possible to get onto the market without middle men. This is undoubtedly something about which I know fairly little, but it certainly also opens up the possibility of living and working in other places than the big centres, where under a different model it was necessary to be present. This reminds me of the fact that now Milan has to deal with all these questions of the trade fairs – like the Salone del Mobile. For it's clear that by now in Milan there are all the ancillary activities of these fairs, which represent an extraordinary quantity of resources, an incredible amount of money. Yet there are also many who are now questioning whether these trade fairs still make sense and whether they are actually so important. We've already seen this to some extent with the Salone del Mobile and the transition from the traditional trade fair, concentrated in big exhibition structures, to the Fuorisalone, that is to say the display of designer products in ordinary spaces spread around the city, often disused industrial spaces, museums, garages or splendid buildings that are not usually accessible. Increasingly the Salone del Mobile is attracting large numbers of people, in part for what can be found away from the bustle of the fair. And now, in my view, the situation is very critical, because in some ways you have to wonder whether it's really necessary … Of late they have been turning more and more into installations rather than exhibitions.

OBRIST   But the beauty of the Fuorisalone is that it has shown us the potential of the city.

BRICOCOLI   That's right, it has been extraordinary: taking you places where you'd never have gone. I think that now it's an open question how much … that is to say, perhaps it has spread out even more. How much is it really necessary to have this concentration in just one week? Putting certain products on show in the physical and digital space has become much easier and I think that there is great fear of this in Milan at the moment.

OBRIST   Tourists generally come to Italy for two motives: for the beauty of its cities, towns and landscape, and for a certain way of life. And these are also the main reasons for Italians to stay in Italy, despite the well-known difficulties of remaining in this country. The cities are major points of social aggregation and great incubators of ideas, full of surprises and chance encounters – and in that sense certainly very different from the logic of the social media, which create bubbles of people more and more like yourself. From this perspective it is important to think about the future of real space in the digital era.

The pandemic and its consequences have provided an opportunity to reconsider cities and regions and make them more equitable. How important is architecture to the healing and improvement of a society and its territory wounded by the pandemic?

BRICOCOLI   There is a book that just came out called *Ricomporre i divari* [Closing the Gaps] that presents the results of a conference which was actually held last year, before the pandemic, and so it has been revised in part. It was a national conference, organised at our department at Milan Polytechnic. The book proposes a sort of exploration and manifesto of how urban and regional planning can act in a relevant way on just these themes of social cohesion and the gap between north and south, between developed and less developed regions. The focus is primarily on public policies, welfare policies, urban and urbanistic ones, policies of regional development. But I think that architecture can certainly do a great deal. There's a lot that has to be done to get it to act in a more incisive and innovative manner with respect to social needs and demands. It depends on what view you take of architecture's role. If we go back to the initial question about the role that beauty can play, I'm sure it can bring incredible qualities. Even in places where the decision might be to renounce development completely and let them collapse totally. So, there can be interventions that demolish, interventions that eliminate, that close things down.

OBRIST   In the future of Italian society there is increasingly going to be a split between those who inherit and own property, and those who have no inheritance and cannot afford to buy their own home on normal wages, and so have to rent. This last segment is going to grow ever larger. We have also spoken of lives lived in multi-locality, where the problem of the home is different. We know that the traditional model of the fixed job in a fixed position and fixed place is becoming the exception. Models of the family are changing, and the layouts of the home ought to reflect these new realities. We are having to deal with an enormous fluidity in living. We are seeing new models of shared dwelling that are emerging from different players: cooperatives, housing movements and enlightened local authorities, but also large digital enterprises.

How do you see the phenomena of cohousing, 'Mietshäusersysndikat' (jointly owned housing cooperatives) or platform urbanism, to name a few?

BRICOCOLI   We have been thinking about this recently. The system of jointly owned housing cooperatives is extraordinary because it shows, for example, how rent can remain very low over the years because all the other costs have been written off. There are some great stories. There's one in particular that I really like. We interviewed the occupants of a jointly owned cooperative in a very central location in Milan. And this gentleman said: 'The people here live a very long time. One member died at the age of 104, another at 98. Because we live a good life here. And everyone thinks that we are at a higher social level, even though in reality our cooperative is called a workers' housing association (*Società Edilizia Abitazioni Operaie* or SEAO). But our advantage is that we don't pay much rent and so we can spend our money differently and in a better way; for example, we can eat fillet steak.' The SEAO is the oldest jointly owned cooperative in Milan. It's a really good story, because it shows what affordability means. If you don't pay much for your home you have money to do many other things. So there is this in the background, and the question is why isn't it done more often? Because there's a lot of other interests. On the one hand owning your own home has now become a real obsession in Italy. And even the latest intervention by the government is now encouraging the provision of mortgages for people under thirty-six. This is an absurd policy. We talk about job fluidity and mobility and you're giving mortgages to people who in any case have the back-up of their parents. And instead of putting resources into employment, you put them into owning homes. On the other hand, there is a property market that is very quick to identify new areas of opportunity. Students, the elderly of course, or temporary accommodation in the city, and so it is working a lot on solutions of this kind as well. Then there are situations that concern fluidity, which in my view are still questions of affordability.

OBRIST   Who does Italy belong to? Who makes the decisions and how does power manifest itself in the urban fabric and what strategies of regulation are there?

BRICOCOLI   It's a complex question, and one where it is always useful to take a comparative perspective, looking at what we know at first-hand about other contexts and countries. In Italy there is a certain section of the population – and this is something that has increased considerably in recent years – that owns much of Italy. There are people who have gradually accumulated house after house. They own houses in several places, in several cities. Many resources instead of being invested in enterprise, in setting up businesses, have been invested in a very conservative way in private property. I find that this marked focus on the private is evident even in those educated and open-minded classes that call themselves progressive. These processes, on the plane of their implications with regard to the functioning of places and regions, have seen a very substantial accumulation of wealth as well. And these are not necessarily the people who govern Italy. It's a private dimension and one that is very little affected by political and governmental decisions. Those who have accumulated a great deal of wealth are fairly distant from many of the country's problems. And then looking closely at what the government is doing, even in Milan there is in my view a marked shift away from the model of the building speculator, of the investor in property, to real-estate development companies that are increasingly intricate and complex and in which the banking system plays an absolutely central role. Central but often opaque and not visible. It's a dimension that leads to a great lack of transparency in decision-making processes: you can't understand, it's really hard to work out what's going on. There is a great deal of difficulty in distinguishing what is public and what is private. In the sense that many public administrations and companies behave in ways that are just like those of a private player. It's as if the necessity to extract value from real estate in the city has become a natural thing. This is true for the public sphere, too. Even public bodies that own property expect to derive economic value from it. And this has now come to be seen as natural in a process in which there can be no doubt that the level of exposure that banks have is absolutely central.

When it comes to governing, public administrations are very subordinate to these powers. For it is those same powers on which a mayor, for example,

MilanoSesto, in the ex-Falck area, May 2022. Credit: Giovanni Hänninen

has to rely for political support. We discussed this recently in a lecture/course that Alessandro Balducci and I organised with colleagues at Sciences Po, Bartlett and the University of Amsterdam, and which saw the participation of students from the different schools. It is a process by which financial activities are acquiring growing importance in the economic system of many European cities and one that, depending on the context, plays out in very different ways. What can certainly be said now is that in Italy all the areas of competence that come into play in the negotiation between public and private have changed profoundly. What used to be relevant with the building speculator were the competences of those who sought to negotiate over the cubic metres, over areas: competences of a technical nature, of urban planning, of architecture … But nowadays, as an official of the Regional Government of Lombardy has said to me: 'We have moved from working on maps to working on Excel files.' And this is really telling. So, it has become very difficult to understand what competences within the public administration are actually available to act on behalf of the public interest in this negotiation with private players that make their decisions on completely different bases. It is possible to exercise control over other aspects, for example environmental quality, open spaces, public spaces. Because the capacity to deal with these is still there to some extent, but they are often almost residual questions with respect to the financial dimension and to major investments. Often this attention paid to these things that are a bit on the sidelines adds even more value, because the quality of public space, the quality of parks and gardens and so on, are all elements that add value to a project whose overall rationale eludes you.

OBRIST In Milan we have seen enormous development schemes with substantial financial flows, where the system of 'star architecture' was used as a marketing ploy for the areas. The promotion of the new intervention in CityLife has found its peak in the Instagram celebration of Chiara Ferragni and Fedez's influencer life in the apartment building designed by Zaha Hadid. We are dealing here with enormous processes of gentrification of the area and commodification of housing.

BRICOCOLI The reference to Ferragni and Fedez makes me think that perhaps we ought to take into account the fact that they are showing off the place where they live. We'll never know if they were sponsored by the property developer, but it's interesting because prior to this none of these figures, not even from the world of entertainment, has ever put on show the place they live in. Certainly not the VIPs of the city. This is not insignificant, considering that the place they live in is CityLife, which has become a symbol, the football players' place … With an imagery all of its own. CityLife is the emblem of these new projects of real-estate development in Milan, but in reality, the first operation of this kind was the Bicocca project. Bicocca was the first case in which an industry at a certain point shut down its production activities and became a real-estate developer. Pirelli set up Pirelli Real Estate to play this role. Thus, it capitalised the areas it owned as real estate and then developed them with a competition of architecture in which the theme was above all how to really develop the area. The fact that a university was brought there, a public institute of higher learning called the University of Milan Bicocca, was a fundamental move in making plausible the transformation of an industrial area into a piece of city with residential functions (something inconceivable at the time) and setting in motion a process of real-estate development in that zone. CityLife is very different. It is fairly clear what happened in the CityLife competition: it was not in any way a choice based on the architecture but a choice of the project that would guarantee the body that owned the areas the greatest economic return. Because those resources had to be used to construct the new trade fair. It makes me think of the case of Hamburg, of HafenCity, which is completely different: there the port had to expand and move outside the city and when the council gave permission for the development of new sites for the port, it acquired all the areas of the old port in order to be able to regulate and exercise direct control over its transformation. In the case of CityLife, in contrast, the trade fair owned areas in the city, but had to move and therefore put most of those areas up for sale along with the possibility to build on them. And so the project that guaranteed the maximum volumes won. I find this interesting with respect to the way more recent competitions have worked as well. The rules have changed completely: these are no longer competitions of architecture, no longer competitions of design. They are competitions in which the economic dimension is much more important. I was talking about this yesterday with my colleagues, among them Cino Zucchi, of whom I think very highly. What he said to all intents and purposes was that the architectural quality has greatly diminished to the advantage of other factors. But I told him that in Vienna for over ten years all the social housing has been built with competitions in which the valuation of the architectural and urban quality accounts for 25% of the points on which projects are assessed while the other 75% are based on social sustainability, energy performance and reduction of costs. It's interesting that architects understand a little better what the role of the architectural project is today and how it fits into the economic processes of urban development. In CityLife it was truly marginal. Perhaps we can say that if Renzo Piano's project (which might have paid greater attention to urban spaces and architectural quality but provided less volume and was certainly less iconic) had won, Fedez and Ferragni would not be living there. For CityLife is highly iconic, and this is another significant theme – what architecture can offer the world of social media: that project is every well suited to it and has been a great success. It has created a different image of the city.

OBRIST It reminds me of that old advertising slogan for the Lancia Y10: Liked by the people who are liked.

BRICOCOLI It's true!!!

OBRIST It was a very astute slogan, and it reminds me of the strategy Berlusconi used to promote Milano 2: the garden city of the TV stars, far away from the classical city, with an internal cable network (Tele Milano) for the inhabitants that became the launch pad for Berlusconi's media empire. Who are the new protagonists of the Milan that is literally being constructed now?

BRICOCOLI Yes, there are some figures who stand out at this moment. Manfredi Catella is the managing director of the company called COIMA, which has developed the Bosco Verticale and the whole Porta Nuova operation. He's a man of finance with a great ability to come up with a well-constructed and convincing narrative. He also heads a foundation named after his father and right now is one of the most influential people in Milan. Mario Abbadessa is the managing director of Hines Italy, a branch of the multinational real-estate company, and he too has taken on an increasingly prominent and visible role in the debate over the future development of the city. These men have profiles different from those of the past, both in terms of image and of that capacity to put forward complex narratives. Then there's a whole front that is not visible, which is that of the banks, which always remain out of sight. They also have very strong connections with national insurance funds, with the Cassa Depositi e Prestiti in Rome. But this is an invisible world and one that is scarcely comprehensible to most people.

OBRIST Do you think this is a new phenomenon for Italy?

BRICOCOLI What there has always been before was the construction of houses for people to live in. In cases of growth many fortunes have been built with different kinds of offer. There was Milano 2, of course, but then there were many other constructors who developed areas too. What we are seeing now is that housing and other buildings are not being constructed for their use, but to tie up and to land investments. Like in finance, with futures betting on the fact that there will be an increase in value. Instead of investing in a business you invest in housing. This explains the growing importance of financial activities. You build houses as if they were shares on the stock exchange: they may not be lived in, what matters is the investment value, not the use value. There are perhaps some elements of resistance in Milan in comparison with other cities where this phenomenon is much stronger. But it's true that it's in the minds of many, so individuals do it too. And the fact is that a lot of people think it's worth doing. Instead of buying a house for your son or daughter, you simply buy houses because you think that their value can increase and so you bet on the city. This creates a circuit. In Vienna it's completely different: I don't think the mayor of Vienna would ever dream of staking his electoral campaign on the claim: 'I assure you that your homes are going to be worth more.' And yet a person representing a large company in the field of social housing told me in an interview: 'But if house prices go up we're happy too, because it means that our homes increase in value.' That's what he said, taking no account of the social impact on the very people for whom their initiatives are intended. It's a mode of conduct of a distinctly private nature, because it means that it's becoming increasingly difficult to create social housing.

OBRIST What potentialities do you see for the transformation of the territory, for instance in post-industrial areas, villages, dispersed cities and the like?

BRICOCOLI But the villages … There has been this debate over the return to living in villages. In my view this can work in some villages but not in others. It's not going to be possible for all villages to have a new future. There are already a lot of villages in Tuscany that have been reborn after being bought up in their entirety by Germans, and there will undoubtedly be others in which investments can be made in a selective way. But I think others are doomed to progressive decay and abandonment. The decline in the population of Italy will in any case be evident. In the dispersed city the quality of living has fallen greatly and a question like the ageing of the population raises some truly critical issues. Imagining forms of reuse of the housing stock in such contexts is difficult, in part because it is all private. It will be hard to succeed in managing life in many of these situations. It requires a great capacity for invention.

OBRIST   Inventiveness will be needed for mobility in the dispersed city too. We are already seeing changes in this respect for traditional cities, too, the ones that were built prior to the invention of the automobile, and where it is easier to replace the model of car ownership with that of sharing. For the dispersed city it becomes more complicated, and the time wasted and money spent on a fluid mobility are considerable. If we calculate the costs of our cars, their insurance, their taxes and their fuel, and the amount of time we don't use them, we would have been able to afford using taxis for the whole of our lives, but above all we could have invented new models of services and sharing.

Perhaps the dilemma in a country increasingly divided between those who inherit something and those who don't, with major changes in the world of work, with growing costs of living and with a global environmental emergency, is strangely that it might just be the environmental and historical beauty which surrounds us that acts as a tranquilliser, and so we move too late to solve the crisis.

Transcript of a conversation that took place in May 2021.

Michael Obrist and Antonietta Putzu in conversation with Gianni Pettena (architect, artist, teacher and pioneer of Radical architecture)

On the road

Gianni Pettena, Ice House. Minneapolis, USA, 1971.

PUTZU — In Italy beauty can be found everywhere, in the fabric of our cities and in the landscape, and forms the usual backdrop to the activities of everyday life. At the same time, more has been built since the Second World War than in all previous eras. These structures rarely attain the characteristics and quality of the buildings and public places of previous centuries. Italy has become a land of *geometri*. [Note: The word loosely translates as 'surveyor'. Unlike in other countries, the Italian surveyor, or *geometra*, is able to design buildings on a modest scale, and of often equally modest quality, without the aid of an architect.] What happens in a society and a country in which beauty is rarely produced as an expression of complexity and contextual interconnection?

PETTENA — I think that the great anonymity of postwar urban expansion is not just an Italian phenomenon but a worldwide one. In the United States, too, it is hard to find examples of urban expansion that are acceptable, that have not been dictated by the logic of investment and profit. Architecture has always been, to some extent, in the hands of investors and politicians. I think it was this anonymity that led to a reaction in my generation. One of the most important schools of those years outside Italy was known as the Austrian Phenomenon. Hans Hollein and Walter Pichler were the main exponents of the movement and they were good friends of mine. At the same time, the Radical movement emerged in Florence out of a critique of the architectural debate of the time and the school of architecture that its members attended. It was a generational critique, of the vision of our fathers. Our fathers had waged wars. In those times everyone's fathers had waged wars and had always sent their sons to fight in them. And towards the end of the Fifties and in the early Sixties, those sons, people like us, had begun to have enough of this blackmail.

An emblematic example of this refusal was the protest of young people against the Vietnam War. This generation of young Americans started to say: 'Dear parents, you have declared this war and you can go and fight it yourselves.' The United States obliged young men to enlist and to go and fight the war in Vietnam. If you did not agree you were a draft dodger and committed a serious offence for which you could be sent to prison. There were two states that took in conscientious objectors: Canada and Sweden. The only two states in the world …
I'm telling you this story in part because, when I'd just turned thirty, I was invited to go and teach in the United States and among my students there were some Vietnam veterans, people who had been in Vietnam and were funded by the state under a programme for the return of veterans to civilian life. And among these students many had problems, including problems of mental balance, while many of the others were exceptional students. I remember one in particular who was of a very high level as a student of architecture.

This protest movement influenced and inspired us here in Europe, too. We had some interesting ideas for museums, for example. And they came from Austria (I'm an Austrophile: some of my blood on my mother's side comes from Vienna). Walter Pichler, for a strange case, came from Birchabruck (Deutschnofen/Nova Ponente in South Tyrol), a village very near Bolzano. Everything that had already been done in those years right at the beginning of the '60s, for example by Hollein and Pichler, is very interesting for its critique of a nondescript expansion which did not interpret the evolution in culture of the time … Many of the exponents of the Austrian Phenomenon were of my generation, just as my generation was represented in Florence. Five years ago, I curated an exhibition at Palazzo Strozzi that was a great success and was called *Utopie Radicali* [Radical Utopias]. It was about what the Radicals did, coming up with a critique of the architectural debate of the time as well as a critique of the school of architecture that they attended in Florence.

OBRIST — It's very interesting what you've said. I was also interested in this generation gap, the one between the generation before yours and your own … You went to university to a place with a very strong historical context, you studied in Florence surrounded by all this heritage and by the enormous collective know-how of the architecture of this city. And what interested us was also, that is, in a certain sense if we

Gianni Pettena, *Carabinieri* performance at the Palazzo Comunale, Novara, 1968.

Gianni Pettena, Tumbleweeds Catcher. Salt Lake City, USA, 1972.

	look now at where people are born on the suburban outskirts of European cities, there is in practice a lack of a context to teach you certain things.
PETTENA	Sure, that's exactly how it is.
OBRIST	You have been working on two levels. You received an education from the cities and from the mountains. And this dual sense of great beauty, that is a curse as well …
PETTENA	Undoubtedly. It's an 'imprinting' …
OBRIST	And it would be interesting to know, too, what you think about the TV, from which a new mass of vulgarity has come, that differs from your reflections on a mass culture which had a starting point, as well as an aim, that was completely different.
PETTENA	The TV of the Sixties was banal too, but it was full of creativity. Even if the shows, the entertainment, were meant for a large and simple audience, great artists often worked on the TV sets. Many young artists of my generation, Pino Pascali, Jannis Kounellis … and then I myself worked not for the television but for theatre groups. Because in those years, even a young architect thought about, and wanted, and was intrigued by this, and by those of the same generation who worked in other disciplines. That is to say, there were no disciplinary boundaries: we were all curious about everything. And so young musicians, filmmakers, actors or theatre directors were a source of inspiration and an opportunity for discussion, for hybridisation of all these experimental experiences. As a generation we were trying to express our point of view in the various disciplines, but it was not very clear what it might be because there were many of us and communication was done through small journals or through journeys we made around Europe as well as in the United States, and so on. And it should be noted, too, that people like Isozaki from Tokyo ended up in Paris in order to find out what was going on there in '68. And then a lot of artists came to Italy. In those years the Venice Biennale was always a place where we met. And the city where everyone ended up after the opening days of the Biennale was Florence. In Florence there was a climate very similar to what happened only every four years at the Venice Biennale, a climate … of exchange of ideas.
OBRIST	How had this climate come about and what changed afterwards?
PETTENA	The climate stemmed from this spontaneous discovery: that we were a generation which was not at all happy with the philosophical and even the linguistic legacy of the vision of the world held by our professors in the faculty of architecture, for instance.
OBRIST	What you're saying is very interesting, and coincides with this reflection on journeys and a personal Grand Tour by some figures in the world of architecture who became stimuli and sources of inspiration for others: if you look, for example, at Bernard Rudofsky, who on leaving Vienna discovered Italy, discovered Procida. He discovered the south and a certain Mediterranean way of thinking, as well, and then this became influential for others like Gio Ponti. The Mediterranean taught Rudofsky and Rudofsky in a certain sense taught Gio Ponti. It was an attempt to find the essentiality of things, of objects, of spaces and their integration into a typically Mediterranean life cycle. How do you view this phenomenon, this quest?
PETTENA	It was a search for the origins. In fact, it was the radicalism of those years that led to the fact that many of us, from Hollein to myself and from Superstudio to Archigram and Peter Eisenman, were labelled as 'Radicals'. We were reconstructing the basis for the interpretation of the world. We felt that our philosophy, the vision that we had, was profoundly different from that of our fathers who had started the Vietnam War and from that of our professors who had been trained between the two world wars and were stuck there. That was their vision, and I think it was a perfectly legitimate vision. It was a rationalistic, functionalist vision that was a reaction against the excesses of the beaux-arts, of art deco, of art nouveau. So, why not, we can say that the generation of those who were in their thirties between the wars reacted by putting architecture 'on a diet'. That is to say that architecture entered the monastery of a religious order that had been founded by Adolf Loos that put architecture on a diet: in other words, it cleaned up the menu of architecture from an excess of ingredients. But we of the postwar period had not suffered because of the war, we were too young … We looked ahead, we wanted everything. We had a vision that had not been influenced by the war. This was the first generation that looked at everything and wanted everything: that was how we interpreted the world. A generation that started to say: 'The architecture that they're teaching us is an architecture on a diet. You can't use colour, you can't use an architectural alphabet that is not strictly functionalist, and strictly rationalist.' But we were in our twenties, bursting with hormones [*laughs*] … What does this mean? It means that every day you have to struggle to bring the rational world and the functional world together. Every day, every morning your education requires you to be rational and control your hormonal impulses. So, architects have become experts at controlling the encounter between the emotional world and the rational world. That's how we can explain why there was this flowering of freedom in the language. [Ettore] Sottsass (as it happens, he had an Austrian

Gianni Pettena, Wearable Chairs. Minneapolis, USA 1970.

mother, he was of Ladin origin like me), despite being twenty-five years older, showed us that with architecture you can make love too. You can introduce both the rational and the emotional world into architecture, and you can get them to coexist. An explosion of freedom, but also an explosion of control of the possibility to bring back onto the menu of architecture all the ingredients, all the dressings, colours, forms, decorations that had been banned by the previous generation.

In this way we can explain, we can try to understand why all these things happened in the '60s. And not just in Italy. In Italy, strangely enough, this happened: the wealth of experimental contributions that originated in Florence spread to Milan with Ettore [Sottsass] who helped us with the first publications because he was already a fairly well-known architect and designer and helped us to get things published in Milan. So, Milan with Alessandro Mendini, with Franco Raggi, and so on, became another place where Radical architecture spread. Then there was Turin and Naples where there were various episodes ... And there was also the dialogue with the rest of the world, wasn't there? In Europe but in the United States too. The United States that have always attracted many Europeans for different reasons, ever since the time at the beginning of the twentieth century when Chicago was the city that represented the future. Since those times when, for example, Frank Paul (who was Austrian) used to draw marvellous cities of the future on the covers of science-fiction pulp magazines. Frank Paul who did wonderful things and is not very well-known, despite being trained as an architect, in both the European and the American architectural debate.

OBRIST We look back at those years of great change, when your generation won back the public space of cities. What you have described to us is the definition of a moment in history and the transformation of a place that today we would perhaps call a truly creative city (but not in a capitalist way) or a great cultural hub and accelerator: Florence ... You Radicals imagined technologies that in the last few decades have become realities which have changed society. How do you view these developments now? The technological transformation that you dreamed of has not only become a physical reality, but the technologies have been made available to everyone. And, looking back, how do you assess this evolution?

PETTENA At the beginning of your question you spoke of public space and that made me think about the fact that Italy has never been a united state until the end of the nineteenth century. There were lots of stamps stuck on the same envelope, right [*laughs*]? All on one peninsula, but there were many small states. And so, in Italy, we have inherited a lot of capitals. The *piazza* that is so Italian, synonymous of collective communication, [Note: The word piazza in Italian is also used to refer to crowds and mobs, to people in the streets.] in a way was born in the

Gianni Pettena, La mia casa all'Elba. 1978

capitals – and in Italy there are many cities that have been capitals, like Rome or Naples, even Palermo. There are cities like Turin that have the formal aspect of a capital, the public buildings, theatres, squares. Turin, Milan, Venice, Padua, Parma, Lucca, Mantua, Urbino … and I could go on. I've mentioned the very important ones that still have this character today, places like Urbino where a sort of periphery has also been added in the form of the university designed by Giancarlo de Carlo. Constructed in the Sixties, it is a piece of architecture that holds a serene dialogue with the historical Urbino. Then there are all these capitals with an identity, a legacy of a state that has a capital and this capital often has a piazza or piazzas among which there is always a main one.

OBRIST Let's talk about this public space, which interests me greatly. In a certain sense your generation, above and beyond its clear demonstration that even 'the private is political', made use of public space in a very conscious way. Today we have a new transformation in the nature of public space. Through social media, the private and the public are overlapping and becoming less clearly separated areas. The commons are lived in but not looked after. Italy is also the country of the neglect of public space and life, even though it is the country that gave the *res publica* its name.

PETTENA That's right, and also today it is not getting the attention it deserves. And there is not even the money: that is, it is not in the interest of the people with money to preserve the *res publica*, the grandeur of the capital, of the various capitals, and this is undoubtedly a problem. You know it is not just in the field of architecture, but of works of art in general that Italy has a fortune that is also a curse. It is a state made up of many small former states that neglect to maintain these treasures as the patrimony of the state. There are all these little former capitals that try in many ways to use a vast number of works of art: sculpture, painting, architecture and so on. In Italy there is such a density of these glorious pre-existences so important to the history of humanity, but Italy as a state does not have this awareness and neither does it have the bureaucratic structure capable of organising the maintenance and correct use of this historical heritage.

And that is why, for example in Venice, there are American as well as European foundations that choose a church, come to an agreement with the owner of the church – very often the Vatican – and say: 'We want to restore both the paintings and the architecture of this church but we want complete independence. You can keep an eye on everything we do, but the choices re design and technical aspects are ours.' So they hire restorers, including Italian ones, but they do it directly, not through building contractors, not through a bureaucracy that tries to make money out of this, whose aim is only to make a profit. On the contrary, the aim of the foundation is the preservation of the cultural heritage.

In Venice, for example, this happens very often. I remember that Hans Hollein, who in '96 was the director of the Architecture Biennale of which I was co-director, brought firms from Vienna: he didn't use Venetian ones. To avoid corruption, to avoid the waste of public money, he took care of things directly, having everything come from Vienna. This means that the negligence of the state is not even the state's responsibility but is due to the lack of a proper state structure. Today, in the midst of the Covid pandemic, with Europe giving us the possibility to improve our economy and state structures, Italy is going to have its last chance to become a state with a proper structure because we don't have one. What we have at this moment is a premier who has a lot of authority also at a European level, Mario Draghi, who has also been president of the European Bank, and has a very strong image in Europe. He has taken on himself the responsibility to give Italy a dignified, decent state structure, acceptable to the country and to Europe, of course. But why am I talking about this? [*laughs*]

PUTZU I just wanted to add a question on the subject of demonstrations, of public space. Italy saw a powerful feminist drive in the Sixties and Seventies …

PETTENA Indeed it did. I was a friend of Carla Lonzi, who wrote a book called *Let's Spit on Hegel*. She was a great art critic, and a central figure in Italian feminism, the co-founder of one of the first feminist organisations in Italy, 'Rivolta Femminile', at the end of the '60s. She was the partner of Pietro Consagra, a very good sculptor of that time.

PUTZU The shift in Italy from a feminism that was in the vanguard in the Sixties and Seventies to the contemporary objectification of women that seems to have taken its cue from the Mediaset empire is disconcerting.

PETTENA Nowadays there is a woman who can be considered as the equivalent of the Carla Lonzi of the '60s: Michela Murgia, who is undoubtedly the most interesting intellectual, and the most severe in promoting an equity of the roles of women and men in every discipline in Italy and elsewhere. Michela Murgia at this moment is a person of the highest quality, who is doing a wonderful work, in my opinion. And she has often been insulted on the social media: Instagram, Facebook, etc.

There is no doubt that in those years, too, there were women who played a crucial role … Katarina Noever, for example, who was the director of the first gallery showing 'Radical' works in Vienna in the mid '60s. It was called Section N and the interior had been designed by Hollein, I believe, together with Walter Pichler. Hollein and Pichler had staged the exhibition in the Nächst St Stephan gallery just a short time before and Katarina Noever became essential in her role of promoter of 'Radical' ideas, organising and bringing together experimental productions from all over Europe.

When I won the Trigon Award in Graz in 1971, I went to Vienna and on my way back to the hotel after dinner I stopped in front of a brightly illuminated shop window which turned out to be Section N. In fact, I walked past it, but then turned back because right in the middle, under the brightest spotlights, there was a piece that I myself had designed. It had been acquired by the gallery and I didn't know it was there. [*laughs*]

Another important woman at that time was Fernanda Pivano, who was married to Ettore Sottsass until 1970. She was very much involved in the American literature of those years: she had translated E.L. Masters' *Spoon River Anthology* as well as Hemingway, Faulkner and Dos Passos. After the war she promoted again the work of Hemingway and all the poets of the so-called Beat Generation, from Kerouac to Gregory Corso to Ferlinghetti … practically everything that was produced in the field of literature by those of my generation or a little older. Fernanda Pivano's foreign connections were also fundamental in drawing international attention to Ettore Sottsass's experimental work. There were a number of couples like them who had different works, but by living together shared their friends and their interests. For what concerns the Radicals, Paola Navone did her graduation thesis at Turin Polytechnic at the beginning of the '70s on the Italian Radicals. She interviewed Archizoom, Superstudio, UFO and myself in Florence. In those days I was already teaching History of Contemporary Architecture at the University of Florence and Paola Navone gave me her thesis to have my opinion, and then she managed to get this thesis published by Casabella under the title *Architettura Radicale*. And there were many other women ... My wife Stefania, who also has often translated the poets of the Beat Generation and has written her own stuff too, and at the same time has been at my side ever since I did my earliest works. For example, when I staged *Carabinieri* in Novara I think it was Stefania that was holding up the R. Her support was not just physical. It's still there now, we still work together. She helps editing my books or articles, for example. She keeps an eye on me and tells me: 'In my opinion what you're saying here is bullshit' [*laughs*]. She knew English very well, while, coming from Bolzano, I knew German. When I was invited to go to the States in 1969, after I had graduated in '68, Stefania took charge of all the correspondence in English because I didn't speak a word. It was not until the contract to go teach in the United States arrived that I did a crash course to turn my German into an improbable English. Which then improved, of course, but still ... So very often, while the man is under the spotlight, there is a great woman behind him, who often also has a parallel activity that shows her own ideas.

OBRIST   Let's go back to the issue of the transformation of society as well as technologies, and of the Radical ideas that have been expressed. Some of these things have become realities, others are still being fought over, and yet others have become dystopian. How do you see now the relationship between technology and society and what do you think of the influence that your generation has had? On the one hand it's a reminder, too, in a way, given that many of the themes that were important to you have fallen by the wayside, and perhaps need to be rediscovered.

PETTENA   Certain themes have been more than mislaid; they do not receive the theoretical attention that we gave them. The characteristic of the Italian Radicals was that the design side and the written side were of equal value. That is to say that what has been written by the Italian Radicals about their desires, about their ideas, including the theoretical, philosophical ones, is worth fifty per cent of their work. They wrote a great deal and drew a great deal and often realised their own work, although it was frequently temporary, as in my case. But they were realisations, materialisations, visualisations that were the result of a theory, of concepts, ideas. So what my generation sees in the work of people who nowadays seem to take their inspiration from the Radicals is a certain lack of theoretical underpinning, which I think is a pity. I often say this when I'm giving a lecture, a Zoom conference for a PhD course at some university or other: 'Please, generation of twenty- and thirty-year-olds, you have the duty as well as, of course, the right to express your ideas. Please do it the way we did at the same age. Because, by doing so, in the end you will make use of us as a reference and we can, at last, go fishing.'

So I am happy, indeed honoured, of the interest that the current generation has in our ideas, in the ideas of those who are now in their eighties. Because the search for a legitimate antecedent with whom one wishes to identify is often very hard. We did it too, respecting and loving the work of Adolf Loos, Frank Lloyd Wright, Le Corbusier and so on. We had these interests as students of architecture, and not just in the field of architecture, and respect, too. However, there was no dialogue with those famous people, while what is great today is that the younger generations of architects want to ask my generation: 'But how did you do these things?'

Speaking about these things, in my view, is useful for staying in contact, but we are perfectly well aware that the situation is now different. However, the energy of those who are now in their thirties and forties is so much greater than the energy we, who are in our eighties, have, that we really hope that the youngsters of today will make it possible for us to retire ... [*laughs*]. Although I myself would be sorry: I don't know how to fish, I prefer chatting with you. Indeed, I find it stimulating, as perhaps you do too. If so, it's the same for me.

OBRIST   We are a society that even before the crisis had to deal with the rise in the cost of housing. Airbnb has become a worldwide success and is making its way into cities everywhere as a platform. Florence is an excellent example of the physical change brought about by a digital platform. Digitalisation is transforming entire industries and regions. Artificial intelligence is both a potential and a threat for the near future. Amidst the acceleration of technological possibilities, we are seeing the emergence of new horizons and some are ready to go beyond them. In your days they went to the moon, now there is talk of possible missions to Mars. How do you see the potentialities and dangers of these aspects, especially after the pandemic?

PETTENA   What happens after the pandemic is something that, as far as Italy is concerned, really depends on the rebuilding of a state structure that has many flaws in the area of justice, in the administration of justice, in the corruption that is largely at a national level but is also international. The corruption of the various branches of the Italian mafia has spread all over Italy. Many local councils in the hinterland of Milan have been influenced by the monopolies, dismissed by the judicial authorities because they have been contaminated by the various mafias that have moved into the Milanese region. These criminal organisations are attracted by profit. In the northern part of Italy, including Tuscany, public administrations have been infiltrated by the mafia. And there is mafia in the Italian parliament, too. The mafia seeks profit and money and now it doesn't use weapons but ... Now, those criminals are all white-collars. Apparently they are people just like everyone else. But they are tools shaped to serve their interest by the mafias who still act with the same violence and have now extended their reach into Germany and France, for example.

The Radicals recently only extended their reach temporarily with two exhibitions in Brussels: one on Superstudio in January, February and March of 2021 and another one, that was a solo exhibition of mine, at the Fondation Hermès. All of this by chance. I knew nothing about the Superstudio exhibit as it was the surviving member of Superstudio, Gian Piero Frassinelli, who had organised the show. It was purely by coincidence that we were in the same city in the same period with an exhibition.

Many of the journalists who are looking at our works are not even thirty yet, and how they react is very interesting because they look at my works of those years according to their own desires. And so, in their enthusiasm or their criticism, it seems that our work, of us Radicals, has the characteristics of an inter-generational bridge. For example, a journalist in Paris wanted to know how come I was interested in nature, in the environment. And my interest in nature dates from the '70s when I interviewed Richard Buckminster Fuller, the 'grandfather' of contemporary environmentalism. I interviewed him three or four times. He was already fighting, then, to defend the planet's ecological balance. And much of my work then, which still has an experimental character today, was precisely on the subject of the relationship between what humanity does and the natural environment. Radical architecture also influenced many of the experiments carried out in the '90s by architects of the generation following ours. As well as in Florence, I taught at the Architectural Association in London, when the director was Alvin Boyarsky, and where the whole world of architecture passed. For example, I met Fuller when he came there to give a lecture. And Bernard Tschumi was teaching there and then brought his students to Florence to chat with us, but this was in the mid '70s. And among Bernard Tschumi's students there was one called Rem, Rem Koolhaas that is, and a young woman called Zaha Hadid. In short, in the mid '70s I often found myself working with Rem and Zaha, who were Tschumi's assistants on a course when he had started to teach at Columbia University in New York. I was a temporary assistant for three or four months at the Architectural Association in London and then went back to Italy while Zaha and Rem were there permanently, of course.

There was Elia Zenghelis, too … And the first to be influenced in his design by the Italian Radicals was Bernard Tschumi, who, when he did the Parc La Villette, openly referred to Archizoom's No-Stop City. In Rem Koolhaas's book *Delirious New York* there's a drawing by his wife Madelon Vriesendorp in which there are very clear quotations of the work of Superstudio.

And I myself have held a dialogue, for example, with James Wines of SITE, who had been inspired by a drawing of mine that had won the Trigon Award in 1971. And then Future Systems and Foreign Office, those two groups of architects who have sometimes quoted, even in a literal way, ideas of architecture coming from the Radicals that were never realised. They were ideas jotted down in a drawing, right? But that ten years later they became sources of inspiration for buildings of the next generation, in a fairly literal fashion and in an often quite creative way. So, in my view, this way of thinking has more influence today on environmentalist strategies. Not just on the context, that can be both natural and already modified by man in previous generations, in previous centuries.

OBRIST This is very interesting with regard to the pandemic, too, and the consequent rediscovery of nature and a new way of life between urban culture through the digital and going to live in more rural settings. In a certain sense it resembles the way you are living now: you're up there in Fiesole with a view of the city, at a fairly idyllic moment and at the same time you're connected with the world …

PETTENA Yes, because I'm ten minutes from the airport, ten minutes from the railway station and ten minutes from the centre of Florence. So, I can choose …

OBRIST But Zoom, too, allows you to live a life that was not possible before. For the post-pandemic discourse, Italy has become even more interesting: it has this enormous quality and in parallel this new connection with the world that opens up a lot of possibilities. In a certain sense you are living in a time that is the synthesis of many utopias.

PETTENA Yes, this is a bit what the youngsters who wrote those reviews of the exhibition in Brussels have seen. It is interesting to see these articles as the most recent reaction to Radical thinking.

OBRIST Where do you see developments that fascinate you in contemporary Italy? Being a visionary, where do you see places, moments, that intrigue you and that you would like to pass on to others. What would you suggest for an alternative Grand Tour of contemporary Italy?

PETTENA Take the museums, for example. The museums are often collecting what wasn't there when I was thirty. The museums are collecting ideas, those of filmmakers, of people in the worlds of theatre, of music. Everything that has been done in a virtual way has been extremely interesting, even if all this gets you very excited over the possibility of making love but you never actually get round to doing it. There's a lot of excitement but in the end, we are all stuck somewhere. I haven't seen my grandchildren for six months, for example … I think the museums are interesting …

I've looked into the real-estate market, and for example, here around Florence quite a few people are escaping from the city and trying to rent or buy something on the hills. But there is also a desire of clients for a larger or better organised house than the ones they have. They want a much more efficient house and if possible one with an outdoor area, be it a terrace or a garden. The real-estate market is making decisive moves in this direction. And then, of course, everyone wants to have a place by the sea or on the mountains where they can retire and work from home. I believe, for example, that the choice I made – and I'm not the only one - to buy a small property here in Fiesole with a view over Florence and not too far away from the airport and the railway station – is one choice that many people are trying to make today. Unfortunately, at the same time there are unauthorised changes in the environment taking place here in Italy, especially in the coastal areas. There's a good degree of anarchy in this effort to ruin the coasts. In fact, I still have a small property on the Isola d'Elba and a week after talking with a journalist from *Le Monde*, she asked me if she could rent my house on the island … That house has an exceptional location because you park the car, walk down thirty steps and arrive at the house. Then you go down another thirty steps from the house and reach the sea, where there is a little harbour for my exclusive use (for which I pay about 500 euros a year).

OBRIST You're talking about your project of an essential Radical house?

PETTENA Yes!

OBRIST Fantastic!

PETTENA And the sunset is right in front. Every evening the sun dies in the water …

OBRIST You started out from the mountains, you became what you are in part through a city, through Florence …

PETTENA … through New York …

OBRIST That's right. But what you were hinting at now is to some extent also a flight from the city. This is in a way the potentially dystopian question of this post-pandemic period. In a certain sense I can understand the desire to escape from the city as a possible reaction in a moment of crisis. On the other hand, we are seeing other developments as a response to the fragmentation of the city. We see the desire to create neighbourhoods, to regain possession of the city and the piazzas of which we spoke earlier. Communities that are organising themselves in a concrete way. How do you see this moment of desire for an exodus from the city, this promise of smart working and living digitally connected to urban or other worlds, immersed in an enchanting landscape or in a small village?

PETTENA It's not even a flight. It's a reorganisation of your way of thinking that requires a reorganisation of your spaces. This is how we could put it: the reorganisation that stems from Covid, from the pandemic, demands a different way of thinking, even in terms of how and where you live. This is very interesting. Just think that when I went to teach at the Architectural Association in London one of my students was a woman who was married to another teacher, Neave Brown, who had built council housing on the edges of a park in London. In Camden they had laid out a park that descended from the hill on which Camden stands, down to the rest of London, which is flatter. On a strip on the edge of this park had been built an estate of fifty council houses. But they had been so well designed that each unit was on two storeys and on the upper floor there was a terrace where you could grow a vegetable garden and a corner where you could even sunbathe in the nude. And this was low-income housing. When this architect took me to see it, the tenants of the various units recognised him and came to thank him. It is the only time I have ever seen the people who live in a place designed by an architect coming out on purpose just to thank him. Low-income, rent-controlled housing of excellent quality. If these units had been on the real-estate market, they would have fetched incredible prices.

OBRIST Given that you've told me that at your age you don't want to retire and go fishing, what dream would you still like to fulfil?

PETTENA I would like to work with different generations, letting them do their things, watching the young people design, make music, theatre and so on. With me standing to one side and saying: 'Watch out! Along this road you're going to come a cropper …' [*laughs*]

Transcript of a conversation that took place in April 2021.

Michael Obrist in conversation with Wilfried Kuehn
(architect, co-founder of Kuehn Malvezzi, full professor of architecture
and Head of the Department for Spatial Design at TU Wien)

On the radical normality of emancipatory alienation

OBRIST When we talk about Italy we focus a lot on words like beauty, corruption and *bel paese* – it's a nation that is surrounded by overused clichés. At the same time, there has been a longstanding effort to understand the entire Mediterranean region as a place to encounter deepness, beauty and emancipation. The Grand Tour was a key element in the education of the upper classes of certain European regions. Through this project, we have tried to go beyond the cliché and to discover something new and unexpected, but highly significant. You decided at a young age to leave Germany to go to Italy and study there, and from this point on a whole reflection on architecture and urbanism began for you. How would you see the term Grand Tour for yourself, as well as in relation to Italy and to the contemporary?

KUEHN I think that, in the north of Europe, people tend to grow up with a *Sehnsucht*, a longing for a place beyond the Alps, that is richer in historical sentiment and possesses an aura of deeper cultural relevance compared to their native region. This impulse to internalise history has persisted for centuries, and for a reason. The south of Europe has produced the most monumental discoveries across such diverse fields as painting, science, banking and architecture, and it was responsible for shaping northern Europe's cultural, social and economic development since the Renaissance's most successful and at once dangerous invention: capitalism. When the power dynamic shifted in the twentieth century, Italy became more and more a tourist destination, finally vulgarising the cultural role of the Grand Tour. At that moment, Italy stopped being this fascinating, far-off country, but rather became something ready there for consumption, a product for the industrialised north.

This tension between admiration and a certain disdain is emblematic for the perception of Italy in the contemporary era. It's fundamental to consider this double life of Italy in the collective consciousness of the north. As a child, when I travelled to Italy, it appeared astounding how culturally rich that country was. All its manmade and strikingly urban environment would speak to you, and not simply as an academic ideal, but something that resonates on a visceral level. In Goethe's diary of his travel to Italy, he reveals how, after crossing the Alps, the first thing he understood upon arriving in Verona was his need for new clothes. He perceived he was not fitting into the Italian environment – and I understood this sense of deficiency very well. On the other hand, Schinkel visits Italy with a more academic focus on classical architecture and to his own surprise falls in love with unforeseen romantic churches of early Christian times and with the simplicity of brick buildings like *fattorie* and *casali*. He understands Italy from an unexpected point of view and finds the country's refinement at a more pedestrian level, in basic and anonymous architecture. The daily life of Italy has an enormous refinement, manifested through a strong sedimentation of knowledge and techniques that are cultivated by repeating them time and again, meanwhile refining them while handing them down to the next generation. There is hardly a difference between building, clothing or cooking in this regard. Paradoxically, despite the very unashamed consumerism of today's Italian society, this precious knowledge lives on and is very much cultivated.

OBRIST Would you agree in saying that the Italian society is quite fractal? If we compare it to the French culture, which is also a very urban one, we might notice that between the most modest place to eat and the meals in the 'court of the king and queen', there is an unbelievable difference. It looks more like a culture of refinement which creates differences. On the other hand, if you go to the most expensive Italian restaurant in Rome and to a normal trattoria you might receive by name the same food, but the first one will be made out of much better ingredients of the same name. There is a capillarity of *sameness* on the territory and a refinement in the fractal itself.

KUEHN I agree with your observation and have always been fascinated by this aspect. Despite being a class-based society, like any other in the Western world, classes reflect one another in Italy in a way that seems almost fractal, indeed. Unlike in England or in France where exclusion between classes is quite prevalent, in Italy there is a form of inclusion by mutual emulation. There will always be a different refinement but the basic cultural elements are the same, which is why everyone in Italy, despite their social class, is enthusiastic about attending football games and enjoys the same food, just on different levels of refinement.

OBRIST Maybe this also made it possible that those who reign are not created by *otherness* but by *sameness*. If we look at Berlusconi's rise to power, it was like a prophecy of what Trump did later in the United States. Their success can be attributed also to their ability to appeal to the similarity to the masses, rather than to their uniqueness. Although being already incredibly rich and powerful, they were able to appeal as 'one of us' to the mass of voters. This is an interesting concept also in the context of urban landscape and architecture, since in the production of cities there is a reproduction of the surrounding territory, and therefore of a certain kind of 'sameness'. Although the *costumi* and the physical icons of each region may change, when you travel to Italy you have a territorial *Hintergrundrauschen* (background noise) of a certain kind of language which is not evident but permeates the ground for what the Italian cities are made of. The repetition of a few iconic models and of a few precise elements, together with the variety in morphology of the cities, shape within the sameness a complete difference.

Going back to what you said before about Goethe's *Italian Journey*, his letters and subsequent writings much later became hugely influential in Germany. The Italian urban culture, with its strong tradition of reflection on objects – whether it be fashion, furniture, architecture and cities – represents a departure from the traditional emphasis on the difference between an intellectual and materialistic culture within German culture, and its suspicion that dealing with *Oberflächen* (surfaces) can lead to an *Oberflächlichkeit* (superficiality). If you look at the German everyday desires, they are about having a little house in the countryside. The anti-urban idea of the forest as the *otherness* in Beuys or Novalis, where another life, a more real one, is happening, where the *'Blaue Blume'* ('blue flower') of German romanticism is hidden (and has never been found), is very present in the German tradition. In Italy, instead, where the consequences of (geo-)politics led to complete urbanisation of the landscape, there is less romanticisation of nature. If we think about the Mediterranean as the Etruscan paradise abundant of resources, sun and food, we could argue that there is no need to create another parallel life of desire, when and where life is already generating everything. On the theatre stage of life, these objects are not just distractions from the essential, but have meaning also by themselves. Only in a culture where 'objects' are already seen as important could Ettore Sottsass and other designers make an anti-design revolution, claiming that those objects were not really needed. In Germany no counter-reaction to an existing presence could be made; on the contrary, the Bauhaus could somehow create design only through the excuse of rationality.

KUEHN The concept of normality is deeply rooted in the Italian culture, characterised by a ritual of creating everydayness without trying to be outstanding, but rather cultivating a constant high level of normality. Everyday life in Italy is based on a good understanding of communication, emphasising the form of *fare bella figura*, accommodating your neighbour, not offending anyone. This culture of diplomacy is reflected in every single object, which should precisely not offend anyone. In northern countries, you could also be not nice, not beautiful, not good to look at, or even be impolite without creating disturbance. It's a cultural difference we might attribute to the fact that Italy has a much longer historical training in urban life and density which makes sameness a rather concrete reality.

When we bring the mastery of highly specific crafts such as silk-making or coin-making to architecture, and we think about what is the city, we find again this emphasis on updating traditions rather than reinventing. Italian modernism, for instance, always focused on improving the historical city rather than making a new one. The theme of repairing and adapting existing structures rather than starting from scratch is extremely relevant in contemporary discussions about adaptive reuse and ecological sustainability. In this sense, Italy could be seen as an avant-garde country, living in close relationship with its past. How can we bring this continuity as an asset together with a more challenging idea of change, as *sameness* comes with a downside, of course: monoculture, ethnic and cultural racism, and fear of the other seem to come along with the celebration of your own cultural techniques as second nature.

OBRIST Rome, for example, was a very transformative landscape, based on the materialistic evidence of a very specific element, which was stone. In the last century, specialisation increased a kind of solipsism also in architecture: every single house is conceived in terms of ownership and personal expression, creating a singular universe by its self, and so a jumble of many components which also makes reuse and recycle much more complicated. The economic growth that in Italy allowed people to have access to cars, or to build their own houses, also created a landscape of fragmentation and insufficiency at all levels. At the beginning of the 2000s, satellites discovered over two million illegal buildings in Italy. We can observe on the same territory tentative ideas like the €1 strategy to reuse collective *'manufatti'* of centuries such as empty villages, and at the same time really evident illegal and criminal acts contaminating the landscape. How do you see the difficulties of operating in such a line of thought?

KUEHN Coming back to what you said before with respect to *otherness*, we could say, for instance, that the way northern people reflect on the forest is a romantic one, while I personally have not encountered much romantic desire in Italy. I always felt that, rather than being romantic and longing for otherness, Italians appreciate realism as a way to deal with concrete facts, and that is a very strong groundwork on which you can build. But the same realism turns cynical when a post-Fascist government is elected, and this kind of ideology quickly evolves into forms of xenophobia and homophobia. Berlusconi's culture itself already embodied these kinds of negative values, and they are now fully ingrained in the political landscape. Like the party of Alleanza Nazionale, which never really managed to break off with the Movimento Sociale Italiano, the current government is still worshipping certain elements that are explicitly Fascist. There is sadly no rupture, no cutting off the Fascist past. How can a country that is so technically meticulous and thus cultivated at the same time be so cynical?

OBRIST Do you relate this to disbelief?

L.O.V.E. by Maurizio Cattelan in front of the Italian Stock Exchange in Milan. Credit: Sinah Hackenberg

KUEHN Indeed, it's like a resignation and a disbelief in almost everything. But it could also be the flipside of realism, and a reason to deal with this condition in a better way. Ultimately, the Renaissance brought us both the emancipated bankers *and* artists. Capitalism came to Italian history with these two options: emancipation from the rural Middle Ages meant that you could become free or become alienated, or even both at the same time.

OBRIST In this book, we tried to find projects which could inspire us, like the Riace model. It can of course be debated, but at least we can say that it was a search for new possibilities within migration and the shrinking of villages in the south; it was an attempt to rebuild a system of dignity. It is interesting to use a neorealistic approach regionally and do what Italy was always great at: investigation and documentation. If we analyse the global success of the TV shows *Gomorrah* or *Suburra*, we notice an attempt to understand spatial and political issues through the media of cinema. When they show very precisely how a trading square for drugs is made, the series is informing us also on a certain kind of urbanism. Rappers from many parts of the world today are going to the Vele di Scampia in Naples wishing to gain credibility: the otherwise pretty hopeless site itself becomes a desiring-machine for a perceived 'realness'. And I think that's interesting, frustrating and challenging at the same time.

KUEHN Yes. In the twentieth century, Italy had the strongest communist party in Europe – revolutionary ideals were always present also, because it is the continent's oldest capitalist country. But a revolution did not happen, and since the Partito Comunista vanished, we have a condition of widespread political resignation. I'm quite convinced that Italy is somehow everyone's future; it is simply more advanced and its cultural development is probably going to unfold everywhere else, at least in Europe.

OBRIST And how do you relate it to architecture?

KUEHN On the one hand, we see Italy as a country that is amazingly sophisticated architecturally, where there is a pervasive quality and respect for its tradition: you will not see Italians tearing down historical buildings as easily as elsewhere in the world. On the other hand, looking at the periphery and the cities from north of Milan up to Switzerland, where the Lega party is the strongest, you understand that there's not even the idea of a plan there. This kind of depressing drama shows that this abusive and alienating system is not sustainable any more. An artistic practice like the one of Maurizio Cattelan for me represents what is strong in Italy right now, telling us that within this absolute realism, you must make very strong gestures. To react and to do something subversive, we need to work within the framework of power instances such as the media, the Catholic Church, even Fascism.

Sottsass embraced this paradigm, without trying to make something 'clean' outside of this order. The architecture practice baukuh is interesting for the same reason. They are embracing this reality in their own way, without romanticising another imaginary world. We must start from the fragments that are there and turn them into something to work with. We cannot overcome what Berlusconi has done to politics, media and culture without digesting it in a critical way. If we consider this as an anticipation of what Trump later did in the United States, the Italian experience might really serve today as a potential model for other countries in order to learn from catastrophe. With the impending ecological crisis, Italy could become a valuable model for cultivating sustainable solutions by integrating historical continuities with advanced techniques. If Italy and Europe more broadly accept their heritage as compromised and in need to be seen from perspectives *other* than their own, there is a chance to reassemble the fragments of our cultural heritage into something innovative and resilient.

Transcript of a conversation that took place in January 2023.

Michael Obrist in conversation with Pier Paolo Tamburelli
(architect, co-founder of baukuh, full professor of architecture and
Head of the Department for Design Theory at TU Wien)

On geography, politics and form

OBRIST I want to start from a historic point of view: the Grand Tour was seen as an informal education based on a journey through a territory. Italy (along with Greece) was one of the main destinations of that tour and continues to provide an inspiring frame of reference. We are trying to look critically at the territory and the idea of the Grand Tour itself. The Last Grand Tour is an attempt to understand our times and Italian society, not just through monuments and icons, but mostly through the new contemporary phenomena and strategies of living which we find in different territories in Italy. We know about the famous *Italian Journey* of Johann Wolfgang von Goethe, a journey which has been a crucial moment for Karl Friedrich Schinkel as well. We know of Italy as a turning point in the work of Louis Kahn, as well as for Robert Venturi. We are now in 2023 – and I am interested in your intellectual reflection about Donato Bramante and Fischer von Erlach, and the attempts of architects to find universality throughout their work. What can we learn today from Italy?

TAMBURELLI Well – being Italian, the Grand Tour, at least the Grand Tour in Italy, is not really possible, because the Grand Tour is, by definition, made to a place that you recognise as 'other'. Not that there are no other possible models and destinations for a Grand Tour because, for instance, Robert Venturi and Denise Scott Brown went on a Grand Tour to Las Vegas. And at the same time, it's also true that, being from northern Italy, it has been possible in the past to consider Rome and Naples the objects of a Grand Tour. You can say that Piranesi spent his entire life in a sort of never-ending Grand Tour in Rome, still remaining a Venetian.

As for Bramante, he was from central Italy, made a very long detour through northern Italy and Milan in particular, and travelled to Rome only afterwards. It is a somehow counterintuitive itinerary if you think of a stereotypical idea of the 'Italian Renaissance'. And because of this strange path, Bramante gets to see ruins in a surprisingly new light, as something urgently near, as a fragment of reality, outside of any classicising nostalgia. And this is very clear in the work of Bramante and not in the work of his contemporaries or of the architects that came after him. For Bramante, Roman ruins were just there, and just there without any pre-defined interpretation (it would not have been like that anymore after Bramante, when it became impossible for his followers to ignore his own understanding of the ruins).

Starting here, from this evidence and this urgency, from this incredibly committed realism, I think it's possible to design your own Grand Tour by engaging in intellectual work as an architect. For instance, for us, at baukuh, it was important to go to Egypt in the early 2010s and see the brutal simplicity and the endless repetition of brick cubes – we were confronted with this incredibly simple architecture, houses repeated over and over and always the same concrete structure filled with bricks that were illegally baked out of the mud of the Nile Valley. Certainly, it is not an unproblematic architectural type, but it has some undeniable strength and we were quite impressed by that. So I guess it's possible to design (or maybe, more modestly, to *find*) your own Grand Tour today – with a lot of caveats and with a lot of framing because it's also quite a colonial practice. The Grand Tour presupposes that there is a place that is somehow a receptacle of culture, but also a receptacle of culture that is somehow lost and that you, the colonial explorer, should recover. So, not so innocent, the Grand Tour!

OBRIST The idea of otherness and the idea of exploration are not so unfamiliar in Italy itself. I think it is very interesting that we think of Italy with a preconception as one country, while its inner condition is vastly different when you look at the extension from north to south, where the north is touching central Europe and the south is settled right in the Mediterranean Sea, which makes the geopolitical situation inherently interesting. Both regions have had an impact on economy and technology for thousands of years, albeit the impact has been quite different in nature. But in that sense Italy becomes a

Poretti Pavilion. By baukuh.
Credit: Stefano Graziani

fascinating manifestation of global forces. And for us, therefore, it's interesting to understand what impact this has on architecture, on the city, and what it does with us as architects.

Being the political person that you are, looking at the world in an enormous transition and then trying to understand an architecture that is able to resist fashion or the fast answers – how would you position the political role of architecture?

TAMBURELLI   With some of the architects that interest me the most there is this capacity to reflect on the geographical and political dimension, this capacity of understanding where exactly you are. I think this is very clear in the case of Fischer von Erlach, who, in my opinion, was not that incredibly interesting as a stylist, as a creator of forms. I think Hildebrand – his rival – was actually better at that. But Fischer was, I think, more conscious of his own role inside a state bureaucracy and capable of understanding the nature of the empire for which he worked, and able to problematise this relation in his amazing, very surprising, book *Entwurff einer historischen Architectur*. Or, to jump to a completely different context, Vilanova Artigas is an architect that is capable of placing himself as a communist architect in the southern part of the world while still belonging to a Western tradition, and using this particular angle to look at classical architecture from a completely different position. And this commitment to 'political auto-cartography' is evident in both their books and their buildings.

Architecture is a way of organising resources, a lot of money, a lot of labour and a lot of materials. This work of organising cannot be separated from certain positions in society, geography and so forth. In Italy, this reflection has been very strong in a certain period of time, certainly during the thirty years after the Second World War. Italy was incredibly interesting as a place of cultural production, entrepreneurial initiative and political elaboration.

Of course, this is a period that is nowadays considered very positive for all of western Europe: the so-called *Trente Glorieuses* – but they were even more glorious in Italy than in other places. And the 'Inglorious Thirties' that came afterwards were even more inglorious in Italy than in other parts of western Europe. Exactly because there was no more this capacity to reflect and to profit from a hybrid condition of a country that is immersed in the Mediterranean Sea in the south, directly in relation with Africa and the Arab world, and directly plugged into central Europe. Italy was consciously a bit different, not your prototypical modern Protestant industrial country (and I say *was*, because this sort of consciousness is unfortunately entirely lost in the contemporary Italian establishment).

Italy in the 1960s was less modern, but also more modern, at least to a certain extent. And the hybrid nature of the country was, I think, looked at with some love by a lot of politicians and intellectuals – Pier Paolo Pasolini, Enrico Mattei, Aldo Moro, even Palmiro Togliatti's very stiff Communist Party was not opposed to it – and by a lot of figures who understood this as an opportunity. Then, around the 1980s, this approach died, fundamentally for a lack of courage of the Italian elite, be it entrepreneurs, politicians or intellectuals. I think this is incredibly evident in the cultural production, where in the end there are less material constraints and the lack of ideas is more evident.

If you try the very unsatisfying initiative of reading contemporary Italian literature (of course, with the exception of Michele Mari), you would run into infinite bad attempts at redoing what American writers were doing twenty years ago. And, obviously, this thing does not work, because that is not where innovation can emerge. There cannot be any innovation without an earnest confrontation with the specific reality of the place where you live and work. And this, in contemporary Italy, would require some courage and, fundamentally, accepting the archaic and provincial (but not only archaic and not only provincial) character of this context. I think a lot of freedom could be gained by learning to look at the Italian context from a global and international perspective. What has been happening in Italy in the last thirty years has been exactly the contrary:

Model of the Scalo Farini Masterplan. By baukuh, Atelier Kempe Thill, Christ & Gantenbein, Lola, Onsitestudio. Credit: Stefano Graziani

OBRIST — trying to bring into the provincial Italian dimensions something that was copied from the international scene (which, by the way, doesn't really require a lot of talent). I think we should do exactly the opposite: use the specificities of the Italian context to readdress global problems.

Reflecting on the production of architecture in Italy, it is evident that history shows us that built structures very much remain through time. The ideology, the social system, the power structures, and even the functional programme which were the starting point behind their construction, might have disappeared, but a lot of monuments, houses, villages and even entire parts of cities survived the passing of time and are becoming cyclically empty structures ready for new interpretations.

The phenomenon of renovation and transformation was always present on the Italian territory, evident in the urban structure of Rome itself, and in masterpieces like Santa Maria degli Angeli e dei Martiri by Michelangelo built of and within the remaining ruins of the former thermae of Diocletian.

Also in this book we have examples of reuse of objects for different means. We investigated in former office buildings which were occupied by desperate citizens in need of homes, becoming new places for a different way of living and trying to be a very specific answer to the latent housing crisis in the big Italian cities. But it became also evident that those projects would not have been so successful if the form of those buildings itself had not been so resilient, by enabling a certain efficiency and capacity for a multitude of programmes and processes.

We could say that architecture, through clever choices in form-giving, can become in a very pragmatic way operational and remain so even longer in time and in use. Not just by looking back at history, but also by reusing and inhabiting already existing architecture, we might find out that certain forms enable a variety of things and might be more resilient than others, or at least more easily adaptable. This still includes the possibility that in the coming decades of adaptation and transformation of buildings we might find out the opposite …

If I look at your reflection and on the collective praxis of baukuh, I see a strong interest in those kinds of questions of form.

TAMBURELLI — Form can be an extremely strong tool. And it's actually, I believe, the only tool that is in the hands of the architect, her or his only weapon. That's also the reason why we normally use simple forms: circles, squares, rectangles, because they are immediately recognised and immediately stored into memory.

I don't think they mean anything. My 'theory of form' on this level is really basic: if you enter into a room that is roughly a square, you recognise that it's roughly a square, nothing more than this. And if you recognise the room as a square, then you also probably remember it better. It's a purely visual thing and not that sophisticated, to be honest. Then, starting from this very basic assumption, it is important to recognise also that architectural form contributes to the establishment of institutions and architecture is a way to institutionalise certain practices. Buildings are quite a powerful 'format', and still very influential. No matter the digital context in which we live, buildings are still very, very influential.

This idea of architectural form (that relates to some basic geometric properties of spaces but does not imply any meaning for those forms, and that sees the production of form as an 'institutional' operation) leads to a 'closed' idea of form. So, against Umberto Eco's idea of the 'open work', I would defend the idea of a 'closed form', something that is the result of a process, that remains, that has fixed properties, that determines a finite set of possibilities, that produces a friction with the context in which it happens to be. And I also think that form is useful because, when you are fed up with it, you can just destroy it and then at least you have something to destroy. That's also why I have always been rather suspicious of these buildings and rhetoric that are deliberately formless, because I think it would be also very difficult to criticise them.

Again, there's a responsibility in form and there is an explicit violence in establishing this form which I

House of Memory. By baukuh. Credit: Stefano Graziani

think is the violence that is associated to civilisation and that we have to deal with and that we can use positively or not. But we shouldn't be afraid of it. I believe in form. I'm a formalist, if you want. But there are all sorts of limitations to it. And I believe in it exactly because it's not everything. I think it's fascinating that certain buildings with certain very precise forms survive over extremely long periods of time, have been transformed and reused but still maintain something. But this is interesting because there's also other buildings that have been smashed and are not there anymore. And some of them were also extremely beautiful. And we – or, at least, me – regret the fact that the Septizodium or the Penn Station do not exist anymore. But that's part of being a building, and a building can be destroyed. And the buildings that have not been destroyed, which is also of value of some sort, acquire more relevance because of that. And I think, in the end, it's a tool – form.

OBRIST In Italy, in certain kinds of urban structures, you could see evidence of 'city first, architecture second', where the architectural objects became an integral part of the city structure and where the urban structure and morphology dictate the framework of the possibilities. And parallel to that, we have produced the *città diffusa* just like everywhere else in Europe. We have this gigantic in-between city stretching from Torino to Venice, along the highway with the fragments of Renaissance cities and '*capannoni*' (sheds), new shopping malls, new areas of leisure and a multitude of singular disconnected objects of houses, etc.

It seems that everyone reacts to those developments with some sort of 'super-pragmatism', because today's situation seems like it is 'too big to fail'. The in-between city is not yet a project, but was mostly a result of the economy and the frameworks of mobility. As the connecting glue between the spots on the territory is a cheap mobility, just the transformations of paradigms and tools in the world of mobility might change it or even create a different territory. Do you see some new urban paradigms emerge?

TAMBURELLI I'm not seeing urban paradigms emerge in contemporary Italy because contemporary Italy is a country that is not growing in demographic terms. So we have a lot of cities that are losing population, but not in a dramatic way like we saw in eastern Germany in the 2000s. It's a slow decrease, almost unnoticeable, but if you go to mid-sized Italian cities, particularly northern Italy, you would notice that something is missing, that the urban life that is supposed to be there is not there anymore. This is interesting because all these cities are shrinking: Cremona, Alessandria,

Trieste and in some places, you can start to see that, if not for the architecture, they should not be called a city anymore. Take Cremona: it has a huge cathedral, a couple of huge monasteries, three or four big palazzi, a city hall, an opera theatre. Everything that defines a city is there, the 'urban apparatus' is far more convincing than in a lot of cities around the world with one million inhabitants, but this city doesn't have the population anymore. The local bourgeoisie is not buying houses for their kids in Cremona anymore; they are buying in Milan or somewhere else. So all of these cities have a really serious identity crisis. Their public building apparatus starts to be unsustainable, the upkeep starts to be a problem, and it's a problem which people tend to deny, a problem that makes them sad and that they want to avoid.

A similar situation occurs in the large stretches of Lombardy and Veneto, where the landscape was shaped by the manufacturing industry. But while the region is still very productive, the industry doesn't use as much space anymore and there are many workshops and warehouses stand empty. These *città diffusa* also have the problem of being actually really ugly. That's one of the things people abroad tend to forget about Italy. Italy can be very beautiful but it's also very ugly. And realising how ugly it is would be great progress, looking dispassionately at all these single-family houses that were built in the 1970s, which are now totally unsustainable from an environmental point of view. They are dispersing an incredible amount of energy, they're literally crumbling, and are also crumbling into the family budget of every single Italian family: the grandparents believed that they could leave a valuable single-family home to their children, but actually they ended up leaving them nothing. This stuff is absolutely worthless. Nobody wants to buy those homes anymore. And so what was probably the biggest part of the financial wealth of the Italian middle class disappeared into almost nothing in the span of fifteen years. I cannot see how this gigantic financial and social and territorial problem can be fixed. Still, for now, not so many people are paying attention to that, at least in the political landscape. It certainly is a topic in academia (Federico Zanfi is doing a great job about this), but it is not a discussion on Italian political TV shows.

The other thing I want to say is a bit separated from that. Before, you mentioned renovation as a new task for architecture in at least western Europe. And I agree with you; all of the competitions we are invited to at this moment are renovations. This is the professional condition nowadays, but it's not really a new condition. Like, for instance, the Renaissance was mainly a very long period of renovation of pre-existing buildings. For example, Palazzo Rucellai is a fusion of two pre-existing buildings and Alberti just did the facade. The Renaissance was a period of change in architecture history that was totally independent from demographic growth and technological progress. The technology of the Renaissance Italian architecture is exactly the same as in Gothic architecture. Nothing changed, only taste. And this is interesting, if you look at it from a contemporary point of view. We are still building with a technique that is, from a structural point of view, that of modern architecture. Of course, we are paying much more attention to the insulation now, but that's it. But this doesn't mean that architecture is not changing. And on that level, the Renaissance situation might be a little bit less alien than we might think. And it would be a fantastic thought experiment to imagine what Alberti or Peruzzi could have done with all these *capannoni* in the countryside.

OBRIST What place would you show to somebody in Italy right now? Where is the place where you could say 'maybe I don't understand it yet, but there is something fundamentally interesting happening'?

TAMBURELLI I think a place that would be interesting to see is Genoa. Genoa lost one third of its population from the 1970s on. In Genoa, dead people are outnumbering newborn babies three times. Genoa was an industrial city, a dry, nasty industrial city – actually it was maybe the only city in Italy where terrorists of the Red Brigades really had some support. The industry was more or less all state-owned. This ugly, polluted, dirty city was still the incredibly beautiful baroque and Renaissance city, but completely forgotten in the dust and not touristic at all. The old harbour was still closed off from the rest of the city until the early 1990s. Then the harbour, the big steel plant and other important chemical plants got privatised in the 1990s. Now, the old harbour is open, there is this intervention by Renzo Piano that gives a relation to the water back to the city, but at the same time, the industrial city died. The private entrepreneurs who got the previously state-owned factories did not invest; slowly all the factories closed. So the city that was once ugly and nasty but alive, now it is pretty but dead. And there are huge problems left; the urban growth of the 1960s massively invaded the surrounding hills, leaving huge geological problems. Genoa is very interesting. It's beautiful and sad, and very interesting.

Transcript of a conversation that took place in January 2023.

Detours to Italomodern

Martin Feiersinger
Werner Feiersinger

In 1984, Gino Valle visited the University of Applied Arts in Vienna and gave a talk. He showed several of his prestigious, pragmatic buildings, as well as a much smaller project, the Casa Rossa in Udine [1]. Something about this house struck a chord with us. It exemplified what Robert Venturi was referring to in *Complexity and Contradiction*, perhaps even more so than the iconic house he designed for his mother. Valle's design might also be considered a variation on the theme of the ordinary house. Shortly thereafter, we came upon a building at the other end of the spectrum, one that looks like a gigantic typewriter. It was La Serra in Ivrea [2], a training centre for Olivetti by Iginio Cappai and Pietro Mainardis. These two poles made us start to think about the diversity of Italy's postwar architecture. How had the buildings of this era stood the test of time? What signs of appropriation could be identified? Did the concepts have an influence on the surroundings? Were the buildings still used as originally planned?

Twenty years later, we began to systematically document buildings throughout northern Italy. When the opportunity to exhibit our photos at AUT, Innsbruck's architecture gallery, arose, our work intensified. At this point we had to find a title for our series of detours on roundabout paths off the beaten track of modernism. Disregarding fiercely contested demarcation lines, we simply called it Italomodern. The first phase, which culminated in the exhibition in Innsbruck in 2011, documented eighty-four projects. A second exhibition there, with 132 additional works, followed four years later. In each case a catalogue was produced.

A variety of journals, monographs and surveys served as the basis for the research. For instance, in *Domus*, no. 801 (1998) we first encountered Giuseppe Pizzigoni's work, an oeuvre with many shifts – moving from neo-classicism to rationalist architecture, then on to studies in geometry and experimentation with thin concrete shells. In 1960, he employed his novel technique for both a church [3] and a pigsty [4].

Our documentation is structured chronologically. Italomodern begins in 1946 with Pizzigoni's Casa Minima in Bergamo [5], a row-house prototype, and culminates thirty years later in Giuseppe Gambirasio and Giorgio Zenoni's elevated courtyard houses in Spotorno [6].

This time span encompasses a remarkable range of groupings and stances: *tendenza organica*, neorealism, Neoliberty, brutalism, various neorationalist positions, as well as technological stances, daring structures and extravagant spatial conceptions. We included some masterpieces by celebrated architects – for instance, the Via Quadronno apartment building in Milan by Angelo Mangiarotti and Bruno Morassutti [7] – but our attention was more often directed to minor works by acclaimed architects and, most often of all, to works by lesser-known architects which, upon completion, received only limited or regional exposure.

Throughout the course of this project, the notion of duality propelled our search and enhanced our understanding of the era's multifaceted architecture scene. In the case of Milan-based Luigi Caccia Dominioni [8/9/10], choosing among his hundreds of completed buildings was a nearly impossible task. Caccia Dominioni once proclaimed that he felt more at home visiting a building site than participating in academic discourse. Yet, with his refined designs of ceramic facades, he established a school of his own. In contrast, Vittorio Giorgini's work consists of just a few buildings, two of which are located right next to each other in Baratti: his own wooden, tree-house-like hexagonal cabin [11] faces his most extreme project, a zoomorphic concrete-shell structure [12]. In 1969, Giorgini moved to New York, where he began a career in academia.

Another pairing of extremes has to do with magnitudes of scale. Luigi Carlo Daneri's gigantic Forte Quezzi housing complex [13] high above Genoa – dubbed *il Biscione* – consists of five serpentine apartment buildings which follow the contours of the hillside. At the other end of the spectrum is a bivouac perched atop the Grignetta [14] designed by Mario Cereghini. His career had two overlapping phases: on Lake Como he was committed to rationalism, while in the mountains he was a contextualist who took cues from local building traditions. For his project on the peak of the Grignetta, however, Cereghini metamorphosed into an engineer. His design of the space-capsule-like bivouac employed prefabricated aluminium panels light enough to be carried to the summit by hikers.

These examples provide a small glimpse of this prolific period – a period characterised above all by playful experimentation, vitality and passion. Perhaps these many detours, taken over the course of a dozen years, amount to a grand tour after all.

This work was originally published in *Domus*, no. 1013, May 2017.

[1] Gino Valle, Casa Rossa, Udine, 1965–66.

[2] Iginio Cappai, Pietro Mainardis, La Serra, Ivrea, 1967–75.

[3] Giuseppe Pizzigoni,
church, Bergamo, 1960–63.

[4] Giuseppe Pizzigoni, pigsty, Torre Pallavicina, 1960–64.

[5] Giuseppe Pizzigoni, Casa Minima, Bergamo, 1946.

[6] Giuseppe Gambirasio, Giorgio Zenoni, residential complex, Spotorno, 1976–83.

[7] Angelo Mangiarotti, Bruno Morassutti, apartment building, Milan, 1960–62.

[8] Luigi Caccia Dominioni, apartment building, Milan, 1955–57.

[9] Luigi Caccia Dominioni, convent, Milan, 1960–63.

[10] Luigi Caccia Dominioni, apartment building, Milan, 1960–61.

[11] Vittorio Giorgini, Hexagon, Baratti, 1957.

[12] Vittorio Giorgini, holiday home, Baratti, 1961–62.

[13] Luigi Carlo Daneri, Forte Quezzi housing complex, Genoa, 1956–68.

[14] Mario Cereghini, bivouac, Grignetta, 1966–67.

The importance of being Ernesto

Shumi Bose
Roberta Marcaccio

1 E. N. Rogers' address was bookended at the close of the exhibition by a lecture from G. E. Kidder Smith, who at the time was preparing the seminal volume *Italy Build* (1953), for which Rogers was to provide the foreword.

2 Transcription of Rogers' speech taken from the article: 'Italian Contemporary Architecture. Opening of the Exhibition at the RIBA, 21 March 1952', in the *RIBA Journal*, April 1952, 210–11. The original catalogue, held at the AA, carries evidence of these difficulties. Its archival content is only partially available (only the introductory texts by Robert Furneaux Jordan and Giulio Carlo Argan appear in the handbook, not the images and comprehensive list of the exhibits) and accompanied by an apologetic caveat 'Because the material has not been received from Italy in time, it is much regretted that it has been found impossible to include in the handbook a list of the exhibits in the Exhibition.'

3 Ibid. *RIBA Journal*.

4 The general opinion of suspicion towards Italian architectural design, and moreover the suspicion towards the open appreciation thereof, has been corroborated in interviews with Joseph Rykwert, John Melvin and others who would have inhabited the concentric circles around architectural academia in the decades following the Second World War.

5 The conflict in depicting the 'Italian' identity can best be apprehended when viewing the content of both exhibitions simultaneously, or as they were shown, in relatively close temporal proximity.

6 A certain nationalistic sentiment – fostered by the Fascist regime – was common amongst the Italian urban middle classes in the early twentieth century and especially characterised the Italian Jewish middle-class, which, on the wave of its success in politics, science, industry, the arts and journalism, moved towards a more complete assimilation. During the first phase of the regime, the Fascist party showed no anti-Semitic sentiments and it is proven that many Italian Jews took part in the 1922 PNF march on Rome and served as ministers in Mussolini's government.

7 'As far as the issue of nationality is concerned, I would prefer and indeed be happier if you were to keep your original one. However it goes without saying that I would never say "no" if this could, in any way, jeopardise the career you have chosen for yourself.' Romeo Rogers to E.N.R., 26 September 1932, BBPR, private correspondence. Source: Luca Molinari, *Continuità: a response to identity crises*. Doctoral dissertation, Delft University of Technology, 2008, 44.

8 Anselmo Bucci to E.N.R., 10 September 1929, BBPR, old correspondence. In ibid., 43.

In the mellow autumn of 1949, an exhibition entitled *Italian Architecture* opened at the Royal Institute of British Architects (RIBA), London. The photographs on display – a collection assembled by Mr Ralph Deakin, Foreign Editor of *The Times* – depicted a somewhat mummified appreciation of the Italian context: grandiose, canonical and romantic examples from Italy's built heritage, encompassing medieval to baroque and Renaissance styles.

Just a few years on, in March 1952, another exhibition with a strikingly similar title – *Italian Contemporary Architecture* – inaugurated in the same premises. Despite the titular echo, the agenda of the two could not have been more different. Curated by Franco Albini and Enrico Peressutti, the 1952 exhibition was the first international show dedicated to Italian modern architecture, showcasing works by Sant'Elia, Terragni, Pagano, Persico, BBPR and De Carlo, to name a few.

Representing the Italian architects – in particular the Italian faction of the Congrès Internationaux d'Architecture Moderne (CIAM) – the architect, editor and educator Ernesto Nathan Rogers of the Milanese office BBPR was called upon to give an opening address.[1] Rogers credited his colleagues with the Herculean task of amassing the works on display, in spite of 'customs barriers, bureaucracies and all the other Philistines who still divided Europe up by fictitious frontiers'[2] and affirmed that the aim of *Italian Contemporary Architecture* was to elucidate some 'thirty years of Italian architecture – the first part of which [...] had been completed in the shadow of political conditions.'[3]

Directing attention towards contemporary Italian cultural production was undoubtedly a sensitive undertaking, following the suspicion related to Italian Fascism – still palpable in London at the time[4] – and the scepticism towards Italy as a protectionist, provincial and underdeveloped field for architecture. With characteristic, almost jocular delivery, Rogers' comments gave bite to the argument presented by the 1952 exhibition, evoking the reality of a nation – and a man – in deep, but vital, conflict with a complex history.[5]

His frontal, mediating role, despite not being one of the curators, is coloured by Rogers' personal entanglements between England and Italy, and as such requires one to unwind several prior decades. Born in 1909 to an Italian mother and a British father, Rogers suffered rather than enjoyed his dual inheritance. Up until his thirties, he had negated the anomalies of his identity – his Jewish origins, dual nationality and erratic youth, spent between Trieste, Zurich, Rome and Milan. In fact, his actions demonstrate an explicit rejection of any obstacle to his feeling at one with the society he was in.[6] Such was Rogers' desire to naturalise as an Italian that he took the formal step of renouncing his British passport, despite the tender consternation of his father.[7] He was extremely reserved on religion and proved to be reluctant to learn the language of his Anglo-Saxon forefathers, as an urgent letter from his art teacher, the painter Anselmo Bucci, shows in 1929:

'Dear disciple, my brief stay in your country has left me an almost civilised person. As you can see I am responding to letters, immediately. I beg you not to get lost in the *alti adagi* but to go to England. In the meantime, you must learn English [...] Learn it immediately. I already have the address of a teacher, a rather mature Irish lady whom I shall seduce (I will introduce you afterwards).'[8]

Prior to the outbreak of the Second World War, Rogers' connections to wider architectural debates were navigated through editorial contributions to the influential journal *Quadrante*, which offered a way into the rationalist networks between Como, Milan and Rome as well as into the international cultural panorama of the CIAM. It was finally through these intellectual pretexts that Rogers travelled to London, in July 1939 (following Italy's decision to promulgate Racial Purity laws in 1938).[9] There is little to record about this primary trip to the land of his forebears; only that the scarcity of prospects led him to return to Italy. Here he remained until 1943, when the worsening of the wartime conditions for Jews – and at the urging of his friends – obliged Rogers to abandon his chosen homeland and seek refuge in Switzerland. The years in exile allowed for a reorientation of his own aspirations and thinking, and a wider interrogation of the Italian interpretation of modernity.

The 1952 exhibition *Italian Contemporary Architecture* ignited a reappraisal of Italian architecture, of which Rogers was the centre; his role as intellectual mediator between the Italian and international scene had gradually consolidated in the years subsequent to his exile. Indeed, the very idea of such an exhibition had been proposed by Robert Furneaux Jordan in 1949, during a period of apparently frenetic exchange between Italy and England, and more specifically between Rogers and the Architectural Association (AA). Moved by the wave of general appreciation and acclaim towards Rogers[10] – who had dazzled as chair of the Educational Commission at the CIAM VII in Bergamo earlier that year – the machinations of Jordan,[11] then-director of the AA, were instrumental in securing a role for Rogers within London's critical and academic discourse.

Following a few false starts and much hyperbole, the first CIAM Summer School took place at the AA between 8 August and 2 September 1949,[12] with Rogers as an invited juror. Open to international students, the course reflected a preoccupation to introduce younger generations to the discourses of the CIAM congresses. The idea was to liberate the education of the young architect from generational oppositions and to allow for an open and free exchange between students, tutors and the practitioners involved. Thus the CIAM Summer School inaugurated, and tested, a new paradigm of pedagogy – one theorised during CIAM VII by the Rogers-led education committee. The model was based on dialectics, teamwork, international exchanges and interdisciplinarity, as well as arguing the necessity for studying the history of architecture, not in isolation but in direct relationship to the immediate problems of design.[13]

Less than a month later, Rogers again returned to London as a visiting tutor, during the first semester of the AA's autumn term. The speed at which Rogers' presence was resumed at the AA reflects a deliberate move (by Jordan) to expose the school to multinational ideas – although internal minutes reveal a certain consternation regarding the teacher's origin, as the following statement testifies: 'The Principal said there was no special significance in the fact that two Italian teachers [the other being Peresutti] were to be engaged for this present, but the chance had presented itself of obtaining two very good men. He asked the council to agree [...]'[14] The notion to bring Rogers back to London was hastened by the unfortunate death of the previously appointed Jaromír Krejcar;[15] for this reason there is no trace of a syllabus. Whether this situation speaks more strongly of the AA's urgency to fill the seat or of Jordan's deliberate championing of a contemporary Italian voice is open to debate, notwithstanding the acclaim and appreciation that Rogers enjoyed at the time. As Pat Crooke, one of Rogers' students, recalls: 'For a large number of AA students, Ernesto's visit was very influential [...] His charisma, in fact, worked on all of us.'[16] The lasting impact of his presence is testified by John Melvin – who studied at the AA in the late 1950s – for whom Rogers' legacy had provided an alternative means of reading historical influence, as opposed to the then-present factions of classicists such as Quinlan Terry, or the proto-brutalist Smithsons.[17]

So successful was Rogers' stay that Jordan made an informal 'exchange' agreement with him, whereby the other BBPR partners would come to the AA in their turn as visiting teachers, while a succession of AA students would each spend a term based at BBPR's Milan studio – a sort of ad-hoc Erasmus exchange. For, in the meantime, BBPR's studio at Via dei Chiostri 2 was fast becoming the Italian base for foreign architects linked to the international CIAM circuit: between just 1947 and 1948, Neutra, Maldonado, Kaufmann Jr, Aalto, Giedion and Roth were received by Peressutti and Belgioioso. AA students, including John F. C. Turner and Crooke, enjoyed 'exchange' stays at BBPR – although the scheme was quietly disbanded soon afterwards.[18]

What Rogers distilled from his encounter with the 'orchestra of students and the chorus of the AA'[19] was a certain 'pre-existing ambience' of dissent. On various occasions, he describes his exchanges with 'the most rebellious, the most obstinate and pretentious students,'[20] such that he refers to them affectionately as 'Mssrs We do not agree'. This 'motto', Rogers explains, means 'We do not agree, because we should like to do it better', and, as he puts it, provides the fundamental key to the 'anti-conformistic spirit of the Modern Movement'.

'We do not agree' would become Rogers' own motto as well as that of BBPR: it indeed suggested that dialectical and agonistic design method – *dubbio metodologico* (systemic doubt) – that distinguishes later practical manifestations of the office's work; as in, for instance, the Torre Velasca or the complex on Piazza Statuto-Corso Francia in Turin. Both projects are the outcome of a tortuous design process of constant interrogation – consecutive approximations and subsequent repentances – as the multiple 'in progress' variations of BBPR designs would testify.

England's cultural, technical and even socio-political milieu provided a consistent background against which Rogers – being both 'of' and outside of it – could constantly measure and mould his own intellectual (and strongly 'Italian') positions over the years.

Reflecting on his experience as a teacher at the AA, Rogers recalls that students expressed a 'persistent critical sense of acute dissatisfaction with every idea acquired, but

---

9. Alberico Belgioioso describes the exact moment in which Rogers learns of the promulgation of Racial Purity laws in 1938. Approaching a nervous breakdown in the streets of Milan, Rogers predicts an apocalyptic end for himself, the Jews and the nation – a somewhat striking reaction, given his measured nature and inexplicable obstinacy, a few years later in 1943, in refusing to acknowledge the worsening of the situation and hesitating to leave the country.

10. To the Bergamo CIAM conference a delegation of students, among them Andrew Derbyshire, was sent to report back to the AA in London. Derbyshire, sentimentally noting the bucolic community life of the pre-industrial setting, took part in the commission for the reform of architectural education, of which Dr Rogers was the chair (by happy accident, he was indeed invited to take the place of Gropius) and Jane Drew the vice president. Dr Rogers, it appears, makes a 'magnificent effort' in marshalling a polyglot agglomeration – fifteen members from the USA, Italy, Switzerland, Belgium, Austria, Holland, England and Norway – to some sort of resolution on the future of architectural education.

11. Robert Furneaux Jordan (1905–78), was principal of the AA between 1949 and 1951. During these years Jordan succeeded in raising the AA's international profile as a progressive, modernist school, with Clement Attlee and Frank Lloyd Wright addressing successive prize-giving ceremonies in 1949 and 1950. Other visitors attracted to the school included Walter Gropius and Alvar Aalto.

12. Initially the CIAM Summer Schools were intended to take place in the cities hosting the CIAM conferences. In practice all the subsequent editions of the CIAM School were held at IUAV in Venice, from 1952 until 1957, with an interruption in 1955. The seminars were directed by Franco Albini, Ignazio Gardella, Ernesto Rogers and Giuseppe Samonà.

13. In the following days, Rogers delivered – to an especially diverse and large audience at the RIBA – the lecture 'Towards a Unity of Plastic Arts', on the subject of collaboration between architects, painters and sculptors. Rogers delivered this paper alongside speakers from all the three arts, such as the artists Graham Sutherland, Roland Penrose, Patrick Heron, the architects Edwin Maxwell Fry, Cornelis van Eesteren, P. Morton Shand, and others.

14. *AA School Committee Minutes Book 1944–1951*, 144, Monday 3 October 1949 (accessed June 2013).

15. Jaromír Krejcar (b. Hundsheim, Austria, 25 July 1895; d. London, 5 October 1949). Together with Karel Teige, Krejcar was one of the main organisers of Devetsil – the group of avant-garde artists, architects and writers active in the 1920s and 1930s. He taught at the technical university in Brno from 1945 to 1948 and then at the AA (1948–49).

16. Email correspondence between Pat Crooke, Andrew Derbyshire and the authors, 3–7 August 2013.

17. John Melvin, interviewed by the authors, 23 July 2013.

18. Ibid. Crooke: With hindsight, I suspect that Ernesto may have entered into this agreement somewhat impulsively, without fully consulting with Belgiojoso and Peresssutti – his Milanese partners who bore the daily brunt of BBPR's busy practice. [...] I was the first of the students to partake in the scheme, and I greatly enjoyed my time in BBPR's beautiful studio (Via dei Chiostri 2) where I worked mainly with Ernesto designing and painting decorative panels for a small Milanese cinema designed by BBPR.

19. Rogers describes the school during a speech in 1949: 'My approach to the AA is rather like a musical crescendo with variations. My first contact was in Bergamo, with two very brilliant students of the School – so brilliant that any school in the world would be very proud, I think, to have them such as ambassadors at such a meeting as the CIAM congress. My second approach was in September, when I was here on a different job and had the great pleasure of meeting Mr Jordan, our Principal, the conductor of the orchestra, and then finally I was able to hear the whole orchestra of students and the chorus of the AA.'
(For the full transcription see *AA Journal 1949–1950*, 127.)

At the foot of the Torre Velasca by BBPR, 1958.
Credit: Antonietta Putzu

all without being able to coagulate thought into form'.[21] A similar 'embarrassment' towards plastic expression is what Rogers finds in the masses of ideology-charged social housing built in Britain during the postwar decades. Even as he praised the British for their 'effort towards the arduous conquest of the house, of humanity and of the instruments for life',[22] Rogers can't help but point out that the serial application of ersatz-modernist solutions 'emptied of spirit' had resulted in dry and uniform formal solutions which had 'no validity in terms of sensitive collective living'.[23]

Conversely, Rogers advocated that new constructions, to be placed into an existing setting, should be evaluated 'case by case', considering circumstances unique to the site of each intervention, and that 'neither planners nor the authorities should base their assumptions on generalisations'.[24] Such an attitude was manifest in those examples of contemporary Italian design on show at the 1952 RIBA exhibition: the outcome of careful negotiation between pre-existing ambience and the new demands of modernity. In Italy, the provision of social housing was not – as in the UK – an absolute priority; indeed, prefabrication and mass manufacture ran somewhat against economic and labour policies of the time. Moreover, as Giulio-Carlo Argan states in the exhibition catalogue, 'in Italy problems of form have always played an extremely important part in the cultural tradition […] political conditions have often made it necessary for ethical questions to be presented in the guise of aesthetic ones, it is a fact that from the earliest days of the Modern Movement, the stylistic problem preceded the ideological one.'

What Rogers, through his travels, teachings and writings, was able to bring forth to international audiences, was the Italian interpretation of modernism. Italy's formally fascinating position could point out the alternatives to England's excessively technocratic direction. At the same time, Rogers' continued exhortations express a hope that Italy's stylistic innovations may be positively 'infected' by English pragmatic humanitarianism. This dialogic method – of posing this against that, to propound an architecture of negotiation – is but a manifestation of the factions of Rogers' own nature, as much as that of the two nations which gave greatest shape to his own positions.[25]

This work was originally published in Pippo Ciorra and Caterina Padoa Schioppa, *Erasmus Effect: Italian Architects Abroad* (Rome: Fondazione MAXXI, 2013).

---

20 Rogers refers to Andrew Derbyshire and John F. C. Turner in the above-mentioned speech at the AA. The affectionate nickname of the 'Mssrs We do not agree' is applied to AA students in a lecture delivered in Venice in 1953 (on the occasion of a later edition of the CIAM Summer School) titled: *Chi siete voi?* (Who are you?) – published in *Venezia Architettura* in the same year. Rogers makes similar allusions in the article 'Tradizione e attualità nel disegno' published in *Zodiac* and in 'Tradition and Modern Design' in the acts of the Seventh International Design Conference in Aspen in 1957, which reappears as an extract in *The Canadian Architect*, in February 1958.

21 'Tradition and Modern Design,' 1957, in *The Aspen Papers*. Extending his observation to the 'Englishmen, from Ruskin to the young men of our time', Rogers accuses the English of 'very often emphasising the moral essence of an artistic object rather than its concrete plastic expression.'

22 'Apologo' (Apologue), in *Domus*, no. 222, September 1947. In England, more than in other countries, the problem of reconstruction had been faced both decidedly and extensively, with a reform of the methods of production in both artistic and industrial spheres.

23 This point recurs in various articles, as for instance in the already mentioned 'Apologo'(Apologue), as well as in 'Appunti sull'Inghilterra e sull'Italia' (Notes on England and Italy), in *Casabella-Continuita*, no. 250, April 1961.

24 Ibid., 11.

25 The authors would like to acknowledge numerous kind contributions of time and counsel, particularly from Mssrs Edward Bottoms, Pat Crooke, Andrew Derbyshire, John Melvin, Manuel Orazi, Joseph Rykwert, Michelangelo Sabatino and Thomas Weaver. Finally we thank Pippo Ciorra and Alessio Rosati for the invitation to submit our humble research.

Deceitful Habits in a Human's Soul

Michael Meier
Christoph Franz

The art and construction work *Deceitful Habits in a Human's Soul* by Michael Meier and Christoph Franz is placed in front of the new building of the Institute for Banking and Finance of the University of Zurich. The work recreates elements from the Trevi Fountain – busts of Triton and Pegasus – newly cast from the metal of ten cent coins thrown into the Roman fountain. The pair are embedded in the building's courtyard, with water flowing from the shell into which Triton blows with inflated cheeks. Rising from the narrow courtyard, they seem oversized and slightly absurd, but the work is tailor-made in that the available budget for art and construction defined how many of the collected coins could be bought at face value from the Roman Caritas (which receives the proceeds from the Trevi Fountain) to be melted down and recast: 8,400 euros, to be exact, or 344.4 kg. *Deceitful Habits in a Human's Soul* was awarded the Prix Visarte 2022.

Deceitful Habits in a Human's Soul. Art and construction, University of Zurich, 2019.
Nickel silver bronze, Euro coins from the Trevi Fountain in Rome.
200 x 409 x 166 cm.

Deceitful Habits in a Human's Soul. By Michael Meier and Christoph Franz. Credit: Susanne Hefti

Tourism in the cracks of the Italian economy

Sarah Gainsforth

1 Paolo Berdini, *La città in vendita. Centri storici e mercato senza regole* (Rome: Donzelli, 2008).

2 Inside Airbnb, Rome, http://insideairbnb.com/rome/ (accessed 15 May 2019).

3 Filippo Celata, *La 'Airbnbificazione' delle città: gli effetti a Roma tra centro e periferia* (Rome: La Sapienza, Dipartimento di metodi e modelli dell'economia, il territorio e la finanza, 2007).

4 Filippo Celata and Barbara Brollo, *#mapparoma27. Airbnb: 15.700 alloggi solo nel 1° Municipio* (Rome: Mapparoma, 2019), https://www.mapparoma.info (accessed 15 February 2023).

5 Antonello Romano, *Il fenomeno Airbnb e la geografia degli host a Roma* (nocodegeography, 2019), https://www.nocodegeography.com (accessed 15 February 2023).

Too many tourists

Bottle caps fill the cracks between the cobblestones in the streets of Trastevere, the once infamous neighbourhood in the heart of Rome. Tourists flock to bars and restaurants, crowding the winding alleyways and banging trolleys up and down narrow staircases to homes no longer inhabited. The area is depopulating. 'In one building, out of ten flats, eight are now vacation rentals,' Stefania Porcelli told me five years ago, when I started investigating the spread of Airbnb in Rome. Porcelli runs the family business, a historic restaurant called Checco er Carrettiere, a stone's throw from Piazza Trilussa. Surrounded by photographs on the walls, she remembered the days when her father handed out a plate of pasta and a banknote to the men leaving Regina Coeli, Rome's jail, round the corner in Via della Lungara. In the following decades, the poor and ill-famed district would change radically.

Between 1951 and 1971 Rome's historic centre lost 54% of its population. Many families were evicted from the small dark homes in Trastevere, while others left willingly in exchange for small buyouts, lured into new homes in more peripheral areas. Trastevere, the second most populous district in the centre, lost almost one third of its inhabitants – dropping from 51,000 to 21,000 residents. Today only 80,000 residents live in the centre of Rome, 20,000 of whom are in Trastevere, with an increase compared to 2001 thanks to an influx of foreigners.[1]

Over the years the district changed as new, richer residents moved in. 'They mixed in and became part of the neighbourhood,' Porcelli explained. The homes in Trastevere were bought and renovated by a much more affluent class of residents and their value increased. 'Then everything changed.' The tourist boom spurred by the 2000 Jubilee and then by the 2008 economic crisis completely transformed Trastevere. 'Small homeowners starting selling or turning their homes into vacation rentals,' Porcelli told me. In recent years, more and more apartments in Trastevere have turned up on Airbnb. And as they did, more and more residents left, their apartments also converting to Airbnb. 'So while in previous decades residents were being replaced by other, more affluent, residents, today residents are being pushed out altogether by a temporary population of tourists.'

According to data from Inside Airbnb,[2] the number of accommodation spaces on the platform in the Italian capital peaked in May 2019, when 30,619 rooms and entire apartments were listed on the website. Of the total listings, 64% were for entire apartments: 20,000 homes in Rome were being rented to tourists on Airbnb; almost 11,000 of these homes were located in the city centre, in the first municipality. After a slight drop in 2020, the number of listings is rising again, while Italy has yet to deal with the issue of short-term rentals, something that has been tolerated by public administrations and promoted by the media. Hence, Italy is one of the few European countries with no regulations in place whatsoever, except for a measure introduced in 2017 for fiscal reasons – a law stating that renting up to four apartments is not considered a commercial activity.

With no regulations in place, until the spread of the Covid-19 pandemic in March 2020, Airbnb was growing in Rome at an annual rate of 8%. However, the historic centre registered far higher rates: in absolute terms, the most central districts saw an increase of 3,355 accommodation spaces between 2016 and 2019 (up 27%).[3] The increase of vacation rentals was such that, in 2019, in some central urban areas, the ratio of beds on Airbnb to residents was one to two.[4] Also, research found that the spread of Airbnb in Rome showed that, alongside a strong spatial concentration of listings in the historic centre, economic benefits were concentrated in the hands of very few hosts.[5] Far from being a tool for 'making ends meet' and aiding an impoverished middle class – as went the claim – Airbnb has become a tool for concentrating wealth and increasing spatial and economic inequality.

Italy's oil

'Tourism is Italy's oil' is a widespread belief in Italy, and a frequent headline in leading national newspapers. Indeed, in 2019 Italy was the fifth most visited country in the world, with 65 million overnight tourist stays

6. Bank of Italy, *Survey on International Tourism*, 5 July 2020, https://www.bancaditalia.it/pubblicazioni/indagine-turismo-internazionale/2020-indagine-turismo-internazionale/statistiche_ITI_05062020.pdf (accessed 15 February 2023).

7. Bank of Italy, *Questioni di Economia e Finanza* (occasional papers) *Turismo in Italia: numeri e potenziale di sviluppo*, July 2019, https://www.bancaditalia.it/pubblicazioni/qef/2019-0505/QEF_505_19.pdf (accessed 15 February 2023).

8. Nomisma, *Terzo rapporto sul mercato immobiliare 2022*, https://www.nomisma.it/terzo-rapporto-nomisma-sul-mercato-immobiliare-novembre-2022/ (accessed 15 February 2023).

9. Federazione Italiana pubblici esercizi, *Osservatorio sul mercato del lavoro nel settore turismo*, XII Rapporto.

10. Istat, *Evoluzione ciclica della produzione industriale e del fatturato in Italia e in Europa*, February 2014, https://www.istat.it/it/files/2014/02/capitolo-1.pdf (accessed 15 February 2023).

11. Comune di Roma, *Annuario Statistico, Cap 2 Le caratteristiche dell'occupazione, anno 2019*, https://www.comune.roma.it/web-resources/cms/documents/CAP_2_Caratteristiche_occupazione_2020.pdf (accessed 15 February 2023).

12. Istat, *Rapporto annuale 2012*.

13. INPS, *Relazione annuale del presidente, XXI Rapporto annuale*, July 2022.

14. *Mi Riconosci? Inchiesta rivela: metà dei lavoratori nel settore culturale guadagna meno di 8 euro l'ora*, https://www.miriconosci.it/inchiesta-rivela-meta-dei-lavoratori-nel-settore-culturale-guadagna-meno-di-8-euro-lora/ (accessed 15 February 2023).

15. Filippo Celata and Antonello Romano, 'Overtourism and Online Short-term Rental Platforms in Italian Cities', *Journal of Sustainable Tourism* 30(5) (2022), 1020–39.

16. Filippo Celata and Antonello Romano, *Spostamenti di popolazione ai tempi del coronavirus* (nocodegeography, 2020), https://www.nocodegeography.com/big-data/spostamenti-popolazione-ai-tempi-del-coronavirus/ (accessed 15 February 2023).

(three million more than in 2018), of which 42 million came from abroad, according to the Bank of Italy.[6] International travel receipts in 2019 reached €44.3 billion, accounting for 41% of service exports. This is a considerable figure. International tourism has grown mainly with holidays in seaside and mountain resorts, while the number of tourists in cities, to which 60% of total holiday spending is attributable, has decreased slightly since 2017. The tourism sector in Italy generates 5% of GDP (13%, including induced activities) and employs 6% of the workforce.[7] Of course, tourism is not an economic sector in its own right, but the sum of activities pertaining to different economic sectors and branches: services, transport, catering, culture, accommodation and so on. From the point of view of the economic impact, according to the Bank of Italy almost one third of the added value generated by tourism in Italy is attributable to the use of homes for tourist rentals. The other economic activities that contribute most to the formation of tourism value added are the hotel, restaurant and transport sectors and, above all, retail trade. The sectors with the highest incidence of tourism are accommodation services, air transport and travel agencies.

However, aside from a strictly economic aspect, the impact of tourism must be measured from other perspectives as well: environmental, social and urban issues are also linked to the growth of tourism. More specifically, they are linked to the absence of public policies guiding the growth of tourism and redistributing tourism expenditure in favour of communities. One third of the added value attributable to tourist rental homes feeds into property income derived from the vacation rental market, a sector with low added value because it produces few jobs, and often precarious and poorly paid ones. This tourist expenditure is captured by homeowners who already enjoy an advantage over those who do not own a second home in an attractive location. Vacation rentals widen this gap: according to the real-estate consultancy firm Nomisma, short-term rentals generate the same profit as a year-long ordinary rental in only 120–130 days.[8] This rent gap leads to a rise in property values in central areas and reduces the stock of homes in the long-term residential market, fuelling a housing crisis.

Another problematic aspect of the tourist economy concerns labour. Tourism is said to create jobs, but these are mostly poorly paid jobs. Trade and tourism employ over 5.4 million workers in Italy, more than the entire manufacturing industry. But 82% of jobs in the tourism sector are categorised as blue-collar and over half are part-time.[9] Also, tourism tends to substitute other economic sectors rather than add to them. Following the 2008 economic crises, when Italy's industrial output shrank by 25%[10] and aggregate domestic demand crumbled under fiscal policy measures, tourism seemed to be the only thing going in Rome, a city that has traditionally lacked an industrial sector. The sectors that recorded the most significant increases in Rome between 2008 and 2019, both in absolute and relative terms, were personal and collective services and business services, which grew by 41.6% and 30.7% respectively, closely followed by hotels and restaurants (28.8%).[11] Between 2004 and 2011, about half of the employment growth in the tertiary sector in Italy was due to the development of hotel, restaurant and domestic services.[12] But, according to the national social security service institute (INPS), 64% of workers in the accommodation and catering sectors are poor.[13] Workers in the culture and arts sectors are not doing any better. A survey conducted in October 2019 found that half of the workers interviewed, many with degrees and doctorates, do not earn more than €8 per hour. Almost 40% of the respondents were earning less than €5,000 per year.[14]

Furthermore, tourism also generates costs. The transformation of so many flats into holiday homes produces social costs in terms of a decay in urban quality and the right to the city. Gentrification due to rising property values and the direct or indirect expulsion of residents from central areas triggers a substantial transformation of the local social and cultural ecology. The replacement of a resident population by a temporary one has also led to the replacement of commercial activities, changing the economic fabric of the historic centre of many cities in Italy to become specialised in tourism-related sectors. So-called food and beverage activities have replaced the commercial establishments needed by residents, and the heart of Rome has become monofunctional.

The effects of the growth of the short-term rental market, however, do not only concern the historic centre. The greatest impact of Airbnb in Rome in terms of depleting the rental housing stock has been in semi-peripheral areas where a population of young people and students usually find cheaper rental accommodation. On a national level, the supply of rented homes started to decrease in 2015, just as demand increased. The supply was even estimated to be negative by 2020, against a growing demand. In 2015, the main real-estate agencies were already attributing the decrease in ordinary supply to the increase in short-term rentals.

<u>Hollow cities</u>

Indeed, the impact that tourism is having on the urban quality of cities such as Rome is impressive. In 2019, homes on Airbnb exceeded those rented to residents in the centres of six cities: Bologna, Florence, Naples, Palermo, Rome and Venice, according to data from Inside Airbnb analysed by the geographer Filippo Celata.[15] Along with residents, neighbourhood shops have disappeared, prices have risen and the continuous flow of tourists has made streets and squares impassable. In a word, historic centres have become uninhabitable.

Before the pandemic, social movements and citizens had already voiced strong concerns about the effects of overtourism (tourist overcrowding) and short-term rentals. But instead of regulating rentals and favouring residents, authorities have spoken only about the need to 'educate' tourists and to focus on 'quality tourism' – a choice of words framing the desire to attract a richer class of tourists than the one brought by low-cost rentals and cheap flights. To combat excessive congestion, mayors have begun to restrict access to parts of the cities. In Florence, Venice and Rome, ordinances have been issued prohibiting tourists, but also residents, from sitting on the steps of monuments. In 2017, the mayor of Florence announced that he would have the steps of churches watered down to prevent tourists from sitting on them. In Venice, gates were set up to regulate access to the historic centre.

The widespread impact of an unregulated growth of short-term rentals became evident in March 2020, when Italy went into lockdown in order to mitigate the spread of the Covid-19 pandemic. The heart of Rome witnessed a 70% drop in population. Similar percentages were registered only in ski resorts.[16] For months Trastevere lay empty and silent, hollowed out, when tourism suddenly came to a halt. The emptying out of the historic centres showed how tourism, a sector time and time again defined as central to the Italian economy, rests on very fragile foundations – suggesting, moreover, the need to review the comparison of tourism with a fossil fuel in a time of environmental crisis.

Over the last decade, numerous cities and natural landscapes in every corner of the planet have undergone profound transformations linked to tourism. The intensive

17   Istat, *Censimento delle popolazioni e della abitazioni, 2019*, http://dati-censimentipermanenti.istat.it/?lang=it (accessed 15 February 2023).

18   Sarah Gainsforth, *Dopo il turismo, riabitare Roma*, DinamoPress, 15 May 2020, https://www.dinamopress.it/news/dopo-turismo-riabitare-roma/ (accessed 15 February 2023).

19   Comune di Roma, 'Linee guida e criteri generali finalizzati all'avvio del Programma Strategico per il superamento della condizione di disagio e della condizione di emergenza abitativa nel territorio capitolino', *Delibera della giunta capitolina*, no. 86, 19 May 2020.

20   *Roma, Unione inquilini boccia Gualtieri: assegnate 70 case*, Askanews, 11 January 2023, https://www.askanews.it/cronaca/2023/01/11/roma-unione-inquilini-boccia-gualtieri-assegnate-70-case-pn_20230111_00184/ (accessed 15 February 2023).

21   Eurostat (2020), *Housing price statistics. House price index*, https://ec.europa.eu. (accessed 15 February 2023).

22   Real-estate values in Italy have risen again only in the past two years, thanks to the highest increase of property purchases in the past fifteen years, according to Nomisma.

23   Enrico Puccini, '*Il mercato immobiliare romano: 10 anni di perdite*', Osservatorio Casa Roma, 2020, https://www.osservatoriocasaroma.com (accessed 15 February 2023).

24   Stefano Sampaolo, '*Tra rendita e nuove logiche di sviluppo: processi adattivi e reattivi di una città alle prese con uno strisciante (e non compreso) declino economico urbano*', in A. Coppola and G. Punziano, eds., *Roma in Transizione. Governo, strategie, metabolismi e quadri di vita di una metropoli* (Rome, Milano: Plan Publisher, 2018).

exploitation of resources has left territories destroyed and polluted, historic centres emptied of inhabitants and overcrowded with tourists, empty homes and streets in different cities all looking and feeling like the same place. These are some of the effects of a process that modifies urban and natural ecosystems, and consumes and erases the characteristics that make tourist destinations attractive.

The collapse of an urban economy heavily reliant on tourism and informal employment took a heavy toll in the Eternal City. Only a handful of restaurants in Trastevere reopened when the restrictions introduced to mitigate the Covid-19 contagion were eased in May 2020. Most commercial activities had switched management multiple times during the past years, as the tourism boom fuelled by cheap Airbnb rentals transformed the old neighbourhood into a tourist resort. Antonio is one of the few restaurant owners to have been working in Trastevere for over a decade. 'It's sad,' he told me. 'Most restaurants didn't reopen for a long time because there were no tourists. But the problem in Trastevere is that there are no residents.' Commercial activities in densely inhabited, more peripheral areas of Rome thrived. But the city centre struggled to come back to life. Rows of closed shutters lined the empty buildings in a neighbourhood gone silent. Alessandro, who runs a bar around the corner from Trastevere's main square, told me that his work routine followed Ryanair's weekly flight schedule to Rome. But in 2020 Trastevere seemed to have gone back to the time when the neighbourhood was dark, poor and dangerous.

A city of empty homes and homeless people

Many homeowners held on until the return of tourists by renting their empty flats on one-year temporary contracts at most. Others sold. But while those 20,000 vacation rentals remained empty, in a city where, according to official data, 166,000 homes are unoccupied,[17] many struggled to pay rent and faced increasing hardship as the city administration struggled to deliver the necessary aid – mainly food stamps and emergency rent subsidies. Many of those facing economic hardship were employed in the tourism sector: the waiters, cooks and baristas, who make up a young, poor and precarious workforce increasingly dependent on family welfare.

Less than 18% of Rome's population lives in rented homes. Applications for rent subsidies submitted in February 2020, before the pandemic, were around 10,000, according to Unione Inquilini (the tenants' union). On 6 May 2020, there were 30,000 applications, but, according to the municipality, the total number of applications would be double that. In fact, one third of renters, 50,000 households, applied for emergency aid, and more than 220,000 Roman families applied for food vouchers.[18] The city administration, whose offices are notoriously understaffed and whose political leaders across different administrations have held a hard-line approach towards the housing crises and poverty in general, failed to meet these demands. Tenants unable to pay rent were added to those already unable to secure a home in the private market before the pandemic.

Rome counts over ninety occupied buildings that provide self-managed emergency housing for approximately 10,000 people. According to the city administration, the housing emergency in Rome concerns 57,000 families, equal to about 200,000 people.[19] Many of them have been waiting for decades for a council house. At the end of December 2022, the city administration published the list of applications for council housing submitted before 31 December 2020 – that is, before the wave of evictions caused by the pandemic, which aggravated an already precarious housing situation for tenants. This showed that 14,349 families applied before 2021 and are on the waiting list for a council house. But, according to Unione Inquilini, 7,681 applications have been excluded – more than 6,000 were classified as inadmissible, while 1,294 were cancelled (179 because the applicant died). Housing allocations are proceeding slowly: according to Unione Inquilini, in the past seventeen months, since Mayor Roberto Gualtieri took office, only seventy houses have been assigned: six houses per month, the worst figure ever.[20] Furthermore, council housing is being sold and privatised. According to the housing expert Enrico Puccini, 20,000 of the 76,000 council houses in Rome will be sold.

For those who cannot access the property ladder, prospects are bleak. According to Puccini, in Italy there is no social housing to speak of. 'What Italians call social housing is merely a rent-to-buy scheme, in which future tenants are selected by private constructors, and the city has no oversight on the process.' The city's plan provides for private constructors to allocate 30% of all newly built homes to people in need on a subsidised rent basis. However, in August 2022, a survey carried out by the city's housing department revealed half of the social housing units are occupied by tenants who lack the minimum requirements to live in them.

Puccini has conducted extensive research on housing in Rome, analysing the scarce data available. What is peculiar about Rome's housing crisis, according to his research, is the fact that it has not been driven solely by rising prices and rents. While many European cities witnessed a 'recovery' of real-estate values beginning in 2013,[21] Italy saw a decrease.[22] Rome recorded an average drop of 27% in rents and 19% in property values from 2008 to 2018.[23] In this context, Airbnb contributed to the stabilisation of property values in the central areas of cities and to widening the gap between central and peripheral house prices: after 2008 central boroughs such as Trastevere survived the market slump relatively unscathed, also thanks to Airbnb, but in areas outside the city centre home prices dropped. 'But evictions continued and spiked in 2016,' Puccini notes. In Rome approximately 9,000 eviction notices are issued each year. He believes that evictions continued to increase after 2008, even when house prices were dropping, because the problem lies also in the job market: 'Tenants simply aren't earning enough to pay rent.' So, what is driving both the housing crisis and the tourism boom is not only real-estate values, but the stagnant economy mainly based on this sector, and low wages.

The tourist market has been used by many owners (as well as by those who have rented houses to sublet them on Airbnb) to buffer the effects of the crisis by reorienting the process of rent extraction around tourism, in the absence of any forms of governance from the city's transformation programme.[24] Rome, and Italy in general, has proven to be particularly suitable for the grafting of a business model centred on real-estate income. Rome's urban economy has thrived on real-estate speculation since the postwar years, when the city expanded to become Italy's largest metropolitan area. But real estate, Puccini points out, needs demand. And Rome's stagnant economy has proven far from attractive. So that demand relies more and more on tourism.

Outside the city centre, with few alternative sectors to real estate and tourism attracting investment, a demographic standstill, high rates of unemployment, and underpaid and precarious labour, especially among the youth who increasingly depend on parents and grandparents, Rome's economy is far from vibrant. To many the city feels forever on the brink of collapsing under mismanagement, public debt, incompetence and plain lack of political vision. 'This is part of the problem: Rome has become dependent on tourism as a natural

[25] Samuel Stein, *Tourism: An Ideology and an Accumulation Strategy*, DinamoPress, 28 January 2020, https://www.dinamopress.it/news/tourism-an-ideology-and-an-accumulation-strategy/ (accessed 15 February 2023).

resource. People adapted to the only thing going: everybody opened a restaurant, a bar, or bought a home to rent on Airbnb,' says Puccini. But the economic shift towards the tourism sector has impoverished Rome in many ways. The growth of tourism and of the related services sector has meant not more wealth, as the tale would have it, but more badly paid and precarious jobs, which translated into too many people struggling to pay rent. It's a vicious circle.

Of course, tourism in itself is not the real issue. The point is the weakness of other sectors in Rome's economy, and the growth of unregulated tourism that is reshaping the city thanks to a planning and management void and the absence of measures for pre- and redistributing wealth and tourism expenditure. Too many city administrations in Italy view tourism as an easy shortcut to compensate for state cuts to public spending, as a means to revive local economies thanks to a foreign demand, in territories made fragile by disinvestment processes. But as Samuel Stein puts it, this is a lazy, short-term growth strategy,[25] replacing other economic sectors instead of adding to them. Not only is this strategy not working, it's widening the gaps.

Two years ago, in the absence of tourism, a choice about Rome's economy could have been made: there could have been an effort to bring back residents to the city centre and foster a more diverse economy. But that did not happen. Meanwhile, the national government was busy compensating tourism-related commercial activities in hollowed-out cities such as Rome, Florence and Venice with public subsidies for the extraordinary drop in demand. No one stopped to reflect on the fact that perhaps this economy is no longer sustainable and should therefore not be subsidised; nor did it occur to those in government that, at a time of climate change, perhaps these drops in demand won't be so extraordinary in the near future. That chance to rethink the urban economy in a long-term, sustainable perspective was lost. And as tourism restarts, not all boats are being lifted. Meanwhile, as the cracks in the tourism economy begin to widen once again, as cities increasingly suffer the effects of climate change also brought on by unsustainable tourism-related practices and enterprises, public debate about the price we are all paying will become inevitable.

Regenerating Rome and Europe through the practice of hospitality

Lorenzo Romito

Myth as a means of navigating towards a possible future

In order to tackle the question of hospitality, I'd like to try to share with you an argument of a mythopoetic nature; in other words, a poetic and not a rational discourse with which to weave, in a unitary and imaginative account, some images symbolic of the aetiological founding and refounding myths of Rome and Europe, together with some often-forgotten historical traces and some emerging aspects of the reality of Rome and the Europe in which we live. Things that we frequently are unable to grasp or refuse to look at.

It is a question of imitating Ariadne and unrolling a thread that can help us find a route towards a possible future, picking our way through the labyrinth of a present that increasingly seems to have no exit …

First of all, I'd like to suggest we see these founding myths not so much as tales of origin – and therefore stories that were concluded forever at some time in the past – but as oracular narrations, enigmatic guides that can be reactivated in order to advance through the non-linear passages of those great and momentous changes that, by restoring circularity to time, can allow us to move from an end to a new beginning.

Understood in this way, myth is able to bend the curve of time, bringing the origin of a city close to its destiny in a circularity that contradicts the linearity of progressive time and makes it possible for the emerging sense of what is happening today to illuminate obscure aspects of the past, turning that mythical time into an ever new one to be interpreted, in order to understand not so much where we have come from as where we are going.

The myths of Rome and Europe

The myths of Rome and Europe, which I am presenting here as complementary, are among those that tell the story of how the forms of collective life are born, decay and are born again, cyclically. We are living in just one of these moments of discontinuity in which a civilisation that has passed its peak is starting to decline and something new is struggling to emerge.

Moments in which the difficulty of glimpsing a future beyond the present becomes social anxiety, an inability to comprehend and to change in the face of a reality that appears unexpectedly foreign, irreducible to an established vision of the world and therefore dangerous.

It is precisely here that recovering and re-enacting myth can help us to grasp how to move ahead and go beyond the limits of our mental patterns, help us to see in change the emerging signs of a new but at the same time ancient sensibility, opening up a passage to a possible, and today invisible, future.

Might not this be precisely the mythopoetic sense of a profound and radical urban regeneration? Hasn't it already happened several times in Rome and Europe?

We are free to regress or evolve, to cling in terror to the things and ideas that we are losing under the blows of change, but we can also venture into the choppy waters of change. It is something that has already been done. Exploring and trying out new forms of coexistence with others and with the environment is possible; it is as risky as it is necessary. And if we embark on that voyage, myth can be a useful compass. At this point I invite you to follow Ariadne's thread and not lose your way in the labyrinth …

Eur(h)ope

In myth, Europe represents in the first place an irrepressible and restless desire to explore and experiment with old-fashioned forms of freedom. In fact, it was curiosity and desire that drove the Asian princess Europa to climb onto the back of Jupiter in the form of a bull and let herself be carried overseas, towards the unknown. In Aeschylus' tragedy, *The Persians*, Europe appears in a dream to Atossa, Xerxes' mother, along with Asia, as a pair of mares that are harnessed to the chariot of the great king, but unruly Europe overturns the chariot, refusing to accept the yoke.

Europe is that desire for freedom which drives us to make the risky and potentially redemptive journey into the unknown, from East to West, towards a promised land, in flight from political oppression, climate change, war and famine, that has always accompanied the unchecked growth of any human civilisation. Europe is that desire for freedom which leads us to set out upon a journey, to emigrate. Does all this remind you of something that is going on now?

The founding journeys of Ancient Europe were the great migrations through the Mediterranean at the end of the Bronze Age, the ones related in Homer's *Odyssey* and Virgil's *Aeneid*, just as the refounding of Europe after the fall of the Roman Empire took place along the routes of pilgrimage that ran across it, redrawing its map: routes leading to Rome, Jerusalem and Santiago de Compostela. And the birth of contemporary, cosmopolitan and cultured Europe was marked by the epic story of a journey, the Grand Tour. A journey to the south in search of the myth of Europe in order to rediscover it and renew its meaning.

Then came the nation states, with their fixed, apparently unchangeable boundaries, and the process of distillation of increasingly monolingual populations, homogenised by the mass media and made sedentary by consumption, and here Europe's journey seems to have ground to a halt. At least until the fall of the Berlin Wall, the consequent wars in the Balkans that got Europe on the move again and the appearance of new Europeans fleeing in search of a better fate.

What is interesting to note is that the myth of Europe, the ideas and geographies it has produced over time, have been continually regenerated through the experience of travel and migration, tracing routes along which to meet and trade, not just in goods but in ideas and knowledge, too. In the process, institutions and spaces have been created to give and receive hospitality and to care for wayfarers, for the production and dissemination of the knowledge they carry with them, along with merchandise.

The history of Europe in this sense is the realisation of a utopia through the formative and transformative experience of travel; in other words of giving and receiving hospitality.

The journey in time of the idea of Europe has produced the infrastructures of material and meaning of a network of cities and territories, constellations that have shaped its geography down the ages. Thus, while the boundaries of Europe have always been uncertain and mutable, the routes of the journeys with which Europe has taken form and along which it has been regenerated over time have been much more durable.

These founding routes are the ones taken today by those pursuing the desire for Europe and seeking to enter and traverse it to reach family, friends and a better life. They are routes along which we are again seeing the emergence of networks of solidarity, new and often clandestine forms of hospitality, places of meeting and exchange between travellers and locals. A developing system that finds it hard to take the form of a possible future; constrained by social rejection and state violence, it struggles against the inability to understand and the attempt to put a stop to this cyclic and necessary process of regeneration of Europe.

The violence of inhospitality, which has also left its mark on the renewed routes of migration towards and across Europe, creates, alongside places of meeting and welcome, places of sacrifice, of conflict and rejection. It is the ensemble of all these places that is redrawing the geography of Europe, altering its *genius loci*. An emerging geography, whose configuration is still hard to comprehend, that is being shaped by thousands of acts of rejection and welcome. They are the places and the painful and heroic vicissitudes of a new people on the march, the new sanctuaries of hospitality and rejection through which the regenerative routes of the Europe to come are unfolding, starting from its *finis terrae*: Lampedusa, Lesbos, Samos, Ceuta, Melilla, Calais …

Xenia, hospitality

On the journey, the encounter with the other is sanctioned by the sacred practice of hospitality, called *xenia* in Greek. Hospitality binds together those who give it and those who receive it and permits the meeting, both useful and sacred, of different worlds, renewing the world through exchange. This is how navigation, agriculture and writing were spread, along with the *polis*, the city itself, a space of sharing and exchange at whose centre, the *agora*, were placed the conflicts and desires of all, so that they were moulded by public dispute and generated laws that could govern Europe's restless desire for freedom.

But we know that this encounter between refugees and natives, between wayfarers and locals, has not always been a happy one. It has given rise and continues to give rise not only to exchanges but also to conflicts. One of the reasons for this is that the *polis*, in its original Greek form, had a limitation: its ethnic character. The encounter with the other was considered sacred but did not entail an openness to hybridisation with the other. It remained restricted to a temporary and asymmetrical circumstance. It did not become a horizontal state of coexistence. It is here that, to complete the myth of Europe, the myth of Rome comes to our aid.

Rome, the Eternal City, not because it shines eternally but because it has always been able to rise again from its ruins. The Universal City, because in its ruins it has been able to shelter the refugees of the world and with them regenerate itself and generate a people always at once new and old; *noantri*, as they say in Rome, we and others together. Let me try to explain …

Roma, Latium and the sacred grove of the Asylum

> 'Rome has no unity, and perhaps has never existed as a unity.
> Roma is a hodgepodge. But it is not just a hodgepodge of repentant brigands in the grove of asylum, or, along the banks of the Tiber, one of she-wolves in brothels. Rome is not just a brew of whores and former assassins, it is also, and above all, a mixture of people from elsewhere.'[1]

Saturn was a refugee and so was the Trojan Aeneas. Romulus and Remus, too, were refugees, floating in a basket down the Tiber. Caracalla must have been aware of this when in 212 CE he granted Roman citizenship to all the inhabitants of the world then known and governed by Rome. Fascism was not aware of it, however, failing in its plan to revive Rome and its glories, constrained as it was by the crude idea, hopefully with no future, of race.

You will certainly know that on Rome's most sacred hill, the Capitoline, stood the sacred grove of the Asylum, perhaps given this name because it was located on the saddle between the two summits of the hill. In this sacred grove room was found for the *others* whom in due time the mythical founder of Rome would be able to unite in the new Roman people.

The sacred grove, and there were many of them in Rome, was mythically part of *Latium*, today's administrative region of Lazio, but always the alter ego of the *urbs*, a wild and holy space because other with respect to the city but necessary so that, through the wild, the spontaneous and the disorderly, Rome could be regenerated and remain Eternal. *Latium*, from the Latin *latere*, 'to be in hiding', just like Saturn, who, driven out by Jupiter, asked for hospitality here from Janus, the guardian of passages, and went on to establish the mythical golden age. An age whose ruins are located

---

1 Michel Serres, *Rome: Le livre des fondations* (Paris: Grasset, 1983), 153.

on the Palatine Hill where, as Virgil recounts, the Trojan refugee Aeneas went to meet the pastoral king Evander, before Rome was born, or perhaps precisely so that Rome would be born, from the ruins of the city returned to the wild, at the hands of refugees.

Latium has a sacred relationship of inescapable reciprocity and interpenetration with Rome. When the time came, it was able to spontaneously take possession of its ruins and make them fertile again, a place of welcome for the future, so that the city could be reborn … If it is going to be eternal Rome can never forget its alter ego Lazio: it keeps it sacred and wild within, and when Rome, in crisis, runs the risk of vanishing, it is in Lazio that it hides in order to rise again.

Inhabiting the ruins together

This is what is happening, once again, in the *Latium* of today, amidst the many forgotten, disused and abandoned areas that cover about half of the municipality's territory and where, outside state control, economic speculation and any institutional purview, forms of plant, animal and human life are taking advantage of the dormancy of the authorities to experiment with new relationships: a chaotic process of becoming in which possible futures often lurk.

We are taught this by the luxuriant resurgence of nature on sites of former industrial exploitation and by the creative experiences of spontaneous reappropriation of disused buildings and industrial ruins by those who have no home, by migrants, the displaced and exiles. It is among these insurgences of wilderness and informal social experiments that we find in Rome today the richest forms of social innovation and the most advanced forms of ecological and multicultural coexistence, going much farther than research and the institutional planning have ever been able to imagine and realise.

So, once more, the traces of a possible future emerge amidst what has been abandoned, amongst those ruins which nature has overrun again and in which the new refugees of the present hide and find hospitality in order to regenerate the city.

For a reciprocal hospitality: sharing the circumstance of lack

In fact, these disused spaces reappropriated by wilderness – other spaces increasingly inhabited by those who are themselves other and excluded from the contemporary world – are the very ones that are becoming the incipient places of a new version of the ancient principle of hospitality.

Here hospitality remains an unconditional principle but loses its asymmetry: those given hospitality are people with no home, often jobless and undocumented. It is precisely this lack that is shared between locals and foreigners and that constitutes the new dimension of horizontality of the act of hospitality. A horizontality that lets hospitality escape its constituent imbalance, between those who give it and those who receive it, making it once again, as in the mythical times of Lavinium and Aeneas, a horizontal and reciprocal practice; not to offer temporary refuge to the stranger in need, but to share that need with the other and make it the prospect of a common desire, the foundation of a new and possible community without origins. A hospitality between the excluded, in a territory that is also excluded and marginal with respect to the city, but that promises to be fertile ground for the rebirth of that city in new forms. Once again, a wild space amongst the ruins of a declining world, a second grove of the Asylum. Thus, the hospitality of the other has become a horizontal practice that offers itself as a means of generating community, not on the basis of language, nationality and presumed blood ties, but on the very idea of hospitality of the other in order to inhabit the ruins of the present together and share the possibility of a new world.

It is in the unregulated and living other space of the wild that homelessness, statelessness and joblessness become *pharmakon*, at once poison and medicine, to be taken together as an act of mutual and horizontal hospitality; ways of exploring new forms of coexistence that only the circumstance of privation seems to make acting-thinking-realising possible today.

Here hospitality becomes a horizontal, reciprocal and common action to escape from the violence of the environmental, economic, political and social relations of the contemporary world, and take refuge in an incipient and wild space-time; an action freed from the bombast and spectacularisation of the event (which would bring it back into the territory of contemporary aesthetics and politics) and reduced to the level of a convivial circumstance, to that horizontal encounter between the different which would otherwise be impossible today. A meeting to be held around the hearth of a lack suffered, chosen or just understood, proposed as a condition for returning to thinking about and acting in order to bring about a possible future, one that lies beyond a present in transit between the economic violence of neoliberalism and the political one of neo-nationalist sovereigntism. A 'convivial circumstance' that might restore the possibility of a new dignity in interpersonal relationships across the borders and walls that are tearing humanity apart today, preventing it from standing up against the horror.

For how long will this possible future have to hide away in the shadows of *Latium*? How and when will it finally become clear that in these years a new Rome is rising amidst the ruins of property speculation and misgovernment? A Rome made up of fragile but advanced forms of coexistence between 'locals' and 'foreigners', between 'humanity' and 'nature', unprecedented environmental, cultural and social forms, seeds of a desirable future founded on a renewed mutual practice of hospitality.

Rome and Europe versus the contemporary

We need the myths of Rome and Europe and their generative energy today in order to escape from an exhausted time that never seems to pass, the apparently perennial time of the contemporary. That contemporary world which to defend itself against the advent of a possible future that might take the present from it is doing everything it can to expel the other, trying to exclude it by building walls, or trying to subjugate it by seducing it with the possibility of success and exploiting it economically. That contemporary culture which with its real time, fruit of a paralysing accelerationism, fights against spontaneity, risk and unpredictability, and that for this reason wants to turn art into a profession, myth into a fairy-tale and ruins into museums. To do so it attempts to place everything under the limelight of a continuous and controlled spectacle, denying life the possibility of finding refuge in the shadows so that it can evolve its way out of an asphyxiating present.

The contemporary, titanic adversary of Rome and Europe is doing its best to prevent Rome, in the shadow of *Latium*, from again hosting possible futures and Europe from crossing the Mediterranean in search of hospitality.

The Alps

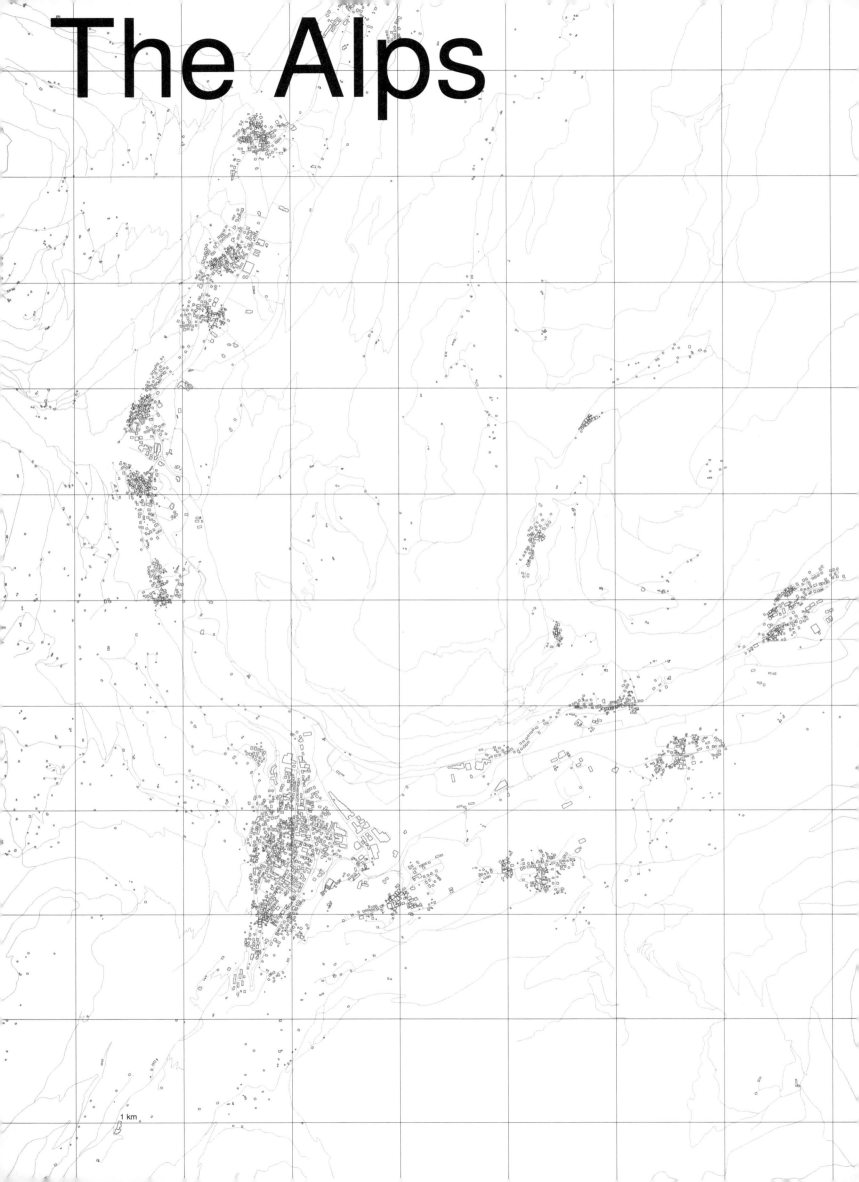

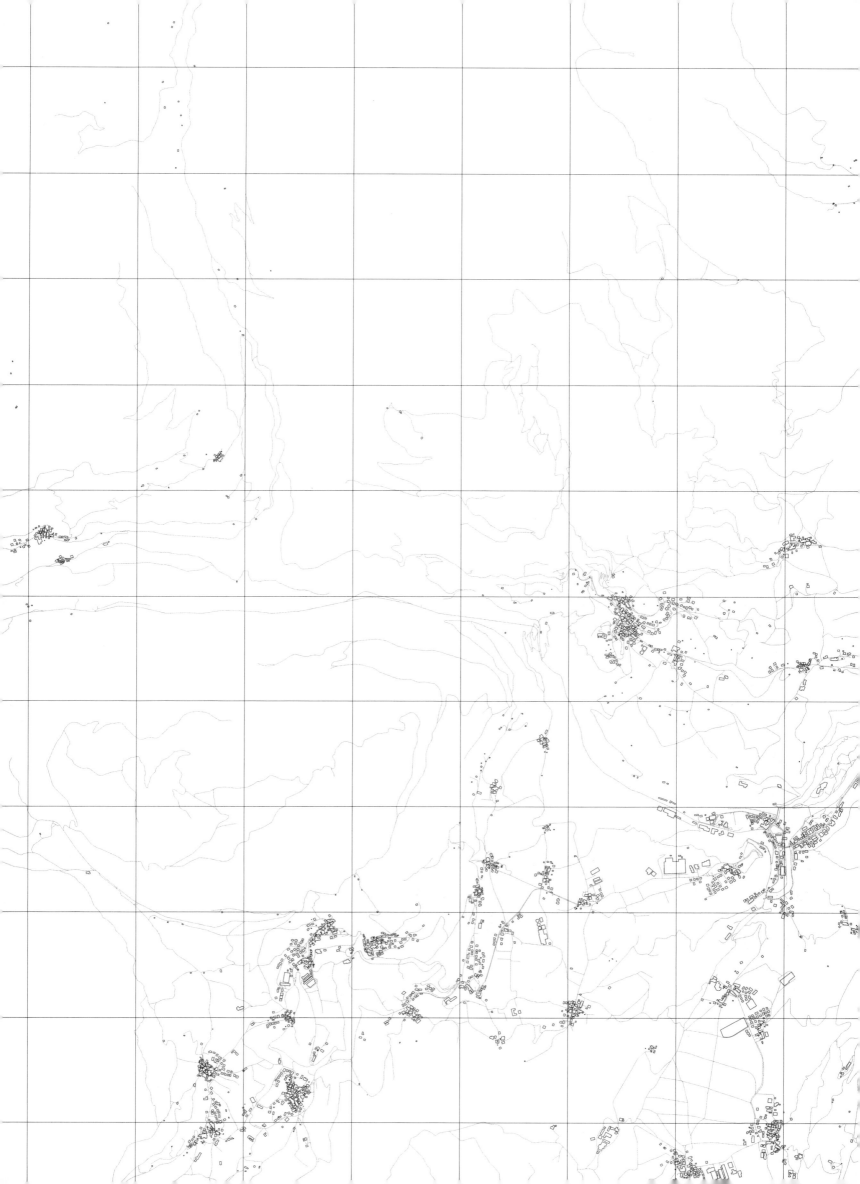

Through the Alps: A photographic account of the changes in the Alpine landscape

Viviana Rubbo
Alessandro Guida
Davide Curatola Soprana
Isabella Sassi Farìas

Text by Viviana Rubbo

045 Credit: Alessandro Guida

1 Eugenio Turri, *Il paesaggio come Teatro. Dal territorio vissuto al territorio rappresentato* (Venice: Marsilio, 1998).

2 Antonio De Rossi, ed., *Ri-abitare l'Italia, le aree interne tra abbandoni e riconquiste* (Rome: Donzelli, 2018).

3 Davide Pettenella, 'Boschi e green economy: un progetto necessario', in De Rossi, ed., *Ri-abitare l'Italia*, 479.

'Photographers have approached the landscape not as detached reproducers of reality, but as spectators who want to change it. In essence, just as has always been the case for painters, by proposing, through their photographs, designs for the landscape, new scenery for our lives. For the world grows old and with it the image we have of it grows old too: in this sense, today it is photographers who make us feel the ageing of the world, the wear and tear to which the everyday is subject, commencing with the backdrops to our stories.'
E. Turri, *Il paesaggio come Teatro*, 1998

Through the Alps is a photographic account of today's mountains, in particular the aspects of their smaller valleys that were, until a few years ago, the favoured destination of seasonal tourism by families. Valleys, too, that are inhabited by communities which live their daily lives in the region and whose challenge is to improve services, with the tenacity of those who have decided to remain where they are. A life that is lived a day at a time, through the perseverance of those who have always been there and through those who have chosen the mountains as their new home, maintaining or rediscovering their resources, renewing the productive and cultural attributes of the location and adapting them to the needs of present and future communities. This is an account that explores a highly variegated space, a succession of anthropic landscapes that are extremely diverse and at the same time very similar: the many cultures and innumerable geological, climatic and environmental contexts, the many elements and many geographies that define this portion of the world that is the Alpine region.

The project sets out to bring a new dimension to the interpretation and perception of the changes that these areas have undergone in recent decades, using a photographic account as a means of in-depth analysis and as a narrative form capable of bringing the local realities to life in an exploration of the contemporary landscape.

Prepared with the involvement and participation of institutional and individual players, and through the efforts of representatives of the associations of architects from ten Alpine provinces, the photographic research started out by putting its ear to the ground, and then going on to examine the signs, traces and characteristics that reflect the history of the area. 'We look at the landscape and become observers of it in different ways,' wrote Eugenio Turri. 'We let the impressions that the sight produces in us sink in or we try to understand, in a semiological sense, what the landscape can reveal to us of the people and the society that identify with it. It's like reading a book […]. Codes of interpretation are needed to help us assign a meaning to what we see. But is it possible to read the landscape then?'[1]

The landscape is the fruit of a layering of histories, cultures, usages and modes of living and working through time, and only a critical understanding of the processes of transformation that have produced it and are moulding it can contribute to developing new imagery able to stimulate exchange and debate over its planning.

Visions, foremost, of an interregional and transalpine breadth that can sustain this context, understood as a complex and many-sided entity; new points of view in support of a revival and a renewed socioeconomic impetus that should start out from the capacity to 'look at these regions for the values and opportunities of life, dwelling and production' contained in them, as Antonio De Rossi put it when speaking more generally of inland areas in the publication *Ri-abitare l'Italia*.[2]

Operationally speaking, the photographic project was the last step in a process of cooperation and sharing of ideas launched in the autumn of 2018 with the Associazione Architetti Arco Alpino (AAA).

The first few months served to make clear the themes of inquiry and the areas of research, which were followed by a preliminary phase of exploration of the regions selected in the form of on-the-spot investigations and guided tours. Having assimilated the fund of information acquired during this first phase, and defined a thematic outline of reference, the photographers then set to work independently, bringing their own perspective to bear on the territory.

From this subjective viewpoint, the collective went on to make a visual synthesis of what are the contemporary mountainscapes of the Italian Alps today. Viewed in this way, photographic research becomes a methodological tool which can be used to interpret the landscape, developing a more conscious and critical understanding of it: the photographic account, used as a narrative language, is able to isolate, compose and recompose the elements of the space, helping thereby to define new narrations for changing regions. It aims to provide an opportunity for the people who live in these places to look again, to discover, or rediscover, their own living space and recognise themselves as inhabitants of the Alps.

The structure of the account

The account that has emerged from this research tackles the complexity of Alpine landscapes through the examination of three main themes:

Forms in space
Resources and production
Mechanisms

Forms in space: inhabiting through time

These are images that recount daily life in the mountains through a gaze that observes the signs of a recent but now vanished past, lingering, along the way, on the forms of dwelling present and on the empty shells of the holiday homes built between the 1970s and 1990s.

Exploring our Alps, we cannot help but start with the communities silenced by depopulation. They are everywhere, small settlements in the lower and mid valley and villages located higher up, inhabited only sporadically and occasionally, or completely forgotten. Examples are the small villages of Bourcet in Val Chisone, Scilironi in Valmalenco, some hamlets of Saint-Nicolas in Val d'Aosta and Poscolle in Val Canale.

This is the legacy of an era that, while physically still present and tangible in the form of ruined buildings, disused quarries, ski lift pylons overgrown with vegetation and closed hotels, belongs to the past. But its traces are clearly visible, still evident. They are the signs of a time, and a very recent one, that exploited the local resources (in the agricultural, industrial and mining sectors), shaping the territory: a time in which the area was made fertile and productive, conduits and installations were constructed, stone was quarried and minerals and metals extracted.

Many of these activities are now at a standstill, closed down or abandoned, and have left behind skeletons of walls and empty shells that need reconsideration but are difficult to convert to other purposes.

In the course of our journey, the memory of a flourishing agricultural society is an element that spans the entire arc of the Italian Alps, uniting the lands of the far east, on the border with Slovenia, with those of the far west, close to France, both through the grandeur of the rural buildings and through the richness and variety of their types. These are the types of barns – *rascard*, *masi*, *tabià* – an architectural heritage of surprising beauty owing to the utilisation of local materials and forms that change from region to region. But inhabiting the landscape is, above all, the life of today, made up of all those familiar, often informal spaces that spring from everyday activities and are on a small scale. They are the spaces of entrance to the village or town, equipped with noticeboards providing information for tourists (or plastered with election posters), along with benches, a drinking fountain and the post box; or the sole commercial enterprise, a hybrid multifunctional space that is a grocery store, café, bar, tobacconist's and newsagent's, sometimes even a surgery. These are the locations of the civic dimensions of a community, a social space, a point of reference for the local inhabitants. Their versatility reflects the spirit of adaptation, the need to consider strategically places that are capable of providing different services and aggregating resources.

But living in the Alps can also be viewed in terms of the continual mingling of individual space and external, collective space: the pylon of an old infrastructure has been turned into a wayside shrine at Jourtousiere in Val Chisone to commemorate the flood of 2000 that spared a house built too close to the bank of the torrent; a football pitch has been laid out in a car park too often left deserted; a small playground has been created on the roof of a garage. These are places of the imagination, an expression of the community that lives in them.

The streets of towns and hamlets outline public space – that is to say 'neighbourhood' space – with a mix of functions. On higher ground, the houses of the villages are wedged into one another, occupying as little as possible of the cultivable land. They gently follow the contours of the ground and comprise passageways, staircases, terraces, small breaks on level ground and then differences again in height. Only in Val di Rabbi and Val Martello do the forms of the buildings assume the dimensions of the large hereditary farms, undivided properties standing in solitary isolation on the slopes.

A common story throughout the Alpine region, without distinction, is the way that the urbanisation of the valley bottom has expanded along the through roads with a markedly urban character, extraneous to the setting of the Alps. The dialogue with the mountains, with geography, seems to have broken down. New proportions, changes of scale, unprecedented building types and materials. The architectural forms do not seek a relationship with the territory, but have turned instead into a hybrid of a composite 'Alpine-rural-urban' nature. Inhabiting has lost its original social and economic dimension and become monofunctional, of chiefly residential character (in the lower and mid valley) or as accommodation for tourists (in the upper valley).

But we have also found examples of survival and resistance, forms of return to and rediscovery of the mountain through the reclamation, and reuse, of existing structures, now converted into people's main homes. The house in the wood at Saint-Nicolas in Val d'Aosta was once a refuge for the workers of the talc mine. Today it has been renovated by a young family that has decided to live in it all year round. At Chasteiran in Val Chisone, the hamlet of Bourcet is the only settlement to have been reclaimed (out of ten of so villages and Alpine pastures that are all in ruins today) and is inhabited permanently by one person who moved there about ten years ago and has now begun to cultivate the steep slopes again, reviving a small-scale agricultural economy and growing potatoes, fruit and vegetables.

There are still families living in hamlets at high altitude, as at Clavel and Gratillon (in Saint-Nicolas), Rima (Val Sermenza) or in Val Tanaro, and who spend all their days in the mountains. These are places in which private space extends outdoors and there is no longer any distinction between inside and outside; the streets and passages leading from one front door to the next become the geography of the community.

When talking about living in the mountains we cannot fail to include the theme of seasonal tourism and the overabundance of holiday homes, a parcelling out of the land for large residential complexes, most of them built between the 1970s and 1990s, that rapidly and radically changed the structure of the Alpine regions. To a greater or lesser extent, this phenomenon has affected all the valleys. Only after the passage of twenty years, and changes in socioeconomic as well as climatic conditions, is the Alpine region now beginning to tackle a not insignificant question: an imposing building stock (in Val d'Aosta alone holiday homes make up 40% of the buildings) of poor quality that is no longer used but has high costs of maintenance and management.

Many questions remain, including:

1. How to deal with the abandonment of the historic and the more recent stock of buildings?
2. What does it mean to construct in the mountains today?
3. What to do with the areas and empty spaces left by activities that have now ceased?
4. How can architecture help us to reconsider the mountains as a dwelling place?

Resources and production: existing systems of production and attributes

The elements that make up the landscape paint a picture of the past and the present, of usages, activities and modes of life in a physical environment that is unique and filled with contrasts: great attractiveness, wealth of resources, inhospitable conditions and extreme fragility.

'The landscape is a form of writing' the author Paolo Cognetti told us in an interview we conducted with him last year. The Alpine landscape that we have travelled through is in fact composed of pastures, clearings, meadows, forests, cultivated woodlands, terraces, water sources, drystone walls, irrigation canals ... All elements that speak of a territory that was once agricultural, and still is in part today.

In the majority of the regions explored (Val Tanaro, Val Chisone, Val d'Otro, Valmalenco, Val Divedro), the fragmentation of land ownership is a major obstacle to the acquisition of larger areas and thus to the revival of a significant agricultural economy. There are some positive examples of small farms, often run by families or individuals, that are trying to recover the land taken over by the forest – which has been advancing relentlessly since agricultural activities started to be abandoned in the mountains in the 1950s – by reviving local crops or introducing new ones. Among them are cultivations of potatoes at Bourcet, in Val Chisone, and in Val d'Otro, lentils in Val Tanaro and strawberries in Val Martello. And then, everywhere, there are vegetable gardens, tiny allotments along the roadside, at the back of houses, in the spaces left over between one property and the next, or isolated in the middle of a meadow. Agriculture in all these valleys was once flourishing and for a long time the primary source of subsistence. On the south-facing slopes, the mountains bear the marks of the crops of the past: the terraces that were used to grow rye, wheat and potatoes.

Today, travelling through the valleys, what you encounter for the most part are arable and livestock farms of small size. There are horse breeders, small greenhouses and Alpine pastures, as well as nurseries for silviculture and fields of freshly mown hay. There are also a number of large stockbreeders (over a hundred head of cattle) with ever more sophisticated facilities and new spaces for the care and shelter of livestock. The model in Alto Adige is more extensive, almost industrial in character, dominated by the system of hereditary farms.

Speaking of agricultural economy and the mountains, we cannot help but give a thought to the question of forestry, in particular in relation to the management and maintenance of woodlands that have expanded greatly, largely due to measures of passive protection and restoration of forest cover introduced in the last century. This resource, a genuine green lung for the country, has been revealed to be ageing, ailing, unstable and vulnerable to weather events of particular violence (such as the Vaia storm of 2018) and thus in need of thinning out, felling and other interventions of silviculture.

Thinking about the maintenance of the woodland resources and felling, we cannot fail to take account of the damage caused by the breakdown of the timber production chain in the mountainous areas of Italy. The theme, highlighted with particular intensity in the valleys of Cadore and Comelico (province of Belluno), raises questions relating to the growing cost of working in the forest combined with a reduction in the real prices of industrial timber, 'in a condition of substantial stability in the productivity of forestry work'.[3] A productivity that has not seen the increases that were hoped for, considering the advances in the mechanisation of felling, logging and transport and the renewal of the infrastructure of forest roads and tracks. When a sawmill closes in a valley of the Italian mountains, the production chain of timber is interrupted and opportunities for employment at all levels downstream of the forestry activity are lost, point out the experts.

The quarrying and working of stone, still an ongoing activity in some regions, is another aspect of the productive dimension of Alpine geography. For centuries material has been extracted, ranging from such ores as zinc and galena in the quarries of Predil (Val Canale), talc (Saint-Nicolas) and cut stones for buildings in the city and street furniture (serpentine in Valmalenco, Laas marble not far from Val di Rabbi and granite in Val Chisone), eating into and eroding the slopes. Where activities have ceased, deep scars have been left behind, wounds in the ground, disfigured profiles and masses of tailings to be managed, raising questions regarding the abandonment of mining activities, the stability of the sections of mountain excavated and the reutilisation and reappropriation of these portions of territory on the part of local communities.

What is left today, now that production has ceased? The new embankment of the river Predil (Val Canale) was built out of the spoils of the mines at Raibl and looks like a work of land art set in a 'geo-mining' park. The mountain is a living element, whose geological forces are in continual evolution, as is demonstrated by the spoil slips in the valleys of Comelico, the erosion in Valmalenco and the gullies of Saint-Nicolas. A fragile mountain that changes inexorably and independently of the techniques of containment brought to bear by humanity. Even the utilisation of water resources makes a connection between the disruptive force of the element and the grandeur of the hydraulic works.

In this context, tourism is an economic activity that pervades the entire arc of the Alps. It becomes almost an autonomous element, disconnected from the environment.

The dimension of tourism really seems to be the common denominator of the Alpine region: the element that, owing to the form and reproducibility of what it has to offer, is repeated across space in a uniform manner. There are the large areas of land set aside for the parking of caravans and campers. There are the road signs that direct and channel tourists along 'pre-established routes'. There are the facilities for entertainment and sport. There are the rest areas at high altitude. These are infrastructures and services that, always the same, pepper and shape the contemporary landscape of tourism. While the character of the places changes, and is always different, the tourist industry requires structures and spaces that are repeated everywhere, identical in appearance. But above all, as the images show, they are elements, activities and facilities completely detached from the context: the mountains are urbanised, modelled, levelled, cleared of trees and infrastructured to make them accessible, globalised and attractive to holidaymakers.

As was pointed out at the beginning, it is necessary to reconsider the Alpine territory in its cultural and productive terms. The contemporary mountains seem today to be a place in search of its calling, poised between a recent past that has produced profound structural changes of an environmental, social and economic character and a rapidly evolving present. There are the difficulties of reviving farming activities as a result of the fragmentation of land ownership, the widespread abandonment of properties, industrial archaeology, the great pits left by mining operations in large portions of territory and, not least, tourism, a demanding machine that runs the risk of imposing one-sided responses that pay little attention to the region and the local dimension.

But today's mountains are also the small villages that are coming back to life, with the introduction of new local production, the phenomenon of new mountain dwellers returning to their origins, the revival of farming, forestry and pastoral activities. Positive dynamics out of which are emerging new modes of living in the mountains, in which small communities, able to find their own values and endogenous qualities again, are trying to shape their future in these territories filled with wonders.

Tourism, too, could bet on the value of the discovery of a region, and thus have a gentler side, more attentive to its locations (like the glacier trail in Val Martello or the opening of the shepherds' huts in Val di Rabbi and Val Martello or the Alpine pastures in Val d'Aosta during the summer season). A tourism that can show its appreciation for the Alpine dimension by recognising the richness of the environment and the spectacular nature of the landscape even when it does not serve as a backdrop to sporting or recreational activities.

Mechanisms

In the process of action and reaction between the peculiarities of the context, the extreme geological dimension of the mountain and the desire to inhabit the Alpine regions – in short, in the dialogue between humanity and nature – the system of mechanisms (infrastructures) serves to support and make possible this coexistence and thus the presence of humans in this hostile environment.

The geologist Emiliano Oddone points out that 'the resilient obstinacy of the mountain peoples has not entirely vanished. It is still handed down weakly, less strongly motivated, but present'. He also says that this aspect may still permit the recovery and comprehension of the sense that there are limits, an essential factor in the coexistence of humanity with the Alpine environment. Oddone the geologist is referring to the aggressive and predatory approach of contemporary society, which has viewed the mountains primarily as an inexhaustible resource, a space to be conquered 'whatever the cost', leading to the construction of buildings in places prone to landslides, along the banks of mountain streams and near gullies filled with spoil slip, with total indifference to any sense of limits. 'To reconcile ourselves with the places it would suffice to take up once again the scaling factors of time, space, masses, the forces at play, proximity and distance, rediscovering our smallness and relativity, but also our role,' concludes Oddone.

In the wholly contemporary effort to master the mountain and its spaces with a multitude of artefacts, the mechanisms are the micro- and macro-infrastructures, all those works that constrain, envelop, cut, counter-slope, support, create connections, bring things closer, cling to the rock and shape landscapes. Things like meshes, pinning, defences, basins for the collection of water, mechanically stabilised earth, humps and retaining walls, as well as small and mysterious devices marked by signs saying 'halt', 'danger'.

These are a series of elements of the landscape that serve to protect a house, a road or an entire community, as in the case of the mechanically stabilised ground above the village of Tossé, in Val di Rabbi, transformed into a walkway, or the Selva di Chambons, in Val Chisone, a true living shield of larches planted to protect the village centuries ago. As are the roads, the retaining walls or the ribs of metal and concrete that are embedded in the rock and attempt to limit, or prevent, the fall of boulders.

This exploration has also looked at the way we conquer space: with winding roads, steep hairpin bends leading to mountaintops, vertiginous trails and platforms, bridges built of stone, wood or metal. They are artifices that facilitate and support the accessibility of places which are very hard to reach. And the car parks, the rest places, often of vast size and used only for a few weeks a year. The mechanisms are all the infrastructures that serve to mediate the human presence in this setting: cableways, pools of water and exchanges for telecommunications.

What emerges from this account is an extremely artificial relationship between humanity and its environment. A world in which we have lost direct knowledge of the territory, that wisdom linked to experience and the collective memory of past events which allowed us to recognise the limits within which to operate with respect for the natural environmental. Today, all too often, living in the Alps no longer has any connection with the geographical space of the mountains. We 'construct' and seek to 'control' nature through an ever more frequent use of technological devices, whose functioning is placed in the hands of technicians responsible for their monitoring (like the micro-elements of the infrastructure for the management of water in Val Tanaro and Val di Rabbi). And this direct and intuitive relationship with the mountain environment and its harshness seems to have been dangerously undermined.

To what kind of landscape have we given rise in the attempt to 'dominate' this environment?

The Alps speak to us of this contradiction: the mountains, a living element, change, evolve, are transformed by gravity, tectonic thrusts, erosion, landslides and spoil slips, while anthropic action moulds the territory, restraining all the 'possible slips of tailings', boring through the rock, cementing the walls, cutting fissures, spanning rivers and torrents and constructing viaducts.

But how do these infrastructures hold a dialogue with the mountains? What impact do they have? Above all, what kind of questions do they raise?

Concluding notes

Through the Alps has been a long journey. An experimental project that has required a great joint effort to take stock of the current state of the Alpine landscape. An initiative that is intended to be a contribution to a necessary and urgent reflection on the future of these territories.

From east to west, we have travelled the roads and paths of Val Tanaro (Cuneo), Val Chisone (Turin), the valley of Saint-Nicolas (Aosta), Val Sermenza and Val d'Otro (Vercelli), Val Divedro (Verbano-Cusio-Ossola), Valmalenco (Sondrio), Val di Rabbi (Trento), Val Martello (Bolzano), the areas between Cadore and Comelico (Belluno) and Val Canale (Udine). It has been first of all a process of discovery, an unusual opportunity to observe these places and immerse ourselves in them, listening to and questioning the people who live in them, people who are familiar with their present and are imagining their future.

A route in stages that has gradually been enriched by encounters with the communities that have welcomed and accompanied us along the way.

A work that has set out to build bridges and, through the images, establish a connection between areas that, when close, often do not know much about each other and, when distant, imagine themselves to be more different than they are.

Out of it has come a cross-section of a large territory, as vast as it is complex in its diversity and in its commonality of intents and challenges. This is a work that aims to recount the way people live in these regions today, which systems of infrastructure pervade the valleys, what signs speak of the activities that go on there, what are the environmental resources that make them unique.

We have tried to do this by drawing attention to the frailty of the woods in Val Canale and the dense meshes of the wire netting used to protect houses in Val Chisone, or the pinning of the mountainside in the deep ravines of the Gola delle Fascette in Val Tanaro, but also marvelling at the sheer walls of the serpentine quarries in Valmalenco and the steep trails of the Val Sermenza.

This project is, above all, an account of the anthropic processes that, especially over the last two centuries, have radically transformed the Alpine landscape. We have set out to use photography to give a voice to the territory and the forms that have modelled and moulded it in recent decades, drawing attention as well to those contexts in which, for a certain period of time, urbanisation has been ill-considered and perhaps too bound by the demands of the tourist industry.

In this photographic account you will find the thousands of kilometres we have travelled by car and on foot, along paths and through hamlets scattered along the ridges, and all the voices and people who have shared with us their vision, allowing us to find out something of their history and their life in the Alps.

Taking this analysis as a starting point, architecture can begin once again to take care of these places by coming up with specific solutions, ones that are capable of reinterpreting them and triggering positive processes of renascence and reappropriation.

001 Credit: Alessandro Guida

012 Credit: Alessandro Guida

017 Credit: Alessandro Guida

015 Credit: Isabella Sassi Farìas

029 Credit: Alessandro Guida

070 Credit: Isabella Sassi Farìas

064 Credit: Alessandro Guida

063 Credit: Alessandro Guida

050 Credit: Isabella Sassi Farìas

046 Credit: Alessandro Guida

053 Credit: Isabella Sassi Farìas

067 Credit: Isabella Sassi Farìas

099 Credit: Alessandro Guida

073 Credit: Alessandro Guida

113 Credit: Davide Curatola Soprana

041 Credit: Alessandro Guida

044 Credit: Davide Curatola Soprana

035 Credit: Davide Curatola Soprana

034 Credit: Alessandro Guida

030 Credit: Davide Curatola Soprana

123 Credit: Alessandro Guida

128 Credit: Alessandro Guida

149 Credit: Davide Curatola Soprana

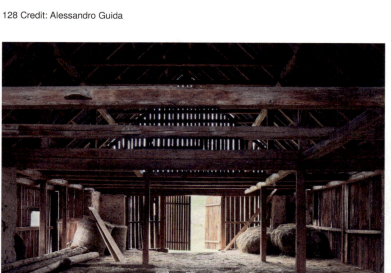

141 Credit: Alessandro Guida

148 Credit: Alessandro Guida

135 Credit: Alessandro Guida

139 Credit: Davide Curatola Soprana

143 Credit: Davide Curatola Soprana

138 Credit: Isabella Sassi Farìas

152 Credit: Davide Curatola Soprana

162 Credit: Alessandro Guida

197 Credit: Isabella Sassi Farias

207 Credit: Isabella Sassi Farias

204 Credit: Isabella Sassi Farias

194 Credit: Alessandro Guida

188 Credit: Isabella Sassi Farias

195 Credit: Alessandro Guida

189 Credit: Davide Curatola Soprana

179 Credit: Alessandro Guida

186 Credit: Davide Curatola Soprana

224 Credit: Isabella Sassi Farias

241 Credit: Alessandro Guida

234 Credit: Alessandro Guida

238 Credit: Alessandro Guida

246 Credit: Isabella Sassi Farias

247 Credit: Isabella Sassi Farias

248 Credit: Isabella Sassi Farias

249 Credit: Alessandro Guida

219 Credit: Davide Curatola Soprana

245 Credit: Alessandro Guida

258 Credit: Isabella Sassi Farìas

269 Credit: Isabella Sassi Farìas

270 Credit: Davide Curatola Soprana

273 Credit: Davide Curatola Soprana

272 Credit: Alessandro Guida

260 Credit: Alessandro Guida

259 Credit: Davide Curatola Soprana

261 Credit: Alessandro Guida

267 Credit: Isabella Sassi Farìas

271 Credit: Alessandro Guida

214 Credit: Alessandro Guida

Through the Alps is a project that was carried out between 2018 and 2020 by the Urban Reports collective on behalf of the Associazione Architetti Arco Alpino (AAA), which has supported and promoted the work. The AAA unites the Ordini degli Architetti PPC of Aosta, Belluno, Bolzano, Cuneo, Novara and Verbano-Cusio-Ossola, Sondrio, Turin, Trento, Udine and Vercelli, with the aim of creating synergies among the participants and coordinating initiatives linked to cultural and professional topics with a significant Alpine connection. It does so with the awareness that the affinities between the geographical characteristics of the mountains of the Alpine region have always given rise to similar problems and requirements, and continue to do so today.

The Urban Reports collective was in operation from 2017 until 2021. Its co-founders and contributors were Alessandro Guida, Davide Curatola Soprana and Isabella Sassi Farìas, architects and photographers (and responsible for the images), and Viviana Rubbo, architect and independent researcher (and author of the texts).

The project can be viewed in its entirety on the Architetti Arco Alpino website: architettiarcoalpino.it

This work was originally published in *Turris Babel 118 Attraverso le Alpi_Quer durch die Alpen* in 2020.

Landscapes

Ursula Aichner

How does the tourist gaze shape the perception of a landscape, and in what built structures does it find expression? The development of tourism and its architecture is closely intertwined with the changing aesthetic perception of a landscape, as can be shown using the example of South Tyrol.

Before we consider the relations between these two things – the perception of landscape and the built structures in which it is reflected – we should begin with the shift in mindset that brought about a new way of looking at the environment, and at the landscape in particular. In his book, *Why is Landscape Beautiful?*, Lucius Burckhardt traces this shift to a specific historical moment in which a marked distinction emerged between city and country, as two sides of a clearly comprehensible spatial structure.[1] City dwellers could perceive the landscape as aesthetic because they were outsiders, not directly dependent on it for their livelihood. And the main way they experienced this environment, before tourism as we know it today became established, was by walking from the city to the countryside. In doing so, they would filter their impressions, match them with the landscapes of memory, processing them into a narrative sequence that was perceived as aesthetic, as landscape.[2] This is relevant because in the modern period – our main focus here – the tendency is to soften the contrast between city and country, the distance between the two being reduced by technological progress and the development of transport infrastructure. And yet, as tourism gathered pace, the position of the outsider would become even more pronounced.

The philosophical reception of the Alpine landscape begins in the Renaissance, with the emergence of the phenomenon of the Grand Tour.[3] To get to Italy, one of the tour's central destinations, it was necessary to cross the Alps. Impossible to conquer physically, and ungraspable by the mind, the mountains exerted a fascination over travellers, inspiring a sense of the sublime, in the aesthetic parlance of the time.[4] The relevance of this, again, is that as the modern era progressed, advances in technology made the previously impassable terrain accessible and tangible, opening up the Alps for tourism as well. In the particular case of South Tyrol, the annexation of the region by Italy in 1919 had a considerable influence on the development of tourism and its architecture. As the Italian state pursued its policy of Italianisation in the interwar years,[5] the transport infrastructure was expanded to encompass the annexed region, in a concerted effort to promote tourism as a new branch of the economy.[6] Through the mediums of print and film, images of the Dolomites were planted in the consciousness of both German and Italian speakers.[7]

Second homes for the summer retreat

If we take a step back and look at the period before the First World War, we find an early form of tourism in the phenomenon of the summer retreat. The attraction of the new, of unknown places – a classic feature of later tourism – did not play a role here: the summer retreat was often spent in the same place year after year. This was also reflected in the type of visitor accommodation, which tended to be private – a second home, as it were.[8] Building on the central motivations of the summer retreat – (physical) recreation and rest – tourism centred around spas and thermal baths established itself in South Tyrol around 1900, mainly at lower altitudes with a mild climate.[9] Typical in this regard is Bad Dreikirchen.[10] The Settaris, a bourgeois family from Germany who always spent their summers here, would buy a large part of the surrounding land to build accommodation for their family members. The resulting ensemble, Briol, though constructed in a modern architectural language in the interwar period, is rooted in – indeed exemplifies – the ideal of the summer retreat.[11]

What is significant here is the site plan, which already has something of an 'urban' character, reflecting a particular understanding of community. Made up of several scattered structures, Briol doesn't just provide a retreat from the outside world, it also allows a degree of privacy within the family units. A certain introversion is also reflected in the architecture; for example, in the Mimi House, the openings

---

1 Lucius Burckhardt, *Why is Landscape Beautiful? The Science of Strollology*, English ed. (Basel: Birkhauser, 2015), 78.

2 Ibid., 83.

3 Susanne Stacher, *Sublime Visionen: Architektur in den Alpen* (Basel: Birkhauser, 2018), 10.

4 Ibid.

5 Ibid., 151.

6 Donatella Strangio, 'Turismo e infrastrutture', in P. Gasser, A. Leonardi, and G. Barth-Scalmani, eds., *Krieg und Tourismus im Spannungsfeld des Ersten Weltkrieges* (Merano: Studienverlag, 2014), 209–29, here 226.

7 Ibid., 37.

8 Michael Wedekind, 'Reisen an den Abgrund', in Gasser et al., *Krieg und Tourismus* (see note 6), 11.

9 Patrick Gasser, 'Vom aufstrebenden "Weltkurort" zum "Weltkriegs-Kurort". Meran im Ersten Weltkrieg', in Gasser et al., *Krieg und Tourismus* (see note 6), 333–59.

10 In addition to the three churches that give the hamlet its name, Bad Dreikirchen in the Eisack Valley in South Tyrol has a medieval inn that was reincarnated as a spa more than 200 years ago.

11 Briol is made up of several buildings by Lois Welzenbacher along with the main house, which was built by Hubert Lanzinger in 1928. The ensemble has been preserved unchanged and is today run as a hotel.

12 Gunda Barth-Scalmani, 'Tourismus und Krieg', in Gasser et al., *Krieg und Tourismus* (see note 6), 34.

13 Lucius Burckhardt, *Warum ist Landschaft schön?* (Berlin: Martin Schmitz Verlag, 2006), 118.

14 Clemens Holzmeister is considered one of Austria's most important twentieth-century architects. Among other things, he was entrusted with the design of many hotels and hospitality buildings that contributed to the development of tourism in German-speaking countries.

15 The Congrès internationaux d'architecture moderne, CIAM for short, were held between 1928 and 1959 and served as a platform for renowned architects to exchange ideas on topics of architecture and urban planning. In 1937 the focus was on 'housing and recreation'.

16 Stacher, *Sublime Visionen* (see note 3), 136.

17 Ibid., 39.

18 Burckhardt, *Warum ist Landschaft schön?* (see note 13), 121.

are reduced to a few small incisions in the body of the building, precisely placed so as to reveal considered views of the landscape. This is combined with a specific way of approaching the buildings that has been preserved to this day. Access by car is reserved for the owners only, so the main approach is on foot. Visitors walk through a wooded area that periodically opens up into clearings that offer views of the buildings and, beyond them, the rugged Dolomites – a study in contrasts. The positioning of the buildings is also significant on a larger scale: the ensemble is located on the opposite side of the valley from the Dolomites, so not in the immediate shadow of the sublime peaks, but on the lovelier slopes, where the panorama of the majestic Dolomites can be admired from a distance. Set against this impressive backdrop, the architecture is restrained, modest in both its external appearance and its interior furnishings, testifying to an intense awareness of the landscape and a certain understanding of our own position in relation to it.

Grand hotels of the emerging tourism

In the interwar period, as was already mentioned, state investment led to the expansion of the transport infrastructure, both the rail network and roads for private motorised transport.[12] With this, the way visitors travelled and approached their destinations changed. Much greater distances were covered in a short time, making it harder to build up a meaningful picture of the landscape. Now, instead of unfolding gradually, all impressions of the journey had to be condensed at the destination into a view that staged the grandeur of the mountains. Hotels were now set right against spectacular mountain backdrops.[13] In these early years of tourism, a holiday in South Tyrol remained the preserve of the well-to-do. This is reflected in the architectural language of the grand hotels, which were designed for guests who would stay for weeks. Here the Hotel Drei Zinnen in Sesto serves as a representative example.

Dating back to 1930, the hotel was the first to be built in an area that is today threaded with tourist structures. The owner, Hans Watschinger, then mayor of Sesto, was instrumental in ensuring that the municipality was annexed to Italy along with the rest of South Tyrol, contrary to the original plan. This suggests a certain openness towards Italy, and so it is not surprising that many Italians became regular guests at his hotel. As architect, however, he chose an Austrian, Clemens Holzmeister.[14] The architectural language of the hotel is modern, but at the same time it incorporates references to traditional vernacular features, as seen in the zoning of the elevation, with a base in natural stone, a white rendered middle part, and a timber apex topped by a gable roof. However, these references are defamiliarised by being reproduced at a different scale, enlarged to create an imposing urban facade turned towards the mountains. On the other side, the hotel is positioned directly on the street. The fact that it is built into the slope means that it is effectively entered at mid-level, developing three storeys upwards as well as downwards. Although the entrance is therefore set relatively low, an impressive view of the Dolomites immediately opens up on entering the lobby. The picture-postcard view is redeemed. The same expansive views are found in the spacious rooms on this level, which are intended for the use of all the guests. In this way, regular visitors formed friendships, creating a sense of community and intimacy that is still palpable today.

The folkloristic experiential world of mass tourism

The modern idea of tourism would only be widely realised after the Second World War, which represented a caesura in every respect. The majority of South Tyrol's lifts and cable cars date from this postwar period. The opening up of the formerly impassable Dolomites by technology was now no longer a selective phenomenon, but one that extended over the entire region. Tourism was no longer just a branch of the economy, but a whole industry. A significant step in this development was the new conception of tourism as a leisure pursuit for the masses. The seeds of this can already be found at CIAM V in 1937,[15] in Le Corbusier's proposal to create ski resorts as recreational parks for city dwellers as part of a larger, region-wide system.[16] The designed habitat took on a much greater scale, extending beyond the conventional boundaries of the city. As recreational areas were drawn into the orbit of the city dweller, the contrast between city and country softened. At the same time, leisure became subject to the same demands for efficiency that applied to work and industrial production. Thus, the landscape became a consumer object, effortlessly accessible to the masses, but also evaluated in the same terms as everyday consumer objects, which are defined by their short-lived character – a source of brief satisfaction, to be rapidly replaced by the next consumer product.[17]

The formal architectural language of the grand hotels, which also reflected their affiliation with an upper-class clientele, became obsolete with the rise of mass tourism. Looking at the architectural structures of the subsequent postwar period, what comes to mind is Burckhardt's term, 'ubiquitous regionalism',[18] critiquing the formalistic treatment, in these mass tourism venues, of elements derived from vernacular architecture. This folkloristic style can be seen as both a logical consequence and an integral part of this total landscape of mass tourism. The hypertypical landscape might be explained as a staged combination of object-like and narrative elements that are put together with a certain intention, or framed for a certain group of consumers. Replacing the narrative unfolding of the landscape, these elements are designed to be read in a specific way, leaving less room for heterogeneity and randomness and ensuring that their aesthetic appeal does not last longer than a single-use consumption.

Aerial photo from 1996. Data: Italian Ministry for Environment, Land and Sea Protection

3.1
space for physical recreation and the landscape of contemplation

chronological classification
- prewar period
- 'Sommerfrische'
- no economic focus

3
tourism and its landscapes

return to Burckhardt — relevance of tourism in relation to landscape
overview Stacher — development of tourism and the sublime in the Alps
consolidation Krieg und Tourismus — South Tyrol-specific

classification in

3.2
space of physical activity and landscape of physical sublimity

Briol example

social
- upper social class of Austria-Hungary

motivation
- recreation
- retreat
- contemplation

spatial
- temporary living
- second residence
- health resorts

architectural
- architectural language of modernism
- 'rescinding' in view of the landscape
- modesty

reference to
- development of tourism in the Alps
- regional differences
- complexity in agreement and comparison of sources

geographical
- in the temperate area

chronological classification
- interwar period

understanding the landscape
the Alps as therapeutic landscape

deceleration ← approach by the visitors — on foot — means of transport

unlike

regular visitors

Hotel Drei Zinnen example

geographical
in immediate vicinity of the mountains

architectural
- majestic facade towards the Dolomites
- architectural language of modernism
- disassociation of traditional forms
- ample communal spaces

social
- upper-class society
- Italian visitors

political
- Italianisation
- implementation of Italian culture

architectural
- grand hotels
- 'destination hotels'
- agreement — forced by fuelled expectations of professionalised travel advertising and visual forms of presentation

economic
tourism as a branch of the economy

through architectural language

geographical touristic discovery of the Dolomites
- supposedly neutral territory
- new narratives
  - stylised as the 'altar' of Italy
  - theatre of war as memory
  - Italy as victorious power

space of consumption and the landscape of dispersion
3.3

chronological classification
- postwar period

economic
tourism as industry

social
accessible to all social classes

technical
infrastructure as area-wide network

South Tyrol proposal

conditions

spatial
territory infused by touristic structures

the hypertypical landscape
operates through
- tangibility and unambiguity
- elements of folkloristic 'Heimatstil'

technical
transport infrastructure
- rail network
- lift facilities
enables focus on winter sports tourism

means of transport condition

perception of landscape
- domination of nature by technological means
- physical experience of domination of nature

based on
CIAM V 1937
Le Corbusier concept
zones of perfect recreation for the working city dweller

its realisation in France
- large urban forms
- inclusion of the rural into the urban system

flattening of the contrast between urban and rural areas

landscape perception
- 'mental' attitude
- passive role of the observer
- the sublime sensation is minimised by the collective experience

implementation of the ideas of modernity in the postwar period

nature as an object of consumption

.Reading the Alps

Alberto Winterle

Living in a place means first of all reading it, understanding it, assimilating it. This is even more evident in the case of a particular natural setting, like that of the Alpine chain, where the possibilities for utilisation of the land are limited.

Looking at the map of the Alps, it is in fact clear how the morphology of the region has conditioned and determined the modes of settlement and exploitation of places. Much of the area is occupied by mountains and forests, while the rest is characterised by slopes that follow the conformation of the valleys. Thus, anthropic space is highly limited and presents conditions that are often hardly conducive to habitation.

In spite of these constraints, the morphology also offers significant opportunities. In particular, the possibility of moving within the space of the valleys in different directions, vertical and horizontal, offers 'innumerable' points of view; that is, a succession of different perspectives on the landscape, whose perception changes continually.

In almost complete contrast with Caspar David Friedrich's famous painting of the *Wanderer Above the Sea of Fog*, which depicts a figure admiring a landscape, but one that is static and aestheticised, the idea of movement in space opens up new visions and scenarios. By moving we have in fact the possibility and opportunity to observe and analyse the transformations of the landscape and the objects that we have inserted in it with different eyes and from different perspectives, capable of revealing to us the true essence of things.

This was the spirit that defined the first Rassegna Architettura Arco Alpino, the survey of the region's architecture that set out to interpret the Alpine chain. It was promoted by the Architetti Arco Alpino association formed at the beginning of 2016 by the associations of architects from Cuneo, Turin, Aosta, Vercelli, Novara and Verbano-Cusio-Ossola, Sondrio, Trento, Bolzano, Belluno and Udine.

The interregional spirit of the association stems from the realisation that it is a unified and recognisable territory, but at the same a very delicate and precious one. The aim is to explore the concrete possibility of analysing the area and coming up with reflections and possible strategies in the light of 'regional empathies'.

This signifies going beyond administrative boundaries and identifying instead situations with social, economic, cultural and obviously 'architectural' characteristics in common. These are areas that are often considered 'peripheral', especially in regions that are not completely mountainous, where the theme of rugged terrain is just one among many. The mountains are a backdrop that appears and disappears from sight according to atmospheric conditions, and in the same manner appears and disappears in regional political priorities as well.

The Rassegna Architettura Arco Alpino consists of twenty-two surveys carried out between 2010 and 2016 in the Italian portion of the geographical area identified by the Alpine Convention and chosen by a jury (made up of Bernardo Bader, Sebastiano Brandolini and Quintus Miller) from 246 candidate projects. From a first interpretation of the interventions, it is evident that the Alpine regions today present a very wide range of cultural, political, social and economic contexts. Something which leads to strongly contrasting phenomena of transformation of the landscape.

In some places the abandonment of the mountains, with the accompanying demographic decline, has led to a risk of losing the important built heritage as well. So interventions have been aimed at making the most of what already exists, and the construction of examples able to serve as a reference for the upgrading of individual buildings and entire villages. In others, however, where a correct balance between anthropic presence and the land has been amply achieved and often even surpassed, the objective is to call a halt to any possible further land take and development of tourism, betting on quality of construction and embarking on a programme of aesthetic and formal research that is capable of becoming of economic value and serving as an element of social identification.

Such phenomena are directly linked to the 'cultural horizons' of reference of each individual context. Evident, in fact, are the close ties that South Tyrol, or Alto Adige as it is called in Italian, has historically maintained with North Tyrol in Austria and with the neighbouring Swiss cantons. Contemporary architecture, as well as research into the most advanced technologies related to the

Casa fd, story of a house not yet finished. Madesimo, Sondrio. By ES-ARCH Architetto Enrico Scaramellini. Credit: Marcello Mariana

sustainability of buildings, are today a common heritage, not only among specialists but also in the general population. Here, therefore, there is clearly a capacity to see the contemporary as something that not only has intrinsic value but can also produce a return in economic terms as well as those of image.

On the other hand, the relations of the eastern Alpine regions with Austria and Slovenia have less effect. Research seems to be the prerogative of a limited number of architects who, with an almost pioneering effort, have succeeded in introducing some interesting examples into the landscape, but which remain isolated cases. In the western Alps the cross-border links with France and Switzerland have deeper cultural and even linguistic roots, but the difficulty of crossing the great massifs in the area may have prevented the sharing and spread of common modes of construction. The focus is on the regeneration of the built heritage rather than on the construction of new buildings, which in some areas is conditioned by the pressure and effects of the tourism-based economy.

The perspective taken by the survey covers all the regions of the Italian Alps, with the aim of comparing the effects and results of the evolution of the contemporary architecture on the same plane. The first question we asked ourselves, in a critical interpretation of the works, is whether the Alpine regions, whose conditions have historically produced a rich set of 'variations on the theme', are today subject to a banal standardisation of models or whether it is still possible to find the richness that we consider to represent an added value. The form of the Alpine regions has in the past constituted a sort of defence, rooted in isolation, of the 'typical' characteristics of places. The difficulties of communication have led to the local development of an empirical research into construction techniques. In spite of very similar physical conditions, as well as models of exploitation of the land and construction of houses, it is in fact possible to find subtle differences that constitute the richness of our built heritage. Just as in language, passing not only from one valley to the next but even from village to village, small variations in vocabulary or phonemes can be recognised, slight differences can be found in construction techniques and decorative details.

Overall, we have been able to observe how examples of the contemporary design of buildings all across the Alpine chain confirm the wealth of differences and small changes of accent that constitute the characteristics of the places that the conditions and the strength of the regions still today, as in the past, continue to reflect, making the works unique and not replicable.

But what significance do works of architecture of quality like the ones selected in the Architettura Arco Alpino survey have in the processes of transformation of the Alpine regions? Are they examples capable of influencing the policies and more generally the culture of a place? In this case it is more difficult to give an answer. With regard to the large number of interventions, both public and private, there is a tendency to come up with responses considered 'traditional' and reassuring rather than go down less familiar and more uncertain roads. In this sense the banalisation of building to serve the needs of Alpine tourism, based on the construction of a fake identity to 'sell' to the people who visit the Alps, can be found in all the different contexts.

What may, however, offer hope are a new critical capacity and an awareness that can help to show how the authenticity of a place is directly linked to the authenticity of the people who live and work in that place.

Thus, we can consider the widespread presence of works of quality in the Alpine regions a positive factor, even if they are of small size and significance, as they become an element of overall enhancement of the landscape. In addition to defining a coherent path to be followed, this serves to highlight the responsibility of individual architects in making their own important contribution, independently of the economic values at play. This regards both single buildings and the space between them: that common space understood as a synthesis between public space and the common good.

The different definition of the projects and the different functional types analysed also underlines the obvious physical, economic and climatic factors that have given rise to them. The conditions on the valley bottom and those in the higher areas of the mountains are in fact very different, to the point where it is possible to identify at least three kinds of mountain: the summit, the part that has remained almost untouched, with a minimal anthropic presence, where interventions are confined chiefly to facilities for excursions in the summer and for winter sports; the middle heights of the mountain, the part devoted chiefly to agriculture and stock farming, which in many cases is seeing a depopulation of the towns and villages; and the residential and productive valley floor with all the problems of an infrastructural nature caused by the greater anthropic pressure and the limited spaces of the valleys.

These contexts are further conditioned by the different modes of use stemming from the seasonal alternation in the possible exploitation of the territory. In fact, the exploitation of the mountain for tourism in the two seasons, winter and summer, entails very different requirements and ways of using the territory. Into this context we must also insert the anticipation of possible modifications in the modes of use and exploitation of the assets that the Alps offer as a consequence of climate change.

If in the end the different situations that characterise the regions of the Alpine chain are clear and legible, at the same time the widespread complexity that is produced today by the themes of habitation remains evident, leading to unpredictable results in some cases. For these reasons we consider it of fundamental importance to continue to observe the evolution of these contexts, comparing projects and experiences and seeking to highlight those processes that are able to generate quality.

Straddling as they do national and international administrative boundaries, therefore, the Alps can continue to be a place of passage, of comparison and of cultural, linguistic, economic and even architectural exchange.

Images from the 2016 Alpine Arc Architecture review and related catalogue, *Turris Babel*, no. 105.

Reconstruction of the Paraloup. By Dario Castellino, Valeria Cottino, Giovanni Barberis, Prof. Daniele Regis. Credit: Leonhard Angerer

Residential unit serving the Albergo Diffuso in Paluzza. By Ceschia e Mentil Architetti Associati. Credit: Alessandra Chemollo

Collective housing, Eppan. By feld72. Credit: Hertha Hurnaus

Wood and the dog. By Studio Errante Architetture. Credit: Studio Errante Architetture

Collective housing, Eppan. By feld72. Credit: Hertha Hurnaus

Reusing the historical architectural heritage inside UNESCO's Dolomites

Gianluca D'Incà Levis

A regenerative vision and practice
for the territory – and for the
Milano Cortina 2026 Winter Olympics

> 'Ingenuity is seeing possibilities
> where others don't.'
> Enrico Mattei

Since 2011, Dolomiti Contemporanee (DC) has been working within the scope of territorial regeneration towards the experimental reactivation of large abandoned or underused sites inside the Dolomites, a UNESCO World Heritage site since 2009. The work involves former plants, factories and villages, or entire territorial areas, hitherto lacking in development and adaptation to contemporary needs.

One example of this process centres on the peculiar building which used to house the former elementary school of Casso, in the Vajont Dam area where, on 9 October 1963, a landslide detached from a mountain, setting off one of the worst tragedies in the history of Italy (the Vajont disaster).

In 2012, the former elementary school building, damaged by that tragic event and, since then, having remained closed for almost half a century, was reopened by DC, which has made it a Centre for the Contemporary Culture of the Mountain and the Landscape. This acts as one of the hubs from which we work on the construction of an intellectual, cultural and functional collaboration for creating a contemporary mountain, one which is neither vapid nor automated or self-cannibalising, one which must never be understood as a mere place of enjoyment (and enjoyment which is mainly stubbornly touristic), but rather is a privileged workshop for people in tune with the environment and the research that is carried out on it. In essence, seeing the mountain as a privileged place wherein to produce and experiment – that is, something very different from a simple place merely to be consumed. We see the mountain itself as a self-transforming construction site. And a construction site is not a cutting board. And a resource is not a bread basket.

Let us consider the symbolic value of DC's presence in the Vajont Dam area. For those who declare that they wish to reopen closed-up spaces, both thinking of the space and critically *meaning* it, this location is extraordinarily emblematic. Here, in 1963, almost 2,000 people died. So, it is not easy to break through this place, still so very marked to this day. It is not easy to declare, in such a place, that culture, art, vision and design are necessary tools, rather than merely decorative ones, through which people renew themselves and their habitat, refounding it when necessary. It is not easy to move beyond the commemorative sentiment gripping the Vajont – which equally must absolutely not always coincide with the identity of these places and those who inhabit them. It is not easy, remaining here; but this is the exact type of place where one must remain when one declares one wants to deal with the regeneration of the landscape and the territory.

Then again for us, here, in the Terre Alte, the High Lands, we want to climb, to scale; and, in fact, we can say it like this, too: DC is a cultural mountaineering project. Scaling is understood, here, with the double meaning of both climbing and measuring things, redefining their value, quality, residual utility, functional transformability. Regenerating lost structures, making a series of new territorial reactors inside the network is, in fact, equivalent to remeasuring the potential and value, and to activating them in a networking practice (with its territorial and extraterritorial alliances, DC has almost 500 partners and supporters, both public and private and related to research, both in Italy and abroad), leading to their recovery.

Former Eni Village Corte di Cadore. The main hall of the Colonia under Mount Antelao. Credit: Giacomo De Donà

Inside the main hall of the Eni Village of Borca. Credit: Giacomo De Donà

Eni Village of Borca. The Colonia ramps in the hypertrophic forest of Borca. Credit: Sergio Casagrande

But we are in the mountains here – pushing the mountain, which means contributing to the co-generation of the Alpine landscape. This landscape is not a gift from God; it does not pre-date humans, it must be built, always responsibly, by humans themselves. So, this scaling which we're referring to is a decisively forward projection, without nostalgia for what remains of the past and for the nostalgia of industrial archaeology.

Let us recall the definition of landscape by Edoardo Gellner, the architect who, in the 1950s, created the Eni Village of Borca di Cadore, another one of the extraordinary sites whose regeneration DC has been working on ever since 2014 (Progettoborca.net): the landscape is the sum of both natural environment and human action.

And so: if one works well, with a vision, on research, then the landscape always moves, rises and is transformed. If one works badly, it is broken. It is paramount to have a will, and the ability to project that will.

Otherwise, these great sites, these amazing factories of the '50s, '60s or '70s, rather than being reborn to new life, will truly die, and will be preyed upon by the atrophying mechanisms of nostalgia, memory or mere heritage protection, instead of being updated, transformed, reactivated.

So, here's the crux of the matter. Inside the Dolomites, as is true for the Alps in general, landscapes that have been preyed upon or disfigured by opaque governance, short-sightedness, as well as the deadly grail of badly managed tourism (leading to overload of both infrastructure and landscape), all suffer, stop, lie still like fossils. Instead, they should be turned inside-out, protected and driven forward (it is not enough to just protect them: they must be moved forward). Significant historical sites (both architecture and heritage in relation to the environment) that have been closed down and extinguished by historical or critical events, these crisis sites, craters of the human landscape, which may show special transformability characteristics (the actual regeneration potential of large real-estate sites must be assessed very carefully before any action is taken in their favour), must be transformed into opportunities.

This activity of rethinking, refounding and refunctionalising critical or problematic sites and contexts is a responsible and necessary action.

So, how do we operate in practice? Since 2011, we have worked on about twenty problematic sites, which are, for those who decide to notice them, precious depressed resources inside the Dolomite Mountains. These sites are striking, in their architecture's relationship with the environmental context, in their history and aesthetics, and in their high residual potential for transformation and regeneration. They are the unresolved sites, those where both policy and public funding for redevelopment projects have failed in their meagre attempts of a restart. They are heritage and, as such, they must be rekindled.

The main institution around which the practice of DC is articulated consists in the residency which animates the regeneration construction sites. The residency is always active within the sites' hubs during the proactive reactivation work phase. Every year, hundreds of artists, architects, designers, researchers, students and environmental experts live and work within the territory, getting to know it directly, and developing with us, in their projects and partnerships, regenerative designs.

DC's experimental and innovative practice is conducted and demonstrated, as well as in the field work on the structures it addresses, through participation in events, platforms, displays, conferences and other initiatives on the themes of urban and Alpine regeneration.

DC participated in the Venice Architecture Biennale XVI (*Arcipelago Italia*, 2018, curated by Mario Cucinella) and XVII (*Resilient Communities*, 2021, curated by Alessandro Melis), on both occasions opening the Italian Pavilion and putting forward its developed themes. In both 2017 and 2018, DC received a special mention from the Italian Ministry of Culture following its participation in the European Council Landscape Prize. In 2013, this concerned Progettoborca (the platform which, as mentioned, since 2014 has been regenerating the extraordinary former Eni Village of Borca di Cadore); in 2020, the recognition came for the vision developed in the Vajont Dam area, in particular for the Two Calls for Vajont, the international competition which will lead to the creation of an anti-commemorative piece on the Vajont Dam (twocalls.net), which, despite being the symbol of the 1963 tragedy, must not be considered eternally as a gravestone, a symbol of death.

Art, contemporary culture, the intellectual elaboration of design and existential models, as well as an unsweetened and non-fatuous image of the mountain … These, together with the vast participatory networks which we utilise every day, are the main tools through which we work on the recovery and rekindling of sites – which aren't dead at all, but dormant, if that. To wake them, sleeping isn't the answer, but rather thinking and doing. It is the *logos*, lo and behold, which guides our action.

At the moment, as everyone is well aware, much is being said about Milano Cortina 2026, and the Milano Cortina 2026 Winter Olympics. Up until now, inside the Dolomites, the work hasn't proceeded well: no planning or ideas, no sensitivity to the issues of regeneration and land saving.

But what are they, the Olympics? Are they useful for the territories in which they take place?

The Olympics are not simply a sporting event, but an opportunity (and therefore also a risk), still, for the host country. Events of this magnitude must help to produce territorial development: ultimately, they must serve this purpose. Infrastructure, visibility, tourism, relaunch trends: the Olympics can be a great inspiration for growth for large areas, and for the entire country.

To be clear: it is the Olympics that, if well managed, should constitute a 'service' in favour of the territory, and not the territory's role to serve the sporting event. Seems simple, right? However, until now, this has not been the case (things have been a little better in Milan, where regeneration has been taken into consideration).

For several years, while networking with both the territory and the universities, we have proposed a solution to the issue of the Olympic Village which must be built in the Dolomites by 2026.

The former Villaggio Eni di Corte, in Borca di Cadore, is 16 kilometres from Cortina d'Ampezzo. This is the great design by Enrico Mattei who, in the 1950s, when he was the president of ENI (Ente Nazionale Idrocarburi or National Fuel Trust), commissioned Edoardo Gellner to create this innovative welfare essay in the heart of the mountains of the Cadore territory. A cradle of modernism and an innovative vision of Italy, the extraordinary creation of Mattei and Gellner (with the collaboration of Carlo Scarpa for Our Lady of the Cadore Church) is, today, still at least three things: the symbol of an era during which Italy worked and truly innovated, permeating the world in culture, architecture, design and business; a work of art, architecture and exceptional environmental sensitivity; a remarkable available square footage, too, which could accommodate thousands of people, and in which is already active, ever since 2014, a major regeneration site, operated by DC together with Proprietà Minoter. This is, more precisely, Progettoborca, a project of functional reconceptualisation of this semi-stranded station.

Since 2014, we have been reflecting publicly on this, as well as on other high-potential sites in the

Former Eni Village Corte di Cadore. Artist in residence, Sandra Hauser. Credit: Giacomo De Donà

Dolomites landscape. For instance, the Trampolino Italia ski-jumping hill in Zuel, a symbol of the 1956 Winter Olympics, and therefore, not only just in theory, a natural torchbearer for the 2026 games.

The former Eni Village, the Trampolino Italia: two extraordinary sites, which the Olympics could help to recover and which, in turn, could make them a less foolish project than they have seemed to be so far. Our idea, in fact, is to 'use' the Olympics to carry out the restoration of these huge sites. So that it may be possible to temporarily host those functions which are essential for the sporting event, as well as the people. Temporarily, of course. Because the idea, and the territorial negotiation (we must reiterate, both cultural and functional – the two terms should be considered as synonyms), is wider and more serious. The restored structures, with the participation of both the public and the private spheres, at the end of the Olympics would become a service and research Dolomiti hub.

The Colonia (summer camp building), one of the structures that make up the Borca Village, alone housed a population of 1,000 people up until the early 1990s. This complex architecture in fact can count over 20,000 square metres of internal space, and is now being used experimentally by DC, which is searching for options for its ultimate recovery. After hosting athletes, then, from 2027 onwards, it could host, on a more long-term basis, a thousand researchers, scholars, creative companies.

The needs of the territory are already intercepted by our practice: they should be catalysed here. The idea, always only vaguely mentioned, of those who, up until now, should have been planning a smart and sustainable Olympics, was this: to create a temporary modular architecture in a free meadow near Cortina d'Ampezzo, and then disassemble it in the aftermath of the sporting event. What an idea! But what about sustainability? Let's see if it changes. We want to change it. Onwards.

Transformation through technology and politics

A Grand Tour through (post-)operaist criticism

Michael Klein

Among the many possibilities of charting a path, of making connections between places and positions to map an itinerary, a tour, that will provide insight into a culture, there seems to me to be a particularly important one that has run, almost invisibly, through an 'Italian' criticism in recent decades. There's always something arbitrary about the stopping points on a tour: they can be continually added to, or curtailed, and their meaning only becomes apparent when one actively seeks them out. The particular route I am referring to leads from Manfredo Tafuri via Giancarlo De Carlo to Silvia Federici and finally to Maurizio Lazzarato. It is, as already mentioned, of an arbitrary nature, in the sense that it could be extended to include other positions, undoubtedly becoming more multilayered and more complex in the process, and undoubtedly more contradictory, too, in the best sense of the word – but that is not the aim here. What holds the tour together, and gives it significance, is the potential that this line of critique opens up for a specific reflection on housing and its architectures – one that requires architecture to be understood in broader terms than the encompassing framework for housing – a reflection that can only be roughly outlined here.

In no way does this tour claim to represent 'Italian' housing. Strictly speaking, it can hardly be understood as an *Italian* Grand Tour. To begin with, its critique does not target anything that appears specifically Italian – rather the opposite: what the individual positions share is an attitude that rejects the idea of a national identity, refusing the definition of an 'Italianness' (*italianità*) and, with it, any attempt to reduce identity along essentialist lines. What they have in common is a *historical* perspective and the emphasis that things could also be different. Nor is the object of their critique exclusively Italian: Manfredo Tafuri, for example, analyses the housing reform pursued by the Social Democratic Party during the Weimar era and the housing programme of so-called Red Vienna; Giancarlo De Carlo discusses the thinking that informed the contributions to the 1929 International Congress for Modern Architecture (CIAM) in Frankfurt, for example, which addressed the theme of *Die Wohnung für das Existenzminimum* (The Dwelling for Minimal Existence) – in other words, strategies of reform aimed at the remediation of the housing shortage or the reorganisation of housing; Silvia Federici formulates a fundamental critique of social conditions with *Wages Against Housework* (even if the text is clearly anchored in the Italian feminist discourse), while Maurizio Lazzarato's *The Making of the Indebted Man* – written when he had already been living in France for decades – contains not a single reference to Italy. In each case, though the critique is not limited to Italy – and, indeed, unfolds outside the country – it indirectly provides an insight into developments in Italy in recent decades. And even if it only partly relates to architecture, all of it – in one way or another – is fundamentally concerned with the household, or, more precisely: the relations of the household to production and reproduction. In this respect, this line of criticism brings together a critical reflection on housing of a kind unseen since Friedrich Engels' polemic on the housing question: the (post-)workerist critique is, moreover, merciless in its attacks on the reforming zeal of the avant-garde (architectural as well as political), rejecting any false romanticism, any conception of a 'heroic' modernism.[1] Such negation is another characteristic of this line of criticism.

Not long after setting up the Institute of History at the Istituto Universitario di Architettura di Venezia (IUAV) in 1968, Manfredo Tafuri began an intensive engagement with the area that was one major vehicle for modernism's attempts to remake society: the housing of the working class. A central theme of the institutional debates of modern architecture, in terms of its content, but only rarely included in its canon, this housing – from Unwin's garden suburbs in Letchworth to the *Siedlungen* of the Weimar Republic or the monumental courtyard blocks of Red Vienna – is a recurring subject in Tafuri's work.[2] His interest, however, is motivated less by a concern to correct an imbalance in the writing of history, and much more by the historical importance that he attributes to architecture as an instrument in the struggle for social change. His verdict on this role, however, is damning: opposing the prevailing social order by means of architecture is a romantic project that can only result in a 'regressive utopia', as Tafuri notes with reference to Red Vienna, probably the most extensive attempt to reform housing on the scale of the city. Such an approach represents little more than a realised ideology – a reality that is staged without making the extensive changes that are actually required.[3]

Forming the backdrop to the historian's engagement are the challenges of the present, for Tafuri's discussion of the architecture of the social democratic parties of the 1920s should be read as a reaction to the Left's disillusion with attempts at reform in postwar Italy, in both the political sphere and in architecture, from the state initiative, INA-Casa, which sought to improve the housing conditions of the working class, to the kind of capitalism with a human face pursued by Adriano Olivetti in Ivrea.

From the perspective of Tafuri, but also of Tronti or Negri, or more precisely of workerism (*operaismo*) as a whole, the reformism of social democracy, as embodied

---

1 Workerism refers to a line of thought that can be traced back to practices that emerged in the early 1960s in Italy and which put emphasis on the subjective and political (i.e., conflictual) practice of social transformation. For a very brief introduction see: Roberto Nigro, 'Workerism', *Krisis*, no. 2 (2018).

2 See, for example, Manfredo Tafuri's *Vienna Rossa: La politica residenziale nella Vienna socialista, 1919–1933* (Milan: Electra Editrice, 1980); 'Socialdemocrazia e città nella Repubblica di Weimar', *Contropiano*, no. 1 (1971), 207–23; and *Architecture and Utopia: Design and Capitalist Development* (Cambridge, MA: MIT Press, 1979).

3 Tafuri, *Vienna Rossa*, 8–10.

Front cover of Manfredo Tafuri, ed., *Vienna Rossa: La politica residenziale nella Vienna socialista, 1919–1933* (Milan: Electa Editrice, 1980).

Front cover of Collettivo internazionale femminista, ed., *Wages for Housework: International Feminist Strategy / Le operaie della casa* (Venice: Marsilio Editori, 1975).

4   Giancarlo De Carlo, 'Architecture's Public', in Peter Blundell Jones, Doina Petrescu and Jeremy Till (Abingdon: Spon Press, 2007), 3–22. The text, which began life as a lecture in Liège in 1969, was first published in *Parametro*.

5   Silvia Federici, 'Wages Against Housework', *The Commoner*, no. 15 (2012), 74–87.

6   Ibid., 77.

7   The initiative goes back to Selma James' and Mariarosa della Costa's discussion of unwaged work and the feminist collective Lotta Femminista, and also includes Brigitte Galtier. Even though this position is influenced by workerism (*operaismo*), Lotta Femminista broke with *potere operaio* as early as 1973 and turned to *autonomia*. See, for example, 'Anna Curcio: Marxist Feminism of Rupture', *Viewpoint Magazine*, 2020.

8   See also Nicole Cox and Silvia Federici, *Counter-Planning from the Kitchen: Wages for Housework, a Perspective on Capital and the Left* (New York: New York Wages for Housework Committee and Falling Wall Press, 1975).

9   Maurizio Lazzarato, *The Making of the Indebted Man* (Los Angeles: Semiotext(e), 2012).

10   T. H. Marshall, *Citizenship and Social Class* (Cambridge: Cambridge University Press, 1950).

---

above all in housing programmes, is little more than a technique to make the capitalist mode of production more efficient. In fact, there had been a fundamental transformation of the logics of capitalist production from the early twentieth century on, driven by a recognition that a partial improvement of conditions led to greater economic efficiency. The inability of the workers' movement to recognise this reorientation, or rather to propose a new strategy to counter it, put it in the worst possible position. By clinging to reformism, the Left manoeuvred itself into a state of political paralysis. This is the starting point for Tafuri's analysis of a modern movement that, for all its overt commitment to the Left, plays into the hands of capital without meaning to do so. For Tafuri, this reveals the problematic nature of any entwining of politics and architectural practice – and the revelation has consequences for his own historical and theoretical practice, which henceforth turns against any simple operative aims.

The new commitment of the modern movement to the renewal of the discipline of architecture is of concern not only to Tafuri but to Giancarlo De Carlo as well. Rather than the institutional nature of housing, his critique focuses above all on the role of the architect and the premise that the construction of mass housing is the means by which modern architecture can bring about a self-renewal, a democratisation of practice. In the text 'Architecture's Public', which crystallises a whole series of his positions, De Carlo questions the 'credibility' of modernism, its capacity to have a concept of the 'public' that embraces all the people who use it, and criticises the elitism that it has inherited from the historical discipline and that it continues to maintain.[4] In its proximity to power, architecture had never really engaged with the actual motivations of planning – a situation that would only become more institutionalised with the rise of bourgeois professionalism, which turned the discipline into a service industry. Modernism, too, as De Carlo makes clear, was primarily concerned with the question of *how,* without devoting much time to *why* ('because the problems of "why" are considered solved once and for all'). Under the rubric *Die Wohnung für das Existenzminimum* (The Dwelling for Minimal Existence) the avant-garde at CIAM II in Frankfurt in 1929 had addressed the question of how best to meet the huge demand for housing that arose with the rapid urbanisation of the early twentieth century. For De Carlo, the response of architecture is as consistent as it is frightening: the industrialised production of a space that, reduced to the bare essentials, soon represents little more than the minimum necessary for subsistence, a proverbial existential minimum. However, more than the existence of the inhabitants and workers, what it secures is the continuation of the prevailing capitalist mode of production, which guarantees the reproduction of labour power without ensuring a quality of life: bound to the logic of the minimum, in the end it upholds nothing but the rationality of scarcity. But what conclusions can be drawn from this experience? This avant-garde approach had made architecture superfluous, when the fortunes of the discipline lay essentially in its indispensability, the fact there is always a need for architecture. Ultimately, De Carlo concludes that architecture is too important to be left to those who create architecture – and couples his demand for a comprehensive democratisation of the discipline to this position.

This turn towards the subject is also followed by feminist discourse, as reflected in Silvia Federici's *Wages Against Housework*, for example.[5] Here, however, the focus is not on the production of the home, but on the everyday life inside it, and thus on reproduction: the activities and social dependencies in the household take centre-stage in the text, making clear the distinction between paid – male-dominated – work and the unwaged, unseen domestic labour that is allocated to women. In this negotiation of the differences between reproductive work and the 'real' work of the man, Federici finds the basis of a system of subordination that insists the place of a woman is in the home, a model of subjectification that would have the woman be dependent on the man, her real task in life amounting to unpaid domestic work. The aim of the demand for wages, however, is not to declare that housework is a job like any other, but rather to draw attention to how this activity has been made a 'natural attribute of the female personality' and invisible.[6] At the same time, Federici shows how this not only puts the woman in a relationship of dependence, but disciplines the male worker who serves the factory, in that 'his' wife, who is fully dependent on his wages, provides him with a service out of love.

The woman thus becomes the servant of both the working class and of capitalism: the relationship of dependence is always a double one, in which the woman as a *lover* serves her husband as a *worker*, on whose income she is dependent and whose wage always already includes the unwaged reproductive work. From this perspective, the political significance of the demand for wages becomes clear. But rather than being an isolated demand, 'Wages Against Housework' is embedded in the International Wages for Housework Campaign (IWFHC) calling for recognition and payment for all caring work, in the home and outside. A grassroots network that came out of the 1970s feminist movement, IWFHC is strongly influenced by the Italian feminist (post-)workerist and autonomist discourse that found expression in the Lotta Femminista collective, for example.[7] Their campaigning takes aim not only at the prevailing social order, but at the traditional line of political critique that sees waged labour as the principal site of the class struggle, overlooking other forms of subjugation.[8] What *Wages Against Housework* makes clear to this day is that, to be progressive, the struggle for social change cannot be limited to the factory, but must encompass everyone, starting from everyday life as a whole.

Maurizio Lazzarato's *The Making of the Indebted Man* could be chosen as the last stop on this tour.[9] Strictly speaking, the essay has nothing to do with architecture; rather, it sketches the contemporary neoliberal condition as one characterised by a specific production of subjectivity, the asymmetrical debtor/creditor relationship. While this form of subjectification is always already inherent in economic relations, as Lazzarato makes clear with reference to Nietzsche on the one hand and Deleuze and Guattari on the other, it only fully unfolds with neoliberalism. At no point does the essay explicitly address housing. And yet the developments that Lazzarato traces, especially in relation to welfare systems and deregulation in Europe, have far-reaching consequences for housing, representing the most significant driver of change in recent decades. Lazzarato's text offers a lens through which to look anew at these developments.

If Tafuri and De Carlo present housing as an extension of the logic of capitalism that uses housing reform as an instrument for optimising efficiency, securing production by improving workers' living conditions – in other words, as a technique of 'public safety' – now the understanding of that safety or security is fundamentally reversed. Whereas the earlier logic was still close to the provision of the welfare state, in the sense of housing as a *social right* of citizens,[10] in recent decades this understanding has given way to the idea of housing as a commodity that is to be traded for profit, and where security can only be found in its economic value. Here, security is a solo undertaking, one that compels the subject to become, as Lazzarato puts it, the

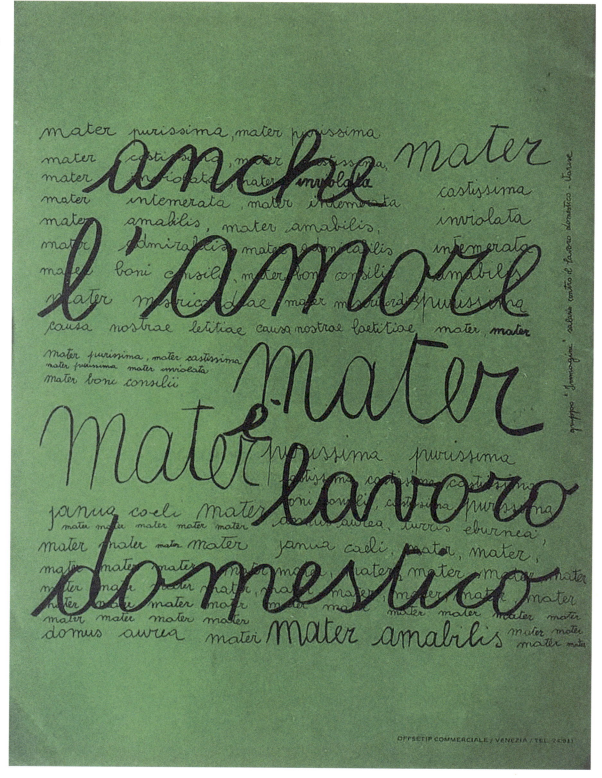

'Anche l'amore è lavoro domestico' (Love is also housework). Back cover of *Le operaie della casa, rivista dell'autonomia femminista*, no. 23 (1976).

11 Lazzarato, *The Making of the Indebted Man* (see note 9), 12.

12 Brett Christophers, *Rentier Capitalism: Who Owns the Economy and Who Pays for It?* (London: Verso, 2020), xvi.

13 The 'Italian' position of post-workerist positioning is thus formulated here less through the lens of a common positive point of reference, and more through a common practice of political rejection *qua* negation, in which subjectivation is assigned a special status.

'entrepreneur' of their 'own misery'.[11] Effectively, there is no real security anymore: in order to provide for their basic needs, the neoliberal subject is compelled to get into debt, to take on a never-ending obligation to repay. Even those who are dependent on state aid cannot simply take advantage of it without offering something in return – this is the new mechanism of debt, as represented by Lazzarato.

The state's provision of social housing – triggered by the housing crisis of the end of the nineteenth century – largely resulted in a devaluation of share capital and a new emphasis on productive capital. Neoliberalism reverses this logic with the return of *rentier capitalism*, whereby payment accrues to 'an economic actor … purely by virtue of controlling something valuable, as Brett Christophers describes the dynamic.[12] Put another way: once more, *ownership* rather than *production* is the driver of profit, making debt an inescapable necessity for everyone.

In Lazzarato's account, the social subject simultaneously endures several forms of dispossession, deprived of public wealth, of participation in decision-making processes and ultimately also of individual agency over how they spend their time, as the creditor/debtor relation imposes a specific regime of time in which the future is equated with the imperative to honour one's debts, to pay them off. Debt erases any possibility of emancipatory change. As a relation of subjectivation, debt is not merely an obligation that acts as an 'external' force on the subject; rather, it invades the body and soul, occupying a person's innermost thoughts, becoming a constant burden. Housing is intimately connected to this new mechanism of debt, as it is often the largest investment a person makes in their life.

None of the positions visited here reflects a naive optimism about the possibilities for change. In relation to housing, the (post-)workerist position is characterised instead by a sometimes vehement rejection of the reformist tendency, as seen with Tafuri, or a disciplinary pragmatism, as De Carlo makes clear. Nor does their critique spare their own movement, speaking uncomfortable truths even to their own disadvantage, as is evident in Federici's feminist position. Admittedly, each of these critiques concedes that these relations are historical and have the potential to be changed. Lazzarato's critique, however, reaches a new level of negation that seems initially to be drained of optimism. The indebted human being is deprived of any possibility for autonomous action, reduced to a mere cog in a complex machinery, leaving hardly any room for the hope that a better world could come about through a purposeful turning of the screws. When Lazzarato speaks of 'machinic enslavement' and subjugation, it becomes clear that the possibility of creating a resistant subjectivity presupposes a radical rejection of the morality of debt: according to Lazzarato, the small reform will not be enough.

At first glance, there seems to be little that is 'Italian' about this position, which follows on from the previous ones – but perhaps the opposite is the case.[13] In Italy, the relatively late experience of industrialisation and urbanisation and the rapid development of Fordism, the resistance to industrial labour, the still patriarchal social structure, the long periods of massive repression of critical opposition, and ultimately also the drastic changes of recent decades, which have involved both the dismantling of the welfare system and the restructuring of the real-estate markets, has made (or rather, kept) the critique of workerism relentlessly honest. Paradoxically, it is often more sober, more direct – and ultimately probably also closer to reality – than its German-speaking and politically institutionalised sister.

Michael Obrist in conversation with Silvia Federici
(scholar, feminist, longtime activist, writer and teacher)

Reproductive work, the body and the politics of the commons

'Enough free work! Wages for housework for the struggle against the first exploitation.' Poster for the 8 March 1974 International Women's Day from the Wages for Housework Committee, Venice.

It has never been clearer that we live in a social system and a social context that is not capable of reproducing our lives. Not only incomes, but life itself has become precarious. Everywhere we turn, we see the great plagues that have haunted humanity and that, presumably, capitalism was to have overcome: hunger, famine, climate change, war and so on. I want to use this confrontation with everyday reality as a determinative frame for this discussion, because the Covid pandemic has made it dramatically present in everybody's lives. Systemic change, creating new social relations, transforming society, even revolutionising it from the bottom up – these have to be on the horizon of every intervention, action and organisation of our everyday life.

As I mentioned, the Covid pandemic has been a window to a reality that was already being experienced intensely by millions of people across the world; as was the knowledge that we live in a society where every structure of the organisation of life and well-being is subordinate to the principle of the private accumulation of wealth. This topic has been at the centre of feminist organising since the beginning of the new phase of feminism in the 1970s. If there is something that stands out from what the feminist movement has contributed to the evolution of the thinking and the vision we have of social change, it is that now we see the issue of reproductive work as being fundamental. Posing this issue at the centre of political thinking and organising has been the window from which we have looked at the world, moving away from the almost exclusive concentration on the factory, industrial work, wages and workday pay.

In fact, there's this other reality – a universe of activities – that has been invisible and taken for granted. The activities of day-to-day reproductive labour are often conceived of in a very reductive manner. When people think of reproductive work, people think of housework, cooking, cleaning and shopping. Whereas anyone with any direct experience of it will tell you that it is work that engages with every aspect of our lives and mobilises all our capacities. It's emotional work; it's sexual work; it's organisational work to address the needs of every person in the family and the community. And all that has been minimised, degraded – and not even been conceived of as work.

Since the beginning of capitalism, from the economic treaties of Adam Smith onwards, when the question of 'what is work' is asked, you will find that reproductive labour is overlooked. It has always been characterised as a sort of personal service – and the effect is that those who have performed those services, which have primarily been women, have been basically forced into a second-class citizenship and made dependent. This has particularly been the case since the turn of the nineteenth century, when the first major long-term reforms of the structure of the family and reproductive work, at least in Europe and in the United States, took place. That is when domestic labour began to be organised specifically and consciously as a function of the production of a workforce. In other words, domestic work was shaped in such a way that it became the daily and lifelong support to the reproduction of the workforce. The real beneficiaries of this work have been not the members of the family, but the employers, the capitalist class, the accumulators of wealth.

So, the fact that we have exposed this universe of exploitation of labour has been extremely important. It has been a major turning point, because it also enabled us to understand that capitalism does not only accumulate labour and wealth, but it also accumulates differences, diversities and hierarchies. In other words, capitalism is able to perpetuate itself by continuously creating hierarchies and dividing those that it exploits. The creation of gender hierarchies, racial hierarchies and colonial hierarchies has been historically one of the main tools capitalism has used to keep its power. We can now recognise, for instance, that coloniality has been a structural character of capitalist development at all stages.

Maria Mies, one of the most important German feminists of the last fifty years, has spoken of 'women as the last colony'. Gender is a form of colony and of course gender intersects with race. This whole hierarchical structure has enabled the capitalist class to delegate to those with more power the control over those sectors of the world-proletariat that have been destined to more intense forms of exploitation. The control and supervision of those with less power has been delegated to the wageworker, who in this capacity has functioned as the representative of the state with regard, for instance, to his wife and children. For generations, capitalism has never had to confront the housewife or the domestic worker directly, as it always could do that through the mediation of the wageworker.

The father, in a sense, has the same role regarding the children as he has to the wife. 'Wait until your father comes home,' we have been told. The father is the name of the law. This has been the function of the nuclear family. It has been a powerful support system for the organisation of work. It has been extremely difficult for women to see the cause of their suffering, dependence and exploitation, because they have not confronted capitalism directly.

The feminist movement, with its tearing of the veil from domestic work and the nuclear family, has made a direct confrontation possible. The goal had been to hide the reality of social relations at work within the family. The feminist movement has played a special role, also, in acknowledging the connection between feminism and the anti-colonial struggle. The struggle against racism and the feminist struggle are not separate movements. We cannot think of a feminist movement that is not, at the same time, a movement against colonialism and against all the forms of exploitation that are happening today.

But we need to create a common ground of struggle. For more than five centuries the capitalist system has been able to accumulate power and exploit populations in every part of the world, utilising all the sciences, sociology, philosophy, law and social sciences. We are confronting the great Hydra, as the Zapatistas would say.

And this is where, for me, the whole question of the commons comes in. Understanding what the commons have been historically is important to understand in what sense the idea of the commons can help us to construct the vision of another society starting from the present, of a society that is just and that is built on cooperation and collective work.

First of all, the word 'commons' is a primarily European word. In Latin America they would speak of '*comunalidad*' (community). 'Commons' refers to a social reality that prevailed in England in the sixteenth and seventeenth centuries and was increasingly destroyed by capitalism. As Marx pointed out in the last chapter of volume one of *Capital* – the famous chapter on the secret of primitive accumulation – the destruction of the commons, and the expulsion of the peasantry in Europe from the lands that they had been cultivating collectively for their reproduction, was the condition for the development of capitalism. This was the nature of the medieval exchange: You get to use the land and then you do labour services on the land of the Lord.

When we speak of commons, we speak of a particular historical reality that for a long, long time, at least since the 1900s, was almost forgotten in Europe. In the seventeenth and eighteenth centuries, the battle for the commons – to reclaim access to forests, grazing grounds, and so on – was the centre of the revolutionary struggle. Later, with industrialisation and the rise of the socialist movement, the key terrain of proletarian struggle was to become wage-work and the wage struggle. By the 1990s, however, the question of the commons has returned to be a key theme in the politics of many social movements, like the Zapatistas …

This is because we have witnessed a new capitalist expansion, comparable to the primitive accumulation drive of the sixteenth and seventeenth centuries, the period that set the conditions for the take-off of the capitalist system. Once again, today, masses of people are being expelled from their homes, from their lands and from their countries. This is why we have huge migratory movements and so many wars. Wars produce clearances, which make mining and agribusiness possible. So, the commons become visible at a moment when millions of people are losing what remains of them.

There is also the ecological connection, because the expulsion of people from the land for the expansion of mining and the conversion of arable land into industrial agriculture comes with a great ecological cost, a climate cost. Much of the warming of the earth is caused by these practices.

But, from a feminist viewpoint, the issue of the commons opens up another perspective: that of rethinking and reorganising our everyday reproduction work in more collective, more cooperative ways, enabling us to overcome the isolation in which we now live. Capitalism has separated women in the organisation of domestic reproduction. The nuclear families in which millions of people, millions of women, have lived, have been a form of enclosure, a form of imprisonment. Women's economic dependence on men, the devaluation of domestic work, the fact that domestic work is not seen as work, and that it is always in a way that isolates us, make this work especially consuming for women.

Domestic work is limitless. You don't have a work time. Your work day stretches all through the day. You don't have Christmas vacations. At Christmas you work ten times more. You don't have a retirement. They say that women live longer than men. I always say, they live longer because they have to help everybody not only to live, but also to die. We never include in the activities of domestic work the work of helping people who are ill and the work of helping people who are dying. Some men and children do housework, but the bulk of the work is still done by women, even when we have another job outside the home.

Applied to reproductive work, the idea of the commons implies a restructuring whereby we break with the isolation in which it is performed today, creating collective forms of reproductive work and with them new social relations, giving us more strength, more power with regard to men and, above all, capital, the state. This means that we also have to reorganise housing and the urban space. In today's urban space everything is organised in such a way that undermines our capacity to come together, to have spaces for collective gatherings and decision-making. We know that the streets of Paris, the great boulevards, were opened up so the tanks could pass through the city after the Paris Commune.

The United States are a fertile ground to understand that kind of politics. For example, the restructuring of the urban space that has taken place in the postwar period with the creation of suburbia was a political programme in every detail. This was a time when the United States was confronting a crisis, with all the returning soldiers from the war, who thought that they had been fighting for democracy and had developed a strong bond with each other. And they knew how to fight. They were coming back expecting something. Apparently, in a number of places, the US government tried to stop the quick repatriation of the troops. Add to that, capitalism was delegitimised, as its support for fascism and even Nazism was well understood. So, they had to pacify the returning soldiers, and giving them a home, organising for them a domestic space far from the places where they worked, making sure that after work they would not congregate with other workers to make trouble, was a major concern. Suburbia was the solution, though those who benefitted from the 'home policy' were primarily white workers.

A home turns a revolutionary into a conservative. That was the thought, and certainly the hope. The home is the quickest programme to erase any desire for change. Putting the home as far away as you can from the workplace meant that, when the workers stopped working, they would not go to a bar and talk politics and unions. They would go home right away, to the suburbs, where their houses would be, all separated from each other, each house a shell. Each house is a cocoon, it's a self-enclosed system of private life. You don't look over to the house of your neighbour; and you'll have a little piece of land in front of the house so that, on Sunday, the worker mows the lawn. So, everything was thought out politically and it is not an accident that the suburbs have been such a centre of conservativism.

We now have to take the opposite path and rethink the house in a way that brings us together and that overcomes the isolation that comes with the domestic organisation of reproductive work. This is the task of the new generation of architects: rethink urban planning, rethink the urban space, the relation between the home and the street. See the street not just as a place for the circulation of people and commodities, but as a place to come together, as a place to have an assembly, as a place where people can actually be present and not just quickly move on to their destination. Rethink the home, the structure of housing, create common spaces, spaces for people to practice collective decision-making and for communities to come together.

The space of the house must be seen as a workspace. How do you cook? Do you cook alone? In the new kind of housing there is only space for one person, which means that all their work must be done alone, in isolation. Today we are witnessing a change, a challenge to the nuclear family. We are beginning to see the development of more extended forms of families. People are coming together, either based on affinities or simply to share the rent, because rents are increasing so much that it becomes difficult to actually have our own apartment. We have, then, to rethink the space of the house from the point of view of the changes that are taking place in the organisation of the family, and the need to include other people, to connect with others in the buildings.

Housing, too, has to be taken out of the market, like healthcare, food and other basic necessities. All these changes will amount to nothing, however, unless we establish that housing is a right and put an end to the fact that people can be thrown out into the streets. In New York, presumably one of the richest towns in the world, you find people literally dying in the streets everywhere. And every day, their number is growing because, especially after Covid, people are losing their jobs and people are forced to live in the streets.

'Commoning' also enhances our possibility of survival in other ways. In many peripheries of cities in Latin America, you will find encampments made by people who were expelled from their lands and forced to urbanise. They take over some land and then build houses, streets, a community. Collective labour allows you to survive. It's the work of establishing streets and keeping them clean; making sure that when it rains, they do not become rivers of mud; the work of helping each other to build a house. In other words: collectivity is realised in the most intense, effective ways in the moments when people have nothing, the moments of crisis, when you think: 'My life depends on yours.' Then, collective labour is the only escape from complete defeat.

We are all in this situation. The threat of losing our home and the threat of a life in isolation from each other is something that is haunting all of us. Thus, the question of the commoning of housing, the commoning of space, is connected in an umbilical way to the commoning of reproductive work and the breaking down of hierarchies. Obviously, it must be supported by a change in the material conditions of our life, by a change in the resources we have available, a change in social priorities concerning the use and distribution of the social wealth and the goals of production.

Last, I want to say that commoning is not just a vision for the future but is a condition of our struggle in the present. I agree with Marx when he says that Communism is the movement that challenges the status quo from day to day. The same is true for the idea of commoning. Our lives are so consuming, so poor in resources, that the making of a struggle can often become another burden. So, it is crucial that when we speak of struggling, we do something that positively changes our lives. Commoning is not only a vision of the future, but a condition for experiencing the principles of the society we want to build in the present. And, to me, there is no better task. There is no better task for us. Wherever we are, whatever we do.

OBRIST Thank you so much, Silvia Federici. It was a short life lesson. I'm very grateful that you pointed out the relation between these sociopolitical questions with architecture and organisation of space and perhaps even the organisation of society itself.

I'm actually in Rome right now, and there are very interesting cases that give me back the hope that things could really change. We are investigating a project of squatters in an old former office building of the state which was sold to Blackstone, one of the big corporate investment companies, that are in possession of, in a real sense of the word, the world. And by squatting and creating something which, in my opinion, is the very idea of autonomy, with the idea of community shaped by a common ground, works like a 'desiring-production' by which people could start to imagine a different world collectively.

And that imagination is a different world from the one that you could imagine while going into solitude, as depicted in Thoreau's Walden.

I am curious to know how you see the production of the commons between Nature, Village and Metropolis?

FEDERICI Well, it's complicated because so much has been done to institute that division.

Negri and Hardt in *Commonwealth* speak of the metropolis as the real place of the commons, the place where the commons are produced. On the opposite side, you have Maria Mies, who sees the city, the metropolis, as parasitic on the village, feeding on nature's commons. The city does not produce its own support, and therefore it's exploitative with regards to the countryside. I think that what we are seeing now are attempts to break down this separation. I am thinking of the movement for communal gardens and urban agriculture. This is restoring the connection with the natural world into our cities. It is a movement that has received a great impulse from the migration of thousands of people from the Global South, from countries where they always had a piece of land, a garden, something in which to plant. Seeing the way things are produced, that carrots do not come in a plastic package, that the kernels come out of the earth, is extremely important.
It is regaining a relationship with the soil, with the growing of things, it is beginning to rediscover needs. It's not a picture that you take on your iPhone as part of a tourist trip, but it's understanding nature as a world of processes that have evolved over billions of years.

In *Beyond the Periphery of the Skin*, I wrote that our bodies do not end where our skin ends. Because our bodies, too, have been conceived as enclosed spaces, as isolated cocoons, by capitalism. And that happened not only by organising all kinds of separation, but by inculcating a conception of the body as a separate thing. The fact that the body is expansive – which explains why we are affected by the music that we hear, why we are affected by people's words – has been largely overlooked. We are affected by relationships. So, our body is not a self-enclosed system, but an open system. The Renaissance idea of the relation between the macrocosm and the microcosm is profoundly true. Because we are not monads in the way Leibniz wrote about, without windows and without doors.

Recuperating our relationship with nature is also transforming our relationship with ourselves. There is a capacity for it that is pre-existing, but we need to actually produce it creatively. And so, opening the city to the natural world is a necessity. I've written about these phenomena occurring in Africa, where the first act of many who are expelled from the countryside and forced to urbanise is to occupy land. Any kind of unused public land is taken over, mostly by women, to plant things in it. This of course requires a struggle to defend the crops from the police, etc. Some analysts of urban cities in Africa say that many cities are turning into garden-cities because so much cultivation is taking place in them. This is a good trend and should occur not only out of desperate necessity but because we need to integrate nature in our life. We need to reconnect with animals not only as pets, and with trees, water, everything. Unfortunately, capitalist development is moving in the opposite direction, even when it pretends to produce clean energy.

I've spoken with women in Brazil who are organising against companies producing wind turbines. They say that now they are beginning to enclose beaches and preventing access to the sea, even for fishers, to plant these wind turbines, presumably for the sake of alternative energies. But in the meantime, they deprive communities of their livelihood, leaving the field free for the great ships who scoop up all the fish for commercial purposes.

OBRIST I find the ideas of self-appropriation and of emancipation are fundamental in your narrative. Growing together, forming a community. I was just thinking that, in Vienna, we have a sort of socialist utopia of ownership of the city and a large amount of housing, granting people a kind of accessibility towards an inner circle of society. This is the origin of the so-called Red Vienna in the 1920s. Today, it generates a welcoming to the poorer parts of society as well as the middle class, but unfortunately not the poorest.

But my question is: Is it possible to establish a state or a city structure as a structure and at the same time be able to create a civic society? Or is the civic society just the product of a fight for autonomy?

FEDERICI Community comes out of struggle. The relationships that people develop in the process of organising in a struggle are those that then shape the organisation of life. A struggle generates a sense of trust, solidarity and understanding, and negotiating the limits of that. Yes, I think it is the struggle that generates the plan.

OBRIST Now, there is all this discussion from left to right about a general basic income. How do you see that concept with regards to the idea of becoming adult, becoming a community through struggle and operating together?

FEDERICI The question is what the basic income actually is. Because there are different versions of it. Let's not forget that the first supporter of the general basic income was Milton Friedman. His idea of the guaranteed basic income was that it would be the end of the 'welfare state'; it would allow the state to stop investing in any form of social reproduction, like pensions, healthcare, education. It would realise the dream of a completely free market. This would come with giving everybody a certain amount of income, certainly very low, at the level of subsistence at best. This was meant as a liberation for the state from any social obligation. But, if the basic income is not associated with access to other forms of social wealth, like housing, healthcare, free education, it may be inconsequential. I am also concerned that we do no not lose sight of the importance of denouncing the devaluation of our reproductive work and the fact that our reproductive work is a pillar of every other form of work, and a major contributor to the capitalist accumulation of wealth.

In other words, seen from the perspective of reproductive work, we can see and make clear that a 'basic income programme' is not a charity, is not a concession by the state to the 'poor'. It would be easy for the state to present the basic income as something that is paid by other workers. This is why our campaign to establish what is reproductive work, how the state has taken advantage of our work and made billions at the cost of women's lives, remains crucial. In Spain some feminists have spoken of 'care income', precisely to underline that it is income we need for the work to reproduce ourselves, which in capitalism is also appropriated by capital and the state.

OBRIST You talked about the history of the commons. We have this concept in the Alps, the 'Almen' which operate on a collective-use basis for the inhabitants to raise their cows and so on. And, obviously, certain kinds of structures have a certain kind of fragility by not being protected.

And here I want to jump to technology – if you look at the internet, it started with the completely naive hope that it would become a common good. But it was penetrated by trolls and by the intelligence agencies, etc. How would you see that?

FEDERICI I want to add that the internet is not a real commons. First of all, in order to produce the technology that makes the internet possible, many commons have been and have to be destroyed across the world. People have to be expropriated of their lands, so that companies may come in to extract the minerals necessary for digital production. We cannot simply look at what can be done with the internet, but what has to be done to produce it.

Digital technology depends on mining. Computers and iPhones are ecological disasters. They require the mining of lithium, coltan, etc. In the Democratic Republic of the Congo, one of the richest regions of the world concerning minerals needed for digital production, they speak of 'blood computers', precisely because, as I said, people's land commons are being destroyed, and inevitably people's lives are being destroyed as well.

We have to think not only of what can be done with the internet; we have to also think, as I wrote in *Re-enchanting the World*, what is the material condition for the production of the internet. So, we cannot say that the internet is a commons while ignoring how it is being produced and the wars this production generates.

Transcript of a talk that was part of the Wohngespräche (Housing Talks) series by the Department of Housing and Design at TU Wien which took place in June 2022.

The hut as an image of the future present

Leonardo Caffo

[1] I develop this concept in L. Caffo, *Velocità di fuga. Sei parole per il contemporaneo* (Turin: Einaudi, 2018).

Everyone in the West feels the desire to escape. Young people are leaving their jobs, many are designing new solutions for an increasingly radical way of living. Escapes to the countryside, to the woods … The need for 'an emergency way out' seems more urgent than ever, whether it be through a return to the hallucinogens of the American counterculture or to meditative practices. In reality, it is always, in any case, a new management of space that contemporaneity is demanding. We could define this trend, stealing a term from astronomy, as a tendency for the velocity of escape,[1] where what emerges – very clearly so even in Italy, to start with a specific territory – is the desire for an alternative to the old models that the not-so-recent capitalism has imposed: family life, classic work, ordinary management of the self in civilised societies.

Epidemic, war, general precariousness. The model of collective salvation produced by the 1970s in the West, by postmodern cultures, seems to have failed. So, what to do? Contemporary times register many discussions on 'escape routes', but it is becoming extremely urgent to devise individual salvation devices. If world and life coincide, as Ludwig Wittgenstein suggests and as we will see shortly, perhaps saving one's own life is a first attempt to discuss the salvation of the world.

To highlight four macro tendencies of contemporary life by recording, so to speak, their categories, we could recognise four paths for salvation:

1. Disconnection from the digital. In spite of the prevailing dominance of meta-webs and social networks, this tendency tells of a widespread will, even among young people, to disconnect and return to 'analogue' life. To make a prophecy: we will design instruments and architectural devices at great expense that will allow mobile phones not to connect. Meanwhile, even here in Italy, the demand to join forces and live in farmhouses, the ever-growing eco-villages and the return to the south, completely transforms the old thinking about 'we will live in the city forever'. On the other hand, Covid must have changed something …

2. The mental escape route through hallucinogens. From ayahuasca and its increasing popularity among young people, to the new mushroom cultures, it expresses a general need to find new ways out of the ordinary mind. This cannot really be all there is. There is a growing awareness that real life is only a part of the true real: how many possibilities of knowledge and wonder have we occluded by not empowering our minds towards new horizons? Again, in Italy, data in hand, we are indulging more and more in alternative possibilities opened up by these substances.

3. The path of mental guidance through meditation, from Zen to yoga – even if often clumsily interpreted by urban cultures – shows the desire to free oneself with thoughts that are less and less anchored to the development of the metropolis and capital, such as Viennese psychoanalysis. In the last year alone, dozens of monasteries have opened in Milan, Rome and Turin to practice different forms of meditation. The space to be reinhabited this time is interior: how can architecture respond to this new journey?

4. And finally micro-communities and anarchy – but that start from a new culture of spaces and return to a reinterpretation of isolation, to which I would like to devote the following words given the general purpose of this work.

One of the most popular accounts on Instagram is called Cabin Porn, named after the editorial project that inspired it. Published by Penguin, it collects the world's most incredible cabins: on mountain furrows, on the banks of rivers, on rocks, climbing in forests, hovering over lava. We are in the age of skyscrapers, it is true, but for many years now the theme of the cabin, which is also that of simple life, has imposed itself as fundamental to contemporary life. In May 2018, an already historic exhibition at Fondazione Prada in Venice called *Machines à penser*, curated by Dieter Roelstraete, analysed the idea that every form of thought and life corresponds to a particular form of space – some lives, as those of Adorno, Wittgenstein and Heidegger, are put in relation to the real cabins in which these philosophers seem to have found the most suitable place for their theories. It is a common

[2] In the sense I speak about in *Vegan. Un manifesto filosofico* (Turin: Einaudi, 2018).

[3] 'Sono apparso alla Madonna', in *Opere* (Milan: Bompiani, 2002), 1155–6.

topos, but nevertheless not over-explored, and perhaps never as actual as today: stories of non-forced and voluntary isolation in order to really learn to think. In such a disheartening present, the pressing question is: how do we save ourselves?

There is a sort of matrix story, the one of Thoreau and his cabin, which is, then, the story of the American literature masterpiece *Walden*. There is the story of Theodore John Kaczynski, better known as the 'Unabomber', a professor of mathematics at Berkley who later became the most wanted terrorist in US history, writing his manifesto 'Industrial Society and its Future' right inside his cabin in Lincoln, Montana. There are diverse stories and cabins, as Le Corbusier's Le Cabanon in Roquebrune-Cap-Martin, France, built in 1951.

It is the myth of the cabin that returns recursively symbolising, above all, the possibility of an emergency exit from everyday life. The spirit of these times imposes a rather urgent reflection on alternative ways of life, because if we stop to observe, the scenario we have before us is not at all reassuring. The average age is dropping again, stress is almost natural, war is everywhere, diseases are increasing, climates are rebelling against man, the world is trembling and too often suggests an abyss. Simplicity as a technique to decrease doing seems to be a solution that is completely internal to the traditional East, of which the imitative passion of the contemporary West – often naive if not ridiculous – is a mirror. This has led to the emergence of yoga between one aperitif and another, door-to-door meditation, and even Tibetan music to listen to in the morning before going to work. A sort of depth for our own use: not even psychoanalysis had succeeded in such a petit-bourgeois project. This is the depth that sinks, to paraphrase a famous phrase by Leonardo Sciascia ('by trying to be deep, one sinks'). Where one might smile, however, a necessary space for reflection opens up. A space that is philosophical in the most technical sense, and which the cabin with all its power recounts: the need to understand another way of living, simpler and more self-care oriented.

Perhaps, especially 'for us', it is wrong to look to an East – currently non-existent except in its most isolated places – if it is simplicity that we seek to understand: there are many Western stories inserted within our vital and daily parameters which can teach us a lot, and that deserve a philosophy that applies to the resolution of a practical and enormous problem: the exit from praxis. The intuition is that no philosophical theory is such if it is not tested through a life practice, and translated into a space of its own. 'Form of life' means the space for that same life. For a 'practice of life' to be such, it must be totally enveloping: it is not a matter of doing something in the 'between' of things, but rather of being that very thing. Michel Foucault's latest courses at the Collège de France are all about exploring the essence of a truly philosophical life: not a life that does philosophy but a life that *is* philosophy. The paradox Foucault arrives at is that a truly philosophical life is only that of the cynic: the one who lives in the present, in immanence and therefore also in violence, and who tends towards total self-presence. Although I do not fully agree with Foucault, I am certain that this new and almost maniacal interest in cabins has its own decisive importance and lies in the wake of this inheritance: the understanding of a simple life, withdrawn without necessarily being isolated, and capable of manifesting concerns only related to the essence of things. A transformation of existence can only be a radical process, and the confrontation between these cabins which, from Thoreau to Wittgenstein, traverse history, is also the most extreme point of this radicalisation: new forms of life through new spaces for life.

The journey into simplicity represented by the idea of the cabin is once again about the value of philosophical research: not a discipline of learning about something, but the transformation of things themselves. Here, philosophy and design meet in a new way. Things are not learnt; they are taken and they become part of us. These attempts to combine thought and architecture are, after all, attempts to disconnect from a 'network' that today seems more present and real than ever. A common acronym is 'IoT' (internet of things). This is the name given to the extension of the internet into the realm of things, of everyday objects but also of physical places. A network that is no longer merely metaphorical but physical, making objects endowed with an intelligence, more or less strong, thanks to the fact that they can communicate data through themselves by accessing aggregated information from others. Many of you will be reading with a SmartWatch on your wrist, indicating when it is time to do some exercise to help lower your blood pressure: you are in the web of things.

There is a common thread linking cabins, even the ones I chose for my book *Four Cabins*. I wrote on the subject (Thoreau, Unabomber, Le Corbusier, Wittgenstein) up to the present state of affairs: what if the net takes over? What if the prophecy known as Stephen Hawking's 'Singularity' brings Philip K. Dick's science fiction literature closer to reality than we can expect: could machines one day evolve to the point where our wills are overthrown? Perhaps the scenario, after the corporeal fragility Covid has imposed on us, is rather about the impossibility of a simple and genuine life in a time when the network has transformed itself from an instrument of consumption into the consumption of its own instruments (us).

This scenario, envisaged to varying degrees by both Thoreau and Kaczynski, could lead to the design of spaces aimed at 'disconnection', of which cabins are the noble ancestors. This is why we are so attracted to them today. But salvation, both in philosophy and architecture, does not mean primitivism. In fact, I would not like the idea of simplicity to be understood as a 'retreat to the past' because these two concepts really have nothing to do with each other. Rather, what happens is that simplicity is the questioning of things that come from the outside and whose reason we ignore: if they weigh down or complicate the only life we have, we have to understand if and how necessary it is to continue dealing with them. Life is really a system of choices, not of expectations. After all, there is a limit to the principle of simplification that is commonly accepted in ontology: if adding hypotheses, assumptions, entities or conditions is necessary for a given principle to work, then simplification must loosen its meshes. The idea of a way out through the contemplation of the 'simple' entails a reflection on how to be in the world while relieving it of everything that is neither necessary nor useful in its contingency.

Simplicity as subtraction – after all, the cabin is a kind of veganism applied to life[2] – leads to the *Absolute* at a moment when linguistic and rational superstructures seem to fade to the advantage of gestures and symbols that belong to domains of meaning, from which we have distanced ourselves. What aims at the Absolute is poetry, mysticism, art or religion – i.e., all activities that deliberately abandon the structure of ordinary language: it is Picasso who invented Cubism to see, by breaking the forms of reality, what lies behind it; it is Carmelo Bene who defined the search for meaning in art as detachment, distance, absence, separateness, illness, delirium, sound and, above all, urgency, life, suffering; the resonance of saying beyond the concept. It is a musical interval of pitch […] it is the abyss that separates oral and written.[3]

Wittgenstein was in constant search of a philosophy that diffuses in life; no wonder, then, that this research comes from one of the supposed fathers (though, as I have already said, misinterpreted) of analytic philosophy:

rigour in the philosophical method is the mirror of the absence of rigour in the world. To be simple is to accept non-sense as an integral part of the life of a meaning generator like the human being: 'Life was a dream, now we are awake.'[4] Wittgenstein is philosophy trying to get out of itself, the paradox of the method in order to do without the method, the non-metaphorical sense of these cabins at the edge of the world where, indeed, the meaning of the world must be outside it. In the world everything is as it is, and everything happens as it happens; there is no value in it – nor, if there were, would it have any value. If there is a value that has value, it must be outside every future and be-as-it-is. For every future and being-ness is accidental. That which makes them non-accidental cannot be in the world, for otherwise it would itself be accidental. It must be outside the world.[5]

The cabin is what is left of the world once you try to place yourself outside the world. It is what remains after the fire, the last vestige of our species once anthropocentrism has been beaten. 'There may be times when reality approaches, others when it recedes. The tide rises or falls, but the sea is always there.'[6] And contrary to what the entire Western tradition in philosophy has maintained, it is not necessary to leave traces, but not to leave them altogether.

In Norway, Wittgenstein looked not so much for the usual way out, but for the way in, into the real. Here, the collapse between life and theory is celebrated – which is the keystone of anticipationism – and it is also here where philosophy is resolved in the project of a cabin, or in the performance of a life that isolates itself from others. The genius, like the cabin, has no community.[7] It is clear that the search for the meaning of life through simplicity is a sad story. It is made up of Thoreau's loneliness, Kaczynski's violence, Le Corbusier's old age and, finally, the inadequacy of the majority world of Wittgenstein who believed 'that only when I am close to death will I see the light of life'.[8] It is the story of anyone who sets out alone on the path of truth. Certainly, Wittgenstein made the goal of philosophy a practice of daily life:

What is the point of studying philosophy, if all it does for you is enable you to express yourself relatively plausibly on some abstruse questions of logic, etc., and if it does not improve your way of thinking about the important issues of everyday life, if it does not make you more aware than any journalist of the dangerous expressions that people of this kind use for their own purposes?[9]

However, I want to articulate better a central point: the practice of extreme life that manifests itself in the construction of the cabin and in the retreat is, as I have repeatedly pointed out, no longer a philosophical language but an artistic one. Many people in philosophy – think of Dewey's famous answer to Benedetto Croce[10] – believe that art cannot be considered as a real form of knowledge, placing it in open contrast with conceptual practice. The problem, however, is that, as Gillo Dorfles states, 'knowledge can be of various degrees and different aspects [...] it is not said that art cannot transmit knowledge of another kind'.[11] Here we must try to make a connection with an important point that emerged in the first part of this book: animal thought. The artistic form of knowledge, far from being defined simply as 'emotional', is first and foremost a privileged way out of the cognitive system of anthropocentrism – forcing it with its own tools, of course, but aiming to free itself from it.

To leap to earth 'again', to abandon the sky that for philosophers is the Platonic world of ideas from which everything began, and which we have struggled so hard to reach, is to attempt the impossible: a human life that is simply a life without any adjectives, in which we, too, like that leaf, can simply breathe in the wonder of our adherence to the world – objects without ideas. The real challenge of cabins, of simplicity, finally of a mature philosophy, is really this: to save us from the damnation of a complex mental life, but also from the idea that the only way out of the world is the violent way of suicide. It was David Pinset who confessed that Wittgenstein told him he 'thought about suicide all the time and was ashamed that he did not have the courage to kill himself'.[12] This should come as no surprise: the link between a way out in life and a way out in death is undeniable. Simplicity, in fact, is an enjoyment of the benefits of death in life – this is how Wittgenstein describes his Norwegian cabin to George E. Moore. Moore wrote about his Norwegian cabin: 'I cannot imagine any other place where I could have worked as I have done here. It must be the quietness and, perhaps, the wonderful landscape. I mean, the quiet seriousness of it.'[13]

A quiet seriousness that is precisely simplicity. Not as an immanent condition, as for a twig or a snail, but as a choice of exit, as for a philosopher. 'At times when everything is going well, we do not think about the weakness of the flesh', writes Wittgenstein under the explicit influence of reading Tolstoy, 'but at the moment of need, then one becomes aware of it. It is then that we turn to the spirit'.[14]

For Wittgenstein, it is clear that life is a text, a sheet of paper on which to write and jot down. The *Tractatus*, in this sense, is an extremely complex autobiography that moves from the period of reason towards that of disillusionment, mysticism and the abandonment to an almost Buddhist flow of things. Text, then, as a practice of life: what else is a diary if not a camera perpetually pointed at those who decide to write it?

The conceptual question is whether and to what extent the cabin can ennoble this detachment from the 'real' world, to the point of a conclusion that leads to an autobiographical posture. It is true – Schopenhauer comes to mind – that the human being is the only animal that is astonished by the very fact of existing. But it is equally true that, once enthusiasm has been reduced to zero, returning to the world may not coincide with liberation from everything we escaped from. Scattered attempts at escape: the *Hütte* on the Todtnauberg inhabited by Martin Heidegger in the Black Forest, the 1951 Roquebrune-Cap-Martin minimal cell or Semper's Caribbean hut, right up to Ruskin's chalet theory. How is this attempt by Wittgenstein different now that we are almost at the end? By analogy, what happens is similar to the difference between 'being poor' and 'possessing nothing' that characterises the canon of the Franciscan rule: if the first thing expresses a lack, the second, on the contrary, manifests a totality or fullness.[15] Thus, Wittgenstein is not in opposition to or distant from the world. Wittgenstein himself has become a world-form: he is not in relation to anything because he is in connection with everything.

---

4 Phrase attributed to Albert Einstein.

5 Ludwig Wittgenstein, *Tractatus Logico-Philosophicus*, cit., § 6.421.

6 Pablo Picasso, quoted in Françoise Gilot and Carlton Lake, *La mia vita con Picasso*, It. trad. by G. and L. Marussi (Rome: Donzelli, 2016), 45.

7 Cf. Gilles A. Tiberghien, *Notes sur la nature, la cabane et quelques autres choses* (Paris: Éditions du Félin, 2005).

8 Michael Nedo, ed., *Wittgenstein. Una biografia per immagini* (Rome: Carocci, 2013), 146.

9 Fabrizio Funtò, ed., *Ludwig Wittgenstein, Diari segreti* (Laterza, 1987), 38.

10 *Journal of Aesthetics*, VI, 1 (1948). Cf. Benedetto Croce, 'Dewey's Aesthetics and the Theory of Knowledge', in *Journal of Aesthetics*, XI, 1 (1952).

11 Gillo Dorfles, 'Arte e percezione visiva', *La mia America* (Milan: Skira, 2018), 227.

12 Ibid., 101.

13 Ibid., 128.

14 Ibid., 139.

15 On this topic, see Giorgio Agamben, *The Highest Poverty: Monastic Rules and Form-of-Life* (Stanford: Stanford UP, 2013).

Michael Obrist in conversation with Lowie Vermeersch
(mobility designer, founder and creative director of Granstudio)

Placemaking through mobility

OBRIST Let's start with one of the basic elements of the Grand Tour: mobility. The Grand Tour was based on mobility, with people and objects moving from one place to another. Mobility was one of the key elements in human history for exchanging ideas and goods, resulting in globalisation. The understanding between the relation of the production of space and the means of mobility is crucial. We are undergoing a period of major changes in the mobility world. How do you see these changes and how will they affect the different spatial and social manifestations in Italy, like the dense metropolitan areas, the little towns, the rural countryside, the in-between city?

VERMEERSCH Before jumping into that question, I would like to go one step back and make sure we have the right picture of Italy. In many cases, mobility is not just the glue between cities, but it's cities that crystallise in between mobility, in between flows of people, matter, energy and ideas. An iconic city like Venice is a good example of this. It originated literally in the water in a moment when mobility over the water was far faster and safer than mobility on land. It emerged in the middle of a flow of food and ideas that connected the East and the rest of Europe. The same goes for Rome, of course. Its position in the middle of the Mediterranean in a moment when ships became good enough to navigate, was crucial for Rome to become much bigger, because all the food could be brought in fast enough over the water to sustain a city of one million people. Thus, cities and societies arise in the middle of mobility or flows. From this point of view, Italy's position fundamentally changed after the discovery of America. It was no longer in the middle of major flows, but peripheral to them.

OBRIST Julius Caesar and Napoleon Bonaparte were travelling with the same speed through territories. Before someone put a little steam machine on rails and then on wheels, the global maximum speed for humans was connected to the power of horses.

You are based in Turin, the first capital of the Kingdom of Italy and in a certain way of the 'Kingdom of Fiat'. It is a city shaped by the car industry. The assembly lines of those car factories were a direct consequence of those established by Henry Ford. They enabled a different kind of mass production for cars and as a consequence their affordability. The workers were not just the producers of those cars, but could become also their first consumers and customers. The workers could now individually find a place to live, independently from public transport like buses, trams and trains, and far away from the factories which needed a huge amount of flexible ground around them for future expansions.

These shaped new forms of cities. From a satellite view you could see the differences. City developments based on train lines produce star-shaped cities, a city shaped on individual mobility creates bubbles. And it is a multitude of bubbles of agglomeration around a highway line from west to east, and vice versa, which forms this new gigantic metropolitan area between Turin and Venice. The new mobility solution for dense cities built before the invention of cars and for the sprawl must be different ones. What new forms of mobility do we need, or do we have to invent, to give an adequate answer to the demands of our time?

VERMEERSCH You touch on some fundamental things here. Mobility in Italy had a huge effect on migration, for example. The large-scale industrial production of cars in the northern city of Turin was a big step away from the artisanal production that had been spread all over Italy until that time. This industrial scale was necessary to make the car affordable and it acted like a huge societal magnet that drew everything into Turin. The city went from 400,000 inhabitants to 1.2 million in approximately thirty years. So that's mobility really changing society. This ultimately gave rise to your point about Ford. Fiat was producing the car so efficiently that it became affordable for the people who worked there. They bought the Fiat 500 on a massive scale and mobilised Italy. This fuelled even more migration and an exodus from the north to the south during the summer periods.

Another consequence of the widespread use of cars was that the connection between geography and the places where people were building and living became less tight-knit. As we saw in the examples of Rome and Venice, before the arrival of the car our built environment was heavily defined by flows of mobility that were closely linked to natural infrastructures such as rivers and seas. The car broke this strong link. That's the sprawl between cities that you referred to. Suddenly, this kind of order, which linked the built environment to the natural infrastructures, exploded. And policies came too late to steer that, especially in a country like Italy, with the unordered sprawl as a consequence.

The second topic you mentioned, about the fact that Caesar had the same speed as Napoleon, is of course because they fundamentally belonged to the same era in terms of energy conversion. An era in which we only managed to master the muscle energy of humans and animals. Only later came the era of industrialisation with the steam engine and combustion engines, generating massive speed increases. In essence, the history of mobility is very much the history of our capacities to master and convert energy.

Now we're entering a different era again, the one of electrification of mobility. This electrification will have a big impact. It will open up many new possibilities and allow for many different and smaller types of vehicles which, until very recently, were not possible. You can compare it to what electrification did to our houses, which are now full of smaller electrified devices.

I think this is a very relevant new opportunity for a country like Italy. Because if you look at Italy from north to south, it now has all these different situations. It has the old cities that were built before there were cars, small boroughs and small villages in the mountains which are sometimes even hard to reach. Additionally, there is a huge car-based sprawl in the middle and a good high-speed train infrastructure. I believe that this diversity of Italy can be a very interesting testing ground to develop new forms of mobility.

And this is relevant because, going forward, we need to create a new kind of diversified mobility that is more context-specific. In the last one hundred years, we had a situation where the car was more or less seen as the one solution that fitted all contexts, whether it was a city centre or a highway. The SUV is the ultimate expression of this 'optimised compromise' or Swiss knife on wheels. But to make progress from here onwards, we should exploit those new opportunities offered by electrification and sharing platforms to create new types of mobility that are better adapted to specific situations. We can then imagine a multi-modal mobility future where we make use of different vehicles based on different places and needs of use, hence offering a more satisfying experience while at the same time being more in harmony with the surroundings.

For example, if you think about the centre of Rome, a car is not the best means of mobility there, as it is not for most city centres. Electric drivetrains, shared use and autonomous technologies will make it possible to create new vehicles and mobility services that enhance the experience of the city rather than destroy it. The 'Mobjects' research project we did is an example of that. From this perspective it's easy to see how I look at the before-mentioned diversity of Italy as a great laboratory for future mobility innovations, much more than societies that have been built basically after the car, like the United States and modern China. In fact, if you look at the mobility narratives that are being defined today in California and China, there is not at all that kind of diversity. The narratives keep concentrating on the car, albeit its electric and autonomous evolution, as a kind of solution for all. But that's not something that will work in Italy and cannot be a complete answer for our future mobility needs.

OBRIST This looks like we need answers which go beyond the given tools and amplify the toolkit of cars, trains, buses, bikes used in urban planning and their relation to each other – all this resulting in a new ecosystem of mobility, creating also an era for new small start-ups and not just gigantic companies.

VERMEERSCH Absolutely. This connects back to my comments about entering a new 'electric' era and stepping away from fossil fuels. Apart from the impact on sustainability – which is currently the main focus and is undoubtedly great – I also look at it knowing what it takes to design vehicles. This is part of the big opportunity I see. Until recently, all vehicles were based on combustion engines. However, making combustion engines has two major limitations. The first from a business and industrial perspective. Developing an engine is very complex, and not many companies can do it because a lot of capital is required. Of course, this creates a very high threshold, which is not inviting for someone who has great ideas but cannot collect that amount of capital to make it work. The second limitation is linked to its geometric constraints. A combustion engine has an inflexible geometry that greatly defines and limits the shape of a vehicle. Now, if you develop an electric vehicle, you can easily purchase electric engines online or off the shelf – thus fundamentally changing the nature of the business. Secondly, due to their smaller size and ability to be integrated into wheels, electric engines allow for much greater geometric freedom. In the same way, battery packs are made up of small battery cells, allowing them to be shaped to different needs. Combining these two advantages opens up possibilities for new, smaller industries.

You can already see it happening. For example, in Turin, they have started producing the Microlino. Whether one likes it or not, it is clear proof of the possibility to start a new business around smaller-scale productions of new types of electric vehicles, away from the large-scale industrialisation that has dominated since the Second World War. I really like to think that this is allowing Italy to reconnect with one of its strengths, which is a type of business that is small enough to work based on human relations and the inventiveness of some people. Just like Dante Giacosa created the original 500. This works differently for the big car manufacturers of today. This seems to fit well with the culture of doing business in Italy. It's enough to look at its industrial history and see that most successes were built around some truly enlightened individuals and operated on a smaller scale than the huge companies that characterise our globalised world.

OBRIST Around the production of mobility tools, we can see two big phenomena in Italy: on one side the big factories of mass production around the cities, mainly in the north around Turin and Milan, and with a few tentatives in the south; and then another high expertise in a more diffuse territory, even in little villages, some of them concentrated in Emilia Romagna in the so-called *terra dei motori* [engine land, ed.] with Ferrari, Lamborghini, Maserati, Pagani, Dallara, Ducati and others. Whereas the big factories became also important places for the social and political movements for the workers' rights, in the latter the overlap between rural culture and high-tech production in these in-between cities becomes an interesting contemporary phenomenon.

VERMEERSCH Lamborghini, in fact, is a great example of two sides of that story. On the one hand, yes, it was a kind of a farmer story, in the sense that Lamborghini was producing tractors, and after he was refused the opportunity to buy a Ferrari he decided to make his own car. Also, Giampaolo Dallara was involved in the engineering of the Lamborghini Miura, still today an absolute reference for beauty in car design. It's very much the story of brilliant people that connected. And so it resonates very much with what I said before. It was often really brilliant people at the centre of these unique things happening. But Lamborghini is also an example of how it's just very,

Production of the Dallara Stradale in the small town Varano de' Melegari. Credit: Granstudio

very hard to be able to still create in the automotive industry without being very big. Today Lamborghini could not be viable anymore from a business point of view if it was totally independent. It's too small for that. Lamborghini is flourishing again since it was bought by Audi and received an injection of capital and gained access to engines and technology. The Lamborghini Urus, for example, is based on an Audi Q8. Here, design and styling serve to maximise visual differences between similar underpinnings. That is a very different approach from what you call being like a shark, which I interpreted as optimising a shape for maximum efficiency within its environment. The Dallara Stradale we designed is maybe one of the last cars designed with that philosophy, far away from marketing and branding, but focused on simply making the car as good and as beautiful as possible with the given technical conditions.

But again, here I'm enthusiastic what new EV drivetrains can bring us in terms of possibilities to make low-volume series. Maybe the business model in which some companies were making running platforms and others were building beautiful shapes over them could come back. But the one thing that cannot come back is the core reason that fuelled the competition between those companies – that is, literally the race to move the limits of speed and performance. When Lamborghini made his first car, going faster was still an expression of progress. Today, electric drivetrains pushed the speed and performance already to the limit of what our organs and tyres can take. So, new motivations will need to be found, and maybe that's partially going back to that image of the shark: finding ways to express a new kind of sustainable performance, and in doing so a new kind of beauty with shapes that are in harmony with the air.

OBRIST A part of the success of these objects of mobility is that, beyond their functionality, they became also objects of desire. Some of them became status symbols. A lot of this is changing now. Mobility objects such as cars are becoming just a part in a bigger mobility ecosystem in which we switch between different means of transport. Sharing becomes a possible answer, and ownership and so on of these specific status symbols might disappear. Fluid mobility models based on sharing work very well in the cities, but we are still missing good answers for the questions of mobility for the sprawl or the rural areas, where the car is still relevant for mobility. The Yellow Vest protests in France were also a symptom of parallel worlds with different problems, where mobility plays an important role. In the countryside the car is still a tool of emancipation and of increasing possibilities for work, culture, leisure. The in-between-city seems too big to let it fail. How do we create sustainable mobility solutions for these complex territories?

VERMEERSCH You touched upon one of the really essential things: we need to define the solution space beyond the object. As long as we apply the new technological possibilities only to the object or the vehicle, we get stuck. The fundamental thing now is to enlarge as a designer our solution space to the full mobility ecosystem, And I know that a system for a designer is maybe not such a nice word. But I don't suggest that you suck away all the elements of beauty and passion. It's just about increasing the solution space while keeping those elements that made the car a success: the fact that we're emotionally involved. We love it, or we hate it – that emotional involvement should remain part of our designs.

But we do need to look at the bigger picture, including beyond the vehicle and also the context,

Mobject 6. Credit: Granstudio

as we mentioned before. We can no longer just focus on the object when we design, as happened basically until now, and then let it loose on the world and see how it goes. When we conceive new mobility means we should be borrowing a little bit from architecture and work in relation to the context. What is good to do in a city? What is good to do in a mountain village? And on a highway?

And then another aspect that you mentioned is of course the big shift to step away from ownership as the only way to access individual vehicles. Today many people still see the world of mobility divided into individually owned vehicles and collective public vehicles. The individual vehicle is your vehicle, only you use it and it's part of who you are. Even if you decide to buy the cheapest one that you can find because you don't care, it's still a way of expressing yourself. On the other hand, public vehicles that you don't own are normally for collective transport. The bus, the tram, the train, such vehicles do not have that connection with self-expression. But more and more those two worlds will overlap. A car that is being shared is public transport, but also an individual vehicle. So, it's not my vehicle, but it is part of my self-expression because I choose that specific shared vehicle. And I choose to share.

So I think there is space for self-expression also beyond ownership. And you already see it. If you look at air travel, almost nobody owns an airplane, but there's a lot of expression into which company you fly with, which loyalty status you have and which lounges you have access to. It's my firm belief that also in non-owned mobility services we will see branding, we will see personal expression, we will see an emotional relationship. In the future there will be many different services for sharing. And if you use one and I use another, it will also be an expression of who we are, how we look at the world and how we deal with our mobility.

OBRIST Italy became world-famous for its car design, and you designed some of these iconic machines. In your education and your work, it is crucial to understand the DNA of a brand, oscillating between continuation of tradition and evolution and sometimes even revolution. That makes car design similar to other disciplines, but also to cultural techniques of the everyday which you find in the Italian territories.

VERMEERSCH It's undeniable that in the Italian design DNA, and definitely in car design, there's something embedded in the culture. I think sensibility, but also giving importance to the visual. What is the visual perception doing to me? That leads to having a different approach. Especially in the first years I came here, it was easier to see that aesthetics were given a lot of importance in the decision-making. The aesthetic attraction had a lot of power inside companies, which is essential to make sure that sometimes you make much more effort to reach a certain shape. If in that moment of the decision-taking aesthetics are seen and felt as important, then those extra technological or investment efforts are more easily made to reach that shape. That's what I've seen happening. My personal perception as part outsider to the Italian culture is that there's just a very strong relationship with the physical presence around you. In the now. What is perceived around you is very much lived, intensely. And that's a bit different from maybe more Nordic cultures who probably will take much more into account 'abstract' elements like strategies, or other concepts which are not felt in the physical now but which you will only feel in the future. My perception is that the sensorial perception of the presence is more easily prevailing over the rational conceptualisation of the future. And beauty, just like food, is expressed very much in that sensorial presence. But Italy seems to struggle to apply this sensitivity to projects and systems on a bigger scale. If you drive today from Turin to Milan and see the new infrastructure built around the high-speed train it seems that that sensibility of elegance and beauty – with a touch of lightness – somehow disappeared.

OBRIST Let's go back to the notion of the mobility ecosystem. Although increasingly seen as a commodity, we should not forget that there is a human right to adequate housing. The prices for renting, owning, building apartments and houses in the urban agglomerations increased very fast in the last decades. As a consequence, we see a growth of the sprawl, where the prices are much cheaper. But this comes at a cost: a lot of time and money spent in mobility. For example, a lot of the workers in the care sector – which becomes more and more crucial for our society – can't afford to live in cities anymore and have to move to the peripheries or even further, with all the consequences we just explained. As mobility and housing are so connected, how can we create a more sustainable and fair society? Should mobility become a common good?

VERMEERSCH   First of all, I fully agree with the idea that mobility should be in that list of common goods. Because mobility is fundamental to life. Only last week somebody told me that 'something in which there's no movement can only be dead. So how much more proof do you want that movement and mobility are fundamental for life'. But if we now go back to that multi-modal future where there are more different types of vehicles and services, services which are more closely related to a specific context … To make that future work I think there's a huge job to be done to find the right balance between private initiative on the one hand and the right guardrails from policies on the other. Because multi-modal mobility can only work well if the connections between different types of mobility means work well. That is the fundamental element.

You and me will only decide to go from A to B using different types of vehicles if the connection between those vehicles or between those services work well, and the overall experience is better than using a single vehicle. But those connections can only work well if there is some kind of broader framework that stimulates different mobility providers and digital platforms to collaborate. A framework that at the same time allows and stimulates also competition.

We spoke before about Lamborghini and Ferrari; that was also a competition between two private companies, but within a very clear framework. The roads were very clear, the rules of traffic were very clear, and so on. So, I think we need both and I think there's a lot of work to be done, because, in my perception, the current framework of laws on vehicles is no longer adapted to current technologies. And those laws are hugely influencing the design and development of new vehicles and mobility services. And where those laws are now based on a definition of different vehicle categories, I think that they should be based more on those different mobility contexts. It's fundamentally different to drive at 130 km an hour on a highway or at 30 km an hour in the city centre. But today we do that with vehicles that comply to the same regulations, funnelling the offerings to the most common denominator. But again, the connection between the different modes is the biggest challenge, not just from a physical point of view, not just for the vehicles, but also from a software point of view. Probably the challenge there is even bigger.

OBRIST   This age of electricity is coming with high costs in the areas where the specific material for batteries and so on is excavated – the exploitation is on an environmental and human level.

VERMEERSCH   You're right that many consequences are not clear yet, and that's also why we should keep the solution space big enough, not attached to a specific technology, but to objectives. Many people forget where batteries come from. You need to pull more or less 200,000 kg of material out of the Earth to obtain enough material to make a car battery. Knowing that there are millions and millions of cars over the world, you start to understand that just making things electric cannot be the solution yet. That's why I believe so much in making vehicles more purpose-specific. If we design vehicles just for those areas where you can go 30 km an hour, of course they can be much, much more efficient and have much, much smaller batteries, I think. It's a good example of how the framework in which we create the future of mobility should not be based on a certain technology – batteries in this case – but on the actual impact on sustainability. That could unleash a rush of creativity similar to that race for speed.

OBRIST   Coming to our last question, and closing the circle with the first one on the Grand Tour. What could we learn from Italy in terms of mobility?

VERMEERSCH   From Italy I learn that mobility solutions in the future need to preserve very much a human scale. If you visit Italy, as you mentioned several times, you have all those cities, those small boroughs, even those in-between areas, which have a scale that is fundamentally very human. So, for me, making a Grand Tour of Italy should be about learning from looking at how life in cities happens at this very human level. It's about all those qualities which we find in those old streets, that create life and the beauty of the public space. It has to do with a certain level of letting go, allowing some lack of control so that unexpected pleasures can seep in. Maybe it's about allowing to live that physical presence in the public space. Now, that is very different from the technology-driven narratives in post-car societies like the United States or eastern China. Here, scenarios are dreamt up about societies full of autonomous cars. But those places do not have those aforementioned qualities. Italy can show us that we need a richer mobility narrative for the future, at least for Europe, with more diversity and human qualities at its centre, not technology. Italy reminds us that new means of mobility will only mean progress if they embrace and foster the human qualities of our public spaces, instead of reducing them to what can be computed by an autonomous algorithm.

Transcript of a conversation that took place in February 2023.

Share screen architecture

Luigi Savio

1. Chitra Ramaswamy, 'Deep fake neighbour wars review – the puerile joy of Idris Elba fighting Kim Kardashian over a wheelbarrow', *The Guardian* (2023, January 26), https://www.theguardian.com/tv-and-radio/2023/jan/26/deep-fake-neighbour-wars-review (accessed 22 February 2023).

2. Bruce Burton, *Theatre Technology* (Nelson ITP, 1998).

3. Katherine Singh, 'What is a content house and does every TikTok star live in one?' www.flare.com, St. Joseph Communications

4. Axel Boëthius and J. B. Ward-Perkins, *Etruscan and Roman Architecture*, Pelican History of Art (Hanrmondsworth, 1970), 379–81.

The year 2023 has opened with the debut on sharing platforms of the New Zealand television show *Neighbours at War*, a work that is absolutely innovative in terms of its script and for the technological component it employed in the production of the episodes. Actors, singers and influencers are part of a grotesque script in which they play a surreal version of themselves.[1] The show is striking for the heavy parody of the show business environment, played, clip after clip, by the same people who are part of it. Expressions are natural but faces remain plastic. The actors are bodies performing facial movements on which the facial physiognomies of the supposedly famous protagonists are mounted simultaneously. The entire show is completely shot using deepfake technology, through which the facial expressions of any face can be simulated, achieving extremely lifelike results.

Neighbours at War is highly relevant content, the offspring of a new family of almost fully automated entertainment products. It is a speciation of a much larger process that hybridises media technology and entertainment. Deepfake fiction represents a benchmark. After it, the role of the actor will perhaps disappear, replaced by the 'figurant' organic mannequin on which to digitally apply the face of people who are famous, or never existed. *Neighbours at War* is the last stage of hybridisation between spectacle and technology, the final stage of a development that began decades earlier, when technological apparatuses such as rotating stages, audio wire broadcasting and lighting effects began to appear in the theatre space.[2] The space of the performance, the physical construction of the acoustic machine that performs by geometry and not by its technological endowment, has long since ceased to exist, pulverised into the multimedia of its contents. Today, even the human component has been set aside, because even it is reproducible in the indeterminacy of its expressiveness.

From the theatre to the smartphone, the process of technological expansion of the architecture of entertainment has undergone several reincarnations and all of them are expressions of a paradigm shift in communication languages. Yet the film, the television set, 'collab houses',[3] are not taken into account by those who study the typological evolution of architecture, almost as if these spaces are not designed. Also, the literature on media only analyses approximately the space of entertainment, and mentions it as a negligible epiphenomenon of something much more relevant – the content. Thus, is it possible in this case to separate the content from its container, and the spectacle from its setting, without incurring major simplifications?

Perhaps from professional strain, the architect's eye tends to fetishise the impact of scenic choices on the success or failure of theatrical art pieces. Perhaps the discourse around the form of the entertainment can be ancillary and negligible when compared with the script or the acting performance. Yet it's evident how much the set designs of some major TV shows have conquered the collective memory of millions of viewers, enriching it with new formal, material ideas on interior design. Scenographic design was not and is not today the mere interpretation of spatial stimuli already present in other types of architecture. These are not merely an assemblage of solutions already seen. They represent an entirely autonomous field of experimentation and, to some extent, one more capable of absorbing the ever-changing instances of the spirit of the times. Consequently, the technological mutation of entertainment and its architecture, cast in a society that constantly produces and devours multimedia content through digital devices, takes on a powerful semantic value, emblematic of the information society and heir to the consumer society.

The following paragraphs examine a selection of events that have guided the evolution of entertainment architecture, attempting to outline the fundamental steps through which the historically determined space of the theatre has changed its connotations in adapting to the drastic changes dictated by the evolution in media technology. From the stage through the television set, the entertainment space has lost its architectural shell, becoming multifaceted and adaptable, capable of filling any context, any place, thanks to its new gaseous state. Today everything is set design.

Entertain, communicate, colonise

There is an extensive literature describing the steps that marked the progressive transformation of theatre architecture, starting with examples such as the Agrippeion and going as far as to take in analysis real cornerstones of theatrical space such as the Festspielhaus in Bayreuth. The typological model of almost all theatre designs from the classical age to the second half of the twentieth century is the odeon,[4] a refined derivation of the *bouleuterion*, the building that in the Greek world housed the boule, the city council. It follows that, likewise the *bouleuterion*, the odeon was designed to allow the encounter of people's ideas, to foster the debate and the individual growth through the collective exchange of knowledge. In other words, the typology of the odeon, a large sloping audience arranged along a semi-circular shape and oriented toward the stage, represented the space around which the ethos of a society was erected. In other words, it was an architectural machine useful

Unleashed, 2018. Credit: (ab)Normal

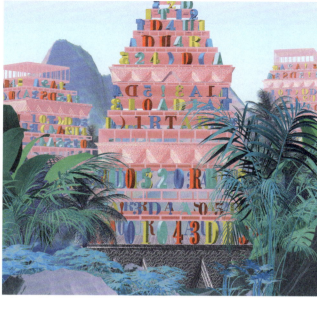
BlueScreen Ziggurat, 2018. Credit: (ab)Normal

Elliot Discovering Some Ammo, 2018. Credit: (ab)Normal

Terra in the Vessel, 2018. Credit: (ab)Normal

5   Pamela Kanwar, *Imperial Simla: The Political Culture of the Raj*, 2nd ed. (New Delhi: Oxford University Press, 2003).

6   Nandi Bhatia, *Acts of Authority/Acts of Resistance: Theater and Politics in Colonial and Postcolonial India* (University of Michigan Press, 2004).

for crystallising the cultural ties of a community through the staging of imaginary stories. Not by chance, the architecture of politics and that of entertainment share the same typological model. It is possible to argue that, historically, the shape of the city has always been organised around certain emergencies; the economic and political life was built around the large institutional buildings, the cultural life around the theatres.

Over the centuries, these great civilisation incubators have been instruments of control and, thus, architectures of colonisation. Just as the Roman amphitheatres are among the elements that defined the cities of the Roman provinces imitating the shape of Rome, there are several examples of replicas of Victorian theatres throughout the former British colonies.

The Gaiety Theatre in Shimla, a perfect expression of the Gothic revival style outside Britain, is one such example.[5] Inside, in a space marked by Corinthian friezes and capitals, not only the most important English plays were staged, but also adaptations of Hindu works pertaining to the traditional Jatra theatre art. Indo-British theatres were places where cultural and political positions clashed with such violence that the British Empire found itself forced in 1876 to enact the Dramatic Performances Act,[6] a legislative instrument through which strict rules were outlined that restricted the writing and staging of native works. Theatre thus became a tool of cultural control and assimilation. Like the British Empire, many other colonial regimes imposed adherence to alien cultural models through the strict supervision on the production and *mise en scène* of content of entertainment. Hence, other medium such as film, television and digital sharing platforms can also be read as tools of cultural control.

Considering the depth of the impact of entertainment spaces in the construction of a society, the lack of attention to the peculiar technological mutations of this kind of architecture is paradoxical.

The understanding of the current structures of power is a process that can't be distinguished from the analysing and understanding of the new communication vectors through which entertainment contents are conveyed. If the language employed by a medium is important, as the direct expression of a cultural hegemony, then also the space in which this communication takes place has a great value. Essentially, understanding the architecture of entertainment helps in understanding the deep nature of the content and, thus, its reasons, its origins.

From theatres to machines

For centuries, the transformations through which spaces for entertainment have evolved have been mostly affected by geometric arrangements, designed to achieve the perfect optical and acoustic enjoyment. These are angular variations, tectonic alterations, compositional and material choices. In other words, absolutely architecture.

7   Burton, *Theatre Technology* (see note 2).

8   Daniel Okrent, *Great Fortune: The Epic of Rockefeller Center* (Penguin Books, 2004).

9   Rem Koolhaas, 'Radio City Music Hall: The Fun Never Sets', in *Delirious New York: A Retroactive Manifesto for Manhattan* (Random House, 2014).

10 John Carpenter, 'The Max Headroom Incident', *Chicago Tribune* (2018, December 17), https://www.chicagotribune.com/business/ct-biz-wttw-max-headroom-30-years-20171122-story.html (accessed 22 February 2023).

Pure architecture, for centuries, generated endless variations of the same model – the odeon – because the content conveyed was essentially always the same. In fact, until the middle of the last century there were very few technological innovations that changed the architecture of entertainment. The typology of the theatre changed slightly on two occasions: when the 'mystic gulf' (the pit housing the accompanying orchestra) was introduced, and when electric lighting was incorporated into the stage shell.[7] Both developments did not change the rigid relational dynamic between stage and spectator in the slightest.

Entertainment, be it high or low, was conveyed as content to be experienced passively, motionless and comfortably sunk into the audience seat. Technology itself, that of major changes, such as artificial lighting, elevators or indoor air conditioning, accentuated the authoritarian characteristics of the spectacles designed to terraform the consciousness of the masses. Cinema is undoubtedly the product of the application of technology to entertainment in order to instigate simultaneous emotions in large groups of people. An emotional control that is far more immersive than the theatrical one for its ability to faithfully reproduce reality. After cinema was invented, amazement, fear, happiness, joy, sadness, became 'palimpsest' emotions, activated at will, and oddly persistent over time. The immersive aspect makes cinema the perfect tool of propaganda and homologation, as it is capable of stimulating hidden emotions through the magic of projection.

However, there are even more extreme examples that have marked, in paradigmatic manner, the drift from architecture to machine that the architecture of the spectacle has undergone.

In 1930 the works on the largest agglomeration of entertainment-related buildings ever constructed, the Rockefeller Center on Sixth Avenue in Manhattan, began.[8] A multitude of cinemas, theatres, recording studios, headquarters of major radio and later television networks coexisting in one single complex. The construction of the Rockefeller Center, the epicentre of North American mass media power, celebrates the marriage of entertainment and technology in one of the most iconic landmarks of Manhattan, the Radio City Music Hall, a tower layering vertically theatrical stages, projection screens, hotels and spaces for body worship, large machine rooms, small private zoos, dressing rooms, restaurants and bars. The RCA soars skyward as a multitude of venues devoted to the satisfaction of the senses, a vortex blurring the consciousness, cleansing it of pre-existing dogmas, and preparing it to embrace the American cultural model.

The main space, the theatre *cavea*, was born directly from the oneiric vision of the entrepreneur who took over the management, Samuel Lionel Rothafel. Roxy, his nickname, drew the theatre's interior as a large sun unpacked in the lighting system of the vaults of the theatre's ceiling. Artificial lighting allowed the staging of real sunsets thanks to the dimmable intensity of the light. The viewer, helpless before this 'artificial sublime', was further stimulated by the diffusion of small doses of laughing gas in the air, which helped to abduct the sensory apparatus within a total work of art.[9]

Those who entered the interior of the RCA tower came out, in other words, completely changed, perhaps dazed, or perhaps invigorated, certainly fulfilled by the wide variety of experiences granted through the technology the tower contained.

Without considering the architectural body, Radio City Music Hall, and more generally the whole of the Rockefeller Center, resembled the feed of any multimedia content platform, representing the embryonic version of the world of digital broadcasting. What was materialised in the RCA through the blending of architecture and technology is now rewritten as a computer code, transmitted through TCP/IP communication protocols and returned in the form of digital images and digital videos.

A screen in every living room,
a living room in every screen

The first screen experienced collectively was the cinema screen. Projection made possible the reproducibility and transportability of content through the flattening of the stage into the dimensionality of the screen. At the beginning of the twentieth century, therefore, a new architectural typology was born, that of the movie theatre, also a distant relative of the original odeon model. Indeed, it is no coincidence that many cinema structures have adopted the namesake. The invention of the cinema, then, certainly represents an important development in entertainment technology. Nevertheless, the invention of the cinema technology did not produce any paradigmatic shift in the design of the spaces for entertainment. In fact, many theatres were adapted to accommodate screens and projectors, becoming therefore real movie theatres.

The fruition of the content essentially has remained unchanged; the helpless spectator who occasionally and collectively takes part in a spectacle. Cinema, in other words, traditionally works for a passive spectator who has no capacity for interaction. Thus, the wall between spectator and actor remains solid. The urban emergence of large covered spaces, where to collectively enjoy works written and directed by a handful of intellectuals who educate and direct the cultural life of communities, still remains standing.

Television completely disrupted this balance. From 1928, cathode ray tube television sets, built following the design of inventor Philo Farnsworth, began to populate domestic environments in the United States and Europe. Within a few years, NBC in America and the BBC in the United Kingdom structured the first weekly television schedules. Living rooms, once inviolate places, spaces dedicated to family intimacy, became portals through which to convey propaganda messages, commercials, news and in-depth programmes. Above all, drawing rooms became small audiences located everywhere on the earth's crust. The space first of the theatre, then of the cinema, once concentrated within large urban boxes, was segmented into endless domestic 'grandstands'. The technology of the cathode ray tube gave rise to a process of penetration of public life into the private dimension of the home, which happens today within digital devices. Television was the first device capable of altering the geography of domestic space, a process that, thanks to smartphones, makes the zoning of the home totally anachronistic.

The architecture of entertainment thus changes, divided between television sets and domestic living rooms.

The spectator's posture, however, remains passive. Television constitutes an extremely hierarchical media that rigidly maintains the distinction between viewer and spectacle. Television sets become attractive representations of the cultural model that television is required to convey. They appear on the screens of all homes, stereotypical living rooms within which actors perform uplifting scenes of daily life, which are supposed to stimulate the mirror neurons of the viewer to assume similar behaviours. Television, democratic technology par excellence, takes on the connotations of a brainwashing machine.

The Max Headroom incident and beyond

After the end of the Second World War, television had really colonised every home. In European houses, the television became synonymous with democracy and progress, the two key words through which the new Western geopolitical system based its success. Television sets in Italian, German or French living rooms reproduced, through the architecture of the television set, allochthonous models of life, more specifically stereotypical of dominant North American thought. Just as European television sets became homologous to the US model, the spaces of homes also began to change shape.

TV represented the perfect instrument of control that magically abducted the passive viewer, blurring their critical capacity. The architecture of entertainment, from theatre to home, allowed a constant and widespread cultural influence on the masses. A demiurgic power, never before experienced, made possible by an iron control of over-the-air transmissions. The space of the airwaves was enriched with political value, and national, state-controlled television broadcasting networks began to emerge.

In 1987 a seemingly inconsequential event happened, but when analysed retroactively, it marked the beginning of a drastic new change.

A group of still-anonymous individuals succeeded in hacking the television schedule of broadcaster WGN-TV (the state of Illinois' controlled broadcasting company) and in penetrating the homes of millions of Americans.[10] They broadcast a few seconds' message with cryptic and self-referential content. They denigrated a few local celebrities, wearing a grotesque mask, a caricature of the fake TV host/automobile Max Headroom. A few moments of sheer madness filtered through the retinas of many viewers. The Max Headroom signal intrusion is an event that has marked the collective memory because of its farcical content and the failure to identify the perpetrators.

Signal pirates remain in the shadows. Although it is part of American popular culture, it is not considered relevant at all. Yet it has given rise to a process of disarticulation of the once granitic distinction between spectator and spectacle. The incident (a term used to define the event) made it clear that, with some notion of physics, the frequency domain was bypassable, making possible for the first time some form of interaction between spectator and spectacle. The mask of little value, the croaky audio, the modified voice, the DIY set design simulating frequency loss (probably staged using awkwardly handled sheet metal) are all telling elements of a perhaps homemade, certainly not professional, context. In other words, this event is the precursor of gonzo content, a specific category of media products produced, interpreted and enjoyed by the author himself, content that gives value to the banality of everyday life. What we call reality TV today, to define globally successful programmes like *Big Brother*, derives exactly from this voyeuristic approach to content creation.

Suddenly the living room expands and, in addition to the spectator's armchair, it incorporates the stage, or rather the television set. The domestic space, now completely desecrated, becomes the setting of the real and thus simultaneously content and container.

Share screen architecture

The examples cited in the preceding paragraphs describe well the path of mutations through which entertainment architecture has been absorbed by the great black hole of domestic space, a category depleted of its meaning consequent to the disappearance of the distinction between public and private. The home and the theatre were merged with the invention of television and reconfigured as a third space, a hybrid place where content was simultaneously produced and enjoyed. The acceleration in the development of mass media technologies has had extremely significant consequences in the form and use of entertainment-related spaces. While the architecture of entertainment no longer exists, whether we talk about fruition or consider entertainment production, we certainly cannot say that entertainment production has suffered declines. In this day and age, it sounds pleonastic to mention that mobile content playback devices such as tablets and smartphones have replaced the architecture by enabling the constant and obsessive enjoyment of entertainment-related content. The very production of entertainment is now accessible to anyone with a smartphone and a profile in any media-sharing platform. One only has to take a look at the demographics of TV and platform viewers to understand that the time of television is nearing its end, and that the primary media used to disseminate entertainment content will be streaming platforms. Those who produce content for platforms such as Twitch or YouTube do so independently, directly from their bedrooms. Thus, the home environment also changes shape and becomes a 'television studio', equipping itself with video cameras and microphones.

The home, for the streamer, is both public and private, and, except for the bed and bathroom, becomes the setting for the tedious and endless spectacle of daily life.

As happened to the theatre scene, flattened to the two-dimensionality of the movie screen, today the house also loses three-dimensionality, reduced to the role of a replaceable background. Nevertheless, the home remains solid in the collective memory as a privileged place of human relations. Domestic space is often used as a scenic device within which to perform pseudo-artistic routines to be shared on platforms such as TikTok and Instagram. Even houses designed specifically as sequences of colourful backdrops are born, within which to contractually bring celebrities from the platform to live in order to create content industrially. Collab houses are anti-domestic houses, looking like space catalogues of wallpaper and trashy lighting, and coming out as photogenic only through the vertical screen of the smartphone. Groups of six to eight teenagers find themselves forcibly sharing intimate spaces, driven by the possibility of increasing followers and consequently income. Neither the designer's touch nor the emotional layering due to the domestic consumption of spaces is felt in these places.

Proceeding by hyperbole, architecture, as a coherent thought about space, seems to no longer exist, because the perceptual three-dimensionality of space no longer exists. Thanks to webcams, we can conveniently experience an infinite number of spaces. What we see inside the screen, however, is only a very small portion of these spaces. The architecture of the screen allows us to observe only fragments, but hardly returns the complexity of the form in its entirety.

However, the architecture of the screen, and thus of entertainment, is an accessible and unpretentious place, a place activated and enjoyed by anyone. Its fragmentariness also corresponds to an enormous potential as a recombinant factor. It is not a predetermined space because it lives by accident. The entertainment of platforms always remains open, ready to be colonised rather than to colonise.

. Riders
not heroes

Ippolito Pestellini Laparelli

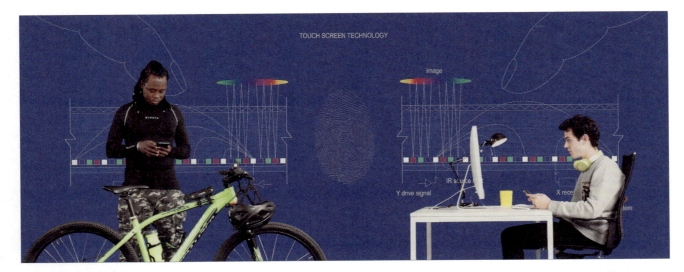

Anatomy of a Delivery, film stills. Credit: 2050+

Extract from an interview with Tim, food delivery rider, Milan, February 2020.

IPL — Hi, what's your name?

TIM — My name is Tim.

IPL — Where do you come from?

TIM — I'm from Aboisso, Ivory Coast.

IPL — How old are you?

TIM — I'm fifty-four.

IPL — Do you have a family?

TIM — Yes, I'm married and we have four daughters – almost a soccer team, ahaha. We live in Mortara, not far from Pavia.

IPL — So, you travel from Pavia every day to Milan?

TIM — Yes. I take the train from Mortara every morning and I come back in the evening with my bike. Many young riders sleep here at the station. There is no affordable housing in Milan.

IPL — How long have you been working as a rider?

TIM — I've been a rider for four years. At the beginning I used to work from Monday to Sunday, over thirteen hours per day. Now I try to work only during peak hours, between one o'clock and three o'clock and then between eight o'clock and nine o'clock in the evening. In between I stay in Milan. I live too far away to go back home.

IPL — What did you do before working as a rider?

TIM — I studied agricultural engineering in Lausanne. I'm a farmer and a designer. I have also trained as a film and sound editor in the audio-visual field to work on movies, radio shows, TV series, etc. In Africa I used to edit films. My dream, though, is to have a ranch. I have bought a four-hectare island where I'm developing a fish farm. You know, in four months I should go back to Africa. The capital of Ivory Coast is Abidjan. The second biggest city is Yamoussoukro, where the biggest cathedral on earth is located. The one in Rome [Saint Peter's Basilica] it's the oldest, the one in Yamoussoukro is the biggest and most beautiful, all in marble ...

IPL — What do you like about being a rider?

TIM — I like being my own boss. At the beginning I especially loved it – I could go on vacation whenever I wanted, without asking any boss. I can just come and go as I wish. I'm paid when I work. You can make good money, you know. When I rode for over ten hours per day, I could earn up to 1,300 euros every two weeks. But it can be dangerous ...

IPL — Have you had any accidents?

TIM — Three! Two are still in front of the judge. I take risks in Milan ... I'm not any longer a boy. I wear a helmet, I use lights ... I'm not ignorant. I have studied. When it rains many riders fall and injure arms and legs. I have seen friends that broke their feet under tramways. Fortunately my papers are in order. I have insurance with my bank and a p.iva [fiscal code]. I

Interview with Tim. Credit: 2050+

would really like to start doing deliveries in Pavia. The city is more quiet and less dangerous.

IPL — Milan has a difficult relationship with bikes, I guess ...

TIM — Milan just doesn't work for bikes. Bikes are becoming more fashionable, but the city is not ready; it's not been designed for bikes. If everyone was riding bikes, there would be more community building ... and it's very healthy, good for your legs, knees and head. Sport keeps you young.

IPL — Do you work well with restaurants?

TIM — Well, they can be mean ... they ask us to wait outside even when it rains and it's very cold. We can wait up to thirty minutes at the door. I always go inside ... in fact, I consider myself a collaborator. I don't let them push me away. At the end of the day, we work together ... I'm not an employee of the restaurant.

IPL — Do you use an app to bike around for deliveries?

TIM — I don't use any maps. I know Milan by heart. The areas of Duomo, Via Washington, Piazza Tripoli, Tre Torri ... by bike we get to know the city better than the Milanese.

IPL — What about your colleagues?

TIM — There are different situations ... some difficult ones ... many should see a doctor ... they have seen people dying at sea ...

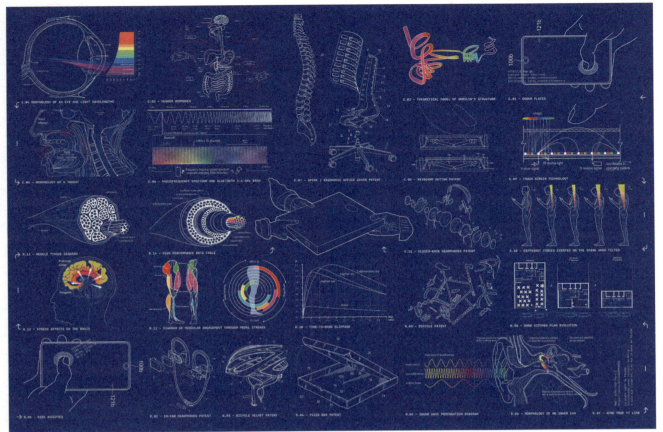

Anatomy of a Delivery, diagram. Credit: 2050+

Living battleground

There are no clear numbers when it comes to assessing how many people work as riders in Italy. According to a report published by the National Institute for Public Policy Analysis (INAPP), based on a survey carried out between March and July 2021 on a sample of over 45,000 individuals aged between eighteen and forty-seven, digital platform workers are little more than 570,000, or 1.3% of the population examined. It is a very broad category, which does not only include riders. One of the most interesting insights brought about by the survey estimates that 274,000 people consider this job as their main activity.[1] It's not clear whether these figures include undocumented migrants working on the account of third parties.

Milan is the national capital of food delivery, with an estimated number of 3,000 riders working across the city. The majority are male, aged between twenty-two and thirty years old. Delivering food is their main source of income, which contradicts the assumption that 'rider equals student with a side job'.

More than half of them are migrants – 40% from Africa, 15% from Asia, 5% from South America. Some have been in Italy for more than two years; others have just arrived, and are often undocumented, which makes them more vulnerable to exploitation and lack of employment protection. Among the *sans-papiers*, getting a thermal backpack for deliveries and a telephone with the app from a fellow-countryman in exchange for money seems the only solution to make a living. On average, they are likely to spend up to fifty hours a week riding their bikes.

Personifications of the precarious nature of digital capitalism, but also of metropolises and their transformation, delivery riders are a living battleground – a conundrum of tensions where the social, economic and spatial impact of platform capitalism, the gig economy, the refugee crisis and the climate meltdown collapse onto a single vulnerable category of digital workers.

This is a phenomenon that is not new but that encompasses the gig economy more widely. Because of the 2008 financial crisis, and in parallel to the surge of techno-capitalist industries, the boom of 'sharing and delivery platforms' has provided the private sphere with powerful market mechanics, enabling the fluid commodification of life. Flexible, web-scale human resourcing drew 'app freelancers' into the gig economy – an unprecedented economic reactivation of latent human assets. A new labour force has emerged, one that is obliged to hire itself out for ever-smaller jobs, where the illusion of empowerment and flexibility conceals what is effectively a total lack of safety net, while big-tech companies are profiting handsomely. Digital platforms employ organisational tools of savage power, masses are atomised – strong-armed into unorganised negotiation, struggling to get decent contracts or basic working conditions.

The asymmetric power relationship between riders and their algorithmic employers is at the base of many of the legal disputes trying to redefine labour jurisdiction addressing an emergent class of digital precariat, in Italy as in the rest of Europe.

In Italy the debate has been intense in the past years. A recent order from the court of Bologna (January 2021) has set a precedent for the rest of Europe, by recognising the discriminatory nature of 'Frank', the algorithm used by Deliveroo to assign job opportunities to riders, following a score based on their reliability and participation. According to the court, 'to treat in the same way those who do not participate in a booked session for futile reasons and those who do not participate because they are on strike (or because they are sick, have a disability, or assist a disabled person or a sick minor, etc.) in practice discriminates the latter, possibly marginalising them from the priority group and thus significantly reducing their future opportunities for access to work'.[2]

Deliveroo has since changed the nature of its algorithms, applying rules that are more linear and fairer for riders, but other companies have not followed suit. Glovo continues to maintain the shift booking system based on a score, even though in 2021 the Privacy Guarantor fined the company 2.6 million euros, urging it to take measures to prevent 'improper or discriminators of reputational mechanisms based on feedback from customers and business partners'. These battles suggest that riders are being and have been treated as cogs of the vast delivery mechanism – more like machines than human beings.

---

1 'Come funzionano gli algoritmi dei rider', il post, 24 November 2022, https://www.ilpost.it/2022/11/24/algoritmi-rider/ (accessed 28 March 2023).

2 Vincenzo Pietrogiovanni, 'Deliveroo and Riders' Strikes: Discriminations in the Age of Algorithms', International Labor Rights Case Law, 3 December 2021, https://brill.com/view/journals/ilrc/7/3/article-p317_317.xml (accessed 28 March 2023).

3 Benjamin Bratton, '18 Lessons of Quarantine Urbanism', *Strelka Mag. Special issue: The Revenge of the Real* (April 2020), https://strelkamag.com/en/article/18-lessonsfrom-quarantine-urbanism.

4 Paul Preciado, 'Learning from the Virus', Artforum (May/June 2020), https://www.artforum.com/print/202005/paul-b-preciado-82823 (accessed 28 March 2023).

5 Evgeny Morozov, 'The Rise of Data and the Death of Politics', *The Guardian* (2014), https://www.theguardian.com/technology/2014/jul/20/rise-of-data-death-of-politics-evgeny-morozov-algorithmic-regulation (accessed 28 March 2023).

6 Preciado, 'Learning from the Virus' (see note 4).

Aside from the progress in terms of labour jurisdiction, the main issue remains the lack of transparency of the algorithms developed by the platforms, which are not made accessible to judges, data scientists or journalists and whose actual mechanics thus remain obscure and inaccessible – in the name of freedom of enterprise and industrial property. A common story across tech platforms, which reverberates and manifests in many forms and scales: from the recent scandals regarding the treatment of users' data by Meta, to the inaccessibility and bluntness of data centres around the world.

Emerging techno-informality

In Italy, as in the rest of southern Europe, the precarity of the gig economy meets the precarity of undocumented migrants in the entangled fight for social justice and better living standards. An emerging informal economy hides in the cracks of platform capitalism, following an old and consolidated model of labour exploitation. A steep increase in the demand of delivery services, propelled by the Covid-19-induced lockdown, combined with the massive presence of undocumented workers, has brought to the surface a number of worrying cases of illegal gangmastering. In the best scenario, these vulnerable groups rely on inner networks and connections – where more individuals share a single account to keep it running at maximum efficiency and profitability. In others, these schemes are operated by intermediaries of large food delivery platforms: these practices recruit undocumented refugees in a state of need and exploit riders by paying a fixed low fare, while forcing them to work during uncomfortable hours, sharing accounts between more riders. A brutal phenomenon, visually embodied by scenes of homeless riders, sleeping next to, or partially inside, their colourful corporate thermal backpacks, turned into occasional micro-shelters.

Described as the 'dark side of the gig economy', this practice is not new, but rather an endemic problem across several food delivery platforms; and it replicates – or even exacerbates, by precipitating it at the speed of data – the illegal exploitation of undocumented workers in the agricultural sector in southern Italy: labour extraction is enabled by the combined effect of exploited illegal migration, the dominance of corporate interests – and the reign of food distribution networks and tech platforms.

Subjects

> 'With the automated order relays, waves of sys-admins and couriers are keeping the world moving when the government cannot. In doing so, the chains of automation have become an emergency public sphere.'[3]

Amid the Covid-19 pandemic, in countries such as Italy that witnessed extreme lockdown measures, society was fractured between those who were confined within their homes and the army of essential workers who kept our social fabric intact. Two categories simultaneously divided and connected by the interface of a mobile phone. Mainstream media has often referred to essential workers as 'heroes', contributing to institutionalising their exceptionality. Food delivery riders, Amazon couriers, and so on, played a huge role in this context: if on one side the sheer increase of their activities ran in parallel with the massive profits performed by tech giants, on the other the visible precarity and fragility of their conditions has made obvious that at the end of the much celebrated 'chains of automation' there are real, struggling people,

and that cities can hardly be understood as operating systems. As much as technology is apparently contributing to shape perfectly smooth existences, we should acknowledge that a simple tap on a screen conceals a chain of sequenced operations, procedures and invisible frictions: a complex system where physical, spatial, biological, mineral, chemical and synthetic regimes are entangled at the speed of light and across scales.

The pandemic has acted as an accelerator, maximising pre-existing forms of violence, while reinforcing the constructions of new techno-subjectivities: on the one hand those confined at home, and on the other the army of essential workers.

> 'The subjects of the neoliberal technical-patriarchal societies that Covid-19 is in the midst of creating do not have skin; they are untouchable; they do not have hands. They do not exchange physical goods, nor do they pay with money. They are digital consumers equipped with credit cards. They do not have lips or tongues. They do not speak directly; they leave a voicemail. They do not gather together, and they do not collectivise. They are radically un-dividual. They do not have faces; they have masks. To exist, their organic bodies are hidden behind an indefinite series of semio-technical mediations, an array of cybernetic prosthesis that work like digital masks: email addresses, Facebook, Instagram, Zoom, and Skype accounts. They are not physical agents but rather tele-producers; they are codes, pixels, bank accounts, doors without names, addresses to which Amazon can send its orders.'[4]

Paul B. Preciado's text resonates with Evgeny Morozov's position on algorithmic regulation[5] as the closest form to a political programme that the tech-giants could conceive – stuck as we are in an endless feedback loop mechanism regulated by algorithmic intelligences that orient our choices, decisions and ideological affiliations. The modern, hyperconnected smart worker – often another member of the digital precariat – lives in a nebulous arena suspended between the digital and the physical, where private blurs into public, and the couch, the city and the planet merge into an unidentified but datafied continuum.

Meanwhile, on the other side of the screen riders keep on riding, stuck into another space, as Preciado continues:

> 'That wage labour is itself an institution of confinement has never been clearer than now, as we witness "essential" workers as de-munised bodies brutally forced into spaces of lethal risk. The essential workers forced to ride are disproportionately low-income, disproportionately migrants, disproportionately racialised bodies. Their forced mobility is also a type of incarceration.'[6]

Riders not heroes

In Milan, among the European cities that were hit the hardest by the virus and where the lockdown restrictions were extreme, riders kept delivering food and other supplies for the entire duration of the quarantine. When the city was totally empty, riders were the only humans who kept moving around what then resembled a ghost town, until their social functions finally started to be recognised. From being invisible, they finally got to be seen, almost by subtraction. Colourful hybrid figures – part humans, part thermal backpacks, part bikes, part data – riders moved unchallenged around the city, while being recorded accidentally by webcams, security cameras and intercoms, and appearing as abstract, de-humanised icons on our mobile devices.

7   Constant Nieuwenhuys, 'New Babylon: The World of Homo Ludens' (1970), https://www.notbored.org/homo-ludens.html (accessed 28 March 2023).

8   Francesca Bria, 'Digital Sovereignty for the People in the Post-Pandemic World', medium.com (2020), https://medium.com/@francescabria/digital-sovereignty-for-the-people-in-the-post-pandemic-world-109472dd736b (accessed 28 March 2023).

The making of our short film dilogy, *Riders Not Heroes*, started around this time, with the intention of investigating the precarious conditions of food delivery riders in Milan. The first chapter specifically makes a strong case for riders as essential workers and a concentrate of tensions lying at the intersection of platform capitalism, gig labour, the refugee crisis and the open spaces of the global pandemic. Milan in this case acted as a prototype of the impact of tech-platforms on any other western European city.

To keep a record of that historical moment, we collaborated with an Italian rider and artist, Lupo Borgonovo. Equipped with GoPros, Lupo was turned into a moving camera, allowing us to experience and film vicariously the empty streets of Milan and the daily routines of riders from an unprecedented perspective.

Built as a desktop movie from an accumulation of the news reels, social media posts, web contents and GoPro footage recorded on the streets during delivery times, the film presents a new urban geography made of flows, invisible communities, spaces and devices that emerged through the impulse of digital platforms.

The riders' city is a mental map of buildings' interiors randomly accessed by those riders, collaged into a single architecture of fragments; it's a map of dangerous shortcuts to complete deliveries at maximum speed and gain competitive advantage over the algorithm scoring your performance; it's a supply chain of basic food ingredients fuelling the invisible networks of dark kitchens – food preparation labs serving several fictitious restaurants existing only on the digital platforms – and emerging in the urban-scape as a hole in the wall; the riders' city is a collection of ethnicities, languages and cultures establishing alliances and networks of solidarity, while also setting clear boundaries; it's a network of train stations acting as occasional dormitories for some, and entry points for those from smaller centres, with fewer job opportunities but lower rents; it's a constellation of urban pockets, from the city centre to the peripheries, where riders rest in small groups, eating chicken and rice, like proper athletes; it's a collection of prosthetic tools – corporate food-boxes, ear pods, helmets, masks, etc. – that act as microarchitectures to mediate and shield riders from the environment they cycle through. The riders' city is a phone communicating and exchanging packs of data across different corporate, state and fiscal sovereignties with servers on the other side of the world, whose mechanics and governance remain largely obscure.

The riders' city is one of the many possible images of the post-city: an agglomerate of flows and of digital and biological bodies in constant negotiation and balancing.

Possible futures

In the meantime, Uber has promised it will be offering food deliveries by drone in multiple countries by 2023. Developments in drone technology are paving the way to a plausible transition to fully automated delivery services, progressively moving the already precarious human gig-labour force into even more uncertain grounds. Automation is progressing and it might turn cities and their skies – at least at our latitudes – into smooth sensing environments marked by machine operations and synthetic cognitive systems. Human friction might be replaced by touchless efficiency, labour by information, protests by coding. Today the fascination towards automation is propelled by corporate promises and visions of greener, more efficient futures, but the full-scale consequences and impacts of such transition remain widely unanticipated – both culturally, socially and spatially.

As we experience an unprecedented technological acceleration, it's important to remember that our social thinking on technology and automation has a long historical trajectory that brings us back to Constant Nieuwenhuys and his 'New Babylon' utopia: a fully automated society where humans would live in floating structures and – by being liberated from the ground and the obligations of the functional city – could dedicate to creative practices and play. In 1970, he would write about his vision: 'New Babylon, perhaps, is not so much a picture of the future as a *leitmotiv*, the conception of an all-comprehensive culture that is hard to comprehend because until now it could not exist, a culture that, for the first time in history, as a consequence of the automation of labour, becomes feasible although we do not yet know what shape it will take, and seems mysterious to us.'[7] While after fifty years we are still debating about the consequences and forms that automation and technology will generate, Nieuwenhuys' vision remains a powerful reminder that the question is still first and foremost political and that technology can't be disentangled from a wider social project.

With corporations such as Uber, Glovo, Siemens, Amazon and the like trying to become the operating systems of the contemporary city, a new model of governance should be sought-after, now more than ever. It is ultimately a matter of politics and of data sovereignty.

'Digital sovereignty means that digital technologies can facilitate the transition from today's digital economy of surveillance capitalism – whereby a handful of US- and China-based corporations battle for global digital supremacy – to a people-centric digital future based on better workers, environmental, and citizens' rights, to bring long-term social innovation.'[8]

The opportunity is to develop a new European model tailored on the scale of the city, offering alternative policies for the democratic governance of digital technology and data sovereignty. A Data Commons future, aimed at aggregating the cumulative intelligence of data shared by citizens for the establishment of collective platforms and for a better offer of services.

What these times really need is a new social contract for the digital society.

Reconnecting civitas and urbs: Making tourists and remote workers temporary urban citizens

Daniele Belleri
Michael Baick
Carlo Ratti

[1] Marco Romano, *L'estetica della città europea. Forme e immagini* (Turin: Einaudi, 1993).

[2] Saskia Sassen, *The Global City: New York, London, Tokyo* (Princeton, NJ: Princeton University Press, 1991).

In August 2019, the Piazza San Marco in Venice was flooded with tourists. They squeezed into selfies in front of the cathedral, bought identical souvenirs, and at times tossed their trash into the canals. Overfed pigeons preyed on the crowd. Every year thousands of Venetians would leave the city, in search of opportunities that the tourist-dominated economy failed to offer. The government planned a controversial 'tourist tax' – a levy to be paid by individual visitors – to mitigate the damage.

In August 2020, the piazza looked very different. Pedestrians stayed several metres apart, plastic souvenirs were replaced by cloth masks, and the canals were eerily clean. The tourists were gone; the Venetian economy risked collapsing. Mayor Luigi Brugnaro, who championed the tourist tax, postponed the measure, lamenting that 'Venice is on its knees'. The tourists' absence proved to be just as jarring as their omnipresence – and the outlook remained uncertain deep into the following year.

In August 2022, the health emergency looked to be finally past us. But what did Venice learn from the pandemic-induced economic disruption? Most importantly, can something be done to avoid going back to square one – that is, to the unsustainable pre-Covid-19 tourism model?

In order to address this issue, we might need to reexamine our understanding of the idea of citizenship – a concept which reached a tipping point following the early 2020s pandemic outbreak. For centuries, most Western societies rested on a couple of assumptions that can no longer be counted on. First: most people live where they belong. Second: the sense of belonging is inextricably tied to one's birthplace. With individuals staying in the same places for years or generations, community and civic participation were easier to foster. In other words, there was a relatively straightforward correspondence between one's physical location – what the ancient Romans called the *urbs*: the built-up component of a city – and the people who rightly inhabit it – the *civitas*.[1]

In the last few decades, an increasing number of people, in different life circumstances, have experienced a severance of the *civitas–urbs* correspondence. Multiple social, economic and technological factors have created this situation. International business interests, more affordable air travel and digitisation, coupled with generally less rigid regional and national borders, have facilitated new connections between distant places, prompting more and more people to look beyond their immediate surroundings – be it for leisure or for work, to satisfy personal ambitions or to flee from undesirable political or environmental conditions. Under the pressure of millions of individuals' uncoordinated decisions, the ultimate outcome is that so many of the *civitates* of our world have been pried apart from their *urbs*.

Nowhere is this happening as dramatically as in big cities, the pivotal nodes of the globalised economy.[2] Our metropolitan centres are filling with tourists, globetrotting commuters, remote workers and ever-growing numbers of migrants. These groups travel across the planet under extremely different circumstances, but they share the common experience of not fitting into the communities where they arrive. Their physical presence, multiplied by the thousands, challenges the correspondence between *urbs* and *civitas* – being in a certain place does not automatically imply being part of its civic society.

The possibility of millions of human beings coming from faraway places to live together might sound to some like the realisation of a cosmopolitan utopia. Undoubtedly, the possibility to decouple one's place of birth from one's destiny has been liberating for multitudes of individuals. However, when looking at this issue on a collective scale, the mismatch between *urbs* and *civitas* generates a series of fundamental social issues and provokes profound social tensions. In different contexts, it can fuel phenomena as diverse as political polarisation and social resentment, urban fragmentation and segregation, or distrust in civic institutions. Populist politicians have been the first to skilfully and selfishly exploit the layperson's sense of unease and fear vis-à-vis this changing reality. How can this vulnerability be repaired?

When we consider the history of cities, we find that the underlying principles are simple. Cities emerged 10,000 years ago, and they succeeded because they brought together a large population with a shared, vested interest in a common space. In these ancient

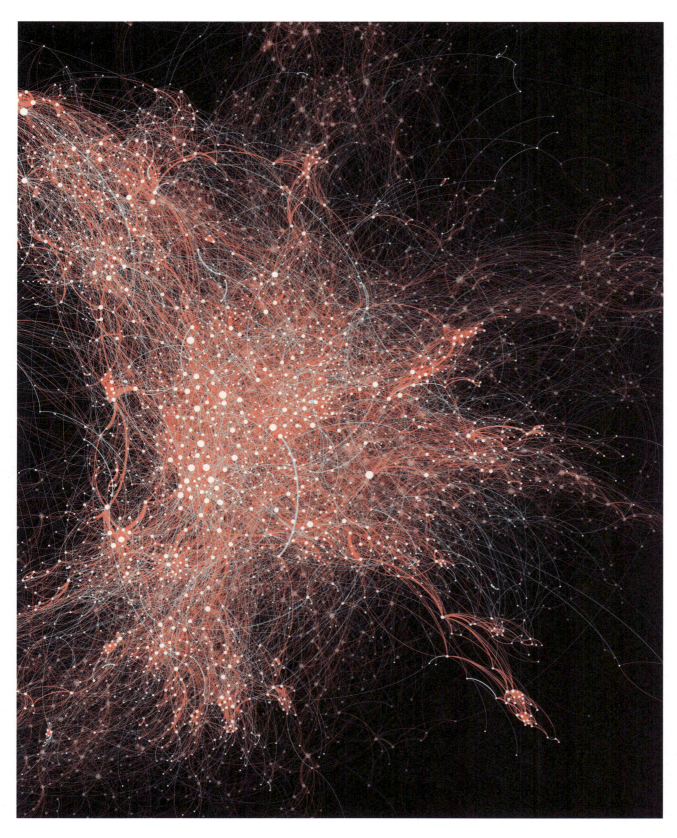

From the outset of the pandemic, our Senseable City Lab at MIT began to study how remote work affects the formation of weak ties. Using anonymous data from the Institute's email servers, we found that students, professors and administrators began to exchange more messages with a smaller group of contacts. In other words, strong ties were becoming stronger and weak ties were falling away.

urban centres, we can see the rudimentary basis of citizenship as a simple exchange: civic contributions for civic freedom. Those with the formal or informal status of 'citizen' are afforded certain rights and advantages, from access to markets to the power of the ballot. As a medieval German adage went: 'the air of the cities makes you free' – and no wonder. Cities would offer far broader horizons than the countryside where peasants struggled to make a living. However, becoming a citizen was not just a question of breathing: that privilege was earned by following certain rules and making critical contributions, from taxes and economic participation to membership in community institutions. It is easy to make these contributions when one lives in a place long-term: a job becomes available, a church surrounds you with holy community, the tax collector knows where to find your door. However, cities have always been less well-equipped to handle new and short-term residents – neither the visitor nor the city they visit is agile enough to collect civic dues and dole out civic privileges. The *civitas* and *urbs* fail to click together, and the new-timers are legally and socially excluded from the rights and responsibilities of citizenship. This failure of connection comes in political, economic and cultural terms.

How can we restore the staying power of citizenship in a world where the experience of rootlessness has become so widespread? Some might dream of a return to the past, when everyone stays in the place where they were born for their entire life. But that is simply not possible: the globe has become deeply bound together, and no realistic return is in sight. Accepting that present trends are likely to continue, a possible solution might lie in rethinking our understanding of the very idea of urban citizenship, with the objective of mending the recently formed rift between *urbs* and *civitas*.

In this text, we sketch a form of 'variable' urban citizenship: legal and cultural paradigms which acknowledge the reality of a highly mobile global population and bring these transient civitates back into

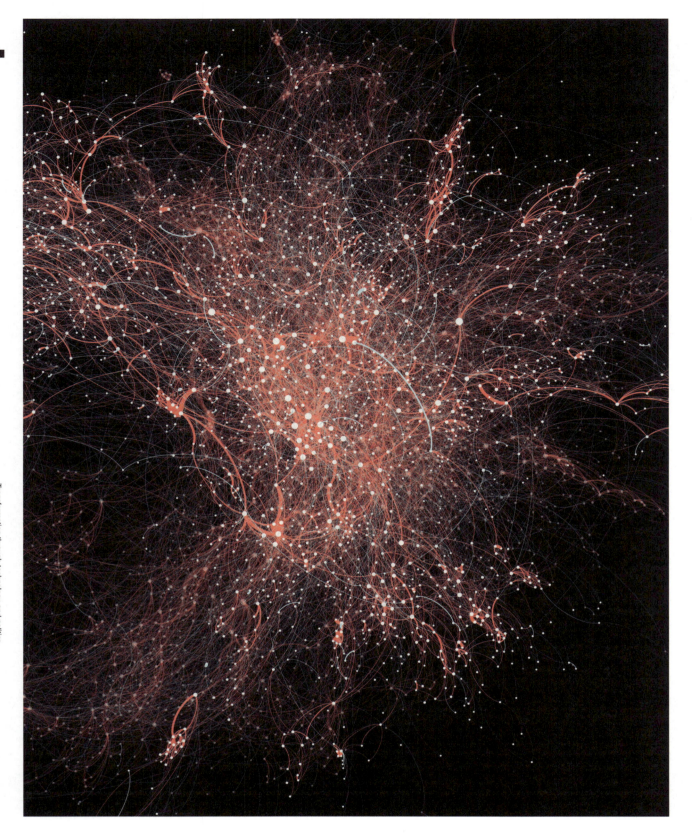

3   Max Roser and Bastian Herre, *Tourism. Our World in Data* (2022), https://ourworldindata.org/tourism (accessed 15 June 2022).

4   Don DeLillo, *The Names* (reissue) (New York: Vintage, 1989).

the embrace of the urbs. To do so, we must think nimbly about the kinds of ways that people can be incorporated into their communities, even if they are new or temporary residents. To flesh out this idea, we will apply it to two groups of people for whom a form of variable citizenship could apply: tourists and remote workers. We imagine policies at the level of the city, focusing on the idea that citizenship is first and foremost lived at the level of one's physically proximate community. While our speculative model touches upon issues studied by multiple disciplines, our first focus is a possible role of designers in reconnecting the *urbs* and the *civitas* through their action on physical space.

First, let us consider the tourist, an individual often imagined to be the exact opposite of a citizen. Tourism is a lucrative business and it has boomed in the era of cheap air travel. The birth of the postwar world is very much the birth of a world of tourists. Global travel has skyrocketed: from 25 million tourists in 1950 to 1.4 billion in 2019.[3] The fragile, local balance between *urbs* and *civitas* can be tragically disrupted by this colossal human flow.

Tourists certainly bring in money but rarely have attachment or commitment to the long-term well-being of the places they visit. 'To be a tourist is to escape accountability', American novelist Don DeLillo famously wrote. 'Errors and failings don't cling to you the way they do back home. You're able to drift across continents and languages, suspending the operation of sound thought … You don't know how to talk to people, how to get anywhere, what the money means, what time it is, what to eat or how to eat it'.[4] DeLillo observes that tourists are granted 'immunities and broad freedoms' in exchange for their cash; this empty transaction is a perversion of the mutually beneficial exchange that defines citizenship. At their worst, hit-and-run tourists disrupt local public life, disrespect local customs, warp local economies and price long-term residents out of their homes.

Resentment against tourists is boiling over. In

the years immediately before the first outbreak of the Covid-19 pandemic, young Catalan activists famously vandalised a tour bus in Barcelona, slashing its tyres and spray-painting 'tourism is killing neighbourhoods' on the windshield. The conflict is especially nasty in cities where tourists outnumber long-term residents. In some cities – especially the ones that are losing population – tourists outnumber residents by a significant ratio. Calculations of the flows of urban visitors can get quite fuzzy due to the difficulty of accounting not just for those who check-in at a hotel or Airbnb, but also for day-trippers. Some estimates have put the figure for pre-pandemic Venice at a staggering 20 million people per year – that is, roughly 350 tourists per resident of the historic city;[5] that number is around twenty in Barcelona[6] and eight-and-a-half in Paris.[7]

How can cities control the torrent of tourists? The municipality of Venice decided to protect its citizens by charging a 'tourist tax' for day-trippers entering the city's historic centre.[8] If tourists do not contribute to the city's life through community membership, Venice could at least extract more monetary value to undo the damage they cause. The funds raised by the tax would, according to the city's mayor, go to cleaning and maintaining security, expenses that are currently upheld by Venetians alone. However, before the tax could be implemented anywhere, Covid-19 struck, bringing international travel to a halt. The planned tax in Venice has been repeatedly delayed and is now scheduled to be implemented in 2023.[9]

The tourist tax contains the rudiments of a citizen-like relationship – paying an extra tax to access the privileges of boating in the canals or strolling through the Piazza San Marco – but the attempt is a narrow one, relying entirely on money as the unit of account for civic goods that cannot be so easily commodified. Squeezing more money out of tourists could raise revenues in the short term, but it cannot address the structural issues that tourists create. Indeed, a more extreme version of the Venetian tax, a relatively small amount of money, might worsen the problems of gentrification by selecting only the wealthiest tourists. If Venice is trying to avoid being Disneyland, raising entrance fees might just turn it into Mar-a-Lago. The flimsiness of a purely transactional relationship was proven during Covid-19 – no tourist felt any roots that would have motivated them to stay in the city that depended on them.

One alternative to address the problems of tourism without the blunt instruments of commodification would be incentivising tourists to settle in cities for longer periods. Almost inherently, a tourist who stays for a few weeks or months rather than a few days becomes more accountable, more like a citizen. Instead of visiting a restaurant once, a longer-term tourist might become a repeat customer who leaves generous tips and makes good conversation with waiting staff. They might learn to speak at a proper volume and support a broader range of commercial activities than hotels, gift shops and tour buses. This would not only be good for the city, it would enhance the experience of travel itself. Rather than moving towards the pessimistic vision of French philosopher Paul Ricœur, who decried how, in the modern world, everywhere 'one finds the same bad movies, the same slot machines, the same plastic or aluminium atrocities',[10] visitors might actually enjoy spending longer periods of time in different cities. We call this model 'pace tourism', and we believe it could help in reconnecting *urbs* and *civitas* in tourist destinations around the world.

The potential of pace tourism is already visible in extant programmes that encourage long stays. Consider another case in Italy, the southern city of Matera, named European Capital of Culture in 2019, which decided to rebrand its tourists as 'temporary citizens'[11] and invite them to help contribute something to the town. As a result, tourism boomed – without some of the seemingly inevitable trade-offs. One could also consider the study-abroad programmes and travelling fellowships adopted by university students across the world. Anchored by host families and other schools, these semester- or year-long stays are transformative without being transactional.

As these examples show, other contributions, beyond the financial, can qualify someone for a form of citizenship without requiring long-term residence. Instead of a monetary tourist tax, what about a civic contribution tax that could come in many other forms? For example, one could become a temporary citizen of Venice for one year in exchange for help with maintenance on its palazzos and stuccos. Young graduates could share digital skills to assist start-ups; retired members of Ingénieurs sans frontières could work to restore the canals. Temporary citizens can become one with the *urbs* with projects that focus on the space itself, giving them the chance to inscribe their lives into the stones themselves – joining with Venetians who have done so for centuries. Moreover, they would learn local customs: their language skills would grow beyond an introductory manual, and they might graduate from visiting restaurants to learning how to cook local cuisine for themselves.

Municipal governments could take action in bringing pace travel to their cities, leveraging the power of online platforms. They could create roles for volunteering and temporary employment, and they could incentivise companies such as Airbnb, or smaller operators, to offer discounts for longer stays. Apps, now ubiquitously embedded with location-based services, can also be programmed to provide incentives based on length of stay and degree of local engagement. These digital tools could be paired with lower-tech strategies, like adding a minimum-stay stipulation to certain tourist visas. The ultimate objective would be to transform tourists from lucrative annoyances to honoured, valued guests.

Another key group to consider is international commuters and remote workers. This demographic travels the world not just to spend money, but first and foremost to earn it.

Fifty years ago, urban theorist Melvin Webber predicted that 'for the first time in history, it might be possible to locate on a mountaintop and to maintain intimate, real-time, and realistic contact'.[12] In 2020, his prophecy came true. Since the first weeks of the Covid-19 crisis, many white-collar workers have discovered that they can do their jobs from anywhere. Connecting digitally with their colleagues, billions of people climbed up the steep, steep sides of the mountaintop.

Once again, this new arrangement puts into question the correspondence between *urbs* and *civitas*. Linking technological progress to social changes, Spanish sociologist Manuel Castells famously wrote about the emergence of an unprecedented 'Space of Flows'.[13] According to Castells, information technology and early digitisation has created a society where wealth and power increasingly bypass physical space. This logic challenges the traditional logic of the 'Space of Places' where localities hold a central position in societal organisation.

When Castells elaborated his theory, many experts shared the opinion that the positive effects of the 'Space of Flows' would outrun any possible negative outcome. In contrast to that, a less optimistic scholar was American historian Christopher Lasch. *In The Revolt of the Elites and the Betrayal of Democracy*,[14] a collection of essays published shortly after his death, the author decried how a threat to American democracy came from its elites, which 'have removed themselves from the common life'.

---

5 Anna Momigliano, 'Venice tourism may never be the same. It could be better', *The New York Times* (2020), https://www.nytimes.com/2020/07/02/travel/venice-coronavirus-tourism.html (accessed 15 June 2022).

6 Lisa Abend, 'Europe made billions from tourists. Now it's turning them away', *Time* (2018), https://time.com/5349533/europe-against-tourists/ (accessed 15 June 2022).

7 Clément Guillou, 'Paris expects 33 million tourists in 2022', *Le Monde* (2022), https://www.lemonde.fr/en/economy/article/2022/06/15/paris-expects-33-million-tourists-in-2022_5986793_19.html (accessed 15 June 2022).

8 Angela Giuffrida, 'Venice pushes ahead with €10 entry fee plan as tourists flock back', *The Guardian* (2022), https://www.theguardian.com/world/2022/apr/19/venice-day-trippers-to-be-charged-up-to-10-to-enter-city (accessed 15 June 2022).

9 Julia Buckley, 'Venice is planning to introduce a tourist tax. Is this a sign of things to come?', *National Geographic* (2022), https://www.nationalgeographic.co.uk/travel/2022/06/venice-is-planning-to-introduce-a-tourist-tax-is-this-a-sign-of-things-to-come (accessed 13 June 2022).

10 Ibid.

11 Matera 2019, 'The Temporary Citizen of Matera 2019', Matera-Basilicata (2019), https://www.matera-basilicata2019.it/en/processes/temporary-citizen.html (accessed 13 June 2022).

12 Melvin M. Webber, 'The Post-city Age', *Daedalus* 97(4) (1968), 1091–110, http://www.jstor.org/stable/20013413.

13 Manuel Castells, *The Informational City: Information Technology, Economic Restructuring, and the Urban-Regional Process* (Oxford: Basil Blackwell, 1989).

14 Christopher Lasch, *The Revolt of the Elites and the Betrayal of Democracy* (New York: W. W. Norton, 1995).

15 Mark S. Granovetter, 'The Strength of Weak Ties', *American Journal of Sociology* 78(6) (1973), 1360–80. http://www.jstor.org/stable/2776392.

16 Martina Mazzarello and Carlo Ratti, 'Leveraging the Use of Digital Technologies to Activate Public Areas and Foster Creativity', in *Intelligent Systems, Control and Automation: Science and Engineering* (Springer International Publishing, 2020), 45–57, https://doi.org/10.1007/978-3-030-56926-6_5.

17 Ray Oldenburg, *The Great Good Place* (New York: Paragon House, 1989).

18 Eric Klinenberg, *Palaces for the People* (New York: Crown, 2018).

19 Ibid.

While the reasons for this phenomenon were manifold, among them was the fact that executives and other high-powered professionals were now operating in a global information market, which allowed them to embrace a regime of international mobility. As a result, these individuals were not tied to any specific location anymore, finding themselves detached from any obligations to the local community. Lasch predicted that, in the long run, this dynamic would increase political polarisation and provoke a detriment of democratic processes and civic trust.

When the book was published, Lasch estimated that the 'elites' made up roughly a fifth of the population of the United States. Since then, and especially with the unexpected acceleration in remote working adoption ushered in by the pandemic, the number of people who had the possibility to leave the physical workspaces and retreat in isolation increased. This group disproportionately comes from the sector of knowledge workers, and while they still may not amount to a majority of residents, as tourists sometimes do, it has reached a size that was unimaginable until a few years ago.

Despite some of the hypothesis mentioned, it was not entirely clear that remote work could necessarily rip apart our civic fabric – that is, until the Covid-19 pandemic gave us the data to confirm the danger. As this massive, unprecedented shift occurred, we gained a once-in-a-lifetime chance to study exactly what effects remote work would have on the individual and societal level.

First, let us characterise social networks using terms developed by the sociologist Mark Granovetter. He divides relationships into two types: the 'strong ties' we maintain with friends and family and the 'weak ties' we form with casual acquaintances.[15] Strong ties yield dense, overlapping networks; your close friends are often close friends with each other. But our weak ties are in many situations even more important, because they connect us to a far broader range of people and completely separate social circles (or 'bubbles', to say it in more internet-friendly terms). Those individuals are more likely to introduce you to new ideas, challenge your preconceptions, and make you aware of the world outside your strong ties. They help us find job opportunities and adapt to new innovations. To put it simply, weak ties are the glue that holds us together as a broader community. Granovetter posited that weak ties are indispensable to a healthy civic life. They are key agents for maintaining trust, enthusiasm and mutual understanding among people of different beliefs. Without them, a society begins to decohere.

From the outset of the pandemic, our Senseable City Lab at MIT began to study how remote work affects the formation of weak ties. Using anonymous data from the Institute's email servers, we found that students, professors and administrators began to exchange more messages with a smaller group of contacts. In other words, strong ties were becoming stronger and weak ties were falling away.[16] This finding fits the anecdotal experiences of many people who were locked down: we dedicated more time to our families at home and to our close friends online. In that same period, our acquaintances slipped through the cracks.

Why does the internet sever weak ties in a way that physical space does not? The key factor to consider is the inevitability and serendipity of the physical world that is impossible to recreate online. The internet allows us to cherry-pick what to see and whom to talk to, a habit only fuelled by the digital algorithms that reinforce our connections with those who most agree with us. Needless to say, in shared offices, buses or sidewalks, we can't screen out weak ties with one click. Indeed, we run into people and ideas we'd never expect.

For these key interactions to take place, we need the common ground of an *urbs* to create the weak ties that bind a *civitas* together.

Yet remote work is clearly here to stay. Short of a Luddite temper tantrum that forces employees to stay in the office and ignore new technology entirely, how can we reincorporate remotely working employees into physical communities? We will need to devise a host of arrangements that coax them back into the social vitality of physical space. The key will lie in adjustments to urban infrastructure, and places to work in particular. The physical office retains its crucial importance in favouring the formation of weak ties, as other shared urban spaces do.

Lasch attributed a part of the *Betrayal of Democracy* to the loss of 'third places' – a term coined by urban sociologist Ray Oldenburg in the 1980s[17] to indicate those spaces beyond the home and workplace that foster spontaneous conversation among citizens of different social classes. This, in turn, echoes the definition of 'social infrastructure' provided by Eric Klinenberg in *Palaces for the People*.[18] In his words:

> 'Infrastructure' is not a term conventionally used to describe the underpinnings of social life. But this is a consequential over-sight, because the built environment – and not just cultural preferences or the existence of voluntary organizations – influences the breadth and depth of our associations … What counts as social infrastructure? I define it capaciously. Public institutions, such as libraries, schools, playgrounds, parks, athletic fields, and swimming pools, are vital parts of the social infrastructure. So too are sidewalks, courtyards, community gardens, and other green spaces that invite people into the public realm. Community organizations, including churches and civic associations, act as social infrastructures when they have an established physical space where people can assemble, as do regularly scheduled markets for food, furniture, clothing, art, and other consumer goods. Commercial establishments can also be important parts of the social infrastructure, particularly when they operate as what the sociologist Ray Oldenburg called "third spaces," places (like cafés, diners, barbershops, and bookstores) where people are welcome to congregate and linger regardless of what they've purchased. Entrepreneurs typically start these kinds of businesses because they want to generate income. But in the process, as close observers of the city such as Jane Jacobs and the Yale ethnographer Elijah Anderson have discovered, they help produce the material foundations for social life.[19]

Although many remote workers come from the private sector, municipal governments cannot leave the effort of creating physical spaces for them to inhabit to the discretion of private co-working firms or spacious cafés with high-speed internet connections. Services and establishments such as WeWork and Starbucks cafés are not necessarily spaces that will create the diversity of encounters and weak ties that are fundamental to the *urbs–civitas* balance.

What forms of public social infrastructure can help to enfold remote workers back into the *urbs* around them? Based on the concept of a *civitas* and *urbs* requiring physical proximity, we should focus on engendering citizenship in whatever place a remote worker spends the most time. The nightmare scenario we wish to avoid is a desolate 'Zoomtown', where everyone spends their days on a computer, participating only in the life of some other place.

How can we imagine a civic space for remote workers? From a designer's perspective, a starting point could be the template of the public library, an institution which developed in the late nineteenth and

20 Sofia Lekka Angelopoulou, 'ALA architects' Oodi central library in Helsinki opens as an indoor extension of public space', Designboom (2018), https://www.designboom.com/architecture/ala-architects-oodi-central-library-helsinki-12-03-2018/ (accessed 14 June 2022).

21 Scott Morgan, 'Taiwan's BAF, Carlo Ratti win design for new National Taiwan Library', Taiwan News (2018), https://www.taiwannews.com.tw/en/news/3537020 (accessed 16 June 2022).

22 Benjamin Barber, *If Mayors Ruled the World. Dysfunctional Nations, Rising Cities* (New Haven: Yale University Press, 2014).

early twentieth centuries with aspirations to help all citizens educate themselves. It would be a mistake to think that the digitalisation of many archives and books has rendered libraries obsolete. In fact, as time has worn on, they became places where people around the world already gather for much more than reading. Wi-fi, public access and other amenities make these attractive, democratic alternatives to private co-working spaces. Now, with the goal of citizenship in mind, architects and planners should strive to imagine further ways to make libraries even more relevant.

From a functional point of view, amenities like conference rooms, fab labs, or spaces for training, and office supply stores have already been incorporated into large-scale libraries around the world, such as the Oodi National Library of Finland, which opened near Helsinki's Central Station in late 2018 to celebrate the country's centenary of independence.[20] Similarly, the extension of the Taiwan National Library, designed by CRA-Carlo Ratti Associati and Bio-Architecture Formosana (BAF), investigated the future role of the library in a digitised society. It centred on the concept of 'Library as a Town'. The new infrastructure would accommodate a variety of functions, including a book museum and a joint archives centre.[21]

Other changes would be programmatic, and should aim to bridge the needs of the local communities with those of the travelling citizens of the digital era. Libraries could offer services to workers on the move like language courses, tax advice, social events and opportunities to enrol in volunteer work. Indeed, they could eventually aspire to become like embassies or community centres for the liminal lives of 'variable citizens', helping them to become more closely tied to the local community and one another. Moreover, so long as libraries also maintain their vital, present functions, they could become a space of social intercourse for permanent and transient populations.

Variable citizenship is much easier to imagine than to implement. While we can fantasise about working around the rigid systems of nation-states, embracing the prospect of 'mayors ruling the world',[22] it will be difficult to tackle issues of taxation, suffrage, government benefits and more. Moreover, the merits of these proposals do not generate political will to be achieved. Green cards, visas and even passports might attract political firestorms. For all of these reasons, any creation of a variable citizenship scheme should be implemented gradually.

In fact, the practical advantages of developing variable citizenship to establish new correspondences between *urbs* and *civitas* might extend beyond the categories of tourists and remote workers. There is a third population that dwarfs the two mentioned here: migrants.

Earlier on, we argued that migrants and tourists, while moving for obviously very different reasons, face similar criticisms about a failure to engage with the local cultures. Here, a robust model of variable citizenship, perhaps developed against lower-stakes populations such as tourists, could help teach an *urbs* to integrate them. While this essay will not engage in the complex task of sketching an extra declension of the variable citizenship scheme that could apply to migrants, this would definitely be worth further exploration, especially as international human flows are poised to increase, further exacerbated by climate crisis-induced conflicts and displacements.

The increasing number of people on the move in our digitised, highly connected world – from tourists to remote-working professionals – is posing fundamental challenges to our cities' social cohesion. In general terms, this tension can be brought back to the severance of the historic correspondence between *urbs* and *civitas*. The speculative proposal of a 'variable citizenship' approach, outlined in this essay, aims to restore this balance, albeit in more flexible ways. Under the constant weight of shifting crises, technological changes and human movements, we must redesign the tools of urban citizenship, while also designing physical spaces that favour social encounters and encourage fruitful exchanges between the more stable populations and the temporary residents. From shifting municipal policies to building next-generation community centres, we have the means to enact a revolutionary, necessary change in how we imagine who belongs where. Ultimately, we may eventually shift the age-old assumption – that people should live in the city where they belong – into its inverse: people can always come to belong where they live.

A longer version of this article was originally published in the *Journal of e-Learning and Knowledge Society*, 18(3) (2022): Special Issue on 'Digital Citizenship'.

Journeys in Italy

Armin Linke

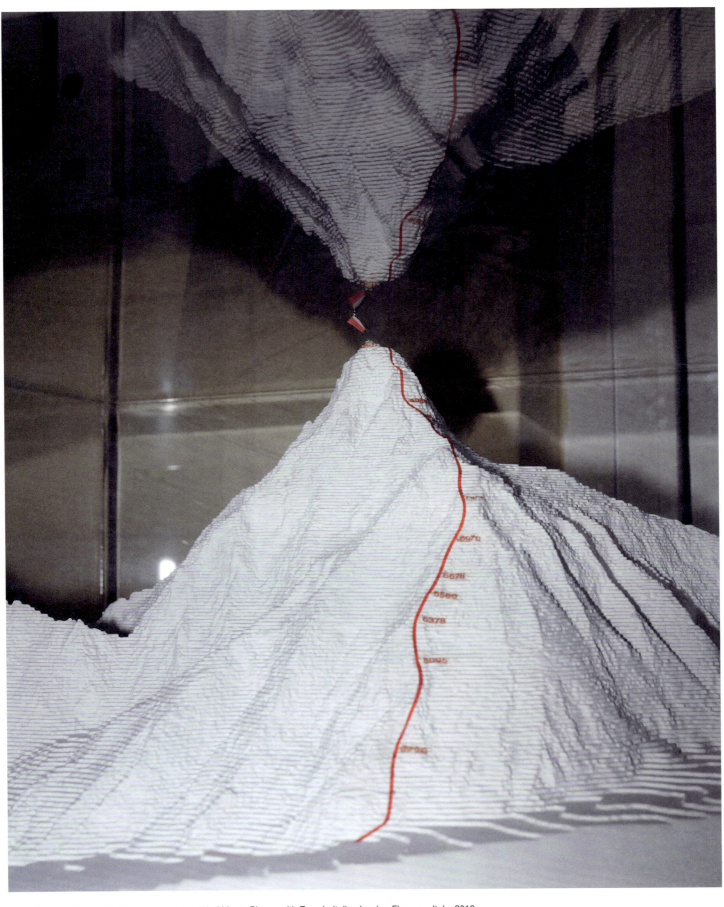

Italian Geographic Military Institute (IGMI), model of Monte Bianco with French–Italian border, Florence, Italy, 2019.

Col de Tende, France/Italy, 2003.

Belvedere Glacier, temporary lake, experiment with fluorescent substance to monitor the flow of water, Monte Rosa (VB), Italy, 2003.

No TAV demonstration against the high speed train, Venaus (TO), Italy, 2005.

Moving cloud, Aosta, Italy, 2000.

G8 summit, Genoa, Italy, 2001.

Mario Fiorentino, Corviale, Rome, Italy, 1998.

Refugee centre, Otranto (LE), Italy, 2002.

Antiquarium, museum, Ercolano (Naples), Italy, 1999.

Torre Vecchia, Rome, Italy, 2003.

Paolo Portoghesi, Vittorio Gigliotti, Sami Mousawi, the Mosque of Rome, Friday prayers in the main hall, Rome, Italy, 2008.

Maria Giuseppina Grasso Cannizzo, holiday home, Noto (SR), Italy, 2012.

Inhabiting the urban realm: Metamorphoses and migrations of contemporary housing types

Cino Zucchi

1 Walter Benjamin, *Das Kunstwerk im Zeitalter seiner technischen Reproduzierbarkeit* (Frankfurt, 1955). [Eng. trans.: *The Work of Art in the Age of Mechanical Reproduction* (New York: Schocken Books, 1968).]

2 Walter Benjamin, *Einbahnstrasse* (Frankfurt, 1955 and 1972–89). [Eng. trans.: *One-way Street and Other Writings* (London and New York: Verso, 1979).]

From 'standardisation' to 'personalisation': the legacy and the betrayal of functionalist principles

Sleeping, washing, studying, preparing food, putting things away, resting after work: the units of activity contained in the circles of 'functionalist' diagrams were supposed to reform the human dwelling to meet objective and universal needs, opposing the morality of the *Neues Wohnen* in both the social hypocrisy of the middle-class home and the squalor of the slums of the industrial metropolis.

But the list of needs that the modern dwelling must satisfy now has to be updated in the light of the new desires and lifestyles of the variegated population of city users. If the rationalist manuals contained the stylised dark outlines of a 'standard' humanity (abstract typical users consistent with the resources of the new clean and sunlit accommodation), the designs for a contemporary dwelling ought perhaps to contain the icons of the diverse virtual population of the Sims or the Metaverse. The concept of the custom-made, of a sometimes extreme 'personalisation', has today brought together the body, the clothing, the domestic environment and even the musical, literary and artistic tastes of residents, transforming the walls of the house into an existential niche governed by the individual choice made possible by the 'dropdown menu'.

The 'liberation of desire' of the Sixties has lost its political overtones and instead has taken on a commercial character, generating a broad range of specific markets targeted by ever more aggressive advertising, where the slogan of 'do your own thing' is paradoxically used to promote the products of global brands.

Whether they like it or not, contemporary housing projects carry in their genetic code many of the results of functionalist and post-functionalist research about mass housing. Ironically, however, the main ideological presupposition of this research, that of an egalitarianism in the positivist mould stemming from the 'universal' character of human needs, has been dropped.

The extreme 'democratisation' of housing proposals for the contemporary metropolis is now taking on new overtones, entering dangerously into resonance with the parallel targeting of market niches by advertisers or the entertainment industry, in the obsession with originality and personalisation that characterises the ever greater diffusion of commodities in mass society.

An awareness of how the city survives individual destinies seems to be the only way of thinking that is capable of laying the foundations for an ethic of resistance to the consumption of the ever-changing images of the 'sex-appeal of the inorganic' described by Walter Benjamin.

'Architecture has always represented the prototype of a work of art the reception of which is consummated by a collectivity in a state of distraction', and, 'its appropriation is accomplished not so much by attention as by habit',[1] once declared Benjamin, who elsewhere urged us to 'live without traces'.[2] Going back to a vision accepting a rather conventional relationship between container and content – not so different in the end from the progressive 'loftisation' of residential space – might constitute a healthy antidote to the suburban atomisation of the fabric that used to make up much of the city we love.

Inside/out or outside/in: the dialectic between the cell and the city

The conflict between the house and outside the urban organism, between the right to individual expression and the conservation of public space – which echoes other typical conflicts between the playful use of the city and the not-in-my-backyard attitude – can perhaps be resolved today through techniques of 'mediation' or the simple creation of an 'interface'. Form arises everywhere there is a need for communication: we could see form as the necessary 'translation' between one system and another, which allows two adjoining realities to hold a dialogue and represent each other.

We realised that the addition of many individual habitats is not able to form a city. The simple movement of the body, which traces and carves out the empty envelope of its living space (from Alexander Klein's

Nuovo Portello, Milan, 2002–08. By CZA Cino Zucchi Architetti, Zucchi & Partners. Credit: Cino Zucchi

diagrams of minimum routes to the organic interior of Friedrich Kiesler's *Endless House*), is not capable of producing true sociability, nor of a true evolution over time of the building substance generated by it. Better, perhaps, to imagine inhabitants as 'hermit crabs', in empirical migration from one shell to another through the orderly trails of the housing ads.

In this sense, the landscape of the *interieur* – from the elegy of the Biedermeier to the protoplasm of IKEA – is not capable of confronting the city directly without destroying it, like a cancerous cell that knows no boundaries and hierarchies among parts. It has to be confined by osmotic membranes that regulate the exchange between the two environments: windows, terraces, balconies, walls, parapets and screens that create microclimates of transition between outside and inside. In this sense, Josep Antoni Coderch's Barceloneta apartment house wrapped in shutters constitutes the common ancestor of many mutant species that have appeared in the urban ecosystem in recent years, collective organisms capable of joint action against the suburban plankton.

The functionalist tradition, in a hypertrophic aspiration to 'sincerity', denied independent formal value to the facades of houses, restricting them to a pretended direct expression of the organisation of the interior. On the contrary, many contemporary designs seem to aspire to the aesthetic paradigm of camouflage so widely used in modern fashion, which is increasingly adapting the functional prostheses of the body (watches, sunglasses, military accessories) to play a 'cosmetic' role. In opposition to the panoptic ideal of the glass house, inhabited by tidy demi-gods, we now have faceless interiors wrapped in 'inhabited screens' of balcony and loggias acting as mediators between the private dimension and the public one.

The space between:
the rediscovery of urbanity and
the environmental emergency

The response to the changing needs and lifestyles of contemporary life generates every day a number of design solutions which are reshaping our living environment. While the historical city built up in time still constitutes a loved backdrop to our daily life, the expansions of the city of the last century often look like the simple addition of 'living units', which are seldom able to produce the comfort and the fascination of traditional urban spaces, where activities live together in a lively mix.

If the last century has been marked by the expansion of the city, today we see more and more a metamorphosis of the urban structure to respond to the evolution of the way we live, work, communicate. All Europe has been marked by the abandonment of large industrial or infrastructural precincts of the first industrial age, whose location and size offer them as among the most interesting opportunities to shape the backdrop to the desire of a 'new urban dwelling', capable of uniting the richness and variety of the urban experience with the environmental qualities of the new suburban quarters.

Today we rediscover the positive qualities of urban density not only for the richness and the variety of the experience, but also in terms of sustainability: an inhabitant of the suburbs consumes twice the electrical energy and three times the petrol of one of the consolidated urban centres.

In giving shape to new dwelling environments, we can blend together all the positive qualities of the modernist research on housing – the search for light and air, optimisation of space, technical performance – with the desire for privacy and environmental quality which brought people toward the suburbs.

To do this, one of the crucial points is a thoughtful design of the 'in-between' spaces, of the interfaces between different scales. The transition from the entirely public dimension of the street to the entirely private one of the room can happen on many levels; these articulations can not only generate interesting small-scale collective spaces at the scale of the neighbourhood, but also an overall richness that creates an articulation between the 'chez soi' of the individual dwelling units and the richness of urban form and common green spaces.

These relation spaces, both at the foot of the building – with a stronger shared function, and the task to define the border between private and public open spaces – and at the various floors all the way to the roof – can acquire today an inhabitable character, and respond to the increasing requests of climatic and energy conservation concerns, becoming sophisticated environmental filters. The growing attention toward sustainability and the desire for private 'outdoor rooms' extending the inner space outward are generating new design themes which can respond to the desire for a new quality of life.

If a cautious experimentalism marks the 'foundation cities' of the new docklands, or the northern European polders like IJburg in Amsterdam or Wasserstadt in Hamburg, the transformation of large disused industrial zones in Italy into residential areas has for the most part been based on a few, disappointing, real-estate models. Even if the happy period following the Second World War can still offer useful lessons on modern living in the urban setting, it is not remotely possible to solve the problems posed today by the constantly changing environment of the multi-ethnic metropolis with the sunny model of the 'functional city' capable of integrating urban fabric and open space.

But the lesson of the housing project is also one of humility and seriousness, in an age that favours formal hyperbole even in the absence of meaning; it requires an attentive, affectionate gaze, one that knows how to work by means of small shifts rather than grand proclamations, pursuing a coherent series of small variations that can lead to unexpected discoveries. Of the new house, of the new city, we would like this: the fact of being at once reassuring and unexpected, capable of articulating the space of relationship and protecting the private dimension that Christopher Alexander saw as a primary necessity in defence of contemporary homogenisation.

Today the question of the form of the common space between housing units appears to be suspended between different objectives. If the modern tradition's policy of the 'satellite quarter' sought to recreate the social solidarity of the village within the new urbanised class, it is not clear what ought to be the social model or the formal paradigm of the connective space keeping together contemporary residential fabrics.

Milanese intermezzo

When we visit a foreign city, the shape and the rhythm of its public spaces, the attire of the people inhabiting its streets and parks, the finer grain of its cobblestones, traffic lights, tree trunks, shop signs leave us an impression that cannot be described in simple terms. We could call it the 'character' of the place; but when we try to grasp it, it seems to dissolve into the thousand fragments of a colourful mosaic. Still, some of the features of an urban landscape generate in us a brighter, longer-lasting impression.

A city that we often perceive as a 'second nature', as something that could be read as a natural event, has nevertheless been made by a series of intentional acts. An architectural design and its realisation are the result of complex forces: the architect's and the client's will, but also the fine net of rules and regulations, the constructive customs, the formal expectations by the public, whose combined action forms a building culture in a given moment of time.

Are the single buildings of a city – be they noteworthy architectural episodes or barely noticed anonymous infills – connected by some common kinship?

If traditional architectural history texts often talk about 'styles' as recognisable galaxies of coherent formal traits, the modern cultural emphasis on the 'author' of a design openly conflicts with this collective reading. Does an underground lineage connect in a thread through time the different buildings of a city, designed by different individuals and built for different, often contrasting goals and needs? Do they belong to a specific formal culture that survives unconsciously through the ages?

Quite differently from many others Italian cities, Milan sits on a plain – the Po River valley – and grew without any strong geographical feature – a river or a complex land contour – which could condition its growth. Its uniform expansion stemming from the original Roman settlement, marked by the radial streets named after the gates pierced in the inner ring of the medieval walls and in the larger polygon of the Spanish walls, is deformed into a heart-shaped figure by the presence of the great infrastructure of the Sforza Castle on the edge of the historical nucleus. All the urban expansions of the nineteenth and twentieth centuries spread out from this structure with a clear urban grammar made of regular grids, tree-lined radial axes, and occasional monumental accents.

This rather simple urban code acts as a unifying pattern holding together a number of quite different 'architectural statements' appearing in the city from the beginning of the nineteenth century. But the marked eclectic character of its architectures quite soon generated a sort of artistic and architectural reaction, a *rappel à l'ordre* grouped around what was known as the 'Novecento' movement. The so-called Ca' Brutta (Ugly House) by Giovanni Muzio is certainly a seminal example of this, with its stripped-bare, 'classical' plaster bas-reliefs which wrap around the two-tone massive facade, following awkward rhythms.

Gio Ponti's Montecatini 1939 office building in via Moscova – with its aluminium windows flush with the facade and the peculiar smooth texture of the cipollino marble slab skin – is among the best examples of the aspiration toward the new themes posed by modernity and the simultaneous capacity of 'grafting' the new buildings on the existing urban fabric.

A large number of realisations of these years show an interesting blend of modernity and tradition; many of them show an urban lexicon that cannot be led back either to the whitewashed radical 'nudity' of northern European functionalism nor to the heavily academic architecture of the Fascist regime.

The centre of Milan has been heavily destroyed by the

Nuovo Portello, Milan, 2002–08. By CZA Cino Zucchi Architetti, Zucchi & Partners. Credit: Cino Zucchi

bombs of August 1943. Many historical landmarks such as the Scala Theatre, the Galleria, Palazzo Marino, the Ca' Granda have been damaged, but also the finer grain of the common fabric which constituted the historical nucleus. If cities which went through a similar fate, like Dresden or Rotterdam, were integrally reconstructed following modernistic urban design criteria, the peculiarity of Milan's 'healing' of the centre after the Second World War is considered today one of the most interesting examples of a mixed strategy capable of consolidating the form of historical open spaces and at the same time insert fragments of modern typology into the existing continuous building mass. Many coordinated interventions on the centre show the actual application of a principle clearly stated by Piero Bottoni, an influential architect and city planner of this period: a lower base following the street line and reinforcing its concave space joint with a higher building slab setback from the street edge and looking for light and air. The buildings by Piero Bottoni in Corso Buenos Aires, Gustavo and Vito Latis and Asnago e Vender ones in via Lanzone, Figini and Pollini in via Broletto, and the cantilevered mass of Luigi Moretti in Corso Italia are interesting examples of this rather original infill strategy.

Residential architecture seems one of the most interesting themes developed by such involved architects as Ignazio Gardella, the Latis brothers, Figini e Pollini, Asnago e Vender, BBPR or Ludovico Magistretti. In this context, the lonely but seminal figure of Luigi Caccia Dominioni – today going through unexpected international attention – stands out for its capacity to respond to the issues of 'modern living' with free-style architectural pieces masterfully inserted into the fabric of the historical city, such as the Corso Italia. But all this quality matured in a social environment of a relatively small dimension, where clients and architects fundamentally belonged to the same social class.

The social unrest of the Seventies, which for some strange reason in Italy seems to have had a peculiar ignition point in the architecture faculties, coincides with the sudden crisis of this well-established social role of the architect, a cultured and creative subject coming from the higher middle-class, and in this sense sharing his/her client's manners and values. Milan's 1980s and 1990s are difficult to describe in terms of architectural realisations, marked as they are by a great paradox: the contrast between the intense architectural debate and intellectual activity and the very low quality of the interventions which transformed the city. The city hosted the editorial boards of some of the most influential architecture magazines – *Casabella*, *Domus*, *Lotus International*, *Abitare*, *Modo*, *Ottagono* and others – and the Italian theoretical production in the matter was followed and discussed in Europe and America; yet famous Milanese architects such as Vittorio Gregotti, Aldo Rossi, Giorgio Grassi, Giancarlo de Carlo, Umberto Riva and others had very little chance to work in their city, which was on the contrary marked by a number of very mediocre buildings. In the long run, this lack of relevant built examples which could exemplify the key issues brought forward by the theoretical debate slowly relegated Milan and its architectural community from the status of an intellectual capital to a sort of weeping province.

This corresponded to a deep mutation of the power relationship between clients, architectural culture, public administration and 'the market': Berlusconi's large residential neighbourhoods of Milano 2 and Milano 3 represent well the detachment between the actual transformation of our city and shared architectural values, which were somehow relegated in small and occasional 'side dishes' in the big city 'banquet'.

Things seem to have got slightly better in terms of final quality at the turn of the new millennium. The tradition of planning instruments put forward by the public – which tried to determine through what is called 'zoning' the form of the city – proved in the long run ineffective, and many lost opportunities are to be ascribed to these restrictions. The case-by-case strategy which followed it, if on one side risked letting financial powers alone determine how and where the city should develop, also permitted the realisation of a number of interventions on many dismissed industrial areas which were left for a long time in their decayed state by the rigidity of the previous rules.

The two bigger urban transformations of Milan's urban landscape of the last ten years, the Varesine-Porta Nuova one and that on the former Fiera Campionaria area renamed CityLife, represent not only a shift in scale but also of architectural and urban modes. Their ambitions, planning procedures and formal horizons stand in a cultural 'middle landscape' which can be barely seen as site-specific in terms of open space morphology, building typology and architectural lexicon. The 'green' concerns – be they sincere goals or just consensus-building strategies – have substituted the urban ones, and the optimistic promises of a new place uniting environmental quality and urban intensity are pursued following a market-oriented approach. As in a blockbuster film with all the right ingredients, the level of their overall craftsmanship is higher than a lot of self-produced counterparts. Yet, without giving too much voice to the huffy apostles of 'tradition', it is true that many citizens feel that something got lost along the way: the formal sophistication and the specificity in response to the site which seemed to be the peculiar characters of Milanese architecture from the 1950s to the 1970s.

Today we are all looking for a global *galateo*, able to translate universal principles of courtesy, consideration for others, capability to listen, and other positive feelings which regulate the relationship between the desire of self-expression and the limitations needed to compose individual acts into a harmonious whole. To do this, we should discriminate the manifestations of self-imposed 'manners' which correspond to deeper feelings from the ones which appear just as adaptive hypocrisies. A strong city is able to metabolise both mediocre and 'bully' architectures in a larger whole, but there is a tipping point where its landscape can become a mere turf for the display of petty individual statements.

If, in fact, the urban expansion of the last century operated on the building types and layouts, the metamorphosis of contemporary Milan is only partially governed by a shared vision of the direction to give to the *Forma Urbis*; indeed, a number of different sites are still unresolved on different scales – empty buildings, abandoned industrial sites, railroad stations or buildings in need of restoration – and present themselves to the intangible forces of finance and politics as opportunities for transformation. In other words, the sites of future changes of the urban fabric are those of its past and present 'weakness'. The situation appears clearer now and somewhat more cohesive from the standpoint of urban and environmental objectives, although the variety of architectural proposals that characterise the main actions of urban reform still do not appear to be guided by any particular shared culture. Where we do observe among them a few common features, these seem due to filtration and data selection through a strict network of regulations that, like an invisible sieve, shapes the structures 'by subtraction'. If, in fact, the architectures of the twentieth century appear still unified by a certain 'set of family traits', today's ones seem to be held together only by the structures of the laws on fire prevention and disability rights. The average quality of the urban and architectural reforms applied in Milan in this new millennium are without a doubt vastly superior to those of the twenty previous years. This has been achieved by applying new methods, rather than by restoring the conditions that produced the Milan of the 'boom' years. The 1980s swept away all the advances in technical and linguistic expertise that still characterised professionalism in the postwar period. What exists today has almost no continuity with so-called 'Milanese culture', whatever could be meant today by that term.

Within this complex ecosystem, an 'entomologist of architectural styles' could attempt a simple Linnaean classification, although any attempt of this kind risks dividing into artificial sectors a field in which the kinships and differences are often not so obvious. In the larger works, the products of a contemporary corporate architecture of Anglo-Saxon origin – in both the more classical and reassuring versions and in the more deformed versions dictated by parametric virtuosity – have formed the cornerstones of this new landscape, altering the skyline from the Po to the Alps before that of the city lying at their feet.

The CityLife skyscrapers (designed by Zaha Hadid, Arata Isozaki and Daniel Libeskind) and those of Porta Nuova (by Cesar Pelli, Pei-Cobb-Freed and Arquitectonica) arise from a design of the ground at their feet that has little or no relation to the canons of 'urban decorum' that have generated an unexpected continuity among the architectures of the past century despite their obvious diversity. But there is no doubt that the efforts of urban reform in which they participate gave rise to new standards of quality operating on several levels – not least that of the design of public spaces according to the canons of a 'new approach to the landscape' – which contrasts with all the disasters created in Milan in the 1980s.

On the other side, a number of projects developed by foreign architectural firms with significant critical and interpretative acuity (such as Sauerbruch and Hutton, David Chipperfield, Grafton Architects, Herzog & de Meuron, Rem Koolhaas, SANAA and others) – have succeeded in establishing a positive relationship and dialectic with the existing form of the city; free of complexes, operating as equals, they have succeeded in reapplying the strategy of grafting onto an existing fabric that we find in those works of our own modern architects in the postwar period that are now destinations for review and study by all Europe.

The real-estate frenzy of recent years has generated a series of opportunities on various scales and has stimulated the ideas of many Italian architects of various generations. The landmark of the Vertical Forest by Stefano Boeri Architetti and of the almost completed UnipolSai Tower by Mario Cucinella Architects are among the most persuasive icons of the new Milan. But the current architectural production of Milanese architects no longer seems to rise from a common language, much less from a 'continuous line'; rather, they seem to reveal an obvious condition of uncertainty, empiricism, even figurative opportunism at times.

In spaces and operations that are more limited in scale, we can find works that demonstrate an increasing interest of an 'Erasmus' generation of now mature architects who received their training in a global framework where they developed highly original theoretical and figurative concepts.

If, on these occasions, they are sometimes limited to

projects for interiors, staging, designing lofts and small additions, and only occasionally have the opportunity to design complete buildings, the cultural milieu created by them through the medium of exchange, sharing and listening to one another has made Milan an important virtual and physical meeting place of European culture.

There exists, right now in Milan, a framework of transformation of quality that is in no way inferior to that of many European capitals; driven by three or four significant opportunities, but also present in bits and pieces in almost the entirety of the city's fabric. The scale of certain abandoned industrial districts has made it possible to launch not only individual replacement constructions, but also concrete actions of micro-urban design; some of these have become workshops of an urban and environmental movement of a new type, which recombines fragments of various types discovered unexpectedly around sequences of collective spaces reinvented out of necessity. On a smaller scale, in a point-by-point transformation that follows the not always predictable mechanisms of 'gentrification', the replacement of buildings changes the aspect of certain districts and penetrates their cells with the gentle virus of an 'architecture of interiors' of excellent level, stimulated by rapid changes among the business activities.

Is there really a 'Milan Model'? If the architects who operate today in Milan do not appear unified by a common culture – but perhaps only by the spread of a 'contagion of ideas' – their clients are in a similar condition of cultural 'opportunism', an indefinable field where a number of seductive slogans (sustainability, smart city, resilience, biodiversity) act as attractors and mediators of the relationship between clients, administrations, professionals, media and the public.

Like jurors on a talent show such as *X Factor*, the powers that choose a subject or a song without reflecting on the long-term consequences are the ones that actually determine the future form of the city. This can generate surprisingly good intuitions – or disastrous errors whose fallout is paid for by the collectivity. On the other hand, the public actor does not seem either equipped or inclined to make architectural evaluations of project proposals, and is often limited to checking numbers, parameters and objectives of a social and environmental character.

The scenario of the new Milan created by the interaction of those forces that now regulate its transformation appears to our eyes a strange mixture of convincing innovations and lazy imitations of international paradigms. The fact that today we look with pride to the Pirelli and the Velasca towers as examples of the 'Italian way of doing skyscrapers' does not change the fact that nothing like them existed within the framework of the ancient city, much less in its nineteenth- and twentieth-century expansion.

History teaches us that the great cities have found ways to digest and integrate diversity, and the city is often more powerful and stronger than its architectures. But it is in its architectures that it reflects itself and it is they that represent it. Gio Ponti said in 1954, in a heartfelt plea to his colleagues of the Building Commission of Milan regarding the Velasca Tower: 'Milan is not threatened by modern architects, it is threatened, instead, by that mass of fatherless construction, lacking in design, that disfigure the new districts so hideously. Milan develops exclusively as a modern city (nor could it be otherwise) and the existence of a valorous and cultured class of modern architects who operate in the city is our highest guarantee.'

It may not be an accident that in contemporary Milan the discomfort that still remains is perceived in the terms of a social and 'environmental' inadequacy. As a city on a plain, lacking in geographical obstacles, it has expanded its web of streets and city blocks through the centuries without being able to include any green islands, without creating any real alternatives to the centre, without aligning new construction with the routes of public transport.

To observe the 'centre' not from a 'periphery' but rather from an archipelago of urban nuclei connected by a tangible and intangible network is the only way to imagine the form of a new metropolis capable of blending urban intensity and environmental quality. The 'resistance' of a city and its irreplaceable particularities should not be seen either as barriers to change or as obstacles on the path to progress, but rather as places with an extraordinary ability to generate differences, as nuclei of quality in the changing landscape of a new urban environment that will somehow have to unite nature and human endeavour in ways that are just starting to become perceptible.

Nomothetic and idiographic:
a personal attitude searching
for shared values

With the background of this physical and social context, and guided by a rather personal path exploring different design directions under a common intellectual denominator, as Cino Zucchi Architetti we were able to test some of the general issues raised above in a series of very specific design occasions of housing complexes in different European and Italian urban contexts. If environmental values have entered permanently, and rightly, into the founding elements of our design process, we don't forget that architecture is a fundamental part of what we could call 'material culture'. Too often today the emphasis is placed solely on the procedure rather than on the final result, and the energy–environmental performance becomes an all-encompassing topic which often distracts from the fundamental theme, that of architectural and urban quality in a broader sense. We must not forget that the urban landscape is made up of the intermediate fabric, of many episodes which must have an individual character but which together must be able to create – like the musicians of an orchestra – a *Sinfonie der Großstadt* (as the title of the documentary by Ruttmann on Berlin 1927).

In the ongoing debate opposing the two complementary models of 'towers in the green' versus the reconstruction of historic blocks, we could argue that the reconstruction of postwar Milan could still lead the way to experiment with on interesting mix of the two. In the housing projects for the Nuovo Portello, the Corte Verde in Porta Nuova and via Valtorta, we have somehow unconsciously applied these principles in an attempt to respond to the two key objectives of the new millennium: the fight against environmental catastrophe and the rediscovery of city as a great 'social contract' capable of making different cultures engage in dialogue. In a metropolis, our next-door neighbour is not necessarily our friend, and contemporary research on so-called co-housing represents only a small part of the problem and often contains simplifications that do not stand up to the natural evolution of people, families and social groups. The collective dimension does not end within the single building, but should perhaps also be considered on the scale of the neighbourhood and the metropolitan one. To reflect on new living spaces, I often show a photograph of my twenty-year-old daughter asleep on the sofa among the symbolic objects of her 'millennial' existence: her smartphone, laptop, an empty cup of coffee, the remains of a Deliveroo meal, an Amazon package. This image represents both the failure of the 'Existenzminimum' housing model divided by functions but also of its contemporary digital 'reinvention'. It invites us to reconsider with fresh eyes the relationship between the new individual dimension – at the same time intimate and connected – and the spaces that host it.

A serious reflection on contemporary housing and its relationship with the city must accept the multi-modal and multi-scalar nature of today's life. At the housing scale, this means rejecting the functionalist determinism that assigned a specific function to each room of the housing. In a broader vision, this means understanding how each housing unit relates in different ways with the size of the neighbourhood (or the city that can be reached on foot in fifteen minutes), with the urban and underground network (defined by the fifty- to sixty-minute journey on public transport) and now also with a continental territory accessible with a journey by plane or fast train.

It is interesting to reflect today on the concept of neighbourhood not only through an architectural and urban project, but also and above all from a socio-cultural point of view: what is the relationship between a part of the city with a relative historical and architectural identity and the communities who live there?

Classical ethnography – often traversed by exoticising or even racist prejudices – has always identified a cultural unit with a geographical one: climate, geography, customs, gastronomy, religion, legends, clothing, children's games, architecture were read in a unified way. But in the contemporary world made fluid and connected by the internet, we see every day the birth of what we could call 'atopic ethnic groups' who find their unity not in belonging to a place but in sharing aesthetic-cultural codes. Vegans, militarists, punks, yuppies are now human categories that we find all over the globe; they show similar psycho-social traits in very distant places, and often strong mutual conflicts within the physical space of a city. The project of a 'city by neighbourhoods', in Milan or elsewhere, cannot and must not have the ambition to 'retopicise' or root in one place these groups linked together by tastes and disgusts. Let's not forget that the step between ideological kinship and a 'gated community' is shorter than it seems. We should favour a 'city of neighbourhoods', or a 'mosaic of subcultures', but not all the way to see identity become social division; we should save the porosity and continuity of the public space that has always distinguished the European city and civil values, and accept that the metropolitan condition cannot assure to everybody the experience of what we call today the fifteen-minute city.

A rather 'romantic' view of the historical city dimension cannot make us blind to the fact that even the definition of *Großstadt* is no longer describing the territorial net; we are presently living it and the design problems we face are in relation to it. Perhaps only the confrontation with the 'different', with the implantation of non-European social customs within the European city-territory, can undermine the all too orderly sequence that has already integrated the varied experiences of 'participatory planning' for some time now. If photographic images of Eastern cities indirectly reveal the failure of the modern ideal of a 'rational' beauty of the big city, the European city may need to metabolise better the mosaic of subcultures which increasingly characterises it, accepting into its well-organised body those vital anomalies that bring the metropolitan dimension to life, according to the prophetic words of Josef Frank: 'So the new architecture will be born of the whole bad taste of our period, of its intricacy, its motleyness and sentimentality, it will be a product of all that is alive and experienced first-hand: at last an art *of the people*, not *for the people*.'[3]

3   Josef Frank, *Architektur als Symbol: Elemente deutschen neuen Bauens* (Vienna: Verlag Anton Schroll & Co., 1931).

Social and free-market housing in via Traiano, former Portello Alfa Romeo area, Milan

As part of the transformation of the industrial enclosure of the former Alfa Romeo factory, within the urban layout imagined by Gino Valle, CZA has designed a fragment of urban fabric mediating between the existing context and the new park.

On the southern side of the area, three linear eight-storey-high buildings take up the textures of the consolidated city by building a continuous urban front along via Traiano. The considerable depth of the volumes is excavated towards the south-west to give an outlook to bathrooms and kitchens: an expansive frame made up of metal profiles unifies the large balconies on the front facing the park. The social housing part is completed by two tall buildings whose staggered position generates a small square to mark the beginning of the boulevard and the visual cone towards the park. The articulated geometry of the openings and recesses of the loggias, the refined combination of colours and materials and the formal variations of elements such as parapets and blinds donate to the complex a strong domestic character.

In a sort of progressive fragmentation of the urban fabric toward the park, the project irregularly arranges three freestanding tower buildings around a common garden: projecting loggias unified by metal frames graft on regular volumes covered in stone of different cuts and colours.

The project is completed by the recovery of the former Alfa Romeo canteen whose facade along via Traiano is maintained and the rest transformed into work spaces. The outcome is a welcoming urban graft, capable of reinterpreting some postwar residential examples – the pitch geometries of the condominium in Piazza Carbonari designed by Caccia Dominioni or the materiality of the facades of Gardella's Borsalino house – and at the same time to engage in dialogue with contemporary European design culture.

Nuovo Portello, Milan, 2002–08. By CZA Cino Zucchi Architetti, Zucchi & Partners. Credit: Cino Zucchi

Housestories: Waiting for the city

Gallaratese housing project by Aldo Rossi. Credit: Paul Sebesta

Project by Johanna Noell.
Workshop: *Italienische Bausteine*
by Antonietta Putzu.
Summer semester 2021 at TU Wien.

Transmedia urbanism: Berlusconi and the birth of targeted difference

Andrés Jaque

1   Boccazzi Varotto Carlo, 'Costruire la RAI. Tecnologia e televisione in Italia dai pionieri al boom economico', in *Nuova Civiltà delle Macchine* (April–June, 2004).

2   John Foot, *Milan Since the Miracle: City, Culture and Identity* (New York: Berg, 2001).

3   Ibid.

4   Gino Moliterno, *Encyclopedia of Contemporary Italian Culture* (London: Routledge, 2000).

5   Roberto Levi, *Le trasmissioni Tv che hanno fatto (o no) l'Italia. Da 'Lascia o raddoppia' al 'Grande Fratello'* (Milan: Rizzoli, 2002).

Accounts of Silvio Berlusconi's power seldom include two of its key sources: namely, architecture and urbanism. Whereas his involvement in media is seen as a momentous constituent of his political trajectory, what is often forgotten is that his particular way of reinventing the relationship between politics and media was an architectural invention, developed and tested through the interiors, buildings, landscapes and urbanism to which he and his team devoted a large part of their time and resources, from the late 1960s to the early 1990s.

In 1968, Italy's future prime minister Silvio Berlusconi, then chair and owner of urban development company Edilnord Centri Residenziali, started to promote Milano 2, a 712,000 m² residential city ten minutes from the centre of Milan. Presented as an alluring and inoffensive mix of rational architecture and vernacular embellishment, Milano 2 embodied a radical urbanism. Conceived as an alternative to the converging and homogenising culture promoted by state-centred postwar European governments, this new urban model would instead segregate society into differentiated clusters of specialised consumption targets. Life in Milano 2 was structured by a cable television service that would grow to become the corporation now known as Mediaset. Milano 2's capacity to integrate the economic, social and political evolution of its inhabitants was fuelled by a series of design strategies meant to coordinate TV programming, interiors, access to commodities and services, architecture and landscaping into what I will call 'transmedia urbanism'. This coordination was intended to render Berlusconi's company as the compulsory node in a new context in which purveyors, consumers, and the links that brought them together, were reinvented.

TV nations

The European national TV networks, such as the BBC (United Kingdom), RTF (France) and RAI (Italy), played a fundamental role in the social articulation of economics and politics of everyday life in Europe's postwar period. While the 1952 European Coal and Steel Community is often considered as the first forerunner of the European Union, the true antecedent was the 1950 organisation that brought together the European national public TV networks, the European Broadcasting Union (EBU). It was precisely these networks that played a role in the social, economic and material reconstruction of postwar Europe, operating within a system where the unifying elements of national societies could be organised from the top-down with the intention of maximising their power of self-production. In this process, RAI was paradigmatic. In January 1954, RAI began broadcasting television programmes from its Milan headquarters at a central position in the city: Corso Sempione. The building included Studio TV3, which was, at the time, the largest television studio in Europe.[1] The headquarters were redesigned by no less a figure than the architect Gio Ponti. Architecture was already an essential factor.

In postwar Italy, television was not watched alone. In 1954, the cost of a TV set was 250,000 lire – three times the annual salary of a secretary. Very few people could afford them. They were found mainly in bars, churches and the living rooms of wealthy families. These places, where television was communally watched, turned into transfamilial spaces of interclass enactments. Control over the television signal was precious, for it brought the power to decide what content would shape collective existence.[2]

RAI worked hand in hand with the Istituto per la Ricostruzione Industriale, a public holding company that owned many of the main industries that shaped everyday life in Italy – from telephones to highways, food to cars, aeroplanes to military weapons. By 1960, 80% of Italy's population watched television, with RAI playing a unique top-down role in unifying Italian society. RAI significantly contributed to the standardisation of language and helped make Italian universally spoken in southern Italy. Moreover, RAI suspended its programmes every evening between 7.30 and 8.45 p.m. to synchronise dinnertime across the country.[3] National schedules were coordinated to ensure rest hours for workers and efficiency in family management. Television delivered a coordinated mass of workers to the nationally centralised industries.

In 1957, RAI began to produce short films to advertise industrial products. The intention of these films was to convey the value of industrial products to audiences who would be rendered into a generic universal public in part by the effect of this commercial TV content. These short films signalled the birth of the TV commercial. The made-in-Milan *Carosello*, a TV show composed of accumulated short commercials, encouraged a common children's bedtime, as it was intended to be watched right beforehand.[4] From 1955 to 1959, Mike Bongiorno hosted *Lascia o raddoppia?*, the most successful Italian TV programme to this day.[5] In this massively popular quiz show, the cultural knowledge of participants was challenged and rewarded, with prizes reaching 5,120,000 lire and with the Fiat 1400 as a consolation prize. The public celebrated the collective achievement of the nation's educational competence week after week, and Bongiorno's language was carefully tailored to make participants and audiences feel as if they were exactly the same: equal citizens or 'ordinary Italians'. Ordinary Italians would simultaneously be the unspecialised consumers and manufacturers of the generic products advertised on television.

This entire process dovetailed with a massive provision of residential units in cities. During the 1950s and 1960s, the number of residential units in Italy increased by 35%, 68% of them built in the thirteen most populous cities. Waves of migration followed a government initiative to concentrate workers in urban areas. The government's aim was to ensure a uniform provision of labour to the factories that were producing goods at a national scale.[6]

In 1968, not only did students protest in Milan, but so did domestic migrant workers, who had come mainly from the south of Italy and who were still attracted by Milan's economic miracle and industrial development. These workers were paid twice the wages that they could earn in their hometowns, but due to the scarcity of affordable housing,[7] their living costs quadrupled. Scandals, such as cuts to Gescal, the government's fund for workers' housing, brought the housing crisis into the streets, where demonstrators demanded more government financing. 'Guerra per la casa' (war for the house) was the name given to the protests by Casabella, the renowned Italian magazine. In January 1970, an editorial exhorted big industry to collaborate and speed up the provision of housing. It argued that the innovation capacity of the nation's industrial muscle should aid in the development of advanced solutions to provide the workers it attracted with places to live.[8] At L'Espresso magazine, architect Bruno Zevi added his voice to the discussion, advocating for the relocation of workers from cities to underdeveloped rural areas, where land was cheaper. All these ideas would rapidly develop into housing projects – but not for the workers.

Milano 2

In 1968, Edilnord acquired the 712,000 m² of land in the municipality of Segrate, where Milano 2 would be constructed, at a bargain price due to the noise pollution of air traffic from the nearby Linate International Airport. Berlusconi's political influence facilitated a reduction of air traffic and the acceptance by left-wing municipal authorities of Milano 2's masterplan. This development was designed not only to supply accommodation for 10,000 inhabitants, but also as a complete urbanism equipped to provide education, fitness, entertainment, idealised nature and, above all, sales. Its 2,600 apartments were placed on the perimeter, with their TV rooms expanding onto big balconies, directed not toward the Milan skyline, but to an inner landscape, with large trees carefully placed to suppress any perception of a neighbouring human presence. Under the direction of the landscape designer Enrico Hoffer, more than 5,000 trees were planted at Milano 2. A significant number of them were already over 12 m tall when they were relocated – among them, fir trees, maples, Japanese red maples, cedars, birches, beeches, gingkoes, magnolias, pine trees, plane trees and lindens.[9] Adjacent dwellings would be screened by a costly and carefully composed biological version of TV snow, an arboreal screen vibrating as the static light noise of unsynchronised TVs.

Milano 2's young design team was led by the then 31-year-old architect Giancarlo Ragazzi, partnered with Giulio Possa and Antonio D'Adamo. The architects paid careful attention to the sectional bifurcation of the design. Milano 2's architecture segregated an aboveground domain for daily human life, characterised by a green landscape crisscrossed by pedestrian and bicycle circulation, from a netherworld of car traffic and underground centralised pipes flowing with utilities and media content controlled by Berlusconi's company, Fininvest. Milano 2 was the outcome of a growing context of Italian companies operating internationally, including Abet Laminati, BTicino, Hoval and Max Meyer. The ideas promoted by these companies aligned with those defended in Casabella's January 1970 issue, which suggested that the development of technologically advanced systems and societies should be specifically applied in new forms of urbanism and architecture.

Producing the Number Ones

From the beginning, Milano 2 was not a project designed to accommodate an existing group of humans, but instead one meant to produce a new type of society. Throughout all media outlets, the development was profusely advertised as 'La Città dei Numeri Uno' (the City of Number Ones). Actors were hired to impersonate the prospective inhabitants in fictional renderings depicting these Number One humans in their City of Number Ones. The Number Ones were not the workers, not even the workers who proved to be exceptional, but neither were they members of the wealthy Milanese society. Number Ones were instead an until-then disconnected sector of ambitious young middle-class, family-oriented executives. They were not working for the national industries governed by the Istituto per la Ricostruzione Industriale, but instead they mainly worked for growing multinational corporations such as IBM, 3M, Siemens and Unilever. These corporations had started to locate their branches in places like Segrate that were more likely to attract middle-class employees and young executives: people, as Berlusconi would present himself, unrelated to Milan's elites or industrial dynasties.[10] Most of these employees were not owners of the companies where they worked, nor did they have personal fortunes, but they were paid high salaries. Milano 2's favourable financing arrangements and low upfront payments enabled them to purchase dwellings of a kind that, in most cases, they could never have afforded in Milan's centre. These employees incarnated the shift from a postwar nation-based Europe to a globalised realm of multinational corporations.

Model apartments were built in the middle of the as yet non-urbanised estate where Milano 2 was to be constructed. They were carefully decorated, photographed and published in the most fashionable international media outlets, including Vogue magazine.[11] From images of fictional Number Ones in these spaces, potential buyers would imagine what it might be like to be Number Ones themselves. This use of printed media set into motion the evolution of the potential subjectivity of Number Ones by the way they were confronted with fictionalised, stylised versions of themselves. These media outlets created a mirror-based dynamic meant to maximise the displacement of daily life into a progression from the actual to the aspirational and vice versa. This dynamic was produced by the fictional architecture of the model apartments where actors performed as Number Ones. These fictions travelled from the fictional settings to magazines and newspapers and eventually to real life. The isolated apartment towers of Milano 2, where the Number Ones would be spatially confined, did not grow out of a city or even the countryside, but rather from media. Milan's new social type, the Number Ones, were segregated spatially, aesthetically and economically from the city, from the rest of society, and from each other. Berlusconi, who involved himself personally in selling the apartments, insistently explained that neither he nor Edilnord had the funds to complete the development, but that funds would be mobilised by a pyramidal financing scheme: those who bought early would get an apartment

---

6 Maurizio Coppo and Marco Cremaschi, eds., Strutture territoriali e questione abitativa (Milan: Franco Angeli, 1994).

7 In Italy, although 26% of new residential units were publically financed in the 1950s, that figure had dropped to less than 6% by the end of 1960s. Coppo and Cremaschi, eds., Strutture territoriali e questione abitativa (see note 6).

8 'Guerra per la casa', Casabella 344 (January 1970), 2–3.

9 P. Ceretti and R. Fantacci, I nostri alberi. Una passeggiata botanica tra le Residenze ed i luoghi d'incontro di Milano 2 (Segrate: Edilnord, 2011).

10 S. E. D'Anna and G. Moncalvo, Berlusconi in Concert (London: Otzium, 1994).

11 Edilnord Centri Residenziali SAS, Milano 2. Una città per vivere (Milan: Edilnord Centri Residenziali, 1976).

Aerial view of Milano 2. Sales Oddity. Milano 2 and the Politics of Direct-to-Home TV Urbanism. Credit: Andrés Jaque / Office for Political Innovation

12 Silvio Berlusconi, in Milano 2 sales brochures (Edilnord Centri Residenziali, Milano, 1970).

13 This consolidation of ownership of the market facilities would remain until the 2000s, when the Fondo Mario Negri sold a large number of the spaces to independent retailers. Source: different property acquisition contracts from commercial space owners examined by the author.

14 Conversations with early Milano 2 apartment buyers. From October 2013 to April 2014.

15 Giancarlo Ragazzi, interview by author, 2014.

16 *Milano 2. Una città per vivere* (see note 11).

that would double its value as others joined in buying the future. From a financial point of view, Milano 2 was sold as the device that would help adventurous early buyers become successful investors.

Escaping urban promiscuity

In the sales brochures, Berlusconi himself encouraged buyers to 'escape from metropolitan chaos – from traffic, crime, immigrants, and workers. From the city itself'.[12] Milano 2's marketing suggested self-banishment from urban promiscuity. Milano 2 provided an additional means to render oneself as a non-worker and as a non-immigrant. Being a Number One was not only a progression to the aspirational, but a departure from urban promiscuity into a realm of class sorting and clarification.

The strategy of offering an escape was paralleled by offering a suburban marketplace within Milano 2, and Edilnord managed to reap a share of the money spent on every good or service that Milano 2's residents purchased on a daily basis. A central part of Edilnord's strategy was to retain ownership of the commercial spaces.[13]

If grey concrete and modern architecture had once embodied the aspirations of Milanese society, now red vernacular seemed to cater to the sensitivities of the emerging Number Ones, who were young enough to enjoy the then-trendy aesthetic context brought about by folk music, picturing themselves in a globalising rural romanticism.[14] Along with the red vernacular came mansard roofs. Milano 2's underground cable TV distribution network ensured TV antennas did not ruin the picturesque atmosphere.[15]

The centre of Milano 2 has never been occupied by the symbolic presence of religious or administrative power but, instead, by the Lago dei Cigni, the Lake of the Swans. The core of Milano 2's infrastructure, which could be perceived as a pleasant architecture celebrating picturesque banality, also contained a sports and business centre, schools, retail, a four-star hotel, and a park that was intended – according to the apartment sales brochures – to allow the children of Number Ones to play Cowboys and Indians and have organised treasure hunts.[16] Together, these elements provided potential buyers of apartments with evidence of the way that Milano 2 would produce Number Ones and their children as competitive, healthy, earnest, aggressive, treasure-seeking and athletic beings, prepared to occupy a position in a socially stratified world. In the way this infrastructure in Milano 2 is used even today, it can still be considered part of Edilnord's project to shape bodies and societies through architecture and urbanism. An important factor in achieving this goal is that part of Milano 2's architecture remains virtually invisible: namely, the underground studios of Mediaset, where the core of Berlusconi's political coordination is concealed, an architecture that needs to be hidden to maximise its political efficacy.

In 1974, Giacomo Properzj and Alceo Moretti started to broadcast amateur programming by tapping into this underground, wired network. Tele Milano had just been born. Unlicensed movies and amateur, self-produced happenings were broadcast from the Jolly Hotel located in Milano 2. The TV station was cheap but successful. It recruited to its official board residents who would help in choosing the content. A programme showing images of women undressing, as male residents of Milano 2 called

Interiors of Milano 2 apartments. Sales Oddity. Milano 2 and the Politics of Direct-to-Home TV Urbanism. Credit: Andrés Jaque / Office for Political Innovation

17 Eugène Saccomano, *Berlusconi: le dossier vérité* (Paris: Parole Et Silence, 1994).

18 Former Tele Milano executive interviewed by author, 2014.

19 F. Colombo, *Le tre stagioni. Problemi dell'Informazione 4* (October/December 1990), 593–7.

20 Gabriele Balbi and Benedetta Prario, 'The History of Fininvest/Mediaset's Media Strategy: 30 Years of Politics, the Market, Technology and Italian society,' *Media Culture & Society* 32(3) (May 2010), 391–409.

21 Paul Ginsborg, *Silvio Berlusconi: Television, Power and Patrimony* (London: Verso, 2004).

22 This information is the result of an ethnography developed by the author in Publitalia's headquarters.

into the station to participate in a quiz game, would rapidly achieve an unexpected success. Not only did it attract viewers, but it also mobilised a particular sector of Milano 2 society, the adult males, and placed them into a differentiated time gap, experienced by its sectored audience as an exclusive late-night TV salon. If RAI homogenised society, gathering the public together into a media space inhabited by generic shows, Tele Milano started to break Milano 2's society into specialised clusters according to the TV content promoted. Whereas RAI coordinated bedtime to ensure national industrial production, Tele Milano kept adult males awake to glean a share of revenue from their phone consumption. Consequently, these men became a group defined by their use of time, their media and their gender practices.

In 1975, Berlusconi's Fininvest became the owner of Tele Milano, seduced by its unexpected success.[17] Edilnord's project to segregate Milan's sectors of mass consumption and solidify control of the interactions and purchases of residents extended to Tele Milano, which would quickly consider its mission increasing Milano-2-based commerce.[18] With a 1976 ruling by the constitutional court of Italy authorising the aerial transmission of private local TV channels, Tele Milano became Tele Milano 58, and then Canale 5, and started to be broadcast over the air, beyond Milano 2.[19] Fininvest purchased local TV channels across the country and, taking advantage of a legal loophole in Italy's aerial transmission regulations, made all the channels broadcast the same content simultaneously, giving birth to what was, in fact, a private national TV network: Mediaset.[20] What had started as a transmedia satellite city expanded into a national transurbanism – one that would produce urban settings in the interaction of actual space with media domains – transferring the segregationist project tested in Milano 2 to the scale of Italy.

Scaling up:
the birth of targeted difference

In the 1980s, Fininvest developed two related initiatives. First, it acquired the retail chain Standa with the intention of controlling this node between distributors and Number Ones, already exiled from urban-market promiscuity. Fininvest's team lacked experience in logistics, and the competence of stronger retail groups made this initiative fail. Second, in 1980 Fininvest created the media agency Publitalia. Within ten years, Publitalia would completely transform urban mediation between production and consumption.[21] Formed to sell TV advertising space for Mediaset, Publitalia developed a different way to recruit advertisers, based on four principles.[22] First, television would no longer be a space for top-down pedagogy, but, instead, a device to bring production and consumption together. Second, TV content would be designed according to advertisers' goals. Third, instead

Milano 2 show apartment. Sales Oddity. Milano 2 and the Politics of
Direct-to-Home TV Urbanism. Credit: Andrés Jaque / Office for Political Innovation

Tele Milano studios in Milano 2, 1976–78. Sales Oddity. Milano 2 and the Politics of Direct-to-Home TV Urbanism. Credit: Andrés Jaque / Office for Political Innovation

Fictional scenario produced by Edilnord portraying 'the Number Ones'. Sales Oddity. Milano 2 and the Politics of Direct-to-Home TV Urbanism.
Credit: Andrés Jaque / Office for Political Innovation

23 Alexander Stille, *The Sack of Rome: Media + Money + Celebrity = Power = Silvio Berlusconi* (New York: Penguin, 2007).

24 Cinzia Padovani, 'Berlusconi on Berlusconi? An Analysis of Digital Terrestrial Television Coverage on Commercial Broadcast News in Italy,' *Discourse & Communication* 6(4) (November 2012), 423–47.

25 Fausto Colombov and Michele Sorice, 'Audience Studies in Italy,' Cost Action IS0906 Transforming Audiences, Transforming Societies (2010). http://www.cost.eu/COST_Actions/isch/IS0906 (accessed 15 November 2016).

of programming to serve generic audiences, content would be designed to attract specific publics – if toys needed to be sold, there would be TV shows for children; if middle-aged males were targeted, there would be late-night shows for them to inhabit. Whereas RAI had promoted urban convergence and the creation of a unified public, Publitalia focused on differentiation and distribution; progressively scaling up what was previously developed as the 2,000-apartment transmedia urbanism of Milano 2 and Tele Milano. Finally, advertisers would not be charged for the amount of time their commercials were broadcast, but for the increase in their sales. Fininvest would get 15% of the increase in sales for companies advertised on Mediaset's channels. Talking of Publitalia's activity, Berlusconi stated: 'I do not sell spaces; I sell sales.'[23] If nation-driven TV-urbanism in the postwar era constructed space and organised society in social classes, Milano 2 instead constructed sales and structured society in consumption targets. By defining and sorting targeted groups, then utilising differentiated channels and timetables and depicting and instigating exemplary subjectivities, consumptions and practices for each individual sector, television would produce urban difference.

Publitalia's project worked. Small local companies such as the furniture manufacturers Aiazzone and Foppap Pedretti, the mattress company Permaflex and fur coat seller Annabella unexpectedly grew when advertised by Mediaset. This success fuelled the expansion of Publitalia. Mediaset's ventures into France, the Netherlands, Spain and other countries were followed by the organisation of new corporations, such as Publifrance, Publiespaña and Publieurope.

In 1984, Publitalia surpassed Sipra, RAI's advertising sales unit, in revenue.[24] That same year, Auditel, the Italian research company that measures television ratings and statistics, was created. For the first time, the demographics of audiences were monitored.[25]

In 1980, Mike Bongiorno, the original host of RAI's biggest hit – *Lascia o raddoppia?* – left RAI to become Mediaset's star presenter. As part of his contract, Bongiorno would live in Milano 2, so he could become part of the community of Number Ones. In contrast to gated communities, Milano 2 welcomed visitors, and it became a popular place to go to see celebrities. The superstars would dwell in penthouses in the Garden Towers, but they could be seen when using the facilities gathered around the lake. The *bellini*, sexy young female models playing secondary roles in TV shows, would occupy apartments on the first floor, where their domestic life could be seen from the gardens.

Transmedia apartments:
mirrored bodies

Mediaset provides a mirrored broadcasted home, an implemented version of the model apartments publicised by *Vogue* magazine that first compelled the Number Ones to buy apartments in Milano 2: a home that has kitchens, mothers, living rooms, sofas, hosts, bedrooms, showers and older brothers. In order to increase the legally regulated maximum percentage of promotional space, advertisements leapt from commercials into TV shows, as promotional segments devoted to sponsors started to be included in Mediaset programmes. Apartments, celebrities, mirrored homes and advertisers

26 M. Golec, 'Optical Constancy, Discontinuity, and Nondiscontinuity in the Eameses' Rough Sketch,' in Mark J. Williams and Adrian W. B. Randolph, eds., *The Educated Eye* (Hanover, NH: Dartmouth College Press, 2011).

constituted a daily-life context to inhabit, one that was not contained in any city, but in an urban enactment resulting from the large corporations' choreography of techno-social interaction.

In the late 1970s, in the underground basement of an ordinary bar in Milano 2, the popular DJ Claudio Cecchetto hosted *Chewing Gum*, a musical TV show. Week after week, Cecchetto brought dancers to populate his basement audience from Milan's disco temple, Divina, where he was resident DJ. With Valerio Lazarov, the 'King of the Zoom Shot', they would edit and broadcast the show in such a way so it would not only bring the best of Milan's nightlife into Milano 2's living rooms, but would also bring the bodily experience of psychedelia and disco dancing to the Number Ones. At the same time that Charles and Ray Eames' *Powers of Ten* (1977) used the zoom to provide universal constancy and 'nondiscontinuity',[26] Lazarov would expand bodies in the living rooms of apartments in Milano 2 by turning these private spaces into centres of disco nightlife. To go out, one could stay at home.

In March 2012, Clemente Russo, a well-known boxer and policeman, made his debut as the main character in the reality show *Fratello Maggiore*, in which he corrected the behaviour of spoiled teenagers by becoming their fictional older brother. In this show on Mediaset's TV channel Italia 1, he can be seen interacting with ordinary people in domestic interiors, where problematic teenagers are asked to reshape their lives according to his suggestions, a process which is scaled up by the way edited images of his life are scrutinised by his Facebook followers, many living in Milano 2 apartments, where they switch on their televisions, check their smartphones, and find him again. There, he wears Dolce & Gabbana and Nike, drinks Bacardi at the Tatanka Club, exercises following *Muscle & Fitness* magazine, consumes Enervit Sport, communicates with a Samsung phone and travels on Alitalia.

Today, Milano 2's banality is incessantly published on Instagram accounts: its swans and its trees, the changing seasons of the grass, its living rooms, cats in front of red vernacular pitched roofs, people in front of TV sets. With more than four million paying subscribers in Italy, Sky-TV, Europe's number one satellite TV platform, currently doubles the number of subscribers to Mediaset Premium digital cable television, Mediaset's satellite television service. Together, Mediaset Premium and Sky-TV, as transnational media platforms, are globalising direct-to-home urbanism, in which the architectural embodiment of the political has been implemented in a way that has so far remained unexplained. The effects of what once started in Milano 2 can be seen everywhere that people consume, and it has become the urbanism we mainly live by.

This work was originally published in *Perspecta 50: Urban Divides* (MIT Press, 2017), 243–51.

Environments of Resistance for Social Individuals

Fosbury Architecture

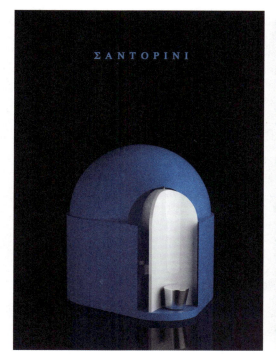

Santorini #bathunit. 2015.
Credit: Fosbury Architecture, Ganzfeld

Bora Bora #bed. 2015.
Credit: Fosbury Architecture, Ganzfeld

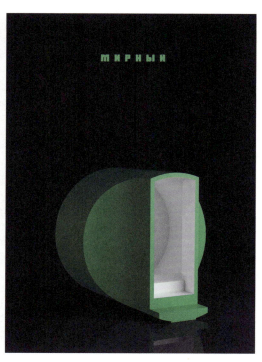

Mirnyj #meditationpod. 2015.
Credit: Fosbury Architecture, Ganzfeld

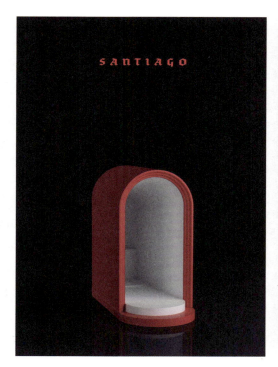

Santiago #pregadio. 2015.
Credit: Fosbury Architecture, Ganzfeld

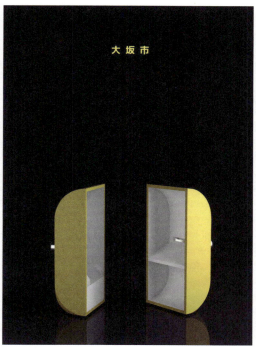

Osaka #studypod. 2015.
Credit: Fosbury Architecture, Ganzfeld

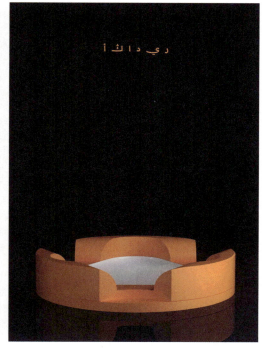

Agadir #conversationpit. 2015.
Credit: Fosbury Architecture, Ganzfeld

The most common piece of furniture is the BILLY bookcase from IKEA. It is estimated that one is sold every ten seconds.[1] We often take it for granted that furniture, as much as painting, sculpture and architecture, reveals the spirit of an era; we even tend to argue that observing how an individual furnishes their own space can help to identify that individual's character. So it sounds at the very least strange that a global and irreversible publishing crisis is corresponding to such a frenetic purchasing of bookcases.

Since 2012, the IKEA catalogue has become, surpassing the Bible, the most widely distributed publication in the world.[2] Created by 250 specialists and translated into twenty-nine languages, more than 200 million copies are distributed each year. It would be limiting to think that the IKEA catalogue is merely able to capture the tastes of the time; it is easier to imagine that it plays an active role in shaping them, seducing us with glossy images of loving parents who smile at their children, blooming cacti, colourful bath mats, scented candles and improbable lampshades. Distributed through formidable marketing efforts, amplified by a pervasive internet presence, the low-price and easy-to-assemble zeitgeist penetrates so deeply into the collective consciousness as to create the illusion that, by combining a finite set of objects, each individual will be able to produce their own very personal and personalised home environment. A mass hallucination, a powerful instrument of control capable of crossing the domestic threshold and undermining the radical ambition of the democratisation of creativity: reabsorbing it in a boring game of combinatorics.[3]

In the current condition of the 'commodification of everything', the border between public and private dissolves until it disintegrates. While the home is becoming more and more a place for work and an instrument of subsistence, domesticity invades every field of human activity, with banks that are camouflaged as lounges, offices as games rooms, and restaurants as kitchens. The work/consume/die human agenda is shifting towards an endless and sneaky productive leisure. Social media has put *otium*[4] to work 24/7, and if the sharing economy has on the one hand completely distorted the housing market, on the other it has converted intimacy into an economic asset.

The home-sharing platforms have produced and broadcast unprecedented physical space, a comfortable, comprehensible, homogeneous and generic geography that allows us to travel from New York to Bali, with stopovers in London and Singapore, without friction. This sterile global landscape is defined by the American freelance journalist Kyle Chayka as AirSpace: 'It's the realm of coffee shops, bars, start-up offices, and co-live/work spaces that share the same hallmarks everywhere you go: a profusion of symbols of comfort and quality, at least to a certain connoisseurial mindset. Minimalist furniture. Craft beer and avocado toast. Reclaimed wood. Industrial lighting. Cortados. Fast internet. Changing places can be as painless as reloading a website. You might not even realise you're not where you started.'[5]

The company that has been able to exploit this panorama better than anyone else is Airbnb. The apartments listed on the website, as if we were in a never-ending IKEA showroom, all look alike. In bright and retouched wide-angle photos, everyone seeks to convey a message of warm domestic uniqueness, combining inexpensive wood furniture with personal items that help to win over potential clients. It is a given that goods today serve to sell oneself more than to tell a story about oneself; to feel at home anywhere is possible – after all, it is almost certain that the host and the guest had their home furnished in the same way. Hence, everybody effectively belonging anywhere.

This contemporary human retreat towards a ubiquitous and reassuring domestic environment recalls a very similar historical moment, both from a political and a socioeconomic point of view: the Biedermeier period. The term (a combination of the adjective *bieder*, which means simple, integral, honest, and *Meier*, one of the most widespread German surnames) was invented as the name of an imaginary character assumed as representative of the middle bourgeoisie without particular interests except those of preserving his private life and domestic intimacy. A sort of *aurea mediocritas*,[6] intended to re-establish, in the habits of life and aspirations, in the simplicity of objects and forms, a balance based on rationality and on the positive consideration of what society could afford in a moment of economic contraction.

From 1815 to 1848, between the Congress of Vienna and the revolutionary upheavals that shook the whole of Europe, at the dawn of the Second Industrial Revolution, the first and genuine taste born and fed by the bourgeois class was the dominant one. Biedermeier furniture soon invaded Europe and prevailed thanks to the large-scale commercialisation, the reduction of production costs, the diffusion of easily exportable affordable models and the invention of product catalogues helping the customers to choose and order. The term that better expresses the atmosphere of this era is *Gemütlichkeit* – yet another German word to describe a place or a state of warmth and friendship, comfort, peace of mind, sense of belonging, wellness and social acceptance.

We are not interested in listing all the positive aspects of this period under analysis; instead, the aim is to highlight how the need for social inclusion in fact contributes to an unprecedented flattening of taste. The sense of bourgeois modesty influenced aristocratic lifestyles and proffered an achievable ambition for the less well-to-do classes. It is at that precise moment that an inexorable erosion of the domestic rituals, peculiar to customs and traditions of each social class, began.

Much like 200 years ago, today's recession and growing social control are leading to frustration for political structures. The consequent fear of the speed of life, the impotence towards the global dynamics and the progressive loss of our privacy due to the digitalisation of the world once again lead to a tactical withdrawal. Sheltered between our four solid, shrinking walls (in Great Britain the average home is now just 925 square feet, barely half the size they were a century ago[7]), and assuming we're even fortunate enough to own our house, we discover that the everyday routine has been cut to the bone, and most activities can be carried out elsewhere, or even in the ether. Given a bathroom, a bed and a computer, the home is now the place to meet friends (Skype), to flirt with one's girlfriend or boyfriend (Facebook), to go to the movies (Netflix), to have sex (YouPorn, provided that someone still uses it), to relax if possible.

What is dissolving today are certainly not the objects, which still enjoy excellent health; what we witness is the dematerialisation of the domestic liturgy linked to them. The transition is perfectly emphasised by Emilio Ambasz in the catalogue of *Italy: The New Domestic Landscape*, in which there emerges a clear distinction between the Object and its counterpart: the Environment.

The Object 'can be stripped of its mystique only if it is tamed, if it is made to assume the role of house pet. Reduced to graspable size, the object no longer intimidates us'. Quite the contrary, the Environment is 'adaptable enough to permit the enactment of different private and communally imagined new events, but at the same time sufficiently fixed to permit the re-enactment of those constant aspects of our individual and social memory.'

---

1   Melia Robinson, 'The 12 most popular IKEA products of all time', Business Insider (2016, 26 September), http://www.businessinsider.com/most-popular-ikea-products-2016-9?IR=T.

2   Harry Wallop, 'Ikea: 25 facts', Daily Telegraph (2012, October 31), http://www.telegraph.co.uk/finance/newsbysector/retailandconsumer/9643122/Ikea-25-facts.html.

3   See the Tumblr called Modern Life Space by Laurel Schwulst: artist, graphic designer and programmer living in New York. In 2011 she started collecting images from apartments listed on Airbnb to find inspiration for her own apartment. Soon after, she discovered that what seemed to be about real people and authenticity had nothing to do with them.

4   From the Latin, the term refers to a precise part of the daily routine free from the occupations of political life and public affairs (*negotia*), which could be dedicated to the care of the house, gardening or to studies.

5   Kyle Chayka, 'Welcome to AirSpace. How Silicon Valley helps spread the same sterile aesthetic across the world', The Verge (2016, August 3), https://www.theverge.com/2016/8/3/12325104/airbnb-aesthetic-global-minimalism-startup-gentrification.

6   From the Latin, the term does not have the derogatory value that the word mediocrity has in the current use, but rather as a means of staying in an intermediate position between the excellent and the bad, between the maximum and the minimum, rejecting any excess.

7   Gerry Peev and Martin Robinson, 'The Incredible Shrinking Houses', Daily Mail (2013, August 21), http://www.dailymail.co.uk/news/article-2398714/The-incredible-shrinking-houses-British-homes-built-just-HALF-size-1920s.html.

And finally, here it is, the main difference between the former and the latter: 'Once a need or a desire is satisfied, the respective artifact or space that served it begins to undergo a process of stylisation. The artifacts, spaces, and ceremonies of the private domain can thus be seen, on the one hand, as directly determined by physiological needs (for example, food), but, on the other hand, they can be seen as icons whose symbolic contents are, in part, intrinsic to them and, in part, culturally assigned as layers of semantic change.'

From the Middle Ages to the present, the Environments of Resistance for Social Individuals are those exceptional 'hard to die' items designed with the sole purpose of accommodating the idiosyncrasies of their occupants. Halfway between an object and a room, their forms are inspired by architecture. They trigger, preserve and perpetuate rituals. They have tectonic value and not just a descriptive or elegiac one. They contain and do not support. They are anthropometric and not zoomorphic. They are monumental and not atmospheric. They are bulky and not market-friendly. Spaces like the alcove, the studiolo, the boudoir, the pregadio, and later the conversation pit, the deprivation tank, the game pod and the peepshow cabin, activate a relationship between life and form that is not fulfilled in mere functional terms, but that challenges life to survive under abnormal conditions – without any ambition to change the habits of anyone other than perhaps those who commissioned them. They do not respond to necessity; they deal with desires.

Tomorrow, shifting towards a world that has developed antibodies against the distortions of Uberisation, all that once was solid will melt into air. In a 3D printable future, the next step of control by the Capital will no longer be the object but the intimate experience. After the adventure packages with bungee jumping included and the trip in the Taiga with fatbikes, the new frontier of entertainment will be to live or experience anonymous pieces of life. The Environments of Resistance for Social Individuals will last as the ultimate spatial epitome of anti-commodification: neither sharable nor affordable, but rather an apotropaic waste of energy, resources, space, time and creativity.

Backgrounds and sequences (or what is missing in contemporary Milan)

Angelo Lunati

Onsitestudio, urban block in Porta Garibaldi, Milan.
Credit: Johan Dehlin

1   Trystan Edwards, *Good and Bad Manners in Architecture* (Phillip Allan & Co, London, 1924).

2   Richard Sennett, 'Thomas Struth's City', in T. Struth, *Unconscious Places* (Munich: Prestel Verlag, 2020), 56.

3   Hermann Czech, 'Der Umbau', in Burkhardt Rukschcio, ed., *Adolf Loos* (Vienna: Albertina, 1989), 159.

Can a haphazard assemblage of buildings, each conceived in isolation, and expressing nothing but its own immediate purpose, really be described as a city?[1]

With this question – still surprising in our actual uncertain cultural condition – Trystan Edwards was speculating over the nature of urbanity in interwar Europe. How could buildings relate in a sequence? Referring to Old Regent Street in London, represented in a print from 1845, before its radical transformation at the end of the nineteenth century, Edwards points out 'the characteristic of the street as a background', in which facades have the 'quality of a wall' and the 'rare combination of diversity and order'. Part of the street's success and charm, he notes, could be attributed to the fact that an 'assemblage of buildings designed to serve the commonalty was here imbued with aristocratic grace'.

Whether in classical or more humble settings, the quality of urbanity embedded in a single piece, or in a sequence, offers resistance to the egotism of isolated presences and a contrast to the 'bugbear of monotony'. The same tension between the singularities and the condition of background informs Thomas Struth's early photographs of ordinary places in European cities: the same feeling of repetition of buildings along streets prevails over the specific detailing of the individual parts. These images argue that, in the city, slightly different forms serve the same functions, but 'modest buildings better serve the streets';[2] the street, made of sequences of singular facts, acts as a continuous background of vibrating presences. In some other photographs, the additive and transformative character intrinsic to the construction of the city is the most relevant quality of the urban space, representing different societies and diverse uses over time within a surprising physical unity. What qualities make groups of urban buildings well behaved?

Building of buildings

The character of European cities has little to do with monumental expression or exceptional presences, but is determined above all by the repetition of buildings along the street or within the block, by the fine grain of singular facts and by their subtle variations. The city, especially the nineteenth-century metropolis, is an 'opus at different scales':[3] those of the block, of the house, and of inner, individual use. Mostly, architectural operations encompass the last two dimensions. Some special buildings, however, have the ability to hold together the first two scales: the urban dimension related to repetition, and that of the individual piece, forged by contingency and adapted to specific circumstances. Such buildings may result either from a synthetic design operation, or from the construction of different elements over time. But in both cases, they can be described as a 'building of buildings'.

A building of buildings is the quintessence of urbanity, as it stands at the intersection between the scale of the single house and that of the collective construction. Articulated in a particular way, it has the capacity to be both a composition of two or more elements and, at the same time, a unitary presence, a single figure. Its well-mannered complexity makes it the opposite of the iconic architectural object. Where the solitary building is abstract, indifferent to these diverse urban dimensions, this special type of building claims a morphological and expressive richness. A building of buildings reacts consistently to the different temporal expressions of the city, combining formal specificity with functional genericity, providing a durable urban response and, equally, the highest degree of adaptability. These buildings are beautiful for many reasons – the assemblage and subtle variation of their facades; the relationship between the repetition of the single element and the typological variation; the richness of uses and the generosity of their interior spaces. Through their intrinsic variety, they already provide a sequence or an articulation, offering a continuous background to the vibrant life of the city, but at the same time asserting their singular expression and elegance.

Precedents

Milan is an anti-monumental city in which modern and ancient architectures are able to coexist in a natural way within a greater 'environmental' unity. Here, different types of these special buildings can be found and may be categorised according to their diverse formal principles, their generative circumstances and, especially, the differences, subtle or radical, between their inner parts. Some seminal cases programmatically encompass different volumetric gestures or ornamental expressions in relation to specific urban situations, such as Lancia and Ponti's conspiratorial duo of Casa-Torre Rasini. In other instances, they produce a multiple tonal continuity, such as the two sequences in Milan by Asnago Vender: the metropolitan version in Via Albricci, made of four pieces built over thirty years, and the mid-rise residential version in Via Senofonte.

Alternatively, they provide diverse articulations resembling historical time and taking to the limit the idea of variation, as happens in Aldo Rossi's block in Schützenstraße, this one in Berlin. On the one side, the rough tectonic and material continuity of Giovanni Muzio's clinker sequence made of three different pieces in Piazza Repubblica; on the other, the delicate stucco and ceramic pairs of Luigi Caccia Dominioni, gracefully set in continuity with the ancient grain of the buildings along the street, engaging with the baroque facade of Santa Maria alla Porta.

Some of these sequences conceptually recall the poor and rough materiality of Rachel Whiteread's shelf sculptures: unruled or precise pieces made of different materials, or else in the same materials but different colours, are set alongside each other, producing playful and intriguing sequences. Whiteread's arrangements generate a subtle energy: a painterly sense of internal motion of colours and shapes animates the composition, resembling Struth's sequences along the street. Akin to a series of humble houses along a street, these different pieces exhibit their modest material differences through their colourful assemblage, ruled by the line of the shelf: possible interpretations of the idea of a building of buildings.

Unexpected resonances

Built within intertwining cultural trajectories, some pairings of Viennese and Milanese buildings indicate possible ways of constructing backgrounds. The urban performance of these buildings is the result of an ever-changing balance between serving the street and introducing a character, defining a background and seeking an expression. Looking carefully at these buildings becomes an attempt to enclose within a picture a close-up of an ornamented detail, and at the same time a depth of field; the surface, the construction and the decoration are not abstract elements in the image, but are comprehensible within a wider space. The candid and ornate surface of Jože Plečnik's Zinshaus and the rounded and chromatically toned one of Giovanni Muzio's Ca' Bruta, the everted red windows in the interior courtyard of Joseph Hoffmann's Klose-Hof and the red

Onsitestudio, urban block in Porta Garibaldi, Milan. Credit: Johan Dehlin

Onsitestudio, urban block in Porta Garibaldi, Milan. Credit: Johan Dehlin

concrete space in front of the long facade of Aldo Rossi's Gallaratese, the corner articulation of the facades of the Looshaus and Gigiotti Zanini's Palazzo Civita, the vertical gap between the volumes of the recent Sergison Bates residential complex at Nordbahnhof and that between the light clinker volumes of Via Giannone's garden by Asnago e Vender, the blue ceramic strips of decorated surfaces in Otto Wagner's Neustiftgasse building sequence together with the icy ones of Caccia Dominioni's Via Nievo residential block. These buildings, coupled by tonal affinity, build a sequence of pendants that generates unexpected resonances and reveals complex relationships able to indicate possible derivations.

Unstableness and resilience

Is it still possible to build specific and durable responses to the different urban conditions and, equally, provide the highest degree of adaptability? How can we enhance a precise atmosphere and at the same time leave room for future change? Can we produce a city accepting social and cultural diversity within a new tolerant coexistence able to last? Within an increasing social uncertainty and cultural heterogeneity, a meaningful combination between the specific engagement of the building with the city and the generosity and openness of its organisation is necessary to introduce a new and powerful idea of resilience.

In Asnago and Vender Via Albricci's block, a virtuous combination of precision and genericity emerges. The powerful unified character of the sequence of four buildings does not arise mechanically from urban planning stipulations, nor can it be attributed to the repetition, with variations, of a pre-set facade composition. Rather, it is the cumulative result of research on the most appropriate characteristics for the construction of the modern city. The unity of the urban block is amplified by the pictorial character of the four facades. A single facade plane tersely borders the urban space, balancing a reduced palette of materials: opaque slabs of Bianco Perlino marble in the bases; polished Chiampo Paglierino marble in the corner volume; shinier sheets of Rosa di Baveno and upper facings in pale clinker at Piazza Velasca.

As in the facades of the Ca' Brutta, the level of the base does not coincide with the commercial level above the ground floor but is free to shift upward, as happens in a forceful way in the building on Piazza Velasca, generating an unusual relationship between the base and the volume of the building and emphasising the facades' pictorial character. The window frames of the facade are always aligned with the pattern of the facing slabs, defining the openings not as autonomous elements but as gaps in a continuous pattern. What is new is the variety with which they are arranged with respect to the vertical plane: jibing with it at the position of the base, but slightly recessed to reveal the thickness of the facade, or forceful shadows at the setbacks of the attic levels. The result is an overall homogeneous character in which the variations we have recognised – the fields of different materials, the thickness between the plane of the cladding and the plane of the window frames, the different sizing and alignment of the openings – are outweighed by the overall sensation of composure.

The corner building between Via Albricci and Piazza Velasca – the most expressive element, with the sweep of its base slightly set back from the curved plane of the facade – is also in keeping with this overall impression. Such a controlled relationship between an overall homogeneous image and the autonomous language of the single piece is the most effective expression of an idea of the city in which the pursuit of a choral effect prevails over the impact of solo efforts. The urban character of the whole series of buildings is expressed through a dual anti-ideological attitude; on one side, the unusual 'anti-functionalist' inversion of the enlargement of the windows moving upwards. So, too, is the autonomy of the functions, and their transformations along time, with respect to the design of the facade. In fact, the new functions to insert in the bourgeois city are commerce, service industries and residences. Via Albricci 8 was originally envisioned as four levels for the offices of the Zanoletti headquarters, with two upper levels for apartments, two per floor. Piazza Velasca has the same four office levels plus three residential floors, each with three apartments. Via Paolo da Cannobio contains seven office levels, while Via Albricci 10 also has seven floors of offices and an upper level for apartments. The facades of the buildings, taken individually, have a controlled vertical arrangement in terms of changes of material, sizing of openings and depth between the plane of the facade and the plane of the glazing; nevertheless, the positioning of the residential spaces in relation to the offices cannot be understood by interpreting these facade variations.

Unlike a functionalist approach, which would systematically indicate the purpose of spaces in keeping with the requirements of lighting and degree of relation with the outside world, here the expression of the building remains independent from the layout of the different activities at the various levels, producing a resiliency related to both the instability of uses over time and the quality of the urban background, continuous but also rich in variations.

Milan 2023

Today the occasion of redefining large abandoned areas in Milan provides a laboratory of experimentation where local and international urban cultures confront each other within an unprecedented series of occasions. The consumerist compulsion combined with the ever increasing economic and social uncertainty characterise this actual dramatic urban transformation, in which the very idea of the city as a place of tolerant and shared culture is put into discussion.

As in other places in Europe, contemporary practice in Milan has turned back to the late-modernist stereotype constructing a city made of buildings that can neither assimilate what is already there nor create a new kind of urban continuity, a consistent background for what is yet to come. Rather than resonate with each other or produce meaningful sequences, these buildings act autonomously, jostling to stand out from the rest, unable to grow old within the city. The unassuming unity that prevailed throughout the construction of the early-twentieth-century modern city has given way to a discordant mix of voices that fail to convey any new idea of cultural continuity. In the areas under redevelopment, scant evidence remains of the anti-ideological, elegantly pragmatic approach that used to allow for a negotiation between the singularity of the object and the articulated unity of the environment. At the same time, the most widespread conception of modernity, among architects committed to the market consensus, seems increasingly to be linked to the ideological use of technological performance or the spectacle of ecological rhetoric.

All the same, our societies may be more atomised than before, our cultures more diverse, but we can still aim to sustain a condition in which buildings are consistently stating their singularity through their architectural expression, while also making meaningful sequences and durable backgrounds.

A possible derivation in Porta Nuova

We like the prosaic and epic character of the city; on one side, the powerful and vivid qualities of continuity and background of the pre-nineteenth-century fabric and the Beruto plan, its streets and blocks; on the other side, the discontinuous character of the productive city and the infrastructural gaps producing large voids in the city. We like to experience how architecture, even within a speculative and fragmentary process of transformation, can take its qualities and character from a specific urban condition and how, at the same time, it can give something back to enhance that urban condition.

A group of three buildings is the result of the transformation of an abandoned L-shaped hotel built in the 1970s, grafted along the border of the compact city in front of the big infrastructural void of Porta Garibaldi train station. The project seeks to skip the narrative of the late-capitalist glazed commercial object by introducing a new robust sequence, deriving its character by combining fruitful indications from their distant precedents with the circumstances related to the necessities of contemporary life: the relation with views and visibility, the energetic performances, the organisation of the common facilities for a workspace.

Resisting a functionalistic approach that would prioritise single unalterable buildings as design objects, as some of the new presences on the other side of the street, the project aims to encompass the complexity of the form, interpreting the grain and hidden qualities of the existing situation: a slightly bended block in front of a small square, a special corner looking for some form of monumentality, an uncompleted garden within the block. The facade articulation combines three slightly different-coloured precast concrete constructions – due to Carrara, Botticino and Zandobbio marble powder – together with a lighter metal-framed piece on the top. The three buildings perform differently to the different orientations and scales, and will be transformed through time so to enhance the diversity between them; hopefully new uses will be discovered in order to enhance the diversities and programmatic articulation between the parts. This becomes the occasion to test how different pieces within one block can naturally be adapted and accommodate diverse programmes, and how a sequence can still behave naturally in the city.

Reclaiming care: Bottom-up feminist spaces in Milan

Florencia Andreola
Azzurra Muzzonigro

1   Aristotle, *Opere*, vol. IX (Bari: Laterza, 1973), 9–14.

2   Joni Seager, *L'atlante Delle Donne* (Turin: AddEditore, 2020).

3   Silvia Federici, *Reincantare il mondo. Femminismo e politica dei commons* (Verona: Ombre Corte, 2018).

4   Source: OECD Gender Institutions and Development Database (2019), oecd.stat.org. See also Moreira da Silva, 'Why you should care about unpaid care work', OECD Development Matters, 18 March 2019, https://oecd-development-matters.org/2019/03/18/why-you-should-care-about-unpaid-care-work/

5   For an accurate analysis of Milanese female work conditions see Lorenza Zanuso, 'Le milanesi al lavoro' in Roberto Cicciomessere et al., eds., *A Milano il lavoro è donna. Il mercato del lavoro milanese in un'ottica di genere* (Milan: EQuIPE, 2020).

6   Data on national female employment rate, source: ISTAT (2020).

Struggling for care in the man-made city

The city, in its materiality as well as in the power relations that underlie it, is the expression of masculine values and needs that have historically defined its spaces: in fact, planning has been a purely masculine prerogative since its origin. Until a few decades ago, even if the current proportions are still indicative of a certain gender imbalance, it was men who imagined the spaces of our cities, responding to the needs of a universal subject considered neutral but which, however, is implicitly male, white, heterosexual, cisgender, able and free from care responsibilities. In the meantime, where were women and what were they doing? Obviously, they were at home, taking care of the education of the children and looking after the house. The space dedicated to them is naturally the domestic one, dealing with the private sphere, or at most places of religious devotion. In ancient Greece, women were considered so much inferior to men that they did not have citizenship, like slaves.[1] If we think that the right to vote was granted to women for the first time in New Zealand in 1893, and in Europe in Finland in 1906,[2] it is immediately evident how our Western culture is deeply rooted in patriarchal values, and which often – if we do not pay specific attention – we do not even realise.

It is good to remember that the growth and articulation of our civilisation in all its expressions, including the development of cities and the capitalist economic system on which global societies are based, was possible thanks to the fact that women were at home taking care of their husbands, the house, the children and the elderly. However, as Silvia Federici explains very clearly, 'the expulsion of reproductive labour from the sphere of economic relations and its deceptive confinement to the sphere of the "private", the "personal" and above all "the feminine", have made it invisible as work, naturalising its exploitation'[3]. In other words: without the invisible and unpaid care work of women, our Western and capitalist civilisation could not have developed.

Thus, even today, 75% of paid and unpaid care work in the world[4] falls on women's shoulders. This involves a very particular use of public services, means of transport and health facilities. Those involved in care work tend to move about following local paths, mostly pedestrianised, made up of interlinked stages related to the multiple daily responsibilities towards those they care for and their domestic duties. Public services supporting childcare – kindergartens, preschools, play areas, places for safe breastfeeding, proximity healthcare services – thus become fundamental safeguards that allow those who deal with care work on a daily basis (still today above all women) to do so by being able to count on a public and accessible welfare network. It is always good to underline, however, that the goal is not so much to define a 'female model' that supports women in carrying out care work in daily life; the point is to put care at the centre of city planning – that is, to observe the patterns, services, networks and infrastructures that care generates in spaces and make them usable by any caregiver, regardless of gender.

Milan is a city that has a much higher female employment rate (67.1%)[5] than other Italian cities (49%)[6] and a fairly widespread network of support services for everyday life care; nevertheless, it has quite wide room for improvement in terms of consideration of the needs of women, of those that are fragile and dependent, of gender minorities, of all those people left at the margins of traditional planning because they are outside the functional paradigm – based, as we have seen, on the universal, neutral and masculine subject.

Furthermore, in the last ten years Milan has been at the epicentre of an unprecedented urban and economic development: *Expo 2015* was the catalyst of a strong wave of real-estate investments that have modified and continue to modify, despite the setback imposed by the pandemic, the face of the city. There are still many relevant 'matches' open from the point of view of urban development: the San Siro area with its new stadium, the former railway yards' sites, the former meat market, the 2026 Milano-Cortina Winter Olympics sites. Such huge urban developments apply a strong economic pressure, especially on the weakest segments of the population in a small European metropolis such as Milan. From this point of view, the question that runs through the current public debate on the city is: Will Milan be able to remain accessible and welcoming to the most vulnerable subjects, socially and economically or, conversely, will it become an increasingly elitist and exclusive city? The role of the public administration is crucial in governing this process. The challenge is to redistribute the value and resources generated by the great transformations through public policies aimed at protecting the weakest groups from the voracity of the market, at enhancing services, investing in social networks, co-creating innovative public policies and practices through listening, and ensuring the active participation of citizens.

What we wonder, therefore, from a gender perspective, is this: Is it possible to imagine and shape a city that puts care at the centre of its own idea of development? Where to start to create an urban environment that focuses on collaboration rather than competition, on inclusion instead of exclusion, on the practice of mutual support rather

Ri-make demonstration against eviction, May 2018. Credit: Ri-make

[7] Some of the cases presented here were already published by the authors in *Tracce Urbane* (2021) and in *Milan Gender Atlas* (2021), edited by LetteraVentidue Edizioni.

[8] For more details see SopraSotto (2019), *Come aprire un nido pirata nel quartiere*. http://soprasottomilano.it/come-aprire-un-nido-pirata-nel-quartiere/

[9] Florencia Andreola and Azzurra Muzzonigro, *Milan Gender Atlas* (Siracusa: LetteraVentidue Edizioni, 2021); interview with Maddalena Fragnito, 128–35.

than on division and isolation? Some signs of this type of approach are already in place: by observing carefully we can find places that are emerging from the bottom-up, grassroots developments, to claim an inclusive, accessible city, where care becomes the driver of a different idea of development. These are heterogeneous places: a pirate kindergarten, a social centre, a shared garden, a so-called 'House of Women'; together they constitute a mosaic of resources that the public administration could look to in order to expand its range of services for the community. They constitute a challenge, a resource, an opportunity not to be missed.[7]

SopraSotto: a pirate kindergarten in the Isola district

Walking through the streets of the Isola district in Milan, a few steps away from the famous towers of the Bosco Verticale (Vertical Forest), if you look carefully you can find a small space of two windows on the street where it is common to find a dozen children sleeping, playing or running around the neighbourhood in their pirate cart. They are the children of the SopraSotto self-managed kindergarten, a nursery that calls itself 'pirate', founded in 2013 by a group of parents who were excluded from the lists to access public nurseries.[8]

In Milan there is a dense and well-distributed network of public and private kindergartens. However, due to the strict rules for accessing the public ones – which penalise those who do not have a fixed-term or permanent job contract – every year between 3,000 and 4,000 children are left out. It is from this particular need of some of those mothers who did not manage to get their children into public kindergartens that the SopraSotto experience was born.

Maddalena Fragnito, besides being an activist and researcher who explores the intersections between art and transfeminism, is one of the founders of this initiative: for this reason, the interview conducted with her within *Milan Gender Atlas*[9] is the main source of this narrative. As well as the urgency of the lack of places in public kindergartens – Fragnito explains – we should consider another alarming fact: the very high percentage of female abandonment of work after the birth of a first child. In fact, nursery schools represent a fundamental welfare device, one which allows families, and especially mothers, to regain possession of their time after pregnancy, and for women not to lose their autonomy, including economic autonomy, which is essential not only for personal fulfilment but also to escape from violent family relationships.

SopraSotto tries to answer these questions by setting up a co-autonomous practice based on the redistribution of care for children in the 0–3 age bracket. On the one hand, this initiative represents a denunciation of the inaccessibility of public nurseries; on the other it is an attempt to create an alternative that is self-managed by a community of parents, educators, girls and boys. SopraSotto therefore gives life to a new model – also from a pedagogical point of view – of nursery school, based on very clear principles.

In the first place, collective care: excluding educators, there are no service figures – everyone does their part in rotation for the good of the whole community. In SopraSotto there are two classes of ten children: the community therefore changes every two years and is made up of twenty children, about forty parents and two educators.

Internal relations are governed by the principle of sharing choices: an educational model based on participation and collaboration; children are educated to be involved and to measure themselves against differences from an early age. Decisions are made by an assembly that also includes children, both for the need to look after them during the time of the meeting, and as an educational choice for the inclusion of the little ones when decisions are made that also, and above all, concern them.

Another important principle on which SopraSotto is based is porosity, which consists of an intense exchange with the neighbourhood: the external activities enter

[10] See http://isolartcenter.org/

[11] For more information see: Isola Art Center, *Fight Specific Isola* (Milan: Archive Books, 2013), http://isolartcenter.org/libro-fight-specific-isola/.

[12] See https://isolapepeverde.org/lassociazione/

the kindergarten in the form of didactic proposals and, vice versa, children leave the kindergarten to make experiences in the neighbourhood. It may happen that the educational proposals arrive from outside, by relatives of the children or by inhabitants and workers of the neighbourhood, and that they take place outside. For example, SopraSotto collaborates with Isola Pepe Verde, a neighbourhood garden where the kindergarten has its own corner, with games and a small plot of land to cultivate; moreover, through crowdfunding, the community has managed to purchase two 'pirate ships', each of which can carry up to ten children, and which allow them to explore the neighbourhood.

What SopraSotto does also is imagine a different relationship between institutions and families: the starting point remains a firm conviction of the need that the school, as well as the nursery, must be anchored to the public dimension, as a safeguard of welfare and equality; at the same time, it tries to question what a public institution could be, how it could evolve to meet the needs of a society in transformation. From this point of view, there is one aspect that SopraSotto strongly emphasises: trust. As a space born outside the institutional frameworks – and therefore with no bureaucratic protocol to refer to – it is essential to put into practice forms of relationships based on transversal and transgenerational mutual trust: trust that comes from time spent together in carrying out specific activities, of care or maintenance of the space in which both adults and children engage.

SopraSotto can therefore be considered a practice strongly characterised by the desire to give new life to obsolete, undersized and heavily bureaucratised public institutions and welfare policies: it offers the example of a self-organised space, a grassroots development, characterised by porosity, strong participation and its relationship with the district. These characteristics would have much to offer in reimagining a public enterprise that does not delegate care entirely to the private sector, nor remain trapped in its own inefficiencies and failings. What places like SopraSotto are asking for is to open a space for equal dialogue with the public institutions: to escape the logic of mere subsidiarity and voluntary work, giving space to forms of self-organisation and collective care from the bottom up. The challenge for the public administration is to intersect these practices with planning: starting from listening to experiences of mutualism and collectivisation of care, it is possible to imagine up-to-date welfare models at an urban and territorial scale that could respond to needs and create spaces of dialogue with citizens.

Isola Pepe Verde:
a shared garden for care

A few steps from the SopraSotto kindergarten in the Isola district there is an empty lot between the houses and the railway that, until a decade ago, was nothing more than an asphalt clearing in which construction waste was accumulated. That was, until an active citizenship group recovered it and turned it into a shared garden. The history of this small part of the city is closely linked to the urban events that led to the transformation of the Porta Nuova-Garibaldi-Varesine area. This, one of the largest urban transformations on a European scale, took place under the pressure of *Expo 2015* and has radically transformed the face of Milan in the last fifteen years. The dense fabric of artisans, small workshops and activities at reasonable prices that had characterised the DNA of the Isola district has been gradually replaced by exclusive skyscrapers, vertical forests, luxury apartments and trendy clubs.

While the whole neighbourhood was a huge open-air construction site, a group of citizens – who mostly came from the movement of artistic resistance to real-estate speculation known as the Isola Art Center,[10] and who had behind them the artist and philosopher Bert Theis, its founder and main inspirer – formed an association to redevelop the disused lot in Via Pepe and presented a proposal to the Municipality of Milan. They asked for a place in which to put into practice another idea of the city, one that was inclusive, protective of the environment and social fragilities. After years of discussions with citizens' associations, in 2012 the municipality recognised the importance of community gardens in recovering abandoned areas and promoting sociality; so, in May 2013, Isola Pepe Verde was recognised as the first community garden in Milan.

We can say with hindsight that the utopian ideals of Isola Art Center have lost ground under the pressure of the enormous flows of money that the great transformation of Porta Nuova brought with it. The movement, which was originally created around the Stecca degli Artigiani – an abandoned building occupied by artists, which was located symbolically and, perhaps even a little cynically, exactly in the place where the two towers of the Vertical Forest now stand – found in Isola Pepe Verde a possibility of existence and resistance. In a certain sense, therefore, the garden represents a symbolic cultural garrison, a small plot of land that has become the ultimate refuge for those who, at the time of the great transformation plans of the city, did not agree, and saw in art the engine and the tool to overturn power relations and implement a daily revolution.[11]

The principles that have animated this place since then – and which are summarised in the statute of the association[12] – focus on the socialisation of environmental care as a value to improve the quality of urban life: the maintenance of greenery is a participatory neighbourhood process, a way to give space and voice to the rights of citizens, in particular to the under-represented subjects – such as the children of the neighbourhood schools – and to socially disadvantaged people. Cooperation and mutual aid are the basis of an open, democratic, participatory process of caring for the city.

Since then, there have been countless activities that have taken place and continue to take place in the community garden of Isola Pepe Verde: from birthday parties to artistic performances, workshops, gardening activities and so on. Anyone can propose an activity, as long as they respect the principles shared by the community, including economic accessibility: it is not permitted to carry out activities that generate profits to be divided among the members or organisers, in favour of usability by everyone.

In this context, the experience of Isola Pepe Verde interests us as it is a concrete representation of an idea of a city that focuses on an expanded concept of care, animated, supported and maintained from the bottom up. The care in the shared garden is expressed in various forms: from caring for plants, to caring for animals – in particular, the garden is the home of a historic community of cats – to caring for neighbourhood social relations. The utopia that animated its birth and continues to feed its existence lives in the possibility of acting as a model for other shared gardens that multiply the spaces for care and sociability, removing them from speculation and profit.

Ri-make: a commons of radical
mutual care

We now move to between Affori and Bruzzano, to an area characterised by a marginal and often problematic condition: a suburban neighbourhood with very limited institutional services and cultural offering, in which numerous migrant families in economic difficulty have settled, with a low schooling rate and often conditions of profound discomfort, from a housing, occupational and social point of view.

Ri-make settled in the territory with the occupation, in its first phase in 2014, of an abandoned bank building; then, following the evacuation of the space in May 2018, it moved to the Omero high school, the only school in the district, which had recently been closed. Today, a notice to demolish the building threatens, once again, the evacuation of the space.

Ri-make is animated by activists who aim to work in the social fractures of the neighbourhood, to mend them, to create an alternative for the inhabitants and to help these people participate in new ways of interacting and of collective exchange. To do this, the network of which Ri-make is part is made up of associations, feminist collectives and anti-violence centres; it does not offer itself as a service for the inhabitants, but as a horizontal platform between the actors involved, one which legitimises the needs of people and works to support the activities that lead to the resolution of these needs on the basis of individual specificities, free from a standardised vision typical of public services.

Over the years, the relationship between Ri-make and the neighbourhood has consolidated thanks to a series of local activities, which have helped to include citizens through leaflets, initiatives in the streets, solidarity lunches, open meetings. The activities of solidarity were at first carried out only by activists, but then also by citizens, in a crescendo of concentric circles.

During the lockdown phase caused by the Covid-19 pandemic, Ri-make chose to intensify an activity that had already existed for a year: the initiative 'You are not alone', conceived to respond to a series of needs unheard and exacerbated by the crisis. The project took shape through the support offered on the aspects related to work, then gradually other activities have become included.

Over time, a specifically gendered need has clearly emerged, in particular regarding those who work in nursing: the pandemic has clearly shown the presence of a systemic problem for this category of healthcare workers, deprived of protection and unable to take time off. On the basis of the needs expressed by this sector, the Ri-make work desk started out from a feminist perspective, because 'if at the heart of the Ri-make project there is the idea of recomposing social fractures through mutualism and of changing things through the struggle and trade union disputes,' activist Marie Moïse tells us, 'the union that has been created over time does not often take into account the specificities of women's jobs, the specific needs of care work, paid or unpaid'.

Part of the 'You are not alone' initiative is also related to the care of children, through 'solidarity babysitting' in explicit support of female workers. Women have been particularly impacted by the health emergency, especially in terms of the overload of care work due to the closure of schools. In the period of greatest impact of the pandemic, the number of families who did not have the opportunity to take care of their children increased significantly, both for purely work and infrastructural reasons (absence of computers, internet, difficulty in managing distance learning, etc.). This initiative was also used mainly by migrant women, cleaning workers or supermarket employees, mothers with disabled children; but also by single men or couples, unable to manage their children due to their working conditions. Ri-make has tried to remedy, as far as possible, the gaps that emerged in Milan, given that during the lockdown the municipality suspended most of its services to families. The help provided also focused on the refurbishment of computers or tablets useful for remote teaching, and supplying internet connections for those who did not have this possibility. The activity of supporting childcare, including help with homework, is characterised by a natural feminist union: it was born around the idea of a collectivisation of care work, historically unrecognised and unpaid or – for those who can afford it – contracted out to categories that do not have the possibility to escape from it. This collectivisation translates into the realisation of mutualistic practices of care, looking for alternatives to the standard parenting idea, in an attempt to overcome the isolation of parenting typical of our society, as well as experimenting with shared forms of care, as a way to give a new meaning to care work and community experience.

The future of Ri-make, despite its evidently positive activity targeting many inhabitants of the neighbourhood, is uncertain. The municipality has ordered the demolition of the occupied school building. It is a policy aimed at making profit out of municipal assets, without considering the civic profitability that Ri-make – as well as many other not officially recognised entities – puts in place.

Throughout the city, but especially in marginal and forgotten neighbourhoods such as the one in which Ri-make is located, the energies of the community that mobilise to respond to unmet needs, as well as highlighting the evident shortcomings of the public sector, represent a precious resource that must be listened to, recognised, and valued. At the basis of the lack of recognition of self-organised groups such as Ri-make, there are certainly political conflicts; however, it would be short-sighted to underestimate their contribution to public action, so often plastered in protocols and procedures that do not enable the formal frameworks for such self-organised bodies, by making them an admissible as well as desirable subject of the public debate. This is certainly an aspect on which it is important to work in order to make public action effective and inclusive of the energies of the territory.

Casa delle Donne: a house for Milanese feminists

We conclude this short journey into the Milan of caregiving from the grassroots with one of the most symbolic places of Milanese feminism: La Casa delle Donne (House of Women).

This place is an important point of reference in the city of Milan for the construction of a gender culture. It was founded as an association in September 2012, based on aspirations shared by many women residents.

A few months after taking office, on 28 September 2011, the Equal Opportunities Commission of the Municipality of Milan, chaired by Anita Sonego, called together the women of the city to express their wishes and requests to the local administration. In that assembly the common need to establish a 'House of Women' in Milan emerged, thus attempting to bridge a serious gap with respect to Italian and European cities: to provide a specific space for women, a point of reference for the constant transmission of experiences and knowledge that favours placing each and every one of them in the city context, a place where respect and value are given to differences due to culture of origin, age, social condition, sexual orientation, cultural positions and policies.

The Casa delle Donne di Milano association was granted a free loan (for two consecutive terms of three years) of the ground floor of the municipal building located in via Marsala 8/10 by the Pisapia council – which, in order to approve the relative resolution, suspended municipal regulations for four years. At the end of 2019, the contract expired, and the Sala Administration declared that it could not continue the loan for use; nevertheless, after a complex and tortuous negotiation, a collaboration agreement which provides for the possibility of free assignment of public spaces to associations deemed to be of social utility was secured. The resolution today provides that half the space will be granted according to the agreement and the other half will be assigned through a public bid with an onerous rent.

Casa delle Donne has a board of seven members and a membership that varies between 500 and 700 people; it is open to all women – men can participate and associate with the blue 'friends of the Casa' card – and is aimed at a very diverse audience precisely because it responds to a criterion of inclusiveness as long as its statute and basic principles are respected against all forms of discrimination. Cyclically, the members of the Casa assemble for a meeting called *Spazio Partecipato* (participated space), where everyone can bring ideas, reflections or criticisms, in addition to the many working groups on the various issues concerning the life of women.

Casa delle Donne represents an important symbolic place for historic Milanese feminism: among the challenges it faces are the generational relay race and intersectionality. It is very important that such a place insists in strengthening the dialogue with younger generations of feminists, with the LGBTQIA* community, with women and gender minorities who have different levels of fragility, broadening their gaze and reinforcing their position as a reference for a vast community mirroring a complex society.

This short journey through the Milanese spaces that represent a concrete experience of a feminist city has intercepted heterogeneous spaces: a kindergarten, a shared garden, an occupied former high school, a women's house. Their genesis, their history, their objectives are very different from each other, but they all stand as effective ways of bringing values such as collective care, mutual aid, cooperation, support of fragilities into play in the city.

In these places it is possible to find the words and resources to give shape and voice to a new, different city: a city that sees care as the engine of the transformation of places, without leaving anyone behind.

Text by Maik Novotny

■ What words will architectural history find to describe the urbanisations of the 2010s and early 2020s when it looks back from a distance of a few decades? The upsurge after the crash of 2008. High-rise residential buildings as cash cows, in the centre and on the edges of town. Prime locations, unique panoramas, optimal transport links, sure-fire investments.

Assets with highway access. Portfolio Urbanism. Suburbs made of concrete gold. Lehman Brothers landscapes.

The images Paul Sebesta captured on his forays through Milan's urban development areas suggest a no-man's-land. But nothing belongs to no-one, especially not here and not now. This land previously belonged to somebody, or perhaps many people – or even everyone. Now it is a someone's-land, but the someone is a no-one. A mailbox in Luxembourg, an account in the Cayman Islands, an investment fund in Seoul.

And yet this architecture cannot cast off the specificity of its material and geographical situation. It may be generic, but in this case it stands not in the milky dust of Hangzhou or the clear morning air of London, but in the soft golden light of a hot northern Italian summer. What am I doing here, it seems to ask itself, nonplussed. Apparently, it has overshot its intended destination. But only by a fraction – it's almost in the right place. Because the high-rise is a Milanese tradition, a more or less well-regulated exception. Out here, though, between the blurred lines of the periphery, at once densified and dispersed, has become something like a shunting station for high-rises, a storage area for scores of exceptions whose rules and regulations are unreadable.

Who lives out here, between the tracks of the Airport Express, the car showrooms, the air-conditioned mega-restaurants next to underground parking garages? Who are the citizens of the Euro-Banana, this multinational zone of affluence that extends northwards from Milan, curving along the Rhine and up to London? Who pays for Portfolio Urbanism, and who profits from it?

In 2008, the year of the financial crash, the Milan-based artist collective Alterazioni Video began their *Incompiuto* project, a photographic documentation of the unfinished landscapes of Italy: highway bridges in a field without a highway, massive sports facilities far from any city, post-human ruined landscapes. Even if the unfinished takes on particularly dramatic forms here, this is not a purely Italian phenomenon, but a political and economic one. Will the city of the 2010s ever be finished; come to that, does it even know what it wants its final form to be?

Perhaps one day it will indeed become a real city, a different kind of city, whose form we cannot envision today. The prognosis is for change from the early 2020s. Sand is getting into the gears of the global construction industry. Interest rates are rising, new buildings are getting shorter. Will the concrete gold in the suburbs become the flotsam of transformation or the emblem of a future city beyond the growth imperative? The urban fringe of today is already the waiting room of post-Portfolio Urbanism.

Someone's-land

Paul Sebesta

Milan

'esterni is a placemaking cultural enterprise that aims to reclaim and create spaces in the city for common use and profit.

In any place, we help the common good come out. In a building we see a meeting place. In a space we see an opportunity for a handshake. In our projects, our starting point is the place itself, whose meaning we always respect. We believe in listening – to history, to stories – and in the power of insight. We believe in profit and in the advantages we can produce for the benefit of all: owners, participants, the community. We think, rethink, create and manage spaces – we are eager to invest in their development.

We use culture, in all its languages. We know how to combine responsibility and lightness, genius and regulations. We feel the urge to do something unexpected, but necessary. Wherever we see an opportunity, in Italy and abroad, we try to show that the best growth is mutual growth – through places.'

esterni

Ideal gatherings

Beniamino Saibene (esterni)

As I said not long ago to the editors of this volume, here at esterni we have never been particularly good at expounding our theories. We have always tried to do theory. So we find ourselves in a bit of a quandary. It will pass.

If the main theme is supposed to be that of inhabiting, then we have to ask ourselves, first of all: What is our habitat, where do we live? The answer that we young inhabitants of Milan came up with, over twenty years ago now, was: in public space. In fact, it seemed to us to make more sense to concentrate on that vast and desolate wasteland than on the multitude of cemetery niches piled one on top of the other in which it appeared to us that our fellow city dwellers had taken refuge, and from which almost every young person has always wanted to escape. Those famous four walls.

So: EVERYBODY OUT!

Rediscovering, reconquering, rethinking our city, our spaces. In the last years of the twentieth century and the early years of the twenty-first, Milan was not known for its beauty, nor for its quality of life. It was not 'attractive'. Milan worked as a brand only when coupled with fashion, opera or football. The city's few attractions, none of them of recent construction (except perhaps the stadium?), could be visited in one day: the Duomo, La Scala, the Castello, the Navigli. Greenery was not much talked about, as if the Milanese were resigned to the colour grey and its few shades. There were no squares. Major events were held indoors. In a nutshell, not many were willing to risk the streets.

But Milan was already known as the Capitale di Design, the 'Capital of Design'. It was our friend the designer Jochen Denzinger who, among others, pointed out to us the contrast between that reputation and the impression of being in an undesigned city, one whose overall design did not seem to be the product of structured thinking (of democratic thinking?). Or perhaps it was; it had the structure of private property. Interior design, for the living room, the kitchen, the bathroom. (Whence the cynical slogan of Duchampian inspiration, Milano Pitale di Design, 'Milan Chamber Pot of Design'.)

The city is for everyone!

Ah, yes? But who knew it? Word needed to go round because the only thing clear to everyone was: you don't throw litter in the street. Was that as far as the sense of commonweal went? Clean pavements, flowerbeds not to be walked on, ordinances stopping people from gathering in the streets at night. Nothing more than 'urban decorum'? In our view, what was needed was to turn the place upside-down, scatter a few pieces of

Credit: All images by esterni

paper (before Facebook, how many flyers!), walk in bare feet on the flowerbeds, dance in the squares, divert the traffic. So, we began to fight, yes really to fight, for the public spaces, first of Milan, then of Italy. To all intents and purposes we became fanatics, intransigent and creative ones, very popular among the young but the butt of frequent reprimands from the municipality: complaints to the police, a lot of fines, brick walls. No funding.

> esterni: 'At least entrust us with some spaces! For example, the Cortile delle Armi, can we hold a party there?'
>
> Council: 'You want the Castello Sforzesco? Certainly not! You can have its moats! Hahaha!'
>
> esterni: '… OK.'

Our battle started with small events; we might call them disruptions, but extraordinarily well-organised and publicised ones. 'A few dozen people sighted along the tracks at Bovisa, a few hundred under the flyover of the ring road, thousands at the Parco Sempione!'

Our projects grew ever larger, with a greater following, more 'participation'. Word of mouth spread faster in the city than particulate pollution. The internet was not yet social, but we didn't let the first emails escape us. In 2005 we sent out our weekly newsletter to almost 50,000 people all over Italy.

And so it was that we went in conquest of public space. A succession of intense projects followed, some at regular intervals, others proposed again in other places around Europe. Initially they attracted the attention of the police, then of journalists, then of young marketing managers. Stolen places: empty car parks, blocked roads, invaded means of public transport … that were transformed for a night, or for a week, changing their function, bringing strangers together, forming memories and a new awareness, introducing people to the city and contributing to a new collective imagination.

> 'Yesterday evening I ended up designing a chair for myself, in the midst of thousands of people who had met up on an expressway, in a tunnel.' Milan.
>
> 'I was on my way home on the tram and what do I see but a band of musicians climb on board? And people on the tram behind were dancing as well. I danced a couple of waltzes and didn't get off. A bar had been set up at the end of the line.' Milan.
>
> 'As part of an experiment they separated me from my friends and put me with some people I didn't know. We walked as far as a sort of hidden garden, where I spent the whole evening. Well, that's how I met my husband.' Milan.

A centrifugal, liberating and exhilarating force drove the city to move differently, going beyond the old routes and more common places and towards new ways of being together. For some years the Salone del Mobile was the ideal testing ground and it only took a moment before swarms of tourists and locals started to go on the adventures we proposed. The idea spread quickly that alongside the Salone del Mobile there could be a mobile salone; that in addition to the magazine *Interni* there could be the group esterni; that after product design we could propose the existence and urgent need for public design. It was the beginning of the fringe events known as the Fuorisalone, which would then spread out into the city, transcending the very idea of design and becoming Milan's main attraction. The projects for public spaces acted as a trigger for that still unexpressed desire, that hidden need, to go out, to mingle, to wander around on foot, by day and by night, discovering new places and people, stories and opportunities. It was something the whole country needed. It wasn't just a reappropriation of spaces, but a need to express oneself, to find things out, to feel part of a community. So one project gave the impetus to the next. With a speed we can only envy today, ideas were turned into experiments in the field. Our workgroup expanded from year to year to cope with the proliferation of projects and subjects tackled: architecture, eyesores, television, people on the move, dirty air, cinema, music, food, adolescence, humanity, power, needs, speculation, public space.

We were received – or we gate-crashed – as architects, designers, city planners, artists, activists, situationists, troublemakers, creatives, entrepreneurs. Most often, though, they called us 'youngsters'. Even when we were past forty. It's an old trick … But we took ourselves quite seriously, enough to stand as candidates for mayors of Milan (2006). Very few votes, but the beauty of being able to propose a programme of 120 projects for the city, many of which we would have the satisfaction of seeing realised … in cities elsewhere in Europe.

At a certain point some of us will have probably thought, OK, cool, but isn't it economically unsound to always take everything down and start again somewhere else? So, we got a place with friends: an eighteenth-century farmhouse between Porta Romana and Calvairate, abandoned and dilapidated, which today is a marvellous, open and pulsating microcosm, the Cascina Cuccagna (www.cuccagna.org). And then we expanded: a disused factory of 12,000 m², '[…] a multifunctional cultural centre that produces social innovation and contamination between arts, enterprises and technology […]', Base Milano (www.base.Milano.it).

So, despite having in a certain sense gone back within those four walls … we are still there. We feel that we inhabit public space. We still have the idea in our head of inventing new spaces and setting up places for the community, of inspiring those communities with the best of intentions, arming them with impatience and strategy, stirring debate, upsetting culture, encouraging talent and know-how. It's a new challenge that aims at the conquest of the Italian stock of historic buildings, unappreciated, betrayed and abandoned. Villages, buildings, factories, villas, barracks … in the big cities, on the coasts, in the mountains. Innumerable properties to be converted in order to recover their urbanistic, historical and civic importance and to unleash their aggregative potential.

Long live restorations for the purpose of conservation, long live gatherings, long live Italy!

Experimental Laboratory Milan

Emanuele Braga

I've been living in Milan for the last thirty years and have been exposed to many of the city's tensions and contradictions in my role as an artist, theorist and activist. I arrived in this city as a university student at the beginning of the 1990s, during a period in which the Socialist administrations of the 1980s had laid the foundations of future urban development under a system of patronage permeated by the new financial players and the ruling class. From the 1990s until the end of the first decade of the millennium, we lived through twenty years of right-wing governments that intensified and institutionalised the mingling of processes of privatisation of public space with welfare services.

This kind of managerial culture fitted well into the symbolic legacy the city had inherited from its past history – on the one hand the capital of the country's productive north, and on the other long the centre of the advanced tertiary sector.

The city of Milan has always been the home of Italian financial capital and of the big media and advertising agencies and publishing houses, as well as an international beacon for the design and fashion industry. These circumstances made Milan a meeting point between a business culture driven strongly by the initiative of the private sector and the transition from industrial Fordism to the new economies of the post-Fordist creative industries within the more general process of globalisation and digital innovation.

In the 1990s I lived in the district of Isola, a fairly central area but separated from the historic centre by a strip of railway tracks leading to the important train and underground station of Garibaldi FS. In those years it was the location par excellence for experimentation and civic activism, with nearly ten squats in a handful of streets. The Centro Sociale Deposito Bulk, the Centro Sociale Pergola, home to hacklabs and the most important projects of digital autonomy, the birthplace of Serpica Naro, which put up critical opposition to the world of fashion, the enormous residential squat Metropolis, the Centro Sociale Garigliano, the V33, the structure known as the Stecca degli Artigiani which served as the base for innumerable projects of critical urbanism, local TV channels and, for me, the even more important project of the Isola Art Center, which was the first to bring to Milan a critical discourse of processes of gentrification on the part of the art world.

In short it was a genuine mecca of Italian activism in the 1990s. This was also the context in which we were able to cultivate urban rituals like the huge demonstrations on Milan May Day parades, organised every year by, among others, the San Precario collective, which in Italy had defined and structured this new subjective condition of job insecurity. A new figure of the exploited within a wider reorganisation of the city's labour market.

I grew up in a district that was a symbol of activism, and the perception of power was palpable and extremely productive and effervescent. But in my view, everything changed at the beginning of the new millennium.

There are traumatic events that have the power to crystallise turning points in history, and two things that happened at the beginning of the millennium led us to change our approach to politics and our perception of the city.

The first was Genoa 2001, where the whole world of the extra-parliamentary left, the activity of the hacklabs, in part channelled into the Indymedia platform, the pervasive and conflictual sphere of the associations, shouting from the rooftops at the social forums that another world was possible, and the anti-globalisation movement in general that had come together in the wake of the protests at the WTO conference in the American city of Seattle, was killed off.

For me, an Italian activist, what happened in those days at the end of July 2001 in Genoa, during the protests against the G8 summit there, was a genuine trauma, a symbolic scar, a wound that was never going to heal. They told us clearly that another world was not possible, on pain of being tortured and charged by the army, in what amounted to a suspension of the rule of law.

The second traumatic event, just a few weeks later, was the attack on the Twin Towers of 11 September 2001, and the beginning of George W. Bush's wars on terrorism in the name of universal Western rights to be exported all over the world.

The symbolic cutting off of the right to political action

Credit: Luca Chiaudano

was very hard to take. On the one hand we had no rights if we wanted to represent an alternative to the model of neoliberal capitalism; on the other that same model had gone to war in the name of the very rights we were being denied at home. On the one hand the Italian state told us there were no rules behind the detentions by the police; on the other it was bombing innocent civilians for motives of geopolitics and energy security with the excuse of exporting those rights in the name of the war against terrorism.

That's how this millennium began for me: Western capitalism had decided to base its political consensus on the criminalisation of dissent. And for a few years we kept quiet, brooding and disoriented. What happened in Milan during that period, the first decade of the millennium, during the mourning over the death of the movements of the 1990s? In the first place the real wave of repression arrived in the city and with it the eviction of many of the *centri sociali*, self-managed social centres. Secondly, the foundations were laid for the grand schemes of transformation of the territory, and in particular for the master plan of Garibaldi Repubblica in the Isola district, and of CityLife adjoining the zone of the trade fair.

In short, they destroyed all the squatted spaces and drew up a development plan to attract the foreign capital of groups like the Texan Hines, along with other old acquaintances like Ligresti, often under the coordination of Manfredi Catella (future Coima group).

Thirdly, but in a more marginal and hushed manner, the foundations were laid for the construction of an intricate system of banking foundations, which on the one hand wished to appear generous by providing funding for the cultural and social sector, and on the other declared themselves ready to tap into the public funds coming from the state-run financial institution Cassa Depositi e Prestiti and the Ministry of the Economy to handle investments in the social housing sector.

In summary, the first ten years of the century started with the repression of activism and self-organisation, processes of unchecked gentrification and the self-promotion of a professed ethical finance disposed to drive compensation for the pouring of concrete by managing and funding the not-for-profit sector and the world of cooperatives.

For many of our analyses, in the first ten years of the century the creative cities were a genuine experimental laboratory at a more global level for the transformation of the labour market. The figure of the multitasking creative, employed on a temporary basis, a self-entrepreneur always on the alert and available right around the clock, often without any real contract and with a low level of contribution to national insurance, eternally waiting for reputational recognition, was an indication of anthropological social change. And this was all the more significant for my community, made up of artists, university students and cultural and social operators.

While for Richard Florida (a lucid neoliberal thinker), in those years a city that could not call itself creative was doomed to disappear from the global economic map, it was also true that in order to be creative the city had to rely on the exploitation of creative people, and therefore re-establish the exploitative relationship between enterprise and labour. And it did so by bypassing simple negotiation with the trade unions while revolutionising the individual at an anthropological level. It was necessary to find a way to make creativity something highly desirable, so as to be able to exploit it as much as possible and ensure that contracts remained on a temporary basis.

And then, to crown this first decade of the millennium, came the financial crisis of 2008. The reaction of European governments was the imposition of a tight squeeze on public spending and the introduction of stability pacts. For the Italian government and citizens, an alliance between the corrupt right and the financial potentates of real estate and the banks marked the beginning of a campaign of attack on public debt and an acceleration of the processes of privatisation. From our viewpoint as artists and temporary workers in Milan, it signified witnessing a drastic cut in public investment and increased insecurity in the private job market. Major public institutions like theatres, museums, libraries, academies and universities were in deep crisis. They were unable to open spaces of production and experimentation, and frequently found themselves threatened with closure, a reduction in staffing, the outsourcing of services and the need to rent out their premises for commercial use, or worse to sell them for conversion into supermarkets. On the other hand, in the private creative industry, it meant a high level of job insecurity in an extremely competitive market that went so far as to ask people to work for free in exchange for exposure.

The only other players were the banking foundations and impact investors, who within programmes of social enterprise funding and a marked bureaucratisation of the process of obtaining credit took the place of the public vocation of the services. But behind these foundations and large cooperative groups were the same banks as were involved in the processes of privatisation and gentrification.

While the wealth distributed through work diminished, public expenditure on welfare was also reduced and house prices went through the roof. Naturally, financial speculators who had invested in the real-estate market were happy and satisfied, but for people living in Milan life has become a nightmare over the last twenty years. A high level of competition, unpaid work, few public services, skyrocketing rents and an increasingly privatised health service. Life for a temporary worker in Milan has meant doing two or three jobs on the same day in different places, some of them off the books, in order to pay the rent for a shared room that swallows up almost half their income.

How has a city of this kind been able to bear the strain? In short, why hasn't everyone fled? Because there is a high turnover. In general, the individual only puts up with it for a few years, and the city fills up cyclically with new arrivals ready to try their luck. In this way students who choose to come to study in Milan's universities from the surrounding area and the rest of Italy, with the support of their families, try to make ends meet through temporary solutions when they've finished their studies, or are milked by the experience of on-the-job training in companies. In the majority of cases they give up after a few years, and leave.

A description of the system of public housing provides a useful backdrop to this scenario. Up until Giuliano Pisapia's first term as mayor (2011–15), the stock of ERP (Edilizia Residenziale Pubblica) in Milan was the exclusive responsibility of ALER, Azienda Lombarda Edilizia Residenziale, the regional agency for public housing. This stock was notoriously poorly managed, and the lack of maintenance made the buildings unassignable, due to sloth, political speculation and corruption. The region of Lombardy has always been governed by the right, and in particular by the Northern League Party, which since the 1990s has defended the interests of the traditionalistic and xenophobic productive north of Italy against immigrants from the south (first of Italy, then of the world). All the right-to-housing movements of Milan were aware that it was not in the interest of a party of this kind to invest in a good public housing service because its users would be made up predominantly of migrants from southern Italy and other countries of the world. For this reason, from the viewpoint of building consensus on the right, the theorem was perfect: by not investing in the social housing where migrants lived, money was saved; and those estates were turned into ghettos in a visibly grave state of decay, making it possible to base electoral campaigns on the great problem of Milan's black, dirty and dangerous ghettos, attracting votes throughout the region. I have to admit that this mix of tactical dysfunctionality, xenophobia and corruption has worked very well and strengthened the far right: it has never (up to now) lost power in the region.

Against this background, Milan was already consolidating a scheme in the first decade of the century: strong branding of the city as a place where there was money, where there was culture and where you could make good; masses of commuters and temporary residents were attracted by this image and willing to work at low cost, investing the family assets accumulated by previous generations in the region outside the city; a concentration of wealth based on live–work in large companies operating as monopolies; inefficient public services that were therefore increasingly delegated to the private sphere, which then charged for them. In my view it was this sort of starkly neoliberal scheme that laid the foundations for a further turn of the screw in the second decade: that of the exponential racialisation of low-paid work, especially in the fields of logistics, the hospitality industry and care.

This was the situation in which we moved from the crisis of 2008 onwards, shaping the agenda of the movement. The international scenario at the beginning of the second decade saw the great uprisings of the Arab Spring, the Occupy Wall Street movement and, in Europe, the demonstrations of 15-M in Spain, the 'Intermittents du Spectacle' movement in France and the protests against austerity and the big central banks.

In the wake of the great victory in the referendum on the privatisation of the public water supply, a movement for the protection of common assets emerged out of the Italian performing arts and artistic sector and grew, leading to a wave of occupations of urban spaces in opposition to processes of privatisation and increasing job insecurity. In 2011 we set up an open assembly of Lavoratori dell'Arte (Art Workers) in Milan that began to consolidate a force which, up until that moment, had acted on an individual and fragmented basis. This assembly asserted the need to reappropriate means of production and urban spaces and to combat the cuts in funding for the creative industries and public institutions. As a first action we decided to occupy the PAC (Padiglione d'Arte Contemporanea), which that season had chosen to rent out the public institution for a lengthy exhibition by PIXAR. For us this was an indictment of the closure of public policy to experimentation on the city's art scene, and the adoption instead of a commercial logic by letting out public institutional space cheaply to an American multinational.

The assembly of Lavoratori dell'Arte grew quickly, its numbers boosted by the arrival of workers from the television and cinema sector, editors from the world of publishing and people involved in video post-production, along with installers, museum guards and students, while the centri sociali and unions began to show an interest. To all it was clear that the boundary lines between one

Credit: Luca Chiaudano

sector and another were very thin. Many people had more than one job and worked in more than one field at a time. Over the following year this assembly of workers on temporary contracts opposing cuts to public spending broadened its scope to the question of the right to the city, acting to fight against processes of gentrification. In Milan the Isola Art Center collective had already raised this problem the previous decade: the strategy of the creative industries was to take on property speculation, which needs a cultural construction of its image in order to sustain these processes. The real-estate interests were mopping up public assets, forcing them to close down and sell up, while branding the city as a hive of underground culture and creativity; and it was always those same interests that constructed luxurious and inaccessible gated communities at the expense of the real needs of the inhabitants and the social fabric. We were faced with a city dotted with abandoned areas, most of them inaccessible because their owners preferred to let them increase in value on the financial markets, and with new de-luxe constructions or shopping malls that offered no compensation; on the contrary, they ate away at social services and public space.

It was for this reason that – with slogans like 'let's take back what is ours' and 'how sad is prudence' – we occupied some of the 700 theatres threatened with conversion into supermarkets and various other empty institutional spaces all over Italy. In the spring of 2012, we decided to occupy the biggest abandoned skyscraper in the centre of Milan, the Torre Galfa opposite the Stazione Centrale, launching the MACAO project. The proprietor of the building was Salvatore Ligresti, a figure symbolic of financial and property speculation and an insurance and banking system that had been in collusion with the Mafia throughout the second half of the twentieth century. Ligresti was a poster child of the smoke-filled rooms of Italy, a friend of Berlusconi, Mediobanca and Cuccia, protagonist of the city plan of the Socialist-run and corrupt Milan of the 1980s. In 2012, when we occupied his skyscraper, this empire was crumbling. Berlusconi had just lost the powers he wielded as prime minister, the great Fonsai-Ligresti insurance and real-estate system was in economic collapse and about to be taken over by the Unipol holding company, which represented the lobby of reference for the area of centre-left politics. At the same time, in 2011 Giuliano Pisapia won the municipal elections, becoming the first centre-left mayor of Milan after twenty years of rule by the right.

The reaction to the birth of MACAO, the new centre for the arts and research that we founded with the occupation of the skyscraper, was impressive. It was perhaps the only true equivalent of the Occupy movement in Italy, with thousands of people camping out around the skyscraper every day to rehash the social contract from its foundations.

The new left-wing politicians who were beginning to govern the city came out in support of MACAO in the skyscraper, along with the main Italian trade unions, and important jurists and constitutionalists in the area of reference of this Constituent Assembly of Common Assets headed by Stefano Rodotà. The basic idea lay in the assertion that there are several passages in the articles of the Italian constitution which declare it to be wholly legitimate for a political movement, with no economic interests, to occupy either public or private property in order to call for its return to a function of public utility.

This was a political point, and not particularly subversive with regard to the law and the state. On the contrary, it sought to bring the law of the state back on its constitutional track, in which the sovereignty of the people prevails over private interests.

This tradition of jurisprudence did not carry much weight, but it had a lot of credit among the country's institutions. It claimed that, since the 1980s, neoliberalism had succeeded in worming its way so deeply into the legislature that it had been able to overturn certain principles of the constitution. All things considered, the laws that govern a city and its development plan are not neutral. They have gradually been modified and distorted by the lobbying of economic interests that have controlled local legislators over the years. The result is that if a public administrator does not privatise and seeks to turn a profit from public assets it is an offence punishable by law, whereas it is considered perfectly normal if they do nothing to house the homeless. The law that shapes the city has been distorted to such a point that there are rights only for those who invest large amounts of capital, while there is no defence of those that have nothing, who on the contrary are criminalised.

In the face of this already accomplished dystopia, we decided to fight to change the laws. Without which everything would be in vain.

It was for this reason that we started in 2012 to propose the introduction of new municipal bylaws in both Naples and Milan. In Milan we worked with a commission made up of representatives of the city council, MACAO, ARCI, the trade unions, the Leoncavallo Self-Managed Public Space and other small associations and assisted by the Neapolitan activists of the Ex Asilo Filangieri. The idea was to draft a municipal framework resolution that would be valid in the whole of the metropolitan territory and define the possibility of demanding the direct management of a public or private asset by an informal assembly of citizens. This kind of bylaw was already in force for the management of small portions of land such as flowerbeds or public gardens, where neighbourhood committees wished to take direct charge. What was lacking was the right of a community of residents to ask to take over the management of whole buildings, preserving their collective civic use for non-exclusive purposes of public utility. In short, we wanted to make it legitimate for communities to redevelop buildings, not for private and exclusive use but maintaining an open assembly and a governance transparent to anyone who wished to participate.

We wanted to oppose the neoliberal drift towards the restriction of public space, proposing a new regulatory framework that would allow it to be governed through self-organisation and social cooperation between those who do not have the backing of large financial capital.

In Naples it was a great success thanks to the mayor at the time, De Magistris. In Milan it was a failure. Although the city council gave its backing to this approach and showed interest in it, it also made sure that the law never really came up for debate until the end of its mandate. When the new mayor, Giuseppe Sala, was elected, he declared that he was no longer interested in the matter. The council passed a law on pacts of cooperation that we regarded as very inadequate with respect to what we considered to be at stake: no transfer of governance, no inclusion of valuable assets or large buildings; in short, a much watered-down and far from revolutionary disposition.

So, what has happened since the centre-left started to govern the city in 2011? What have been the real changes on the urban planning level, and what has been the social impact of three terms and over ten years of progressive administration by the centre-left?
Not much, I would say.

Following the cultural surge of MACAO, Milan City Council started to favour the entrustment of abandoned public spaces for projects of investment in hybrid enterprises, in part commercial and in part with a social impact and the ability to provide services. Out of this came many projects of art and culture in what were once farmhouses, post-industrial spaces, swimming pools and former garages. Base, Mare Culturale Urbano, Santeria Social Club, Ostello Bello, Cinema Armenia, Cascina Cuccagna … and a multitude of smaller projects all over Milan. The city seemed to be undergoing a new renaissance. Even on the housing front the council laid claim to the direct management of part of the Aler building stock, and sought to facilitate investment by private banking foundations in the construction of new social housing and students' residences.

The line taken by the progressive democratic administrations on the centre-left that have followed one another from 2011 until the present day (2023) has I believe been in essence this: they wanted to make the city attractive in the eyes of major investors, and asked them in exchange to guarantee social justice. This kind of position has in fact been very well expressed by the figure who has led the city over the last two terms: Giuseppe Sala. A dynamic manager, able to speak the language of national and international business, but one who never misses an opportunity to declare his concern for the rights of the poorest, for the environment and for gender rights. The problem is that this recipe does not work. The politicians who claim to be able to attract private investors and get them to serve public and social interests always end up subjugating the public to the interests of the private.

The social movements have criticised this approach on many occasions: however much people may hope that it works, in reality neoliberal policies never lead to social equity. And the figures speak for themselves. If foreign investment rises in a city, the privatisation of public assets increases, but so do rents, while waiting lists for public housing grow longer, evictions continue at a relentless pace and average incomes fall. This means that the public administration is incapable of defending the interests of the public against plunder by the private. According to the latest report on the income of the residents of Milan, one person in four is living beneath the poverty line. Literally, this signifies that while almost everyone is pretending to be doing well so as not to be seen as losers, many of the city's inhabitants, while everything around them glitters, are unable to make ends meet.

The cultural organisations entrusted with public space by the municipality have over the years increasingly turned it into restaurants, pubs and premises rented out for conventions of the business-oriented lobby. The myth of doing business as much as is needed to provide cultural and social services does not hold water. The truth is that taking care of the renovation and maintenance of large buildings on the free market means obtaining bank loans of millions of euros with interest rates at 6% or 7%, and this determines the amortisation plans. To get a return on the investments made, no art centre, no community centre, no social housing or student residence is able to keep its prices low or be sustainable without charging commercial rents and commoditising its products.

For this reason, in the case of MACAO, we proposed in 2018 buying the building, constructing a co-ownership founded on communal shareholding. We wanted to show that it was people, and not banks, who were capable of delivering buildings from the process of privatisation, making them legally common assets, forever taken off the market. But the municipality would not agree to sell it because the offer, while in the millions, was not considered lucrative enough, and our capital was not sufficient. In addition, the municipal secretary refused to take the social impact into account. In short, if you want to lay hands on a building in a very expensive city, the only thing that matters is money. You have to be a large real-estate company or you can't be trusted. And that's written into administrative law, which of course protects those who do business, not those acting in defence of the weakest and for the benefit of all.

The story of MACAO made this contradiction very clear when compared with C40's Reinventing Cities programme. In 2020, the whole of the area formerly occupied by Milan's fruit and vegetable market, in which the MACAO building was located, was put out for tender under the C40 programme. This coordinates the privatisation of public space in a number of big cities at a global level, seeking out private consortia willing to propose projects of urban regeneration with a high environmental and social impact. All the consortia that submitted a tender tried to involve MACAO in their investment projects, and for this reason we were given access to the economic plans underpinning these investments. Our conditions for cooperation were a minimal level of investment in support of MACAO for the infrastructural regularisation of the building and the transfer to MACAO of management control in the long term, in order to be able to continue with an autonomous, accessible programme of public utility.

None of the consortia was able to meet these conditions. None of the projects was able to fund MACAO without inserting in the amortisation plans a fairly onerous commercial rent, or without asking to play a part in our governance, thereby acquiring the power to exercise control over the building's management. This led us to take a stand on the greenwashing that paints a great deal of contemporary business-oriented urban regeneration. The risk was that of reproducing a process of what we have dubbed green gentrification. The private sphere has jumped on the bandwagon of environmental sustainability, zero emissions, the short supply chain and the circular economy, but then produces services like student residences, gyms and schools only for wealthy whites. Cities are turned into enclosures with organic vegetable markets, high-tech buildings with a lot of glass and greenery, surrounded by tracks for joggers and charging points for electric vehicles, all of it tailored for upper middle-class whites, with only minimal sops to the poorest of the poor.

And this is the Milan that is entering the third decade of the new millennium: a renewed skyline, effervescent from the cultural viewpoint, polycentric with a multitude of small squares gentrified by places that cater to the young; but with unaffordable house prices, a majority of the inhabitants are compelled to take insecure and badly paid jobs, and very few social or public spaces have really escaped the blackmail of being used as commercial enterprises as well. While the public housing stock is being constantly eroded rather than expanded, notwithstanding the exponential increase in demand.

The left-wing governments of the city have demonstrated on many occasions that they are incapable of subordinating private interests to the public one. Indeed, every time they announce that they have attracted private investment in order to be able to put more funding into public services, the opposite has happened. Private enterprises have used the centre-left to take possession of public space and then impose their own conditions, worsening the situation from the perspective of social and environmental justice.

For all these motives, in the last few years we have laid down some guidelines on how to emerge from this vortex in which the same elements are continually mixed up: processes of privatisation, inflation, high rents and high bills, lack of environmentally sustainable structural interventions, such as free and energy-efficient public transport, commercialisation of cultural, educational and health services, fall in incomes against the background of a substantial increase in poorly paid and insecure jobs.

What are needed first of all are direct public interventions in the fields of housing, culture, education, health and income. These were the slogans raised in the streets during the pandemic in Milan and in particular during our occupation of the Teatro Piccolo in 2021.

We have to puncture the false dream that the private can bring in the money that the public does not have to put into welfare. And this is possible only if the public sphere manages a substantial portion of services through direct investment.

Secondly, we need to strengthen cooperative enterprise and grassroots associations and organisations based on the commons, loosening the grip of the fake support for the cooperative movement offered by the self-styled ethical finance lobby and the banking foundations. We have to make it clear that, when the social and environmental impact is that of major capital investment masked by benevolent and cooperative foundations, the result is nothing but green gentrification, greenwashing, social washing and pinkwashing.

In the third place, and following the example of referendum campaigns like the one conducted successfully in Berlin in favour of expropriations to control the cost of rents, we ought to be proposing legislative actions that will allow the public to exercise control over the dynamics of the private.

This is the key to everything: defence of and increased investment in the public welfare service, oversight (and not wooing) of the private sphere and support for a healthy and grassroots cooperative movement.

Fourthly, the city should stop seeing itself as a driving model, sucking in all the energy and economic resources of the region. Instead of concentrating ever more unsustainable and contradictory forces in its vortex, it should be triggering the reverse process by which resources are redistributed from the centre to the provinces and the surrounding areas.

Without taking these steps I do not think it possible to imagine another city, a city at last no longer neoliberal but ecosystem-based, on pain of implosion in its structural unsustainability.

. I am here to learn

Sophie Schaffer
Alexandra Torggler

The project explores a bleak future after a complete recontextualisation of the spatial and social fabric. How can the ruins of capitalism be used to create a potential that serves the common good and at the same time turns the architectural development into a beneficial change? The answer, in this case, relies on an all-knowing artificial intelligence that is capable of shaping not only a society but also a whole ecosystem. The relationship of humanity with nature has become both parasitic and symbiotic, and the arising conflicts in both ruins and dwelling spaces require an artificial and ever-learning entity that can act as a mediator.

'I am here to learn' is an imagination of ruins of shopping malls becoming spaces of harmonic coexistence, where people live alongside rats, fungi and vegetation, and where a romantic but virtual reality bleeds into a brutal system.

Project by Alexandra Torggler and Sophie Schaffer.
Design studio: *Post-Pandemic City* by Lorenza Baroncelli and Michael Obrist. Summer semester 2021 at TU Wien.

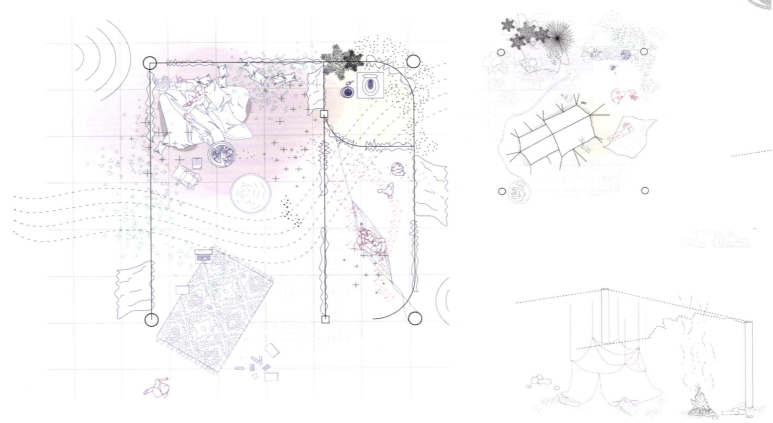

Flat 4: textile separation

Flat 1: tent shelter

Dead malls

Final image

The System 1. Mycelium, 2. Nervus cellula, 3. Fungus, 4. Daucus carota, 5. Homo sapiens, 6. Araneae,
7. Insecta, 8. Fallopia japonica, 9. Floris, 10. Rosa, 11. Microtus Arvalis, 12. Papaver rhoeas, 13. Odonata, 14. Technologia

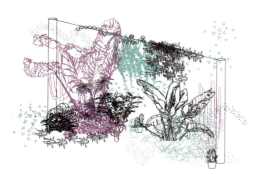

Flat 5: plant separation

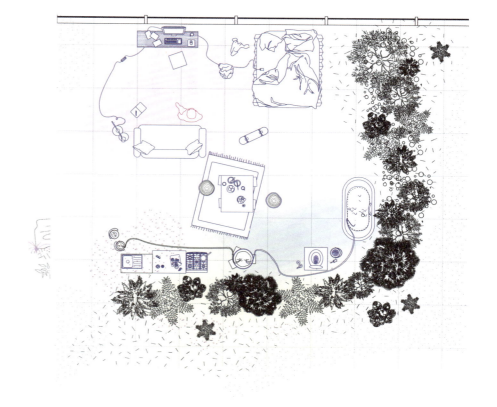

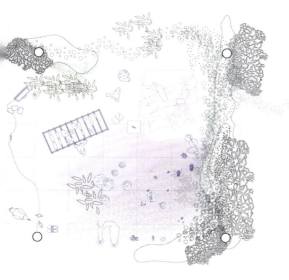

Flat 3: mycel wall

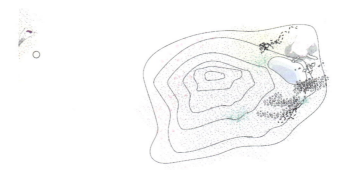

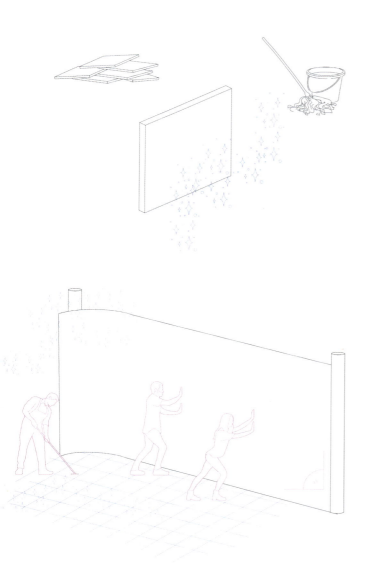

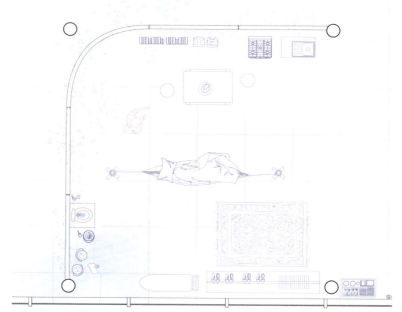

Flat 6: clean elements

Periphery

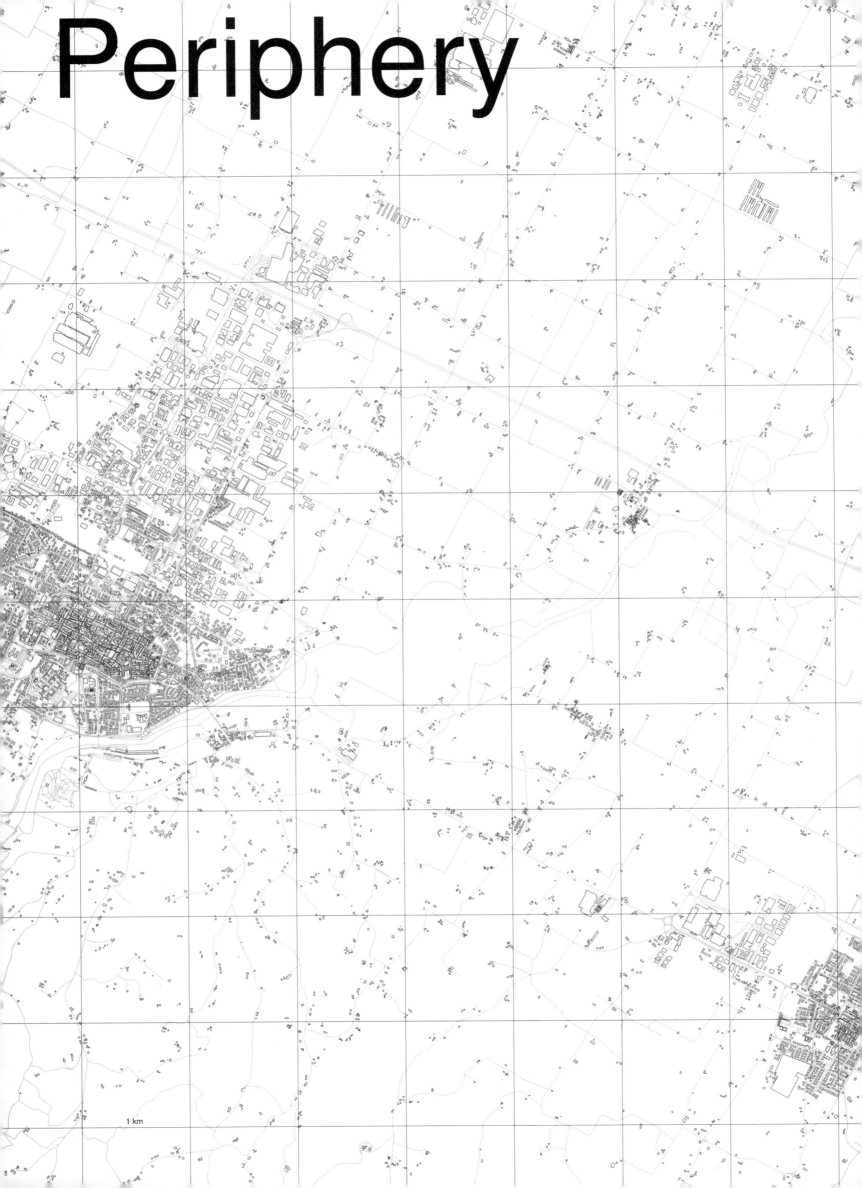

1 km

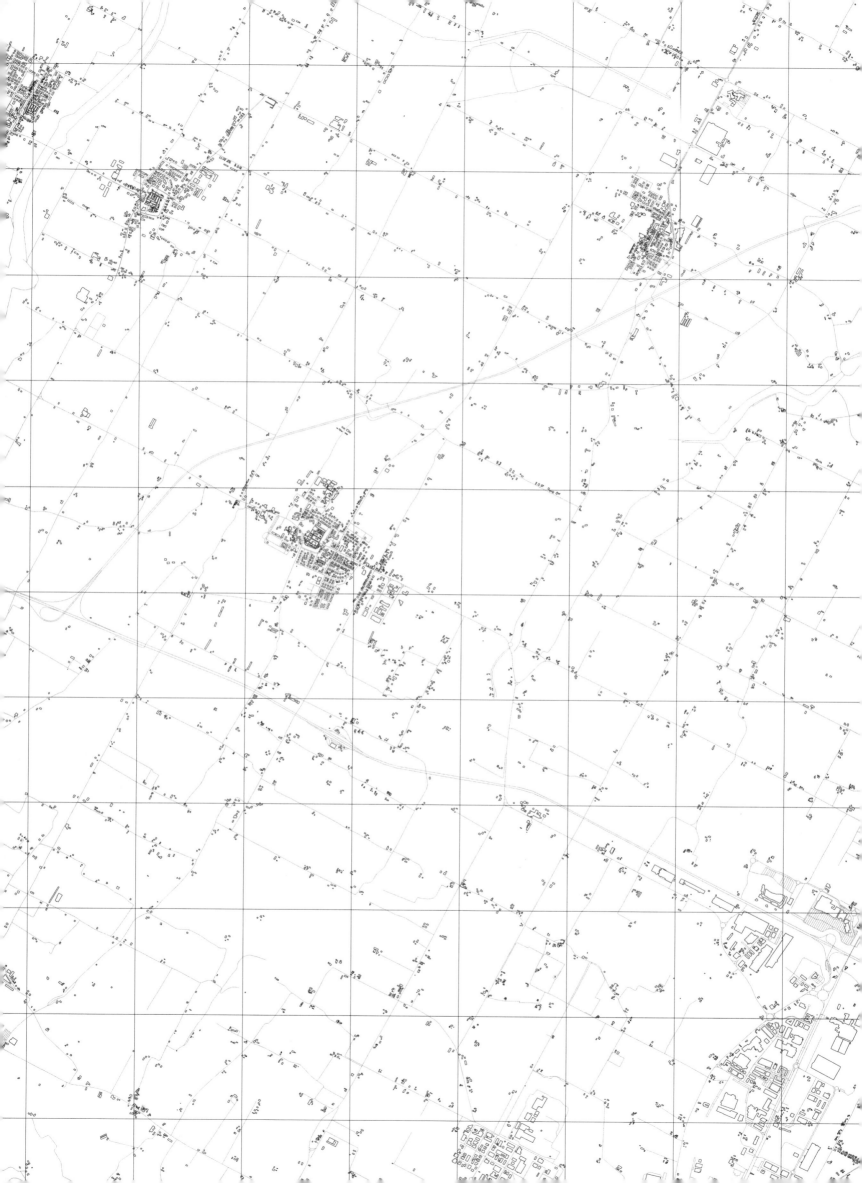

Michael Obrist in conversation with Paola Viganò
(architect, urbanist and full professor of urban design
at EPFL in Lausanne and IUAV in Venice)

Laboratories of the transition

Bicycle tour with students from IUAV; square in Maerne (VE), Italy, 2005. Credit: Armin Linke

OBRIST: What do you see as the weaknesses and strengths of the diffuse city in this time of the pandemic crisis, particularly in relation to the traditional city? What do you think can and should be strengthened now?

VIGANÒ: In Italy there's been a debate around how the pandemic has shown the advantages of diffuse cities – the benefits of private gardens, of being close to big open spaces, when people living in small apartments in traditional city centres felt trapped. For many this was an opportunity to reassess the idea of the diffuse city. But I didn't need the pandemic to think about its qualities. The diffuse city is a human settlement, it's part of our history. Rather than attempting a moral judgement, we should see it as a specific culture or way of using space. Historically, for many poor and marginal regions it was a means of emancipation, a chance to develop without having to wait for major investment from the state. More recently, with climate change and the lessons of the pandemic, both its good and its bad aspects have become more apparent.

During the pandemic some 50% of Switzerland's population worked from home. This is a massive shift, a prompt to rethink the possibilities of some of the more remote areas. But we also need to bear in mind that the diffuse city is very much a product of the age of non-renewable energy. At the moment the cost of the new 'pandemic lifestyle', in terms of energy consumption, massively working from home, is just not clear. According to some calculations, it's even higher than pre-Covid, when people were regularly taking flights and so on.

Given the continuing existence of both the compact city and the diffuse city, I think we need to try to valorise their distinctive qualities, resolve the problems that are particular to each of them. People living in compact cities found the lockdowns very hard – they became acutely aware of the fragmented nature of public space and the lack of connection with the landscape. Up to then, I think we'd really underestimated our need for the outdoors. Very often cities are not adapted to that need, which goes beyond the question of fresh air, of cycling somewhere rather than using the car. It's really a deep-rooted physical and psychological need. We need to put our feet on the ground to understand our place in life.

The philosopher André Gorz made a clear distinction between scientific ecology and political ecology. Scientific ecology pretends you can solve all the problems – *if* you have strong authorities to impose rules on citizens. Political ecology is based on a different ethics: it attempts to establish a new relation between the individual and society, between people and nature. How do we live in this territory that we consider as a subject and not only as an object to be exploited? The way we perceive the landscape changed drastically during the pandemic. We're now in a time to rethink the biopolitical dimension of space; the ecological and socioeconomic transition might require a new biopolitical project.

OBRIST: I think the interesting thing about the city is the way its complexities overlap with the development of individual lives. How can we create the same kind of life-defining complexity within the system of the diffuse city, which has traditionally been based on mobility?

VIGANÒ: But that raises a question about the sense of urbanity in the contemporary city. Imagine that 50% of the inhabitants of Milan now work from home. What happens to the life of the city if the people who use it evaporate? Today, a large part of the urban experience is based solely on consumption. It's a fact, and it calls for a radical reconsideration. I don't know exactly what people are thinking – maybe some are simply hoping that everything will soon go back to 'normal' – but I have the impression there's a lot of questioning going on. I suppose this 'political ecology' new awareness will have durable consequences.

OBRIST: Let's talk about the opposition of the two models of the city. Do you see digitalisation as a threat to the power of the diffuse city?

VIGANÒ: I don't think so. On the contrary, digitalisation can be an opportunity to redress some of the weaknesses of the diffuse city. But that depends on our approach: do we treat it on a par with the compact city, or do we see it as a mistake? There's the radical view that says we should demolish everything built in this way. That's not my position. For me, the diffuse city is the product of an immense collective effort in terms of infrastructure and embodied energy, and I think we need to respect that. It's also interesting to have different possibilities for inhabiting a territory. The digital economy has a lot of potential to regenerate this kind of city, and to some extent this regeneration is already happening. Renewable energy systems are being installed, houses are being insulated, people are trying out new types of mobility, new kinds of organisational services. There's a lot of ongoing investment in the city, although many cities in Europe have reached the limits of their urban expansion and we're now reworking an existing urban space.

OBRIST: But as you said, more profound change will require a rethinking of the city's political-economic structure. How would you go about this?

VIGANÒ: As architects, I think we can contribute at the level of the imaginary: we can work to change the image people have of the city and its future transformations. It's very important to establish a dialogue, to take people with you at a time of profound change. There is a fundamental cultural and anthropological dimension in the transition. We also need to stay open to different viewpoints, rather than following a single line of thought. Interestingly, it's easier to open a dialogue when you're talking about very concrete changes – for example, about the length and width of a cycle route. Ideological differences can be set aside when it's a simple question of: 'Do you want a bike lane that stops after 500 m or do you want to cycle for 40 km?' Perhaps I'm naive, but I think our drawings and our words have a certain power to connect with the public.

And, on the other hand, as architects we also have strong connections with those who are changing the city in concrete ways – the powerful people working in city administrations, who are responsible for traffic planning, water management, greening, commerce … They very rarely work together, even if that would seem to be the most obvious basis for making reasonable decisions. So I see it as our responsibility to participate in this debate, even if it can be exhausting. And then, as architects, we also have the capacity to produce projects that are innovative not only spatially but on many different levels – socially, ecologically, economically. But I'd be interested to know more from you about the situation in Vienna. How are these ecological transitions viewed?

OBRIST It's a political question. Unlike Milan, say, where the city resonates with the Lombardy region, here the boundaries of the city and the region are the same. So everything has to be planned, resolved, within a rather small territory. On the plus side, the governing coalition between the left-wing SPÖ and the Greens [which ended in November 2020] put us in a stronger position than most in relation to ecological issues. The situation is helped further by the huge amount of housing production that is controlled (or even owned) by the city itself. In Vienna 'social housing' can be seen more as a kind of 'societal housing'. It's built for a broad range of society, not just the poorer segments, but also the middle classes, as part of a larger sociopolitical strategy for emancipating citizens. Within this system the city puts social and ecological sustainability at the top of the agenda, alongside economic and architectural questions.

VIGANÒ In the past decades, especially in Europe, there was no real thinking about decentralisation and the idea that you could have the same rights as a citizen regardless of where you lived. From a certain moment in the 1980s the focus was instead on the concentration and reinforcement of the biggest cities, with the result that we now have vast swathes of marginal territories that have been hollowed out economically – more than half of Germany, the whole of the Apennines, as well as the south of Italy and huge parts of England and Scotland. We have to get rid of this strange idea that everything has to be in one dense place. It was never the case in the past, but is a fairly recent idea connected to a certain political and financial project that has now clearly shown its limits.

In my recent research on the Horizontal Metropolis, which is reflected in three different publications, I've considered the phenomenon of extended urbanisation, proposing a vision to foster horizontal relations among territories, stressing and designing horizontal links. Horizontality means that you can live in different parts of a territory and have the same rights – that you don't have to move to a big city because it's the only place you can find work. There's a question of balance connected to the question of decentralisation, specifically the hierarchy of power relations. From many different points of views – transport, distribution of services, of employment – territories could be organised less hierarchically. We have a long tradition of thinking about alternative ways of organising cities and territories. I'm currently working with Martina Barcelloni on an anthology that shows the continuity of this tradition almost up to the present day. More recently, however, this discourse has been neglected. We thought we needed more top-down government to solve our problems. But when you're creating bigger hospitals, schools and services, and at the same time closing smaller structures and railway lines, it's clear you're creating marginal areas. This could be countered with a horizontal project that also addresses the difficult questions of climate change and the ecological crisis.

OBRIST How can digitalisation and its tools contribute to these horizontal connections across the diffuse territory? What happens when work and the university come into our homes? We have students who decided for economic reasons not even to come to Vienna during the pandemic – as well as Erasmus scholars who are having a very strange, isolated moment in their lives, with zero contact with other students. Every innovation creates its own beauty and its own possibilities, but also its own difficulties and unintended consequences. I'm thinking about the element of surprise, the potential for unplanned encounters, that are a fundamental part of the experience of the city.

What do you think are the ingredients that are important right now? What is the potential of the different technologies that we're developing?

VIGANÒ It's a difficult question. During lockdown I would ask students how they felt. Many had psychological issues, but one student said he was very well, indeed he'd never felt so free. The difference was that he was following the course from a small house in the mountains. This example shows there are potentially huge benefits to be gained if we can find the right balance between working remotely and being together with others. The conventional workplace can seem rigid, confining. Maintaining the kind of flexibility we've enjoyed recently would be very beneficial for everyone.

The technologies are difficult to gauge. We don't know exactly how they'll play out. But what I do know is that many of the problems of the diffuse city relate to its infrastructure. Before we can speak of energy consumption, there's a huge amount of infrastructure that we need to rethink. We could stop selling gas boilers today, but this technological shift needs to go hand in hand with an infrastructural transformation if we want to avoid creating systems that ultimately negate our environmental goals. In any case, I think we have to accept that the diffuse city is ageing and define a collective position towards it. Do we want to maintain these areas? If we do go in that direction, it will call for a close reading of their conditions and their rationale – their problems as well as their positive contribution towards the quality of life.

This interview was originally published in Paola Viganò and Michael Obrist, 'Laboratories of transition', *ARCHDIPLOMA 2021: A Repository of Ideas. Regenerate a Territory* (Sonderzahl Verlag, 2021), 9–17.

The spaceships of the Po Valley: The rise and fall of northern Italy's suburbia and of its architectural masterpieces

Alessandro Benetti
Martina Motta

Villa Clerici under construction, 1966. Credit: Studio Carlo Moretti

1. The event was briefly covered by the local press, mostly online. See for instance: Chiara Lazzati, 'Villa Clerici lascia il posto alle patatine fritte', *Legnano News*, published online on 3 August 2016. Link: shorturl.at/cfmtx (accessed 8 December 2022).

2. As of December 2022, the building is still standing. On the project for the detached houses in Cusago (1972–74), see some general titles on Renzo Piano's work, such as Fulvio Irace, ed., *Renzo Piano. Le città visibili* (Milan: Mondadori Electa, 2007). See also the buildings' presentation on the website of *Lombardia Beni Culturali. Architettura in Lombardia dal 1945 a oggi*, a survey of the region's relevant architectures from the last eight decades. Link: shorturl.at/cmnAS (accessed 8 December 2022).

3. To promote the practice of 'south working', companies are implementing specific services and maps about the *presidi di comunità* (which loosely translates into 'community centres'). In this regard, see: https://www.southworking.org/

4. Paolo Scrivano, 'Signs of Americanization in Italian Domestic Life: Italy's Postwar Conversion to Consumerism', *Journal of Contemporary History* 40(2) (2005), 323–4.

5. *Ville moderne in pianura* (Milan: Gorlich editore, 1968), 4. The book is a review of several dozen villas from well-known and lesser-known architects, most of which are located in the suburban areas of the Po Valley.

6. For a general introduction on these topics, see for instance: Luciano Patetta, *Scritti sull'architettura del Rinascimento* (Milan: Maggioli Editore, 2008); and David Watkin, *Morality and Architecture: The Development of a Theme in Architectural History and Theory from the Gothic Revival to the Modern Movement* (Chicago: University of Chicago Press, 1984).

Driving a Lancia, living in a 'Renzo Piano': the broken dreams of northern Italy's suburbia

Villa Clerici, an elaborate architectural *folie* from the late Sixties, and a masterpiece by local architect Carlo Moretti, once stood proudly along the highway leading from Legnano to Milan, the regional capital. It then lay abandoned for more than four decades, deserted by the heirs of its first inhabitants. It cut an obscure, ever more derelict presence in the twilight landscape, sharply contrasting with the glittering lights of the nearby mall, multiplex and the hectic traffic on the surrounding flyovers. When it was eventually demolished in 2016 and replaced by the dull shed of a Burger King fast-food restaurant, the event passed in silence, just a few local connoisseurs regretting the loss.[1] At about the same time, in Cusago, also in the outskirts of Milan, a huge public outcry greeted the controversial decision – not yet implemented at time of writing – to pull down one of the surviving detached houses designed in the Seventies by world-famous architect Renzo Piano, to make space for some generic residential development.[2] Moretti's villa and Piano's house are anything but isolated cases. All around the Po Valley a sizeable heritage of modernist and late-modernist single-family houses is in danger. The once triumphant homes of a rampant, wealthy, cultivated middle-class of professionals and entrepreneurs – the type that would drive a Lancia and live in a 'Renzo Piano' – seem to have fallen from favour once and for all. Clumsily altered and renovated, or in most cases neglected, abandoned and eventually destroyed, their doomed fate testifies to the profound socioeconomic and cultural transformations of northern Italy's suburbia.

This short text provides, in the first instance, a few key elements on the history of their rise and fall between the 1950s and the 1980s, framing it in a broader context. Links are established with the large-scale urban transformations of those decades, with the centuries-long history of the typology of the villa, and with the evolutions of the national architectural and domestic culture. Second, and more importantly, the aim of this text is to point out what are today the potential threats to this heritage, in order to raise awareness and hopefully contribute to its preservation. What is the future, if any, for these forgotten spaceships of the Po Valley?

The Yankees and the Romans: the suburban villa at the crossroads of spatial and cultural models of different origin

Sales in the first of seven Levittown settlements in the United States started in 1947. These neighbourhoods were the brainchild of entrepreneur William J. Levitt, who claimed that he was providing families with an essential component of the American Dream, the 'home sweet home', just as General Motors provided them with cars. Indeed, a car-based comparison may help cast light on a crucial difference, in terms of their architectures, between the US hyper-standardised residential suburbias and their Italian counterpart, which started developing more intensely from the mid-1950s. While the Italian middle-classes preferred the sporty Alfa Romeo and luxurious Lancia to the copy-pasted Chevy, Pontiac and Oldsmobile, so too they yearned for a house of the same exclusiveness and originality. Hence, contrary to what happened in Levittown, the new part of the city which was being born in northern Italy 'expressed an assortment of individual desires more than new physical configurations, a sort of large urban continuum made unit by unit […] produced by the crowd of individual actions, and the frantic search for distinctiveness'.[3] These are the reflections by the authors of *X Milan* about the city's metropolitan area, but they can easily apply to many areas of the Po Valley. As a result, all of the buildings tried to be unique, and the villas were no exception to this. This and other factors resulted in major conceptual and economic investment in their design. An increasing privatisation of the country's society, for instance, added to the traditional Catholic-inspired and familistic approach in prioritising the domestic space, considered as the household's nest, over all other shared spaces. As Paolo Scrivano writes on the symbolic value that domesticity acquired in the immediate postwar years, 'in an effort to confront fascism's populist myth of the masses, citizenship was symbolically redefined in terms of domesticity, in a way that signalled a shift in social life from public to private. In this context, kitchens or living rooms increasingly took over from courtyards, streets or *piazze*'.[4]

At the crossroads of these phenomena, starting from the 1950s, the suburban villa comes under the spotlight as a much-coveted type of residence. Many of the features that ensure its success are inspired by its namesake archetype from Roman times. In fact, since ancient times, the villa has been interpreted as an emanation of the city itself, an effective stress management device capable of balancing its vices and excesses. In the suburbs of the second half of the twentieth century, the villa is conceived as a 'satellite', too: it is at the villa that its inhabitants can experiment freely with their interpretation of the modern way of living, based on a well-balanced mix of the traditional dichotomy of *otium* versus *negotium* (leisure versus business). *Ville moderne in pianura*, a manual from 1968, describes the state-of-the-art villa as 'comfortable and rational, close enough to the city centre, where its owner runs his business, but yet quite rural as to allow a complete isolation from what the city entails in terms of traffic, noise, pollution, etcetera'.[5] The fence of each modernist villa encloses not only the actual building but also a complementary natural element for the family's private use. This landscape *in vitro* balances the loss of an authentic relationship to the rural surroundings, which Roman and Palladian villas could claim. It furthermore cuts off all links to the outside world, allowing the villa to function as a totally secluded island of peace and commodity. Thanks to their illusory isolation, throughout history villas have often been regarded as a blank canvas to experiment with original architectural languages, which rejected the predominant style of the cities of their time. This was carried out by either trying to reproduce styles from the past or creating one *ex novo*: the *ville* of antiquity informed the shape of their heirs during the Renaissance, while British architects of the seventeenth century were highly fond of the Palladian style.[6] In continuity with this tradition, the villas of the Po Valley from the 1950s and 1960s often provided a privileged space for modern and late-modern architectural experimentation.

From villa to *villetta*: the 1970s suburban craze and the triumph of quantity over quality

The long-gone Villa Clerici in Legnano, completed in 1969, was in many regards archetypal of this experimental attitude. Its author, Carlo Moretti (Milan, 1931)[7] had already designed other remarkable villas in the same area, including one in Gallarate. Featured in *Domus* in March 1960, it stood out for its horizontality, for the use of exposed concrete and for its almost entirely glazed facades. On that occasion, the editors would comment on it insisting on the seamless visual continuity between inside and outside, home and landscape: 'The house is an incessant sequence of transparencies and perspectives, an invitation to pace it (on an even plan,

The inauguration of Villa Clerici, 1969. Credit: Studio Carlo Moretti

7 As of December 2022, Moretti still leads his own firm, based in Cassano Magnano, between Milan and Varese. In the 1960s and the 1970s, his work was featured in such magazines as *Domus* and *L'Architettura Cronache e Storia*. In more recent years, he has authored a few books and articles on his proposals for utopian architectures and cities. See for instance: Carlo Moretti, *Verso la città che non c'è* (Milan: L'Archivolto, 2007). For a more recent analysis of his work, see Alessandro Benetti, 'Memorabile, eppure dimenticato. Carlo Moretti, professionista visionario', Domusweb, published online on 10 February 2020. Link: https://www.domusweb.it/it/architettura/2020/01/23/memorabile-eppure-dimenticato-carlo-moretti-professionista-visionario.html (accessed 8 December 2022).

8 'Una casa "dentro" la collina', *Domus*, no. 436 (March 1960), 7.

9 The clients and owners of the villa, a doctor and an entrepreneur, were prominent figures of the local bourgeoisie and would host frequent and crowded parties, as reported to the authors by several local sources.

uphill or downhill), a concatenation of glazed spaces, either opening towards the outside or enclosed, where "outside" and "inside" merge and blur within each other.'[8] Nevertheless, nowhere did Moretti prove his genius more than in Legnano's Villa Clerici, ground-breaking in its technical, spatial and formal plans. An elevated rectangular platform rested uniquely on four angular pillars, shaped as pyramids. This unprecedented, bold structural solution, taking the potential of pre-stressed reinforced concrete to the limit, required original calculations and countless on-site adaptations. The unobstructed ground-floor space was crossed by a single-ramp staircase leading up to the house's main entrance, and conceived initially as a drawbridge. A service stair, circular and wrapped in a transparent envelope, gave access to the underground garage. The actual house stood over the platform, the different rooms corresponding to as many volumes of elementary geometrical shapes. The centre of the domestic life was the open-air stepped *teatrino* ('little theatre'), which most rooms overlooked, and where frequent parties and spectacles were organised during the summer.[9] In his own words, Moretti had designed a house that would 'float above the fog',[10] which was still very common in the region at the time. Critics and architectural magazines did not grant Villa Clerici the recognition that it deserved for its originality and charm. Furthermore, the untimely death of one of the owners led to its abandonment just a few years after its completion.

It is cited here as a case in point of an outstanding design for a single-family house in northern Italy's suburbia of those years. First-tier Milanese-based architects and lesser-known practitioners from all around the province worked alongside enlightened clients, mostly progressive self-made men who contributed in their different capacities to the region's economic boom, to deliver countless innovative house projects. Such acknowledged masters as Franco Albini, Gianni Avon, Luigi Caccia Dominioni, Ignazio Gardella and Vico Magistretti were often engaged in this process. In fact, while the season of the *professionismo colto*[11] of northern Italy and particularly of Milan has mostly been identified up to present with the typology of the city apartment block, a parallel history has still to be written which focuses on the suburban villa. For the dissemination of villas in a larger territory, this would possibly include in the main narratives on the *professionismo* – revolving around the remarkably high average quality of ordinary architecture of the time – the trajectories of practitioners working in more peripheral contexts, too.

The golden age of the suburban villa was bound not to last. Starting from the early Seventies, as migration flows from the city to its suburbs increased steadily, the need for a mass production of single-family houses emerged. By that time, the tragic upheavals of Italy's late-twentieth-century history were redefining the ambitions and fears of suburbia, with the troublesome age of terrorism and protest taking over the naive optimism of the postwar years and several economic crises systematically challenging the very survival of its middle-class inhabitants. Architects and most often *geometri*[12] frequently gave up quality and exclusiveness in favour of quantity and repetition: the so-called *villetta* was born, accompanied by an update of its owners' lifestyle. In the words of Luigi Trentin, 'the cult of the *villetta* included the search for an isolated enclave, private property at all costs, dramatic reduction of adjacent spaces and full exploitation of all available lots outside the city centres. The exploding real estate industry and its strict rules were leading the process.'[13] A juxtaposition between the city and the suburban house was still longed for but no longer possible in practical terms: the spreading of the *villette*, and the general densification of northern Italy's suburbia, marked the

Carlo Moretti, study models for
Villa Clerici, Legnano, 1965.
Credit: Studio Carlo Moretti

10 The authors first met Moretti in 2008, on the occasion of a workshop held at the Faculty of Architecture at the Politecnico di Milano, Bovisa. A first interview took place at Moretti's office in January 2008, and was conducted by Giulia Celentano, Margherita Locatelli and Simone Zanni.

11 The term *professionismo colto*, which loosely translates as 'cultivated practice', defines in the first place the approach of a group of Milanese architects active in the 1950s and 1960s, of bourgeois origins and primarily working for a bourgeois clientele. They associated a pragmatic, commission-based attitude to a remarkable level of experimentation and refinement. For general information on this topic, see for instance the studies by Maria Vittoria Capitanucci, such as: *Il professionismo colto nel dopoguerra* (Milan: Solferino Edizioni, 2015).

12 The word loosely translates as 'surveyor'. Unlike in other countries, the Italian surveyor, or *geometra*, is able to design buildings on a modest scale, and of often equally modest quality, without the aid of an architect.

13 Luigi Trentin, 'Abitare in villa, lavorare in città: due architetture di Luciano Brunella', in Bruno Bosetti, Angelo Del Corso and Luigi Trentin, eds., *Una stagione breve. Le architetture di Luciano Brunella* (Varese: Ordine degli Architetti di Varese, 2012), 37.

14 Rem Koolhaas, *The Generic City* (New York: Monacelli Press, 1995).

15 The first local case of Covid-19 was identified in Italy near Lodi, at the core of the Po Valley, on 20 February 2020. The state of emergency had been declared already on 31 January, but it was enforced with stricter rules about self-isolation starting from 8 March.

16 Francesco D'Abbraccio, Andrea Facchetti, Emanuele Galesi and Filippo Minelli, *Atlante dei Classici Padani*. (Brescia: Krisis Publishing, 2015).

17 Ibid.

end of any idyllic dream. This evolution was not only about sizes: as everybody was rushing to build as much as they could, the polished architectural language of modernism was rapidly taken over by lavish and extravagant postmodern fantasies. Rem Koolhaas, in his famous essay from 1995 on *The Generic City*, goes straight to the point by claiming that the style of choice of suburbia is postmodern and will always remain so,[14] which is also true in the case of the Po Valley nowadays. Each chapter of this short architectural story resulted in rapid obsolescence, and frequent abandonment, of the previous one's main characters.

By the early Seventies, the modernist *ville*, outdated both in style and dimensions, were swiftly ousted by the jaunty *villette*, which also rapidly aged. With their sadly vintage allure, they still stand today as a reminiscence of the excessively standardised mode of living which they embodied.

Construction sites and ghosts:
the possible futures of the spaceships
of the Po Valley

Until the declaration of the state of the pandemic emergency in March 2020, and the subsequent imperative for everyone to barricade themselves in their homes,[15] one could go as far as to claim that northern Italy's suburbia laid largely 'unfinished, abandoned, mummified'.[16] In the words of artist Filippo Minelli from the years 2010, 'the archaeology of the macropolis' was 'a guided tour through business failures, surrounded by the ruins of the present and by entire rows of decaying urban corpses, into a morbid set up which addresses its viewers by yelling at them: "Remember: you're already dead!"'[17] As evocative and somehow sublime as this portrait can be, it nonetheless ends up betraying a reality of things which has significantly evolved in other directions ever since. Padania was and is not Detroit; it is transforming but it's far from shrinking. We can safely assess today that, during the pandemic, the house proved to be a crucial space for a critical reflection on extractive capitalism and its markets. As post-apocalyptic urban landscapes were emerging, interiors were packed with people that *had to* keep agonising architectures alive: the intercoms and bells rung by Amazon delivery people, the forced joyful gatherings on balconies and terraces, those who were experimenting with new recipes in the kitchen and the leveraged workers, staring twenty-four hours a day into their computer screens. This was true also for the Po Valley, and might have significantly contributed to averting any Detroit-like scenario.

Over the years following the strictest lockdowns and until today, housing has been at the epicentre of different phenomena, which are redefining once again the identity of the Po Valley's landscape. While the pandemic brought 'back to the fold' both students and workers, fleeing large cities and their skyrocketing rents, the post-pandemic period registered the permanent resettlement of many people, leaving the metropolis to get a home elsewhere that would be roomier, with a garden or a view, possibly of a bunch of trees. Some took advantage of this historic turn to reinhabit villages or to head back to warmer southern provinces. Several EU-sponsored 'green' incentives, such as the 110% Ecobonus and Sismabonus to be requested for buildings in need of improving their energy performances, combined with advantages for the purchase of low-emission cars, as well as with investment on digital infrastructures such as mobile networks, to give suburbia a so-called sizzling vibe. The suburban house is back on track as a retreat, this time from an external world that is losing steam: hostile in terms of climate, prohibitively expensive, insanely work-oriented. For all these reasons, while until

very recently a process of rapid consumption of the Po Valley's built stock of single-family houses took place under everyone's eyes, things might have taken quite a different turn. A new focus of debate has arisen, and a fundamental question to answer: which role could the suburban villa, *villetta*, or even *rifugio*, play in the near future?

This is a tough topic to approach, though. In addition to being scattered across a vast territory, this heritage is extremely composite and multifaceted, often subject to biases and misconceptions, which makes it even more difficult to assess its overall value. Moreover, the reflection at the architectural scale of the single-family house can by no means be disconnected from the landscape it has colonised and produced. On a morphological level, the reading of maps and navigation on Google Street View clearly show that large parts of the territory have been fenced off to serve as secluded open-air playgrounds for private homes, increasingly watched over by the latest models of security cameras. Still, the landscape produced by this spontaneous accumulation of architectural objects has paradoxically taken on a collective value, as the most relevant representation of half a century of social, economic and cultural development – and decline. Thus, the importance of this huge number of isolated buildings is not diminished but rather amplified by referring to its larger context.

Architects and urban designers are faced with a tantalising challenge. Whether they read this heritage as the remnants of a former Virgilian paradise, now exploded into countless hidden oases, as an embryonic city than was never actually born – or that might be on the verge of being reborn – or else they recognise this hybrid condition as its main potential, tailor-made strategies are required. These should prevent both its total disappearance and the threat of its selective museification, mimicking the current condition of many so-called historic centres in the Western world. A new practice of event-based consumption is establishing itself, amongst other things, giving the opportunity for private visitors to pay for and enjoy a specific villa for a limited amount of time. A contemporary, anti-ideological approach is desirable, one which gives up the traditional qualitative distinctions between high and low architecture and deals more with a global vision of suburbia as a cultural document. A collective, glowing, boisterous construction activity is enlivening the suburban stillness with bonuses, opportunities, speculations of the day. On the other hand are the former bourgeoisie's oversized, obsolete, often ostentatious dream vessels that fade into the spring mists, which protect them as precious evidence of a long-gone past. These UFOs of enigmatic beauty are the spaceships of the Po Valley.

This work was originally published in Alessandro Benetti and Martina Motta, 'The Forgotten Spaceships of the Po Valley: The Rise and Fall of Northern Italy's Suburbia from the Perspective of a Modernist Masterpiece', *Failed Architecture* (2016).

Villa Clerici, 2014. Credit: Alessandro Benetti

Villeggiatura: The contemporary retreat

Isabel Köhler

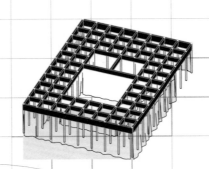

The villa in European history is really an invention of the antique world. Wealthy urban citizens of Rome discovered the countryside as a place of muse, 'honest' work, culture, education, the *otium* (leisure) opposed to the *negotium* (roughly translated as 'business').

The villa (sub)urbana came into being. Only a few original villas are preserved, but they remain today in literary traditions.

In the Renaissance, an era that cited antiquity, the villa experienced a new surge in popularity – now conceived in the spirit of Renaissance principles. The villa is less a building than an idea, a form, a medium. The villa is not subject to the influences of evolving societies and technologies – in fact, the opposite is true: evolving societies and technologies are virtually subjects of the villa.

Throughout history, the villa has expressed human thoughts, abilities, fantasies and ideas. The villa is a place of universal human needs and a manifestation of an imaginary life of human beings. The rural area oscillates in our perceptions from a space that one leaves due to its 'crampedness', or the limited professional possibilities it offers, to a space of longing in which a different, nature-related life can take place. The truth is not just in the middle, but in a superposition of complexities and realities. With the push of digitisation and changes in production, mobility and living conditions, new opportunities are currently emerging for rural areas.

In this project, the idea of the villa is broken down into its components. These components are the constant basic framework of the villa, its principles, the pillars on which it stands.

Their contents, on the other hand, are variable and contemporary. It is a dissection of an ideal and the consideration of possible individual parts. Spaces or functions are more rigid than actions and are already a resulting conclusion. Thus, at the beginning of Villeggiatura, there are first actions of a digital–analogue reality that lead to possible spaces or places.

The project is composed as a series of digital and analogue interventions in a Cartesian space, forming a collection of scenes that are 'performed' in the form of a fictional story. A fictional and relational landscape emerges, one that contemplates the contemporary phenomena of a digital–analogue intertwined reality.

Project by Isabel Caroline Köhler.
Design studio: *The Analogue and the Digital: 'Country Life' Revisited* by Michael Obrist and Ole Schilling.
Summer semester 2021 at TU Wien.

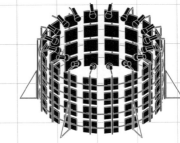

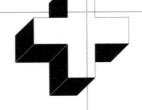

Housestories: #casasperimentale

Casa Sperimentale in Fregene, by Guiseppe Perugini, Uga de Plaissaint and Raynaldo de Perugini, 1968–75. Credit: Philipp Stauss

Sabaudia

Lotte Schreiber

Text by Alexandra Seibel

At the beginning of the 1930s, Benito Mussolini drained the Pontine Marshes, or Agro Pontino, south of Rome. The Fascists accomplished what generations since antiquity had failed to achieve, and their land reclamation enabled the founding of five cities, including Sabaudia. Sabaudia was conceived as a model city intended to showcase Italy's Rational architecture, and it ultimately solidified architectonically into a Fascist utopia caught between classicism and modernism. Over the years, even leftist intellectuals like Pier Paolo Pasolini grew to admire Mussolini's propagandistic structures, suggesting that this Fascist architecture did not violate Italy's pristine landscape and people. Lotte Schreiber cites statements by Pasolini, who regularly summered at a beach house with a view of Sabaudia: 'There is nothing Fascist to be found in Sabaudia, aside from a few facades.'

The filmmaker repeatedly tests the veracity of this statement as she observantly captures the faces of various Sabaudia residents looking directly into her camera, filmically resembling still photographs. Schreiber charismatically visualises a force-field outlined by Mussolini's authoritarian architectural visions, Pasolini's attempted reconciliation from the perspective of a mythic Marxist folk culture of resistance, and Sabaudia's current incarnation as a historically blind tourist magnet.

From the start, Homer's lament, 'Where goest thou, unhappy man?' accompanies the historically charged black-and-white shots of a seemingly near-mystical marsh landscape. Its complete demystification as achieved by the Fascists is conveyed by subsequent forest shots in colour. In a concise exchange between black-and-white images underscored by audio recordings of a speech by Mussolini, and colour shots of contemporary urban life in Sabaudia with its inhospitable architecture, Schreiber creates a formally beautiful and historically powerful portrait of a landscape and a city.

Sabaudia. Credit: sixpackfilm/Lotte Schreiber

Original title: *Sabaudia*
Director: Lotte Schreiber
Year: 2018
Country: Austria
Duration: 24 min

Periphery and freedom

Lorenza Baroncelli

In 1996, Marc Augé spoke for the first time about non-places. They are many and diverse. Motorways, road junctions, airports, means of transport, shopping centres, refugee camps, waiting rooms, lifts. Spaces where millions of people collide with each other without communication, driven by the frenetic desire to consume and speed up their daily lives. Spaces that have built our suburbs as opposed to the historic city.

And so we grew up, scattered all over the world, in working-class neighbourhoods made up of reinforced concrete buildings, prefabricated schools, car parks that became meeting points for us as youth with nothing to do. In neighbourhoods where retail gradually disappeared and social control was replaced by gates and cameras. When in 2000 the news showed us the clashes in the French banlieues, who among us did not think that those neighbourhoods resembled our own?

As some would say: 'It's the same the world over' (*tutto il mondo è paese*).

I lived in Roma 70, in the southeastern suburbs of Rome. A neighbourhood planned in the 1970s but only built in the late 1980s, due to corruption and bribes. I remember as if it were only yesterday when they embedded glass spikes in the walls of the car park to prevent 'drug dealers' from meeting in front of our building. Or when we started to be allowed to take the bus, on Saturday afternoons, how we met up to go to McDonald's in the nearest neighbourhood to spend our free time. Supermodernity (as Augé calls it) versus history. Control versus freedom. Conformism versus identity.

And yet, even though for many years, urban planners, architects, sociologists, anthropologists and politicians have demonised non-places, and with them our suburbs, it is precisely there that we have built our identity. Today we are working hard to regenerate those places. A bit like when you go to a psychologist to process a trauma or, as Zerocalcare would say in the 2021 series *Tear Along the Dotted Line*, when you try to turn a scar into something beautiful: 'The scar doesn't go away, it's like a medal that no one can take away from you.' (*La cicatrice non passa, è come una medaglia che nessuno ti può portare via.*)

And so, as we scramble to regenerate the suburbs, to make counterculture the dominant culture, streetwear haute couture, we fail to realise that non-places no longer exist in our cities, but are moving elsewhere. Into the net.

The oxymoron place/non-place has now become physical/digital, or rather self/non-self.

On the net we live illusory experiences – our self is mediated by our digital image. And so, if in the 1990s non-places were the space of conformism, today control, supermodernity, live in the metaverse.

The critical problems of these new non-places are various. The most obvious are related to information privacy, because the companies involved are likely to collect users' personal information through their wearable devices and interactions. Facebook, for example, is planning new forms of targeted advertising within the metaverse, raising further concerns about the spread of misinformation as well as the loss of personal privacy.

User addiction and problematic use of social media are perhaps the risks that catch our attention, or at least mine. Internet addiction disorder, social media and video game addiction – these will all have physical and mental repercussions over an extended period of time, such as depression, anxiety and even obesity. Experts are concerned that this new digital reality could be used as an 'escape'. The metaverse will have a great social impact because it will have the ability to algorithmically adapt virtual worlds according to each person's beliefs, further distorting users' perceptions of reality with illusory content created to maintain or increase their engagement. A new fake world where everyone will feel reassured and comforted by being like everyone else.

Today we are building our new digital peripheries. Eventually these digital non-places will be replaced by the places of the future, just as they were once in the past. And then we will start again, in a continuous wave that leads human beings to constantly lose and find themselves in their own history.

Site Specific Roma. Courtesy of Yancey Richardson Gallery. Credit: Olivo Barbieri

Periphery

Venice

1 km

The Venice Syndrome

Andreas Pichler

Venice – that is pure romance, the longing of all Europeans, the dream of all Americans, the wish of many Chinese. But the most beautiful city in the world becomes a ghost town in the evening: whole quarters are empty, long since abandoned by their inhabitants; these uninhabited walls serve the business of a myth.

Due to the enormous influx of tourists, the city becomes uninhabitable. Venice's urban life of its own has almost collapsed, it hardly exists anymore.

A requiem for a still grandiose city. A lesson in how public property becomes the prey of the few. A hymn to the last Venetians, their wit and their heart.

The Venice Syndrome
Original title: *Das Venedig Prinzip*
Director: Andreas Pichler
Year: 2012
Country: Germany, Austria, Italy
Duration: 82 min

IT IS ESTIMATED THAT BY THE YEAR 2030 THE CITY WILL NOT HAVE A SINGLE RESIDENT.

Venetian impressions: Lines of flight from the terrace-city

Marco Baravalle

Ranjit Kandalgaonkar,
A History From Below.
Woodcut on Fabriano
Rosaspina paper, 2021.

The terrace-city: quality food, shitty life

What if Venice really became a museum? You just have to understand the type – maybe like the Museum of Alexandria, the one Ptolemy had dedicated to the Muses, to study, to international exchange. A museum as a meeting place, a *dispositif* to foster cooperation of brains and not just tourist consumption.

Instead, everything seems there to be devoured or is allowed to be devoured.

The city of records, the Biennale of records, the civic museums that open for tourists and close when the tourists are not there (as happened in 2021). All boundaries have disappeared between the hotel room at 250 euros (the cheapest you could find), the vaporetto at 9.50 euros, the kilometre-long queue to see art, and art itself. In Venice, the dream of the avant-garde is reversed – art does not disappear into revolutionised life, but into the abstraction of capital (and so many still delude themselves that they have it in front of them).

The use value of heritage, of fields, of buildings has retreated somewhere, there at the back, behind exchange value, hypertrophied to the point of occupying the whole scene.

They want to put a ticketing system into the city. Venice with a ticket … Will it have double sittings like restaurants? First round at 7.30 in the evening, second at 9? Venice, with the ticket (preferably pre-purchased), finally manifests as the fulfilment of a metamorphosis, becomes an event itself; but when 'event' ceases to be the name of something that breaks the routine, it turns into its opposite, into the name of the everydayness of extractivism, of the new normal of value extraction, fuelled by small and large rentiers.

Some imaginative architect in the 1970s designed modular cities inspired by the supermarket and the parking lot. Someone else later described the space of postmodernity as 'junk space', a global continuum of glass and steel membranes, escalators and air conditioning. The module that Venice imposes as the matrix of the global tourist city is the terrace. Chairs-umbrellas-tables-spritz-fingerfood-bill-chairs-umbrellas-tables-spritz-fingerfood-bill … To infinity in space.

Slow food is enlisted: quality food, shit life

The temporality of the global tourist city is that of a flooded digestive system, a social gastric reflux, an inflamed colon defecating crowds of tourists (and in shit you struggle to live). Who better to govern (or rather guard) this eternal rumination than the current mayor, an entrepreneur of temporary employment and entertainment. If shit were gold … And it is, for those who make money from it.

Where does tourism end? Where do those other things called city, culture, art, public space, politics begin? They are no longer 'other things'; those who do not understand this are deluding themselves. And they are deluding themselves that by evoking them, as in the past, something will change.

Lines of flight 1: the port and the hospital

What is a port? It is a junction within a *hydrarchy*. From above, hydrarchy is grasped as imperial control over the waters, a *dispostif* for putting the submerged part of the globe to profit, now more central than ever in an age of logistical capitalism. But hydrarchy, as historians of piracy teach, is also that set of patterns of self-government, rebellion and lines of escape traced by seafarers, pirates, insubordinate women, runaway slaves, the poor and so on.

Porto Marghera, the industrial port of Venice that developed in the 1920s as one of the centres of gravity of the modern project for Venice, was for decades the main polluter of the Lagoon, but it was, at the same time, the working-class heart of the city. As the petrochemical industry declined and the tourist industry advanced, the centre of gravity shifted again from Marghera to the Stazione Marittima (i.e., that portion of the port located in the historic city), which, until 2021 (when the struggles of the No Grandi Navi committee convinced UNESCO and the government to ban the wreakers of havoc), housed cruise ships and carried out related logistics.

What would happen if the Marittima transformed from an institution serving extractivism to an institution of care? For *Le mostre della Laguna*, an exhibition curated by Sale Docks in 2021, Ranjit Kandalgaonkar imagined the Marittima being replaced by the (never realised) hospital that Le Corbusier designed for Venice in the early 1960s, shortly before his death. In his woodcut, the Indian artist depicts three levels. At the bottom are the typical Venetian ancestral foundations, pointed poles of larch or fir that sink into the *caranto* (a layer of solid clay under the surface slough), a necessary base for the Istrian stone walls that will support the actual building. The middle level is occupied by the outline of the present Stazione Marittima (until recently, as we know, a cruise port). At the highest level, on the other hand, the outline of Le Corbusier's hospital, conceived for the *sestiere* of Cannaregio and left on paper, is suspended.

The modern returns here not as the failure of a utopia, but as the utopia of care against the process of touristification that progressively empties the city of its inhabitants. This emptying, in recent decades, has been matched by a parallel demobilisation of healthcare institutions: the Civil Hospital is defunded, departments and services are closing, there is a shortage of staff; primary care physicians are in short supply; mental health services are closing. The relationship between health services and the territory is weakening. The buzzwords are privatisation and centralisation. Buzzwords that cost a notable number of lives during the pandemic.

The smeared lions: iconoclasm in the touristified city

A nocturnal crime: one evening in 2018, four university students (three of them enrolled at the local Academy of Fine Arts), on their way home, daub the mane of one of the two marble lions that stand guard over the little square of the same name, next to the Basilica at the northeastern end of St. Mark's Square. The 'social media sphere' is outraged; enraged stances of the authorities follow, from the mayor to the regional president. The perpetrators are identified, denounced, and the school threatens expulsion.

For Venetians, those two marble lions have a special sentimental value. For generations, in fact, it has been customary for children passing through to stop there, not to admire them, but to ride them bareback, once hoisted on their backs by their parents. Monuments to be used, not just contemplated.

Yet, in Venice, tourism continues to expel residents; fewer and fewer people, fewer and fewer parents, fewer and fewer children. Not only that, fewer and fewer residents (unless they work there) pass by St. Mark's Square and see it as a socially viable part of the city.

The bad conscience of institutions and the dullness of school leaders are well represented by the eagerness to punish the iconoclastic students and in the disinterest (or inability) to question the causes of iconoclasm. I do

Le Mostra della Laguna, exhibition, Sale Docks, 2021, Venice. Credit: Veronica Badolin

not want to suggest that the students were as clear-headed as the Black Lives Matter activists when they were tearing down statues of slavers and colonisers, yet the problem is not always in the monument itself – as a monument not only projects certain hierarchies onto the surrounding space but also catalyses its status.

Lines of flight 2: a night game of football

Gestures of careless iconoclasm strike cultural heritage (which in Venice is at one with the city) when the latter loses its meaning, when, all traces of resignifying use having evaporated, it disappears from the emotional maps of those who experience the city.

I arrived in Venice as a university student in the year 1999–2000 and lived the first two years in a students' residence (*collegio*). Still in the new millennium, the tenants of that residence handed down a tradition: at least once a year, usually at the close of a particularly lively evening, taking advantage of the darkness and strong in numbers, we would move to St. Mark's Square for a ball game.

St. Mark's is not a football field, but that tradition was more than the tailspin of a dying student spirit (*goliardia*). Our game was an act of occupation (albeit temporary), a performance of reappropriation of that space already completely taken away from life, expropriated by tourist extractivism.

Play, philosophers say, is a rituality that returns to use what is separated in the sphere of the sacred. Of course, to trace this radical character, one must look elsewhere than to the gambling industry, televised games or professional sports. Perhaps our epic runs on the wing framed by the Procuratie Vecchie, our (scalene) triangulations and shots spiked from the disconnections of the *masegni* (the stones forming the floor of the square), were so many acts of profanation of a space that tourist religion had sequestered, perimetered as its own sacred place.

Thus, through profanation, I gave meaning to that portion of the city. Thus, the square entered my emotional map. Thus, a youthful nocturnal ritual that common sense would probably categorise as a symptom of 'degradation' (*degrado*) is actually an act of love, care and resignification.

Instead, as if to confirm the disaster of Venice's neoliberal governance, in the days following the defacement by the students, photos circulated online depicting the two lion cubs surrounded by sinewy local police officers.

Rem Koolhaas and a slipper

OMA, Rem Koolhaas's architectural firm, designed the interior of Venice's most expensive shopping mall, housed by the Fondaco dei Tedeschi, a few steps from the Rialto Bridge. A space without quality, where the reference to the historic commercial destination (it was, originally, the place reserved for the trade of German merchants) and to trade as the key to the cosmopolitanism of Venice in the past, is a ridiculous anachronism. Today's Fondaco, if anything, serves a form of commerce that sanctions the dissolution of all relational opportunity in the oligopoly of brands. Above all, OMA missed the opportunity to draw the necessary conclusions from the reduction of architecture to the cosmetics of a financial transaction; rather, it pathetically seeks to legitimise the latter by alluding to its own intervention as a further stage in the 'accumulation of authenticities' that characterise the building's transformations since the fifteenth century.

It is, in any case, a place reserved for extra-rich tourists where Venetians (apart, perhaps, from the extra-rich) do not set foot; and let us gloss over the affair of the privatisation of the Fondaco, a public building sold to Benetton, and now managed by Bernard Arnault's multinational luxury company LVMH.

A few years ago I happened to see a photograph of a 'product of excellence' for sale in said mall. A slipper (cost, around 300 euros) on which a gondola was embroidered. Only the gondolier was placed at the bow (instead of at the stern) and was rowing in the opposite direction to the correct direction of travel. To clarify the point: like embroidering a car in which the driver, placed in the engine compartment, was seated facing in the reverse direction.

I wondered why such a basically mundane image had struck me so much. Upon reflection I realised the reason: because there is no mistake, it is not *wrong*. Instead, it is a realistic depiction of what a gondola actually is today. As soon as it leaves the *squero* (the shipyard where it is manufactured), it ceases to be the fruit of an ancient craftsmanship (by the way, now an integral part of the tourist experience itself), to become a sign-commodity, no more and no less. If, as Wolfgang Scheppe states, Venice has become a real abstraction, a social mechanism in which 'abstract principles of exchange' dominate the concrete dimension, then the boat symbolic of the Lagoon does not escape such principles. The gondola *is* a several hundred euro slipper, good for the Saudis, Chinese, Russians or Americans who can afford it.

The gondola escapes abstraction only when it is *traghetto*; that is, at those two or three points overlooking the Grand Canal where, still, gondoliers shuttle from one bank to the other, carrying residents and non-residents, for a few cents and a few euros, respectively.

Lines of flight 3: a virus, an octopus, a brill, a cormorant, two dolphins

In pursuing the growth paradigm, capitalism bases its reproduction on infinite expansion. In the relentless retraction of the frontier of accumulation, wildernesses shrink, increasing promiscuity between human and non-human animals in spaces such as industrial farms and wet markets, encouraging contact with unknown viruses, spillovers and new epidemics.

The spread of the Covid-19 virus has dramatically highlighted the interdependence of bodies and, at the same time, opened the stage for different bodies. In Venice, these peeped out from the waters of the canals in the lockdown months, when tourism suddenly ceased, along with the movement of motor boats. It took only a few weeks to spot two dolphins at the mouth of the Grand Canal, opposite Punta della Dogana; a respectably sized octopus clinging to the *fondamenta* near Piazzale Roma; and I myself, one morning, witnessed a cormorant re-emerging from the waters of Fondamenta della Misericordia with (what seemed to me) a large brill in its beak.

A local biologist interviewed said that these sightings were due to the easing of anthropogenic pressure. When all space ceases to be occupied by human bodies, non-human bodies manifest. They do not, however, replace what was full with something more full; rather, they punctuate, emerge, appear, cross, float, surface, anchor, explore.

These glimpses of the post-human city are not glimpses of the future, so much as, rather, flashbacks of a history: the history of Venice itself in which only through skilful human intervention, the Lagoon was not transformed (as it would naturally be) into an arm of the sea, or, conversely, into a stretch of marshy land. What does this mean? That the Lagoon is not nature surrounding the city and, diametrically, the built-up islands are not artifice opposite to nature. Lagoon and city are one system; more, they are the same matter, they share one destiny. Only their skilful combination gave birth to that thing called Venice, only their final separation can decree its end. At the same time, however, built Venice and Lagoon have different properties. It is Venetian society that, for more than a millennium, has governed the encounter between city and nature by constructing it as a history of managing a balance, as an internal dialectic of the same matter.

Today, the touristification of the city is a symptom of the crisis of this caring action; neoliberal governance embodies a new dualism of substance that not only undermines life (understood as the life of residents), but also undermines the Lagoon, which, as we have seen, is at one with the city.

The octopus at Piazzale Roma comes to remind us of two things. First, that non-human bodies still have not surrendered to anthropogenic pressure. Second, that their presence should not surprise us. Never more so than in Venice, we are made of the same matter.

Lines of flight 4: staying, or of radical permanence

The term flight here certainly does not allude to the abandonment of the historic city, but to that set of forms of life and imagination (in perpetual renewal) that escape or antagonise the neoliberal grip. One flees by inventing ways to stay, not by running away. Individual tactics, collective games, artworks, appearance of non-human bodies, but also – and above all – radical political organisation. Elsewhere I have written that the Venice Biennale should free itself from a certain regime of mobility that I have called *neoliberal nomadism* and build alliances with forms *of radical permanence*. A fortiori, this applies to the city as a whole.

Despite the tourist siege and the neoliberal policies that foster it, kids continue to throw balls at the walls of the churches that dot the *campi* and people continue to organise assemblies in public spaces, to set up paths of mobilisation and resistance. Such pathways are crucial because they are potentially *instituting*. They are, that is, capable of endowing the city with counter-spaces and alter-institutions (social centres, climate justice movements, committees, networks of occupied houses, student collectives, observatories, Italian schools for migrants, and so on) that not only propel struggles, but that, by existing, change the experience of this city. They draw a map and a set of city ways that allow those who practise them to meet, organise and breathe. The goal is not to create niches for oneself in a doomed system – the horizon is always that of the transformation of the present state of things – but it would be difficult to sustain this enterprise if one could not experience, here and now, that other desired city that, though only in flashes, already exists in the moment of its collective construction.

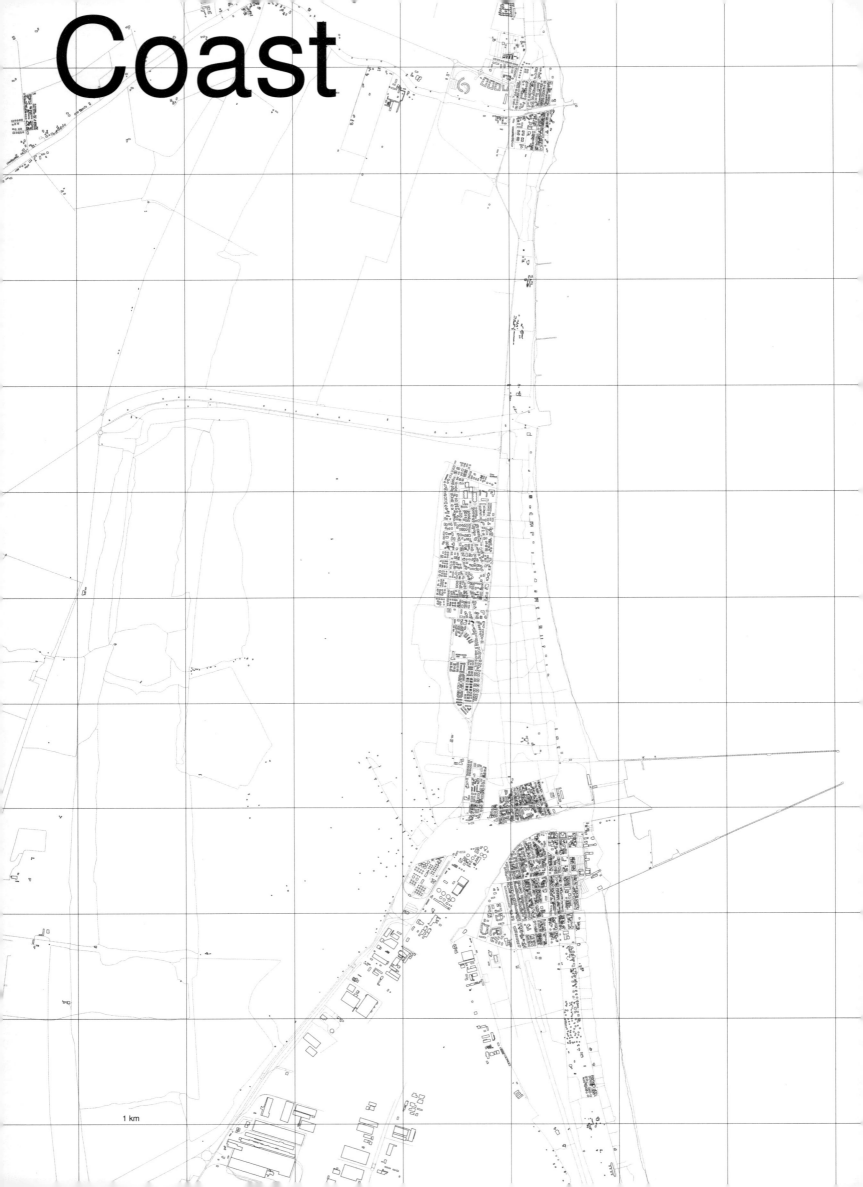
Coast

1 km

The Adriatic: An ancient door to a new world order

Manuel Orazi
Marco Vanucci

Mouth of the River Conca between Misano Adriatico and Cattolica (Romagna, Italy), 2005. Credit: Guido Guidi

'All history must be mobilised if one would understand the present.' – Fernand Braudel

During an official visit to Kazakhstan, in September 2013, the President of the People's Republic of China, Xi Jinping, announced a global infrastructure strategy adopted by the Chinese government called the 'Belt and Road Initiative' (BRI), formerly known in English as the 'One Belt One Road'. This vision was addressing the infrastructural gap between the Far East and the West by projecting a strategic masterplan to develop new terrestrial and maritime trade routes between the Asian and the European continents. The plan aimed at constructing 'a unified large market and [to] make full use of both international and domestic markets, through cultural exchange and integration, to enhance mutual understanding and trust of member nations, resulting in an innovative pattern of capital inflows, talent pools, and technology databases'.

While the BRI involves moving goods from the polluting large merchant ships that transit the Suez Canal to the new land route that connects over seventy countries, the project includes the strengthening of the Maritime Silk Road, which is already the preferred route for more than half of all containers in the world.[1]

The terminal of this programme is invariably the Adriatic corridor and the North Adriatic region. There, alongside many historical and industrial cities, is Trieste, the northern Italian hub with its international free port and its rail connection to Central Europe and the North Sea.

The Chinese geostrategic masterplan offers a unique opportunity to rethink the Adriatic region, its cities and port infrastructures.[2] However, rather than a new scenario, the BRI represents a return to a dimension the Adriatic region played for many centuries: that of the gateway to the East, a role the Adriatic had since the time of Marco Polo. For over a thousand years, in fact, La Serenissima, the Republic of Venice, established its wealth and dominance as a commercial superpower by expanding its trading relations with Asia and the Middle East. It's not a coincidence that the Venetian Patron was coming from the East as the painting by Gentile and Giovanni Bellini, St. Mark Preaching in Alexandria (1504–07), perfectly explains; St. Mark's Basilica was founded in the ninth century to house the corpse of the Evangelist after Venetian merchants stole it from Alexandria in Egypt.

Thus, the Adriatic Sea, otherwise called for centuries the Gulf of Venice, was considered the door to the Levant, the border between Western civilisation and the East. John Ruskin observed: 'Opposite in their character and mission, alike in their magnificence of energy, they came from the North and from the South, the glacier torrent and the lava stream: they met and contended over the wreck of the Roman empire; and the very centre of the struggle, the point of pause of both, the dead water of the opposite eddies, charged with embayed fragments of the Roman wreck, is Venice. The Doge's Palace of Venice contains the three elements in exactly equal proportions – the Roman, Lombard, and Arab. It is the central building of the world.'[3]

Yet, the history of Venice and its gulf was overlooked by modern history. While the Fascist regime grossly manipulated the history of the ancient Venetian colonies in the Levant, the trading activities of the Repubblica were superficially interpreted as the precursor of modern capitalism and therefore ideologically dismissed.

However, Venice was an exception among nations, founded on the sea, a capability derived mostly from Byzantium. The 'Stato da mar' (state of the sea) was formed from an archipelago of islands (Crete, Euboea, Cyprus, Corfu) and ports of call (Istria, Dalmatia, parts of Montenegro and Albania, Morea) up to Constantinople – where there was a Venetian quarter.[4] The history of the sea, more than the one of the lands, evades historiographical cliché and prejudices. As opposed to the land, the sea doesn't leave any trace[5] and yet its history, the history of maritime trading and exchange, is better suited to help us understand the richness of multiculturalism – a richness that has been consciously hidden by twentieth-century nationalism. According to David Abulafia, in the Middle Ages the Italian identity all around the Mediterranean was mostly defined by the Venetian and Genovese merchants and their interaction with trading partners and people. At the same time, what was unique in Italian cities, particularly in Venice, was a sense of belonging that involved not just Venetians but also recent immigrants or settlers coming from foreign places.[6]

Multicultural cities, ports and new typologies

Known in the past as *sinus*, inlet or gulf, while the Romans called it *mare superum* (as opposed to the *mare inferum*, the Tyrrhenian), the Adriatic Sea has been described as a sea of intimacy.[7] Since the Romans, the Adriatic had played a central role in the commercial exchange between the different peoples and tribes that inhabit its shores: the frequent trade between the Romans and Illyria (the current region of the Balkans), the Byzantine, the Ottomans, they all benefited and strived thanks to the maritime connections they established with neighbouring cities and populations.

The wealth of commercial activities shaped the Adriatic coastline: Trieste, Aquileia, Ravenna, Rimini, Pesaro, Fano, Senigallia, Ancona, to name but a few cities on the Italian coast; Pula, Rijeka, Zadar, Sibenik, Split, Dubrovnik in Croatia; Bar in Montenegro; Durrës and Vlorë in Albania – all of them have names in Italian, too. All these cities had been part of a stable relationship with the Venetian Republic for centuries until its fall. In the extraordinary map of Venice made by Jacopo de' Barbari in 1500, at the centre of the city in the *bacino marciano* there is Neptune, the marine god who was then 'Venetianised'. Similarly, in the last years of the Repubblica (eighteenth century), Giambattista Tiepolo represented Venice in the Doge's Palace as the 'Queen of the Adriatic Sea'.[8]

It is thanks to this dynamic environment that the early Renaissance was rooted along the Italian Adriatic coast. Around the mid-fifteenth century, the Duke Federico II da Montefeltro hired Luciano Laurana, an expert builder from Dalmatia, to build the Ducal Palace in Urbino. Laurana, who is known to have collaborated with Leon Battista Alberti in Mantua and was also flanked by Francesco di Giorgio Martini in Urbino, was called *schiavone*, an Italian ethnonym literally meaning 'slavs' in old Venetian. In the nearby Loreto, the Basilica della Santa Casa, designed by Giuliano Da Sangallo, Donato Bramante and Luigi Vanvitelli, enshrines the house in which the Virgin Mary is believed by Catholics to have lived. The legend claims that the house was flown by angels from Nazareth to Trsat, a suburb of Rijeka in Croatia, then to Ancona before arriving at Loreto.

However, the fervid trading established by the Republic of Venice gave birth to new architectural typologies along the Adriatic as well as in the many ports and cities across the Mediterranean and beyond. The *fondaco* was a building (or a complex of buildings) of medieval origin which, in the seaside towns, served as a warehouse and often also as accommodation for foreign merchants. The term is present in all the old languages of the Levant and beyond – in Turkish *funduq* means warehouse, meanwhile *fhondac* is tavern; there are also *hanı, wakala, milaton, phoundax*.[9] The Venetians established *fondaci* all around the Mediterranean, the Black Sea and, in turn, built a few in Venice to host their

---

1 Manuel Orazi and Marco Vanucci, *Log*, no. 53 (2022), cover story.

2 The Architectural Association Visiting School Adriatica is the first masterclass studying and discussing the urbanisation along the Adriatic coastline. The first edition was held in Riccione in July 2021 and focused, among other things, on the repurposing and transformation of the offshore oil platforms which form an archipelago of nearly a hundred maritime infrastructures that are being decommissioned or at the end of their lifecycle: see www.aadriatica.eu

3 John Ruskin, *The Stones of Venice* (1851).

4 The Turkish name of Pera, Beyoğlu, is a modification by folk etymology of the Venetian ambassadorial title of Bailo, whose palazzo was the most important building in this quarter.

5 'The earth is, like our own skin, fated to carry the scars of ancient wounds', Fernand Braudel, *The Mediterranean and the Mediterranean World in the Age of Philip II* (Berkeley: University of California Press, 1996).

6 David Abulafia, 'Gli italiani fuori d'Italia', in Gabriella Airaldi, ed., *Gli orizzonti aperti. Profili del mercante medievale* (Turin: Scriptorium, 1997), 175–98. See also idem, *The Great Sea: A Human History of the Mediterranean* (London: Penguin, 2011).

7 Predrag Matvejević, *Mediterranean: A Cultural Landscape* (Berkeley: University of California Press, 1999).

8 See the painting Neptune Offers Gifts to Venice (1740–45).

9 Ennio Concina, *Fondaci. Architettura, arte e mercatura fra Levante, Venezia e Alemagna* (Venice: Marsilio, 2001). Cf. idem, *A History of Venetian Architecture*, trans. Judith Landry (Cambridge: Cambridge University Press, 1998).

10 Donatella Calabi, *The Market and the City: Square, Street and Architecture in Early Modern Europe* (Aldershot: Ashgate, 2004).

11 Donatella Calabi, *Venice, the Jews, and Europe: 1516–2016* (Venice: Marsilio, 2016). The Venetian ghetto was the first in the world; it hosts five synagogues and Jews from northern Europe, Spain and the Levant. The word spread world-wide also for other minorities.

12 Robert Venturi and Denise Scott Brown, *Architecture as Signs and Systems: For a Mannerist Time* (Cambridge, MA: Harvard University Press, 2004), 96–7.

13 Cyriac of Ancona, *Later Travels*, trans. and ed. Edward W. Bodnar with Clive Foss (Cambridge, MA: Harvard University Press, 2003).

14 Lotte Labowsky, *Bessarion's Library and the Biblioteca Marciana. Six Early Inventories* (Rome: Edizioni di storia e letteratura, 1979).

15 Carlo Ginzburg, *The Enigma of Piero. Piero della Francesca: The Baptism, the Arezzo Cycle, the Flagellation* (London: Verso, 1985).

trading partners: the *Fondaco dei Tedeschi* or *Fondaco dei Turchi* (Turks was used to refer to anyone from the Middle or Far East just as Germans referred to any northern merchants from the Netherlands, Flanders, Scandinavian countries or Central Europe) are just a few examples and a testimony to the many relationships the Adriatic Sea fostered between different continents and civilisations. According to Donatella Calabi, the *fondaco* is basically an island in the city, a peculiar market inside a wider merchant area and an instrument of control of prices imposed by the Repubblica.[10]

The *lazzaretto*, on the other hand, was a place where goods and people from countries of possible contagion had to stay for a certain amount of time, often forty days (hence the term *quarantena*) before being released. The term *lazzaretto* has a twofold etymology: on the one hand, it comes from the leper Lazarus – the protagonist of the Gospel parable – venerated as the protector of people suffering from leprosy. On the other hand, it recalls the first lazaret, that of Santa Maria di Nazareth in Venice (otherwise called Lazzaretto Vecchio), whose name has been transformed from Nazareth to *nazaretto* in *lazzaretto*. They were temporary hospitals that were set up to avoid an epidemic of plague, thus anti-pandemic architectural devices.

In 1468, on the island called Lazzaretto Nuovo, a new structure was created to collect and examine the goods and people suspected of being infected with plague disease. A similar function was attributed to the island of San Lazzaro degli Armeni. This island has been the point of reference for the Armenian diaspora before the foundation of the modern state of Armenia (1991), after the dissolution of the Soviet Union. Armenians were among the minorities linked to commerce, together with the Greeks and Jews, such that they were present in every relevant port in the Adriatic and the Mediterranean. In Venice this is particularly evident in the toponomastics: San Lazzaro degli Armeni, Ghetto degli Ebrei[11] (Jews); San Giorgio dei Greci (Greeks); Scuola degli Albanesi (Albanians); Riva degli Schiavoni (Slavics); and the already mentioned Fondaco dei Turchi and Tedeschi. Thus, Venice represents a model for contemporary globalisation: it's always been a melting pot with different languages and dialects transferred to its architecture. If we look carefully at St. Mark's Square we won't find any 'Venetian style', but a juxtaposition of different references: the Byzantine stones of the Basilica (full of Arabian influences because the body of St. Mark was found in Alexandria of Egypt), the Tuscan-Roman Renaissance of the Jacopo Sansovino's Library, the peculiar late Gothic of the Doge's Palace and of the Procuratie Vecchie, the mannerist-baroque touch of Vincenzo Scamozzi and Baldassarre Longhena to the Procuratie Nuove, the French neoclassical of the Napoleonic Wing (Procuratie Nuovissime), the orientalism of Caffè Florian (where coffee was first imported from Turkey and served filtered in Europe), the eclectic reconstruction of the Campanile – and so on. It is no coincidence that Robert Venturi and Denise Scott Brown found it their favourite square, provided with 'the richness at a pedestrian scale of combined styles of commercial, civic, and religious architecture of the piazza'.[12]

A lazaret was present in every relevant Adriatic port, but probably the most impressive is in Ancona. The city, a stronghold port that used to have relative autonomy inside the Papal State, had its own *lazzaretto*. In 1733, Pope Clemente XII Corsini commissioned the rococo architect Luigi Vanvitelli to design a new infrastructure so that the port could adapt to the new needs of the trading city. The neoclassical architect did not simply build a new complex but instead created a new artificial island within which a sophisticated pentagonal structure was erected to provide space for people and goods. At the centre of the courtyard, Vanvitelli designed the *tempietto* dedicated to San Rocco, protector of plague victims. The same Pope managed to restore the operability of the other Adriatic port of the Papal State, Ravenna, promoting the development of Canale Corsini, which at that time was in decline due to its occlusion. In order to relaunch commerce after almost two centuries of decline, Clemente XII introduced also the '*porto franco*' in Ancona (1732), imitating the free-trade zone in Trieste which was introduced by the Austrian Emperor Charles VI (1719). The strategy of eliminating taxes for a weekend encouraged the creation of an annual fair in Senigallia which, as Alfred de Musset recounted in his writings, attracted merchants from the internal regions, from northern Italy and the Levant.

'Reviving things long dead and forgotten'

Beside trading, the Adriatic has also been the site of intense cultural exchange between Greek and Roman culture and, later, between the classic tradition and humanism.

Ciriaco de' Pizzicolli, also known as Cyriacus or Cyriac of Ancona, is traditionally considered the founder of antiquarian science and played a pivotal role in shaping Western humanist culture and its self-conscious tie to the classical tradition.

In the fifteenth century, Cyriacus was a prolific recorder of Greek and Roman antiquities, particularly inscriptions and archaeological documents. These finds were used as a currency or 'cultural capital' that he established among financiers, aristocrats, the military and prelates with whom he came into contact in the course of his life and through his travels.

His mercantile nature and philological passion enabled him to transform a vague curiosity of the European ruling classes for antiquity into a cultural paradigm at the base of the modern concept of archaeology. He would seek support for his activities as a way to save the heritage of the classical tradition preserved by the Byzantine Empire that was endangered by the Turkish invasion.[13]

Cyriacus created a new way of thinking about classicism in relation to the political needs of his time; he packaged and presented it as a 'restoration' of the authentic classical tradition. In fewer than thirty years, he brought new attention to the classical tradition, developing a widespread sensitivity for ancient Greek culture in the Western ruling classes, making it become perceived as the 'cultural capital' of Western civilisation. Cyriacus most likely acted as the agent of Cardinal Basilio Bessarion, who was the main theorist of this idea: to create a new brand for the Byzantine Empire, at that time in search of alliances and economic support in the West to face the threats posed by the Ottoman Turks. Bessarion was the promoter of the Concilius of Ferrara and Florence (1438–39) and was actively campaigning to cement the relationship between the Latin and the Orthodox churches and to unite them against the aggressiveness of the Ottomans to the Byzantine Empire.

The political project of Bessarion was aimed at transforming the Western perception of the Byzantine Empire as the repository of the classical tradition which constituted the foundation of Western civilisation. At the end of his life, he donated his precious library rich with Greek and Latin manuscripts of the classics to Venice,[14] as he considered it the last bastion of Greek civilisation and the only state at war with the Turks. This explains why Bessarion might be one of the characters in the enigmatic *Flagellation of Christ* by Piero della Francesca in Urbino.[15] Born in Trabzon around 1400, Bessarion died in Ravenna, the former seat of the Byzantine governor of Italy, in 1472.

Watershed between the Adriatic and the Black Sea basin, Bernina Pass (Grisons, Switzerland), 2022. Credit: Paolo Rosselli

16 'munus renovandae vetustatis, vel ab interitu potius vindicandae': Cyriac of Ancona, Life and Early Travels, trans. and ed. Charles Mitchell, Edward W. Bodnar, and Clive Foss (Cambridge, MA: Harvard University Press, 2015), App. III, Lett. I, n. 1.

17 Christopher Montagu Woodhouse, Gemistos Plethon: The Last of the Hellenes (Oxford: Clarendon Press, 1986).

18 Manfredo Tafuri, Venice and the Renaissance (Cambridge, MA: MIT Press, 1985), ch. II.

Cyriacus was a creative executor of Bessarion's vision. He expressed interest in the aim to 'Renew, or rather resurrect antiquity',[16] as he wrote, manifesting his neo-pagan faith.

Bessarion had in turn been a pupil of another key figure for Cyriacus' religious and political culture: the Greek Neoplatonic philosopher Georgius Gemistus Pletho – who was also present in Florence in 1439 playing an active role in the reintroduction of Platonism into the Western world.[17] The effects of neo-Byzantinism in Venetian architecture, particularly in San Salvador, were studied by Manfredo Tafuri.[18]

Cyriacus was familiar with the House of Malatesta. It is possible that he had some weight in the formation of the young Sigismund, who had Leon Battista Alberti design the Malatesta memorial monument: the Tempio Malatestiano in Rimini is an extremely unorthodox Catholic church, in fact a 'temple' and one of the most important buildings of the Renaissance. Thus, it's no coincidence that Sigismund later became a great admirer of Pletone; he invited him to Rimini in 1460 and stole his mortal remains from Mistrà, in 1466, to place them as a sacred relic in the arches of the Malatesta temple. Cyriacus was also one of the pioneers of the studies on triumphal arches and, according to his biographers, it was the triumphal arch in Ancona that ultimately triggered his interest in antiquity and led him to interpret, imitate, copy, emulate or quote these specific antique models on both sides of the Adriatic.

There's no reason to doubt that Cyriacus' work influenced Leon Battista Alberti. We know that they met in Ferrara, where Alberti designed the arched pedestal for the equestrian monument to Niccolo III d'Este (1393–1441) called the Arco del Cavallo, when Cyriacus was there acting as judge. They also certainly met in Rimini, where Alberti asked Cyriacus to see the books of sketching and annotations on the Greek monuments, epigraphy and decoration taken in years of travels in the Oriental Roman Empire, in Alexandria in Egypt and in the Levant. Cyriacus was the last Western man who would see the Parthenon and the real elephants along the Nile – which were the family crest of the Malatesta.

From the Adriatic to the court of the Ming dynasty

The old Silk Road travelled by Marco Polo was directed to China because of the silk and spices which were transported to the West from Southeast Asia, China and India. China was the only country in classical times where farmers and weavers had developed techniques for producing high-quality silk fabrics.

Another seminal figure in bridging the West to the East via the Adriatic Sea and beyond was the Jesuit priest and humanist Matteo Ricci. It is from the shore of the Adriatic, precisely from the town of Macerata, that, in 1578, Ricci set to sea in the direction of China. As one of the founding figures of the Jesuit China missions, Ricci embarked on the evangelical mission to bring Catholicism to the heart of the Ming dynasty. Ricci started from Lisbon, approached China via Macau (then a Portuguese colony), where he studied Chinese language and customs, and settled in Zhaoqing, at the invitation of the governor Wang Pan, who had heard of Ricci's skill as a mathematician and cartographer. Moreover, he composed the first European-style world map in Chinese, called Da Ying Quan Tu (Complete Map of the Great World), where China was placed in the middle of the map.

Then, in 1601, Ricci was asked to be an adviser to the imperial court of the Wanli Emperor, and became the

19 Matteo Ricci, *On Friendship. One Hundred Maxims for a Chinese Prince*, trans. Timothy Billings (New York: Columbia University Press, 2009).

20 Filippo Mignini, ed., *New Perspectives in the Studies on Matteo Ricci* (Macerata: Quodlibet, 2019).

21 Jonathan Spence, *The Memory Palace of Matteo Ricci* (London: Penguin, 1985).

22 Egidio Ivetic, *History of the Adriatic: A Sea and Its Civilization* (Cambridge: Polity Press, 2022).

23 Giorgio Fuà, 'Rural industrialization in later developed countries: The case of Northeast and Central Italy', *Banca Nazionale del Lavoro Quarterly Review*, no. 147 (December 1983).

24 Federico Fellini, *The Clowns*, 1970.

first Westerner to be invited into the Forbidden City. This honour was in recognition of Ricci's scientific abilities. The emperor granted him patronage and supported Ricci's completion of the *Zhifang Waiji*, China's first global atlas.

With the help of his colleague and collaborator Xu Guangqi, a Chinese agronomist, astronomer, mathematician, politician and writer, Ricci translated several classic Western texts into Chinese, most notably an anthology about friendship,[19] and the first part of Euclid's *Elements*, as well as several Chinese Confucian texts into Latin. During his mission in Asia, he found that Chinese culture was strongly intertwined with Confucianism, so he decided to use Chinese concepts to explain Christianity; he aligned himself with the Confucian intellectual elite literati, and even adopted their mode of dress and a local name, Li Madou. Ricci did not explain the Catholic faith as entirely foreign or new; instead, he explained Christianity as the completion of the Chinese belief in God.[20] In this way Ricci was very subtle: he demonstrated his good intentions without any colonial purpose, thus founding a precious cultural bridge with an insular Chinese culture by agreeing to live the rest of his life in Beijing. At that time, strangers could enter the capital but, once settled in, they could not leave it. However, Ricci's policy of dialogue with the local culture was not appreciated by the Vatican that just had established the Counter-Reformation. This is the reason why his writings were translated full of censorship and his great work was really only discovered in the twentieth century.[21]

Today, the Adriatic basin is still a frontier between the old European continent and the opportunities offered by the new Asian superpowers. At the same time, the urbanisation along its ridge, across Veneto Emilia Romagna and Marche, represents a unique, and all too often overlooked, laboratory to study the evolution of the contemporary European city. The fragmentation of the urban texture, the coexistence of irreconcilable traits and the diffuse sprawl reflect the uncertain and precarious nature of the contemporary urban and sub-urban condition.

The Italian side of the Adriatic has always been a perfect landing for refugees: up until the unification of Italy (1861) and the construction of the Adriatic railway (1863–72), this side of the peninsula was not considered as split between North and South. Dante Alighieri considered it still horizontal like in the *Tabula Peutingeriana* (a copy of the thirteenth century, of a possible Roman road map). The Arch of Trajan in Ancona was literally considered the door to the Levant. For centuries, Greeks, Armenians, Jews, Albanians, Slavs, Syrians, established enclaves along the Adriatic to escape from wars, as well as being attracted by a scarcely populated fertile land. The main cities were established far from the shore which was often characterised by marshes (and therefore by the spread of malaria) and were more vulnerable due to the raids of the Saracens. For this reason, the lands near the sea were practically a marginal no-man's land. Vice versa, the ports had no need for streets or railways as they were already connected to the sea. The city port fully embraced its border condition which was to be covered or removed by the ideology of the nation-state. In the eighteenth century, the Austro-Hungarian Empire started to project its power toward the Adriatic, which became soon an obsession for the Habsburgs: the Südbahnhof in Vienna and the Miramare Castle in Trieste (residency of the Archduke Ferdinand Maximilian and later of Maximilian I of Mexico) are two examples of this effort to establish a presence on the Adriatic by attracting the Mittel-European middle class – thanks, also, to the new infrastructures.[22]

The Adriatic city: recent past and future prospects

During the second half of the last century the Italian east coast experienced an economic growth thanks to the combined effect of industrialisation, mostly by small and medium-sized manufacturing enterprises, and the touristic exploitation of the coastline. The formal and informal settlements of the 1920s and '30s were repurposed and absorbed into a diffuse network of hotels, ephemeral and multifunctional structures, clubs, beaches and theme parks. Mostly built in the postwar period, this urban continuum has determined the leisurely character along the coast. Since the 1960s the Romagna coast became the epicentre of mass tourism, affordable, motorised, full of seasonal events. Federico Fellini's *I vitelloni* (1953) indicated the great gap between the Rimini full of tourists, workers and summer parties and the melancholic and provincial winter atmosphere when the city is almost deserted. A few years later, in the midst of the economic boom, *L'ombrellone* (1965) by Dino Risi – his first movie in full colour – registered the 'anthropological mutation' of Italian society due to consumerism and the new rhythms of life.

Up to the present day, the industrious inland and the laid-back coastline are the two faces of the same coin. Between these polarities the Adriatic city unfolds relentlessly across different regions, provinces, counties and municipalities: holiday resorts, city-state, historic city, industrial compounds, logistic infrastructures, amusement parks, urban fringes, agricultural land, density and unrestricted growth, etc. Despite its apparently chaotic prosperity, the Adriatic city has developed out of a rather specific set of socioeconomic and historical circumstances.[23]

Nevertheless, the general character of a land for exiles is still very present. While the distance from the great cities (Rome, Florence, Milan, Naples) is augmented by the Apennines, the distance from ordinary city life is enhanced by the suspended time of the holidays where one could dress and behave in a totally different way. This new condition allowed the testing of new modern typologies of leisure. During the Fascist era, summer colonies for children were designed by Adalberto Libera in Civitanova Marche (1935) and Giuseppe Vaccaro in Cesenatico (1938). The cinematic masterpiece *Ossessione* (1942), by Luchino Visconti, begins around the River Po and ends with a dramatic escape to Ancona. Some of the first discotheques in Europe, such as L'altromondo by Piero Derossi (1967) in Rimini and the Woodpecker (1966) by Filippo Monti in Milano Marittima, were constructed as pop shelters exploring uses for new materials such as polymer plastic and fibreglass. At the same time, the marginal areas along the Adriatic also became home for Gypsy communities, Roma and Sinti, and alternative art collectives such as the Mutoids (Mutoid Waste Company) which escaped consumerism by recycling metals and turning them into work of art. The Romagna region is also the homeland to itinerant activities like the circus whose families often come from here, and from which Fellini drew inspiration for his cinema.[24]

The gay culture appeared on the Adriatic thanks to the writer Pier Vittorio Tondelli, who is considered the main postmodern Italian novelist and who published *Altri libertini* (1980) and *Rimini* (1985). Tondelli was also the first to see how the main cities along the Adriatic coast would form, thanks to the sprawl, an urban continuum, a linear city.

Here, we also find two opposite ideas of city elaborated by two of the great masters of Italian modern architecture: Giancarlo De Carlo in Urbino and Carlo Aymonino in Pesaro. Two architects, planners and friends who worked together in the Spine Bianche district

Kamenari–Lepetane ferry boat (Montenegro), 2023.
Credit: Romane Bourgeois

Lošinj, Kvarner Gulf, Croatia, 2022. Credit: Stefano Graziani

Adriatic Sea (staged) Dancing People (Ravenna: Danilo Montanari Editore, 2016). Credit: Olivo Barbieri

Porto Recanati (Marche, Italy), 1984. Credit: Luigi Ghirri

Lošinj (Kvarner Gulf, Croatia), 2022. Credit: Stefano Graziani

25 Giancarlo De Carlo, *Urbino: The History of a City and Plans for its Development* (Cambridge, MA, MIT Press, 1970).

26 The model for Aymonino and his fellow and friend Aldo Rossi was on the other side of the Adriatic: Diocletian's Palace in Split, 'History offers, in its events, an architecture-city and the alternate use of different typologies', A. Rossi, *L'architettura della ragione come architettura di tendenza* (1969), now in idem, *Scritti scelti sull'architettura e la città 1956–1972*, Rosaldo Bonicalzi, ed. (Macerata: Quodlibet, 2012), 348.

27 Pesaro and Urbino are part of the same province and are at only 35 km distance, see M. Feiersinger and W. Feiersinger, *Italomodern 2. Architecture in Northern Italy 1946–1976* (Zurich: Park Books, 2016).

28 'Finally what makes a State recognizable is the fact that we accept, in one way or another, that it exists. And that together with us someone else, State or individual, starts to do the same,' Graziano Graziani, *Atlante delle micronazioni* (Macerata: Quodlibet, 2015), 12.

29 Tradition holds that Saint Marinus was a Dalmatian stonemason by trade who came from the island of Arba (today Rab), on the other side of the Adriatic Sea escaping Diocletian's persecutions.

30 Robert D. Kaplan, *Adriatic: A Concert of Civilizations at the End of the Modern Age* (London: Penguin Books, 2022).

in Matera in the Fifties, became colleagues at IUAV in Venice in the Sixties, and finally separated ideologically in the Seventies. On the one hand was De Carlo, who, informed by his experience in Team X, worked and studied the city of Urbino, once a centre of the first Renaissance.[25] On the other hand was Aymonino's typological and morphological approach to the industrial coastal city of Pesaro.[26] Urbino and Pesaro are so near and yet so territorially opposed. It's not a coincidence that the Feiersinger brothers stopped there their surprising investigations on modern Italian architecture from Austria toward the south.[27]

The Adriatic was also the site of utopic projects and revolutionary visions. In 1974, Kisho Kurokawa was commissioned to plan a unification of the cities of Vasto and San Salvo in the Abruzzo region. The plan would have produced a metropolitan area of about 70,000 people, at the time one of the largest in the mid-Adriatic region, specifically designed to accommodate the city's growth over time.

Around the same time, the national economic programme, titled Progetto 80, envisioned the development of the 'Adriatic corridor' into a vast urbanised area of 80,000 km² and one promoting a truly metropolitan vision: a territorial city.

Micronations

In the second half of the twentieth century, the Adriatic 'utopia' took even more radical forms. In 1945, Enrico Mattei was appointed (by the National Liberation Committee) to the leadership of the national oil company AGIP, established by the Fascist regime, with the clear task to dismantle it. Mattei, instead, restructured the company and turned it into one of the most important national assets. Having found that the Po Valley and the Adriatic were rich with oil and methane, Mattei bid on Italy's energetic self-sufficiency.

In 1960, Eni – 'Ente Nazionale Idrocarburi' (the National Hydrocarbons Board) – developed the first extracting platform in the Adriatic in front of Porto Corsini, in Ravenna. About 130 platforms were built in the Adriatic for the extraction of methane (Ravenna, Cervia, Rimini, Pesaro and all the way to Pescara).

Nevertheless, the dream of offshore self-sufficiency was not bound to be limited to the state-owned energy infrastructure.

In 1968, the engineer Giorgio Rosa designed, financed and built an artificial island in front of the coast of Rimini, in international waters to escape the control of the Italian authorities, and declared the independence of the Respubliko de la Insulo de la Rozoj (the Republic of the Island of Roses in Esperanto, the official language of the island), a short-lived micronation.[28]

These two stories represent the passage between the social and economic programming of the new democratic state of the Fifties and Sixties to the autarchic self-organisation of the Seventies.

Social experimentation, however, was not new to the Adriatic.

The city-state of Republic of San Marino[29] reminds us that micronations were once upon a time very much diffused. Max Weber, in his posthumously published book *Die Stadt* (1921), wrote that in the Italian Middle Ages even small communities were considered both economic and political entities with their own institutions, administrative offices and military constitution: the *comune* was a state within another state, an archetypical political organism, consciously and deliberately illegitimate and revolutionary.

In fact, the cities that claimed their autonomy from a larger state (Venice, the Papal State, Ottoman Empire, Austria) presented emblems of freedom in their flags: a cavalier for Ancona and Zadar, Saint Blaise for Ragusa/Dubrovnik and so on.

The Rose Island was a utopian project halfway between naval engineering and political experimentation that became a symbol of autarchic freedom and escape from traditional society, a space of self-determination that captured the spirit of an era and, once again, the endemic libertarian vocation of the Adriatic.

According to Robert D. Kaplan, the future of the eastern Adriatic cities, along the Balkan peninsula, could lie in the return to the condition of city-states, free to trade with foreign partners, not dissimilar from Dubai or Singapore.

That wouldn't be a new condition, but a return to the original nature of the Adriatic Sea.[30]

Respubliko de la Insulo de la Rozoj, the steel platform off the coast of Rimini. Credit: Mondadori Portfolio

Text by Ippolito Pestellini Laparelli

Because the night

Architecture research has an awkward relationship with the night. It usually emerges in the views of artificially lit buildings, city skylines or spectacular bird's-eye views, leaving the impression that architectural space at night can only be witnessed from a far distance or from above, like an image on a postcard. There are rare exceptions to this platonic experience of the night: the pictures and videos taken by Robert Venturi and Denise Scott Brown on their night rides in Las Vegas come to mind first. But in general, architects are used to looking at cities and buildings in daylight, with their clear forms and sharp edges reliably dictating and framing the flow of responsible daily productivity.

One has to turn to other disciplines – cinema primarily – to experience the narrative of space by night, its particular activities and atmospheres. At night the status quo is reversed, the most intimate desires are unveiled, creativity reaches unexpected and progressive domains, and the collective takes other forms and places for its representation. Life at night is extreme and essential at the same time. The spaces that characterise it are defined by light, sound, temperature, smoke, colour, bodies, actions … more than rigid geometries, walls, well-defined edges and impenetrable surfaces.

A different architectural narrative is necessary to understand the spaces of the night and the fundamental rituals they stage: a space able to reconcile the dynamic relationship between body, culture and place. In Monditalia at the 2014 Venice Architecture Biennale, the works of Catharine Rossi, Felicity Scott with Mark Wasiuta, and Giovanna Silva have succeeded in finding and representing that narrative. In an interview, Gianni de Michelis, the former Italian foreign minister, has said: 'Nightclubs were a means of anticipating social and cultural trends'; in another interview, Claudio Coccoluto, Italian superstar DJ, tells us: 'A club microcosm embodies contemporary society; it provides the most realistic insight into youth culture.'

Between the end of the 1960s and the early 2000s, nightclubs in Italy, as in the rest of Europe, were the outposts of progressive social and cultural change, acting as the experimental labs of an evolving society. Giovanna Silva's parabola for Monditalia stretches across almost five decades and different seasons of Italian nightlife, through interviews and archival materials, landing in the present moment with an impressive series of photographs on the current flattened aesthetic and social role of some of the most iconic Italian discos. Silva's perspective is both historical and anthropological, tracing a parkour through the time and space of Italian society, where architecture emerges among the protagonists of the night in different phases.

In the late 1960s, interest in architecture of the night increased with the experiments of the young radicals from Florence: in the heap of radical creativity, Mach 2 by Superstudio and Space Electronic by Gruppo 9999 were among the very few examples of built radical architecture, embodying the idea that discos should be 'a home for everything, from rock music, to theatre and visual arts' (Carlo Caldini, member of Gruppo 9999, architect of Space Electronic). They were multimedia environments designed to be flexible, technologically advanced and adaptable through time, built with new materials, more similar to experimental theatres than nightclubs. In Turin, Piero Derossi launched the Piper with similar ambitions, turning his venue into a meeting point for emerging artists of that generation (among them Pistoletto and Schifano), reinventing nightlife through an unprecedented mixed cultural programme and experimental architecture, and transforming the club into a social factory. Piper – its original version and replicas – soon became a brand for music and innovative architecture.

By the end of the 1970s the new model of the Riviera Romagnola emerged as the result of collaboration between creative business and artists and performers. Discos were temples, both physically and figuratively, attracting thousands of punters for their night rituals gathering around the DJ priest. Architectural devices such as the iconic Pyramid of Cocoricò – a techno version of the Louvre Pyramid – contributed to the strong identity of these discos and reinforced a sense of community of clubbers with their clubs.

Through architectural statements, the launch of new music trends such as house and techno, and through massive communication campaigns, the disco-temples became places where the wider culture and the private body could integrate and thrive, in constantly changing environments. Moving up north, in Brescia, the Number One in the early 1990s – a venue of large black-and-white checkerboard floors – became the Italian temple of hardcore, importing from northern Europe the extreme Gabber house movement, 170 bpm hardcore music with its ultimate increase in electronic music tempo: a final attempt to push music and dance beyond the limits in a rush before the eruption of the internet onto the world scene. With this phase came the raves, the abandonment of designed discos in favour of found spaces – from warehouses to parking garages to open fields – a new nomadic and ubiquitous culture that turned any location able to host large numbers into a temporary club. The social ritual is re-enacted over and over, independently from its origins, around the globe – from Naples, to Ibiza, Berlin, Barcelona, Tokyo or San Paulo.

The rest is recent history – very little has happened in the past ten years. The impact of technology has dissolved the body as it lost ground to social networks and remote connections, and with this dissolution those places dedicated to celebrating the collective encounter of bodies, through the designed or provisional medium of architecture, have lost their relevance. Phone applications open the doors of clubs for remote, individual experiences. A night at a disco can be experienced today comfortably from our own couch …

Looking at Giovanna Silva's dynamic and captivating pictures of the present status of discos, one might feel nostalgic, and even wonder if we are witnessing the ultimate finale of the disco era, the end of communal physical exuberance, and maybe the end of the collective in general; at the same time, on another level they radiate an inevitable sense of euphoria, a common understanding that we should never renounce the possibilities of solid physical spaces as a medium for escape.

In an ideal generational bridge, Silva's work speaks of youth culture and their spaces across multiple generations, mobilising visual memories and facts. If discos were a means to anticipate cultural and social change, a visual and historical analysis of their spaces might well tell us in which direction we are moving.

This project was part of the 2014 Venice Architecture Biennale and was published in *Nightswimming: Discotheques from the 1960s to the Present* (Bedford Press, 2015).

Nightswimming: Discotheques from the 1960s to the present

Giovanna Silva
Chiara Carpenter

Pyramid, Cocoricò, Riccione. 2014. Credit: Giovanna Silva

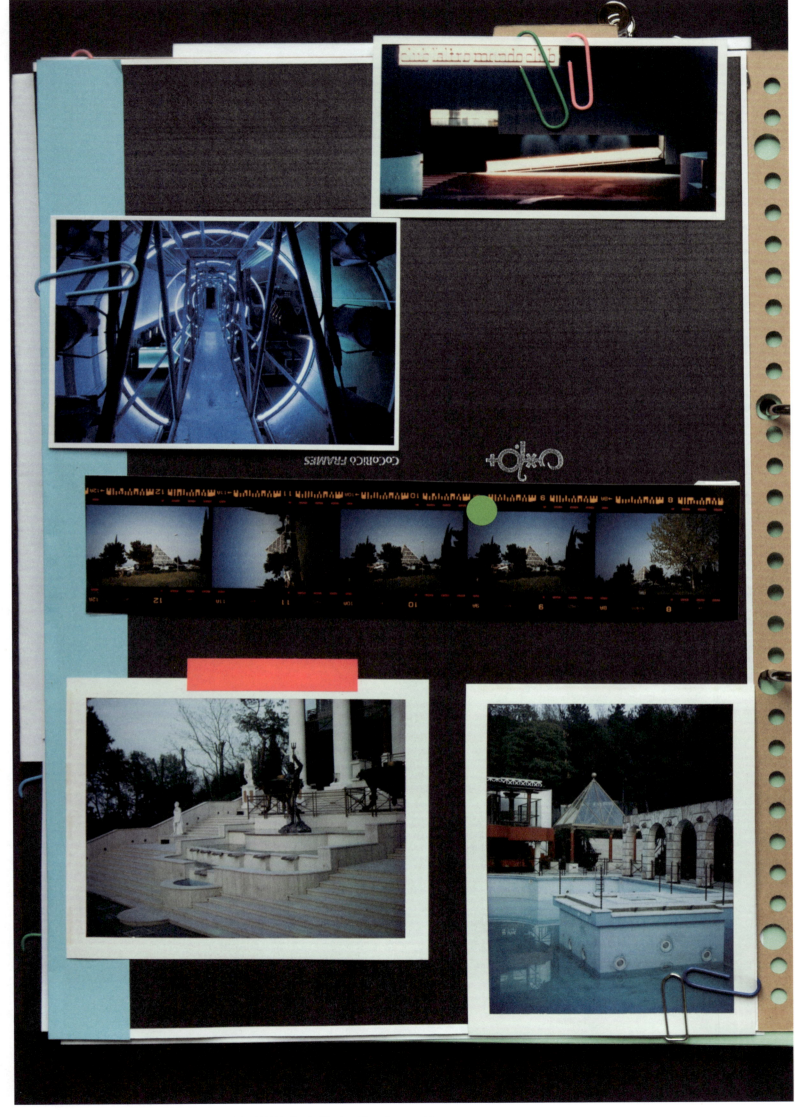

'Nightswimming', booklet published on the occasion of the 2014 Venice Architecture Biennale, page 14.

Cocoricò, Riccione. 2014. Credit: Giovanna Silva

Cocoricò, Riccione. 2014. Credit: Giovanna Silva

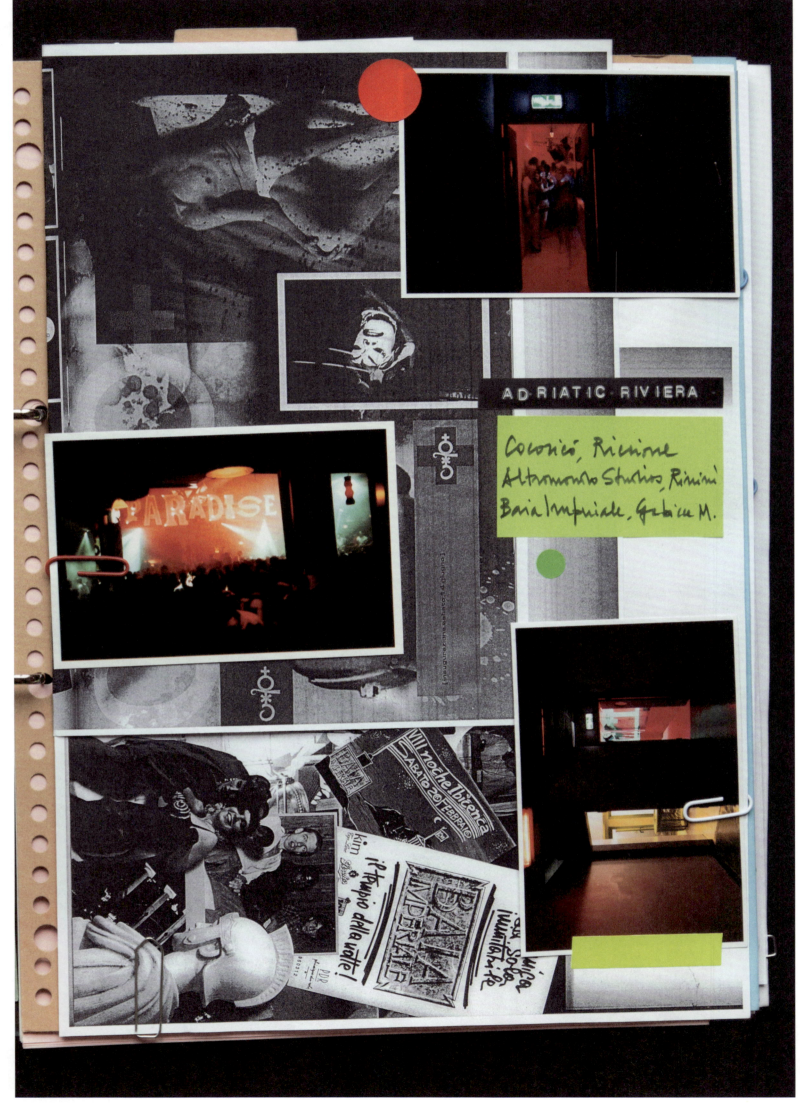

'Nightswimming', booklet published on the occasion of the 2014 Venice Architecture Biennale, page 13.

'Nightswimming', booklet published on the occasion of the 2014 Venice Architecture Biennale, page 7.

Inner Areas

1 km

Community and welfare houses: Experiences and projects in Italy starting from the margin

Antonio De Rossi
Laura Mascino

Massimo Crotti, Antonio De Rossi, Marie-Pierre Forsans, Studio GSP, Centro culturale Lou Pourtoun, Borgata Sant'Antonio-Miribrart, Ostana. Credit: Laura Cantarella

[1] Antonio De Rossi, ed., *Riabitare l'Italia. Le aree interne tra abbandoni e riconquiste* (Rome: Donzelli, 2018).

> 'I am located in the margin. I make a definite distinction between that marginality which is imposed by oppressive structures and that marginality one chooses as site of resistance – as location of radical openness and possibility.'
> bell hooks, *Choosing the Margin as a Space of Radical Openness*, 1990

Never have the mountains and disadvantaged areas of Italy been as much in vogue as they are today, being at the centre of a debate in the media and a topic of public discussion. Of course, the pandemic has acted as an accelerator. But in reality this is a question that goes way back, the product of a change of image and a cultural reworking of the planning of the Italian territory that in the last few years has received some concrete boosts, from the policies introduced by the National Strategy for Disadvantaged Areas to the hundreds of spontaneous experiences of regeneration that are to be found in villages and towns all over the peninsula.

The pandemic has short-circuited the crises of recent years – environmental and economic, but also that of the space generated by the development models of recent decades – with the emergence of new values and visions for the disadvantaged areas. The health debacle has made plain the extent to which the spatial and territorial dimension has been expelled for some time from the policies of this country, reduced to a mere diagrammatic and abstract space. A 'non-physicality of things' that also permeates the philosophies of smart working or of replicable best practices, in accordance with the idea that it is sufficient to stick to a procedure in order to handle the complexity of the contemporary world.

The abstraction from physical space has permitted those actions of *concentration* (of excellence), *separation* (from the territory) and *specialisation* (of function) that have been the mark of the recent transformations of our country. Perhaps it is no coincidence that the polycrisis has been felt most deeply in those intermediate territories that have been the main targets of sector-specific policies.

This growing awareness has only served to bring the problem of disadvantaged areas further to the fore. Thus, in the early months of the crisis we saw interventions that talked of getting villages in the disadvantaged areas 'adopted' by their metropolitan cities, arguing that the future of the country lies in the regions on the margins and no longer in urbanised areas.

Apart from the widespread wishful thinking that characterises these positions – which rarely ask themselves the question of how, and above all with what economic and social aims, limiting themselves to a world made up basically of pretty pictures – what is striking is the imagery underpinning such reflections, which always seems to be rooted in an oppositional and dichotomous vision of the areas, rather than an idea of cooperation and concurrence. Either/or instead of both/and. Either the city or the countryside/mountains. Either the 'centres' or the 'peripheries'. Or again the idea of metropolitan reality 'helping out' the disadvantaged areas, as if they were empty shells, with no communities, plans or desires, just their natural and historical heritage.

And yet these years have shown how the frontier of innovation has often come to lie right along the lines of the margins: projects of regeneration on a cultural basis, community cooperatives, processes of resettlement. To be sure, these are experiments as fragile as the places in which they occur. But in them the spatial dimension plays an active and unprecedented role, one that ought to be observed with attention precisely because of the new openings it can offer, including with respect to increasingly paralysed urban contexts.

Unfortunately, in the responses provided up to now, that paradigm of the technical solution devoid of any physical dimension which has guided the country in recent decades continues to prevail. And yet the crisis demonstrates just how decisive a priority the spatialisation, the territorialisation of policies, is today. The pandemic has in fact shown that the areas which have the greatest resilience are the ones where a high degree of variety and interdependence of the parts is combined with specific environmental characteristics. It is evident that the disadvantaged areas have cards to play in this game. But this signifies redefining in radical terms many of the policies applied to these areas, which have almost always centred on a capitalisation of local resources and their exploitation for the purposes of tourism that is at bottom 'urbanocentric'. We need to look at things the other way round, as we tried to explain in the jointly authored book *Riabitare l'Italia*, published by Donzelli in 2018:[1] not from the centre towards the periphery, but starting from the margin. From the idea that these should not be merely places of *consumption* (of nature, of scenery, of traditions), but first of all areas of *production*: of new cultures, of social innovations, of rural know-how and practices, of renewed ways of ensuring people's welfare and interacting with the environment.

All this, however, runs the risk of remaining an abstract statement of principle if the underlying cultures and imagery do not change. Paradoxically this country, notwithstanding the incredible variety of its landscape, has never cultivated an idea of integration of its parts. New metro-mountain and metro-rural visions are needed, founded on the interdependence of the different territorial systems and their cooperation.

And what is needed, above all, is a new idea of regional habitability. We must stop talking about hospitals, schools, roads. Instead, we should be talking about health, educational communities, the right to mobility and access to information. Getting away from the taxonomy of preconstituted objects and the abstract vision of minimal thresholds, and reconstructing models of infrastructure and welfare on the basis of the specific characteristics of areas. Innovating and contaminating.

From this point of view, the crisis has revealed the senselessness of the sclerotic debate conducted for years over the contrast between large- and small-scale works of 'infrastructuring', where the term itself seems to have turned into a sort of metaphysical fetish detached from the reality of the areas it inhabits. What this country requires is a grand project of re-infrastructuring on different scales that is able to bring together the dimensions of logistics, the environment and welfare.

But to avoid the disadvantaged areas becoming yet another proposition of the Italian road to development centred on building things, a radical cultural change is needed. Here, there is very little to construct. If anything, there is an immense fixed regional capital, made up of villages and farming and riverine systems, of forests and minor infrastructures, which awaits reinterpretation, reuse, maintenance and innovation.

For some time now we have been pondering the possibility, when operating in concrete situations and contexts, that the work of planning around the margins might permit the emergence of a different vision of the practice of architecture, deeply embedded in the materiality of things, regions, communities and processes. As bell hooks puts it, the margin is a heuristic space in which to practise forms of radical opening up to possibilities. There are many disciplines – from the historical social ones to the scientific – that in recent years have chosen to focus on the space of the margin, of the fringe, as a place of inquiry and research.

Among the many experiences of regeneration under way along the fringes of the disadvantaged areas, the best reveal precisely how the architectural project can function as a new root of production in relation to regional assets. Moving away from a merely culturalist and capitalising understanding of the problem, the palimpsest inherited, in the course of the act of regeneration, regains its material and concrete value, becoming a decisive player in processes of reactivation. The physical projects, the buildings, are no longer just an expression of functional and developmental aspirations, but become proactive, serving as locomotives of the regenerative processes. A work of architecture whose value no longer lies solely in its intentions, but in the effectiveness of the results and thus in the effects produced. A regenerative work of design that places the accent more on interpretation than on transformation-construction, and that makes social, cultural and economic dimensions intersect continually, from within the processes, and therefore has more need of the figure of the *bricoleur* and the mediator than that of a traditional designer. Innovation on a cultural basis, new forms of agriculture and welfare and green and techno-rural economies are at the root of these processes of reactivation.

The infrastructuring of communities as an accelerator of regeneration

In all this, particular attention is reserved, from the planning perspective, for the experimentation of new community structures, of unprecedented models of what are known in Italy as *case del welfare*, or 'welfare houses', which combine various aspects of the social services and represent – as experiences in the field have demonstrated – necessary and important incubators, in the intertwining of practices and the physical dimension, of processes of revitalisation and regeneration. Spaces of experimentation in which to reconfigure – shaping them to meet the needs of the community but also with a view to innovation – those taxonomies and segmentations in the provision of services of an urbanocentric character and twentieth-century origin that revealed all their problematic issues and limits in the period of the pandemic and in the processes of decline within communities.

The effects of the pandemic, and more generally the changes in cultural vision of the last few years with respect to the way in which we look at disadvantaged rural and mountainous areas, are in fact leading to a redefinition of important themes such as social relations in communities or regional welfare services. This redefinition pervades public debate, but it also plays a part in a multitude of 'grassroots' experiments and experiences that are emerging here and there in the mountainous and rural regions of the country; even making its way into public policy, as in the case – to take a few examples – of the community nursing programme and the new conceptions of educational spaces introduced under the National Strategy for Disadvantaged Areas, or again the Case della Salute envisaged by the NRRP (National Recovery and Resilience Plan).

In this multitude of cases, certain characteristics and elements seem to recur:

1. The superseding of the idea of 'minimal thresholds' of population and users, taking cognisance of the different characters of these areas.
2. The need to develop specific and pertinent, place-based models of welfare services, tailored to the needs of communities and the characteristics of the areas.
3. The abandonment of the strict sectorial subdivision in the provision of services of an urban character in favour of the synergies and interactions that were historically typical of these areas.
4. The question of intergenerationality viewed as a positive factor.
5. Experimentation with forms of technological innovation (telemedicine, etc.) in the supply of services in disadvantaged rural and mountainous areas, through modes of adaptive transfer suited to the specific character of places.

However, the factor of greatest novelty, together with these points, is the idea – as can be inferred from the experiences and experiments in the field – that the question of services and welfare in local communities should not remain confined to a matter of organisation and delivery, but become an active vector of processes of revitalisation and regeneration.

Support services for people in need and to achieve work–life balance for families, training and educational facilities, activities connected with health and welfare, cultural infrastructures, social housing in support of resettlement processes, along with co-working spaces and incubators of new local economies, the commercial structures needed to make places habitable; these are viewed therefore not in terms of the guarantee and provision of basic services to citizens, but as systems of social innovation able to generate new forms of sociality, economy and culture.

It is a change of perspective, discernible, as has been said, in the experiments in course, that can be truly significant. Places that not only deliver services, but activate and produce new ways of creating a community, new forms of welfare, entrepreneurship, knowledge and local know-how. And that above all can function as accelerators of processes of regeneration. It is no coincidence that novel forms of management are also being developed around these experiments, which in addition to the public sector are increasingly seeing the involvement and active and proactive contribution of the communities themselves, of organisations in the not-for-profit sector, of community cooperatives and of forms of public–private partnership. A suitability and pertinence that therefore does not concern solely the forms and types of services, but organisational cultures and forms of management.

In all this, the physical and spatial dimension is not irrelevant. This is an aspect that is often forgotten or underestimated, in the belief that the central and most important factor is essentially the delivery of services. The most interesting and innovative experiments under way in Italy and elsewhere in Europe are showing instead how the localisation component, the ability to establish relations with the surrounding region and the quality of the interventions play a decisive and strategic role in processes of revitalisation and regeneration.

From the perspective of settlement and localisation it is in fact a question of creating 'focal points' around which to develop generative triggers, while on the physical and architectural scale it is important to work on interaction and concurrence, overcoming the usual separation and segmentation and fostering that quality and beauty of spaces that are indispensable premises for a sense of identity and of belonging to a place. Decisive, above all, is the capacity of these spaces to create a 'critical mass', bringing together different generations and people and providing services not from a specialist perspective but from one of integrated construction of the habitability of the place. Instead, it is often thought that the delivery and distribution of services to a number of villages or settlements in the same area can ensure greater opportunities of access and utilisation by the population, but this runs the risk of losing the multiplier effect of the critical mass.

This theme, on which a number of experiments are being conducted today in the disadvantaged rural and mountainous areas under the names of Case di Comunità, Case del Welfare and others, is not a new one, having been explored in experiences of self-organi-

Massimo Crotti, Antonio De Rossi, Marie-Pierre Forsans, Studio GSP, Centro culturale Lou Pourtoun, Borgata Sant'Antonio-Miribrart, Ostana. Credit: Laura Cantarella

sation of regions in the past. For instance, the health and education network established in the nineteenth century in the Waldensian valleys of Piedmont – hospitals, Beckwith schools, and so on – and the community and village houses to be found in many settlements in the Alps and Apennines, a policy that continues today with the creation of *Dorfhäuser* in South Tyrol, multifunctional structures at the service of villages in the disadvantaged valleys. A history that, in the light of contemporary developments, is worth exploring and analysing.

Planning experiments on the ground

At Turin Polytechnic we have long been practising forms of applied planning research in close coordination with local communities and regional bodies. Such practice does not merely answer to the vital need for the university to go out into the field to carry out a reality check of the effectiveness of methodologies and means. Above all, it performs an experimental and heuristic function: maintaining the connection between the results of research and the dynamics of change in society, opening up new and unexplored questions and visions in the light of this dialectic and contributing to the development and progress of local ecosystems, of which academic structures are an integral part.

So it is not a simple activity of transfer or a third mission for social ends, but a work of socio-spatial mediation that in its initiation and implementation is also a practice of scientific conceptualisation. It is at bottom what our founding fathers – from Quintino Sella onwards – were doing in support of the construction of the recently unified state.

All the while with an extremely particular, specific value of the know-how of architecture and the disciplines that deal with the physical dimension of areas: the spatialising of planning and design intentions and policies of transformation, with the aim of prefiguring their effects and permitting public discussion of the possible outcome. And an idea of architecture that is not just civil but above all productive, and that perhaps also foreshadows a new way of thinking about the profession, in which being there and confrontation with the existing are decisive questions.

What follows is a brief description of some of the experiences in course along the difficult margins – but filled with openings and possibilities – of the disadvantaged rural and mountainous areas of our country.

Ostana, community houses and welfare infrastructure for resettlement

Ostana is a town in the upper Po Valley, at the foot of Monviso, that in 1921 had 1,200 inhabitants but whose population declined steeply over the course of the twentieth century, like that of all the Occitan valleys. In 1985 one of the first projects of revitalisation in Italy was launched here. This turned on making the most of the local history and resources. The town started to attract attention and visitors, but this did not halt its depopulation: by the end of the century Ostana had only five permanent residents. It was evident that something different was needed. In 2003 a second phase in the process of revitalisation began: this time it entailed setting up welfare services to encourage resettlement, facilities for the new local micro-economies and the production – not just consumption – of culture. With the support of Turin Polytechnic a series of spaces were created for the community: the Lou Pourtoun cultural centre, the Mizoun de la Villo – Casa Alpina del Welfare and the Valentin co-housing project, as well as structures for new farming activities and sustainable tourism. A sort of infrastructuring of welfare and new economies that has played a decisive part in the rebirth of the town. Many of these structures are run by the Viso a Viso community cooperative, providing services to the population. Today Ostana has over fifty inhabitants, many of them young families with children with a high level of education. A place that, after running the risk of dying, symbolises the possibility of a new way of living in the mountains.

Centro culturale Lou Pourtoun project: Massimo Crotti and Antonio De Rossi (Turin Polytechnic), Marie-Pierre Forsans, Studio GSP; Mizoun de la Villo project: Massimo Crotti and Antonio De Rossi (Turin Polytechnic), Luisella Dutto.

Community houses and services in the Casermette di Moncenisio

Moncenisio is a village in the upper Val Cenischia, close to the pass and lake of Mont Cenis and just a few metres from the French border, that for a long time has been top of the list of the smallest municipalities in Italy. Some years ago a process of revitalisation of the place commenced, with the setting up of an ecomuseum devoted to the subject of borderlands in collaboration with the Diocesan Museum of Susa and with the creation of several new accommodation facilities. Histories and memories have been at the centre of an effort to raise its cultural profile. But today the municipality of Moncenisio has set itself new goals: the creation of spaces for community life and cultural production and of services for the well-being of the inhabitants and visitors with a view to their integration with the structures that already exist. Out of these premises has emerged the project for the upgrading of the Casermette or former barracks of the Guardia di Finanza, a set of spaces located in an Alpine garden that will permit, from a so-called 'metro-mountain' perspective, new forms of sociality and a new quality of life for the local community and visitors.

Project: Antonio De Rossi, Laura Mascino and Matteo Tempestini of Turin Polytechnic; Edoardo Schiari and Maicol Guiguet.

The network of community and welfare services of Dossena

At Dossena, a locality situated between the Val Brembana and the Val Serina in the province of Bergamo, an entire generation of young people between the ages of twenty and thirty has decided not to leave the place, and to engage collectively in its administration and in the local community cooperative of I Raìs in an effort to bring the town back to life. A large number of cultural initiatives and programmes to boost tourism and the economy have been put in place in recent years, attracting considerable public funding. But here, too, as elsewhere, it was realised that the promotion of the town risked being insufficient if work was not also done on the creation of welfare services and facilities for the community. And so, alongside the museum and the new Tibetan-style bridge, the network of trails and the rehabilitation of the former bird-trapping post called the 'Roccolo', various projects with sociocultural aims have been launched: the new library, a nursery school for children aged between two and four and a music school for children from two to six, both run by the local community cooperative, the Casa Renato devoted to intergenerational dynamics with spaces for the young and old that functions as a genuine community house, the ambitious project for turning the former Albergo Mirasole into a new cultural and social centre for the town. With the support of Turin Polytechnic, and in collaboration with local planners, an operation has been carried out to put all the plans online with the aim of constructing a network of community and welfare services for Dossena.

General regeneration project: Antonio De Rossi and Laura Mascino.

The community house of Gagliano Aterno as a means of regeneration

At Gagliano Aterno, a town with around 250 inhabitants in the Valle Subequana, Abruzzo, the rate of decline has been accelerated by the earthquake of 2009. Recently, a process of revitalisation and regeneration of the place has got under way, launched by the local council together with the group of young anthropologists called Montagne in Movimento. The resources allocated to repair the damage caused by the quake are being used for a project of reappraisal of Gagliano Aterno, aimed not just at its material reconstruction, but at the creation of social and welfare facilities and structures from an integrated perspective, in which the restoration of the Monastery of Santa Chiara and the realisation of the new Municipal Operations Centre will function as infrastructure for regeneration and resettlement services in the town: spaces for children and families, for cultural production, for new local micro-economies, for sports facilities and above all for community activities and events. A large community house in the centre of town, set up with the support of Turin Polytechnic and local professionals, aspires to be a place able to drive the process of regeneration, which also envisages the creation of an energy community.

Centro Operativo Comunale – Casa Comunitaria project: Antonio De Rossi, Laura Mascino, Matteo Tempestini (Turin Polytechnic), Vincenzo Durantini, Francesco Eusani.

The Caserma of Usseglio as a space of metro-mountain services

Usseglio is a town in the upper Viù Valley, one of the Lanzo Valleys. A place that, in spite of suffering from the decline and depopulation common to all mountainous areas, has been able to maintain some of its strength, partly owing to its long tradition of welcoming tourists. It is clear to the community, however, that it is necessary to diversify its vision of development, and to rely as well on new activities and sectors able to keep the population in place and, if possible, attract new inhabitants. The opportunity to make a move in this direction has been provided by the acquisition by the state of the Caserma Rocciamelone, a former barracks that consists of a series of buildings located in a small park. A work group has been established, made up of the municipality of Usseglio, the metropolitan city of Turin, the Association of Friends of the Civic Museum of Usseglio, the University and Polytechnic of Turin and the two Consortia of Mountain Communities of the Lanzo Valleys, with the support of UNCEM (Unione nazionale dei comuni, comunità ed enti montani). This has drawn up a plan for the barracks centred strongly on the social and welfare values of the new way of life in the mountains. There are spaces for services, and workshop and educational facilities for the residents of the town, but also for the inhabitants of the entire metropolitan region, as in the case of the facilities devoted to mountain therapy for psychophysical well-being, with a view to characterising Usseglio as a place of exchange between mountains and city from the perspective of the metro-mountain.

Project: the architect Loredana Iacopino, with the consultancy of Antonio De Rossi (Turin Polytechnic) and Filippo Barbera (Turin University).

Massimo Crotti, Antonio De Rossi, Marie-Pierre Forsans, Studio GSP, Centro culturale Lou Pourtoun, Borgata Sant'Antonio-Miribrart, Ostana. Credit: Laura Cantarella

Further reading:

Filippo Barbera and Antonio De Rossi, eds., *Metromontagna: Un progetto per riabitare l'Italia* (Rome: Donzelli, 2021).

Antonio De Rossi, ed., *Riabitare l'Italia. Le aree interne tra abbandoni e riconquiste* (Rome: Donzelli, 2018).

Antonio De Rossi and Laura Mascino, entries 'Patrimonio' and 'Rigenerazione' in Domenico Cersosimo and Carmine Donzelli, eds., *Manifesto per riabitare l'Italia* (Rome: Donzelli, 2020).

Antonio De Rossi and Laura Mascino, 'Territorio / Territory – Per un progetto metromontano' / 'Promoting a metro-mountain project', *Domus*, no. 1052 (2020).

Massimo Crotti, Antonio De Rossi, Luisella Dutto, Mizoun de la Villo – Casa Alpina del Welfare, Ostana.
Credit: Laura Cantarella

Massimo Crotti, Antonio De Rossi, Luisella Dutto, Mizoun de la Villo – Casa alpina del welfare, Ostana.
Credit: Laura Cantarella

Letter on paesologia

Franco Arminio

To the friends of the
Temporary Community

After dedicating five books to the subject, perhaps the time has come for me to try to sum up in a few words just what *paesologia* is.[1]

The first thing that needs to be said is that *paesologia* is a discipline rooted in the land and in the flesh. The flesh of the observer, the land that is observed. A form of fluctuating attention in which the observer and the subject of observation often end up exchanging roles. And then it is the land looking at the flesh, the land inquiring into the moods of whoever is looking at it.

What is needed is an idea of the self disconnected from the classical and reassuring little habits of the Cartesian ego. We are just as exposed to the vagaries of the weather as a tree, as a roadman's house. We are not a fortress from which to peer at the infantile disaster of the world; we are not adults sheltered from the draughts that come from below, the draughts of childhood and of Thanatos.

Yesterday an architect friend told me he would like to train as a *paesologo*. He said that the perspective of *paesologia* comprised everything that he did and that he was not very comfortable with defining himself as an architect. It is the same reason why I do not feel at ease describing myself as a writer or even a poet. These words seem to speak of experiences too different from my own. What sense does it have for someone to define me in the same way as Moccia? With *paesologia* I head off somewhere else, I define a place filled with foxes and buzzards, broken street lamps, stray dogs, cats, old men on benches, old women wandering the street clutching bags. This territory is the drop of blood on the slide. But there's no need for a microscope. The view is broadened by anxiety, by the fear of remaining in the crater of your own body, a crater that trembles, has always trembled.

Paesologia is not a new human science; it is a way of paying attention to the outside – intense attention because it is temporary, because *paesologi* start from the depths of their body and return to them continually. Their gaze requires them to balance on their presumed non-existence, a perennial attempt to come into the world that appears never to be completely successful. But in this reaching out can be sensed the grace, the confused swirl of things that lie outside, the immense expanse of creatures deposited in the happy hell of the round earth.

For me it makes no sense today to be writers, sociologists, architects … There is no sense even in defining ourselves as human beings. We are called upon to listen to the air and the air tells that the things we know are nails made of plaster on which we can hang nothing.

Paesologia is a defenceless discipline, but it has not surrendered. It does not go on marches or turn academic tricks. It lines up details, advances, retreats, stumbles, and perhaps it is through this stumbling that it is able to go farther inside, to get closer to things.

The *paesologo* has no plans for the salvation of *paesi*, does not defend parochialisms, dialects, rancorous whinings, the craving for confidences and intimacies. Sometimes the *paesologo* becomes combative, gets angry, demands protection for the beings and things that are located up there, far away from the ravings of the plains, but this strand of ardour is immediately intertwined with one of sadness. *Paesologi* go to *paesi* looking for despair and find themselves with a smidgen of bliss in their hands: it might be a step, a new house or an old one; it might be the sight of a castle or a walnut tree; it might be an empty square or an alley with the hum of a TV set. *Paesologia* has no remedies for curing things, but takes care to look, to wander around aimlessly, to linger or even leave hastily. There are no rules, no questionnaires to fill in. There's no formulary to prepare. You go out, you leave for a few hours the prison of your home, the prison of your profession. You go to the most out-of-the-way and disconsolate places and you always find something. You fill yourself up because the world makes sense only where it is emptier; the world is bearable only in its cracks, in its neglected spaces, in the places where the steamroller of consumption and production has run into some rock that won't crumble.

It won't always be like that. *Paesologia* is a temporary science. It could not have existed a hundred years ago and it will not exist in a hundred years. In a century the *paesi* will have taken a clearer turn. They'll be dead or they'll be alive and kicking, and then they will no longer have this twilight air that makes them so distinctive. A small window has opened and through this window the *paese* is showing us the delirium and glory of being in the world.

Go to the *paesi*, then, to the towns, villages and countryside, go to where there is no one around. Take care to believe in the wasted beauty of the *paesaggio*, the landscape. Go and drink from the remote fountains of the breath.

---

[1] *Paesologia* is a word coined by Franco Arminio from the Italian *paese*, which can mean countryside, town or village.

Searching for the 'Italian code'

Lukas Spreitzer

The work is a reflection on the multilayered realities defining Italy. It opens up the perspective from the repetitive models of late modernism in search of an answer for the question of housing for the 'many' – from the new models of the *borghi* in the overlapping of the digital and the vernacular (depicted is Colletta di Castelbianco) to a new way of reorganising the spatial fabric to resonate with the changes in society.

Project by Lukas Spreitzer.
Design studio: *Grand Tour Italy* by Michael Obrist and Antonietta Putzu.
Workshop: *Drawing Architecture: Italian Collages* by Bernadette Krejs.
Summer semester 2019 at TU Wien.

Repetition of modernism

The vernacular

Searching for the 'Italian code'

Towards a critical rurality

Iain Chambers

The challenge of new rurality proposes a new figure of thought, a modality of thinking and associated practices, that carries us beyond the inherited divisions of town and country, urban and rural, industrial and agricultural. A series of overflows and contaminations – the cellphone in the countryside, natural foodstuffs in the supermarket, satellite television in the mountain village, the weekend cottage retreat – invite us to rethink such categories and their assumed distinctiveness. To fold inherited categories and their associated territories into other critical narratives is to expose their premises to unsuspected questions and transport them into unguaranteed spaces. Local tradition – rural and urban – is crossed by the social transformations and historical transits of translation. And it is in the crossings and cuts elaborated in the passage of artistic languages, in their exploratory excess and errancy, we most sharply encounter this new cartography. For here, we are consistently called upon to evaluate the ordinary, the presumptions of our everyday world, in the light of the extra-ordinary, to register an aesthetics that also transmits ethics.

To embark on emergent rurality, we must reconsider such consistently abused terms as 'tradition' and 'identity'. We must expose them to a movement, so our critical landscape acquires new forms and possibilities. Against the sedimented logic of a 'passive revolution' (Antonio Gramsci) sustained by insidious stereotypes of 'common sense', it is necessary to interrupt a continuity that promotes the static understanding of historical processes and cultural forms, condemning us to be prisoners of an uncontrollable destiny. To enter the folds of the narrative and move along lines disseminated by intervals and interruptions that negate the linear banality of historicism is to propose a diverse poetics (and politics) of time. Following various sounds and signs, it becomes possible to cut up and sound out the terrain, the territory, and the transit of lives lived and yet to come to expose new dimensions, viewpoints and lines of observation. After all, the rural world is never homogeneous. It, too, proposes diverse tracks and traces, desires and deviations, that confound the placid image projected in the dynamics of urban life.

There also exists the question of scale. In the impossibility of indicating where the 'local' concludes and the 'external' commences, there emerges a series of intertwinings that render each and every place a knot, a node, in a network suspended and sustained in what are ultimately planetary processes. In these mobile geographies, a web of relations bends and folds distance, proposing various proximities and perspectives: new and unexpected. In this manner, a new rurality offers a discontinuous understanding of history. The past is not cancelled but reassembled in a more mobile and contingent set of responses to the present. The past becomes a living present, a group of interrogations, traces and testimonies that persist and live on; these potentially interrupt the presumption that the past is really over, dead and buried. As an 'eternal return' that provokes a sense of time always open to the unresolved and to the survival of what is presumed to have been overcome and cancelled, the critical cut of discontinuity (concerning the linearity of explanations we are expected to accept) requires that we crack apart the old debate between tradition and modernity, and transform it into another language.

Gramsci's radical twist and transformation on the question are pivotal to our concerns. Refusing the linear logic of historicism in which modernity was merely the successful overcoming of tradition, Gramsci shifted the whole debate 180 degrees. Insisting on the power of culture (and the culture of power), he argued in terms of relations between hegemonic and subaltern social formations in which tradition and modernity are distributed and decanted in multiple practices and places. Religion, superstition, custom and habit are not the property or prerogative of any single formation but are elaborated in diverse forces and forms. To be recognised in modernity can draw upon the oldest traditions' appeal to seemingly timeless truths secured in the soil. Still, their recognition is also the registration of their pertinence to modernity as they survive and sustain themselves in the transit of historical translation. As instances of translation and transit, such elements of tradition find themselves *within* modernity. They may well be marginalised, negated and repressed, but, like the unconscious, they are there.

Understanding traditions from within the formations of modernity permits us to abandon thinking *of* the South as an object and to begin, as Franco Cassano suggests, thinking *with* the South as a subject, perhaps subaltern, but always as an integral and active part of modernity. With this perspective, it becomes possible to enter the folds of the landscape and there render it less provincial. In this, an altogether more open prospect, we can also return to such vital concepts as 'territory' and 'identity' in reconfiguring our sense of history and culture as open-ended processes and not as stable objects already framed in pre-existing interpretations. The landscape at this point becomes a living archive, fluid and mobile, home to a series of processes caught in nets that, like all nets, are also full of holes that suggest further opportunities, movement and transit. This dynamic heterotopia provokes a *critical rurality*. Here we find ourselves beyond the instrumental 'solutions' of politics in the living problematics of a culture that becomes the primary means for reappropriating a territory, a history, a life.

To return to the languages of errancy and excess, to the grammar of art … Listening to the soundscapes modulated in the jazz saxophone of a local musician, where the improvised flights of the blues cross the landscape, repeating its histories in another key, we hear a truth, sustained in sound, that exceeds sociological explanation. From the rich opacity of sound emerges a diverse modernity – heterogeneous, multiple and multilateral: a migrating and creolising modernity. In the end, we confront modernity that, exceeding our domesticating desires, propels us into a territory still to be mapped and traversed.

The Million Donkey Hotel

feld72

Million Donkey Hotel.
By feld72. Credit: Hertha
Hurnaus

Credit: Hertha Hurnaus

Credit: Hertha Hurnaus

Credit: Hertha Hurnaus

Can you build a hotel in twenty-four days?

In 2005, 73% of the population of Europe lived in cities, and this figure was growing. This sort of percentage not only means the constant growth of (in-between) cities but also – and above all – the disappearance of the cultural and natural landscapes familiar to us. In a complexity of connections that we possibly are not aware of, the future of these zones that are threatened with extinction also represent Europe's future.

Migration and its consequences are also the theme of 'The Million Donkey Hotel', a project by feld72 carried out for the Villaggio dell'Arte by the Paesesaggio workgroup. In August 2005 a group of national and international artists was invited to address questions of identity, territory, social space and landscape in the Matese Regional Park near Naples by means of art projects involving the participation of the local population. The artists were required to live locally for one month, to work together with the local population and to draw all materials used from the local villages to stimulate the micro-economy of the region.

Prata Sannita is a village divided into two, consisting of a medieval '*borgo*', known as the Prata Inferiore, which cascades down a hill from a castle, and a newer part, the Prata Superiore, which owes its structure above all to the victory of the motor car and other promises of modernism. In the course of the last century Prata Inferiore was dramatically affected by migration caused by poverty and is now only a small part of the village, inhabited by a minority made up mostly of elderly people, and with a very large number of empty buildings, some of which are already in ruins. How could these two clearly separated areas of the village be linked again? How and for whom could the qualities of the almost sculptural spatial landscape be experienced once again? How can spaces that stand for loss become a self-confident part of a new Prata Sannita? How can a 'free of' lead to a 'free to'?

Prata Sannita is seen in its entirety as a large, scattered hotel that still has rooms available: the abandoned rooms. These are not regarded as bearers of memories but as potential for the future. They become cells in a larger entity and the entire area of Prata Sannita is perceived as a single action space. The first adaptation of three spatial units (and a special 'bathroom') to form 'hotel rooms' distanced from everyday life was the start to making the spaces usable once again; but this time for a nomad not driven by worries about a better future – the traveller. The rooms were individualised and given specific themes and atmospheres based on migration and memory. Through the intervention, the local residents were to be stimulated to understand, in a second phase, the other abandoned rooms as further building blocks of this hyper-real hotel and to reactivate them accordingly.

The Million Donkey Hotel at the same time became an extension of public space – in the 'off-season' the hotel rooms could also be used by the Pratesi. Through the impressive involvement of up to forty volunteers in the village (with an estimated 4,300 hours on site) it was possible to implement the Million Donkey Hotel despite the very tight time framework (one month with design practically on site), a low budget (10,000 euros) and the use of only the simplest means.

Thanks to the great success, feld72 were invited back the following year. The work in 2006 was focused primarily on public space – for example, a ruined house in the immediate proximity of the completed hotel rooms was converted into a literal 'stair-house' (amphitheatre) – and an association was set up. The Million Donkey Hotel is now organised by a small group of 'local heroes' who were involved in its building.

Credit: Hertha Hurnaus

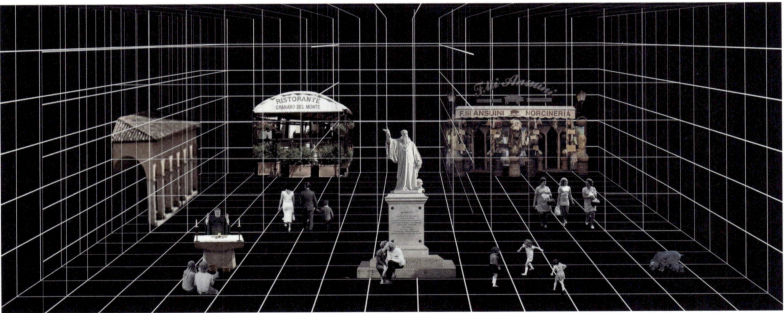

Projects by Julian Graf and Isabel Caroline Köhler.
Design studio: *The Grammar of Reconstruction* by Christina Lenart.
Winter semester 2019 at TU Wien.

The grammar of reconstruction

<u>Conservarium</u>
Julian Graf

Norcia, a small municipality in the province of Perugia, was shaken by an earthquake in 2016. A large part of the old town became unusable, forcing local institutions to close. It was only after almost two years that they found a new place, secluded outside the city.

Besides the immediate need for shelter after a catastrophe, it is equally important to create space for coming together and for everyday rituals, routines and habits.

The *conservarium* is a proposal for a flexible, temporary space that supports the residents in the various tasks of reconstruction.

The *conservarium* is intended to protect the key spatial elements which are essential to guarantee public life in the municipality.

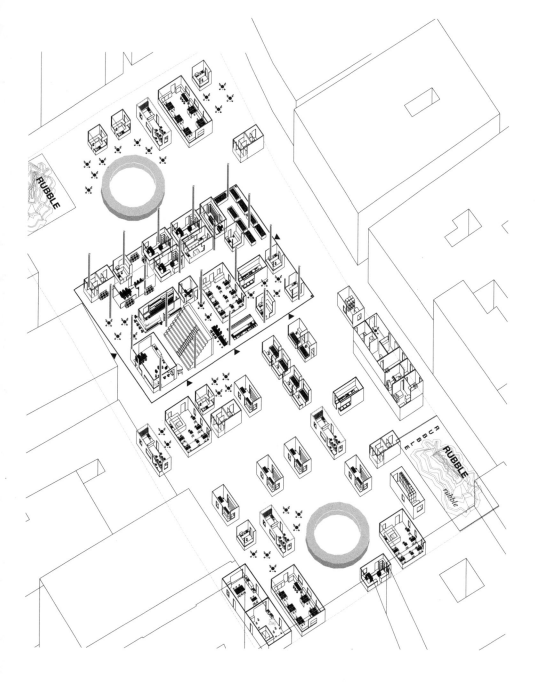

<u>Offset – free space
as a binding element</u>
Isabel Köhler

The identity of a person and a place are interrelated. The person helps the place to find its identity, and the place helps the person. Once this connection is broken – as in the case of a disaster such as an earthquake – it is a difficult and long process to re-establish it. This is exemplified by the situation in L'Aquila, which ten years after the earthquake still seems not to have found its way back to some kind of urban life.

The aim of this urban and social strategy is to keep this connection alive. On the one hand, to drive processes 'from within' and, on the other, to connect them to urban life.

The open spaces serve this purpose. Paths and squares are the first things that can be made usable again. They hold potential or space for functions that keep the city alive and drive it forward. It is an intermediate stage between habit and new beginning. A distancing of the inhabitants from their city is prevented or at least reduced.

An offset of the city is created by shifting the public functions from the unusable buildings to replacement structures which are now occupying the public space and become the new attractors for social life. The built typologies form a cross-section of the functions that are essential for urban life and should thereby give the locals as much space as possible for cultural and identity formation.

Il bello, il brutto, il cattivo

The aesthetics of beauty

Caroline Faber
Roswitha Goy
Julia Maretzki
Theresa Reiter

Throughout history, there has been a constant search for universally valid rules for beauty in architecture. Can beauty be measured at all on the basis of fixed parameters? A close examination and analysis of well-known examples of Italian architecture is an indispensable method of research.

On the basis of architectural and urbanistic icons, an attempt was made to show the parameters of beauty and how they have changed over the course of time. These buildings, squares and places of public life have had a decisive influence on the understanding of beauty in architecture.

In examining these examples, patterns are revealed that attempt to explain visually perceptible beauty. The architectural icons chosen illustrate, both in their wholeness and in their details, the design principles of harmony, tension, symmetry, rhythm, proportion, golden ratio, rules of scale or hierarchy.

By meticulously drawing the icons and analysing the essential design elements, it is possible to derive supposedly universal principles of beauty. The Italian icons are examined both in their wholeness and in their detail.

The collage method illustrates the narrative, autonoetic strength of this pictorial form. Image fragments alter perception through collisions, super-impositions, disturbances and gaps. Theses and questions are taken to extremes and specifically challenge perception.

The Italian code of the aesthetics of beauty is composed of the application of well-known design principles and the meticulous composition of structural elements. This emerges from an interplay of context, detail and identity. These fragments occur coherently, often overlap and partially condition each other – they have a decisive influence on the perception of buildings.

Based on this recognition of the multilayered factors in the creation of beauty, three spaces of varying quality were designed. The beauty of these spaces is only revealed when they are combined to form a whole. The combination creates meeting zones, paths and squares. These components constitute different cities through subtle accumulation. Hidden, moving and polarising spaces can be recognised in any joined urban system. This possibility is the key to a new code: the aesthetics of beauty.

Project by Caroline Faber, Roswitha Goy, Julia Maretzki and Theresa Reiter.
Design studio: *Grand Tour Italy* by Michael Obrist and Antonietta Putzu. Summer semester 2019 at TU Wien.

City of squares

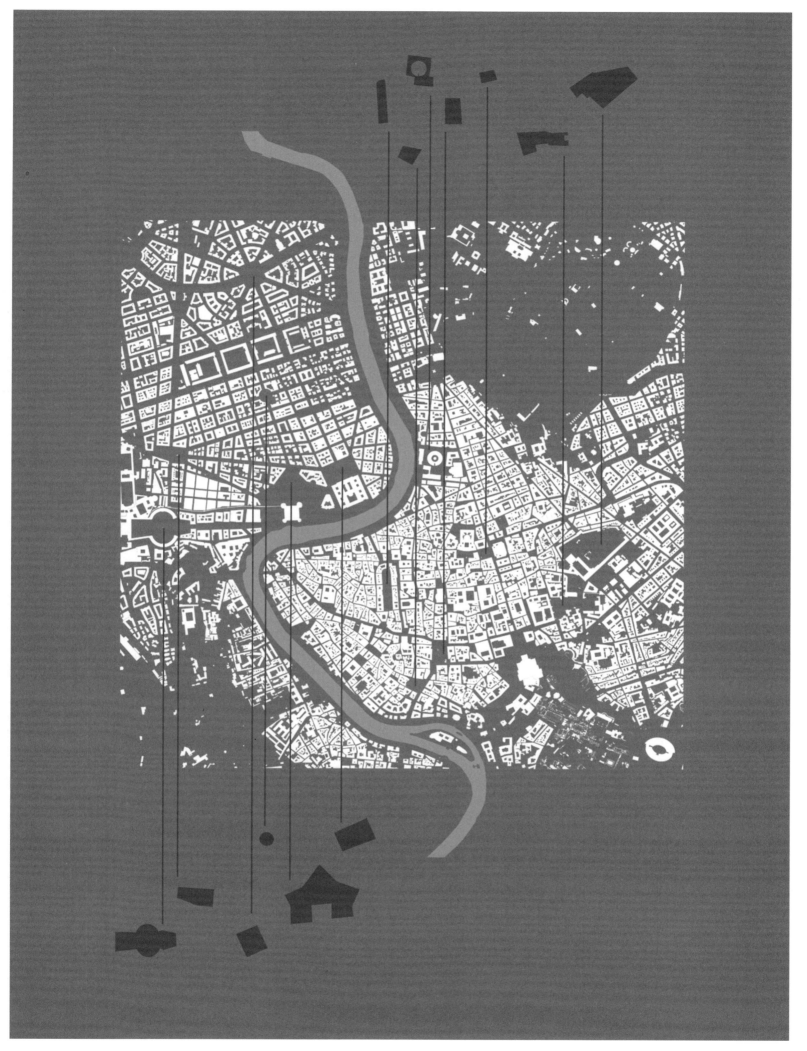

Visualisation of city of squares

 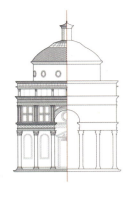 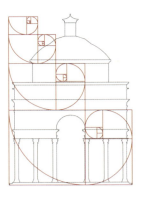 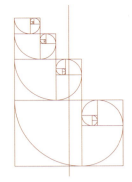

Cappella Pazzi

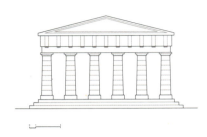 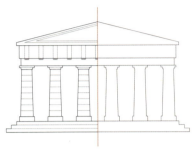 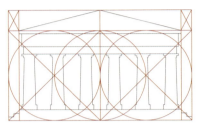 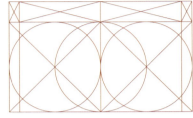

Tempio di Segesta

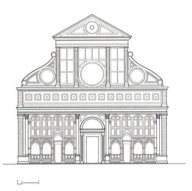 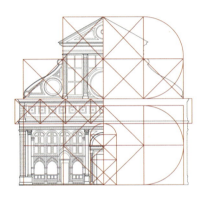 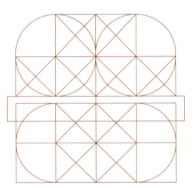 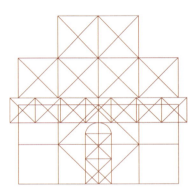

Santa Maria Novella

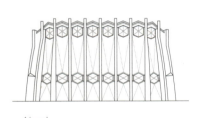 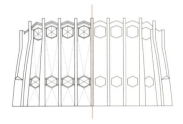 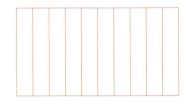 

Sinagoga di Livorno

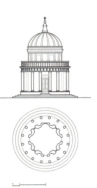 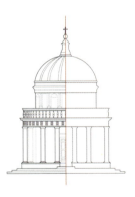 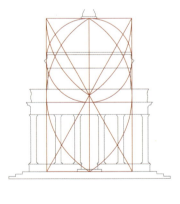 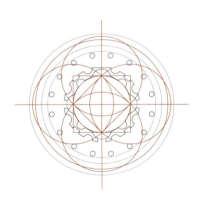

Tempietto del Bramante

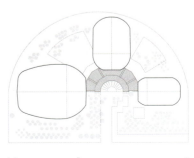 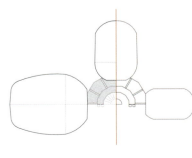 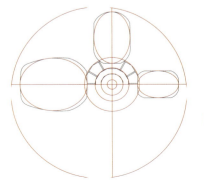 

Auditorium Parco della Musica

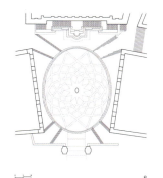 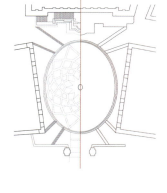 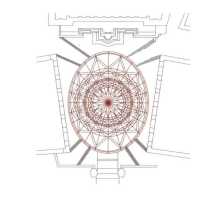 

Piazza del Campidoglio

 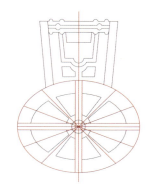 

Piazza San Pietro

  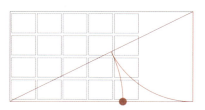

Casa del Fascio

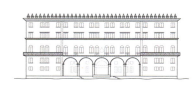  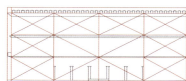 

Fondaco dei Tedeschi

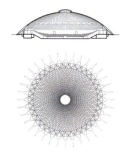 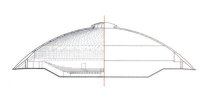

Palazzetto dello Sport

 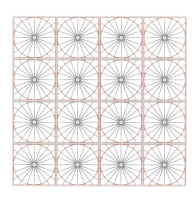 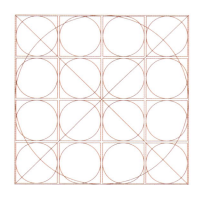 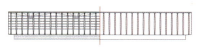

Palazzo del Lavoro

Il bello, il brutto, il cattivo

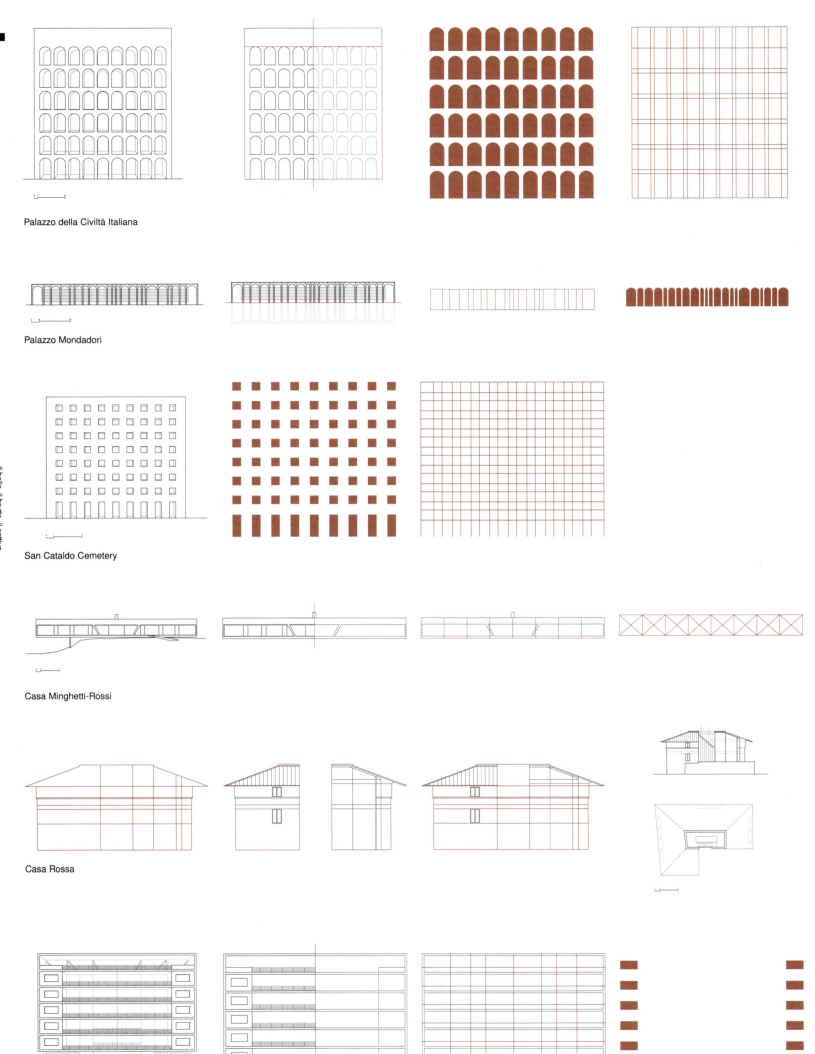

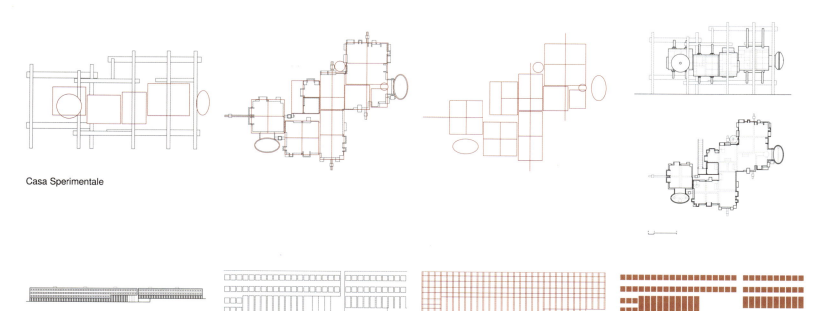

Casa Sperimentale

Complesso Gallaratese

Palazzo del Te

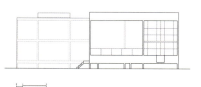

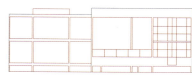

Pavillon de l'Esprit Nouveau

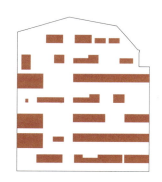

Piazza Carbonari

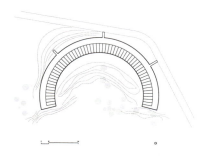
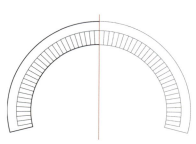
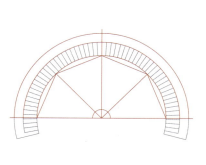
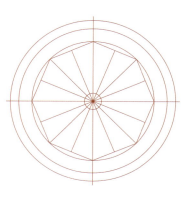

Unità Residenziale Ovest

Visualisation of context,
architecture and nature

Il bello, il brutto, il cattivo

330

City of voids, aerial view of Florence

Visualisation of
Italian code multiplied

Il bello, il brutto, il cattivo

■ The hidden space – the invisible beauty. An introverted space, the conscious moment makes this the centre of our world.

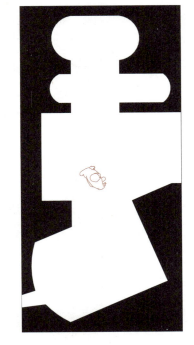

The moving space – the beautiful as the attribute of the situational. Through physical movement, the sequence of space can be grasped in its entirety.

The polarising space – the beautiful as provocation. A characteristic that instrumentalises the exaggeratedly beautiful and the sublime. A game of scale.

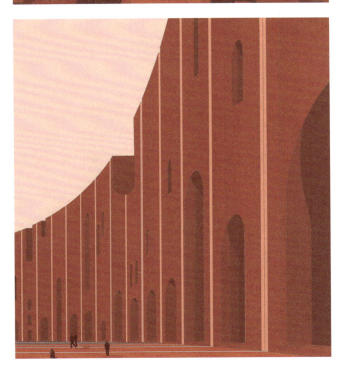

Codes – the evolved city

Codes – the radical city

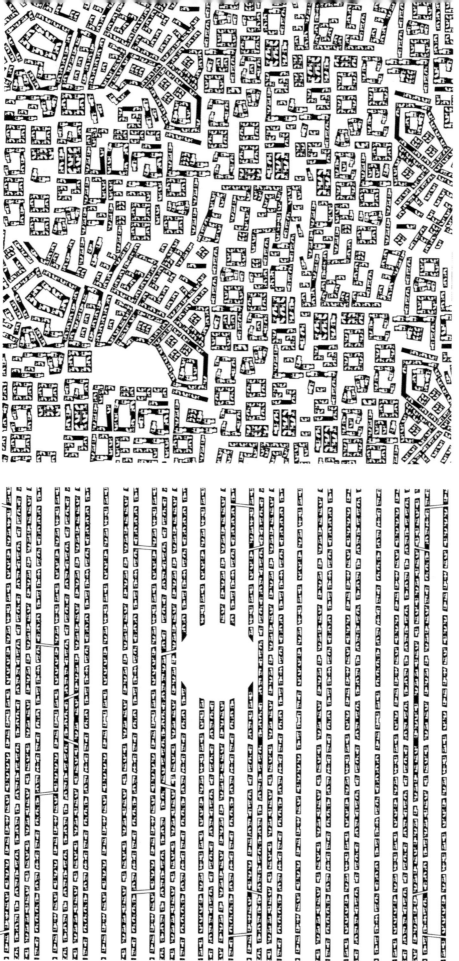

Il bello, il brutto, il cattivo

The evolved city

The evolved city

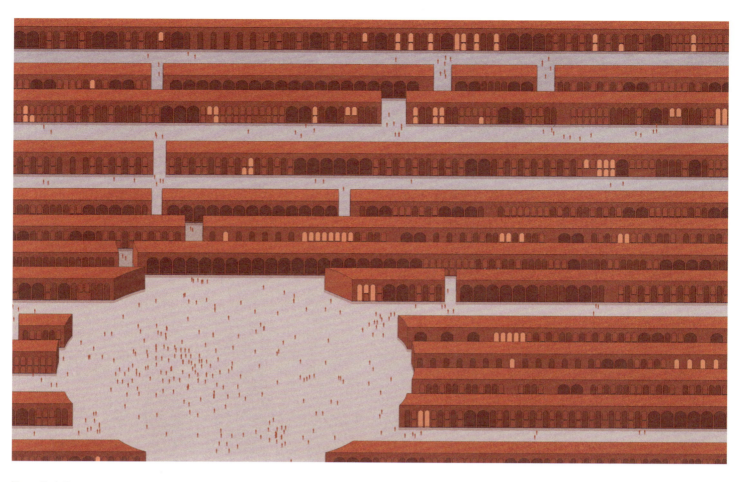

The radical city

The radical city

Una casa all'Italiana: The emergence of the vernacular

Antonietta Putzu

Villa Malaparte by Adalberto Libera, Capri 1938. Credit: Bruno Melis

'[B]ut I also think that it is quintessentially Italian without being an idea of Italy. It's just Italy' – this is how director Luca Guadagnino describes Crema, a quiet and picturesque small town an hour's drive from Milan that was one of the main locations for his film *Call Me by Your Name*.[1] He explains his choice by invoking the 'authentic' found quality of this place, which is characterised by its walkability, its centuries-old urban fabric and its cultural richness. As a counterpoint, he refers to the Hollywood productions that often show only an idea of Italy, a fake image, whereas for him 'it's important you make the thing that looks the most correct and the most real'.[2] In *I Am Love*, *Call Me by Your Name* and *A Bigger Splash*, he narrates territories and characteristic typologies of *abitare all'Italiana* (Italian living). The rationalist Villa Necchi Campiglio in Milan, the Renaissance Villa Albergoni in the Cremona countryside and a vernacular *dammuso* on the island of Pantelleria:[3] these three residential typologies and their landscapes constitute a fragmentary echo of the Grand Tour.

The films take us into the lives and living spaces of the (haute) bourgeoisie. Spaces, objects, costume design, the framing of the bodies in relation to the space, from the interior to the city or the landscape – all are meticulously (re)constructed, staged and sublimated. The film sets are eclectic constructs, haptic and visual archives of sorts, whose authenticity is reinforced by intentional stylistic inconsistencies and imperfections.

I Am Love takes place in Milan in the early 2000s. The villa is located near the Duomo and was built in the rationalist style in the early 1930s by Piero Portaluppi. It is shown as an opulent *machine à représenter* for the wealth and reach of a patriarchal industrialist family, the Recchis. By contrast, the country residence of the academic family in *Call Me by Your Name* bears the marks of more convivial and casual use, with scuffed antique upholstered furniture.

In *A Bigger Splash*, the protagonists inhabit a *dammuso*, an archaic house typology of Pantelleria, for the duration of a summer. The whitewashed, cavernous interiors contrast with the harsh landscape of the island. It is this work that makes the most explicit reference to a (geopolitical) reality outside the refined film narrative. We see the island through the eyes and needs of the vacationing protagonists: the openness of the landscape, the secret restaurant tucked away in the hills, the pleasurable lounging around the private pool, all elements of a leisurely summer. But the island, just 60 km from the Tunisian coast, is a significant port of call for migrants.

The intersection of these realities is shown almost incidentally, in a scene where two of the main characters, Penelope and Paul, are startled when they come across a small group of migrants in the remote hills (and vice versa). As a poetic aside, a subtle reference to Jean Luc Godard's 1963 film *Le Mépris* and its architectural protagonist the Villa Malaparte[4] is staged. In a key scene, Tilda Swinton – playing Marianne, a recovering rock star – stands on the vaulted roof of the *dammuso*: the endless sky behind her, her pose and her clothes all echo Brigitte Bardot on the sundeck of the inaccessible icon by Adalberto Libera.

Guadagnino calls these films his *Desiderio* – longing, yearning, desire – trilogy. The name is apt not only in terms of their respective plots; paradigmatically, it pays sublimated homage to three coveted typologies of the Italian way of life.

The magazine *Domus*, founded by Gio Ponti in 1928, played a leading role in the dissemination of this lifestyle, using images and drawings, along with concise multilingual texts, to picture and define modern domestic environments for both the Italian middle-class readership and the international architectural scene. The title, *Domus*, was the programme: the culture, objects, architectures and spaces of domesticity, from the coffee set to the Milanese apartment building, were all (re)presented. Readers were offered not just a frame of reference for a cultivated life, but instructions on how to live. *Domus* was both a commercial agent and an educational tool for the new way of living *all'italiana*.

The transformation of the relationship between house and landscape – in particular the coast – can also be traced in the pages of *Domus* over the decades. In the presentation of 'Una villa in Riviera' from 1928, the sea was still a faraway element of the landscape, the terrace of the house offering only a distant view of the curving coastline.[5] A few years later, the first *casa al mare* was announced in the table of contents; in this new typology, the sea was no longer an element of a contemplative landscape, but a habitable place. This newcomer would be regularly illustrated and referenced during the 1930s. In 1937, Bernard Rudofsky published for the first time in *Domus*, presenting a 'Villa for Positano and other coasts' co-authored with Luigi Cosenza.[6] Set on a cliff, just above the sea, this was an 'ideal residence', a prototype that could be widely replicated, given sufficient right-minded clients: 'And for this ideal client they [the architects, ed.] worked conscientiously without polemical ideas and without utopias', the manifesto-like project description declares.[7] An attached list of construction costs promotes the house as an affordable consumer item. And yet, despite their discursive and formal references to the simplicity of the Mediterranean way of life and its vernacular building traditions, these villas were reserved for the elite, as Michelangelo Sabatino points out: 'To be sure, enthusiasm for the Mediterranean was spurred primarily by the "leisure class", who commissioned weekend and vacation homes along the Adriatic, Ionian, Mediterranean, and Tyrrhenian seas.'[8]

In the same year as they published their prototypical villa for Positano, Rudofsky and Cosenza completed the Villa Oro in Posillipo near Naples. The house, the main residence of a doctor, is unmistakably influenced by Rudofsky's documenting of traditional buildings in the Mediterranean: formed of white rendered cubes of varying sizes, it sits on a steep cliff overlooking the sea. In the tradition of the Grand Tour, Rudofsky travelled to Santorini as early as the 1920s, and wrote his dissertation on 'a primitive type of concrete construction in the southern Cyclades' while he was living on the island. His fascination with the vernacular was informed by a holistic, anthropological approach to architecture and by a critique of the dogmas of modernism and an appreciation of the inherent connection between architecture, landscape and production. He was one of the first to document and research buildings outside the canon of architecture – so-called vernacular buildings – and to bring them to the notice of a wider public with an exhibition, *Architecture Without Architects*, at MoMA in New York in the 1960s.[9] Long before that, however, traditional architecture was a reference in architectural and political discourse: in the VI Milan Triennale of 1936, the exhibition *Architettura rurale nel bacino del Mediterraneo* attempted to co-opt rural Mediterranean architecture for Fascist ideals; after the end of the war, it was the basis for the neorealist current of Italian reconstruction.

In the catalogue for the MoMA show, Rudofsky wrote about Positano: 'Positano changed within a few years from a simple fishing town – it was an important harbour some five hundred years ago – to a luxurious resort, without destroying the local architecture.'[10] The transformation from a complex environment that had evolved over centuries to a site of tourist consumption is dealt with in a single sentence. This narrative ignores the socioeconomic crisis that hit rural and southern Italy particularly hard in the postwar years, when precarious working and living conditions forced a large part of the local population to abandon the landscapes and rural

---

1 Colin Crummy, 'Italian Summer: Guadagnino's Film, *Call Me by Your Name*', *Vice*, 25 October 2017.

2 Ibid.

3 The term *dammuso* derives from the Sicilian word *dammusu*, meaning 'vault', and refers to a stone architectural structure of Arab origin. It is the traditional house on the island of Pantelleria.

4 Godard's 1963 film offers the only opportunity – apart from short commercials for various luxury brands – to see the interiors and vistas of this icon of Italian modernism.

5 Luigi Brunati, 'Alberto Francini, Una villa in Riviera', *Domus*, no. 2 (1928), 22–5.

6 Luigi Cosenza and Bernard Rudofsky, 'Una villa per Positano e per … altri Lidi', *Domus*, no. 109 (1937), 10–17.

7 Ibid.

8 Michelangelo Sabatino, 'The Politics of *Mediterraneità* in Italian Modernist Architecture', in Jean-François Lejeune and Michelangelo Sabatino. eds., *Modern Architecture and the Mediterranean: Vernacular Dialogues and Contested Identities* (Abingdon: Routledge, 2010), 58.

9 Bernard Rudofsky, *Architecture Without Architects: A Short Introduction to Non-Pedigree Architecture* (New York: Museum of Modern Art, 1964).

10 Ibid., 37.

architecture praised by Rudofsky. Internal migration led to a massive increase in the labour force in the cities of Italy and made possible the *miracolo economico*, which mainly benefited the industrialised north.

In the period from 1945 to 1985, over eight million Italians left the country, with 400,000 emigrating in the peak year of 1961 alone. The exodus would slow drastically in the early 1970s, with the recession that affected many industrialised countries of emigration. Up to then, the industrialised north, and in particular Milan, experienced a huge revival of economic and cultural fortunes, which was reflected in the production of architecture and design that became key reference points in the international architectural discourse. At the same time, as the south emptied out, the Mediterranean was opened up to tourism and *non-pedigree* architecture found its way into the image of Italy, becoming a globally recognisable, marketable product. John Steinbeck's piece in *Harper's Bazaar* in 1954 – 'Positano bites deep. It is a dream place that isn't quite real when you are there and becomes beckoningly real after you have gone.' – made the coastal village a dream destination for many Americans.

Guadagnino's trilogy loosely picks up where Steinbeck left off, painting a picture of a privileged Italian social milieu and the places and architectures and residential typologies associated with them.

The dwelling in *A Bigger Splash* is not in the same category as the urban villa or the country residence, which were conceived and built for and in a continuous, hegemonic context. Previously a place of production, whose aesthetics were shaped by collective consensus and the need to eke a livelihood from the landscape, the *dammuso* was increasingly transformed from the 'other' into a desirable place of leisure consumption, its image remade in the postwar period both by socioeconomic upheaval and by inclusion in the architectural discourse and increased representation in mainstream culture. Guadagnino's *A Bigger Splash* pays homage to 'a physical artefact which contains within itself the continuously evolving social and technological situation in which it was built',[11] and which was transformed by its resilience – functional and aesthetic – from a marginalised housing typology into a characteristic *casa all'Italiana*.

11 Adam Caruso, *The Feeling of Things* (Barcelona: Ediciones Polígrafa, 2008), 53.

Elements of the Italian city

Andrea Di Tommaso
Fit Phuong

Piazza, /piàz·za/

A free area, more or less spacious, square, rectangular, circular, polygonal, which opens into an urban fabric, at the end of a street and more often at the intersection of several streets, and which, limited by buildings, often architecturally important, and sometimes embellished by gardens, monuments, fountains, has the urban function of facilitating the movement […], to give access to public buildings, to serve as a meeting place for citizens, often constituting the centre of economic and political life of the city or country.

Source: https://www.treccani.it/vocabolario/piazza/

Portico, /pòr·ti·co/

An environment limited, on at least one of its sides, by a series of columns or pillars, and along the other sides by continuous walls, even interrupted by doors or windows; it is a covered passage along the streets and around squares, courtyards, sometimes representing a distinctive architectural element of facades or sides of buildings.

Source: https://www.treccani.it/vocabolario/portico/

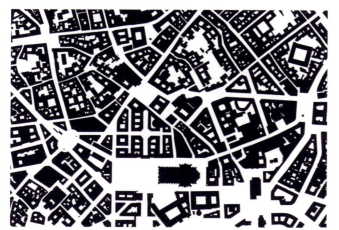

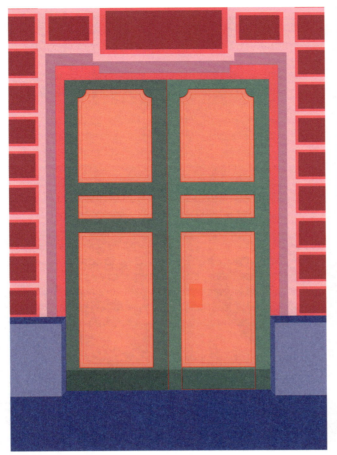

Portóne, /por·tò·ne/

A large door that serves as a main entrance or for the entry of vehicles into a building and that, both as a room and as a closing window, is particularly impressive and often enriched with decorative elements of various kinds in monumental buildings.

Source: https://www.treccani.it/vocabolario/portone/

Androne, /an·dró·ne/

a. Under the ancient Greeks, in the broad sense, the part of the house reserved for men only.
b. In ancient Rome, a corridor of disengagement between the environments of men's meeting rooms and the rooms of the women, and of access to the apartments of the hosts.
c. In modern architecture, the room of passage from the entrance door of the house to the stairs and the courtyard.
d. In military architecture, the passage under the parapet that connects the floor of the fortress with the moat.

Source: https://www.treccani.it/vocabolario/androne/

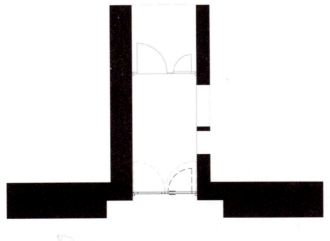
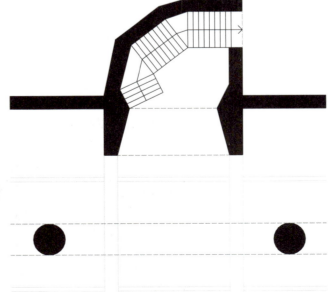

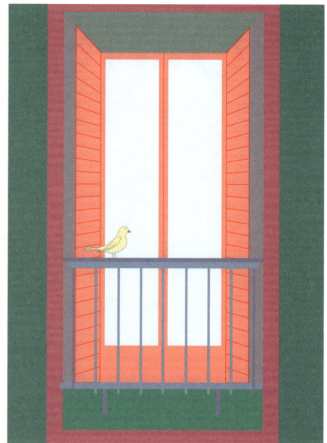

Cortile, /cor·tì·le/

A portion of an open area between factory buildings intended to provide air and light to the interior, to the passage of people, or to other functions. For example, a 'palagio' with a beautiful and big cortile in the middle (Boccaccio); the cortile of Palazzo Vecchio, in Florence; or in the cortile of a school, the windows overlooking the courtyard.

Source: https://www.treccani.it/vocabolario/cortile/

Balcone, /bal·có·ne/

Architectural feature consisting of a structure generally protruding from the facade of the building to form a shelf accessible through one or more French windows and surrounded by a parapet or masonry balustrade or a metal railing.

Source: https://www.treccani.it/vocabolario/balcone/

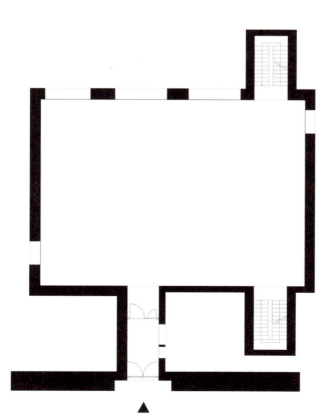
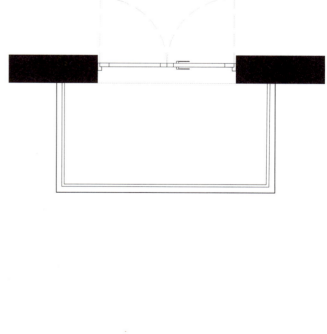

Rome

Roman bigness: Large-scale architecture as a design tool in Rome

Diego Martínez

How does the idea of a new architectural grand scale fit with Rome? At first glance, Rome's large scale appears chaotically built on foundations of former grandeur. Always in relation to remaining structures of antiquity and the palimpsest of a contradictory history. If you widen your gaze, a heterogeneous picture emerges, composed of layers of a city with many histories and many faces. Big architecture and projects present themselves as a collection of self-contained yet territorially delineated islands.

This work explores this approach in three designs. They form new islands in the sea of the Roman palimpsest and are exemplary antitheses to the prevailing conditions. As Rebel Islands, they present an architectural hypothesis of the city that combines formal elements and basic features of parasitic practice into laboratories of alternative housing and urban models.

Diploma thesis by Diego Martinéz.
Supervision by Michael Obrist.
Summer semester 2023 at TU Wien.

Palazzo del Popolo.
Alternative imaginary for the
Palazzo della Civiltà Italiana.

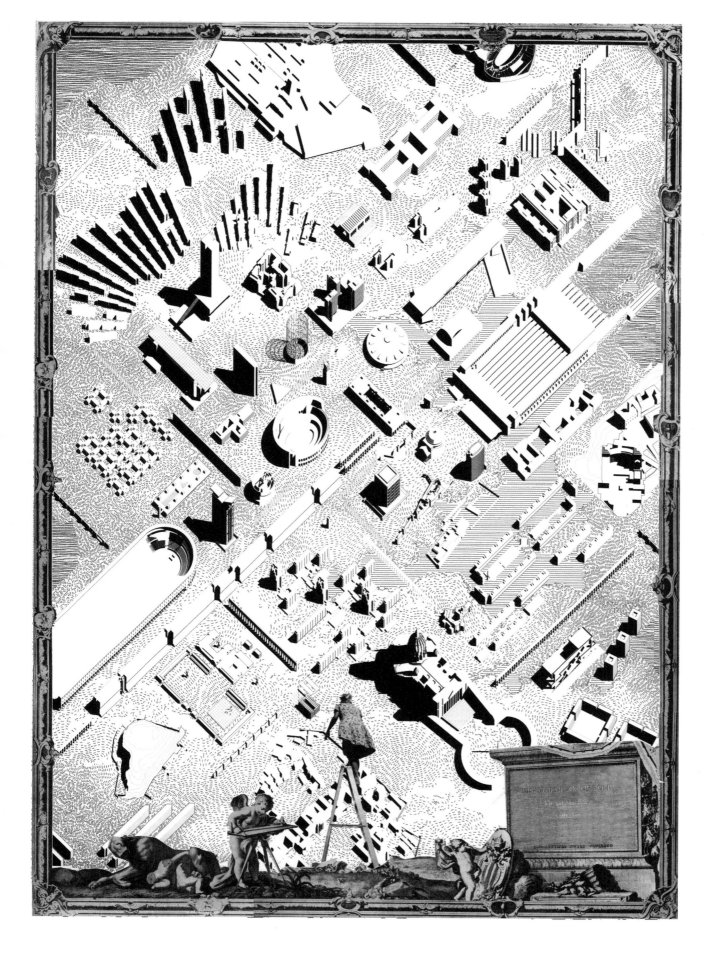

TORRI LIGINI
TOWER ISLAND

Design 1: Tower Island – Torri Ex Ministero delle Finanze. Perspective.

MERCATI GENERALI
ROMANO OSTIENSE

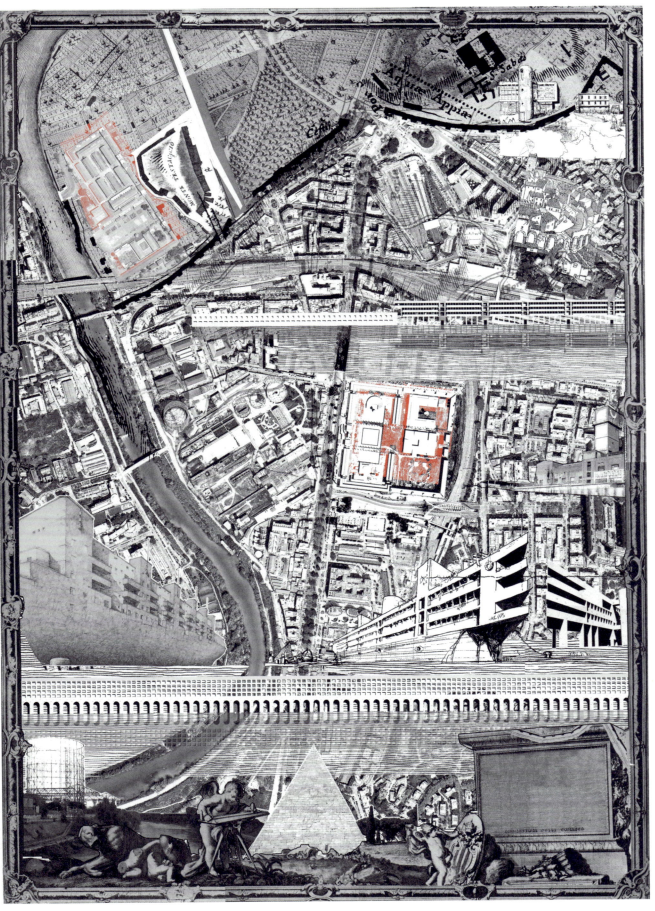

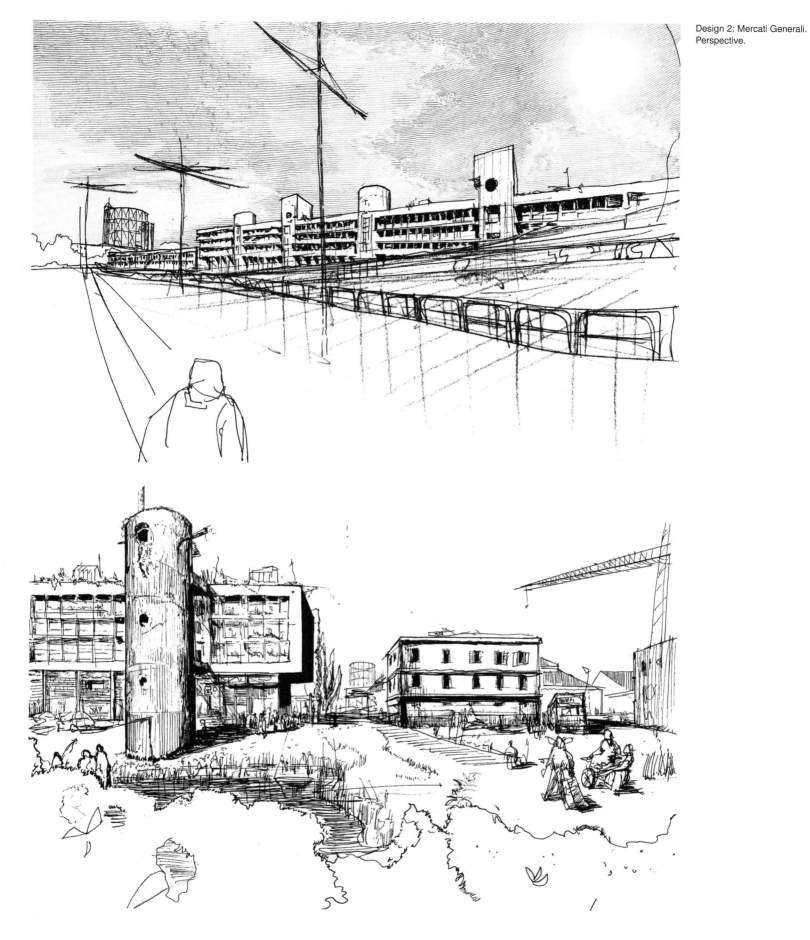

Design 2: Mercati Generali. Perspective.

As above, so below: A large-scale solution for conflictive conditions

Marek Nowicki
Diego Martinéz

The Roman quarter of San Lorenzo: through the clash of typologies, stylistic eras, uses and temporal overlaps, an area for living as well as for nightlife, we see issues that are typical for places just outside the ordinary tourist zones. Despite – or because of – this, the area gains in attraction and produces rising costs of housing and levels of gentrification.

The 2019 design studio *Rome – The Fight for Housing* by Michael Obrist poses the question of whether a living space can be created here that allows for multifunctional public uses and overlays while at the same time preserving the uniqueness of Rome and San Lorenzo.

The plot at the Via dei Lucani, not far away from the ancient Porta Maggiore, is an in-between-land that borders train tracks, the old city wall as well as the *Tangenziale* (a major elevated street). It is an uncontrolled place of resistance, filled with small-scale production such as car workshops, social centres with creative elements and empty, undefined zones which in the last years have been affected by crime. It is a potential space of change for the whole *quartiere*.

With its clear elements, the chosen large-scale structure stands in opposition to the multifaceted, meandering design process. Instead of a common thread and a finite design solution, many approaches are followed and more questions are raised.

The versatile language of the work allows for interpretation and brings contradictions and contrasts to the fore. Historical works and influences are juxtaposed with representations of the design project, allowing for subjective interpretation by the viewer. It is to be understood as an unfinished approach within which one can take many paths to get closer to the genius loci of Rome.

Project by Marek Nowicki and Diego Martinéz.
Design studio: *The Fight for Housing* by Michael Obrist.
Summer semester 2019 at TU Wien.

Perspective from below

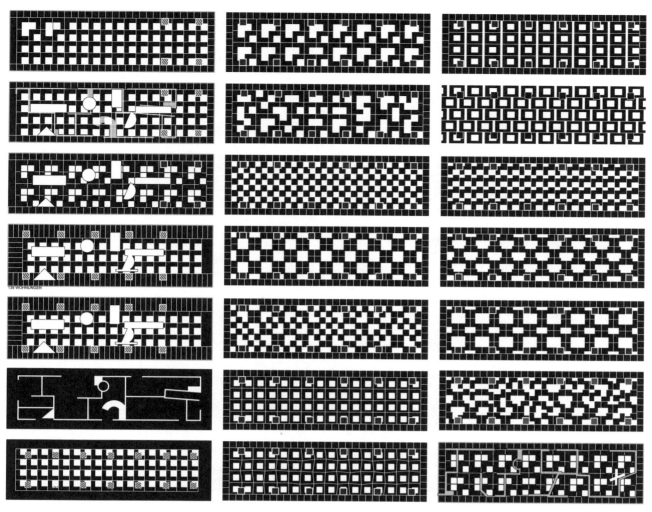

Housing Pattern

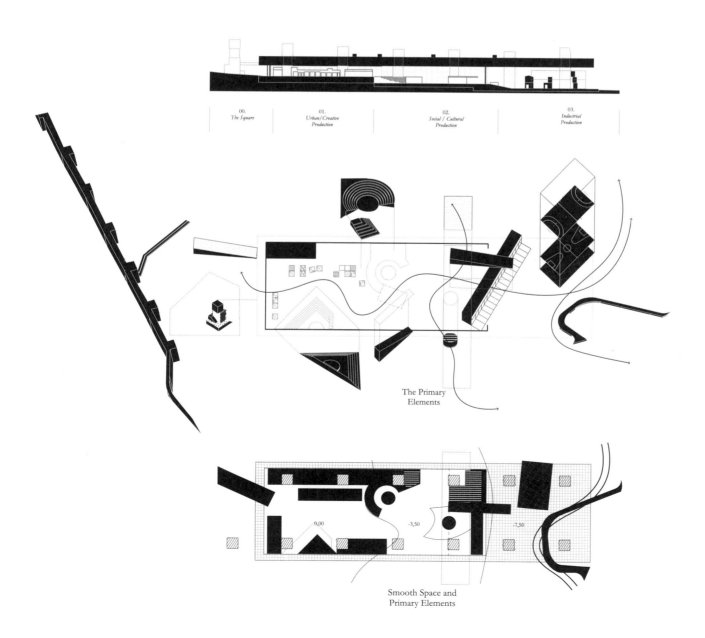

00.	01.	02.	03.
The Square	*Urban / Creative Production*	*Social / Cultural Production*	*Industrial Production*

The Primary Elements

Smooth Space and Primary Elements

AS ABOVE SO BELOW

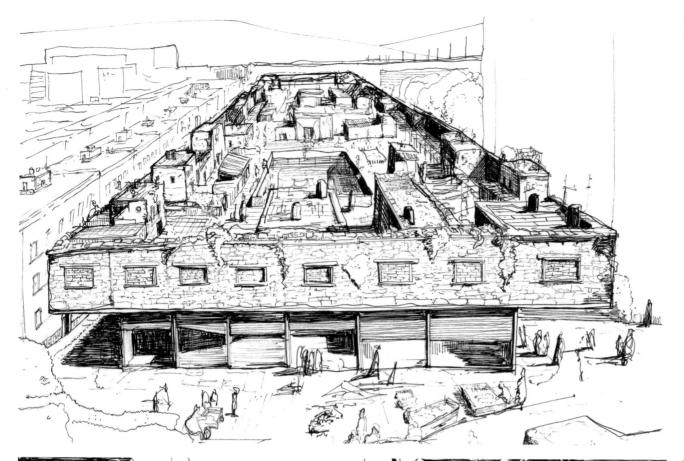

Perspective from above

Market perspective

'Architecture after the architects' future concept

Rome: Does Pasolini still live here? Amongst shanties, tower blocks, Roma camps and squats

Francesco Careri

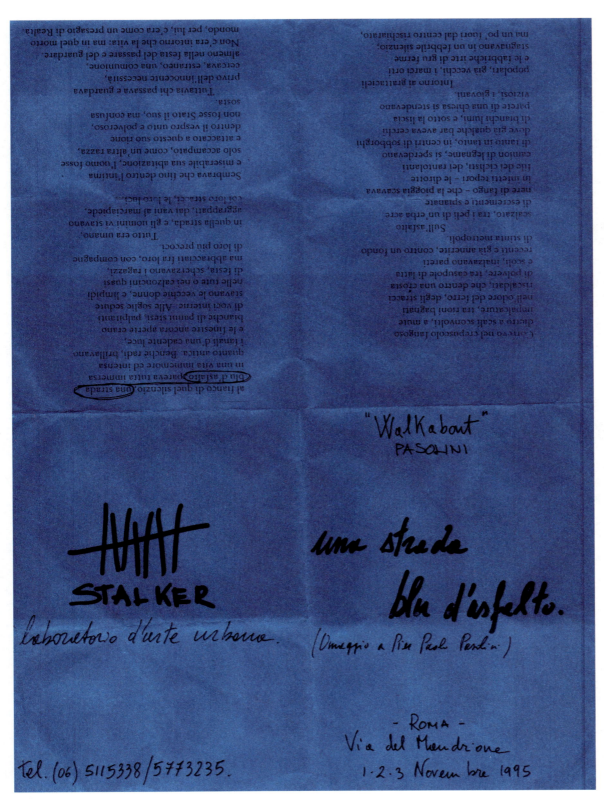

Stalker, Walkabout Pasolini, Rome 1995, original flyer. Courtesy of Stalker Archive

[1] The three articles have been translated into English under the titles 'The City's True Face', 'The Shantytowns' and 'The Concentration Camps'. See P. P. Pasolini, *Stories from the City of God: Sketches and Chronicles of Rome, 1950–1956* (see note 3). The inquiry 'Viaggio per Roma e dintorni' conducted by *Vie Nuove* was published on 24 May 1958.

[2] The story of the *borgate*, or working-class housing estates on the outskirts of the city, is told in Giovanni Berlinguer and Piero Della Seta, *Borgate di Roma* (Rome: Editori Riuniti, 1960 and 1976). Out of these first explorations came a famous inquiry into the situation of the *Borgate Romane* conducted by the anthropologist Franco Cagnetta and with photographic documentation by Franco Pinna, along with Giovanni Berlinguer's studies of food and health and Giorgio Nataletti and Diego Carpitella's first ethnomusicological studies.

[3] Pier Paolo Pasolini, 'Il fronte della Città', *Vie Nuove*, Rome, 24 May 1958. Trans. into English by Marina Harss as 'The City's True Face', in P. P. Pasolini, *Stories from the City of God: Sketches and Chronicles of Rome, 1950–1956*, ed. Walter Siti (New York: Other Press, 2003), 165–70.

[4] On Stalker in the early years of its activity in Rome, see: Flaminia Gennari, 'Progett/Azioni: tra i nuovi esploratori della città contemporanea', *Flash Art*, no. 200 (1996), 62–4; Emanuela de Cecco, 'Non volendo aggiungere altre cose al mondo', *Flash Art*, no. 200 (1996), 64; Lorenzo Romito, 'Stalker', in Peter Lang, ed., *Suburban Discipline* (New York: Princeton Architectural Press, 1997), 130–41; Francesco Careri, 'Rome, archipel fractal, voyage dans les combles de la ville', *Techniques & Architecture*, no. 427 (Paris, 1996), 84–7; Stalker, *A Travers les Territoires Actuels / Attraverso i Territori Attuali* (Paris: Jean Michel Place, 2000).

This year, 2022, has seen the centenary of the birth of Pier Paolo Pasolini, poet, film director, writer and journalist, who was an attentive observer of the social and urban changes that transformed the face of Rome between the 1950s and 1970s. His violent death in 1975, on the beach at Ostia, is one of the many Italian mysteries that are still shrouded in judicial fog. After the Spontaneous City of *baracche* and *tuguri*, of shacks and shantytowns, Pasolini was not able to see the new 'concentration camps' for the people in the brutalist housing estates of the Public City. And even if he had been able to foresee the arrival of boats crammed with migrants, he could not have imagined the Hybrid City that was created by the squats organised by the housing-rights movements. This article discusses the Rome described in Pasolini's essays and sets out to interweave it with the author's own experiences with the Stalker collective and then with the Department of Architecture at Roma Tre University.

The Spontaneous City

On 24 May 1958 *Vie Nuove*, the magazine of the Italian Communist Party, published Pier Paolo Pasolini's '*Viaggio dentro Roma e dintorni*', made up of three articles on the recent urban and social transformations of Rome: '*Il fronte della Città*', '*I tuguri*' and '*I campi di concentramento*'.[1] Two years earlier, in March 1956, there had been a heavy snowfall that had completely isolated the new informal settlements which had sprung up on the outskirts of the city from the centre. Thousands of people suddenly found themselves left out in the cold, without food or water. The first to come to their aid was a group of communist intellectuals that included Pier Paolo Pasolini, Elsa Morante and Alberto Moravia.[2]

The 'Journey through Rome and its environs' published in *Vie Nuove* arose from that context and had the aim of goading the world of politics and culture into doing something. The article '*Il fronte della Città*' – which begins with a series of questions, 'What is Rome? Which is Rome? Where does Rome begin and end?' – continues with a description of the 'eruption of building' on the fringes of the city, where the new tower blocks of the property speculators were advancing rapidly, eating up the countryside, where migrants from the south were constructing their *tuguri* or shantytowns alongside the *zingari* or Romani camps and where the new 'concentration camps' were being built for the poor. Pasolini describes the experience of a hypothetical tourist coming to visit the ancient monuments of the Eternal City, who from the window of his train or coach gazes distractedly at the revelation of a 'Rome that is unknown to tourists, ignored by the right-minded, nonexistent on maps':

Before his unseeing eyes, clusters of hovels will fly by, expanses of shacks like Bedouin camps, collapsed ruins of mansions and sumptuous cinemas, ex-farmhouses compressed between high-rise buildings, dikes with high walls, narrow muddy alleyways, and sudden empty spaces, empty lots and small fields with a few heads of livestock. Beyond all of this, in the burned or muddy countryside, marked by little hills, ditches, old pits, plateaus, sewers, ruins, trash piles and dumps, lies the true face of the city.[3]

In those years there was a close relationship between the front of the constructed city and the nature of the Roman countryside, still incredibly intact at the foot of those high-rises. That nature was immediately turned into lived space: football pitches, paths leading to other housing estates, caves in which to play at war, farmhouses to sneak off to and make love, ditches to wash and hang out clothes. Groups of children and youths entered and exited from that front in a daily toing and froing between inside and outside, between city and countryside. They lived in the open margin as a space in continuity with the new housing that had just violated it. But over the following years those spaces were gradually forgotten. Middle-class affluence turned them into places synonymous with poverty and prostitution, the paths filled with brambles and became impassable. From the 1980s onwards, disused factories and fields left with no one to cultivate them were added to those derelict spaces and, as the new public housing estates were built, the shantytowns slowly began to disappear. The only inhabitants left in those areas of urban countryside were Roma refugees fleeing the Balkans and the first migrants arriving from the Global South. The rest of the territory was essentially deserted, forgotten, out of sight and mind of politicians and citizens.

In the mid-1990s I was involved in the birth of Stalker, a collective of architects, artists, activists and idlers with which we started to walk along those margins in search of *territori attuali*, interstitial and marginal areas, abandoned spaces or spaces undergoing transformation.[4] Those abandoned spaces were our city, a fertile land, an 'urban amnesia' in which to dream of a new relationship between art, nature and metropolis. They attracted us as zones of hybridisation between the urban and the wild. They were empty gaps left between the built-up areas, *terrains vagues* waiting to be understood, spaces of freedom in which to experiment with new forms of creativity.

In October 1995 we made our first 'transurbance' on foot, an initiatory journey of adventure and discovery, and on our return painted a map – the *Planisfero Roma* – and wrote a *Manifesto*. We wanted to present the city in the form of an archipelago, with urban continents separated from one another by seas, gulfs and coves of empty space. Inviting the residents of the city to lose themselves in order to be able to get to know them without cultural prejudices. We walked for four days and three nights without ever going home, sleeping in tents, wading through the mud, following paths through the brambles and trying always to stay in a wild space, extending the gaps and connecting them up with new paths. We attempted to avoid asphalt and always walk on bare ground, with 'the front of the city' always present in the background. Pasolini was in our steps; we knew that we were in *his* city and we mixed his gaze up with those of the Situationists, Robert Smithson and above all Tarkovsky, for the 'Zone' was also a mystical space and the nature was the mutant one of his film *Stalker*, from which we had taken our name. We had decided to immerse ourselves in it, sure that we would find something important there, that not everything had already been said and mapped, that we too were worthy of recounting our present city, certain that the Selva, the Forest, would save us, because as Hölderlin put it, 'where the danger is, also grows the saving power'. Almost all of us were architects, but we weren't interested in drawing up plans and constructing buildings. What we found far more interesting was the appearance of new spaces amidst the indifference of the city, abandoned spaces, 'nonexistent on maps'. The last item in our *Manifesto* is in fact 'The Abandonment':

The attempt at defining and controlling the entire territory, mirage of our western culture, just when it seemed most likely to realise itself, gives forth its first water. The first cracks have opened in the very hearts of our system: the large cities. The forest that at one time surrounded cities and villages, where bears and wolves, but also the nightmares would hide, where the fantasies and the very idea of liberty itself were shoved far from the city, put into the corners, restricted and in an unbelievable act of clemency, protected. And here it is now that that same forest rises again, exactly there in the cities where the

5 *The Stalker Manifesto*, written by Lorenzo Romito in January 1996, is published in several languages on the website http://digilander.libero.it/stalkerlab/tarkowsky/manifesto/manifest.htm.

6 The festival was organised by the Dark Camera & Art Department, a group of architecture students set up like Stalker during the occupation of the Faculty of Architecture in 1990 at the time of the student movement called 'la Pantera'.

7 On this theme it is worth recalling Cecilia Mangini's 1969 film *Domani vincerò*, which tells the story of how the Gypsies of the Mandrione changed from horsemen into boxers; the two 1978 RAI documentaries by Gianni Serra, *Al margine* and *Essere zingari al Mandrione*; and the exhibitions *Crescere zingaro al Mandrione* and *Zingaro a tre anni* curated by Angelina Linda Zammataro.

8 Pier Paolo Pasolini, 'I tuguri', *Vie Nuove*, 24 May 1958. Trans. into English by Marina Harss as 'The Shantytowns of Rome', in Pasolini, *Stories from the City of God* (see note 3), 177–82.

9 The poem dates from 1951 and was published for the first time in *itinerari* in 1953 and then in the collection *Dai Diari 1943–1953. Poesia con letteratura*. See Walter Siti, ed., Pier Paolo Pasolini, *Tutte le opere*, vol. 1, 'I Meridiani' series (Milan: Arnoldo Mondadori, 2003), 754–5. It is translated into English by Stephen Sartarelli, ed., *The Selected Poetry of Pier Paolo Pasolini: A Bilingual Edition* (Chicago: University of Chicago Press, 2014), 146.

10 Bruce Chatwin, *The Songlines* (Franklin Center, PA: Franklin Library, 1987).

11 Stalker's action Walkabout Pasolini was published under the title 'Stalker, via del Mandrione', in the monographic issue on Pier Paolo Pasolini, entitled PPP, of the magazine *Initiales*, no. 7 (2016), Ecole Nationale Supérieure des Beaux-Arts de Lyon, 98–9.

12 For more information see: http://articiviche.blogspot.com/.

13 Pier Paolo Pasolini, *Trasumanar e organizzar* (Milan: Garzanti, 1971). The poem has been translated into English by Stephen Sartarelli as 'Lines from the Testament', in Sartarelli, ed., *The Selected Poetry* (see note 9), 386.

territory's systems of appropriation and control are most ancient and crumbling. Given the impossibility of total human control, the cement under which the forests were covered has cracked open, the earth flowers in new and unpredictable forms, preparing to contest with its human occupants the domination of space, from the scrap-heaps and beyond. To forecast the unforecastable, to save the coming into being of the 'Actual Territories', means to abandon them. For abandonment is the maximum form of a cure for that which has developed outside human will and plan.[5]

A month after the tour of Rome we were back in the street again, this time in an explicit tribute paid to Pier Paolo Pasolini on the occasion of the festival '*La Passione: Pasolini al Mandrione*',[6] marking the twentieth anniversary of his death. We spent days with mops and buckets of blue paint in our hands, using them to colour 300 metres of the asphalt of Via del Mandrione, a narrow and winding street that runs alongside the ancient Acqua Felice where it enters Rome. Via del Mandrione in 1995 was no longer the one in the photos that Henri Cartier-Bresson had taken in 1959, nor that of the lyrics of the song 'Cristo al Mandrione' which Pasolini had written for Laura Betti and Gabriella Ferri, and yet today it is still a decidedly Pasolinian place. It is a street hemmed in by the aqueduct and the railway that, despite its transformation into a district of little houses with gardens, retains an ambience that has never succeeded in completely erasing its past. The aqueduct was an infrastructure able to provide shelter and water and from the 1940s to the 1980s had taken the form of a long spine against which abutted a shantytown. In 1943 the families evacuated from the district of San Lorenzo, bombed by the Americans, had taken refuge there. Later it had become a place of prostitution and Romani communities, the famous 'gypsies of the Mandrione'.[7] In his '*Viaggio dentro Roma e dintorni*' published in *Vie Nuove*, Pasolini describes the *tuguri* or shantytowns of the Mandrione in detail and concludes:

> I remember one day, driving by the Mandrione shantytown with two friends from Bologna. They were horrified at the sight of a group of children, between the ages of two and four or five, playing in the mud in front of their hovels. They were dressed in rags, one of them wearing a little animal skin that he had found who knows where, like a savage. They ran to and fro, without even the sense of order imposed by a game. They moved around as if blind in those few square feet where they had been born and where they had always lived, knowing only the shack where they slept and the two feet of mud where they played. [...] The pure vitality which is at the core of these souls is the combination of evil in its purest form and good in its purest form: violence and goodness, depravity and innocence, despite everything. And for this reason something can, and must, be done for them.[8]

Once the asphalt had been painted, the perception of that space was completely altered. By day people in cars found themselves driving along a strip of blue, not knowing whether it was a new kind of road marking or how they ought to behave. In the evening, though, the street was closed to traffic for the festival and we scattered hundreds of little pieces of blue paper on the blue asphalt. On one side there was the title of the action, *Walkabout Pasolini: Una strada blu d'asfalto (omaggio a Pier Paolo Pasolini)*; on the other side Pasolini's poem '*Correvo nel crepuscolo fangoso*'[9] in which we had underlined the phrase 'a blue asphalt street':

> [...]
> Around already old low-income high-rises, rotting gardens and construction sites bristling with motionless cranes stagnated in feverish silence. But a bit outside the lamp-lit center, beside the silence, a blue asphalt street appeared wholly immersed in a life as oblivious and intense as it was ancient. [...]

In the poem the blue was that of the sky reflected on the wet road after the rain had just stopped, but in our case the street really was blue and skirted the arches of the aqueduct, where it was still possible to see the remains of the majolica tiles and plaster of the shacks in which that 'life as oblivious and intense as it was ancient' had been lived. The title *Walkabout* was a reference to the ritual wanderings of Australian Aborigines described by Chatwin in *The Songlines*.[10] For us it was important to stress the act of walking as an aesthetic and ritual activity. We wanted to get the public to walk on that surreal road and we wanted every single person to read the poem alone as they walked past the arches. We wanted to get across the idea of Pasolini the walker, recalling him as an itinerant poet who went around exploring the crudest and at the same time most human cracks in the fabric of the city.[11]

In 2006, when I became a university lecturer, I taught for the first time a peripatetic course in which we explored the city the way I had learnt with Stalker. The course, which still exists and is called Arti Civiche, 'Civic Arts', is held once a week, with the whole day spent walking.[12] The first year we decided to go on foot from the former slaughterhouse, where the Faculty of Architecture is located, to the seaplane base at Ostia where Pier Paolo Pasolini had been killed. My *Ragazzi di vita* were fifteen-odd male and female students ready for anything. We walked through the fields next to the built-up city, just as in many of the scenes in *Mamma Roma* and *Accattone*. At last we were out of the university's lecture halls and had the whole day at our disposal to get lost, climb over gates, play with space, talk to people. We didn't even refrain from acts of pure vandalism, such as knocking down the bricks that closed the doors and windows of abandoned farmhouses and pushing a dumped car against a wall so hard that its windows exploded from the force of the collision.

Between one adventure and the next we stopped to read poems and passages from the *Stories from the City of God*. Many of Pasolini's poems about Rome are linked to walking. They are accounts of neighbourhoods and streets, of seductions, in which the city seems to be an exciting jungle filled with dangers and solitude. Even if they were written after his return home, the steps he took amidst the smells and sounds of those places can still be heard in the background. Arriving at the location of his murder, we read a poem from the collection *Trasumanar e organizzar* that seemed to have been written precisely for us:[13]

> You have to be very strong to love solitude; you need good legs and uncommon stamina; you can't easily catch cold, flu, or sore throat; you can't be afraid of muggers or murderers; if you have to walk all afternoon or even all evening you must know how to do this without noticing; there's nowhere to sit, especially in winter; the wind blows over the wet grass and there are big rocks, wet and muddy, amidst the garbage; there's really no comfort at all, no doubt about that, except in the fact that you've got a whole day and a night ahead of you, with no obligations or constraints of any sort. Sex is a pretext. No matter how many encounters you may have – and even in winter, in the windswept streets, between garbage heaps against a background of buildings, there are many – they are only moments of loneliness; [...]

Stalker, *Planisfero Roma*, Rome 1995, route map. Courtesy of Stalker Archive

LAC Laboratorio Arti Civiche, the Metropoliz rocket, 2011. Credit: Luca Ventura, courtesy of Stalker Archive

14 For more information: https://suilettidelfiume.wordpress.com/.

15 The situation of the Roma in Rome in those years has been described in Francesco Careri and Lorenzo Romito's book, *Stalker-ON / Campus Rom* (Matera: Altrimedia edizioni, 2017). The reader is also recommended Fabrizio Boni and Giorgio de Finis' film, *C'era una volta Savorengo Ker* (2011), which can be viewed at https://www.iridaproduzioni.com/produzioni-video/savorengo-ker-documentario/.

16 Pier Paolo Pasolini, 'I campi di concentramento', *Vie Nuove*, 24 May 1958. Trans. into English by Marina Harss as 'The Concentration Camps', in Pasolini, *Stories from the City of God* (see note 3), 171–6.

17 The reference is to Piero Brunello's book, *L'urbanistica del disprezzo: campi rom e società italiana* (Rome: Manifestolibri, 1996).

18 On these themes see: Alberto Clementi and Francesco Perego, eds., *La metropoli spontanea. Il caso di Roma* (Bari: Dedalo, 1983); Vezio De Lucia, *Se questa è una città* (Rome: Editori Riuniti, 1989); Franco Martinelli, *Roma Nuova: Borgate Spontanee r insediamenti pubblici* (Milan: FrancoAngeli, 1990).

19 On these themes see Ludovico Quaroni, 'Il paese dei barocchi', *Casabella-Continuità*, no. 215 (1957).

20 A book that is helpful in understanding the transformations in Roman urban planning is Italo Insolera's *Roma moderna: Un secolo di Storia urbanistica* (Turin: Einaudi, 1962), of which the latest edition, updated by Paolo Berdini, is recommended: *Roma moderna. Da Napoleone I al XXI secolo* (Turin: Einaudi, 2011).

No supper or lunch or worldly satisfaction can compare to an endless walk down impoverished street, where you need to be wretched and strong, a brother to dogs.

The following year, we walked from the seaplane base in Ostia along the banks of the river in order to describe them in an *Atlas of Informal Dwelling on the Tiber*.[14] We encountered shacks of all kinds, sometimes isolated, at others in small groups or in immense shantytowns with hundreds of people living in them. It felt like the years had been rolled back, because the last shantytowns had vanished in the 1980s. But Rome was again full of *tuguri*, although instead of Italian migrants from the rural areas of the south, they were inhabited by foreign immigrants from all over the world, usually adults, and of course the Roma with their children, the only ones who had always been there. We spent a whole semester meeting these people in order to try to understand and to express our indignation in poetry.

That image of children playing in the mud in front of their huts can still unfortunately be seen today. But these places are no longer visited by engaged intellectuals as they were after the great snowfall of 1956. The only people who go there today are the police, social workers, members of voluntary organisations and, when a crime has been committed, journalists, before the bulldozers arrive to destroy everything, the homes of the culprit and the homes of those whose only fault has been living nearby. With the result that the *tuguri* are rebuilt just a few metres away, alongside the remains of demolished shacks piled up by the bulldozers. The problem is always moved and never solved. It is dredged up only to suit the needs of election campaigns for which it is the defenceless who pay the price. As usual the war on poverty is waged against the poor, whether the government is of the right or the left.

As we walked along the Tiber, Mayor Veltroni, from the centre-left, had begun the construction of new mono-ethnic concentration camps, reserved solely for Romani, dubbing them 'Villages of Solidarity'. They were not new housing estates but camps for undesirables, true states of exception out of the city's sight, sometimes without a supply of drinking water. The houses were tin boxes and the density extremely high: the housing standard was four square metres a person when the law required seventeen. His successor as mayor, Alemanno of the far right, saw this as a very avant-garde project and decided to expand it and beef it up by placing private armed guards at the entrance and surrounding the area with barbed wire and CCTV cameras: preventive imprisonment for those whose only crime was being poor and Romani.[15]

The Public City

The article 'I campi di concentramento' in *Vie Nuove*[16] is a brief history of the 'town-planning of contempt',[17] in which Pasolini describes the *borgate Romane* or working-class housing estates, dividing them between 'authorised' and 'unauthorised' ones.[18] The unauthorised settlements were the ones built along the consular roads after the war, where the Italian migrants had brought with them 'a habit of seriousness and rural dignity typical of an ancient province'. They were clusters of little white-washed houses like 'Bedouin villages', that subsequently evolved into neighbourhoods of small villas and blocks of flats built without planning permission which have gradually been legalised and provided with services.

The official estates, on the other hand, were the ones 'built by the municipality, apparently deliberately, to concentrate in them the poor, the undesirable'. The first official estates had been the *borgate* built after the demolitions carried out by the Fascist regime in the historic centre, when 'large numbers of the Roman *lumpenproletariat*, teeming in the centre, in the old districts that were demolished, were deported to the middle of the countryside, to isolated estates, built not coincidentally like barracks or prisons'.

In contrast to the chaotic and irregular urban structure of the unauthorised estates, in the official ones geometry ruled and the style was an obsessive repetition of uniform and standardised houses and courtyards. The second generation of official estates was the one that Pasolini saw in the 1950s and served as a backdrop to his novels *Una vita violenta* and *Ragazzi di vita*: 'the Christian Democrat *borgate* are identical to the Fascist ones, because the relationship that is established between the State and the poor is identical: an authoritarian and paternalistic relationship, profoundly inhuman in its religious mystification.' What had changed in the Christian Democrat estates, with respect to the Fascist ones, was the density and the height of the blocks of flats, always identical but arranged diagonally to make the most of the sunlight. These were the neorealist estates like the Quarticciolo, the Tuscolano and the Tiburtino, where the style of northern European rationalist architecture was at times hybridised with a more rural and vernacular one that in Pasolini's view bestowed on them 'a romantic and coquettish air'.[19]

On 2 November 1975 Pasolini was barbarically murdered at the seaplane base in Ostia. His death remains one of those great mysteries of Italian history in which are implicated the so-called 'rogue' secret services, the P2 masonic lodge and the management of ENI, about which Pasolini was writing a book entitled *Il Petrolio*. In that year architects and left-wing administrators were working on the new Piani per l'Edilizia Economica e Popolare (PEEP, 'Plans for Subsidised and Public Housing'),[20] the third generation of *borgate ufficiali* that Pasolini did not have the time to see: Corviale, Tor Bella Monaca, Laurentino 38, Vigne Nuove and the other large housing estates of the public city where the former shanty dwellers described in the *Viaggio dentro Roma e dintorni* ended up living. I can imagine that Pasolini would have seen the birth of these estates as a new generation of concentration camps for the poor. They were planned to be self-sufficient and should have been equipped with services and infrastructure, but remained for years gigantic satellites disconnected from the city. The society homogenised by the neoliberalism of which Pasolini had seen the birth in embryo had turned citizens into consumers and the proletariat into an aspiring bourgeoisie. In the last years of his life he had said that there was no more hope for Rome. When he was asked in an interview to try to anthropomorphise the city, he had replied:

I would assign it a gender that is neither male nor female. But that special gender that is the gender of children and adolescents. […] The kind of spirit that stems from a non-moralistic conception of the world. And so not Christian either. The spirit of someone who has his own morality of a Stoic-Epicurean type that has survived, let's say, Catholicism. […] Rome is the least Catholic city in the world. It used to be a great working-class capital. Of the proletariat and the lumpenproletariat. No longer now that it has become a petit bourgeois city. Today the teenager of the suburbs gets on his scooter and comes to the *centre*. Nor does he say any longer, like he used to, I'm going *into* Rome. The centre has come to them. […] Before the men and women of the suburbs had no inferiority complex about the fact of not belonging to the so-called privileged class. They felt the injustice of poverty, but had no envy of the rich, of the well-to-do. Indeed they almost regarded them

Stalker, Walkabout Pasolini, Rome 1995. Credit: Francesco Careri, courtesy of Stalker Archive

Porto Fluviale, the Developers Ship, murals by Blu 2015. Credit: Francesco Careri

Stalker, *Pranzo Boario*, Rome 1999. Credit: Romolo Ottaviani, courtesy of Stalker Archive

Stalker, *Attraverso i Territori Attuali*, Rome 1995. Credit: Lorenzo Romito, courtesy of Stalker Archive

21 Luigi Sommaruga, 'Intervista a Pier Paolo Pasolini', *il Messaggero*, 9 June 1973.

22 Francesco Careri and Didier Laroque, 'Problèmes de la grande dimension: Corviale, la plus longue erreur du monde', *L'Architecture d'Aujourd'hui*, no. 273 (1991), 105–10.

23 *Immaginare Corviale* was a project of Stalker/Osservatorio Nomade, curated by the Fondazione Adriano Olivetti on behalf of Rome City Council – Office of Social Policies for the Suburbs, Local Development and Labour; Department 19 – Policies for the Development and Reclamation of the Suburbs; in collaboration with the Laboratorio Territoriale Corviale Roma Ovest.

24 The project has been published in Bartolomeo Pietromarchi and Flaminia Gennari eds., *Osservatorio Nomade. Immaginare Corviale: Pratiche estetiche per la città contemporanea* (Milan: Bruno Mondadori, 2006), and numerous magazines including *Lotus International*, no. 124, *a+u*, no. 420 and *Domus*, no. 886. The materials have been shown at exhibitions in various countries, including the first Beijing Architecture Biennale in 2004, the exhibition *The Naked City* in Orléans for Archilab in 2004, the exhibition *DynamiCity* at the NAI in Rotterdam in 2005, the exhibition *Spam Arq* at the MAC in Santiago, Chile, in 2006 and the exhibition *Non basta ricordare* at the MAXXI in Rome in 2013.

25 Pier Paolo Pasolini, *Scritti Corsari* (Milan: Garzanti, 1977), 24.

as inferior beings, incapable of subscribing to their philosophy. But today everyone has this inferiority complex. If you observe the young members of the lower classes you will see that they no longer seek to assert themselves for what they are, but try to blend in.[21]

Almost fifty years have passed since Pasolini's death and society has changed. The city has swallowed the countryside and neoliberalism, in spite of the continual state of emergency as a result of economic crises, wars and pandemics, has crushed almost every form of resistance, producing ever more undesirables and impoverishing the petit bourgeois class that had abandoned the shanties for the *palazzoni*, as the Romans call those grey housing estates, made up of nondescript buildings constructed of raw reinforced concrete, brutal and brutalist. Model estates built and at once abandoned, first by the architects who had conceived them, then by the administrations that were supposed to manage them, and finally by the city, which has turned away in order not to look at them. Pieces of city left to the architectural debate, to exploitation by the political parties, to the control of the police, to social workers and to the goodwill of their inhabitants, who with great effort have succeeded in preventing them from exploding. After the first twenty years of neglect the *palazzoni* once again became a subject of debate by planners, and since the early 2000s have been the target of new policies of urban reclamation in an attempt to provide them with services of education, transport and health. Today it is no longer just undesirables who live here. There is also a middle class that has organised itself into associations and committees and rejects the stereotypes and simplifications of the media, which paint these housing complexes simply as 'monstrosities' to be demolished.

Corviale is the most famous of these *palazzoni*, and the Romans call it *il Serpentone*, 'the Giant Snake', even though there is nothing sinuous about it as it is a single linear building stretching for a kilometre. The first time I entered it was in 1990 to write an article for *L'Architecture d'Aujourd'hui*.[22] Corviale had been inhabited for seven years, but the means to get there were lacking: 10,000 people deported to the middle of the Roman Campagna. The article was called 'Corviale, the longest mistake in the world' and ended with the words of someone who lived there: 'Dear architects never make a mistake like this. Don't make this mistake again,' I was twenty-three years old, a student of architecture, and our professors, even though megastructures were no longer in fashion, taught us to stay within the confines of the discipline, among the drawing boards and far away from the city and from people. That article was full of stereotypes and words that I would no longer use today, but it took a very clear critical stand: 'The city cannot be reduced to architecture and architecture to a work of art filled with flats [...]. Architecture must not play with the life of the poor people and subject them to experiments.' Art, architecture and social experimentation were terms that needed radical review. Poetry had to return to the territory to criticise and transform society. Pasolini was dead but his city was still there and someone had to sort it out.

In 2004 I went back with Stalker/Osservatorio Nomade and no longer asked myself whether Corviale had been a mistake or not. It was simply there and it was necessary to deal with the place. The intention was to explore it, free from prejudice and from the positions of the academic debate. By this time people had been living in it for twenty years and as artists we had been called on by the Fondazione Olivetti to 'Imagine Corviale'.[23] Osservatorio Nomade was a network of artists and researchers that Lorenzo Romito had established around Stalker in 2002. A map of the players reveals the strategy of the project and the roles of participants, clients, inhabitants, artists and architects. It is a diagram with three major groupings: *ON/Field*, i.e., artistic projects operating in the field; *ON/UniverCity*, the workshop conducted by groups of young architects; *ON/Network*, our television, the flyers and the bulletins that kept Corviale and the city abreast of what we were doing.[24]

We had found our headquarters with the project entitled '*Storie Comuni*' (Common Stories), when Matteo Fraterno and Cesare Pietroiusti succeeded in persuading Loredana, a woman living by herself in a large apartment in the Terzo Lotto of the Corviale, to put us up temporarily. Here we invited to dinner, along with her friends, some of the people who had been involved in the birth of Corviale, such as Renato Nicolini, Achille Bonito Oliva and Stefano Fiorentino, the son of Mario, architect of *il Serpentone*. Having a base inside the building allowed us to go around not as visitors but as 'Loredana's guests', and this changed everything. The first thing we realised was that the inhabitants were ashamed of saying they lived in Corviale. Although it had become a 'normal' estate, with the same problems as all the outlying areas of Rome, Corviale was still a monstrosity in the city's eyes. Its stereotyped image had been used as the setting of some famous TV programmes, and the national news broadcasts showed its image every time there was a story about the outskirts of any Italian city. The media had built a whole world of violence, drug-taking and social deprivation around that obsolete image. Pasolini's words in the *Scritti Corsari* on the bourgeois transformation of society and the power of the media come to mind again:

> The responsibility of television is enormous, not, of course, as a 'technical medium', but as an instrument of power and as power itself. Because it is not only a space through which messages circulate, but also a centre for the processing of messages. It constitutes the space where a mentality is shaped that, without it, would not know where to put itself. It is through the spirit of television that the spirit of the new power is made concretely manifest.[25]

Television and the media had created the mask of Corviale's monstrosity, so it was necessary to use the media to try to remove it. Taking back the power of the media for ourselves with *Corviale Network*, we presented a completely new image of *il Serpentone* in the whole region of Rome. We had realised that if the media were used playfully and poetically they could transform reality more than any project of architecture.

Corviale is also famous for the squatted homes of the *Piano Libero*, or 'Free Floor', where new Pasolinian *tuguri* run right through the building in the place where its designer had envisaged locating shops and common spaces in the manner of Le Corbusier. If in the imagination of the city's population Corviale was Rome's Bronx, the fourth floor was the Bronx's Bronx. At ATER, the proprietor of the building, they didn't have the faintest idea who lived there. For them they were illegal occupants who were stealing electricity, heating and water from the people to whom they had been allotted. The outside of the *Piano Libero* is characterised by small unplastered blocks of concrete, sheets of metal and aluminium-framed windows: a linear favela that cuts horizontally across the concrete structure. But when the students rang the doorbell and were invited inside, they found themselves first in large common spaces equipped with TV sets, sofas and ping-pong tables that were run by groups of neighbours, and then once they had entered the homes encountered cosy living rooms, kitchens and bathrooms in which large sums of money had been invested. Many of the squatters were children of the people flats had been allocated to, who, once they had started a family, had decided to move into those shops that had never been opened. Others had bought them from their previous occupants, while others still rented them from the Mafiosi of the moment. All, or almost all, had established a dignified way of life for themselves that was completely invisible from the outside. What they wanted was to make their situation legal, to have a home at last.

In 2006 I continued to work on the *Piano Libero* for the new Neighbourhood Contracts in which ATER had involved Roma Tre University. This was an experimental programme for the 'realisation of housing of various types, intended for special categories, i.e., assigned to those among the current occupants who had title'. The *Piano Libero* was the place from which to start in order to give the whole estate a new prospect, the negative image to be turned into a positive reality able to meet the needs of the inhabitants, tailoring the project to suit the families. So, together with the inhabitants, we criticised the preliminary plan drawn up by ATER, modifying the sizes and number of the flats to make room for single-parent families and young couples. We proposed the maintenance of the interfamilial common spaces and the existing ties between neighbours. A committee was set up that proposed a project based on shifts, dividing the work up into phases because, its members asserted, they were never going to leave until they had been assigned a new flat.

At this moment I am still working at Corviale through Roma Tre' Laboratorio di Città,[26] a community facility supported since 2018 by the region of Lazio as a social and cultural complement to the new interventions of urban regeneration: the architect Guendalina Salimei's Chilometro Verde, the architect Laura Peretti's Crossing Corviale and the new Integrated Urban Plan to be implemented with the funds of the NRRP (National Recovery and Resilience Plan) made available by Europe for the revival of the country following the coronavirus pandemic. A process of regularisation of the squats on the *Piano Libero* is in fact under way, using a Special Notification to identify the families with the requisites for the assignment of public housing.[27]

The Laboratorio di Città faces onto a small square in which arts and crafts associations are located, and within a short space of time the desire emerged to regularise not just the accommodation but all the commercial spaces that are currently occupied. These efforts could not be limited to the *Piano Libero*. It was necessary to take advantage of the moment to tackle all the problems together and not separately, following the logic of the funding. We immediately launched an artistic process capable of preserving the memories of the occupied floor, not just as a commemoration but also as psychological compensation and means of helping people to work through their removal from their home and the inevitable change in their living conditions. The relationship of trust we had established allowed us to enter people's homes and listen to their stories, as well as photograph and survey the flats. The materials we have put on display speak of well-looked-after homes encrusted with memories, with drawings on their walls made by children who have now grown up and left. Spaces that time has made it possible to personalise, turning them into homes. The exhibition, mounted in one of Corviale's common rooms, has become a permanent museum and is an implicit public recognition of people's capacity to produce autonomous solutions to their own housing needs, through an alternative narrative to the ones criminalising or victimising the occupants that currently predominate in the public sphere.

The Hybrid (Mestizo) City

> Blue-eyed Alì, one of many sons of sons, shall descend from Algiers on sailboats and rowboats. With him shall be thousands of men with tiny bodies and the eyes of wretched dogs of the fathers on boats launched in the Realms of Hunger. With them they shall bring little children, and bread and cheese […] They shall land at Crotone or Palmi by the millions, dressed in Asian rags and American shirts. […] – they shall destroy Rome and on her ruins they shall lay the seed of Ancient History. Then with the Pope and all the sacraments they shall go like gypsies up, to the West and North with the red banners of Trotsky in the wind …[28]

Pasolini's *Prophecy* has inexorably come true. The migratory movements that have crossed the waters of the Mediterranean for millennia have resumed with full force. More and more foreigners continue to cross the borders and take their turns in inhabiting the ruins of Rome, building themselves a shelter like the ones in those old prints in which the painters of the Grand Tour showed the Colosseum filled with shacks, with clothing hung out to dry between the arches.[29] Blue-eyed Alì lives here, sleeping under the bridges, bedding down near the stations, and when at last he finds work is not able to afford a home in which to start a family. But perhaps there is something that was not foreseen in Pasolini's prophecy. Thousands of people have refused to be segregated and deported to the farthest outskirts of the city and instead have squatted disused buildings, cutting off revenue from those in power.

Over the last twenty years the housing-rights movements have attained extraordinary dimensions. They have been able to tap into the influx of migrants and, turning ruins into homes, have created a network of squats that comprises more than a hundred large properties where over 10,000 homeless people live. The encounters between temporary workers, students and families of migrants from Latin America, Africa and Eastern Europe have produced hitherto completely unknown models of dwelling.

These new intercultural complexes are developing innovative forms of cohabitation, bringing different approaches to the housing crisis together synergistically as well as responding to the need for temporary accommodation on the part of people in transit. In contrast to the system of institutional 'reception', which categorises people on the basis of their origin and rights and spaces them out in different homogeneous and hermetically sealed containers, in the squats everything is in contact and hybridised. The people who live here do not just belong to the category of those caught up in the housing crisis, on waiting lists for subsidised accommodation for years. There are also people with different life aims and desires who do not fall within the scope of any housing policy: refugees and asylum seekers driven out of the institutional system of reception centres; those who have come to the end of the time limit for getting their papers in order; the ones known as *dublinati* in Italy, who are sent back to the country from elsewhere in Europe under the rules of the Treaty of Dublin; economic migrants in transit, who prefer not to be registered in Italy and are trying to get to northern Europe; and the many who have established relationships and found work in Italy but are forced to go underground because asylum is not granted to people of their nationality.

And a fact truly worthy of note, the squats have been the first to include the Roma in this babel of cultures from all over the world, breaking down that undeclared apartheid which has always excluded this European minority not only from the institutions but also from the struggles against them. After a great deal of initial

---

26 The Laboratorio di Città is made up of Sara Braschi, Giovanni Caudo, Francesco Careri, Fabrizio Finucci, Maria Rocco and Sofia Sebastianelli.

27 The project envisages the realisation of 103 flats where 135 families live today. The Department of Housing Policy of the Municipality of Rome, following the Special Notification of 2016 reserved for the residents of the *Piano Libero*, approved the list of households allocated a home (out of 135 families, seventy-three requests were received, forty-seven of which were admitted and twenty-six rejected). The amnesty approved by the Regional Government of Lazio with law 27/2006IS is also still in force.

28 Pier Paolo Pasolini, *Profezia*, in *Poesia in forma di rosa* (Milan: Garzanti, 1964); reprinted in *Alì dagli occhi azzurri* (1965). The poem has been translated into English by Stephen Sartarelli as Prophecy, in Sartarelli, ed., *The Selected Poetry* (see note 9), 371–5.

29 On the theme of ruins, foreigners and the refounding of Rome through hospitality, it is worth recalling Stalker's project *Tra le Rovine del Contemporaneo*, carried out during the Studio Roma artistic residence at the Istituto Svizzero in Rome in 2016; and the project by Stalker and NoWorking *Xeneide – il dono dell'Altro. Miti, Pratiche, poetiche dell'ospitalità* in 2017. See Lorenzo Romito, 'Walking out of the Contemporary', in Miodrag Mitrasinovic, ed., *Concurrent Urbanities: Designing Infrastructures of Inclusion* (Abingdon, UK: Routledge, 2015).

30 See Irene Di Noto and Giorgio de Finis, *R/home. Diritto all'abitare dovere capitale* (Rome: Bordeaux Edizioni, 2018).

31 Pier Paolo Pasolini, *Vie Nuove*, no. 17, 29 April 1965.

32 See Laboratorio CIRCO, *CIRCO: Un immaginario di città ospitale* (Rome: Bordeaux Edizioni, 2021). The workshop was set up within the Department of Architecture of Roma Tre University and along with the author its participants are Fabrizio Finucci, Chiara Luchetti, Alberto Marzo, Sara Monaco, Enrico Perini, Serena Olcuire and Maria Rocco (https://laboratoriocirco.wordpress.com/).

33 It involves participation in the PINQuA competition on the Quality of Housing of the Ministry of Infrastructure, sent out to the municipalities of Italy, to which the City Council of Rome, headed by Mayor Raggi, decided to respond in an innovative way, obtaining entirely public funding of 11 million euros. The project has been endorsed by the squatters and by a considerable number of institutional actors, including three ministries, three universities, the three levels of the regional, municipal and local administrations and fifteen local associations interested in taking part in the process.

34 See Roma Capitale, Delibera Giunta Capitolina, DGC-43-2021, CUP no. J83D21000030001, Allegato A – Relazione.

resistance due to mutual prejudices, today there are Roma in many squats and they are no longer regarded as 'Romani squatters', but squatters just like all the others.

The squats also house other non-residential forms of urban life that would not easily find room in the city ruled by the market. In many cases, in fact, they have a 'private-living' part on the upper floors and a 'public-social' part at street level, where they become visible and permeable and offer services and spaces for meetings, concerts, social eateries, carpentry shops, cycle repair shops, sports facilities and craft workshops, involving not only the world of the voluntary associations and possible local allies, but also those of institutional culture, the universities and contemporary art. The three main Roman movements – BPM, Coordinamento and Action – although facing enormous difficulties and internal contradictions – realise on a daily basis the paradigm of a hospitable, inclusive and intergenerational city, where another culture and another vision of the world are produced, a model of assembly-based self-management and mutual hospitality that the institutions responsible for housing and reception would find it hard to reproduce. Here the popular cultures brought by the migrants have hybridised with what remains of the local cultures of opposition, laying claim together no longer solely to the right to housing, but to the right to the city.[30]

The opening scene of the film *Uccellacci e uccellini* (*The Hawks and the Sparrows*) was supposed to have been set in a circus and was the story of an untameable eagle. The scene ends with the French tamer, played by the famous actor Totò, after multiple failed attempts, turning into a bird and flying away. The episode, which was called '*L'aigle*' (The Eagle) and then renamed '*Totò al circo*', was discarded during the editing of the film, but a subtitled film clip and Pasolini's first screenplay have survived:

> The backdrop to the fable is the crisis in Western liberalism and, in this case, Parisian rationalism. M. Cournot is a tamer from a famous French circus who has come to Rome. He is giving an interview to some Italian journalists, whom of course he despises: what does he announce? The beginning of a sensational enterprise: the taming of the Eagle.[31]

Pasolini's circus does not have the atmosphere of Federico Fellini's films, of that magical and dreamlike spaceship of trumpets, lights, drumrolls and Gypsy freedom, but is a place of taming and the untameable. A place of contradiction between what wishes to remain informal and spontaneous and its institutionalisation in a formal and rational system.

For some years I have been working with a group of young researchers at Roma Tre on the CIRCO project, an acronym of Casa Irrinunciabile per la Ricreazione Civica e l'Ospitalità (Indispensable Home for Civic Recreation and Hospitality). It is a project that tries to enter into this contradiction. It is a proposal of housing policies for the city of Rome that has come out of what we have observed in the squats, and that is driven by the new crisis resulting from the pushback of migrants to the borders of Europe. In fact the project was born in the autumn of 2017 and consists in turning disused building stock into a metropolitan network of intercultural blocks of flats founded on Hospitality: a hospitable city that aims to situate itself exactly in the gap between domestic and institutional, between legal and illegal, between formal and informal, proposing to the institutions that they experiment with innovative spaces in which hospitality is conceived as a fertile opportunity for the city.

The acronym is an explicit reference to the imagery of Fellini's circus, to the nomad who brings into the city an atmosphere that is unreal and magical, but decidedly foreign to the sedentary city. An itinerant universe that installs itself in the city's wastelands and that includes and puts on show strange and different figures like the dwarf, the clown and the fat lady. The circus is the nomad proud of his difference, wearing an architecture different from other buildings, one that is mobile and as colourful as the skirt of a Gypsy woman. It is the socially acceptable nomad, the different among us and yet familiar. It is the space of the Other for which we feel an archaic necessity. It is indispensable, untameable, unshakeable. It is that contradiction of which there has always been need: a place able to reveal its otherness, its potential conflict, its power of provocation, turning them into regenerative energies. Without submitting to the conditions of state or municipal hospitality, the circus sets out to be a normo-generative architecture, a network of places of continual experimentation that instead of being subjected to rules is capable of proposing new rules for everyone. The first step in the research was the drawing up of several public maps: that of institutional reception, that of the squats and the resistant city and that of the abandoned and underutilised buildings in which it would be possible to realise CIRCO, such as military barracks, train sheds, cinemas, theatres, schools, sports facilities, healthcare centres, church properties and disused factories.

Later, the potential inhabitants of a circus were identified, and it became clear that a huge number of different people could cohabit with those already present in the squats, favouring hybridisation and sociocultural diversity: the elderly, out-of-town students, expats, seasonal workers, young temporary workers, artists, activists, volunteer social workers, even tourists interested in staying in a strange social guesthouse where they could make their own skills available.[32]

The institutions have recently opened up the possibility of experimenting with a prototype of hospitable space at a civic level through the regularisation of a squat.[33] It is a project that envisages the 'participatory reclamation of the artistic and social heritage' of Porto Fluviale, a former military barracks occupied since 2003 by the Coordinamento Cittadino Lotta per la Casa, with the aim of 'rehabilitating a listed building, giving a new function to a disused building without further land take and with a view to sustainability and densification; increasing the stock of social housing; reducing the housing shortage through a process of social integration of a squat; providing the neighbourhood with a new public space; utilising innovative modes of management; activating a participatory process; increasing social diversity, understood as an antidote to the processes of gentrification underway in the neighbourhood and making the most of the social proximity of heterogeneous groups'.[34]

Porto Fluviale is in fact a very well-known building in the city. It is regarded as a monument by both the Cultural Heritage Service and the housing-rights movements. It is an icon recognisable by the murals of the street artist Blu, which have made the building famous all over the world. The project envisages the reclamation and realisation of new units of public housing to be allotted to the current squatters and the rehabilitation of the existing sociocultural spaces on the ground floor, which will then be reassigned to the workshops that are using them now and to other municipal services. Fifty-six households of thirteen different nationalities live in the squatted building, most of them from Latin America, the countries of the Maghreb, eastern Europe and Italy. More than sixty children have been born and raised here, attending the local schools, and today many of them are adults. The municipality has recognised it to be a community that, while the cause of conflicts at an urban level, has developed internally some unprecedented and innovative forms of intercultural coexistence, as well as opening itself up to the neighbourhood with performances and social activities. The process of inclusion, through the transition from unauthorised occupants to legal tenants of public housing, is intended to put an end to years of conflict, and will entail carrying out, as in the case of Corviale, an official census of the families and then the opening of a Special Notification that will check the possession of the requisites for access to public housing and assign the new accommodation. Also envisaged is a system of successive phases of construction that will allow the inhabitants to remain in the building for the entire duration of the work.

On the ground floor there are a large courtyard and many semi-public spaces and sociocultural activities. The interior is currently only accessible through a street door or from the tea room that connects inside and outside. For many years the outside world was perceived as hostile and the building had remained shut up like a fort, obliged to defend itself against the continual threat of eviction. But then commenced a process of opening up, whose stages have been discussed at length in assemblies of the occupants. In fact the squats are like islands of a parallel sovereignty where it is not the rules of the state that hold, but those of the assembly.

The first step was to turn the internal car park into a communal courtyard: a creation of semi-public space for themselves that has produced playgrounds for small children, football pitches for the bigger ones and volleyball courts for the grown-ups, a barbecue area and spaces for eating on the occasion of the ever-growing number of events proposed by associations from the world outside.

But the turning point came in 2010 with the opening of a tea room directly on the street: a visible, permeable and well-kept space, frequented by people who on entering started to understand a world often remote from their middle-class imagination. It is not just a place for drinking tea. As soon as you go in it is evident that it is a community-run, almost family-run, enterprise, with the feel of the lounge in someone's home. The tea room communicates with both the street and the courtyard, so it is a sort of filter, where outsiders who have earned greater trust can pass through and participate in the life of the intercultural community. Different degrees of intimacy make it possible to penetrate more and more spaces and establish more relationships, until you get the impression of having gained enough trust to feel that you are a welcome guest.

It was through that door that the group of lecturers and researchers of the Laboratorio CIRCO made its entrance. Over the last ten years it has carried out many artistic actions and taught university courses in collaboration with the residents in that courtyard, producing a marine imagery of flying and swinging boats and painting the entrance as the threshold of another world. On the occasion of the PINQuA competition, the university initiated with the students and the most active part of the community the process of participation and co-design that led to the winning of the competition. In the project the internal courtyard will continue to be used as a place in which to celebrate political initiatives and the festivals of different cultures around the world, and at the suggestion of the district council of the VIII Municipio will be turned into a public plaza with additional activities currently absent from the area: a weekly market for locally sourced produce; an easy-access help desk for women who are victims of violence; an integrated intergenerational space with a playroom and services for senior citizens; facilities for distance learning, reskilling, coding and a study room set up in collaboration with the Roma Tre University that is open around the clock.

As I write, the project for the transformation of Porto Fluviale is getting under way and if it is carried out without any betrayal of the intentions will have a great capacity for introducing innovations into future urban policies on the housing crisis and the reception of migrants. Rome is in fact still a city of ruins and foreigners, filled with empty buildings, a place of distortions in the property market and services never opened, abandoned or left in a state of perennial construction, and of Pasolinian figures from all over the world. The housing-rights movements have indicated a possible way forward and future administrations ought to take it. Cities need threshold spaces on an urban scale, grey zones that are not completely tameable, protected by the world of voluntary work and counter-power, where a hybrid popular culture can develop its own vision of the world, subverting the conditionings of the dominant culture.

That anthropological mutation which Pasolini saw as an imminent catastrophe has in fact occurred and is continuing. Social and cultural homogenisation is still advancing like the front of the city, and first the media revolution, and then the digital one, have completely altered the fabric of society. Even the Roma, the most loath to give up their age-old culture, are starting to renounce their pride in showing themselves to be different so as to blend in. But some pockets of resistance survive, or rather are evolving. If you venture past the mask of the media and walk off the map you can come into contact with those worlds 'unknown to tourists, ignored by the right-minded' where the saving power still grows. The author is profoundly convinced that getting lost like brothers to dogs in the cracks in the fabric of Rome is still an Odyssey worthy of song.

An earlier version of this text was published in Spanish in Francesco Careri, 'Walkabout Pasolini', in María Bastianes and Andrés Catalán, ed. and trans., *Pier Paolo Pasolini, Maravillosa y mísera ciudad* (Barcelona: Ultramarinos, 2022), 222–37.

Housestories: Good idea, wrong site?

The Corviale – a 958-m-long megastructure in the southwest periphery of Rome – was built between 1975 and 1982 according to plans by architect Mario Fiorentino. Pictured is a montage of the building in Rome's centre. Collage by Costanza Zeni. Inspired by works by Marlene Lötsch and Alexandrina Chergarska.

An elsewhere to discover otherness

Giorgio de Finis

Twelve years ago, in 2011, 200 squatters, migrants and people with temporary jobs from all over the world (including from Italy, because the poor are not just imported), who were occupying the former Fiorucci salami factory on Via Prenestina in Rome, agreed to take part in a magical realism project on the theme of the Moon: building a big rocket, leaving Earth and ushering in the age of exoplanetary migration … a way of saying to the city that had pushed them into the margins, the Rome that had become an expulsive and hostile metropolis: 'You are not chasing me away, it's me that's leaving!'

This was the *Space Metropoliz* project, which we described as a cinematic and artistic device to emphasise that cinema could create a 'playful situation', of the kind that art creates, which is always an aspiration to freedom. For a year, the project involved artists, philosophers, astronomers and astronauts (including Umberto Guidoni, the first European to visit the International Space Station) in our 'mestizo city'.

Two years after the factory's occupation, the place was taking the first steps towards becoming a community, and the squatters had already united around the need to claim their civil rights, first of which was having a roof over their heads.

The Museo dell'Altro e dell'Altrove di Metropoliz (MAAM, Metropoliz Museum of the Other and Elsewhere) was set up a few months after we had finished shooting our film. Like an hourglass, the rocket had turned upside-down in the sky, landing again in the place from which it had been launched, from that moment a land of fertile utopias. The Moon was the Elsewhere evoked by the name of this short-circuit between the highest point of the city (the museum, the place where precious things are stored) and its lowest point, the dust under the carpet, the squat, the slum (which I discovered in Rome with amazement on my return from a trip to Mumbai, economic capital of the fifth-largest economy in the world with eleven million people, out of sixteen, living in shacks made of cardboard and sheet metal).

What happened in the ten years from the birth of MAAM on 23 April 2012, from the creation of the Facebook page announcing its opening, defining it as the third museum of contemporary art in the capital (a rival to MAXXI and MACRO)?

MAAM's collection began with the artistic debris of *Space Metropoliz*, the telescope on the tower created by artist Gian Maria Tosatti (who in 2022 will represent the Italian Pavilion at the Venice Biennale and who has been appointed director of the next edition of the Rome Quadriennale), the walls painted by Lucamaleonte, Hogre and Sten & Lex, the lunar surface realised by Collettiva Geologika and of course the great rocket, a bit favela, built by the inhabitants (see www.spacemetropoliz.com).

Among MAAM's goals there was the creation of a barricade of art in order to defend Metropoliz and its people, a contribution to upgrading their common spaces, fighting the enclave effect of a place that needed to protect itself by shutting up behind a gate – and not least an attempt to find a new way of practising art and social design, one based on collaboration and generosity.

The first room that the museum realised was the children's recreation centre, entrusted to painter Veronica Montanino. It took a year to fix the roof and finish the work, which was opened on Epiphany in 2013. A big party for the Befana[1] was reserved for the youngest … and yet the kids' reaction to that giant colourful painting sliding across the walls and the floor was violent. Kicks, screams and punches were aimed at this blob that intended perhaps to swallow them up, but was playfully inviting them to enter a world made of colours and imagination. (The explanation I came up with for this violent reaction – which was only initial as it afterwards became their playroom – was that the wall which Veronica had painted in brilliant colours had suddenly revealed all the rest of the building to be a grey and crumbling ruin.)

That work was soon joined by many others; artists began to flock to the place, passing on the baton and transforming this urban ruin into the Lascaux cave of the third millennium. The first 'inhabited' museum on Planet Earth, as we like to describe it, now boasts over 600 works of art.

When Roman rapper Piotta shot his (first) music video, he made skilful use of a Steadicam. It was the best way to communicate the nature of this collective

[1] In Italian folklore, the Befana (pronounced [beˈfaːna]) is an old woman who delivers gifts to children throughout Italy on Epiphany Eve (the night of January 5) in a similar way to Santa Claus or the Three Magi Kings; https://en.wikipedia.org/wiki/Befana.

Michelangelo Pistoletto, Venere degli stracci, 2015. Credit: Giorgio Benni

Sten & Lex, In alto, 2011. Credit: Giorgio Benni

work that is also a single piece, an unbroken strip of continuity that accompanies you as you move through the space, a great harlequin cloak celebrating the value of diversity and encounters. This is what catches off-guard the visitors who come to see what it's like to live in a squat and don't expect to be surrounded by a number of artworks, shaking their certainties and prejudices (we all have them), just as those who come to visit a museum don't expect to see laundry hung out to dry, to hear the cries of children and to smell the odours of cooking.

MAAM has come a long way in a decade. Marc Augé defined it as a 'super-place'. The deputy mayor Luca Bergamo found it so interesting (for the city's cultural growth) that he did not limit himself to visit and promote it, but entrusted to the author of this essay the direction of Rome's museum of contemporary art, MACRO, which was changed into an 'asylum', bringing into the heart of the capital the experience born in Via Prenestina 913 (today another museum is looking to MAAM as a paradigmatic example of what the outskirts of the city can produce in terms of urban regeneration, of surprise, of vitality, the RIF – Museo delle Periferie).

And yet the sword of Damocles of forced eviction looms ever more threateningly over this unique and probably inimitable phenomenon, which we have recently decided to put forward as a candidate for the status of UNESCO intangible cultural heritage. With the 'NUNESCO campaign', the museum has playfully presented its (self-)candidature that also stems from the desire of inhabitants and activists to protect Metropoliz, recognising MAAM as their inalienable and worthy home, rejecting any possible individual solution aimed at putting an end to a collective and communitarian journey. We firmly believe that without MAAM, Rome and the world would lose a place that is a manifesto, a hope, a utopian and concrete image speaking of a different, inclusive, plural, fair and self-managed city, and of a social, generous and relational art, capable of constructing, by drawing on the logic of the gift, a communal space.

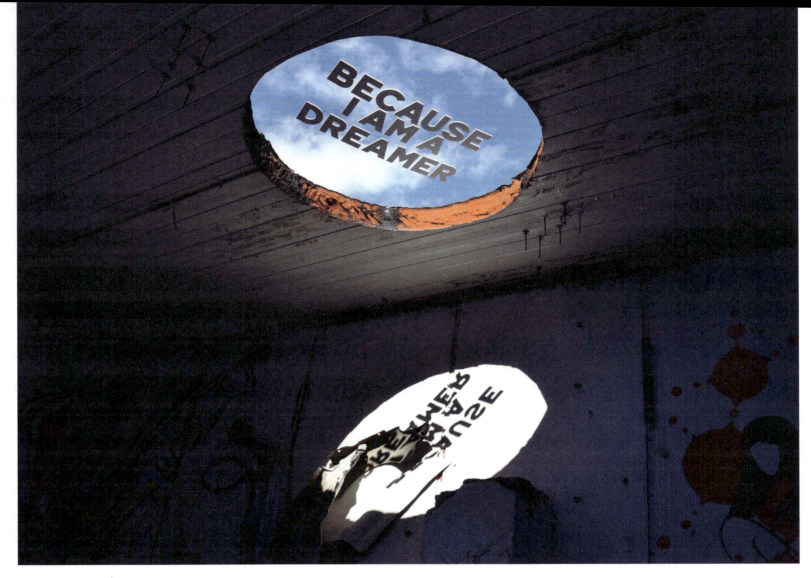

Gianluca Fiorentini, Because I am a Dreamer, 2021. Credit: Gianluca Fiorentini

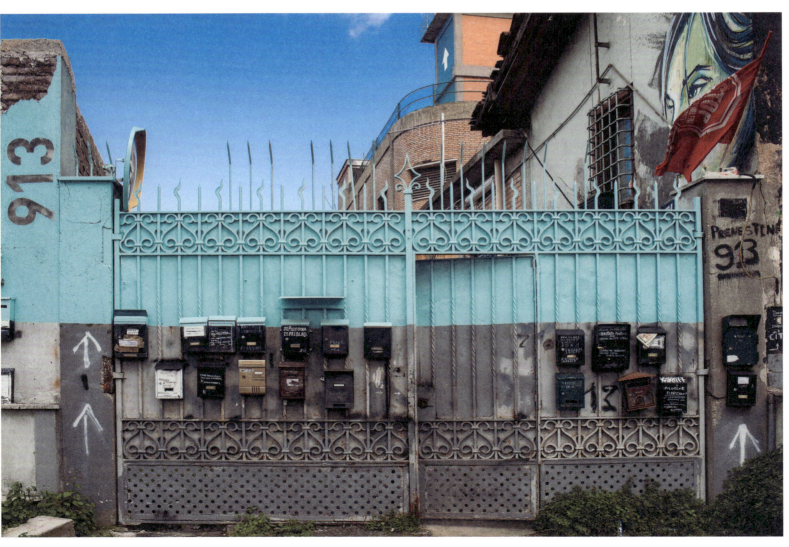

Davide D'Elia, 913, 2013. Credit: Giorgio Benni

Mauro Cuppone, Fart, 2013. Credit: Giorgio Benni

Alice Pasquini, Senza titolo, Intervento per la ludoteca di Metropoliz, 2013. Credit: Giorgio Benni

. Hypothesis Rome

Giulia Fiocca
Lorenzo Romito

By 'chasm' we understand a collapse, a rift revealing a latent state of crisis that instantly connects spatio-temporal spheres and dimensions that are usually separate, distinct. The chasm makes visible what was not visible, and it can cause what was taken to be established, definite, sure to vanish into thin air. This generates a level of uncertainty and ungovernability, of completely new relations and processes, which sweep away the status quo, opening up a gulf of possibilities between what can no longer be and what is unexpectedly about to occur. An uncontrollable process of becoming which it would be difficult if not impossible, and in any case risky, not to confront.

The current propensity is to repress, shut down, dismiss what has (unexpectedly?) happened. But that is not, nor has ever been, the way things work: how can we try to handle this unforeseen relationship between what has instantaneously become irremediably past and what irrepressibly and unpredictably clears the way for a future as different as it is dicey?

In Rome, we could say, the chasm is the founding space of the city, the *mundus*: physical, political and spiritual centre dug out as foundation in the centre of what was going to become the city-world.

> The word *mundus* actually represents the passage from the subterranean to the celestial and vice versa, i.e. the vertical connection between the two dimensions of below and above. Therefore, the *mundus* can lead to the underworld and, at the same time, [be] thought of as upside down, correspond to the opening that turns towards the vault of heaven. In other words, there is a reciprocal relationship between the two dimensions: the *mundus* from the depths leads to the world of the living and, conversely, from the light it leads to the darkness of the abyss, [...] However, ancient sources distinguish two different [*mundi*]: the city's foundation pit and the *Mundus Cereris* pit, which connects the world of the dead with that of the living and which is not necessarily dug during the urban construction ritual. The two cavities have often been confused and, consequently, homologated. The misunderstanding arose from the geographical location of the foundation pit of the city of Rome.
> (Roberta Esposito, 'Mundus. Fundus. *The pit that connects the subterranean and the celestial*')

The question of the *mundus* immediately raises uncertainties, admitting of different interpretations. Besides, we are moving between the scanty traces of archaeology and the liberty of interpretation of myth, which, through the accidents of history, can be used to renew its meaning.

With Stalker, we have explored, inhabited, celebrated and named many *mundi* in Rome: holes in space-time through which possible worlds can be glimpsed. Often they are small chasms hidden from daily view by neglect and wild nature. At other times they are sensational but soon forgotten events, areas blocked from view by obstructions, distractions or prohibitions, imperceptible tears in the tissue of the city's skin that give rise in the shadows to new and unknown microcosms. And it is just these microcosms generated by chasms that interest us, probably because Rome is incredibly familiar with the collapses in space-time that are chasms or sinkholes.

> 'Rome: 1526 sinkholes have been registered by ISPRA, the eastern zone is the worst affected'
> (Fabio Grilli, *RomaToday*, 13 June 2022)

> 'Rome is sinking, ISPRA has published its new study: the southern zone is the most exposed to sinkholes'
> (Fabio Grilli, *RomaToday*, 3 August 2022)

These are just two of the more recent newspaper articles that speak of how Rome is sinking. Sinkholes are opening up ever more frequently in the asphalt of busy streets, stemming from the weight of the traffic and the increasing heavy downpours of rain in recent times. The causes are many and diverse, from the city's geological conformation, abounding in natural and artificial cavities, to the presence of a large amount of water underground and the ways, both official and informal, in which it has been built, at times without an adequate geological survey. The ground in Rome is mostly volcanic, containing pozzolana and various kinds of tuff, materials used to construct the city since Roman times, and so the subsurface is filled with tunnels and cavities that have been put to the most diverse uses over the centuries: catacombs for the Christians, hideouts in wartime, refuges for those who have no right of citizenship today, ideal places for the cultivation of mushrooms.

If we turn our view of Rome upside-down by looking at it from below the level of the ground, we find a city full of voids. ISPRA's geological map of underground Rome[1] tells us of the constant risk of sinkholes and subsidence, but it also opens up endless imaginary vistas, glimpses of mystery and, at the same time, possibility: another subterranean, invisible Rome, an Eternal City that conceals different levels of history. This is the Rome that interests us, the one that is transformed in order to survive the passage of time at every slippage of the ground. It is of this other world, at times subterranean and at others just barred off and hidden, that we have chosen to be witnesses, defenders, storytellers, activists, connoisseurs … inhabitants.

Rome is the field of research and action, the territory from which to learn

In recent years with Stalker and the SUN (Scuola di Urbanesimo Nomade)[2] we have been collaborating with social and cultural forces particularly active in the defence, comprehension and collective use of these places and the emerging communities that are trying to make them habitable, supporting them in their struggle for survival and recognition of their right to exist.

Protests at the Lago Bullicante, 2021. Credit: Pierre Kattar

1   ISPRA, Istituto Superiore per la Protezione e la Ricerca Ambientale (Italian Institute for Environmental Protection and Research): https://www.isprambiente.gov.it/en/ispra-services/cartography/map-of-the-underground-cavities-of-rome?set_language=en (accessed 26 February 2023).

2   The School of Nomadic Urbanism is an informal course of mutual education launched in 2017 offering training in social creativity and in collective, explorative and experimental action. Those who take part are invited to be present, to respect others, women as well as men, to pay attention to places and listen to the people who live in them, to take part in conviviality and creative interaction with the repressed, the unexpected, the excluded and the strange. The school – itinerant, convivial and playful, in the open and open to all, with or without a degree or a residence permit – aims to explore lost or repressed memories, visible and invisible realities, possible and desirable imageries with which to re-establish relations between people, communities and places in an attempt to rouse a common space-time above and beyond the dreariness of an exhausted contemporary era.

We have focused our attention on two kinds of emerging ecosystems that are strategic for the rebirth of Rome:

- The ecosystems emerging out of the spontaneous reappropriation by nature of sites subjected to exploitation and speculation. The spaces of spontaneous resurgence of the wilderness in the city are often degraded and damaged ones, places in ruins. They are places that, thanks to their abandonment and the creative reaction of nature, constitute today the epicentres of a spontaneous process of renaturing and biodiversity that is fundamental for the city. Fragile, often unfamiliar places lacking adequate public safeguards, like the former SNIA Viscosa factory, where an attempt at property speculation in 1992 has left behind the skeleton of a shopping centre in the middle of a lake, created as a result of the rupture of an aquifer, called Lago Bullicante.

- The sites of multicultural coexistence stemming from the decision of the right-to-housing movements to occupy disused public buildings in the process of 'securitisation', i.e., those buildings put on the market to reduce public debt, and that are characterised by a very high percentage of migrants who could find nowhere else to live. These buildings have a configuration with an abundance of entrance halls, auditoriums, garages and spaces for 'public' use on the lower floors and offices in the upper ones. While the offices and the presence of shared bathrooms on these floors constitute an obstacle to their adaptation for living purposes, the ample supply of common spaces on the lower ones has permitted the squats to house, as in the cases of Spin Time and Porto Fluviale, social and cultural activities and associations and local services for the people living in them, as well as services provided for the neighbourhood by the occupiers. Notwithstanding the continual and comprehensible tension between those who live in and those who use these spaces, these situations represent the most complex and spontaneous responses to the prospect of 'urban regeneration', i.e., to the transformation of the need for housing that is under way and to the necessity to provide neighbourhoods with common spaces for the handling of social problems and the local production of culture.

Lago Bullicante

In 1990, a construction company bought the entire area of the disused SNIA Viscosa artificial silk factory, demolished some of the blocks and started to build a shopping centre where the city plan did not permit construction. In the process of excavating three storeys of underground parking, to a depth of about 10 metres, the underlying aquifer was ruptured and the entire surrounding area of Largo Preneste was flooded. The consequence was the formation of a body of water that covered an area of just under a hectare around the reinforced-concrete structure that was under construction, preventing its completion. Thus was created the Lago Ex-SNIA, collectively renamed Lago Bullicante in 2019. Over the years, the absence of human activities has led to the emergence of a natural ecosystem around the spring in a district of high population density, a refuge for species of animals and plants that, left undisturbed for decades, have adapted to living with the waste and ruins left by humanity. Nature left to its own devices has generated a 'new urban wilderness'. Be they former industrial, agricultural or military sites, unfinished constructions, exploited, abandoned places, waiting for a use to be found or just left over, Rome is full of them. Among them, Lago Bullicante is an emblematic place, one where it was the power of water, unleashed by human violence inflicted on the environment, that gave rise to a new and evolving urban landscape as a spontaneous and effective response by nature itself to the loss of biodiversity that we are experiencing.

While it is true that it is only the absence of human beings that has made possible the creation of an urban wilderness, it is also true that the emerging natural state has also had, in this particular case, a decisive social character. A community of people has formed, grown, learnt and become aware of the importance of this place for the area and for the city as a whole, observing it, inhabiting it, experiencing it at first-hand and defending it.

It is more than thirty years that the self-organised community has been fighting to defend the site of the former factory from property speculation in order to preserve, as a common heritage, one of the last empty plots of land in the district. Over time, the demands have come to take on an ever-greater awareness of the ecological role of the place. Those who frequent and defend the lake have grasped the privilege and the opportunity to be witnesses to and protagonists of a process that aspires to rediscover a lost contact with nature, sensing at the same time the social, political and cultural responsibility of fostering a new alliance with it.

For some years we have been participating as Stalker in the Forum Territoriale Permanente Parco delle Energie, which is the meeting point, initially set up by the Ex-SNIA social centre and the Pigneto-Prenestino neighbourhood committee, for the different social forces of the district and the city. Through the monthly assembly, attended by residents, activists, researchers, artists and local administrators, the Forum manages and looks after the entire Parco delle Energie, which currently comprises the area of Lago Bullicante and the public park, officially recognised in 1997, in which the Casa del Parco, with its Sala Ovale for community activities, the historical archives and children's recreation centre, is located.

The Forum is a laboratory of experimentation and exchange of ideas for the development of strategies for dealing with political and administrative bodies, as well as actions of protest and other creative and collective activities. At the Forum experts collaborate with researchers and with research and educational institutes on study of the site, identifying complex and appropriate responses to the problems raised by its use and protection and preparing a joint project for the future of the area. Fundamental activities have included the mapping of its fauna and flora, studies of the water system and environmental monitoring, as well as initiatives aimed at exploring the possibilities and limits of the creative relationship that can be established with nature, of a genuine 'education in urban wilderness'. Meetings on participatory planning, assemblies, rallies outside institutional offices, conferences and study meetings with activists, politicians and researchers, including foreign ones, interventions by artists, and of course occasions of conviviality: these are the many faces of the political activity carried out by the community of the lake. An important aspect is the mutual and intergenerational educational process that is conducted through teaching activities for schools and others, connected with the industrial history of the area and naturalistic topics. Near the lake there is also an apiary that, in addition to introducing people to the world of bees and producing excellent honey, is an indicator of the ecosystem's health.

Documentation of the intertwining of the natural and anthropic history of the place is kept at the Centro di

Flooded construction at the Ex-SNIA area, now Lago Bullicante, 2021. Credit: Pierre Kattar

Documentazione Maria Baccante – Archivio Storico della Viscosa, which houses original papers and documents from the factory, rescued from their abandonment by the inhabitants of the area in the mid-1990s. The documentation centre is becoming, through a public process of sharing of stories and records, an important piece in the construction of the collective memory of this urban community.

The activity of the Forum is a struggle still in course: on the one hand with the institutions, in an effort to get the still privately owned area expropriated and recognised in its entirety as a natural monument; on the other with the owners of the land, always ready to proceed with new speculative operations. The Forum has a very clear idea of what kind of urban scheme is possible for this place. That scheme is the combination of everything that has already happened, what nature has re-created over the years and what the inhabitants have done to protect it. Understanding that the project is already under way, that it is the fruit of situated knowledge accumulated through the experience of defending and taking care of the site, that the agency of the spontaneous and emerging ecosystem is the principal planner and that it is therefore not the fruit solely of human will and cannot be implemented within the framework of regulations that would place limitations on the creative process make this a struggle/project/operation of a profoundly innovative character.

The MAd'O, Museo dell'Atto d'Ospitalità, at Spin Time Labs

The squatting of buildings by the right-to-housing movements continues today, amidst great difficulties and conflicts, to be the only valid alternative in Rome to the shortcomings of the institutional social system of emergency housing, and at the same time a unique experiment in multicultural and intergenerational cohabitation based on self-organisation. In addition, they are places that promote a different vision of society which no institution currently seems able to imagine. The fact that today the right-to-housing movements bring together people from different cultures – Italians but above all foreigners – excluded from the right to a roof over their heads, makes them genuine workshops in which the future and the coexistence of diverse cultures are being forged. In particular, the more central public buildings like Spin Time and Porto Fluviale constitute the only intelligent planning response to the urban desert produced by gentrification and touristification in the historic centre. They are buildings that today house social and cultural activities of collective interest, turning these squats into potential hubs of the social life of entire neighbourhoods, as has happened at the Esquiline with the building on Via Santa Croce: the squat in which 450 people from twenty-seven different countries live together with social and cultural entities gathered around Spin Time Labs, which is also the main promoter of the district's so-called Polo Civico, a network that for over a year has been linking up a broad range of social and cultural associations and bodies. Thanks to this mix of cultures, spaces and relationships, these squats are not self-enclosed ghettos but true experimental laboratories of new forms of dwelling, hospitality and management of common assets.

At Spin Time there is also MAd'O, the Museo dell'Atto d'Ospitalità (Museum of the Act of Hospitality), set up by Stalker along with several other bodies, to play a part in the implementation of this complex project/process of coexistence. The occasion was provided, in July 2020, by Sébastien Thiéry of the French collective PEROU (Pôle d'Exploration des Ressources Urbaines). Sébastien was given a study grant at the French Academy in Rome at Villa Medici, where he proposed as a research project the compilation of a dossier for the inclusion of the Act of Hospitality on the UNESCO lists of intangible cultural heritage. A series of documents and images donated by photographers from various countries recording spontaneous acts of hospitality towards migrants were selected at a workshop in Villa Medici to serve as the basis for the dossier to be presented

Protests at the Lago Bullicante, 2021. Credit: Pierre Kattar

Model by Nadja Muck. Work from the design studio *Living Ruins* by Christian Nuhsbaumer at the Research Unit of Housing and Design at TU Wien.
Credit: Paul Sebesta

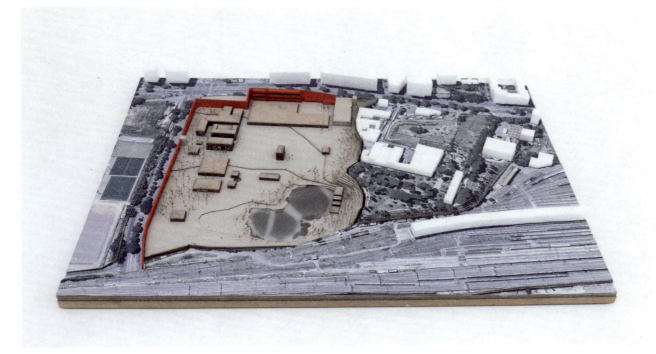

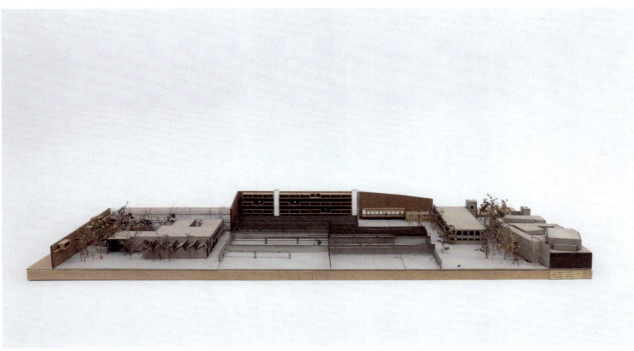

Model by Philip Unger: The Dissolving Border. The wall around Lago Ex-SNIA is dissolved and understood as its own typology. New and communal programmes form an opportunity to experience the city where there used to be a border.
Work from the design studio *Living Ruins* by Christian Nuhsbaumer at the Research Unit of Housing and Design at TU Wien.
Credit: Paul Sebesta

to UNESCO. In addition to PEROU and Stalker, the participants in the workshop were Spin Wide Shot, at the time the photographic lab of Spin Time, *Scomodo*, a magazine for young people based at Spin Time, and a number of the squatters of Santa Croce. The images chosen were printed on wooden placards and, on the occasion of the annual exhibition of the *pensionnaires* at Villa Medici, carried in procession along the Via Felice (a road linking the Villa Medici and Spin Time, laid out in the baroque era by Pope Sixtus V, in the world Felice Peretti) to Spin Time, in the squat on Via di Santa Croce, recognised as a place symbolic of hospitality in Rome. The placards have been put on display in the new space dedicated to MAd'O and constitute the first nucleus of its archives.

MAd'O is intended to be a space of possibility, devoted to the encounter between the people squatting the building on Via di Santa Croce, the neighbourhood, the city and the world. An artistic and cultural means of supporting the political struggle of those who have no home and very often not even the right of citizenship and of trying to find another way of living together in places that would otherwise be abandoned. A space in which to experiment with the practice of mutual hospitality, where there is no difference between host and guest.

So here we have started to hold exhibitions, meetings, book presentations and discussions of the practice of hospitality and the different cultures that cohabit in the occupied building. A space where women, men and children who come from far away can find a familiar place for their own festivals and celebrations. The objective of the MAd'O is to get the inhabitants and their experience to play a leading part in the creation of a living museum, where hospitality is investigated as a cultural practice at the same time as being practised. Already, with the preparation of the space set aside for a museum, consideration has been given to fostering an exchange with the women and men who live in the building, to learn about and share their different ideas and practices of hospitality. A slow process, one that takes time, which can provide an opportunity to get to know and document – partly through the experience of Women Crossing, a theatre workshop with the women of Spin Time, and AMM, Archive of Migrant Memories – life stories, histories and geographies of hospitality given, received or refused. Thus the renovation of the space has also served as an occasion for the production of the first contents of the Museum of the Act of Hospitality, where what is emerging is not just a unique space of intra- and transcultural production, but an archive of the repressed memories of immigration in the city.

Hypothesis Rome, a sympoietic eco/mytho-system

These two places, the Lago Bullicante and the MAd'O, constitute the main workshops for the development of new forms of coexistence, overcoming the socially imposed limitations on the citizenship of 'foreigners' and on nature in the city. Routes to the establishment of a possible society to come.

For some years they have been at the centre of the research/action on the city that we are carrying out with Stalker and the Scuola di Urbanesimo Nomade, where artistic action is indistinguishable from social activism and educational experimentation. Chasms into which Stalker has sunk almost to the point of disappearing, only to re-emerge where and when it is useful and effective to make ourselves visible in order to support struggles and practices necessary to the attainment of a desirable future. Over the last three years two projects, La Zattera and Spontaneamente, have allowed us to obtain the resources and means needed to start a public debate, involving local and international, institutional and informal actors; an experimentation with educational and spatial practices that turn around the staging of public actions which we call *Circostanze* or Circumstances:

The *Circostanza*, an opening out of the times and spaces to which a place belongs, is a means of public and creative involvement, aimed at keeping in effect the character of disadaptation to the places passed through that becomes a position from which to act on/think about the possible generated by the re-emergence of lost memories, and their weaving into new narrations. On the human plane the *Circostanza* is also the convivial and creative occasion for a possible meeting between places and people ever more divided by social, economic and cultural conditions that today wall us off from a desirable and happy coexistence.

At present we are also working on binding these two emerging urban dimensions together in a single eco-mythological narration that, harking back to the founding myth of Rome, sees it rising again from its own ruins, reappropriated by the wilderness, the Latium, an alter ego necessary to the survival of the city, in which the excluded and the foreign can find hospitality and refound Rome, just as happened in the sacred grove of the Asylum on the Capitol. Wilderness, traces of the past, survivors and new inhabitants who together constitute the ingredients for an alchemical transmutation; a cyclic regeneration of the city in forms that are both new and old, allowing it – eternal city? – to be born again at the end of a life cycle.

We have called this prospect Hypothesis Rome: Rome is a complex form of life, a sympoietic ecosystem, with an emerging organisation of its own capable of evolving spontaneously and regenerating itself. A system whose natural history depends on the success of the ecological relationship between human and non-human, on a possible scheme of co-evolution between the biological and the social whose feasibility and limitations characterise its many declines and rebirths, from the ecological perspective its resilience, from the mythological one its eternity. An eco/mytho-system, therefore, in which the human component has a fundamental role but does not dominate.

A Rome has always existed and still exists that spontaneously discloses possible worlds to come amidst the ruins of burnt-out civilisations and cultures, unwittingly playing host to emerging environments and lifeforms, the spontaneous and unexpected consequences of its own failures. A hidden and eternal Rome, not because it is eternally shining, but because among the ruins run wild of its multiple declines it has always found room for an encounter between survivors and foreign refugees, reconstituting each time the possibility of yet another future. Not according to a linear logic of progress and domination of the other but following a nonlinear and circular logic, that of life itself, of the regeneration of relations with the other, be it the past, the natural environment or the stranger.

.Spin Time Lab

Zara Pfeifer

Text by Gerald Weber

■ It was originally intended to be modern Italy's showcase urban project after the Second World War: the Don Bosco housing project on the southern edge of Rome. Although planned while Mussolini was in power, Don Bosco matches the modernist style of the 1950s and 1960s and is wholly in harmony with the spirit of postwar reconstruction. As it is comparable to housing projects in other large European cities, this development demonstrates the gap between socio-political utopias of the modern age and their reality in a virulent manner.

Schreiber's works are cartographic portrayals in film form in which she attempts to translate the formal languages of landscape or architecture into that of cinematography. This process was also applied to *Borgate*: Schreiber consistently transfers Don Bosco, which was designed by the city's urban planning department, into rigidly framed images and sequences of serial montage.

In the interplay of these mainly static shots and relaxed pans across facades and structural details, combined with quotes from Pasolini and Fellini to Antonioni, *Borgate* produces a visual and acoustic showcase of failed urban utopias.

This animation is reinforced by abrupt intrusions of video fragments in violent motion, resembling what seem to be splinters from a 'real space' in the aesthetic filmic space.

In contrast to Antonioni's men about town, for example, whose psychological crises are reflected in the *objets trouvés*, wide streets, two-dimensional facades and empty suburban squares, Schreiber searches for and finds precise details and total views of these outlying urban zones for the purpose of dealing with the crisis of the modern age itself.

Original title: *Borgate*
Director: Lotte Schreiber
Year: 2008
Country: Austria
Duration: 15 min

Borgate

Lotte Schreiber

Borgate. Credit: sixpackfilm/Lotte Schreiber

Borgate. Credit: sixpackfilm/Lotte Schreiber

Roman notes: The free life of elements of architecture

Simone Capra

[1] AMO and Rem Koolhaas, *Countryside. A Report*, catalogue of the exhibition *Countryside, The Future* at MoMA, New York, February 2020–February 2021 (Cologne: Taschen, 2020).

Environmental scenarios

Ever since the first studies of the planet's health were made public in the second half of the twentieth century, people have started to become more aware of the problems posed by climate change. Consequently, the need to come up with adequate responses to these environmental challenges has opened up a wide-ranging debate in the last few decades over the sustainability of human activities. This public discussion has inevitably brought with it a general reappraisal of the disciplines and sciences that study and organise the modes of human settlement on the earth.

In those fields concerned with the organisation of inhabited space, a great deal of attention has been paid to the technological themes of the applied sciences, with an attempt to deal with the climate-altering effects of pollution and the artificialisation of the environment using a remedy based paradoxically on a further degree of artificialisation.

From this point of view, many lines of research have focused on renewing the disciplinary fields of mechanical engineering and energy production, both from a practical and professional perspective and in the area of academic training. A great deal of effort has gone in to reimagining the envelope and machinery of buildings, such as air-conditioning systems and the consumption and waste of energy. This approach has so far had the upper hand, in part due to the fact that less has been heard from architects and urban planners – with a few notable exceptions – on the theme of sustainability.

Continuity versus autonomy

If, however, we shift our viewpoint and look at the transformations that have taken place over the last century from the perspective of the urban dimension, we can see that this progressive artificialisation of the land has been the result of the greatest expansion of the urban phenomenon ever to have occurred on the surface of the planet, with the emergence of huge agglomerations, some of which have reached populations of 30 million and more. This unprecedented and extremely rapid process of land take, still under way, has led to the juxtaposition of species-specific environments and biotopes that were previously distant, to new forms of conflict between the human species and others species of animals and plants, to a different interpretation of what the city is and what remains outside it.

In the early months of 2020, during the lockdown imposed by the pandemic – itself probably due to phenomena of spillover resulting from the contiguity of anthropic systems with natural ones – AMO (the research, branding and publication studio of the OMA architectural practice) and Rem Koolhaas opened an exhibition called *Countryside, The Future*[1] in New York. The curators put on show a hybrid and roboticised version of agricultural production, debunking with their images the myth and authenticity of an arcadia-refuge outside the space of the city. The countryside is just a different productive district of the city with a different rate of automation/artificialisation.

In this sense, the urban expansions of the second half of the twentieth century and the first decades of the twenty-first have redefined the relationship between built environment, countryside and wilderness, potentially establishing an urban continuum with different degrees of artificialisation, inside which survive geographical accidents such as natural reserves of biodiversity.

On a different scale, the modern city, born out of the principle of the *tabula rasa* and the dream of an orderly sequence of areas of land created by means of zoning, resembles, a century later, that urban continuum of the historical city which planners had set their sights on superseding.

Illusion of the *tabula rasa*: for a new model of the approach to the existing city

According to the principle of the *tabula rasa*, the city of the new man was to be erected for the new man, showing a complete lack of concern for the historical city or even proposing its erasure.

The analytical and figurative model utilised by Le Corbusier to interpret the historical city, applied in the

2 Here we are referring to the figurative procedures used to extract abstract volumes from the continuous fabric of the historical city, relying on the expedient of photomontage. See the illustrations in Le Corbusier, *Vers une architecture* (Paris: Crès, 1923.)

3 Le Corbusier, Plan Voisin for Paris, 1925.

4 Rem Koolhaas, *The Generic City* (New York: Monacelli Press, 1995).

5 In Italy a broad interpretation of conservation subjects to verification of cultural interest – and thus of the obligation to preserve – everything built over seventy years ago and designed by an architect who is no longer alive.

experiments presented in *Vers une architecture*,[2] was taken as an operating model from the time of the suggestions of the Plan Voisin,[3] a new grid superimposed on a pre-existing city razed to the ground, ignoring its topography, the natural system of the drainage of water from the land and even the adaptation of human life to its environment over centuries of anthropisation. Like the Arch of Constantine in *Vers une architecture*, some monuments were isolated and preserved as vestiges of the vanished city. On the one hand, the city of the new man; on the other, the historical city. On the one hand, the modern city for production and work; on the other, the city of heritage preservation for leisure and the emerging phenomenon of mass tourism.

Exactly a century after the publication of this fabled text, and given the impossibility of destroying all the city centres of Europe, the only practical approach that planners have managed to come up with – and for the moment this remains the case – is that of a twofold expansion. On the one hand, increasing the area of the modern city to find locations for the new functions of work; on the other, expanding the perimeter of the preservation and restoration of what is recognised as the historical city.

The point here is not to produce a far too belated critique of Le Corbusier and early modernism, but to set that work against the background of its time. The upheavals of the early twentieth century demanded an approach by antithesis: if the historical city was adapted to topographical factors, the new city had to be an abstract grid; if the historical city was made up of multifunctional buildings, the new city had to organise functions separately into homogeneous zones.

What we want to stress here is that the training of architects and urban planners and their box of tools for interpretation and design are still the offspring of the *tabula rasa* – that is, of that early twentieth-century dichotomy, when there is no longer an outside to be colonised or an existing city to be preserved as a whole.

The proposition we want to make here is that, within a hypothetical continuum, the challenges faced by the designers of inhabited space are those of preserving the areas of cultivable land and natural wilderness, safeguarding their biodiversity. As a consequence, the tools that will open up unprecedented scenarios for new architects are the ones that allow them to work on and in areas that have already been anthropised – that is, on the transformation of the already urbanised and the remodelling of the already built.

Going beyond the obligatory formulas of urban substitution, where the existing city blocks further processes of evolution, what was said above signifies being able to figure out programmes of urban renewal based on forms of transformation by addition and adaptation – that is, those that can start out from stratifications of the existing palimpsest, from processes of densification of the gaps, or on the contrary from processes of incision for the reopening of public spaces of social mediation.

From what has just been described, it is clear that the operations of urban regeneration we are beginning to imagine in Europe potentially share characteristics of continuity and similarity with the processes of transformation of the historical city. Addition, adaptation and incision are just some of the means utilised by the architects of the past who operated in the fabric of the historical, pre-industrial city. If we look at these models, we find masses of tools that can be updated and used for the reinvention and transformation of the generic city.[4]

Constructing on the already urbanised entails an operation of revision of what is meant by historical city, as we can longer be content with a classification of the concept of *historical* that is based today solely on the principle of its age and that potentially extends the city to be preserved ad infinitum.[5]

If we accept that reducing the anthropic footprint means moving towards zero consumption of land, and therefore working on already built-up areas, architects are going to need to bring back into play a critical approach to the existing city that has been suspended for over a century and that in the separation of the disciplines of the planning of space has been entrusted solely to the category of architect-restorers.

So, intervening in the existing signifies not settling for a suspension of judgment with regard to what has been classed as historical, but going back to making selective choices: what to preserve, what to demolish, what to transform, and thus what to hybridise and densify.

This operative approach is in the first place an interpretative approach that entails the proposal of an academic training which moves towards a holistic conception of the city, the territory and the human structures built in them – including learning from the immense catalogue of the pre-modern historical city.

On the subject of great works of literature, Italo Calvino wrote In *Why Read the Classics*[6] of the importance of rereading, because while the book has remained the same, we who are rereading it and the context around us have changed. The classics are those writings that however well we think we know them, reveal themselves to be *original, unexpected and innovative* on each rereading.

Paraphrasing Calvino's lessons and substituting the word work for that of book, we can go back and reread Rome as a collective work and great classic of inhabited space that has produced specific forms of dwelling and strategies for the constitution of the urban phenomenon, according to principles of adaptation to the topographical and historical substratum.

From this rereading it is possible to extract a catalogue of spatial, interpretative and design operations to be rediscovered in the process of transformation and regeneration of what already exists.

Rome as catalogue: the elements

'A classic is a work that comes before other classics; but those who have read other classics first immediately recognise its place in the genealogy of classic works.' (Calvino, 1995).

Archetypes: the problem of the Tabularium

For centuries, Roman architects, and the foreign ones who arrived in Rome as holders of scholarships at the academies, or following the itineraries of the Grand Tour, tried their hands at the theme of the reconstruction of the building of the Tabularium, the structure of the Roman State that at the end of the republican civil war between Marius and Silla was erected to house the tablets on which the law was engraved. As an architectural expression of the foundation of the state, the Tabularium presented – for the first time in known Roman history – the political manifesto of Greek entablature framing the Etruscan arch, an architectural synthesis of the unification of the Mediterranean world under the Roman aegis: the Tabularium became a myth. As such it was positioned on the (slopes of the) Capitol and formed a scenic backdrop to the valley of the Forum along the Via Sacra, and at the same time the base of the saddle of the Capitol Hill.

The potency of its conception and the ambiguity of the location of its ruins, incorporated into the rear of the complex of palaces on the Capitol, have for a long time been a problem of typological interpretation that has tested generations of European architects, from the

6   Italo Calvino, *Why Read the Classics*, trans. Martin Mclaughlin (London: Jonathan Cape, 1999).

7   See Andrea Carandini, ed., *Atlas of Ancient Rome* (Princeton, NJ: Princeton University Press, 2017).

8   On the experiment of hybridising nature and architecture, the writings of Paolo Portoghesi are fundamental: *Nature and Architecture*, trans. Erika G. Young (Milan: Skira, 2000).

9   In this essay we have looked at the element of the facade as a means of adaptation of the design, but we could have picked any other. It suffices to think of the inhabited wall and the research commenced by Luigi Moretti in *Spazio* in 1953 or the stair and its confrontation with the urban – the aforementioned stair of the Capitol or the steps of Piazza di Spagna. This essay presents an excerpt from broader research into Rome that owes a debt to the joint work carried out in the Teaching Unit of the Rome Program, Iowa State University, with the architects Consuelo Nuñez Ciuffa and Lavinia Minciacchi and that has been further developed in the lectures for TU Wien. This text is an extract from a forthcoming publication, Readers are referred to the results of the whole programme of research for the investigation and analysis of the other elements.

Jacopo Lauro (?), reconstruction of Ancient Capitolium, in Famiano Nardini, *Roma antica di Famiano Nardini alla santita' di N.S. Clemente XI*, Rome, 1666.

reaffirmation of the classical in the Renaissance onwards.

The difficulty of the theme lay not so much in the reconstruction of the classical language used as in the question of the typological characteristics of the building and its location on the cliff. What was the base of the Capitol, what was its crown, if there was more than one level – and in that case how were they organised?

Paradoxically, the person who came closest to the original structure, as has been corroborated by the studies of the archaeologist Andrea Carandini,[7] was Famiano Nardini in the seventeenth century with his fanciful reconstructions of the ancient Capitol (illustrated in an etching by Jacopo Lauro): in a many-towered version of the Capitol, a hill turned into a castle with a series of terraces facing onto the Via Sacra, the Tabularium is just a porticoed facade on a geographical scale that opens onto the valley of the Forum. The Tabularium is the facade of a cliff. The Tabularium is a facade that contains the inhabited space within its thickness. Above the Tabularium there is no roof, but the square that is today Michelangelo's Piazza del Campidoglio.

So the theme to be resolved was one of interpretation: the architecture was not erected on the ground, from the bottom up, but along the side of the cliff and beneath the level of the square.

For an architect who thought of a space suitable for construction as a horizontal site on which to found the building, there was nothing behind the facade. For the architects of republican Rome, there was the foundation of Roman space and the birth of the idea of architecture in section.

The theme that emerges on the Capitol is the uninhibited use of the elements of architecture that make up the canonical building: facade, stairs, internal partitions, floor slabs, roof. In this case, the facade was an architectural element used as a means of artificialising the natural setting. It was not the natural state that was erased by a process of *tabula rasa* in order to turn the topography into a neutral plane on which to erect the building, but the building that was exploded in order to find the single element best suited to the complex geographical situation. This method was applied to the various components and portions of the hill (the saddle that became a square, the slope that was urbanised in the stair of the Capitol, etc.). It was a hybrid in which nature and architecture were fused.[8]

The second aspect that emerges from the vision of the Tabularium, and one that was correctly interpreted in Lauro's fanciful drawings, is the expansion of the object to the scale of the city and the landscape as a figurative element independent of the walls and adjacent substructures.

The scale of the facade and its independence of the context permitted a direct dialogue between the architectural element and the urban landscape, without the mediation of the building as it had been conceived in its entirety. The expansion of the element's scale also brought an increase in its depth. This thickness immediately became inhabited space. The elements were hollow spaces.

The process of artificialisation of the environment and of Rome becoming a city was conceived by dissecting the building into its basic elements, which were then applied directly to the given geographical and topographical situation.

Dissected in this way, the architecture serves on an urban scale as an instrument of stratification, reinterpretation and densification of what already existed. What existed coincided initially with the natural topography, and subsequently with the layers of history transformed into a geographical substratum.[9] The city proceeds by additive formulas that densify the existing space. Each element is a hollow space inhabited in its thickness.

The facade as it has been presented is a mask; it faces outwards. Through the reinterpretations of it made in the Renaissance, the archetype of the Tabularium was able to become a model to be copied and reproduced. The element, free from typological connotations, was flexible and could be adapted to different contexts.

In the second half of the sixteenth century, Giorgio Vasari applied the theme of the facade not to a geographical situation but to a pre-existing urban fabric of medieval derivation. The street running from the Arno to the Palazzo della Signoria was regularised with a new, continuous facade running along three sides that framed the river. Behind the facade, the thickness of the building

[10] The reference is to the projects of the Tour Bois-le-Prêtre, Paris, 2011, and the Quartier du Grand Parc, Bordeaux, 2016.

is variable, filling the gaps between the structures of the medieval fabric and the straight line of the facade; in it were located the offices for the new magistracies. The interstice is an inhabited hollow space. The rhythmical pattern of the facades imparts a sense of order to the public space and at the same time responds to the pre-existing streets that end at it. The facade masks a portion of the city.

If, according to Calvino's adage, it is possible to recognise a genealogy through a classic, making a leap in time, these approaches to design can also be discerned in the works of contemporary architects. The project of the Nieto Sobejano practice for the extension of the San Telmo Museum in San Sebastian can rightly be said to belong to this category. The hollow space hidden behind the slender facade created with a digital cutting machine houses museum functions and the filled interstice is once again the gap between a facade and a geographical feature, the foot of the hill between the city's two gulfs on which the castle stands.

It is also possible to examine some of the work of the Lacaton & Vassal agency under this lens. In the experiments carried out in Paris and Bordeaux,[10] in what is almost a Vasarian rereading of the theme of the facade, the element, in its independence – even structural in Bordeaux – is juxtaposed with public housing from the 1970s, taking up again the additive principle of urban renewal in historical cities, in the absence of costly demolitions and with the aim of creating spaces for habitation without expelling the inhabitants.

An intervention for new magistrates' offices in Florence, an intervention to create new museum spaces and an intervention of expansion of public housing: the method of the dissection of architecture and its elements is adaptable to different functional and programmatic necessities of composition of the city and to interventions on different scales.

Paradoxically, a possible overcoming of the deadlock produced by the imprinting of the modern city and the continual colonisation of natural areas viewed as a *tabula rasa* can come from the rereading of the historical city and from one of the many possible lessons of its archetype Rome.

Inhabiting Rome

Lorenzo Romito

Rome is a place that has been inhabited for an almost infinite length of time. It is – has been – city, village, city-world. Each of its refoundations over time has occurred on the ruins of the past; this has been done in an effort to erase its origins in the hope of avoiding its end. As Michel Serres so clearly explained, Rome is incomprehensible to itself, a black hole, a space-time of transit between eras and civilisations that succeed one another, a forging of the curvature of time, of that reverse time in which decline leaves space and time for the rise of a new world.

At the antipodes of this obscure and secret bending of time, which over millenary cycles replaces origin with rebirth, Rome has become city, urban model of a new age, and the map of the equilibrium it has attained a compass with which to orient the very idea of a city in the world, of city-world.

This seasonal perpetuation through the winters of history makes Rome not so much a city as a form of life, one which at different stages – gene, body, environment – is inhabited by the human as well, but is not properly speaking a product of human will and action. The humanity that is part of it, that inhabits it and is inhabited by it, participates in the transformation of this complex life form precisely by living in it and cohabiting with it.

Architectural projects and urban plans, when they do not constitute penetrating syntheses inspired and informed by a superhuman process of intelligent and creative becoming, are a grandiloquent and monumental expression of human self-referentiality; of arrogant thirst for power, something of which Rome is also an image, seeking to mark out a new, impossible domain, fated soon to fall into ruin, only to be mineralised by human and non-human habitation, refuge of the possible, infrastructure of what is to come, warning of the presence of time, nostalgia for the past and desire for the future.

Thus, it is time, another wintery time, that hides in order to take the living city from autumn to spring, to avert end and beginning, to turn the worn-out body of the decaying city into the fertile ground of the city to come. Time and the spontaneity of life are the great planners of Rome. Those who inhabit it and those who are inhabited by it work on it, metabolise it, contributing to that continual transformation that is the project of time. An inhabiting and being inhabited by Rome that is change: struggle, adaptation, coexistence, co-evolution.

What are the spatial and temporal boundaries of Rome if it is has the ambiguous substance of endlessness? In the process of its becoming, it has been almost nothing and almost everything; so, what is Rome? Today the terms Capital, Outskirts, Historic Centre are taken as the forms in which to frame Rome's problems and the planning responses needed to deal with them – but are they adequate, useful terms?

If we use the image of the black hole, of time curving back on itself, we are able to visualise the question of the boundaries of Rome: there are none. There are margins, folds in space-time, zones of contact and exchange, where time accumulates, relations are intensified, losing definition and generating unprecedented configurations, edges on which space-time slides into the black hole. They are margins, folds, encrustations that cannot be reduced to the clarity of boundaries. The Aurelian Walls, built already too late to defend the city from its decline, and the Grande Raccordo Anulare (or 'great ring road'), also a failure in its effort to contain modern urban expansion, are the proof. Rome gave its citizenship to the world in an attempt to coincide with it. Useless the effort made by Fascism which, unable to keep the shanty dwellers outside the city, took away their citizenship in an attempt to exclude them, just as the effort to do the same with 'immigrants' today is a failure.

Rome expands and shrinks. Its material and immaterial space takes the shape of a vision of the world only to disappear into the past. Rome has no boundaries, but it has margins. It is margin, a borderland between city and nature, between East and West, between Europe and the Mediterranean, between past and future. A confluence of different ecosystems that get mixed up in Rome, between sea and mountains, between two volcanic systems and the waters that spring from them, flowing into two rivers. No one is foreign in Rome, because everyone is. It has no boundaries nor beginning, there is no autochthony nor polis. In its recesses it hosts and cyclically gives citizenship to every possible otherness in order to outlive the usual end of every identity: it is inhabited by the past with its ruins, by the wilderness that takes over the ruins, by the foreigners who make this uninhabitable space inhabitable. That is what happened in the sacred grove of the asylum where foreigners gathered to found – once again? – the city on the inhabitable hill of the Capitol.

We lack the history of the last, of the least, which we need to understand Rome, as well as a history of the city as history of its environment. Rome is city and nature, its citizens residents and outsiders.

So to think about Rome we have to remove boundaries and definitions, explore its margins, which are also boundless, making them the workshops in which to forge a common desire of future, between becoming and what is to come, between how many we are and how many we are becoming, gaining experience of everything that needs to be reconsidered in the world today: the relations between human and non-human, between city and nature, between citizens and foreigners. It is not politics that decides and determines, but a mechanism that sees planning as failure and spontaneity as a process on which it feeds.

Rome has been colonised by ideas that do not belong to it, like those of Centre, Outskirts, Capital and Metropolis, just as the ecological idea of polis, political space of the human in opposition to the rest of the living world, the economic one of capitalism and the political one of nation, the aesthetic one of contemporaneity, exclusive space of real time, perennially present, decontextualised by the flow of time, fed by the frenzied consumption of the

[1] The *Circostanza*, opening out of the times and spaces to which a place belongs, is a means of public and creative involvement, aimed at keeping in effect the character of disadaptation to the places passed through that becomes a position from which to act on/think about the possible generated by the re-emergence of lost memories, and their weaving into new narrations. On the human plane the *Circostanza* is also the convivial and creative occasion for a possible meeting between places and people ever more divided by social, economic and cultural conditions that today wall us off from a desirable and happy coexistence.

past and the future, do not belong to it. Ideas that Rome tries to include, like any otherness, to metabolise in order to turn them into ruins, reducing their devastating impact. So those who are rejected, excluded, subjugated, create a city by inhabiting uninhabitable ruins, making them habitable, in a continual activity that spontaneously and unintentionally generates the world that is going to come.

Is this a perspective that can be shared? A narration that can be used to interpret the time that we live in and the forms that Rome has assumed and may still assume? In this unpredictable process of becoming, large tracts of which are hidden and incomprehensible (just like the Rome of the origins or of the Middle Ages), what might be the role of the planner, artist or architect, alongside that of the inhabitants who work there, inhabiting it, in the face of the continual subterranean and vital transformation of Rome? I have been trying to answer this question in the twenty-eight years of my activity as Stalker.

Should the planner inhabit Rome in order to be inhabited by it, by that involuntary know-how, typical of fungal hyphae, but also by the fact of remaining an outsider, of distrusting one's own confidence and one's knowledge of a city that does not know itself …

Should the planner/Stalker rediscover, explore and reconnect, narrating to the present times and places that are phantom, inoperative, in order to grasp the traces of the past and the signs of the living that inhabit its present, listening to them and taking care of them, finding narrations and rituals that make this structure an expression of the process of becoming of a place, seeking to make the uninhabitable habitable, forming a community to come, a conscious gathering of strangers that celebrate the umpteenth beginning without origin …

It is hard to turn this narration into a planning paradigm. I will try to provide examples through the editorials that I wrote to accompany the *Circostanze* (Circumstances),[1] actions of the Zattera project (2020–23) organised with my partner Giulia Fiocca for Stalker, wandering around repressed spaces and times of Rome together with an informal educational community, the SUN, Scuola di Urbanesimo Nomade (the School of Nomadic Urbanism).

Circostanza No. 1: Borghetto
Prenestino, 31 January 2021
I hope Yusuf comes …

I hope Yusuf comes to this public *Circostanza* to recall the Borghetto Prenestino, a 'circumstance' that occurred forty years after that last party to mark the burial of every trace of the epic refuge whose story had begun in 1930. In those days in May 1980, when victory was celebrated in the very long struggle to allow its residents to move from their shacks into council houses, the proposal was made to turn the area of the biggest shantytown in Rome into a park named after Pier Paolo Pasolini. In an interview published in *l'Unità*, however, Ninetto Davoli suggested that the memory of the settlement be preserved and that the park be called the 'Borghetto Pasolini'; and to underline the disorientation resulting from the demolition of the *borghetto*, added that it would be a good idea to have the surreal road signs of *Uccellacci uccellini* in the park: Cuba 13,257 km, Istanbul 4,253 km … We have added another: Manila 10,384 km. It was from Manila that the plane which crashed on a piece of wasteland on 14 January 1954 came. The pilot heroically avoided the houses and shacks, so that only the people on board died; but all of them. Today, on the site of the tragedy, the traces of a recent fire amidst the remains of an encampment that did not even have the dignity of a shantytown evoke the wreckage of the plane, accidentally stirring that lost memory in our imagination; a memory that we would like to restore to the forgetful city and, if they wish, to the Filipino community that did not yet exist at the time, thereby delivering the place from neglect and the event from oblivion.

I hope Yusuf comes in particular because, in a twist of fate, the first families of shanty dwellers who constructed the Borghetto Prenestina, using the 'experimental' and extremely cheap technique of self-building, also came from the place where Yusuf lived until a short time ago, under the iron bridge over the Tiber. There have been shacks beneath it for ninety years now.

I hope Yusuf comes because he too has decided, now that he has a roof over his head, to turn the location of his long-suffering residence, the shanty on the Tiber, into a garden, and we and some art students are helping him. I think he is doing it to regain the freedom to be able to forget by turning that place from hell into paradise.

It is important to remember – how many important things we have forgotten, absentmindedly, or even refused to recall – just as it is important to remember to leave people free to forget what they find too hard to remember. This combination of the collective need to remember in order to understand and to change, and the personal desire to be able to forget the suffering of the past, seems to give a circular shape to time, turning it into a disc, one that if well-made and thrown with force can clear the way to a possible future for us again. A way that in the society in which we live, where the proactive mechanism of memory seems to have been disabled, was assumed to have been lost, at least until the arrival of the pandemic.

How much we still need to discover and understand in the recesses of our city … That until forty years ago there were shacks everywhere in Rome, then there were no longer any and now they have appeared again; that the Italians have moved from the shanties into council houses and the Roma, Italian and foreign, into camps; that from 1939 to 1961 those who came from the countryside were not guaranteed the right to live in the city and that since 2009 the same violence is being used against undocumented foreigners; that many people recall life in the shantytowns with more pleasure than in the large public housing complexes, stages in an exodus that over the space of 150 years has emptied the city, turning into an endless periphery … That there are certain stories many didn't want to tell then, and don't want to tell now …

Memory and learning are inseparable. It is important to remember in order to understand that the largest informal settlement in the city had an institutional origin. In fact, the Borghetto Prenestino was born in the shadow of and partly within an official housing estate of the Fascist period, just as the institution of the Roma camps has become the infrastructure for the reappearance of the shantytowns. Places of forced and discriminated habitation for the last, for the bottom of the heap, obliged to live in the spaces of rejection specially designed for them by the experts of academia and the institution.

And it is precisely when social creativity driven by the need to survive despite the institutional rejection of rights generates new forms of life and sociality, invents possible futures of coexistence, transforming and adapting the coercive spaces of the institution, that the latter reacts with anger and tries to erase every trace, all memory. And it is only when it does not succeed that out of these collective processes of emancipation and struggle society is able to regenerate and evolve. It was in the Borghetto Prenestino, and many other places like it in Rome, that were born the struggle of the right-to-housing movements, the struggle for the abolition of special classes for the disabled and for an alternative education, the capacity of political and social forces of different natures and creeds to form a united front. It was in the Borghetto Prenestino that Ninetto Davoli and Pier Paolo Pasolini met, that a new, at once realist and surreal art took shape, profoundly renewing Italian culture and allowing it to tackle important social and political challenges.

How to recall the sorrows and joys of this erased and scattered community? How can we help those who experienced that past repressed by everyone to forget except by getting to know it and recognising it and making it public? How and what to remember? What can we learn from this history? How to make sure that to fifty years of struggle for the right to housing are not going to be added another forty of privation and suffering? This is what has happened to those who, from 1980 to the present day, have been moved from the shanties into equally exclusionary and ghettoising council housing, even if with a bathroom and central heating …

In search of a possible future in the forest of repressed memories

With the School of Nomadic Urbanism, we ventured into the forest of repressed memories, wandering around on largely abandoned terrain where diverse forms of life, including human ones, still seek shelter today in the depths of a resurgence of the wild. We saw a kestrel and a pheasant, found a thicket of broom, a grove of holm oaks and lots of trees of heaven. We listened to Piero, to his stories of a carefree childhood among the shacks, his irreverent familiarity with those strange and later legendary personages who frequented the Borghetto, from Mother Teresa of Calcutta to Pasolini. We met the few people who live in that marginal place, wondering how they do it, what they know about it. They pointed out traces, while others we discovered, like the entrances to an extensive underground system; someone said that it went as far as San Giovanni. We found vestiges of an ancient catacomb, used as a quarry, where the children of the Borghetto confront the darkness as a game.

Here, outside control and planning, bodies with different needs, memories and imaginations continue to establish involuntary and highly imaginative relations, as improbable as they are necessary and creative, that revive the genius loci, hidden in the wilderness, whose voice we tried to hear.

It is into the depths of this repressed history that we feel the need to have re-emerge in the present those sunken roots, the subterranean mycorrhizal network which can draw on the struggles of the past to feed the ones needed today in order to bring back a possible future. Only an ecological use of the memory can allow us to renew these subterranean traces and try to make them shared and public.

We have a huge need for this wild space in our cities today, and no city is as generous as Rome in generating it, having itself been generated by the wilderness as the many place names derived from trees record: the Caelian Hill took its original name (*Querquetulanus mons*) from *Quercus*, the oak; the Viminal from *Salix viminalis*, the willow or osier; the Fagutal from *Fagus*, the beech; and the Esquiline may come from *aesculus*, the Latin name for the Italian or winter oak.

The forest has given names and a location to the city, so let us take care of it. Why not entrust the memories we have unearthed to the creativity of the forest, so that it can guard them and keep them alive? So that a forest of memories is born, so that every shack that was there finds a tree to remind us of it, so that a wood can commemorate the victims of the plane crash.

In Rome the forest or *selva*, Latium, is the *spazio selvatico* or wild space for the asylum of the Other, the alien, the spontaneous, the unexpected, so that the Other together with what remains of Us can give rise to a renewed *Noialtri* (Roman slang for us, literally us-others), thereby taking part in the birth, always the rebirth, of this city, which perhaps only for this reason is eternal.

Circostanza No. 2: The wilderness traverses Roma Mundus Subterraneus 14 February 2021. Stories of mushrooms, abysses, phantoms and other rifts between Rome and Latium

For this *Circostanza* we could not fail to take note of the circumstance that today, 14 February 2021, St Valentine's Day, coincides with the season of Carnival, two feasts in one. Both have remote and forgotten origins, ancient and Roman, savage and alien to us: St Valentine's Day in the festival of Lupercalia, the Carnival in the celebrations of Saturnalia.

They are festivities that in the Roman era comprised the winter months that the Romans initially did not even measure, being another time, a reversed, wild, subterranean time in which it was feared that the souls of the dead would leave the underworld to wander in procession and that barren and untilled land would no longer become fertile again. A time that started with Saturnalia, celebrated between 17 and 21 December, a solstice festival during which Saturn, like Proserpine, sank into the Mundus Subterraneus, and from god of the harvest became a hidden god of the underworld, making way for January, the month of Janus, god of beginnings. And concluded with Lupercalia, an orgiastic festival of fertility in the middle of the month of February, dedicated to purification from the spectres of the winter, while waiting for spring; a festival at which Febris, goddess of fevers, was venerated too, honoured for keeping malaria at bay. A celebration so licentious that Pope Gelasius I tried to suppress it in the fifth century, seeking to replace it first with the feast of St Phebronia, a Syrian martyr, and then with that of St Valentine.

For several days during the festivity of Saturnalia a sacred and subversive inversion of social roles took place: the Mundus inversus, in which slaves masqueraded as free men. Among them one was chosen to be king and dressed as Saturn, cloaked in red, the colour of the gods, and acting as custodian of the souls of the dead in the underworld and protector of the harvest. In the Lupercalia, which brought this other space-time to a conclusion, young men who had regressed to a savage state after sacrificing a goat set off from the Lupercal, the cave dedicated to Faunus Lupercus in which the she-wolf had suckled Romulus and Remus, and then ran back there along the boundary of Roma Quadrata, the Palatine Hill, dispensing fertility to women by touching them with strips from the hide of the animal that had just been sacrificed.

Saturnalia and Lupercalia comprised that wintertime of the apparent end that always threatens and announces the rebirth of spring. A time that was not measurable, neither linear nor entropic, like the time that leads from the beginning to the end, from order to disorder, but a reverse and negentropic, risky and creative time, that from the end can lead back to the beginning, from disorder to order; the time in which Saturn, hiding in the underworld, regenerates life.

They are festivities that concern the city's sacred relationship with the Other, spaces and times extraneous to the city but that Rome does not exclude: the other time of Saturn and the other space of the wilderness, symbolised by Faunus-Lupercus. The outsider and the savage, both as risky as is necessary to a city that aspires to eternity, in order for time to reverse its course and return to the beginning, negating its origin as well as its end. Could this be the meaning of Saturn, i.e., Latium, hidden in a cave beneath Rome to ensure its eternal splendour?

So, let us take advantage of this circumstance to turn, if we are allowed, the world upside-down.
We will move on foot between the ground and the underground of a hidden, vanished, invisible Rome, in that alter ego in which the city of Janus – god of the passages that bring opposites together – hides to be reborn: Latium, which has always given refuge to repressed memories and informal practices amongst its uncultivated spaces. So that from all this Rome can be reborn again.

We will try to inhabit the different and reversed times in which it has been salvific and insalubrious forest, wilderness. We will meet the new guardians of the gates between the two worlds, celebrating that reverse time which gives the last kings and queens back the power to regenerate the land after the long winter of an alien modernity that has turned it into exploited periphery. We will honour them, listen to them and then ask them to give us access to that subterranean network where the passage between Rome's past and future is revealed, where the ghosts of a history that no one has wanted to write have been relegated, where mycelial webs work continuously and silently on weaving relationships between different species into an inextricable tangle of mutual aid, once again offering hope of surviving the imminent, possible, mass extinction. Mythology and mycology will guide us through that labyrinth where the connection between Rome's past and future seems to have been lost, in the attempt to bind together again unrelated histories that still today feed the phantoms of a past and a present to which we do not yet know how to put an end. We will attempt to ritually circumscribe the epoch-making winter of the contemporary era, evoking a genius loci that will infuse us with the hope of finding a way to a different future.

To carry on with this carnivalesque and subversive babbling we have to move away from the idea of order that becomes disorder and towards the prospect of a more complex order that emerges from disorder through an exploration of the repressed, of its phantoms. To do so we must bring into question the whole contemporary history of Rome, 150 years that constitute a brief interlude in the millennia of its existence rather than its destiny as a capital.

Circostanza No.3: Along the Strada Felice [literally the Happy Road] towards worldwide citizenship, 28 February 2021

The possibility that we would like to unleash with this *Circostanza* is the necessary and urgent one of a common condition for citizens of Rome as well as the world. We will try to do it along a single straight road, the Strada Felice that Felice Peretti, Pope Sixtus V, traced within a stellar design that reinvented Rome.

We will walk along the stretch that runs through the whole of the Esquiline Hill, between Porta Maggiore and Santa Maria Maggiore where the sumptuous villas, monasteries, vegetable gardens, vineyards and pleasure gardens of what had become, for the second time, the most beautiful city in the world. A heritage erased by the property speculation of Umbertine Rome with its extraneous and magniloquent royal place names. Names not pertinent to the no longer foreign colours and scents that fill it today, nor to the painful memories of what really took place there but does not yet have a name.

Only a few months ago we first walked along the Strada Felice from Villa Medici to Spin Time (a multi-cultural squat), holding placards with the photos collected by PEROU (Pole d'Exploration de Resources Urbaines) to propose to UNESCO the Act of Hospitality as an intangible cultural heritage of humanity. From that collection of photos was born the MAd'O or CAd'O, the soon to be opened house/museum of the Act of Hospitality.

Ten years ago, though, after the disastrous clashes with the police at the demonstration held on 15 October 2011, a small group of people camped out for a month in Piazza Santa Croce in Gerusalemme to join the planetwide protest of Occupy Wall Street and then moved along the Strada Felice in a straight line from Santa Croce in Gerusalemme to Piazza del Popolo. This was on 11.11.11.

It is a road that must also have been followed by those first Asian migrants who, like so many other Romans since the unification of Italy, were driven out of the historic city and gathered among the ruins of the former Pantanella pasta factory. Renamed Shish Mahal, it was the place where alongside thousands of migrants Don Luigi Di Liegro, Dino Frisullo and Sher Khan engaged in one of the first battles in the bitter struggle, still under way, to obtain equality of rights for Italians and foreigners. It is partly for this reason that the hostel for the homeless Luigi Di Liegro founded at Stazione Termini has been named after him, that the area in front of the Ararat squat, in Campo Boario, has been named Largo Dino Frisullo, being the location of his longest battle alongside the Kurds, and that today we are dedicating to Sher Khan the corner of Piazza Vittorio in which he froze to death, like too many others, in the hope that the city council will eventually do the same. There is work to do on the toponymy of the Esquiline, but it's nice to know that the memory of Willy Duarte, murdered just a few months ago, will soon be preserved in a renewed Piazza Pepe.

The Strada Felice must have also been the route taken by the coffin of the first ambassador of the Congo, come to plead before Pope Paul V for the rights denied to the others, to the different and to the lost. Reaching the city in 1606 after a dramatic journey, and dying of exhaustion shortly after that long-awaited arrival, he was buried in Santa Maria Maggiore, with a funeral in grand style which should have been the ceremony to welcome him.

For the ancient Romans tomorrow, the first of March, zero discrimination day, marked the beginning of the new year. It is the month of Mars, the god of war, and on the site where Santa Maria Maggiore now stands, which was then the grove and later the temple of Juno Lucina, was celebrated the Matronalia, the festival of all women and the celebration of their power to bring wars to an end, as they had done in the one between the Sabines and the Romans. Just as men did in the Saturnalia, women inverted their social role by preparing a meal for the household slaves, before going in a procession to honour the goddess of fertility, Lucina, she who brings children into the light, on the very spot where Christians were going to house the sacred relics of Jesus' crib, relics that the Strada Felice connects with those of his cross, in Santa Croce.

We too will walk along this road and on it traverse thirty years of struggle against exclusion, discrimination and racism. We will carry with us the hope of a finally worldwide citizenship, like the one that, for the first and only time in history, Caracalla granted in 212 CE. We will walk through the sites of struggle, of suffering and joy, of the memories and desires that can today offer us the prospect of a *strada felice*, a happy road to be taken, on foot at last, in a reborn natural setting, filled with fruit and recollections.

<u>Circostanza No. 4: Ostiensistan,
a haven on the Silk Road,
28 November 2021</u>

To visit Ostiensistan, memory and imagination are needed, but above all presence. It is necessary to uncover its traces, the routes of access hidden between the tables of the restaurants and bars of a fashionable neighbourhood, ignoring the many distractions that divert most people from the intention. You need to look farther, find the sources of memory scattered here and there around the area. You need to get to know their custodians, ask them questions and listen to them with patience, help them to reorganise their archives. Ostiensistan is a nomadic space. Things are unlikely to still be in the same place they were last time, and on each occasion it assumes the form of a carpet in which the warp is made of stories, of things that actually happened, and the weft of desires. Desires that, interwoven with memories, reveal in the reality of the neighbourhood an imagery which starts to occupy reality and subvert it, drawing on the precise recollections and the passion that only the desire to gain access to a possible world can stir. A good way to start the journey is to roam around the Stazione Ostiense, waiting, trying to take your mind off an ever more unpresentable present, recognising and getting to know a *mosafer*, following him and hoping he will tell his story.

Mosaferan, 'travellers', is the proud name adopted by the many children and young people who, fleeing from lands torn by years of strife, have set out on foot along the Silk Road, the age-old route linking East and West. Arriving in Rome in their thousands, after admiring Bruce Lee's house, or the Colosseum as we call it, from the windows of the no. 175 bus from Termini, they reached the Stazione Ostiense, convinced that Karzai was going to pay for their ticket. Epic and fragile figures, the *mosaferan* will open the gates of Ostiensistan for anyone who has the opportunity to listen to their adventurous, premature and traumatic experiences of flight. First, in a deafening and icy silence, the *ajay*, 'grandmothers', as the Afghans called them respectfully, in spite of the indifference and hostility of society and the institutions, found it natural to take care of these very young travellers camped out in the desert of the Stazione Ostiense. We will ask the *mosaferan*, who have grown up Italian, and their *ajay* to tell us what happened there just ten, twenty years ago. We will listen to them. Anyone who enters Ostiensistan is duty bound to share and keep alive the memory of the loving as well as bitter and painful relationship between *ajay* and *mosaferan*, a still unpaid debt with history for a society that has chosen not to see.

If you're lucky the *mosaferan* will take you along platform 15, where they slept in the open and many of them fell sick, between an attempt at flight and a turning back from and to France, up and down on the Rome–Ventimiglia train, which left from there and returned every day. You will realise you are in Ostiensistan if the platform appears to your eyes to be the colour of lapis lazuli and you slowly start to make out the young people nestling one against the other, sleeping to the sound of a marvellous lullaby. A monument of the most delicate forms will appear to you amongst the initially ephemeral but bombastic ones of the Stazione Ostiense, built of scaffolding pipes, wood and plaster, a ridiculous set staged for the ill-omened meeting, on 3 May 1938, between Hitler and Mussolini. Perhaps they, too, will appear to you, amidst Chaplinesque mimics, brutalised crowds and pompous cardboard colonnades, while plotting yet another devastation of Europe. The road under the tracks was built to lead to the 1990 World Cup, when the station was doubled in size, creating a gigantic air terminal whose urgent construction cost a number of workers their lives. In total there were twenty-four deaths and 678 work accidents during the preparations for Italy '90, as well as three stations built in Rome and never used. The air terminal, where, in 1995, we presented Stalker's first journey through the disused and abandoned areas of the city, sleeping there for a night in order to fit out the great empty space with hundreds of toilet rolls and discovering that hundreds of people were already sleeping in the baggage hall. The Farneto underground station that we passed through on that first tour before it was occupied by Fascists, and that of Vigna Clara, where the tour started and ended after four days of walking.

For those who do not have access to Ostiensistan, the air terminal has become an international food centre where thousands of people can eat all sort of things at all sorts of prices, without having any possibility of imagining or remembering where they are. The epicentre of a transformation that in the space of a few years has seen Ostiense become the district with the highest seating capacity of any restaurant in Europe and, as they say in Rome, *der monno*, in the world. But there are still a lot of abandoned places in Ostiensistan, among the old disused factories. Like the deserts on the Silk Road, those who pass through them run the risk of falling prey to hallucinations. Thus, Calvino's invisible cities might appear to them: that of science and technology, that of the young dreamed by the emir Veltroni and designed by a very great architect who has preferred to remain anonymous. If and when you wake up, you will finally be able to see that, in Rome, it is not plans that design the city, but the consequences of their almost constant failure.

Ostiensistan appears right there, with its oases in the middle of the desert, among the ruins of those failed dreams taken over by the creative uprising of nature, inhabited by semi-nomadic communities that meet up there and around the fire tell biological stories of natural resurgences and social stories of alternative and innovative uses, of political and civil commitment to the rights of people, of the community and of the environment, of the difficult construction of a common possibility. Stories that have arisen spontaneously, unplanned, amidst the ruins of an unpresentable present. These oases are fragile socio-ecosystems in the making, traces and signals of the future to be remembered, cared for and defended from the voracious dreams of those in power who continually threaten to swallow them up. For Ostiensistan is the Rome that has always been reborn from the bottom up, a wild, hybrid place. Some are still living stories while others tell of vanished worlds. They are stories from which we can learn how to turn our gaze on the future, with determination and desire. Among these oases are hidden important archives, like those of the Global Village, the Mario Mieli Circle of Homosexual Culture, the Pirateria di Porto, Alexis, the Grassroots Community of San Paolo, the Porto Fluviale; experiments in socialisation and in turning the desire for a different future into practice; treasures for which no map exists.

Here will appear to the luckiest of us the time in which Ostiense and Ostiensistan have learned to coexist, when the memories of the artistic and social movements have penetrated and completed the archives of collective memory, where the places in which these stories have been acted out and told have become the theatre in which they can be understood: oases and sites for the ecological and social construction of a different future, one no longer delegated to homogenising and destructive economies and policies, but shared between human and non-human beings, where the necessary and vital relationship between places to be reinhabited and communities to be reinvented can be reconstructed.

This is Ostiensistan, a network of oases in what threatens to turn into an urban desert, inhabited by wildlife and foreign communities, landing place for Afghan refugees as well as for the Kurds who, in 1999, in the former slaughterhouse, in collaboration with Stalker and many other bodies, set up the Ararat sociocultural centre, the first and still the only embassy of the many communities living in exile in Rome. A world generated by a unique interweaving of social, cultural and artistic practices. An experience that today we would like to share with the Afghan communities, so that they, too, can have an embassy in exile. We have called it the school of Herat, where old and new refugees from Afghanistan can meet each other and the city in order to give expression to the cultural richness and diversity of their places of origin. And, through unique skills like the painting of miniatures and weaving of carpets, render their presence no longer an awkward occasion for charity, but a great opportunity of cultural enrichment for the whole city, at the very moment that a renewed religious fascism is once again forcing into flight those who are most able to love and create, above all women and artists.

Circostanza No. 5: How to deceive
a time without memory or
imagination, 19 December 2021

Do you know the Stazione Cavour? In Rome? No, not the Metro B station on Via Cavour, nor Piazza Cavour, on the other side of the Tiber. It's easy to get them mixed up. Another place entirely, named after Cavour only ten years ago: the new Tiburtina station, opened in 2011, the year in which the 150th anniversary of the unification of Italy was celebrated, right in the middle of what we might call the forgetful two decades that stretched from 2000 to 2021.

Two decades of colonisation of the world on the part of the Contemporary, an aesthetic invention of the dominant culture aimed at making the present its own global as well as eternal domain. Twenty years in which momentous challenges have turned into unsolved and ever more unsolvable problems. Twenty years of eternal present, in which the future has slipped through our fingers and the past has grown remote. Twenty years in which the struggles against inequalities, for the protection of the environment, for the rights of women and minorities, have turned into wars: on terrorism, on the environment, on the poor, on migrants, on the virus.

Commencing on a political level in 2001 with the war on terrorism (11 September) and the repression of the anti-globalisation movement (20 July), on an aesthetic and technological one a bit earlier with the opening of the Guggenheim Museum in Bilbao (18 October 1997) and the appearance of the first smartphone (also in 1997). Twenty years in which the history that was thought to have ended broke into a run instead, but we didn't notice. We weren't able to do anything – caught between fear and distraction – but kill time on our smartphones, on planes and on high-speed trains, in the seductive and dissuasive waiting rooms of history created for us by contemporary architecture. The fixed and mobile, real and virtual means of the acceleration that has led to us forgetting.

The Stazione Tiburtina is one of those places, of which there are few in Rome, a city resistant to the contemporary and its architecture, that are more likely to fall into ruin and be overrun by nature again than to be finished, victims like the Tower of Babel of their arrogance, as has happened to the Sports City complex and the former wholesale market. The Stazione Tiburtina, like the Nuvola at the EUR, battles between life and death, between the difficulty of adapting to a time that is starting to turn its back on it and the hope that its time, without environmental or economic or physical limits, will be able to establish itself again and here too. In particular, it seems that the Stazione Tiburtina cannot manage the ambiguity typical of contemporary architecture which allows it at once to seduce and distract the good and dissuade and reject the wicked, those who have no worldwide safe conduct.

The new Stazione Tiburtina is in fact a hostile and repellent work of architecture for all the travellers that pass through it. Only those who get off the train have access to the tunnel leading straight to the Metro. Anyone who wants to take the train instead is repelled by backward-revolving turnstiles and directed by armed members of the security service to the gallery suspended at a height of 14 metres, going up three long flights of escalators and down two more (9.50 m) before reaching the level of the platforms. A distance that, with its up and downs, is equivalent to six or seven storeys of a block of flats. A trip that takes an excessive amount of time and, when you're late and in a hurry, generates anxiety, then anger and, if you miss your train, frustration.

A station created to stage a performance, somewhere between the real and the virtual, but the zigzagging, intended to distil the railway's customers and distance them from real life, is exasperating. Thus, the balance between attractiveness for passengers and dissuasion of others from entering breaks down and the station reveals its hostile side to everyone, although with varying degrees of sadism. For regular passengers the cost is just an extra five minutes, but for those it wants to exclude, no bathrooms or benches, no possibility of sheltering from the cold and rain, cost what it may, even life itself.

Some of the most brutal and hypocritical means of repulsion are the new flower boxes located at the entrance to Piazzale Spadolini, where for years the immigrants in transit that perverse European laws force to remain undocumented in Italy before trying to reach destinations elsewhere have been sleeping in their hundreds.

'New flower' is the translation into English of Addis Ababa, the city subjected to the horrific massacre perpetrated by the Italians in response to the attempted assassination of Graziani, between 19 and 21 February 1937. But Italians have no memory of the unspeakable things they did in their colonial history. If they could learn to remember, perhaps they would no longer be able to so thoughtlessly wall up three storeys of never-used underground car park to prevent its use by crowds of migrants in transit, without feeling like criminals. Those car parks under Piazzale Spadolini are one of the many places proposed to the railways and the institutions by the solidarity association Baobab Experience in order to make Tiburtina a station no longer so hostile and repellent for migrants; here, since 2015, Baobab has been offering them hot meals, blankets and today vaccines as well, and has continued to do so even after forty-one clearances. In six years, it has helped about 95,000 immigrants, a sort of Italian Ellis Island that, when this hostile time is over, will have to have a place of commemoration right here at Tiburtina. Today there is only a low wall of containment, far enough away from the station not to have been repainted, on which it is still possible to read the handwritten traces of their passage in Arabic and English.

We are living in a time so forgetful that already, or still, no one knows that for ten years the station has been dedicated to Cavour. And the immense memorial, over 20 metres high, at the entrance to the station is of no use at all. Nowadays the more we see the less we remember. The monument is built of COR-TEN steel, an extremely contemporary material, with a worn, oxidised air, but impervious to the corrosion of time. It is impossible from below to read the whole of the two long speeches by Cavour that are engraved on it and that look like an endless flood of words; words that could make the observer dizzy and stir other memories, far more deeply rooted in the past of this place of transit, and other kinds of imagery that would help us to emerge from the waiting room of the history.

So, rummaging through the rhetoric, the first words I read between the lines are … Di Segni, the name of the Jewish woman who manages to escape from the Stazione Tiburtina in Elsa Morante's *La storia*. It was 16 October 1943, date of the deportation of the Jews of Rome, despatched from Tiburtina's platform 1, crammed into twenty-eight goods wagons heading for the death camps. A memory so grievous, deep and collective, that of 16 October 1943, that the Stazione Tiburtina ought to be dedicated to it entirely. The proposal was made in January 2012 by Rutelli, the former mayor, and the city's mayor Alemanno and the region's governor Zingaretti immediately paid lip service to it; rather too late of course, given that it was they who had inaugurated the monument and the dedication to Cavour along with the president of the Republic just a few months earlier.

So I go on seeking between the lines of that speech, growing more and more interesting, other key words to evoke the repressed memories of the station … I find Kerba: outside the door, in the old depots of the station on the apparently wrong side of history, a residential, cultural and political experience took place between 2003 and 2005 that indissolubly linked the community of immigrants from the Horn of Africa to the Città Tiburtina, which stretches from the station as far as the link road on the street of the same name. It was known to the newspapers as Hotel Africa, but we would like it to go down in history under the name given to it by its inhabitants, Kerba, the Arabic for 'ruined building'. It was a fundamental turning point in the recent history of migrations in the city, an experience of self-management shared between communities in exile from different countries, often in conflict with one another or internally.

The clearance of this small informal settlement, enlivened by shops and restaurants, gave the go-ahead for the criminal strategy of reception implemented by the city of Rome, which with great continuity, from the mayoral mandate of Veltroni to that of Alemanno, would be known for a decade as Mafia Capitale. But above all, and this is less well-known, it transformed the migratory experience of many people into an urban ordeal that afflicted this part of the city, from Via Cupa to Ponte Mammolo, from Via Collatina to Via Scorticabove, and that reached its dramatic climax in August 2017 with the clearance of Piazza Indipendenza by force. A peregrination that is beginning to take on the substance of urban history. A history, that of the tribulations of the community from the Horn of Africa in Rome, which we have started to reconstruct with its protagonists in a relationship of reciprocity that is allowing us to draw the map of a common consciousness of how unjust and violent remains the connection between this country and that part of Africa.

So Tiburtina remains a border station, just as the Bahnhof Berlin Friedrichstraße was during the Cold War. Not so much the border between the city and its outskirts, which the macho gesture of an immense girder suspended in the air was intended to rhetorically reconnect, but a barred gate between the city and the standardised and globalised contemporary world, and the city and world that have been excluded and are its victims; between colonisers and colonised.

But every great station is a station that is able to receive everyone, and can only be born out of the breaking down of the boundary that runs through it today, as happened to the station of Friedrichstraße when Germany was reunited. So that that space, liberated from the spatial frills of hostility and bulimic consumption, can rediscover the unitary character of its original design, before it was infested with fake shopping shacks and *chevaux de frise*; and the yellow waiting rooms suspended in the air will no longer serve to kill a time that doesn't want to pass, but become, since they have no other use, the workshops in which to construct a hospitable future together, reminding us of the right to citizenship.

For several months, thousands of migrants have been gathering in the snowy woods on the border between Poland and Belorussia. Anyone who leaves their home to help them is subjected to reprisals by the Polish police. The best way to help these people has become to stay at home, but hang a green lantern in the window as a signal of invitation to enter. In the face of the horror to which a time without memory can lead, we invite you to walk through the Stazione Tiburtina with a green lantern that will allow us to see what is still invisible to most people.

Migration

Carina Sacher in conversation with Irene Di Noto, a BPM activist; Valerio Muscella, photographer of the web documentary *4 Stelle Hotel*; and Leroy S.P.Q.R'DAM, a trained architect and one of the first squatters in the hotel

4 Stelle Hotel: From non-place to self-organised plug-in city

1 Figures as of October 2019.

2 4 Stelle is pronounced '*quattro stelle*' in Italian

The collective reappropriation of unused buildings in public and private ownership is a direct critique of prevailing housing policies and the real-estate industry – and a fundamental, everyday practice for movements fighting for social justice and the right to housing. Blocchi Precari Metropolitani (Precarious Metropolitan Blocks) or BPM, founded in 2007, is one of the largest movements for housing rights in Rome, creating places to live through squatting. Working with other collectives and grassroots groups, they organise demonstrations and campaigns to resist forced evictions and demand political rights.

In the aftermath of the 2007–08 financial crisis, various movements came together under the name Tsunami Tour and occupied dozens of buildings in Rome on three dates in December 2012, April 2013 and October 2013. One of these buildings is the Eurostar Congress and Conference Hotel in the eastern suburb of Tor Sapienza, built in 2000 and abruptly abandoned just eleven years later, after which it was taken over by the commercial bank UniCredit. Since December 2012 the former four-star hotel has been home to 520 people, including 160 minors, from eighteen countries.[1] Not far from the 4 Stelle Hotel[2] is the abandoned salami factory, Metropoliz, where around 200 people have been living since 2009. With its numerous activities and the MAAM (Museo dell'Altro e dell'Altrove di Metropoliz, or Metropoliz Museum of the Other and the Elsewhere), Metropoliz is an important public space in a neighbourhood that lacks essential infrastructure.

Credit: Valerio Muscella

Credit: Valerio Muscella

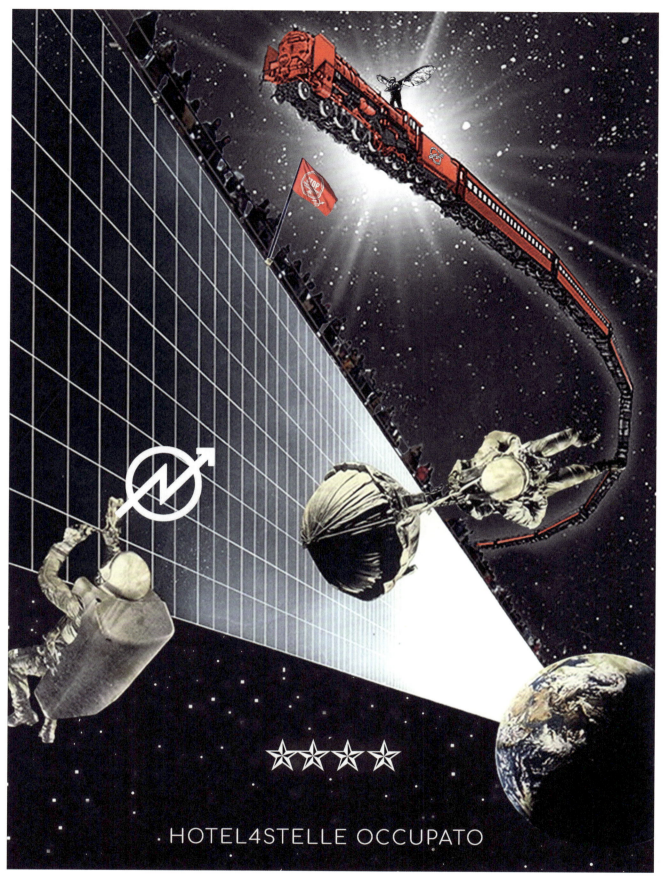

Credit: Leroy S.P.Q.R'DAM

3   In Italian: *Riprendiamoci la città!*

4   Piano Casa was enacted by decree on 28 March 2014 and passed as law in May 2014. Article 5 is titled 'Fight against the abusive occupation of buildings' (*Lotta all'occupazione abusiva di immobili*).

5   Addition by Irene Di Noto, June 2022: 'The law in question is the resolution of the Council of Lazio (Law no. 18 of 15 January 2014). It remained unimplemented in Rome, unlike in other provinces. The 197 million earmarked for 764 public housing units in Rome were not used to address the housing emergency, as required by the terms of the resolution, but were instead used to settle the debts of the Lazio region. The continuous campaigning of the movement and trade unions for the right to housing led to the adoption of Regional Law no. 1 of 27 February 2020 which regularised the position of those who occupied public housing up to 2014 (the date when Article 5 came into force) and introduced a rule allocating 35% of public housing to squatters of occupied buildings as a solution to the evictions.'

6   Metropoliz and 4 Stelle are still occupied and now rank first and sixth respectively on the new list of eviction targets published in April 2022.

SACHER   The financial crisis of 2007–08 and the bursting of the real-estate bubble intensified the housing shortage in Rome. This was also the moment when Blocchi Precari Metropolitani was formed. Can you describe the changes you've seen in the housing situation since the early days of your activism, and the increasing importance of squatting as a tactic in recent years?

DI NOTO   BPM essentially understands the housing crisis as part of a broader social crisis caused by neoliberalism. The poor and the socially precarious are being denied the right to the city, with measures becoming even more restrictive since the financial crash. Between 2012 and 2014 BPM reappropriated dozens of buildings along with other right-to-housing collectives. Our constant activism, and the squats especially, have played an essential role in providing dignified housing solutions for thousands of people, creating communities that are resilient and diverse. The squats, in particular, represent an alternative way of living – a society oriented towards use value, which is able to give new life to unused buildings. In addition, we continue to engage with local, regional and national institutions, pushing for structural policies that will go beyond this crisis management of a permanent housing shortage and resist real-estate speculation.

MUSCELLA   From the point of view of the campaigns, it could be said that the years from 2012 to 2014 were a kind of golden age. At every demonstration, thousands of people from all kinds of backgrounds came together under the slogan 'Let's take back the city!'[3] Collectively, there was a feeling that we had the necessary momentum to change the situation and have an impact on the city. This energy then spread to other cities like Florence, Pisa and Bologna.

LEROY S.P.Q.R'DAM   The Tsunami Tours took both the police and the city authorities by surprise. For me, they were the best moments in the process of occupying the buildings, involving many secret meetings in advance. When it all began, we were very excited. We saw ourselves as on the attack, rather than in a defensive position. We believed we could make a difference to the housing situation.

DI NOTO   In May 2014, as part of its housing development plan, the Italian government passed Article 5,[4] which criminalises squatting and prohibits activism in this area. The aim is to further marginalise the people in this situation. For example, it's now illegal to give the address of a squatted building as your place of residence, which has major consequences, not just in terms of access to the education and health systems, but also for the renewal of visas for refugees and migrants. New occupations have become virtually impossible, as there's a special police unit that clamps down on them almost instantly. We had successful negotiations with the various bodies involved in steering housing policy in Rome and the Lazio region and got a law passed to convert squats into public housing. But nothing has come from it yet.[5] Instead, the forced evictions of squatted buildings go on as before. In July 2019, the Ministry of the Interior published its hit list of twenty-three addresses that it wants vacated next year. Metropoliz was second on the list, the 4 Stelle Hotel fourth.[6]

SACHER   What do you see as the main reasons for the profound housing crisis in Rome?

DI NOTO   Over the last two decades, housing has essentially disappeared from the political agenda. Instead, it's the construction companies and financial holding companies that influence urban politics. Over the years, we've seen a retreat of the state and local governments from housing policy, from the liberalisation of the housing market since 1998 to the sale of public assets from the early 2000s on. Neoliberal policies seek to abolish social housing as a right. In this context, even social services, legal advice and aid agencies refer to squatting as a temporary, emergency solution. It's a paradox that we're having to use structures that are considered illegal to solve problems that the authorities cannot deal with. We often ask ourselves how we can avoid becoming a social safety net – because we can't allow those in power to shirk their responsibilities.

SACHER   More and more segments of society are being affected by the difficulties in either accessing housing or remaining in the free housing market. The make-up of the population of the squats is more diverse than it was in the 1970s and 1980s. What trends are currently emerging?

7   Addition by Irene Di Noto, June 2022: 'The direct relationship between occupations and the realisation of public housing plans ends in the 1990s. After the solutions to the evictions have been found extemporaneously. We are trying to reverse this trend, fighting for an extraordinary plan of public housing – of at least 60,000 flats by 2022 – above all through the recovery of public and private buildings.'

8   According to Irene Di Noto, nothing changed between the interview in autumn 2019 and summer 2022.

9   In Italy, housing policy is the responsibility of the Ministry of Infrastructure.

DI NOTO   The current composition of the squats is very different from how it was forty or fifty years ago. Back then the squatters were internal migrants, lower-class Italian families, mainly from Abruzzo or Calabria. In the early 2000s, when the housing crisis flared up again, they were almost all refugees, migrants, many of them recently arrived. The 2007–08 crisis then saw the increasing impoverishment of the middle class and the emergence of the working poor. At the same time as house prices rose, countless jobs were cut, so many Italians and migrants were evicted from their homes because they couldn't pay their mortgages or were bankrupt. With the Arab Spring and the destabilisation of Libya, many refugees left the inadequate reception system and occupied properties instead. Another new development in recent years has been the way Roma people have taken up squatting. When the taboo was broken, so to speak, at Metropoliz in 2009, other Roma families also began to choose this path to oppose discriminatory policies. But even though the portion of Italian families has increased with the crisis, some 80% of the people in squats are still refugees, migrants.

SACHER   What has been the effect on squatting of these various factors – the composition of the population, the specific Roman context of a handful of influential actors, and current politics?

DI NOTO   Unlike in the past, when resistance led to the allocation of public housing, squatters today have no prospect of getting social housing.[7] This means people are aware that they're going to be spending a long time together. So, they consider the squatted building as their home, except for those who continue their migration path towards northern Europe after clearing the bureaucratic hurdles.

SACHER   The 4 Stelle Hotel is one of the biggest squats in Rome. Of the 700 people who arrived at the Eurostar Congress and Conference Hotel on the day of the Tsunami Tour, around 520 of them have made it their home. What were the first steps in appropriating such a large structure? How were the rooms allocated and the common spaces created?

LEROY S.P.Q.R'DAM   At the beginning, for almost three months, everyone had to stay together on the ground floor for reasons of security. If there's an attempt at eviction, it's easier to defend the place that way.

MUSCELLA   Securing the building with barricades was one of the first shared activities, along with the manning of the checkpoints at the entrance and the lookouts on the roof, to warn if the police were coming. Everyone had to get involved, with no exceptions. In their six-hour shifts, people from different countries with different languages and religions started to get to know each other. But besides this first step, which was organised by BPM, the inhabitants started to self-organise and work together in line with their particular abilities. Different groups took on responsibility for cleaning or for the electricity supply, for example. This grassroots exchange promoted interaction between the residents. It was mainly the children who mediated between families, as they were the only ones who spoke clear Italian. The Italian lessons organised by volunteers were another collective activity. And from the beginning, there was also cooking. I remember one woman from Morocco who baked bread, not just for her family but also for celebrations and for those who had to go to work early in the morning. Then other kitchens opened, for South American, Eritrean-Ethiopian and East European food. During these three months, however, the problems also multiplied, as the residents were practically living on top of each other.

LEROY S.P.Q.R'DAM   Then, in March, each nucleus – that's what we call a family or unit – was given their own space. Depending on their size, this was either a hotel suite or one or two rooms. The allocation was decided by BPM. People were so happy when they heard their name and room number being called out. The whole room applauded every single time a key was handed over. It was as if they had all won the lottery. As with any building occupation, the common rooms and spaces are shaped by the inhabitants themselves, their passions, interests and desires. So, every squat is different because the people are different. The common spaces were created because there was a need for some functions. For example, the gym in the conference hall was the idea of a young man who is a boxer and wanted to teach boxing to the others. There's also a football field that was initiated by the children.

SACHER   How does the 4 Stelle Hotel, with its hotel typology, 238-room capacity and existing facilities such as meeting spaces, restaurants and furnished units,

	compare with other occupations, for example of office buildings, public facilities or industrial sites?
LEROY S.P.Q.R'DAM	It's like the plug-in city of Archigram. It's a big structure with many capsules that can be filled with functions. There are two different types of capsules: the hotel rooms on the upper floors and the former service areas on the ground floor along with the parking garage and the large conference hall in the basement. Converting the hotel rooms into apartments was easy. They were already equipped with toilets. Some families have added a second sink for the kitchen and for cooking they use bottled gas. So the biggest job was to connect each room to the water supply. The rooms are very flexible because the drywall partitions can be knocked through to connect two rooms, one of which is used as a living/dining room, with the toilet converted into a kitchen, while the other serves as a bedroom, as before. With a factory or office building it's much more difficult, because you usually have large, open spaces or halls, with the toilets concentrated in just a few places. So before you do anything else you have to build the partition walls and re-route the pipework. The structure of the hotel lends itself more easily to squatting. Here, the ground floor could be readily transformed into communal spaces: for example, the former meeting rooms now host the collective, the old conference space has been turned into the gym and there's an information desk in place of the reception. Each room has windows and is already supplied with electricity. Only the industrial kitchen was never used, for safety reasons. The same applies to the lifts.
SACHER	In a neighbourhood with poor infrastructure, what role does the spatial proximity of Metropoliz and the 4 Stelle Hotel play for the people living in the squats?
LEROY S.P.Q.R'DAM	Unlike Metropoliz, the 4 Stelle is not on the main road, so it's less visible. Metropoliz is also more involved in the neighbourhood because of its activities. But there is a strong connection and solidarity between the two places. For example, children from 4 Stelle attend the homework club at Metropoliz that has been organised by a student collective. In emergencies, like the fire at 4 Stelle in November 2018, or when there's a risk of eviction, people help each other.
DI NOTO	Although the 4 Stelle is spatially isolated, people have developed a strong sense of community and have good connections with the outside world, through school or work. Squats are secular, even though different religions are practised. They celebrate their traditional festivals together. For example, Muslims celebrate Christmas with Orthodox Christians.
SACHER	How would you describe the 4 Stelle Hotel today, after seven years of occupation?
MUSCELLA	The constant threat of eviction clearly affects the stability of a place. The social pressure, the isolation, the criminalisation and marginalisation enforced by the municipality – for example, through the simple gesture of not providing any garbage bins – have an impact on the people who live there, inevitably making coexistence more difficult. Nevertheless, spaces are still shared, common activities still take place and new ones are proposed. Squats are dynamic, always moving and never staying the same. This dynamic, unpredictable quality is the very essence of squatting with people from different countries and with different backgrounds. It's about encouraging people to create their own spaces of possibility, to gain self-determination, to decide for themselves how they want to live and live together, and in doing so they also have the right to fail – it's in their hands. Of course, if a community space is not taken care of, it will deteriorate. Some of the activities, like the gym or the collective kitchens, are still there, others have changed.
SACHER	In Rome there are some 12,000 people living in around ninety squatted buildings. What influence do right-to-housing collectives and other grass-roots movements have on housing policy at a regional and a national level?
DI NOTO	Currently, the new governing coalition of the Democratic Party and the Five-Star Movement is working on a national housing programme with a budget of one billion euros, which is clearly not enough![8] Together with other activist groups, BPM attended a meeting with the Ministry of Infrastructure[9] in mid-October 2019 to understand how this money will be spent. There are so many new buildings that have been built by private companies for speculative purposes, and they remain empty. We demand

that the public authorities buy them up – for the cost of construction, and no more – and convert them into public housing. In addition, we're continuing to campaign for the abolition of Article 5 of the housing development plan. We're currently at a crossroads: either the government decides to go ahead with the next round of evictions in the face of resistance from the activist groups, or it stops this plan and works on a housing policy that is coherent and does not rely on crisis management. In the meantime, our movements are ready to resist any further attempts at eviction under the banner 'By any means necessary!'

Blocchi Precari Metropolitani calls for a complete rethink of the approach to squatting and in this sense advocates for an extraordinary housing programme that aims to create 60,000 living units by the end of 2022, in particular through the conversion of unused public and private buildings.

This interview was first published in *dérive*, no. 78, January–March 2020; interview from autumn 2019 updated for this publication.

Credit: Leroy S.P.Q.R'DAM

Social regeneration versus urban rent

Irene Di Noto

On 6 December 2012 the Housing Rights Movements, together with a number of student unions, launched a new wave of squats in the city of Rome with the so-called 'Tsunami Tour for the right to housing'. Hijacking the Five Star Movement's campaign, they shattered the deafening silence on the housing question by taking over contemporaneously ten abandoned buildings in various parts of the city, allowing 2,000 people (10,000 over the course of the following three 'tsunamis') to put a roof over their heads, but above all drawing everyone's attention to the theme of growing social inequality in a city with over 20,000 families waiting for affordable housing and more than 200,000 vacant flats.

Those were the years, in fact, in which the effects of the slump made themselves felt, resulting in a steep rise in the number of evictions for inability to pay the rent with the involvement of the police force.

When we talk of empty buildings, it is worth pointing out that these are properties owned by banks and financial holding companies waiting to see if there is any possibility of an increase in their value, just as it is worth making it clear that those who occupy them, in contrast to what is claimed by the smear campaigns conducted by media outlets owned by the same interested parties, are not taking away anyone else's rights. We are talking, in fact, about people who are already on the municipal list for the assignment of public housing.

Thus, the question raised by the 'tsunamis' and encapsulated in the slogan 'let's take back the city' has gone beyond the mere dimension of housing, turning inevitably into that of the denial of the right to the city to thousands of people, while Rome remains in the hands of private finance.

In opposition to the idea of a speculative regeneration, the Housing Rights Movements have proposed not only utilising spaces converted for use as housing or for social and cultural ends but also making the most of the communities that have been formed, while preventing the appearance of new volumes of concrete and dysfunctions in the territory. It may seem banal, but squatting acts as a real lifesaver for those who have been evicted, whether they are Italians and longstanding immigrants who have had to deal with the economic crisis of 2007–08 or people who have arrived in Rome fleeing from war and poverty. Amidst the endless difficulties of a precarious life and a cohabitation not chosen but dictated by necessity, occupied and autonomously run spaces represent in fact a possibility to overcome loneliness, get back into the game and even try to imagine a different tomorrow in which you are no longer forced to choose between paying the rent and the fees for your children's education.

Instead of recognising the political and social value of these experiences, over the course of these years the threats of forced removal have intensified and some decidedly aggressive legislation has been approved, waging a war against the poor in the name of security and order.

Following the eviction of the squatters in Via Cardinal Capranica in the district of Primavalle in July 2019, with all the contradictions that it brought to the surface, the conflict over the occupations is still under way. According to the schedule of evictions drawn up by the Prefecture, at least four more ought to be carried out by the end of 2020, including the building on Via del Caravaggio, much in the news these days, and immediately afterwards the disused factory of Metropoliz.

What is at stake, from our point of view, is the public city, which has to withstand repeated attacks from a neoliberalist vision that grants citizenship on the basis of wealth, leaving the poor on the margins and indeed seeking to inculpate and medicalise them.

In this sense the responses to the clearance of Cardinal Capranica, with the rhetoric about assistance to the vulnerable utilised in shameless fashion, already laid bare the punitive and paternalistic attitude of the city council towards the evicted in the days preceding the police operations. In a nutshell: there is no recognition of the right to housing but an imposed condition of vulnerability that entails the willingness of people to accept their failure as individuals, an evident inability to look after themselves and the consequent acceptance of welfare that takes the form of beds in dormitories and reception centres where they can neither receive visitors nor cook. The state of emergency, which becomes permanent, puts the economy of the reception business on a sound footing, with the cost per 'guest' of 20 euros a day. And with the prospect that the people receiving welfare will have to go back to renting on the free market, with a contribution of just over 500 euros from the municipality. But the municipality is considered an unreliable payer and so offers no guarantees to landlords; something, moreover, that even the people who do have a pay packet to show in their support are unable to do either.

Of the seventy-eight family units evicted, only twenty accepted assistance from the municipality, while the others chose to carry on their battle for the right to decent housing, moving into squats in the north of Rome, which are also allowing people to remain in the area where they have lived for twenty years.

To understand the reason for this choice, all you have to do is pay a visit to the reception centre in Piazza delle Gardenie at Centocelle, where there are around fifteen households from Cardinal Capranica in a permanent state of waiting for news that something is being done for them, and who are threatened at the end of every month with being thrown out onto the street. Including the children who every day face a two-hour bus ride to take them to schools in Primavalle.

The atmosphere in the squats is quite different. Without wishing to paint a falsely romantic picture, we can undoubtedly say that these are communities engaged in a fight where solidarity and mutual aid are the rule, for if it is impossible to make it on your own then it is necessary to organise things together. Putting aside selfishness and inflexibility, questioning your own habits,

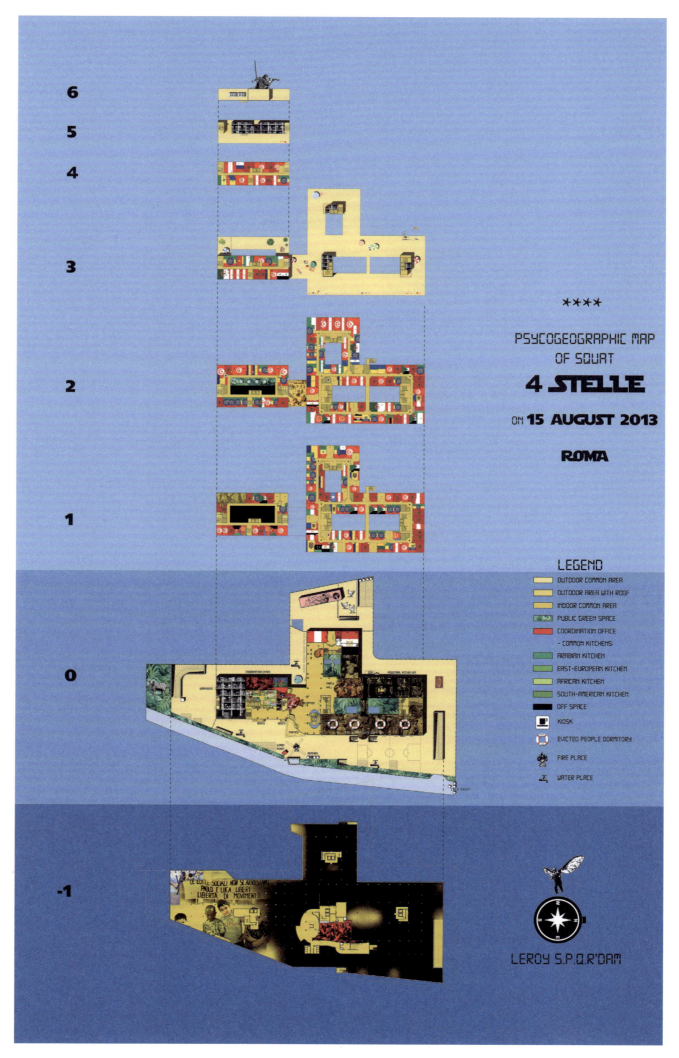

Credit: Leroy S.P.Q.R'DAM

going along with shared rules of coexistence and with responsibilities that cannot be shifted onto others.

The fact is that it is a choice which, however freely made, is dictated by necessity; but it is also one that presents opportunities.

From the story of Malika, inhabitant of the former four-star hotel Eurostars Roma Congress at no. 944 Via Prenestina – occupied on that same day of 6 December 2012 – it is clear that, notwithstanding her efforts to rent a flat, her financial difficulties and problems with her health, together with a certain racism on the part of landlords, have left her with no choice but to seek refuge with her husband and children in the occupied hotel, taken in by a community of which she has become an active member.

A place where over 500 people live and support one another, amidst myriad difficulties, in a battle for dignity. In fact, the 4 Stelle Hotel has overcome some stiff tests, from the resistance to two attempts at clearance to an accidental fire whose consequences have been dealt with collectively, including reconstruction of the damaged parts.

Obviously, just as in the best-run blocks of flats, there have been inevitable problems of coexistence and high-handedness in such a complex situation. But it is one where everything has been handled and overcome on the basis of each person's awareness of the need to forcefully defend the small measure of security they have won.

A hard life but an opportunity, too, especially for the children and the teenagers, the true strength of the occupied hotel. Both in the relationship they have established with the neighbourhood, through attending the schools, taking part in after-school activities and frequenting sports and cultural centres, and in the capacity to take care of the common spaces in which they are growing up together. They are children with the same stimuli and desires as their peers, who have had to deal with difficult situations (eviction, the fear of clearance, the fire) but have had the possibility to work through these events collectively. They are children fully conscious of the 'anomalous' situation in which they find themselves but who have no intention of being left behind the others.

This is the value of the squats: in an anaesthetised city, obsessed with control and prohibitions and where the poor are treated as a problem of public order, these self-organised housing experiences represent on the one hand resistance to social injustice and the arrogance of speculators and on the other a possibility. The possibility that the city itself will not cease to be seen as a public space, inhabitable by and accessible to the many diversities that constitute its true wealth.

Privatised push-back of the Nivin

Charles Heller

A reconstruction of events by Forensic Oceanography, affiliated to the Forensic Architecture agency, Goldsmiths, University of London

In November 2018, five months after Matteo Salvini was made Italy's Interior Minister and began to close the country's ports to rescued migrants, a group of ninety-three migrants was forcefully returned to Libya after they were 'rescued' by the Nivin, a merchant ship flying the Panamanian flag, in violation of their rights and in breach of international refugee law.

The migrants' boat was first sighted in the Libyan Search and Rescue (SAR) zone by a Spanish surveillance aircraft, part of Operation EUNAVFOR MED – Sophia, the EU's anti-smuggling mission. The EUNAVFOR MED – Sophia command passed information to the Italian and Libyan Coast Guards to facilitate the interception and 'pull-back' of the vessel to Libya. However, as the Libyan Coast Guard (LYCG) patrol vessels were unable to perform this task, the Italian Coast Guard (ICG) directly contacted the nearby Nivin 'on behalf of the Libyan Coast Guard', and tasked it with rescue.

LYCG later assumed coordination of the operation, communicating from an Italian navy ship moored in Tripoli, and, after the Nivin performed the rescue, directed it towards Libya.

While the passengers were initially told they would be brought to Italy, when they realised they were being returned to Libya, they locked themselves in the hold of the ship. A standoff ensued in the port of Misrata, which lasted ten days, until the captured passengers were violently removed from the vessel by Libyan security forces, detained, and subjected to multiple forms of ill-treatment, including torture.

This case exemplifies a recurrent practice that we refer to as 'privatised push-back'. This new strategy has been implemented by Italy, in collaboration with the LYCG, since mid-2018, as a new mode of delegated rescue, intended to enforce border control and contain the movement of migrants from the Global South seeking to reach Europe.

Using georeferencing and Automatic Identification System (AIS) tracking data, Forensic Oceanography reconstructed the trajectories of the migrants' vessel and the Nivin. Tracking data was cross-referenced with the testimonies of passengers, the reports by rescue NGO WatchTheMed's 'Alarm Phone', a civilian hotline for migrants in need of emergency rescue, a report by the owner of the Nivin, which he shared with a civilian rescue organisation, the testimonies of MSF-France staff in Libya, an interview with a high-ranking LYCG official, official responses and leaked reports from EUNAVFOR MED.

Together, these pieces of evidence corroborate one other, and together they form and clarify an overall picture: a system of strategic delegation of rescue, operated by a complex of European actors for the purpose of border enforcement.

When the first – and preferred – mode of this strategic delegation, which operates through LYCG interception and pull-back of the migrants, did not succeed, those actors, including the Maritime Rescue Co-ordination Centre in Rome, opted for a second mode: privatised push-back, implemented through the LYCG and the merchant ship.

Despite the impression of coordination between European actors and the LYCG, control and coordination of such operations remains constantly within the firm hands of European – and, in particular, Italian – actors.

In this case, the outcome of the strategy was to deny migrants fleeing Libya the right to leave and request protection in Italy, returning them to a country in which they have faced grave violations. Through this action, Italy has breached its obligation of non-refoulement, one of the cornerstones of international refugee law.

The report 'Forensic Oceanography: The Nivin Case: Migrants' Resistance to Italy's Strategy of Privatized Push-back' is an investigation into this case and new pattern of practice.

The full report can be read here: https://forensic-architecture.org/investigation/nivin

The map shows the trajectory of the migrants' boat and the Automatic Identification System (AIS) tracks of other vessels in the vicinity.

The Nivin's AIS track is interrupted between 20:42 UTC on 7 November and 13:35 UTC on 8 November 2018. During this time, the Nivin's AIS transponder was either not functioning or was intentionally turned off.

The AIS data also shows that, at approximately the same distance from the migrants' position while it was in distress, was a second merchant vessel, the Omega Star, which was heading towards Malta. Two georeferenced locations concerning the migrants' boat are highlighted:

A) 18:10 UTC, 7.11.2018: 33°39'N 014°39'E. Position sent by ICG to the Nivin at 19:39 UTC.

B) 03:06 UTC, 08.11.2018: 33°58'N 014°40'E. Position sent by the migrants in distress to the Alarm Phone and corresponding to the location of rescue.

Credit: Forensic Oceanography

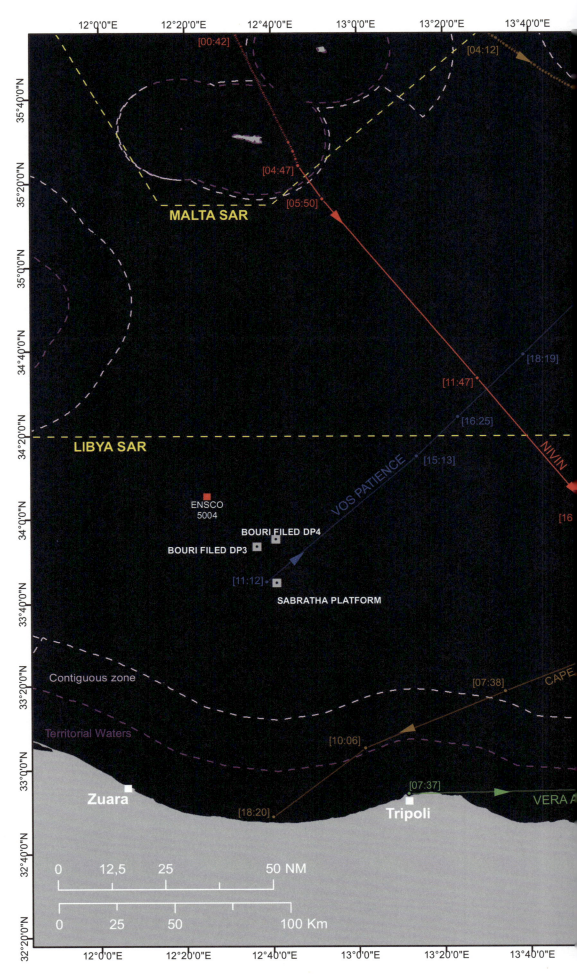

Credit: Forensic Oceanography

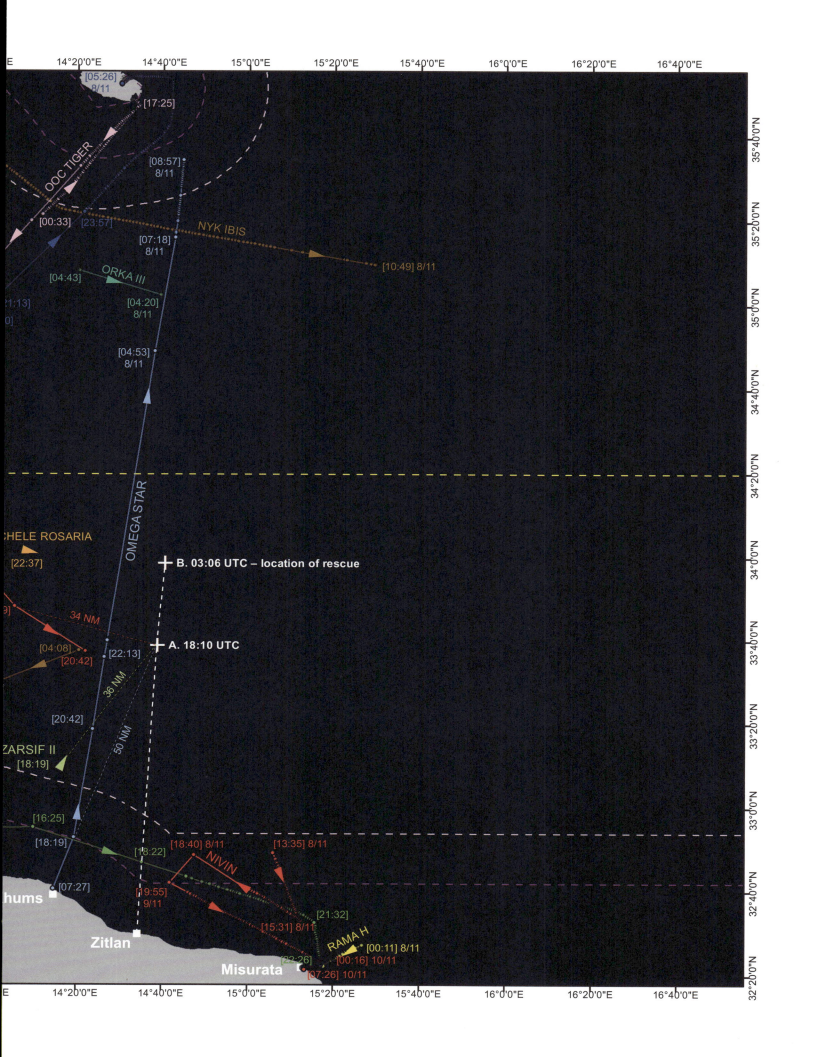

Life on the edge: Migrants in Italy

Alessandro Penso

This work explores the situation for migrants, asylum-seekers and refugees, particularly those from Africa, in Italy since 2010. Most wish to continue their journey on to countries that are more welcoming or where they already speak the language or have relatives. Instead, they find themselves stuck in or sent back to Italy in accordance with the Dublin Regulation, the European agreement under which all requests for protection must be handled by the EU member country of first arrival.

Italy has been the main entry country for African migrants arriving by sea in recent years, but it has also seen a constant flow of arrivals, including from the Middle East and South Asia, via the Balkans route. The government has never enacted a proper integration plan, and the number of people living in illegality and/or grave precarity has skyrocketed. Political decisions have favoured an alarmist approach that has seen the creation of Extraordinary Reception Centres, where migrants can be stuck for years while waiting for their applications to be processed. These centres make up the vast majority of reception facilities and do not provide support services such as language classes or chances for integration. Once a decision on their request has been made, applicants exit the system and things become even harder.

Many, whether their request is successful or not, end up living in squats and informal settlements, some of which have become ghettos where the lack of sanitation is dire. To survive they are often forced to accept jobs that pay a pittance, such as in the agricultural sector, where they can earn as little as 3 euros an hour. Recent statistics refute the notion of an 'invasion', yet for many Italians who are still not used to living side by side with migrants, this idea is growing, supported by increasingly race-based politics and now a governing coalition involving the far right that has refused European support and made cuts to the few existing programmes that offer help to migrants and refugees.

Gorizia. Credit: Alessandro Penso

Foggia. Credit: Alessandro Penso

Borgo Mezzanone. Credit: Alessandro Penso

Bari. Credit: Alessandro Penso

Rome. Credit: Alessandro Penso

The Riace model and the Domenico Lucano case: Is another world possible?

Alice Lomonaco

1 Annalisa Camilli, *Internazionale*, 8 October 2021.

2 Mimmo Lucano, *Il fuorilegge* (Milan: Feltrinelli, 2020).

3 *Il Manifesto*, 3 October 2021.

This work was originally published in *Welcoming Spaces* (2021), https://www.welcomingspaces.eu/project-partners-2/.

On 30 September 2021, the court of Locri in Reggio Calabria sentenced the former mayor of Riace, Domenico Lucano, to thirteen years and two months in prison. The judges accused him of criminal association aimed at aiding and abetting irregular immigration, abuse of office, fraud, extortion, embezzlement, bid-rigging and ideological falsification. In addition, he was ordered to return €500,000 of European funds. The severity of this sentence has been described as unexpected and unusual.[1] The court of Locri doubled the penalty requested by the Public Prosecutor's Office, accusing Lucano of being the head of a criminal association for the purpose of aggravated fraud and embezzlement – that is, using funds allocated for the reception of migrants for other purposes.

Domenico Lucano was mayor of Riace from 2004 to 2018 (until he was suspended), and had become known internationally for his pro-migrant reception position. The Riace model was based on a vision of an alternative and welcoming society in which everyone, regardless of origin, language or culture, participates in the life of a community in order to find their place, as he describes in his book *Il fuorilegge*.[2]

Like many other municipalities in Calabria and southern Italy, Riace has been marked by a strong emigration of its inhabitants, who after the Second World War left one of the poorest areas in Europe in search of new life opportunities in northern Italy and abroad. In 1951 the population of Riace was 2,331, but depopulation continued inexorably until the 1980s, when 1,668 residents remained. To fight the depopulation of Riace and deal with global migration, Mayor Lucano opted for an integration of migrants into the life of the village, leading to a considerable increase in the population (from 1,610 in 2001 to 1,869 in 2021, with a peak of 2,345 residents in 2016). Through the recovery of uninhabited houses, renovation of infrastructure and investment in local crafts, the local economy was rehabilitated. This also made it possible to support the education and training of migrants, demonstrating that 'another world is possible'.

The Riace model had been recognised by the United Nations High Commission for Refugees (UNHCR), attracting international interest and inspiring numerous reception projects in Italy and abroad. Lucano's work paved a different path to the depopulation of villages, imagining an alternative for a region that is a 'land of consumption'[3] and typically dependent on the economic growth of central and northern regions.

The Riace model was a symbol of redemption of the margins. First, the territorial margins of a region such as Calabria, which paid for its entry into modernity by providing cheap arms for industrial development in the north of Italy and Europe. Second, the human margins – as migrants are often considered – creating alliances and development projects for a solidarity-centred, sustainable and innovative renaissance. Lucano's legal troubles began in 2018, when he was placed under house arrest and suspended from his position as mayor. Two weeks later, the Court of Re-examination of Reggio Calabria banned him from staying in Riace, as an alternative to house arrest. The Riace reception project was closed a month after Lucano's arrest, although the Council of State later ruled in favour of the appeal filed by the mayor. The council defined the closure of the reception centre as illegitimate and the behaviour of the Ministry of the Interior as 'hostile' towards Lucano, having dismantled a project that he had supported and financed until a few months earlier.

In 2019, Lucano was indicted, as the Public Prosecutor's Office accused him of arranging a marriage of convenience. At the basis of the accusation was a telephone conversation in which Lucano talks about the possibility of obtaining citizenship for a woman who had been denied asylum three times, by marrying a Riace inhabitant. The Public Prosecutor's Office also accused him of illegally assigning waste collection services, between 2012 and 2016, to two cooperatives – which employed migrants – that were not registered in the regional register (as required by law), and without inviting tenders. The court, in fact, had found no evidence of 'fraudulent behaviour' by the former mayor in awarding services to those cooperatives.

Lucano was then also accused of fraud because some migrants lived in apartments that were not certified as 'habitable'. In 2019, he received a further notice of indictment for issuing identity documents to an Eritrean woman and her infant son who were not in possession of a residence permit. As Lucano explained during an interview in Riace in June 2021, it was part of his idea of integration, a political idea of reception. In his words: 'But they were the ones who called me, they were the ones who asked me to take in so many people, humans, because they had nowhere to put them … and I took them in … I committed a crime of humanity'.

Lucano's 'outlawed' actions were consciously carried out in contravention of laws that he considered unjust and detrimental to the rights of immigrants and inhabitants of Riace. These actions did not provide him with any personal or political benefit. Lucano's legal sentence also seems to be a vicious attack on a project that has successfully shown the potential of regenerating shrinking areas by establishing welcoming spaces.

Planning Riace: Urban regeneration and reception

Giorgio Sokoll

1   *Sistema di protezione per richiedenti asilo e rifugiati* (System of Protection for Asylum Seekers and Refugees).

2   *Sistema di protezione per titolari di protezione internazionale e per i minori stranieri non accompagnati* (System of Protection for Beneficiaries of International Protection and for Unaccompanied Foreign Minors).

3   'Riace, rigenerazione urbana e accoglienza', experimental degree thesis, the result of research work carried out between January and December 2016. Experience in the field, analysis of direct and indirect sources, interviews conducted with migrants, local residents and representatives of institutions and study of urban and architectural spaces have proved to be useful means of comprehension of the model of reception applied in Riace, defining as a result guidelines for the implementation of a model of urban regeneration and reception to be proposed in similar areas. Department of Architecture, Roma Tre University. Supervisors: F. Careri, F. Finucci and A.F.L. Baratta.

Over the last three years the system for the reception of immigrants in Riace has undergone a crisis. In 2017 the allocation of funds (reimbursements) was frozen over inconsistencies in accounting. Today it seems that associations such as È stato il vento and ReCoSol are restoring part of the system, utilising awards and donations to support businesses and rents. Many of the new residents have stayed, having put down roots in the town, producing new generations and making themselves independent of the model of subsistence.

Riace represents the possibility of obtaining a virtuous solution from the meeting of two problems. Simply getting two critical phenomena that are affecting the country – depopulation and immigration – to offset one another brings an advantage: one is part of the solution to the other. The difficulties faced by people living in small towns is leading to demographic decline.

According to Legambiente, there are 2,430 municipalities in Italy, with a total population of about 3.5 million, whose survival is threatened. The abandonment of small towns and villages is slow, linked to the progressive political, economic, social and cultural decline of entire regions. The big cities promise to meet contemporary needs, driving a process of abandonment of the small municipalities, which still lack the strategies and resources needed to check it. On the other hand, owing to its geographical position and configuration, Italy is subject to a substantial level of immigration.

The national regulations relative to the phenomenon have been expanded over time, often in an attempt to deal with emergencies. When speaking of Riace we make reference to the SPRAR,[1] which has now become the SIPROM[2] and applies only to those who have already been granted asylum and to unaccompanied foreign minors. This system of second-level reception is based on the concept of empowerment of migrants, something that can be achieved through their integration into the fabric of society. The idea is that their stay in the reception facility, and above all their presence in the area, make it easier for them to acquire a new local identity, favouring their emancipation from the support system of the first level of reception. So, the region seems to be the common element between the reception of immigrants and depopulation.

The solution to these two problems requires an intervention supported by well-defined socioeconomic strategies and the money needed to implement them. The SPRAR funds were utilised in Riace to finance reception, but also reached the local inhabitants thanks to the activities and initiatives through which the integration of migrants was affected: upgrading of buildings, support of the local economy with redistribution of the funds in 'local money', a waste-sorting service, new jobs, schools, clinics.

In fact, Riace's model of urban regeneration envisaged the renewal being of use to a range of people, to their mutual benefit: the solutions offered were not circumscribed but aimed instead at the reactivation of economic and productive cycles within the community, activities rooted in the identity of the area but handicapped by depopulation, through the addition of human and economic resources. Only through a joint operation that involves local players as well is it possible to generate a circular system that will safeguard the cultural identity of these places.

Research into the way the system of urban regeneration and reception functions[3] has revealed that there are some minimal requisites of human, social and regional potential if the programme is to be a success.

For example, a homogeneous distribution of inhabitants in the historic centre has helped to consolidate its social system and free it from areas at risk of exclusion. On the practical plane, a medium level of education of the town's population has made it possible to provide the training needed for the development of the system for management of the project. The presence of childcare services and primary schools has facilitated integration of the families of migrants into the local context. From this perspective, the involvement of social groups and networks that are already present is fundamental, as they are able to spark off processes of inclusion, cohesion, cooperation, participation, information and communication. The main players are bodies that are well-established in the area, already points of reference for the local residents. Places of socialisation and recreation were identified by surveying spaces of public or private aggregation such as squares, clubs and cultural associations.

Riace shows how the insertion of new spaces of reception has to take the presence of these activities into account, intertwining the social life of migrants with the existing one. The shops located in the town have made it easy to obtain the majority of basic necessities, uniting daily life and urban space.

The cooperation groups linked to events staged in the town are a nerve centre of local life. Thanks to an active and inclusive collaboration, locals have been made aware of the project, while integration of the migrants has been facilitated by involving them in the traditional activities of the area. In order to function correctly, a project of regeneration and reception should also take regional, urban and residential characteristics into account. The analysis carried out has adopted both qualitative criteria (identification of assets of historic and cultural interest) and quantitative ones (identification of empty buildings), taking into consideration the location of each property and its state of repair and integrity.

In this way attention has been drawn to the things on which to place an emphasis in the prospect of a future intervention of rehabilitation and to which buildings, for their location or type, are suited to residential or service functions. Study of the historic centre has shown how architectural and urban factors favour a form of 'obligatory socialisation'.

Riace is a town constructed in the likeness of the farming community that inhabited it: like many of the smaller municipalities of the south, it still reflects the collective nature of the working and social habits of the past. For example, rooms on the ground floor (called *menzanini* in Calabria), previously used for the joint work of women, are now lived in. These spaces require the opening of doors onto the street for reasons of illumination and ventilation, establishing a direct relationship between domestic intimacy and urban life. Thus, the close proximity to adjoining houses, the presence of people of different origins in the same building and the location of some parts of the home on the street are elements favourable to interaction between the inhabitants and the creation of a social community.

At the urban level, the historic centre of Riace is characterised by a centripetal fabric. The public spaces are barycentric, the urban functions are concentrated in Via Roma, the central street. Movement through the streets is more intense near to the places where the migrants are housed, and the predominance of pedestrian or narrow roads slows the flow of traffic, favouring the meeting of people. All the everyday activities take place in the town, inside the walls that originally circumscribed it or between the valleys that still define its natural boundary, preventing any sprawl of the settlement.

Riace Marina, on the contrary, an expansion of the town along the coast of the Ionian Sea over the last century, presents factors unfavourable to implementation of the project. The analysis has revealed a fragmentation and dispersion of the settlement and a large stock of unused buildings, given the seasonal character of its frequentation. This diminishes both the possibility of people meeting and the perception of an aggregative fabric, weakening the project. According to information obtained from local residents, during the last elections the inhabitants of Riace Marina, where the project had struggled to take root, were in favour of abolition of the system of reception, unlike their fellow townspeople in Riace Superiore, where the project had yielded better results.

Of course, there is a form of design and planning within this programme, too. Fundamental is a study of the place that does not stop at mapping and observation from above. Along with the macro-scale that outlines the identity of towns and cities, it is essential to enter progressively into domestic space: an investigation of the micro-scale reveals the diversity of individuals that is able to foster potentialities. So, it is not a matter of mere urban or architectural analysis: any material sign should be read and interpreted in relation to the social fabric, in a mode of research that requires an interdisciplinary approach. Riace shows how an implementation of the model of reception attentive to the socio-spatial problems of the area contributes to the upkeep of the town and its architectural heritage, giving a positive impulse to the local economy thanks to the presence of new residents and their purchasing power, and to valuable initiatives of urban regeneration.

. Built on Sand

feld72

The participative project 'Built on Sand' from 2012 deals with the informal settlements in the estuary of the Isozone, near the industrial city of Monfalcone. The river is considered a nature reserve, although it is characterised by a seemingly chaotic assemblage of huts, cottages and bungalows. The settlements are abandoned, made uninhabitable by a storm and by new administrative restrictions. It is only a matter of time before these testimonies of an anarchist building culture will disappear from the scene.

The narrative around migration surrounding the shipbuilding industry and care work reveals itself through the walk. The participants delve deeper into a strange, almost surreal world through the superimposition of formal and informal, stories of labour and exploitation, speculation and economic opportunism. At the end, they find themselves in an active role in the finale on the sandy beach of Monfalcone.

Credits: Johannes Puch and feld72

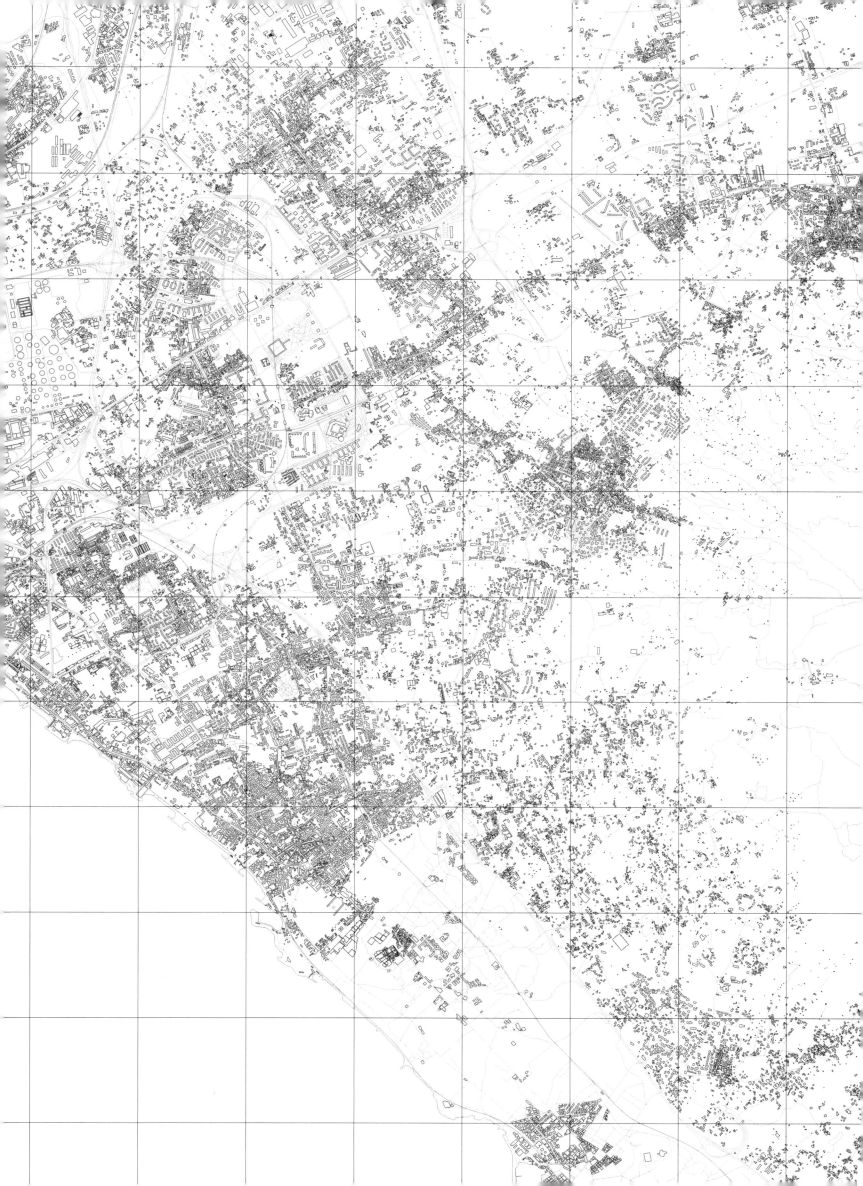

Naples, hybrid city: The Quartieri Spagnoli

Giovanni Laino

A privileged place

The area of the Quartieri Spagnoli, or 'Spanish Quarters', is a part of the urban centre of Naples that consists of an orthogonal grid of streets. It is located behind the city hall and on a slope running down from the hill on which stands the Certosa di San Martino to Via Toledo, an important street opened in the mid-sixteenth century by Don Pedro da Toledo on the layout of what had previously been a city wall.

There are over 170 blocks (constructions bounded by four streets), with four, five or six storeys above ground. Some of them are occupied by single blocks of flats, but it is more common for them to be divided into several buildings, with independent entrances and staircases (more than one block of flats on the same lot).[1]

In a number of cases, they are small buildings with a narrow staircase and standard floors of one or two rooms (about 50–70 m²). Overall, the roughly 500 blocks of flats contain some 3,000 households, making up a total of around 15,000 people.[2] Many of the people in need live in the 900 so-called *bassi*. These are street-level flats with one or two rooms and small bathrooms and kitchens, which alternate, on the ground floors of the buildings, with the entrances to 150 single-family homes located on the mezzanine floors. The variety and vitality of the area also stems from the presence of 250 craft workshops, 360 shops and other activities, as well as 196 storage facilities and 223 garages.[3]

Over the years reuse of the building stock has been very intense, as a result both of restoration and maintenance work carried out on entire constructions and of a process of subdivision of the flats on a massive scale – almost always unauthorised – that has broken up in plan and elevation many of the larger apartments present in the housing stock of the area. Even the facades of the blocks of flats, with their variegated set of balconies, windows, additions and fixtures of all kinds, reflect the high level of micro-transformations and the intensity of utilisation of the building stock. These works have been carried out to improve the living conditions of pre-existing family units, to house new types of inhabitants (students, singles) and as a consequence of the slow and unseen process of gentrification that has transformed the social profile of the groups present in some parts of the area.

Back in 2001 I proposed a sort of sociological joke to try to paint a picture of the ways of life that had been emerging in the area for a long time. I believe that in spite of a constant trend of transformation and adaptation to the dynamics of change in the local living conditions and to globalisation, the characterisation is still very realistic. The nuclei of coexistence in the Quartieri Spagnoli can be subdivided into three fundamental social groups, to which some new tribes have been added in recent years.

The largest group consists of the *Eduardians*,[4] basically 'sound' families that often rent their homes and whose members have a low level of education, work for their living (often doing short-term and informal jobs, or are low-skilled public employees), involved in popular culture and – as in Eduardo De Filippo's plays – get caught up only sporadically in experiences of deviant behaviour. In general, these inhabitants do not live their lives in the street.

The *Vivianian* families, on the other hand, are far more visible. The women and children in particular spend more time in the street and establish usually informal networks that are often irregular or occasionally totally illegal. In many of these families, which not infrequently suffer from chronic social exclusion, the symptoms of alienation (truancy, lack of working experience, giving birth at an early age, dependence on welfare, experiences of imprisonment, family trauma and promiscuity) are recurrent. The many teenagers and youths who ride their mopeds around the streets, usually without a helmet, belong to this group. Also belonging to this group are a hundred or so families who have members involved in the activities of the Camorra – although recent years have seen a reduction in this – or have committed crimes.

The third group is perhaps the least numerous and above all the least visible: a low and middle class of workers, often public employees, who live in the area more as temporary residents than as inhabitants and find it difficult to put up with the uses (and abuses) of the other groups. While the children of the first two groups move out only reluctantly when they marry, generally to degraded districts on the outskirts of the city, young members of the low and middle class associate social advancement with migration to other areas. Obviously, there are many family networks that span at least two of these groups.

While the presence of these three groups has remained substantially the same over the years, even after the earthquake in 1980, without any evident signs of upheaval, the arrival of three other social groups presents a scenario of change and possible social polarisation in the future.

After the first twenty years of the new century, it can be said that the number of immigrants, legal and illegal, is growing. They are the new tenants of the *bassi* abandoned by the Neapolitans, or utilised by prostitutes up until the 1990s. Some ground-floor premises are used as storerooms for immigrant street vendors. A number of families, however, after years of sacrifice, have succeeded in putting down roots and renting better accommodation than the *bassi*. According to the most recent field research, some of it carried out since the Covid-19 pandemic, the number of these families is growing both in the flats – especially the ground-floor *bassi* – and in commercial activities. The Chamber of Commerce has registered hundreds of people who have declared themselves to be street vendors and we have ourselves found over fifty premises used to sell food and/or household cleaning products.[5]

---

[1] The main studies published on the area of the Quartieri Spagnoli are Giovanni Laino, *Il cavallo di Napoli. I quartieri spagnoli* (Milan: Franco Angeli, 1984); Teresa Colletta, 'Napoli: La cartografia pre-catastale', *Storia della città*, nos. 34–35 (Electa Periodici, 1985), 5–178; Michele Capobianco, *Un progetto per Napoli. I quartieri spagnoli* (Rome: Officina Edizioni, 1987); Salvatore Bisogni, ed., *Napoli: Montecalvario questione aperta* (Naples: Clean Edizioni, 1994); and Italo Ferraro, *Napoli. Atlante della città storica. Quartieri spagnoli e rione carità* (Naples: Oikos Edizioni, 2004).

[2] These estimates may differ in relation to the area for which the calculations are made, given that the Quartieri Spagnoli do not have an administratively defined boundary.

[3] The data are fairly accurate, although subject to variation as a result of changes in use and the degree of error in the survey, which is updated periodically. The figures quoted here date from 2020.

[4] The reference for the Eduardian families is to the writings of the famous playwright Eduardo De Filippo. The model of the Vivianian families, on the other hand, refers to the dramatist Raffaele Viviani, who in the first half of the twentieth century wrote many plays in which he represented scenes from the life of the Neapolitan urban underclass.

[5] Giovanni Laino, 'Immigrazione straniera e attività commerciali, a Napoli', *Territorio*, no. 100 (2022), 104–29.

Nationality	Fixed location	Street traders	Addresses with more than one street trader	No. of street traders with VAT registrations at the same address				With VAT no.	% concentration
				2	3	4	5 ≤		
Pakistan	18	62	10	10	6	8	6	30	48.4
Bangladesh	14	171	39	30	24	12	82	148	86.5
Sri Lanka	9	38	5	8	0	0	5	13	34.2
China	3	39	8	14	0	0	0	14	35.9
	44	310	Total no. of the four nationalities in QS area						
	587	3,484	Total no. of the four nationalities in Naples						
	7	9	% QS of Naples						

Table 1. Numbers of foreign traders in the Quartieri Spagnoli (QS) by nationality and numbers of street traders present at the same address. Source: Chamber of Commerce data, 2020 (see note 5).

6   This particular fragmentation and over-utilisation of ground-floor premises on the part of immigrants is even more evident in other working-class areas in the centre of Naples, especially in the areas around the railway station. In the Quartieri Spagnoli, however, no cases have been found of people of different origin living on the same premises.

7   Between 1991 and 2011 the percentage of owned property in the Montecalvario neighbourhood increased by 10% (from 38.9 to 48.9%). This is in line with that of other working-class districts of the centre and higher than in the outer suburbs.

8   An estimate of around 400 adverts for short-term rented properties in the Montecalvaio neighbourhood is given in Gaia Del Giudice, *La casa come asset finanziario*, PhD diss., Department of Architecture of the University of Naples Federico II, 2021.

Table 1 presents some very interesting figures with regard to the location of foreigners registered as street traders with the Chamber of Commerce in 2020. The most numerous groups are the ones from the four countries indicated. In many cases immigrants live in the *bassi*, as families or more often in temporary groups of cohabitation, while also using the space to store the stall from which they sell their generally cheap goods. The presence of several immigrants who make their living as traders at the same address is a reflection of the fact that these ground-floor premises function as homes with very small sleeping, bathing and cooking areas, and also serve as storerooms and/or contact addresses for people from the same country.

There is a markedly greater concentration of Bangladeshi in the area. Perhaps these are cases where street traders who arrived first have been joined by others from the same country who arrived later. For the Sri Lankans, except in one case, we can suppose that it is more likely that the *bassi* are used as residences in which the occupant or a relative is registered as a street vendor.[6] In the same survey as was cited in note 5 more than fifty premises were found to be in use as minimarkets selling food and household cleaning products, which now make up a web of local commercial activities that has in part replaced the old commercial network, without any upheavals or expulsions. The people who run the minimarkets have done this by using the same suppliers, selling mid-range merchandise for a widely distributed popular market and offering deferred payment to housewives who ask for this kind of service. In these stores it is rare to find goods typical of ethnic shops. They are always small supermarkets that stay open for many hours.

Here, too, the porosity of the building fabric and the social context is evident, along with the complexity and variety of the modes of integration of foreigners coming from different countries.

For some years now a new and less numerous group has been settling in the area: the new middle class of resident house owners who, partly due to the degradation of the surroundings and some of the building stock, are able to buy and renovate flats at prices they can afford,[7] accepting the need to put up with some local diseconomies in exchange for the advantage of being located in the urban centre and leading a kind of neighbourhood life attractive to those who like the vitality of the old city better than the modernist one. And with the installation of more lifts, what up until the 1970s had been garrets often of medium size, with terraces and panoramic windows, homes previously left to the lower middle class owing to the inconvenience of the many stairs to be climbed on foot, have, over the last thirty years, gradually been renovated and made more desirable for a better-off segment of the population.

With the significant growth in tourism since 2015 that, after the grave crisis of the first two years of Covid-19, has regained its intensity in 2022, in the Quartieri Spagnoli, too, especially at certain times of year and in the lower part of the area, another metropolitan type can be found: that of Italian and foreign tourists. Both those who sleep for a few nights in the hundreds of flats turned into B&Bs,[8] in holiday homes and in the two hotels present in the area, and those who come to the Quartieri Spagnoli on tours of just a few hours, to dine in the lower part, which has seen a considerable increase in the number of pizzerias and restaurants, or to visit a small area of ruined buildings turned into an altar in memory of Diego Armando Maradona.

After the pandemic the urban scene of the Quartieri Spagnoli seems to be fulfilling a hope expressed by Luigi De Magistris (mayor of Naples from 2010 to 2021), who in 2011 proposed turning the area into a Neapolitan-style Montmartre, filled with more and more restaurants and small clubs. Following the pandemic these pizzerias or restaurants, occupying the space in wholly informal and extensive ways, now offer lunches and dinners or drinks for the local young people who frequent the area from the evening until the wee hours of the morning, making the Quartieri Spagnoli a centre of nightlife. In the part higher up, in particular, while showing signs of a slow but constant transformation on a small scale, the area does not seem to have lost its distinctive characteristics, still presenting the appearance of a very lively and densely populated neighbourhood, with somewhat less of a variety of functions than in past decades.

The craft industry, even though it has been in sharp decline in recent decades, is still a characteristic

[9] The small shrine of St. Mary Frances of the Five Wounds is visited by many women who believe that sitting on a chair present in the church – where Mary Frances used to rest in order to find relief while she suffered from the pain of her stigmata – will help them to overcome infertility and have children.

[10] The Associazione Quartieri Spagnoli has been operating since 1986, providing assistance for children and families in need. In 2013 the FOQUS, Fondazione Quartieri Spagnoli, housed in a former monastery in the middle of the area, set up an important centre of education and services which has received a lot of coverage in the national media. Then there is an association that runs a small local youth orchestra and several parish-based voluntary services, as well as sports clubs and private radios.

[11] It is known that the percentage of families receiving this economic support is much higher in the south as a whole, and in particular the region of Campania, than it is in the regions of the north.

feature of the area. When compared with the data of the last forty years, however, there are clear signs of slow change. The most evident of these is the crisis in a significant manufacturing district where in the 1970s and '80s the leather and fur workshops used to employ over 600 people. There are also fewer artisans working on the maintenance of the building stock (carpenters, blacksmiths, plumbers, joiners). As a consequence of the growth in tourism, the last few years have seen a large increase in the number of restaurants and pizzerias, especially in the lower part of the district, as well as in the availability of rooms for B&B or for holiday homes. The entrepreneurs who have started up new trattorias or similar enterprises are often people who were already operating in the area.

The three parish churches, the home of St. Mary Frances which attracts many devout visitors,[9] the social clubs (which have diminished in number over the decades), the very few places where local women still play tombola in the evening and at night, a small number of important organisations in the not-for-profit sector[10] and some new meeting places set up informally by enterprising immigrants are only partially able to counter the forces of social disintegration that affect, in particular, children and young people, women and the elderly living alone. While the habit of turning to loan sharks to cope with periods of economic difficulty is still widespread, prostitution – which used to be common in the lower part of the area – and the economy that fed off it have now almost completely disappeared.

The criminal organisations that in the 1980s in particular had shown themselves to have a great power of aggregation and ability to marshal human and economic resources are less influential now.

Many of those who were not killed in clashes between rival bands are in jail and the activities that presumably continue are much less visible in the area, even though, when working in the community centres, it is not uncommon to come across families that – among many other problems – have the still-young head of the household in prison, or even in the cemetery, killed in the conflict between rival bands. From the figures on the number of people subject to remand orders as an alternative to imprisonment, it can be noted that, unlike in many other cities, the presence of people in Naples under house arrest or the obligation to report every day to a police station is substantial not just in the outlying suburbs (as is the case everywhere) but also in the working-class neighbourhoods of the centre, which can rightly be regarded as inner suburbs. The Quartieri Spagnoli is one of these fragile areas. Various fairly unusual and folkloristic activities continue, but despite the persistence of popular cultural customs, the influx of new inhabitants who lead more familiar and metropolitan lifestyles seems to be growing ever stronger.

The urban scene

The sight of working or unemployed men playing cards at an improvised table in the afternoons, very common up until the 1980s, is now fairly rare. Overall, in fact, the scene in the street has changed, although the habit of invading public space has persisted, for instance with cars or the tables of the many new restaurants, preventing passage through some of the alleys. What can still be seen are the processions of small groups that parade dressed in white with flags, standards and small baldachins. They are devotees of the Madonna dell'Arco who, drawing people's attention with the sound of small bands of musicians, collect funds for the annual procession to the sanctuary of the same name.

The sight that has grown more frequent, in the lower part of the area, is that of tables set up on the pavement outside some place that offers drinks, snacks or meals, a reaction to the growing numbers of tourists attracted by the area's reputation for local colour. Guided tours of the *bassi* or particular shops and workshops have even been organised: the one known as the '*bassi* tour' takes visitors to see a few typical locations that present a picturesque if somewhat contrived image of life in the neighbourhood. Then there are two more attractions that in recent years have been luring many people from outside the district: the aforementioned area of ruins that has been turned into a shrine for the veneration of Diego Armando Maradona and the Fondazione FOQUS, which attracts instead visitors interested in the experiment of the community hub installed in the former monastery or in cultural activities (debates, open-air cinema) that draw in the public from other parts of the city.

As for the voting habits of the population – which is, however, widely disenchanted, with some groups directly involved and/or implicated in networks of patronage – the centre-left coalition won the local elections of October 2021. The winner of the general election of September 2022, with over 80% of the votes, was – like everywhere else in the city – the Five Star Movement, considered the champion of the programme of universal basic income introduced in recent years.[11]

From general surveys of usage, it can be deduced that the area is split in two. The lower area, between Via Toledo and the sixth street parallel to it as you climb uphill (Vico II in Montecalvario), and the rest of the zone that rises towards Corso Vittorio Emanuele. While the first part, closer to Via Toledo, is more densely occupied by commercial enterprises, to a large and increasing extent pizzerias, restaurants and the like, the part higher up is still relatively unaffected by the new activities linked to the strong growth in tourism the area has seen over at least the last ten years.

Owing to the predominance of housing that is cheap, or at least good value for a location in the city centre, it has been, from its foundation to the present day, a district inhabited largely by the working class, along with a few other strata of the population, members of the lower middle class, temporary residents and foreign immigrants. The premises on the ground floor of the buildings are still put to a great variety of uses, and a lot goes on in the streets, which are not very wide and often occupied by parked cars and scooters, as well as other improper activities. All this, together with the habit of using the area outside the home as a buffer zone between public and private space, determines a particular milieu: a teeming, often crowded scene, that is reminiscent in some ways of the markets to be seen in African cities.

In the working-class districts of Naples, signs of tradition and of the impact of globalisation and modernisation are both present. The result of this process of modernisation, which is always relatively slow, is that of a hybridisation in the medium or long term. The city acts like a sponge that, thanks to its peculiar capacity for acceptance and absorption of the new, digests these novel presences, adapting to them and reshaping, without any particular trauma, its socioeconomic and spatial landscape in a way that does not erase the more profound characteristics of pre-existing ways of life.

Politics

We can gain a better understanding of the characteristics of the context if we bear in mind a series of factors that can be deduced from the effect that public policies have had on the area.

As a planner working since the end of the 1970s on behalf of an association committed to combatting poverty and promoting human rights, I have had a privileged vantage point. In the late 1990s I collaborated with the municipality and since then have kept a close eye on local politics. This has allowed me to gain a broader perspective.

A turning point in the life and politics of the area – and the whole of the urban centre – was the earthquake of 1980 that led to many of the buildings being declared unfit for use. The work of repairing the buildings took more than ten years, and there were cases of collapse due to neglect and the lack of maintenance, but, overall, most of the constructions have been rehabilitated and almost all the housing stock has been subjected to a constant effort of upkeep.

The earthquake was important for another reason, too. In the 1980s around 20,000 housing units were constructed under an extraordinary programme of public building and, thanks to the availability of this new stock, many families obtained homes in outlying districts or municipalities of the province of Naples, abandoning the *bassi* in which they had previously lived or their houses they had shared. So, it was for this reason, too, that the population density in the area was reduced and a number of families were moved out of the urban centre.

At the end of the 1980s proposals of widespread and intensive intervention were suggested for the entire city by Regno del Possibile[12] and NeoNapoli.[13] The two proposals gathered strong coalitions determined to promote interventions that would not have excluded the urban renovation of significant parts of the city centre.

Against the background of both the criticism of the extraordinary intervention following the earthquake and the implications of the judicial investigations of members of the local business community and the political elite, the management of urban transformation remained in limbo up until the early 1990s and was left in the hands of individual enterprises, always on a very small scale and often irregular if not illegal. At the end of the 1980s a general process of legitimation was set in motion for initiatives of various kinds that sought to build on indications from European countries which had adopted more effective policies for the regeneration of failing districts than Italy. Contemporaneously many interventions were made to rehabilitate whole buildings, along with the first signs of a possible experimentation with social policies that could lead to schemes and services never hitherto attempted in the cities of the south.

Since the mid-1990s, withthe passing of certain laws, many not-for-profit organisations have gained a significant role in shaping the policies adopted with regard to run-down neighbourhoods, thanks to an activism that had no rivals, at least up until that time. This marked the beginning of a phase in which, with these grass-roots initiatives, it was 'the projects that drove the policies'. From the end of that decade, however, the whole country entered a different and more mature, although problematic and ambiguous, phase in which it was 'the policies that drove the projects', in the sense that many initiatives seem to have been prompted chiefly by the availability of funding.

In keeping with this scenario, from the end of the 1980s the Quartieri Spagnoli, too, saw, in part thanks to the activities of an otherwise weak and 'Lilliputian' not-for-profit sector, the arrival of a certain amount of resources, legitimising and reinforcing initiatives and projects that have to some extent filled gaps in the local model of welfare.

At the end of the 1990s, the work of the Associazione Quartieri Spagnoli (AQS),[14] whose members had been operating as an informal group since 1978, led to the adoption, in consultation with the operators of the municipal social services and the more dynamic members of staff of the five schools serving the neighbourhood, of an area coordination plan to provide assistance to families in difficulty and teenagers, as well as to help in the shaping of local policies. The services launched by the municipality were consolidated later, but without overcoming a sectional attitude that prevents a truly integrated approach to the handling of social needs.

The solicitations of the AQS, together with other favourable circumstances, made it possible to attract the resources needed for significant initiatives of an innovative character. Thanks to the work of the association, in fact, as far back as the early 1990s the European Union, the Ministry of the Interior and the municipality of Naples allocated resources for projects of educational integration and activities preceding vocational training. The implementation of this kind of project with the support of good networking and the constitution of a sort of local coalition for development made the area capable of attracting and credibly managing additional resources.

From the 1990s up until the first decade of the twenty-first century, innovative policies were implemented, thanks to the favourable attitude of local politicians (during much of the period Antonio Bassolino was mayor of the city). These included the launch of several European programmes (from Quartiers en Crise to the PIC Urban[15]), a first reopening of the complex of what was originally the convent of the Trinità delle Monache and then the Military Hospital, which between 1994 and the present has been partly renovated but is still underexploited, and an attempt to come up with a policy for upgrading of the *bassi* as proposed by those in charge of the Si.Re.Na. programme that Mayor De Magistris (2011–21) would later abolish.

The political vicissitudes that the Quartieri Spagnoli have had to deal with over the last twenty-five years are a reflection of a broader problem. According to some administrators and many academics, the build-up of social capital, policies to encourage human development and the non-residual welfare provided through a reasonable expansion of the system of opportunities are, and should be, substantially secondary with respect to the need to produce more immediately and materially visible results: cleaning up the urban environment through the restoration of the facades of buildings and in particular their ground floors, street lighting, restaurant tables on the pavements … In the imagination of many people – including technicians and administrators of progressive coalitions – development is still directly and strongly connected with building work, with the physical transformation of neighbourhoods. With the drawing up of local plans, even the policy of the social services – in concomitance, too, with the programming imposed by the application of the new reform of the services (Law 328/2000) – has been based on a traditional approach of systemic planning, limiting consultation to the admittance of representatives of the not-for-profit to only very occasional meetings. With all of them taking by and large an isotropic view of the territory, ignoring the differences and asymmetries between parts and sections of its components, institutionalising practices of local development and impoverishing the possibly innovative outcome of the initiatives.

In the early 1990s, by circumventing the red tape of regional procedures for the utilisation of European funds allocated for vocational training (which is still beset today by the limitations of a conception as sclerotic as it is bureaucratised and inefficient), a way was found to make use of the funds available for community initiatives of an innovative character: the three programmes to combat poverty and the first launch of the Integra, Horizon and NOW initiatives. Up until the second half of the 1990s in the Quartieri Spagnoli, as in almost all the other districts in distress, there were no other policies (apart from traditional and always very poor-quality and patchy endeavours of social welfare and urban upkeep). In 1991 a phase commenced in which the efforts of the first

---

12 The Regno del Possibile, or 'Realm of the Possible', is the name that was given to an association set up by the Banco di Napoli and local businessmen with the intention of carrying out studies and research aimed at the guidance of a wide-ranging process of reclamation of the historic centre of Naples. Two books with the same title presenting these studies and other pertinent research were brought out by the Studi Centro Storico Napoli in 1986. See: Studi Centro Storico Napoli, ed., *Il regno del possibile, Analisi e prospettive per il futuro di Napoli* (Milan: Edizioni del Sole 24 Ore, 1986).

13 NeoNapoli was a later initiative promoted by the Minister for Finance and Economic Planning at the time, Cirino Pomicino, who got a group of expert consultants to write a series of essays discussing the possibilities for a comprehensive relaunching of the city's planning policy.

14 The AQS is a not-for-profit organisation, formerly established in 1986, of which the author was one of the founders, see: https://www.associazionequartierispagnoli.it. See, too, Giovanni Laino, ed., *Quartieri Spagnoli. Note da quaranta anni di lavoro dell'Associazione* (Naples: Monitor, 2018).

15 For information on the PIC Urban (Urban Community Initiative Programme) of Naples see Giovanni Laino, 'Il programma Urban in Italia', *Archivio di Studi Urbani e Regionale*, no. 66 (Milan: Franco Angeli, 1999), 69–97. This text obviously reflects the position of the author, who played a significant role in the planning and implementation of these policies, both in the PIC Urban and for Naples' first Municipal Plan for Children, as well as for the experimentation with the introduction of a Minimum Integration Income programme in the city. See, too, Pier Carlo Palermo, ed., *Il programma Urban e l'innovazione delle politiche urbane. Il senso dell'esperienza: interpretazioni e proposte* (Milan: Franco Angeli, 2002).

Quartieri Spagnoli, 2016. Credit: Stefano Paolo

Credit: Sinah Hackenberg

associations and spontaneous groups led to the proposal and realisation of exemplary initiatives that would constitute a broad range of projects and stimulate the development of policies. In the late 1990s alone, in fact, and with the Municipal Plan for Children in particular, new measures on behalf of families – of which the most important was the experimentation of the Minimum Integration Income programme – and the realisation of some of the procedures of the PIC Urban, a framework was established of social and economic policies that were sensitive to the questions of integration and sought to improve the living conditions of the disadvantaged population.

From the mid-1990s, especially with the PIC Urban and the projects funded under Law 285/97, several experiments with social and economic policies came out of the area that have been taken as models for other districts or cities: training programmes and the activity of street educators, the public tender for an incentive for craft activities, things like the Maestro di Strada, Nidi di Mamme, Chance, Sportello Sociale and Sportello Lavoro projects, the prototype of the Laboratori di Educativa Territoriale (local education workshops, still today one of the few enduring policies of the municipality of Naples to have been put into effect in every district of the city), the tutors for fostering, the training programmes for socialisation at work and the services for the employability of young people on the margins of the education system.

The funds of the PIC Urban for the Quartieri Spagnoli were used to rehabilitate an abandoned nursery school, turning it into a centre of social and educational services for mothers, children and young people. Over the following years the city's mayors, Jervolino and De Magistris, chose to locate municipal offices in the structure, undoing years of work that had drawn on some of the most innovative ideas coming from elsewhere in Europe.

It is now evident that, while in the early 1990s local grassroots activity of an integrated character was a sort of borderland in which, notwithstanding the pluralism and the odd blunder, you found yourself working alongside other 'activists', with the evolution of the problems and with a number of successes achieved by project teams in the many social programmes implemented all over Europe, people are now operating in social niche markets, where the various players have a position and a mission aimed at corporate consolidation – first and foremost – rather than enhancement of the social bond through affirmative action on the behalf of disadvantaged groups. Even the involvement of the public administration has changed, in the sense that whereas representatives of the local government would previously be 'brought into' these processes, today, owing both to a greater awareness and to the realisation that social work in the community provides an opportunity to build consensus and to manage resources that are not so risible anymore, there is no longer a willingness on their part to leave room for the role that some activists of the non-profit organisations had carved out for themselves in the past. Overall, there are many elements to support an argument that may be of validity well beyond Naples: the institutions, while involved in innovative processes, tend to learn nothing, proposing once again, even after years have passed, approaches of a conformist nature, without favouring any real subsidiarity for the more competent forces of the not-for-profit sector.

Conclusions

Until the age of eleven I lived in ground-floor flats in the area. Then I moved into a small house with a panoramic view, allowing me to observe for twenty years the vitality of the alleys from above, the teeming of life in the garrets, on the roofs. I learned with some annoyance to put up with the din of the fireworks that are let off at any hour, even a minute before midnight, to celebrate birthdays and name days of girlfriends living in the neighbourhood or for other purposes that are to tell the truth still unknown to me.

While frequenting circles outside the district I began, in the mid-1970s, to do voluntary work there, cooperating with a pioneering community providing accommodation for minors that a rather crazy Jesuit had set up in the heart of the Quartieri Spagnoli.

Later, on the day in March 1978 when they found the body of Aldo Moro, I was helping a house painter to put up wallpaper in the premises occupied by the group of people who would go on to found the AQS in 1986. In those years, in addition to two artisans, in the final section of the long alley three *bassi* were used by prostitutes, while a family lived in the last one. Over forty years later, just one of the sons of one of the artisans is still working there with his own son, who used to play football as a child with the groups of the association. Almost all my other neighbours in the alley have died or moved elsewhere. In one of the *bassi* there is a young family and in the one opposite an elderly local woman, while the other two are occupied by immigrants who share the street with parked cars and the only surviving workshop, that of a carpenter. Along with other people, I have witnessed the unfolding of many stories, while my own has changed. Existence has a great capacity for surprise, and recently I have returned to live on the same terraces, where I have found a different world.[16]

While I prefer ground floors as a way of getting to know the life, the social networks and the goings-on in a neighbourhood, there are in reality other vantage points that make it possible to grasp other, important dimensions. Perhaps the planner who wants to gain a better understanding of the different aspects of life in a particular place, with the hope of perceiving elements that go beyond the surface, ought to be a bit of a lift operator, able to go up and down, passing through with others, whether tenants or visitors, not just the places but also the initiatives and policies that affect an area.

In the first half of the 1990s the AQS formulated and implemented a variety of initiatives of protection, prevention and preparation for social integration, based on the C.Ri.S.I. (Cantiere per la Riqualificazione Sociale Integrata) model of intervention, harbinger, although not the only one, of an approach that in other contexts would come to be known in Italy as that of the *cantieri sociali*, literally 'social construction sites'.[17] These were followed by all the programmes carried out in partnership with the municipality or with a number of foundations that selected projects for funding.

A first reflection from the perspective of this rich range of experiences pertains to factors that in hindsight can be considered to have been essential to the efficacy of the work done by the AQS. The putting down of roots in the territory (viewed as 'thrownness', with no time limits), the ability to connect people and flows of different origins and identities (local and not, members of the underclass, researchers and 'out-of-the-ordinary' people), together with the constant commitment of certain professional figures permanently involved in the mission and the willingness to go through a very long phase of integration and listening without any particular end in view: these are all factors that were undoubtedly at work in the past, and that can be directly linked to the success of the initiatives. On other occasions I have made reference to methodological factors (low threshold, active offer, harm reduction and caring for life, a propensity for interaction and social entrepreneurship and a sometimes unreasonable determination). In the background, as promotors of what was a sort of local development agency, we were inspired by an implicit theory of the privileged place, which can perhaps be considered a particular version of a tendency much more common among all those who have over the years been involved in local initiatives on a non-occasional basis. In other Italian contexts the echo of Danilo Dolci's experience of community development had spread – with due distinctions and variation of characteristics – amongst single, small movements, leading to the setting up in Naples of the Casa dello Scugnizzo, the Associazione Rinascita Napoli and the Mensa dei Bambini Proletari.[18] But on the basis of the vision of Critical Christianity,[19] which placed at the centre of private life sharing and civil solidarity with social groups that were particularly present in certain areas of the city, as some other small groups had also done – the members of the AQS started out from the conviction that in order to give meaning and credibility to their civil and political engagement it was necessary to insert themselves in some of the human networks of that territory. All these initiatives were devised outside traditional forms of political engagement, within parties and groups. In fact, one of the distinctive features shared by all these experiences is the conviction of their protagonists that the place on which they were focusing was never a centre, but rather a periphery, a territory of exclusion. It was the cultural premise, the positioning – not without ideological aspects – that made it possible to argue over the years to come that the search for the elements needed for a credible policy for the periphery was feasible only on the basis of a significant rooting in the periphery of politics.

Only in the first twenty years of the twenty-first century, in interaction with all the other phenomena that have generated the context on different scales, has it become necessary to yield to the logic of projects, of the imagination and realisation of a prospect of development of the social bond, of the 'community' to be reinvented. This is in part because, for a variety of reasons, the shards of what had previously existed (modes, traditions and habits of life, social roles and frameworks of values) no longer appear so precious.

Against the backdrop of the question of local initiatives of development, in addition to a whole series of criteria that can more credibly promise the attainment of high levels of efficacy,[20] there is a more general question pertaining to the forms used for the framing and conceptual construction of projects. Many operators, including activists in local groups, have adopted a mode for the gathering of suggestions, and treatment of ideas, that entails an absolute predominance of the ideational plane, with a marked bias towards what can be seen as beautiful, new, captivating … Generally, previsions of a deterministic kind are assumed and taken for granted in imagining the connections (always regarded as certain) between problems and solutions, supply and demand, operators, means, resources and users.

Some passages of this text have already been published in the first article referenced in note 20, but have been revised and updated here.

---

16 An article in which I present an analysis of the events of the last sixty years that have affected the lives of the families in the building in which I live is in the course of publication in English.

17 One book which inspired the founders of the magazine *Cantieri Sociali* was Giancarlo Paba, *Luoghi comuni* (Milan: Franco Angeli, 1999).

18 These are well-known experiences in Naples. They have been talked or written about by Geppino Fiorenza, Goffredo Fofin and Fabrizia Ramondino, who all played a leading part in some of them, while remaining attentive and sensitive observers of the local situation: see Geppino Fiorenza, 'Prima di tutto i bambini ! Dalla Mensa dei bambini proletari ad AsCenDer', in Attilio Belli, ed., *Napoli 1990–2050* (Naples: Guida Editori, 2022), 189–202; and Goffredo Fofi, *Le nozze coi fichi secchi* (Naples: L'Ancora del Mediterraneo, 1999).
For information on the Associazione Quartieri Spagnoli, see, too, Giovanni Laino, 'Associazione Quartieri Spagnoli. Una storia locale nel flusso', in Attilio Belli, ed., *Napoli 1990–2050* (as above), 203–18. On the Mensa dei Bambini Proletari see Fiorenza, 'Prima di tutto i bambini!' (as above).

19 The founding members of the AQS were united by their connection with the network of religious communities inspired by Charles de Foucauld.

20 For a brief enumeration of some of these criteria see Giovanni Laino, 'Il cantiere dei Quartieri Spagnoli di Napoli', *Territorio*, no. 19 (2001), 25–31; and 'Condizioni per l'efficacia dei programmi di riqualificazione nell'ottica dello sviluppo locale', in *ASUR*, no. 70 (2001).

In 'city making', there is the city

Umberto Napolitano
LAN Architecture
Cyrille Weiner

1 Francesco Milizia, *Principj di architettura civile* (Finale Ligure: De' Rossi, 1781). '*Anche senza sontuose costruzioni, le città possono apparire belle e ispirare grazia. Si deve però ammettere che una bellissima città è innanzitutto una buona architettura.*'

'Even without sumptuous buildings, cities could be beautiful and inspire grace. It must however be admitted that a beautiful city is first and foremost a good architecture.'[1]

The primary objective of the study *Napoli Super Modern* was to determine how the architecture examined could teach us something about modes of considering the contemporary city. The investigation, carried out through drawing and analysis, aimed to demonstrate the validity of our intuitions arising from observation and experience, and to clearly reveal the unanimous will of a generation of architects in support of a specific idea of the city.

Each of the eighteen buildings presented in the study, built in Naples between 1930 and 1960, contributed to the transformation of the city as a physical environment, and today each continues to contribute to the transformation of the city as human environment. Their morphologic qualities, whether formal or functional, draw on the heritage of the city in order to serve the city. These buildings reveal another face of modernity, one that doesn't conflict with historical progress but that, on the contrary, relies on history in order to contribute to a coherent urban narrative. The city becomes simultaneously the tool, the ingredient and the product of the project. The city makes the city makes the city … to say it *à la* Gertrude Stein.

The evolution of this selection of buildings over time reveals both successes and failures. If the latter relate to a lack of anticipation in predicting the transformations of such a complex territory, and especially the cultural deficiencies it denotes, the successes encourage us to reconsider the city starting from architecture.

Architecture is the only instrument we have for rethinking our cities, and architecture is as much an art as it is an occupation. We have tried to extrapolate from the buildings analysed in this book that which belongs to the occupation, the figures that have permitted the translation of desires and ideas into spatial acts. Nevertheless, each of these figures – concrete facts or abstraction, tangible realities or products of the mind – already held the conviction and the certainty that the city is the point of departure and arrival of architecture. To understand cities we must walk a path in between these disjointed realities, and the project must echo this trajectory and describe it in the resulting traces. This idiosyncratic approach to the project, which was not necessarily typical of modernist production of the mid-twentieth century, is nevertheless employed in the works studied here: the environment transforms the building so that the building, in return, transforms the environment.

To the question 'What is the city of tomorrow?', we would like to reply that it is above all that of yesterday. If the city is a process – and as such is also an evolution, a mutation, a transformation – it is only by intervening in the city that we will succeed in its reinvention. We don't wish to feed a nostalgia for the past, but to understand the opportunity being offered to us, at this specific point in time, to gain an increased awareness of the environmental impact of built landscape on our lives.

The project of the city must now ensure several fundamental states of equilibrium: that between density and viability, between nature and the built, between permanence and resilience, between sobriety and diversity, between the connectivity of long and short distances, between identity and universality, between intensity and a welcoming urbanism, between attractiveness and inclusiveness.

Architecture is nothing more than the result of a process that acts on the resources of a given environment by displacing them and transforming them; and, at a time when cities are questioning their territorial identity, the idea is gaining ground that it is architecture, more than other disciplines, that is able to interpret the complexity of the territory in order to re-establish or propose a new and sustainable equilibrium.

Shortened version of a text that was originally published in *LAN – Benoit Jallon and Umberto Napolitano, Napoli Super Modern* (Zurich: Park Books, 2020). Photos by Cyrille Weiner, from the series *Napoli Super Modern*.

Social housing in the Rione Cesare Battisti, Luigi Cosenza, 2020. Credit: Cyrille Weiner

Ponte di Tappia designed by Raffaello Salvatori, 2020. Credit: Cyrille Weiner

The Società Cattolica Assicurazioni skyscraper, Stefania Filo Speziale, Carlo Chiurazzi, Giorgio di Simone, 2020. Credit: Cyrille Weiner

Clinica Mediterranea, Sirio Giametta, 2020. Credit: Cyrille Weiner

Naples: A porous modernity

Iain Chambers

Under the volcano

'The word "history" stands written on the countenance of nature in the characters of transience.'
Walter Benjamin, *The Origin of German Tragic Drama*[1]

'I remember that my heart finally broke in Naples. Not over a girl or a thing, but over an idea. When I was little, they'd told me I should be proud to be an American. And I suppose I was, though I saw no reason I should applaud every time I saw the flag in a newsreel. But I did believe that the American way of life was an idea holy in itself, an idea of freedom bestowed by intelligent citizens on one another. Yet after a little while in Naples I found out that America was a country just like any other, except she had more material wealth and more advanced plumbing.'
John Horne Burns, *The Gallery*[2]

To speak in and of Naples is to feel bound to an overwhelmingly historicised place. The evidence is irrefutable: a gaping hole in Piazza Bellini reveals the Greek walls of Neapolis; the ubiquity of baroque buildings; the disrepair and decomposition of antique streets and irregularly paved alleys. All this material evidence of the passage of time seemingly provides an immediate set of explanations. After all, this is what the hundreds of books on the city tell me again and again. It is also what the local account, suitably crossed with Oriental and Greco-Roman myths, and then amplified in folkloristic details, also provides. The Sirens (Homer's adoption of a Phoenician myth) and the passage of Ulysses between Capri and the tip of the bay at Punto Campanile, the Sybil of Cuma and the entrance to the underworld at Lake Averno in the nearby Phlegraean Fields, traces of the Asiatic cult of Mithras, the adoption and solace of souls in Purgatory through the polishing and personal care of skulls in the city's underground cemeteries – all deepen and disseminate the mystery. In this narrative Naples emerges, in Curzio Malaparte's words, as a survivor from an 'antique, pre-Christian world, that has remained intact on the surfaces of modernity'.[3] Evoked against the timeless intensities of the Mediterranean Sea and a slumbering volcano, such accounts colour, if only tangentially explain, the textures and temper of the contemporary city, its sedimented reason and unfolding rationale, its passionate geography and psychosomatic philosophy.

Naples is a multifaceted city attached to the edge of southern Europe. As such it has often provided a favourite site for examining the loose ends of a European formation, where civil society and the state seemingly wither away in the chaos of its streets and the snarled-up complexities of its institutions. For it is here that the urban web tends to come undone and expose a living museum of archaic fragments, customs and practices. Yesterday its ruined landscape was the source of the romantic sublime (Goethe, Turner), or later of a disenchanted capitalism (Benjamin, Sohn-Rethel). Today it increasingly attracts the gaze of anthropologists as they retreat from previous peripheries to consider Europe's own internal frontiers and the peculiar rituals of its native populations. Yet Naples is not simply the laboratory of the archaic or a zoo of arrested urban development. Its crumbling historical core toasting in the sun has also been abruptly interrupted by the modern skyline punctuation of a commercial and administrative centre that was conceived in Tokyo, complete with mirrored-windowed high-rise office blocks and external express elevators.

With its violent mixture of antiquated street rites and global design capitalism, Naples confronts us as a riddle. Its sphinx-like qualities, reflecting back what we hope, and fear, to see, disclose an unstable hubris dissected by different cultures and historical rhythms. Until recently a precarious water supply and an erratic public transport system serviced seventeenth-century streets and sewers blocked with the traffic of the twentieth century.

Male youth pissing in the night-time streets. Is this just a generational bloody-mindedness or expression of the banal fact that there are very few public toilets in Italian cities? Perhaps the absence of 'public' toilets is itself indicative of an understanding of the relationship between one's private body and the community of public zones, between the fanatical securing of personal purity and an indifference to public filth and the anonymous character of civic space? Neapolitans consume five times more water than the inhabitants of Paris; not only bodies, but also floors, are washed daily. Although managed by capital the city seems frequently to be out of control. Only an exasperated individualism, everyone free to invent his or her own highway code and building legislation, manages to leave its mark. Yet it works: the rubbish is collected each and every night, the litter-strewn streets are swept each morning, good quality drinking water arrives in your home, a modern subway system is slowly creeping under the town.

Still, the modern myth of the rational organisation of urban space, of production, labour and profit, continues to be interrupted, decomposed and deviated by innumerable pockets of social resistance, mercantilism, barter, corruption and crime that frequently cross-fertilise each other: the corner deal concluded on the cellular

---

[1] Walter Benjamin, *The Origin of German Tragic Drama* (London: Verso, 1990), 177.

[2] John Horne Burns, *The Gallery* (London: Secker and Warburg, 1948), 48.

[3] Curzio Malaparte, *La pelle* (Milan: Mondadori, 2001), 34.

4 Giuliana Bruno, *Street Walking on a Ruined Map. Cultural Theory and the City Films of Elvira Notari* (Princeton: Princeton University Press, 1993).

5 Predrag Matvejević, *Mediterranean: A Cultural Landscape*, trans. Michael Henry Heim (Berkeley: University of California Press, 1999).

6 Benjamin, *The Origin of German Tragic Drama* (see note 1).

phone, black market couriers on their scooters, the buying and selling of favours, the institutionalised bribe. This is the tangled undergrowth of another city, and of a cultural formation that loses its strands in the labyrinth of kinship, street culture, local identity, popular memory and urban folklore.

To be open to this dimension, to the collective narration of identities and the exchange of memories that pass under the name of 'Napoli', is clearly to abandon the possibility of conducting all these threads into a single conduit, a unique narrative able to explain such details. Of course, we can employ terms like 'uneven development', the 'backwardness' of southern Italy, and refer to the local, national and international concatenations of mixed temporalities, of structural inequalities disseminated in specific historical and political formations, but the particular syntax of these conditions, their 'Neapolitan' mix, can only find inconclusive explanations in these categories. Perhaps, rather than seeking to 'resolve' such questions, it might be instructive first to absorb them in a manner that might suggest another sense of the city and the urban and historical style it exposes. For Naples certainly proposes its own particular configuration of modern life. Here conflicts and contradictions are uncovered, sometimes brutally, and often violently registered. This is a manner of being contemporary that is strikingly different from those institutional proposals that persistently mask social, economic and cultural tensions behind the glass and steel facades of an official modernity that simply exorcises and consigns to the 'market' what it cannot absorb and manage.

To follow the twists and turns of the city's intestines, to enter what the late-eighteenth-century Neapolitan journalist Matilde Serao referred to as its 'belly', and to proceed along its winding streets, is to register what, in reference to the silent cinema of the Neapolitan film director Elvira Notari, was disparagingly termed a 'mad body language'.[4] For here one's own uncertain trajectory and that of the ill-defined urban corpus are mutually integrated and interrogated. The insistent physicality of the streets, daubed by decay and disregard, accompanied by the aggressive overspill of private effluence into public matters – from street rubbish to raised voices seeding a potential public drama – draw you into the city's interior, transforming a walk in the street into an unscripted performance for all its participants.

The street as spectacle, as simultaneously the space of a performance and a mass public, is what no doubt links the figure of Pulcinella (who apparently first appears in 1609 at the Stanza della Commedia in Via Medina) to the great twentieth-century Neapolitan comic Totò. The intertwining of public and private in the theatrics of street humour signals the modern wrenching away of entertainment from aristocratic clutches (there is a similar parabola in the shift of opera from court to theatre in the seventeenth century) and the growth of modern urban mass culture. Initially a cabaret and theatrical performer in the 1930s, Totò went on in the postwar period to appear in innumerable comedy films (some brilliant, some mediocre, but all unequivocally marked by his presence). A somewhat aloof, even contorted personality, marked with a tragic streak that Pasolini sought to explore, Totò's comic seriousness ineluctably caught the absurdity of an official rhetoric that was unable to contain the turbulence of postwar Italy.

Totò's popular but pungent art transformed the banter of the alley and the street into a metaphysics of the human condition. His hyper-intelligent dismantling of the formal pomposity of institutional oratory – both Italian and Neapolitan – carried his audience to the slippery edge of acceptable sense. In his mouth, language punned and punished to an extreme in syntactical hyperbole and linguistic overkill falls apart to reveal the joins, the glue and the gaps that the official facade and the rigid stereotype seek to paper over. A contorted body, a mobile face, an illogical expression break through the phrase; language is pushed out of place and the limits of sense are registered and then rendered poetical. The very 'now' of a performative body, its accumulated tics and specificities, ridicules the legislative pretensions of imposed norms and empty abstractions. In the cynical wisdom of what, underneath it all, was a tragic humour, Totò, in the deliberate ambiguity of his language and the exaggerated ambulation of his body, has become fully identified with the city itself. In a profound sense, to have seen one of his major films – for example, *Guardie e ladri*, *Totò, Peppino e la malafemmina* or *Siamo uomini o caporal?* – is already to have visited the city and inadvertently touched some of its deeper chords.

An architecture of transit

'The inhabitants of the Mediterranean belong more to a city than to a state or a nation.'
Predrag Matvejević, *Mediterranean: A Cultural Landscape*[5]

Like many Mediterranean cities, Naples refers to itself and its local hinterland long before the nation state appears in its sense of identity. Even the Nativity scene becomes a Neapolitan scene. The papier-mâché models and ceramic figures of biblical Bethlehem that constitute the Christmas *presepe* are invariably populated with local market figures, piazzas and pizzas. Two myths are fused into a miniaturised language of representation in which the religious and the secular, the past and the present, the distant and the immediate, the dead and the living, share the same world. Once a capital, Naples has become an ex-centric city without an obvious compass. Seemingly robbed of its destiny, its trajectory has been blocked by a loss that it appears incapable of confronting and working out. As a defunct centre, a victim of history and a corpse, the city is perpetually ready to 'enter into the homeland of allegory'.[6] The visceral gestures of self-referentiality – and the *presepe* and a local literature deeply self-absorbed in the city's dissolution and imminent demise are only the most documented exposure of this daily narrative – continue to propose all the pathos of that loss. This is to appreciate that there is no overall project or unifying design able to encompass the Neapolitan experience. It is a story that can be caught in fragments, in the economy of disorder, in the cathartic laughter induced by a tragic comedy, in the flickering half-light of a seemingly ineluctable decay.

Paradoxically, as a built environment, an architectural reality, a historical testament, the sense of the city continues to be represented as though it were homogeneous: the teleology of temporal stratification has at all costs to be respected and conserved. There seems to be little interest in the idea of re-proposing elements from the past and relocating them in the present, that is of provocatively re-citing them in order to re-site the city. Faced with demands for urban renewal, architects and planners invariably find themselves locked in the problem of conserving the past which, in turn, leads to the blocking of architectural renovation. It ought to be possible, on the contrary, to respect the past in a diverse fashion – that is, not in a closed logic but rather through a more complex engagement with its undeniable presence. Surely there exists the possibility of a contemporary architecture that recovers such traces and which subverts the problem of bowing before an implacable historicism and the divisive logic of the 'past' and the 'present'? Yesterday it was the 'baroque', today it is the 'modern': this simply leads to a debate between the baroque and the modern in which to preserve the baroque it becomes impossible

7 Ermanno Rea, *Mistero napoletano* (Turin: Einaudi, 1995).

8 Alfred Sohn-Rethel, *Napoli, la filosofia del rotto* (Naples: Alessandra Caròla Editrice, 1991).

9 Benjamin, *The Origin of German Tragic Drama* (see note 1), 177–8.

10 Christine Buci-Glucksmann, *La raison baroque* (Paris: Galilée, 1983), 71.

to consider the modern. It ought to be possible to conceive of the modern and modernity in a multiple manner so as to return the traces and interrogations of the past to the present. This would be to learn from the critical evidence deposited in the city itself.

The social and cultural problems of the historical centre continue to be architecturally dominated by the ideological insistence of conservation, even when sometimes it might be more beneficial simply to eliminate a crumbling building in order to create an open space or green zone. Naples has the lowest amount of recreational space and parks in the whole of Europe, and probably in the First World. It has very few 'lungs' and has a lot of difficulty in 'breathing'. That is why, when observing some of these decaying buildings, often accentuated by the effects of the 1980 earthquake, it would seem better, despite all the difficulties of resolving the personal situation of those who live there, to remove the building, not in order to build again but rather to change the use of that space by leaving it open, unbuilt. Maria Cerreta, an architectural friend, tells me that this approach has rarely been considered. The temptation is always to fill space, never to leave it empty. This, associated with the lengthy processes such interventions require, means that the historical centre is full of ghost-like building sites and precarious edifices that are literally propped up by scaffolding. Given the length of time involved this often means to live in a building that will never be fully renovated and will never 'return' to its 'original' state.

As a propped-up environment, a propped-up city, an uncertain ambient that experiences continual mutation, Naples inadvertently suggests a more transitory sense of habitation. There are many major cities in the world, not necessarily occidental, such as Cairo and Rio de Janeiro, where large segments of the population live in a transitory habitat, in buildings that the inhabitants themselves are architecturally responsible for, creating housing that employs urban detritus for their building materials. This is not to suggest that the damaged and decayed buildings of Naples are of this order, but to think about a temporal and transitory architecture is also an invitation to reconsider how one might inhabit urban space in a more flexible fashion as opposed to the static logic of the historical 'palazzo' deeply rooted in time and the terrain.

Critical city

'The evidence appears banal, beneath the threshold of our intelligence, while on the contrary it is strikingly beyond it.'
Ermanno Rea, *Mistero napoletano*[7]

As with all cities, rational explanations are drawn from the evolution of the urban settlement in time. Geography and history are distilled into a coherent framework, occasionally seeded with accidental forces, that advances the continuity of development. A certain inevitability is secreted in the account: the present state of the city somehow already exists in embryonic form in the instance of its foundation. There is a progression that initiates with birth and concludes in the maturation of the present. Cities only die in antiquity. This, however, is only one particular manner of collecting and remembering the past. The history of a city could also be narrated through discontinuities, temporary states and transitory configurations: invasions, destruction, disasters – all the uncertainties that attend an uncontrollable nature and irreverent time. Naples, for example, certainly lends itself to this latter form of telling. The desire for stability, as the desire for survival, perhaps blinds us to these other dimensions, these other senses.

Writing in the 1920s the German visitor Alfred Sohn-Rethel noted:

The city lived under Vesuvius, and its existence was therefore constantly threatened. As a consequence, it participated in the diffusion of the technical and economic development of Europe in piecemeal fashion, because it was impossible to know whether the year would not be interrupted by a catastrophe.[8]

Experienced in this fashion the city is not simply a physical reality, the sum of its collective histories, memories and monuments, but is rather more aptly apprehended in the instance of what the Situationists called psychogeography: the practice of mental and physical drifting that leads to rewriting the urban text in terms of a desire that snares the unexpected and the incalculable in the immediacy of a situation. The instructive value of Naples, both socially and aesthetically (and are they really so easily divisible?), may lie not in its pretended uniqueness but rather in its capacity for dispersal, for losing itself and thereby escaping the predictable. Here the city does not stand for a firm, rational and unique referent, but slips through conventional schema to propose a floating semantics, drifting through a hundred interpretations, a thousand stories. Its meaning flows beyond the rough physicality of its streets into the interior architecture that provides the scaffolding of the imaginary.

This imaginary place, like all dream material, promotes a language that calls for a mode of interpretation. Alfred Sohn-Rethel's linking of the city to the idea of catastrophe, to imminent destruction and decay, draws us into the language of the ruin, the language of the baroque. Naples is fundamentally a baroque city. This is how Walter Benjamin, who wrote much of his book on the baroque theatre of mourning in 1925 while staying on Capri and frequently visiting the city, comments on the centrality of the ruin in the figural economy of the baroque:

In the ruin history has physically merged into the setting. And in this guise history does not assume the form of the process of eternal life so much as that of irresistible decay. Allegory thereby declares itself to be beyond beauty. Allegories are, in the realm of thoughts, what ruins are in the realm of things. This explains the baroque cult of the ruins.[9]

It is, as Christine Buci-Glucksmann notes, in the allegorical style of the baroque, in its insistence on ruin and decay, in the shrivelling-up of history and life, that the 'maximum energy emerges due to it being a corpse'.[10]

To live under the volcano in a constant reminder of one's mortality: is that the key to the city's schizophrenic energy, its language of exultation and despair, its extremes of physical violence and mental resignation? In Naples you are constantly aware of not simply living an urban experience, but also of living urban life as a problem, as an interrogation, as a provocation. As an unfolding negation of the assumed inevitability of 'progress', the city continually proposes physical and philosophical foundations that are stymied by the principles of stability. Hence, lived as a predicament, rather than as a planned environment, Naples presents itself as a *critical* city. Its innumerable seventeenth-century buildings are silent witnesses to the continuing disruption of linear development as urban and architectural design dissolve into sounds, streets and bodies that do not readily bend to the structural stability sought by the modern will. Inhabiting the baroque motif of the ruin, positioned in the precincts of progress, always on the threshold of disaster and decay, Naples is perhaps emblematic of the city in crisis, of the *city as crisis*. The self-conscious pathos of its language, its composite but insistent style, betrays the multiple

11 Iain Chambers, *Culture after Humanism* (London: Routledge, 2001), 129.

12 Giuseppe Montesano, *Nel corpo di Napoli* (Milan: Mondadori, 1998).

13 For a literary recreation of the life of Muhammad Al-Idrisi in *Siqilliya* and the court of Sultan Rujar (the Norman Roger II) in Palermo, see Tariq Ali, *A Sultan in Palermo* (London: Verso Books, 2005).

histories and memories that swell up in the rupture and revenge of signification, leaving us with a profoundly metropolitan interrogation of the enigma of what Heidegger once called the nebulous quality of life.

A desired historical continuity frequently obfuscates the complexity of the past which lies in those loose ends and uncoordinated strands of unfinished business that are always ready to snare the present; all those lives, voices, projects, patterns and occasions that somehow failed to register, or are only permitted a marginal presence in the consistency of the present-day tale. Here the incoherent, the silent, the banished, exist only as noise, as background static, as unheeded disturbance. The unilateral nature of time, the inevitability of progress, the implacable determinism of a destiny ruled by the past seduces us into accepting a unique understanding. It is seemingly only our individual ignorance that prevents us from reaching out to grasp the wholeness of history. But contemporary voices, invariably arriving from elsewhere, have suggested that time is not so homogeneous, that both collective and individual lives are not so continuous; a heterogeneity, sustained by silent and excluded witnesses, draws us into listening to the other side of history, both to the histories of others and to another history. This latter tale leads us to abandon the longing for a single coherence; it forces us to recognise in the narration the act of repression that accompanies every representation as the price of coherence.

Some years ago I wrote:

> Writing in 1924, Walter Benjamin and Asja Lacis noted, in what has subsequently become a much-cited commentary, that the city of Naples consists in a 'porous architecture'. Its principal building material is the yellow *tufo*, volcanic matter emerging out of the maritime depths and solidifying on contact with sea water. Transformed into habitation, this porous rock returns buildings to the dampness of their origins. In this dramatic encounter with the archaic elements (earth, air, fire and water) there already lies the incalculable extremes that co-ordinate the Neapolitan quotidian. The crumbling *tufo*, child of the violent marriage between volcano and sea, fire and water, is symptomatic of the unstable edifice that is the city.[11]

Applied to the physical and metaphysical sense of the city, the idea of porosity can be extended to include its historical and cultural formation. Porous matter absorbs whatever it encounters, it soaks up external elements while maintaining its initial form. It embodies and incorporates foreign elements and external pressures. The history of Naples is also, and perhaps most significantly, the history of such processes. Naples has hosted innumerable invasions, incursions, overlords and political delegations over the last millennium. Conquered and occupied many times, in the end it is invariably the conqueror who is subdued and ends up paying tribute to the internal rhythms and autochthonous design of the city.

Unruly histories

> 'Landrò always found himself contrary to something or somebody, and it seemed that his main worry was that of being always able to say no, to negate every possibility of anything positive or affirmative.'
> Giuseppe Montesano, *Nel corpo di Napoli* [12]

The original settlement of the future city was inaugurated by the colonising Greek Cumini (themselves apparently from the island of Rhodes). They established Palaepolis on the hill of Pizzofalcone. In the fifth century there was the establishment of the second settlement of Neapolis further to the east in the present-day historical centre; the most obvious traces are in Piazza Bellini, and in the subterranean classroom or *Aula delle Mura Greche* in the Orientale University in Piazza San Domenico Maggiore. As a Greek city, Naples was a favoured choice for Romans, both of the Republic and the Empire, desiring a 'classical' education. The language of the city was Greek, Greek were the festivals, the modalities of civic administration and the education system. It was also here, to Villa Lucullo (once home to Virgil and today the fortified complex of Castel dell'Ovo), that Odoacre dispatched Romolo Augustolo to end his days as the last Roman Emperor.

In the sixth century Naples was a Byzantine city where religious institutions were both Latin and Greek. The city was bilingual; only in the eighth century did Latin replace Greek as the official language of the now autonomous duchy which was only nominally linked to distant Constantinople. Fear of losing their new won independence led the Neapolitan dukes to solicit aid from Arab forces in both Sicily and North Africa against a possible Byzantine return. This, in turn, led to increasing Arab incursions in southern and central Italy, including the sack of Rome in 846. At Vico Equense, half an hour's drive south of Naples there is a *Torre Saracense*; built as a fortification by Arab raiders, today it is a sophisticated restaurant. Further south, Sicily was under the dominion of Berber powers from North Africa and the Emirs of the Egyptian dynasty of the Fatimidi until the arrival of the Normans in 1061, who, in turn, became turbaned monarchs. Al-Idrisi, resident at the court of Palermo, dedicated his important geographical treatise in Arabic, *Kitab Rujar* or *Amusements for those who long to traverse the horizon*, to the Norman Roger II.[13] Roger's wife, Elvira, was daughter of Alfonso VI of Castile and his Arab wife Zaida; Roger's grandson, the Arab-speaking Holy Roman Emperor Frederick II, founder, in 1224, of the University of Naples, was to reinstall the Muslim call to prayer in the Christian-controlled city of Jerusalem, and to deploy Arab cavalry to defeat the Lombard League. Under the Norman monarchy in Naples the commercial area outside the city walls was known as the *moricino*, for it was there that the Moors or Arab merchants lived. It is perhaps in this profounder sense, in its historical debt to the southern and eastern Mediterranean, rather than in the supercilious and racialised stereotypes imposed by the Piedmont commanders who took over the city in 1860, that Naples is an 'oriental' city. Its own creolised past casts a critical light into the internal formation of a future Europe that has persistently sought to counteract such southern and oriental 'roots'. Such negations perhaps also explain the city's own neurotic relationship to modernity, in which an imposed inferiority is often worked up into the persistent mannerisms of uncritical local pride.

Naples is famously a city framed by the sea, the sun and a volcano. Beyond such immediacies, rendered commonplace in a hundred descriptions, a thousand songs, ten thousand photos and postcards, these natural referents reveal themselves to be a perpetual reminder of what our anthropocentric understandings often fail to register. The earthquake, the threat of volcanic eruption, or simply the perpetual accompaniment of the sea, register the limits and continual interrogation of a self-absorbed humanity. Beneath the indifferent glare of sunlight, unsolicited accidents and natural hazards are invariably considered marginal and insignificant in the unfolding narrative of immediate lives. Nevertheless, if reintroduced into the account, the 'natural' dimension of history renders the social security of the earlier narrative altogether more fragile and transitory; that is, altogether more 'historical' in the deeper, temporal and tellurian, sense of the term. For here history is not merely the story of selected human events; it is also the testimony of an unfolding and unforeseeable terrestrial transit.

The figure of the city, with its sedimented strata of previous lives and memories, was a favourite metaphor of Freud's for the unconscious, and Naples is certainly a city that believes in the talking cure. It repeatedly refers to itself, offering up the scene of endless analysis. Perpetually constructing and reassuring itself in words, the city itself is continually exposed in laments for the past and fantasies for the future, while the present often passes unattended, abandoned, like the peeling walls of its buildings. Self-absorbed, as though blocked in what Lacan refers to as the mirror-phase – the glance of Narcissus that avoids the void, the abyss (Vesuvius?): the other that might challenge its presumed uniqueness, its identity – Naples, witnessed from elsewhere, also becomes the laboratory of a critical configuration.

For the city, despite all its specific details and provincial claims on experience, cannot avoid acquiring a part in other stories, other idioms, other possibilities. It is ineluctably transformed from being a self-referring monument to becoming an urban intersection, a rendezvous, a site of transit, in an altogether wider network. Set loose from its moorings, the city drifts into other accounts. Its parochial hold on reality is compromised by economic and cultural forces that are also being narrated elsewhere: in a global economy that is simultaneously signalled in the world stock exchanges, the world drug market and contemporary patterns of international migration.

Walking in the city I follow narrow alleys that turn inwards towards the piazza, a church, or bring me to monuments set up in the name of death and disaster: the decorated *guglie* or obelisks that commemorate volcanic eruptions, earthquakes and plagues. Only rarely do streets direct me towards the opening of the sea. It is as though the city draws its energies from the darkness, the shadows, sucking the light out of things in an irrepressible self-reflection that serves to illuminate its passion for self-centredness. The sea remains an accessory, an appendage from which fish once arrived and urban effluence is now dispatched. Naples is above all a vertical city, reflected in its archaeological sedimentation and social stratification. The class ladder commences with one-room dwellings on the streets – *i bassi* – to arrive at the attics and terraces of the professional classes and splinters of aristocracy still clinging to the heights. The sea and sky are caught in snatches, the lateral (democratic?) view is rarely permitted; the gaze is either bounded by narrow streets or else directed skywards towards secular and religious authority.

Probably the aspect that most immediately strikes a visitor, a stranger, is that Naples is a city that exists above all in the conundrum of noise, in the 'incessant shouting of that paranoid city' (Tomasi di Lampedusa). Added to the constant murmur that a local *intellighenzia* spins in literary lamentations and critical conservatism are the sounds that arise from the street between the interminable acceleration of scooters and angry car horns: the shout of the fishmonger; the cries of greeting; the passing trucks and megaphoned voices offering watermelons, children's toys, glassware and pirate cassettes of Neapolitan song; the fruit seller who publicly commences on his wares and their supposedly low prices in the third person: '*Che belle pesche. Duemila lire … ma questo è pazzo!*' (What fine peaches. Only two thousand lire … but this guy's mad); the itinerant seller of wild berries at seven in the July morning whose acute cry fills the empty alley. These lacerations of silence attest to the physical punctuation of space by the voice, the body. It is also the body that provides a fundamental gestured grammar in which hands become interrogative beaks, arms tormented signals, and faces contorted masks. A pre-linguistic economy erupts in urban space to reveal among the sounds a certain distrust of words, their promise of explanation and their custody of reason.

The hidden plan of the city lies in an architecture of introspection that is revealed not only in crumbling edifices and grim-coated facades, but also in the taciturn faces and sceptical sentiments of its inhabitants. Here, where the linearity of time spirals out into diverse tempos, the residual, the archaic and the pre-modern can turn out to be emergent when visceral details and distortions undermine the dreamed-of purity of rational planning and functional design. In its art of getting by (*arrangiarsi*), making do and rearranging available elements as props for a fragile urban existence, the presence of Naples – as a European, a Mediterranean and a contemporary metropolis – proposes an eternal return to the inscrutable lexicon of modern urban life, to the contingencies of an unstable language in which all city dwellers are set and configured. Here, to return to the underlying connection between criticism and crisis, Naples is also a potential paradigm of the city *after* modernity, of what, in the wake of that dream, survives and lives on. Connected in its uneven rhythms and volatile habits to other non-occidental cities and an emerging metropolitan worldliness, Naples proposes an *interruption* and *interrogation* of our inherited understanding of urban life, architecture and planning. Participating in progress without being fully absorbed in its agenda, Naples, as a composite space, reintroduces the uneven and the unplanned, the contingent, the historical. Viewed and, above all, lived in this manner, the interrogation posed by Naples returns the question of the city to the relationship between politics and poetics in determining our sense of the ethical and aesthetical; that is, our sense of the possible and imagining our location within it. Beyond the numbing sentence of rationalism, was that not what modernity itself once sought to achieve?

What, elsewhere, is invariably forgotten and overlooked, in Naples remains strikingly evident. Every city involves a pact, a settlement, between human occupation and the physical site in which it is located. There exists an ill-understood relationship between the geography and the sensibility of a city. Every city develops an unconscious trauma with its location: London on the Thames, Los Angeles in the desert, Moscow on the steppes. The site of a city is invariably both a source of attraction and repulsion, for visitors and inhabitants alike. Wherever it is located, the geographical location of the city is also the subsequent source of a sedimented, emotional map. In its combination of natural setting and psychosomatic elaboration, every city is therefore also the historical realisation of a human allegory. If Naples shares this condition with all cities, it is in the *explicit concentration* of these elemental forces that it perhaps appears atypical.

The instability of the ground upon which buildings are erected and over which human traffic moves, the proximity of the volcano, the indifference of a timeless sun and sea, have all contributed to a ubiquitous pessimism in which, as the Neapolitan writer Raffaele La Capria eloquently puts it, the *topos* rapidly slides into *pathos*. Naples is *La Città del Sole*, and Tommaso Campanella was to spend more than twenty years imprisoned in its three castles – Castel Sant'Elmo, Castel dell'Ovo and Maschio Angiovino – while, between torture, he composed this utopic text. In such a charged setting, a human presence is tolerated but not essential. In this disquieting geography a deathly uncertainty coalesces around an almost Bartlebyesque affirmation of the individual and collective refusal to choose. Here the 'barometer fails to register and the compass goes crazy'; one makes contact with a rarefied immobility such as that of 'the equivocal smile that appears on the face of the dead' (Anna Maria Ortese). Destiny, rather than decision, has the upper hand. Still, if this might explain the seeming arrest of so much of the city's official culture and thought – its conservatism and nostalgia for the 'lost harmony' of a vague and mythologised past – it also nurtures a widespread scepticism that refuses the superficial optimism of those, invariably from more northern climes, who believe they are predestined for 'progress'. In a negation that is often simply condensed in a visceral 'no', the seamless temporality of modernity is rent by a disquieting refusal to accept its confident prophecies. As the site of a compressed and concentrated urbanity – some parts of the city have the same population density as Hong Kong – where modernity is squeezed into the custody of seventeenth-century streets and archaic rituals, in the end Naples, rather than announcing a slide into a stereotypical vision of the 'Third World', perhaps reveals less about its own obvious shortcomings and more about the limits and illusions of modernity itself.

For the details, the psychogeographic and allegorical particularities of Neapolitan life, also represent a local version of a far vaster configuration. Ultimately, the formation of a city like Naples is inseparable from its historical location in a Mediterranean, and, ultimately, a worldly setting. Amongst the clearest symptoms is the immigrant labour force that lives in the city and hinterland. In Naples the vast majority of immigrant domestic female labour once came from Cape Verde, Somalia and the Philippines; more recently it has been supplemented by immigration from Ukraine and Sri Lanka, while male labour employed in agricultural and street vending largely comes from West Africa and China. Chinese labour is also predominant in the semi-clandestine clothing industries in the satellite towns at the foot of Vesuvius. To hear Arabic in the buses, Chinese on the streets, observe the turbans, scarves and vivid patterns of the cotton dresses of women from East Africa at the post office sending money home, is to recognise an urban future destined to transform local coordinates.

If Naples is unwillingly thrust into the critical and global limelight of metropolitan enquiry it also donates its own form of questioning: a particular contribution to the simultaneous formation of concentration and dispersal, that *Unheimlichkeit* or uncanny recognition of the visceral proximity of the foreign and the strange – perhaps the profoundest symptom of modern life – that consistently doubles and displaces urban geometry with the unruly histories of the repressed and the inauguration of displacement. The city itself is frequently reviled for seeming to be precariously placed at the limit of Europe and modern urban life, clinging intermittently to those more ordered lifestyles associated with London, Paris, Milan and New York. Yet, in its seeming proximity to the more 'typical' world cities and civic clutter of Cairo, Sao Paolo, Mumbai and Lagos, this Mediterranean city also paradoxically finds itself drawn into proximity with the cosmopolitan composition of a Los Angeles or a London as its own internal history comes increasingly to be intersected by the intrusion of extra-European immigration and the imposition of global capital reworking its local concerns. Here, in the space of these 'new powers and expanded intercourse on the part of individuals' (Karl Marx), where we are forcefully invited to rethink the spatial division of centre and periphery, of 'First' and 'Third' worlds, the specific historical and cultural configuration of Naples acquires a new and unexpected insistence.

Interrupted narratives

> 'Build your cities on the slopes of Vesuvius! Send your ships out into uncharted seas!'
> Friedrich Nietzsche, *The Gay Science* [14]

Living under a volcano – the 'furious giant, rebel of the sky' (Girolamo Fontanella) of Neapolitan baroque poetry – that is always on the verge of eruption (the last one occurred in March 1944 and the next, with a projection of a catastrophic eruption and a death toll of 80,000 is well 'overdue'), the violent persistence of Arcadian forces is periodically underlined by seismic events. Such reminders are mirrored in a ubiquitous uncertainty and the resigned acceptance of decay that accompanies mortality. While waiting in a doctor's waiting room, one inevitably overhears the muttered phrase '*Siamo nati per morire*': 'We are born in order to die'. The fundamental pessimism revealed in this phrase – saturated with historical determinism as well as the unsuspected Heideggerian insistence that the sense of our lives arises from our potential death – condenses in a phrase the mental style and wisdom of the city. In this sense, Naples is both architecturally and existentially a profoundly baroque city. I have always been struck how in Naples a person's height is often referred to as though the body is in a horizontal state: a tall person is considered not to be 'tall' but 'long' – as though just born or already laid out on the mortuary slab. The circularity of birth and death is, of course, a profoundly seventeenth-century motif, and it is this circular, baroque, manner of thought that perhaps best captures the worldly and ironic relationship of Neapolitans and their city to modernity.

Walter Benjamin, as theorist of the baroque, of the allegorical and of a fragmentary modernity, clearly haunts such descriptions. To insist on the allegorical fashioning of the city is to insist that every explanation is transitory, mortal and forever incomplete. To express and experience the city in this manner is to render its enigmatic quality emblematic. This path is not chosen to deepen the mystery of arcane mythologies, populated by Sirens, sibyls, martyrs and neo-pagan cults of the dead, but rather in order to render explicit and problematic the modernist desire for a conclusive transparency secured in another myth: that of the teleological inevitability of 'progress'. For all its parochial concerns, Naples here emerges from its local coordinates to query and disturb the projected homogeneity of the blueprint born in the anxious midst of metropolitan powers desirous of a seamless symmetry.

The city, of course, is certainly not a homogeneous place. Every city is the site of collective and contested memories. To represent a city is not only to describe its physical form and material details; it is also to enter the altogether more immaterial passages proposed by memory, myth and legend. The city is an immense archive that betrays the unconscious architecture of historical trauma: of what is simultaneously represented and repressed. To read it and seek an explanation is to register an enigma. If we attempt to exhaust the meaning of the city, to render it transparent, it turns out, as Poe reminds us in 'A Man of the Crowd', to be a text whose secret cannot be told. The city proposes a narrative that is inexorable, relentless; it is a tale that exceeds the sequential logic of writing and the conclusive evidence of a document. The voices, bodies and lives that compose the urban script move in diverse directions, and render every narrative provisional, every history susceptible to a further telling. The transitory image that gels in a photo and lacks any pretence of explanation is perhaps a more fitting modality of representation than that proposed by writing. For the immediacy of the instantaneous 'now' caught in a photograph is saturated with time and simultaneously the testimony of its passage. In such images the past both invades and exceeds the present. In turn, this both encourages and interrogates our desire for interpretation, and brings us back to writing.

Against a local, often folkloristic, orthodoxy that fosters a predictable vision composed of sun, mandolins and pizza, or the altogether more refined metaphysics of the timeless sublime of 'a splendid day' (*Che bella giornata!*) evoked by Raffaele La Capria, there are the memories, the dead lives and labour inscribed in the

---

14 Friedrich Nietzsche, *A Nietzsche Reader* (Harmondsworth: Penguin, 1977), 208.

15 Giuliana Bruno, *Atlas of Emotion* (London: Verso, 2002).

16 Walter Benjamin, *The Arcades Project*, trans. Howard Eiland and Kevin McLaughlin (Cambridge, MA: Harvard University Press, 1999).

17 Franco Cassano, *Il pensiero meridiano* (Rome-Bari: Laterza, 1996), 25.

streets, sounds, languages and life of contemporary Naples that continue to contest a predictable accounting of both the past and the present. The latter potentially render the city a stranger to itself.

February 1724: the Jesuit priest Matteo Ripa leaves China aboard an East India Company vessel accompanied by four young Chinese males bound for Naples and the subsequent establishment of the 'Chinese College' in the city, later to become the Istituto Universitario Orientale. On the sixth of May in the following year the four Chinese students, popularly known as 'Turks', witnessed the annual liquefying of the blood of the city's patron saint – San Gennaro – in the cathedral. The college itself, where today I teach, was intended to promote both the ecclesiastical and commercial interests of the Holy Roman Empire in India and China, and to provide instruction in Chinese for members of the Ostend Company established by the Holy Roman Emperor Charles VI in 1722 in order to contest the hegemony of the English and Dutch companies in Asia. The company will be dissolved five years later, crushed by English and Dutch commercial opposition. Real 'Turks', however, whether in the form of corsairs from the Barbary coast or in the direct presence of the Ottoman empire itself, were deeply entrenched as the privileged figures for feared strangers and an alternative political and religious hegemony that continued to patrol the Mediterranean even after the Catholic naval victory of Lepanto in October 1571. In fact, Istanbul rebuilt its fleet within a year, held on to the island of Cyprus, and a century later laid siege to Vienna. Venice meanwhile slid into its long decline and Spain increasingly turned its attention to the exploitation of the New World. In everyday contemporary Neapolitan parlance, to be 'taken by the Turks' means to be seized by panic.

The city is most obviously the material repository of historical memory. As such, it is the primal archive of that shared but ragged discontinuity that presents us with our 'selves'. The city, its buildings and spaces, its tastes and sounds, all deposited in the physical and poignant languages of locality and place, is not merely a crypt conserving dead matter; it is also witness to the disquieting ambiguity of who we 'are' and what we might become.

But what type of memory is this? After Freud, we know that historical memory, like all memory, is a selective process, dependent on language as the factor of truth. Memory depends on a language of representation and repression, of choice and displacement, of expression and oblivion. Sometimes it is necessary to forget in order to survive. Yet what is forgotten remains an essential part of the story. So, the memories and forgetting deposited in the city of Naples, and the languages that seek to retrieve them, ultimately circulate without the guarantee of either continuity or conclusion. While the inventory of 'facts' and 'documents' apparently establishes the historical archive, it is the altogether more unstable language of interpretation that sustains them. It is here in our relationship with the dead, and in our awareness of a past that is simultaneously represented and repressed, that a more open and ethical understanding of the present is expressed. Explanations always remain susceptible to interpellation by the past. In this space the knowledge and authority of historiography finds itself on an unstable terrain, appealing to uncertain foundations, for it is here interrogated by the very processes it seeks to explain. Unavoidable corpses lie between the pages of each and every homogeneous accounting of time.

The past, like memory, the unconscious and language, overflows rational arrest. The city, its languages and lexicon, exceeds such a confinement. It is the failure of a historicist reason to engage with the living potlatch of the city – what the past offers up as an excessive gift that exceeds reification in a stable historical object – which suggests that historical knowledge is ultimately subordinate to a more extensive reasoning. What I have learnt from living in Naples is that the explanatory frames of historiography, sociology and anthropology are clearly insufficient. The city as an allegorical tangle, an entwined knot of language, dialect and idiolect, of sound, sign and souls, and Naples is a supreme example, punctures the analytical picture that seeks to immobilise and render the 'city' explicit in an imposed coherence.

This is not to suggest that the city therefore remains a mystery, a riddle beyond the frontier of understanding; rather, it is to suggest that the city itself, its complexity and seeming indecipherability, proposes a diverse sense of 'understanding'; one that requires us to supplement a taxonomic cartography with an 'atlas of emotion'.[15] To understand, to take stock, to seek to possess and to register the perspiring skin and mutating body of the city, is perhaps to appreciate that 'sense' is both corporeal and temporal: it ultimately resides in the ambulatory body that contains and sustains the transport of our thought. This is to suggest a way, a direction, the movement of sense, rather than a stable semantics that seeks the impossible goal of critical distance. Sense is not what is, but is rather what becomes; it emerges in transit, in the unguarded transfer of language, and in the passage of bodies in time that circumscribe, transform and produce space in the particularities of a place. To register what escapes the immediacy of reason, what remains asymmetrical, is to acknowledge what remains out of joint, negated, and invariably repressed. To bend attention to this subterranean and subaltern telling is to disperse the authority of history by other narratives, by forms of telling that transgress, while traversing, the relentless sequential rhythm of 'progress'.

So, the 'sense' of Naples is not to be found solely in a series of historical, sociological and anthropological verdicts. The city is obviously not only authorised in this manner. The seemingly implacable assurance of these and other institutional voices are not ignored, but are rather heard while under way, seeking to register and sound out a city that refuses to be read as though it were a definitive script. The city presents itself as the site of an inconclusive passage that we can explore, experience, exhume, but never fully explain. It is this that draws us on, step after step, street after street, ready to be side-tracked, distracted and deviated – like Walter Benjamin's 'botanist on the asphalt' – by the details, and then, finally, to recognise in the detour the making of our selves and the infinitely layered world we inhabit.[16]

Writing the city is also to be written by the city, suspended in a narration without pretence to finality. In Naples such fashionable open-endedness is historically accompanied, as in every city on the sea, by the horizontal slash of infinity suggested by a marine horizon. From the sea, novelty, foreigners and invaders arrive, towards the horizon the desired stability of sense slips away. The definitive is destined to unforeseen drift: 'the break in the horizon produced by the sea prevents thought from arriving at a definitive state and power from fixing itself in the immobility of a personal patrimony.'[17] This does not mean to be left reading a merely subjective account. What is sought in the city, in the rude hospitality of its languages, is the sense of a critical constellation able to portray Naples in its simultaneous uniqueness and connection to the worldly landscape of a differentiated modernity that ultimately frames us all.

Finally, how should I write and view this city: as a travelogue, from the point of view of the stranger, or as an inhabitant? How to avoid the superficial eye and the imposition of an external measure, fruit of an imperial formation? Whatever posture I adopt I find myself within

18   This Caravaggesque sensibility and aesthetic is brilliantly evoked in Derek Jarman's film, *Caravaggio* (1986).

19   Gilles Deleuze, *The Fold: Leibniz and the Baroque*, trans. Tom Conley (Minneapolis: University of Minnesota Press, 1992).

20   Louis Marin, *To Destroy Painting*, trans. Mette Hjort (Chicago: University of Chicago Press, 1995), 15.

21   Ibid., 102–3.

22   Ibid., 164.

the long tradition of these questions and gestures. For this city is also my home.

The subverted eye

Coming in off the narrow, shadowy street, full of people, rain, small shops and urban decay, and stepping into the brightly lit greys and whites of the octagonal structure of the church of Pio Monte della Misericordia in Via Tribunali, is a shocking experience. It is as if to step dramatically out of one world into another, out of ragged chaos into a stilled order. As with all uncanny experiences, the disarming familiarity of both dimensions sucks me into the dramatic milieu of the city. In the wink of an eye, I am thrust into startling proximity with one of the greatest paintings of the European baroque. Caravaggio's *Sette opere di misericordia/Seven Works of Mercy* (1606, Chiesa Pio Monte della Misericordia, Naples) is a large canvas, almost four metres by three. It lies brooding over the altar and, despite the competition of other large works, including paintings by Luca Giordano and Battista Caracciolo, completely dominates the church.

The seven works of mercy, that is the six works enumerated by Christ in St Matthew's Gospel, plus the additional but very pertinent burial of the dead for a plague-ridden sixteenth-century Naples, are immersed in a dramatic slice of then contemporary street life. Bodies are creased by shafts of light and enveloped in folds of darkness. A woman succours an old man with milk from her naked breast, the arched back of a bare body, the Madonna and child protected by the outstretched wings of an angel gaze on the abject details of this urban scene. The painting is framed by angles. There is no simple or obvious centre, but rather an agitated constellation of attention. The eye is not drawn in, but drawn across the canvas in a series of trajectories that refuse to coalesce in a single point of unity. The bodies that populate this space are bodies of light seemingly distributed in a casual and quotidian manner, looming out of the shadows sustained by layers and layers of darkness. Their faces and looks propose a series of intersections that cut across the privileged perspective of the viewer's gaze. The viewer is de-centred, his or her centrality displaced. Instead of the eye travelling into the picture towards a hypothetical vanishing point, the pictures invade the eye: disturbing, deviating and dissecting its habitual line of vision. Attention is unfolded across the canvas in multiple directions. We are drawn into the undulations of clothing, flesh, faces and the wings of an angel: all suspended in varying quantities of darkness.[18]

If the painting and the church represent the triumphal affirmation of the Counter-Reformation, they also, and above all, recall the complex composition of an emerging metropolis. Naples was the second city in Europe after Paris, and the second in the Mediterranean after Istanbul. Host, as Peter Robb reminds us, to some 10,000 foreign slaves, perched on the edge of a Mediterranean Sea that had witnessed the temporary defeat of Ottoman hegemony only a few decades earlier, Naples, a colonial city ruled from Madrid, was suspended in the traffic between multiple worlds, both old and new. Its very diet was being radically transformed by the Americas: tomatoes, chilli pepper, subsequently potatoes, beans, chocolate, peppers, squash – all ingredients to be added to the earlier Arab contribution of citrus fruits, coffee, aubergine and rice, and all destined for the formation of the 'traditional' Mediterranean diet.

Continuing my walk along Via Tribunali is to continue to wander in a gallery of baroque churches, buildings, hidden gardens, stumbling into skulls and bones sculptured in bronze on the side of the street, fresh flowers thrust between the grinning molars: the Chiesa delle Anime del Purgatorio (one of the innumerable signatures of the baroque architectural giant Cosimo Fanzago responsible for works that run from churches and palazzi to the massive, incomplete Palazzo Donn'Anna whose brooding presence dominates the sea at Mergellina). The street itself, the civic trace of the original Greek plan, cuts the ancient city in half – *Spaccanapoli* – as if a physical metaphor for the dualism that characterises both the baroque and, in an altogether more repressed fashion, modernity. In the unresolved division between mind and body, terrestrial decay and celestial perfection, between darkness and light, the framing of thought, and life, comes to be suspended in a fluctuating and ambiguous balance: caught between the flat, tabular frame of reason and the infinite spread and interlayered folds of the body of becoming.

As suggestively caught in the Italian translation of Gilles Deleuze's book on the baroque, between a *spiegare* (to explain, expound, unfold) and a *piegare* (to fold, wrap, crease) there emerges the *spiegamento* (the explication, the spreading out, the unfolding).[19] Contrary to the fixed point of Cartesian rationalism there is the mutable point of view revealed by the body, where to explain is to disclose a complexity to be subsequently traced in the folds, creases and envelopment of the world. In this sense the centrality of rhetoric to the baroque world, and hence to Naples, is not an idle or 'ornamental' matter. The art of seeing and comprehending has to be sensually assembled, it is diverse from abstract knowledge or mere information. In the violent instability of the Counter-Reformation and the uncertain world of a new social, political, geographical and scientific order, knowledge demands conviction, a mute consensus is insufficient. Sometimes the construction, whether in architecture, theatre or thought, leans more towards the light, sometimes more towards the shadows; invariably it recognises its hybrid provenance in both. The constraints of mortality are inscribed as much in the abstraction of rational flights as in the vivid immediacy of bodies and light obliquely pictured in Caravaggio: temporarily caught but not centred, falling away, out of the frame.

It is in the art of Caravaggio that we most persistently encounter the uncertain sense of stability and certitude; his paintings open a window on the seemingly inexplicable and indecipherable hubris of this fundamentally baroque city. Here the perspective of mimesis and the desired transparency of reason sought in representation are subverted and the doubts of depiction announced. The neo-classicist Poussin declared that Caravaggio had come into the world in order to destroy painting. Frustrating a rationalist appropriation inscribed in the pleasurable measure of classical order and interpretation, Caravaggio's manner of painting directly 'from life' threatened the nobility of the gaze (*theoria*) by offering what was seen and felt, rather than what reason composed and condoned. The deadly beauty of theory, the conclusive, crypt-like configuration of discourse and the rationalism of representation that render the world legible and read for possession, are destroyed by Caravaggio turning the gaze inwards on itself and the mortal framing it announces.[20] With Caravaggio, as Louis Marin points out, we encounter not the truth of the object represented, but the truth of the representation. Eliminating distance and trapping the eye in appearance, all occurs on the surface of the painting; on the plane where the outside and inside coincide in a blurred and indecidable boundary. It is here that the outside and inside are at their most intense and attain their greatest power, a power so overwhelming it cannot be resisted.[21]

The 'idea' of painting as faithful mimesis, as 'true' to nature, as a historical judgment and critical prospect, is

23 Norman Lewis, *Naples '44. An Intelligence Officer in the Italian Labyrinth* (New York: Carroll & Graf, 2005), 137.

replaced by the act of painting in which 'the moment of sight erupts within representation'. Marin concludes: what looms out of the black space of these canvases is that 'the self-reflexive moment within Caravaggio's paintings reveals painting to be a representation without basis, without foundations.' In Caravaggio, 'the glance is a gesture of pointing, a wordless "this" that does away with supplementary discourses and description, striking here and now.'²² In its violent affirmation, this temperament announces the precarious space of the emergence of the modern urban world, and anticipates what in later centuries will be referred to as 'mass culture'.

Rubbish

At every corner, and dotted along the streets occupying valuable parking space, are the rubbish bins. These are large metal containers, on wheels, and opened, if the rigid plastic cover has not been destroyed, with a foot pedal. Household rubbish is supposed to be deposited in these containers only after seven in the evening; this acquires a certain urgency in the summer months when high temperatures and organic decomposition augment street smells. The rule is rarely respected. During the night, and quite remarkably nearly every night, the containers are individually hooked to the back of a large rubbish truck and then mechanically hoisted into the air to deposit their contents in the vehicle for crushing and eventual transfer to the tips.

It is said, but also corroborated by investigative journalism, that this metropolitan rubbish, both its collection and the management of its disposal in often unauthorised landfills, is in the hands of local crime syndicates: the camorra. Many of these illicit rubbish tips continue to operate, often accepting illicit toxic materials from elsewhere in Italy. Paradoxically, many of the official sites, owing to saturation, have been closed. For several months in the spring of 2001 this led to a crisis with mountains of rubbish rotting in giant plastic bags on the streets. Subsequently it was all dispatched by train to Düsseldorf where its incineration supplied energy to the German city's power grid. Since then, often amid an opposition that represented ecological, but perhaps also other, more shady, interests, the regional authority has begun to propose similar energy recycling plants that will supply the local grid, provide employment and guarantee an ecologically more sustainable disposal of rubbish.

The sociological and historical explanation of the Neapolitan camorra sets them apart from the Sicilian mafia. The latter initially emerged in a rural context. The camorra is fundamentally an urban phenomenon, product of the popular masses housed in the overcrowded and politically abandoned quarters of the city. The economic and social security of the street, its management and 'policing', fell into the hands of those willing to use the violence required to create an 'order' amenable to their family and clan interests. From being a local counter-power, managing the hidden economy of organised street crime, prostitution, extortion and the price-fixing of the fruit and vegetable markets, the camorra, with its Sicilian and Calabrian cousins, and often in collaboration, has developed into a modern financial organisation with significant social and political clout.

After the closure of the free port of Tangiers and the subsequent shift of the contraband tobacco trade to the northern side of the Mediterranean, the camorra in the Campania region grew in the 1970s in economical and organisational scale. The Neapolitan port of Mergellina, as elsewhere up and down the coast, was full of high-speed boats. With their cargo of cigarettes unloaded from ships in extra-territorial waters, these streamlined blue craft were able to outstrip the cutters of the local Customs in their dash for the shore. In Naples alone more than 4,000 boats were directly involved in the night trips off-shore, and around 50,000 people operated in the contraband cigarette business. Organised crime also made further gains in the early 1980s, above all in the construction industry, after the earthquake of 1980. The power of organised crime was rendered explicit with the direct intervention of the boss Raffaele Cutolo and his Nuova Camorra Organizzata on behalf of the Christian Democrat Party in obtaining the release of the local politician Ciro Cirillo from the Red Brigades. The camorra simultaneously earned both half the ransom money and significant institutional and political goodwill. Four decades previously, towards the end of the Second World War in occupied Naples, the English intelligence officer Norman Lewis had this to say:

> Genovese, according to Edwards, was not, as described on our files, ex-secretary to Al Capone, nor was he even a Sicilian, but had been born in the village of Ricigliano, near Potenza. He had been second-in-command of a New York mafia 'family' headed by Lucky Luciano, Edwards said, and had succeeded to its leadership when Luciano was gaoled, after which he had been acknowledged as the head of all the American mafia. Shortly before the outbreak of war Genovese had returned to Italy to escape a murder indictment in the US, had become a friend of Mussolini's, and then, with the Duce's fall, transferred his allegiance to Allied Military Government, where he was now seen as the power behind the scenes. Genovese controlled the sindacos [mayors] in most towns within fifty miles of Naples.²³

On 5 July 1950 the 28-year-old Sicilian bandit Salvatore Giuliano was killed, not in a shoot-out with the Carabinieri as the official account announces, but in his sleep, betrayed and executed by his lieutenant and cousin Gaspare Pisciotta (later poisoned in prison after claiming his responsibility for Giuliano's death). Giuliano's death marks the closure of the initial chapter of postwar Italy in which the complex political, cultural and economic reassembling of national reconstruction is shadowed and permeated by the insertion of the mafia and the camorra, not to speak of elements of the Fascist regime recruited in the new 'war' against communism, into the historical equation. In the same month seven years previously, Anglo-American troops had invaded Sicily. The Americans chose to reanimate their historical links with Italy (more than four million, predominantly from southern Italy, had permanently emigrated to the United States in the previous seventy years) by deploying Italo-American personnel in the Italian campaign and, above all, by cynically activating the international networking of the mafia (along with the Catholic Church and the Masons) in preparing the invasion and the subsequent postwar administration. In January 1946, Charles 'Lucky' Luciano was released from a United States prison and dispatched to Italy. Although Luciano, head of the New York mafia, had been condemned to over thirty years' imprisonment in 1936, Thomas Dewey, governor of the State of New York, accepted the board of parole's verdict, which has subsequently been revealed to have been motivated by the secret collaboration between the mafia and the United States Navy in the preparations leading up to the Allied invasion of Sicily.

Charles Poletti, a successful Italo-American lawyer, was dispatched to Palermo as Military Governor of Sicily. Among the mayors of the liberated towns Poletti immediately nominated were several noted mafia chiefs. In the turbulence of postwar southern Italy, characterised by feudal property rights and a disoriented and alarmed bourgeoisie faced with peasants hungry for land, re-emerging unions and the threat of the 'reds', the

24 Ibid., 137–8.

'trinity' (Pisciotta's own term for this unholy alliance) of militarised policing, mafia and banditry served to maintain an existing order all over the Mezzogiorno through the judicious dispersal of violence. In 1947 Giuliano and his band machine-gunned the May Day march of peasants at Portella della Ginestra, leaving eight dead and thirty wounded. Three years later his services were no longer required. Isolated from the concerns and councils of the mafia, by now a folkloristic embarrassment to the local oligarchy and the public face of government, Giuliano was an abandoned bandit with ninety-seven warrants for arrest, accused of 300 crimes and held responsible for the deaths of peasants, private citizens and eighty-seven police officers. His ultimate undoing was his lack of integration in the postwar settlement.

This has certainly not been the case of the capillary association of the mafia, the camorra and the Calabrian 'Ndrangheta, with their ability to organise the economic and political control of rural territories and urban fiefdoms. Such organisations only give vent to highly publicised violence when the calculated logic of their economic, territorial and political power is threatened. Violent deaths, and they have been hundreds over the last three decades, express the constant struggle between organised bands, associations and alliances for territorial control and subsequent economic power. Codified in a perverse sense of 'honour', and respectfully serviced by a conspiracy of silence (*omertà*), the power of organised crime not only reaches far into the recesses of civic, political and economic activities but has successfully transformed itself into becoming an integral and, implicitly, accepted part of their textures. In their own, very particular, manner they represent a specific contribution to the ongoing configuration of civil society. As a local building industry boss intent on 'sacking' the postwar city with illegal building projects and quick profits, Rod Steiger, as Edoardo Nottola, vividly captures in a suitably histrionic performance the tentacled reach of corruption and political interests in Francesco Rosi's classic film, *Le mani sulla città* (1963). Rosi has also graphically recreated the official and unofficial *imbroglio* of both the earlier Guliano and the Luciano affairs in his films *Salvatore Giuliano* (1962) and *Lucky Luciano* (1974)

In this rhizomatic extension of power coursing through the grey areas of legality, a community of interests, favours and unspoken collusion is stitched together. The details and denouncements of local corruption and criminal activity rarely come from resident journalists who are themselves often imbricated in the context and the collusion of the community. If it does, it invariably concludes in death, as the young freelance journalist Giancarlo Sini, sometime contributor to the Neapolitan daily *Il Mattino*, discovered to his cost in 1985.

Emerging out of the local logic of territorial control and a political spoils system, organised crime is today a complex global business. Its tentacles connect the heroin street fix in the Neapolitan periphery of Secondigliano, the nightly rubbish trucks passing down the street, to the building industry, and such major state interventions as the massive reconstruction of housing and infrastructure in the Neapolitan hinterland after the earthquake of 1980 that left more than 3,000 dead and thousands homeless. Right now, organised crime is burrowing into the bids and contracting around the ongoing construction of the Italian high speed railway system, and was all set for the proposed suspension bridge across the Straits of Messina before it was cancelled. From here the network reaches out to the international commerce in drugs, contraband arms and the laundering of illicit gains in the financial paradises of global capital. Back in wartime Naples, here is Norman Lewis once more:

> What was to be done? Nothing, Edwards said. The CIC [Counter-Intelligence Corps] had soon learned to steer clear of any racket in which Genovese had a finger – and his finger was in most. Too many American officers had been chosen to go on the Italian campaign because they were of Italian descent. For this reason, it was hoped that they might easily adapt to the environment, and this they had done all too well. The American-Italians in AMG [Allied Military Government] reigned supreme and knew how to close their ranks when threatened from without. An American CIC agent who had cottoned on to the fact that the notorious Genovese was in virtual control of Naples and set out to investigate his present activities, soon found himself isolated and powerless, and all the reward he had had for his pains was loss of promotion.[24]

What ultimately emerges from this 'dirty' landscape, from this *monnezza* of illicit power, is not merely the complex intertwining of mafia and politics, of crime, business and government, but, above all, the external, Allied and, in particular, American management of the postwar Italian scenario. Local authority, in the form of mafia power and earlier Fascist officialdom, was promoted and protected by the Allied forces. In an emerging Cold War climate intent on containing and rolling back the 'red' menace, such a strategy ensured that public and political institutions experienced a sustained continuity. The Fascist state and its personnel were neither dismantled nor reformed. The OSS officer James Jesus Angleton, a Republican Mason and later responsible for the CIA desk for Israel and Italy, rushed north in the dying months of the war to save Prince Junio Valerio Borghese, head of the notorious X^a MAS battalion of the Fascist Republic of Salò, from execution by the partisans. Both Borghese and his lieutenants were recruited by the OSS as agents of United States intelligence. Fifteen years later Borghese attempted a right-wing coup. If, in 1945, 'liberation' and 'democracy' were the official bywords, for the OSS, incubator of the future CIA, it would be a hidden league, forged in the symbiotic networks of mafia, masonry, Fascism and the Catholic Church, that was to secure the authority of order and an enduring political settlement. This 'third force', to evoke Graham Greene's *The Quiet American,* subsequently cast its net over Italian civil and political society. That force has never been eradicated.

Philosophical haunts

From Vatolla, a small village perched up in the mountains of Cilento, some eighty kilometres to the south-east of Naples as the crow flies, one looks out of the studio window of Palazzo Vargas across the Sele plain with its buffalo and mozzarella. Your eyes are drawn towards Capri and the Bay of Naples; a vision that traverses the Greek temples of Paestum and its striking depiction of the world beyond in the remarkable painted Tomb of the Diver. This was the view, no doubt tinged with nostalgia, that entertained the city's most famous philosopher, Giambattista Vico (1668–1744), in his eleven-year sojourn as tutor to the children of Domenico Rocca, Marchese of Vatolla. Unlike most Italian intellectuals of both his own and subsequent generations, Vico had no other means than his own intellectual wits on which to survive.

Very much a Neapolitan, Vico was obsessed with the problematic nature of historical processes. In his writings, a native sense of destiny, whether endorsed by religious or rationalist dogma, was challenged by the innovative idea that history was an ongoing cultural elaboration: the product of human imagination and labour. Further, Vico went on to radically extend the idea of 'history' from a narrow concern with political figures and military events to include every aspect of human life. In his striking modern understanding of history as a symbolic and social construction, Vico reminds us, despite the irresistible faith in 'progress', that history is not an arrow slicing through empty time, but is rather the untidy and incomplete testament of lives lived in a worldly frame. Naples itself, in its buildings, streets, sounds and prospects, is witness to the perpetual process of historical sedimentation, detritus and contingent configurations; witness to lives that inevitably remain irreducible to the unilateral concerns of a singular purpose or perspective. Here history slips beyond teleology into testimony; bearing witness, it does not present us with an implacable destiny, but rather envelopes us in a persistent interrogation of our condition.

The city is not a stable archive, housing the accumulation of dead documents and established facts; rather, it proposes the unruly and unmapped (even unmappable) topography of time. In the immediacy of bodies and sense, of cultural traces and physical constraints, history as epistemology – that is, as a theory of knowledge and progress – is invaded, interrupted and displaced by a complex, often indecipherable ontology, that the discipline of history invariably fails or refuses to register. To experience Naples as a historical challenge, one that persistently queries the desire, design and discipline of historiography is, in truth, to query the very premises of representation and the assumed relationship between language and event (once again, we are drawn into the baroque and the layered folds of darkness that sustain Caravaggio's art). The experience of Naples suggests the translation of that tradition, and its institutionalised knowledge, into an engagement with the prospect that history occurs *within* language; that, in a profound sense, the language of history is the history of language. This is to border the syntax of representation with the shadow of our responsibility for repression: the very language that seeks to illuminate and render the world transparent, as though it were a beam of light, produces the shadows that constitutes its obscure margins.

If it is from a backward glance that future scenarios are constructed, then considering how the 'past' is constituted becomes imperative in deciphering the sense we wish to bestow on this city. Walking its streets, seeking shade from the piercing rays of the sun, feeling the almost tangible qualities of the spiral of time, we are faced with the choice of either remaining prisoners of an implacable past, and hence of time itself, or else of returning to that inheritance in order to remember and interpret it in a manner that frees the present for further possibilities. This is a question that not only, and most obviously, invests modern historiography; it is a debate that has persistently contributed to the very making of modern, everyday Naples as a physical and metaphysical edifice. The city, after all, has been home to both Giambattista Vico and Benedetto Croce. In the respective works of these two thinkers, it is possible to enumerate a divergence of historical understanding that invests both the very sense of 'history' and, as a consequence, of the city itself.

Vico conducted a continual critique of Cartesian rationalism and its universal point of view, insisting on its circumscribed applicability to social and human affairs. Against the arbitrary insistence on an a priori truth articulated in our abstractions, Vico proposed a limited human consciousness unable to render nature fully transparent to its will. That Vico drew upon an esoteric vitalism to contest the mechanical logic and triumphant rationalism of the then very actual scientific revolution does not diminish the pertinence of his critique of the will to universal uniformity that the new epistemology sought to secure. After all, his contemporary, Isaac Newton, was deeply inspired by the cabbala and the magic of numbers in his own rationalising endeavours.

Where Vico's arguments achieve their forceful synthesis is in his opus *Principi d'una scienza nuova dintorno alla natura delle nazioni* (1725) which, along with its various amendments, is generally known as *Scienza nuova*. In this work Vico proposes a science of history in which human activity and truth are conjoined in the institutions of language, laws and myths, and is authored by human beings. In this key, the distinction between abstract philosophical 'truths' and immediate philological 'facts' is overcome and absorbed in the socialised activities of humankind. Vico insisted on a poetic understanding, distilled in myth, magic and non-rationalised understanding, that depends on the power of language and the centrality of metaphor in the articulation of knowledge and, hence, in the writing and reception of history. Such a perspective is destined to irritate and interrogate the heady rationalism of intellectual formations self-absorbed in proposing their doctrines and 'civilisation'. The Neapolitan philosopher persistently argued against the presumed superiority of rationalism confronted with ancient beliefs, as though the latter were without sense; hence his rejection of the idea that the archaic is somehow external and foreign to modernity itself (a criticism that more recently has been effectively echoed in the anthropological work of Ernesto De Martino and in the cinema and poetics of Pier Paolo Pasolini). In his grounding of thought and truth in time, in his location of interpretation within contingent, historical and cultural framings, Vico evoked both interdisciplinary study and the concerns of modern cultural anthropology. Drawing critical attention to the precariousness of culture and reason, Vico's work proposes a sustained critique of rationalism through excavating a reasoning that is not merely logical in intent nor unilateral in affect.

So, if, as Vico argues, history is the product of human activity and therefore only humans can ever 'know' history, they can, at the same time, never fully know or 'possess' it. At this point there emerges the critical imperative of reading knowledge against knowledge; just as books are about other books, so knowledge emerges on a relational and contested terrain. Perhaps the most significant testimony to the modern pertinence of Vico's thought is to be found in the prison writings of Antonio Gramsci and his incisive analyses of the formation of modern Italy, and, more recently, in the critical revaluation of historiographical thinking proposed in Hayden White's excavation of the structuring tropes deployed in recovering the past and 'representing' it.

After Vatolla, Vico returned to Naples to take up the Chair of Rhetoric at the University of Naples where he taught from 1699. The original site of the University of Naples, founded to contest the power of Bologna, and frequented by Thomas Aquinas, is unknown, but it was almost certainly in the historical heart of the city. Today, its main entrance is on Corso Umberto, a modern avenue created in the late 1880s as part of the '*risanamento*', or cleaning up, of the city after the cholera outbreak of 1884 that struck down more than 7,000 Neapolitans. It was here, in a generalised European climate of 'inventing' traditions, that Francesco De Sanctis, subsequently Minister for Education, elaborated and authorised an organic national literary canon with his *Storia della letteratura italiana* (1871). Here, too, one can view the plaque in the entrance hall to the university commemorating those 'non-Aryan' teachers expelled from the education system in the wake of the racial laws of 1938. Ten minutes' stroll away in Via Semmola (now Via Benedetto Croce), at number 12, is the fourteenth-century Palazzo Filomarino, with is massive baroque doorway by the eighteenth-century architect Ferdinando Sanfelice. Here Benedetto Croce lived much of his life. It is with Croce that we encounter another version of 'history', one that superficially pursues Vico's concern with our temporal framing, but which ultimately delivers a radically different verdict on our historical state. It has been Croce's vision that has acquired the hegemonic status of critical common sense. The disquieting responsibility of registering a limited rationality, of acknowledging a circumscribed knowledge in writing history and evoking the past – bequeathed by Vico and sharply reinforced in Hayden White's recent critical work – hardly finds an echo in modern Neapolitan and Italian historiography.

Croce believed in an 'absolute historicism' for which life and reality are nothing other than history. But here history is not so much the temporal articulation of social and symbolic life as the history of the individualised, and ultimately infinite, manifestations of the ahistorical immanence of the human spirit. This vapid destination for historical sense, mediated through the thousand details, anecdotes and principled lives that Croce lovingly evokes in his many histories of Naples, is cousin to Croce's aesthetics. In both cases, 'history' and 'art' are presented in the idealistic determinism of self-regulating categories, impervious to radical problematisation and critical appropriation. In both cases, we find ourselves conversing with what turns out to be a disembodied absolute. For Croce the work of art is totally autonomous from all other human activities; art proposes an unconditional, disinterested and self-sufficient image whose character is universal. Similarly, if for Croce historical consciousness is the unique form of theoretical validity, the problematic nature of what constitutes 'history', how it comes to be recognised, authorised and narrated, is consigned to the implacable authority of a human 'spirit' that sustains, in a sort of secular religiosity, what is ultimately an incontestable framing of the world.

The positivism of 'progress', guaranteed by the presumed linearity of time and the unfolding development of a 'freedom' that is realised in the identity between history and spirit, seals historical explanation in an autonomous, self-sustaining semantics. This idealistic grammar, however, can be dispersed, the idea of 'progress' can be put on ice, and the 'logic' of 'history' can be opened up to interrogation by those expelled from the account; that is, by those 'without history' who have been structurally excluded from, or simply obliterated by, 'progress'. Here, as Dipesh Chakrabarty reminds us, there emerges what is most profoundly 'underdeveloped' in the occidental awareness and elaboration of history and its 'modernity'. Many, and invariably without choice, continue to live this temporality differently, inhabiting a plurality of histories and powers that constitute an altogether more complex, ragged, heterogeneous, non-linear modernity.

Yet the 'victims' of an inevitable 'progress' are not only and most dramatically those who have paid, and are paying, with their lives. There are also those who continue to propose and live this stunted vision. Here history is not considered to involve interrogations, endings, beginnings, partial, partisan and always incomplete understandings, only the perpetual unfolding of a 'passive revolution' (to adopt the eighteenth-century Neapolitan historian Vincenzo Cuoco's critical warning) that continues to confirm the status quo.

Moving now to a building in which this drama has been most vividly etched, we find ourselves in the octagonal courtyard of the Palazzo Serra di Cassano at Monte di Dio, with its external winged staircase also designed by Ferdinando Sanfelice. The main door to the building opens on to Via Egiziaca a Pizzofalcone, where I myself live. Here, almost eight centuries ago, Frederick II hunted with his falcons (Falcon Peak: Pizzo Falcone). The massive metal portal, however, has remained closed ever since that fatal day in 1799 when the Duke of Cassano decided to close the palace doors that faced the Royal Palace in protest after the decapitation of his son Gennaro Serra, Duke of Cassano. Gennaro Serra, along with hundreds of other liberal aristocrats, intellectuals and radicals who participated in the revolution and subsequently short-lived Neapolitan Republic of 1799, lost his life following the bloody restoration of the Bourbon monarchy.

After five turbulent months the city had been retaken by a peasant army led by Cardinal Ruffo, while the reinstallation of the Bourbon regime was directly supervised by Horatio Nelson from the flagship of the British fleet at anchor in the bay. The short-lived republic is today still overwhelmingly discussed in terms of the errors, weaknesses and characteristics of the local liberal bourgeoisie (brilliantly recreated around the figure of Eleonara Pimentel de Fonseca in Enzo Striano's *Il Resto di Niente*). It is in the mummified logic of a missed moment and the tragedy of a 'lost harmony' (Raffaele La Capria) that explanation is sought, rather than in the altogether more extensive light provided by the swell of revolutions that swept around both sides of the modern Atlantic world between the 1770s and the 1820s, from the United States to France, Ireland and Naples, while simultaneously swelling up in the Caribbean in the successful slave revolt that led to the foundation of the black republic of Haiti, to crest in the subsequent wave that swept over Latin America. This was an epoch that was characterised by expanding colonialism, capitalism and industrialism, all girded together by the political economy of the Atlantic slave trade. It was also a period dominated by the Napoleonic wars and a struggle for global hegemony that witnessed the simultaneous presence of the British fleet in the Indian Ocean, the North Atlantic and Oceania, as well as in the Mediterranean and the Bay of Naples. The history of the Neapolitan Republic is also an integral part of this wider, contested world.

Still, those doors, with the exception of a brief opening for the bicentenary one morning in 1999 in the presence of the left-wing mayor of the city Antonio Bassolino, have remained closed ever since. Today, climbing the stairs up to the Italian Institute of Philosophical Studies on the first floor of the building, the visitor cannot avoid the massive tablet announcing the names of the 'Martyrs of 1799' (a similar commemoration flanks both sides of the main entrance to the town hall in Piazza Municipio). In the gesture of the sealed doorway time is frozen, like the names of the hundreds of martyrs etched in marble, as though it were a hermetically closed event that somehow devours the present and all possible futures. The revolutionary 'failure' of 1799 has not only stained subsequent Neapolitan history, but also effectively sealed the city's destiny. The failure to recognise its location in the historical dynamics of a wider, ultimately planetary, atlas of power, condemns '1799' to being the site of a subaltern malaise, never the source of an alternative or counter-hegemonic history.

It is as though Naples is left suspended in time, robbed of a future, unable to bury its dead and effectively mourn its past in a manner that would transform what was once blocked and negated into a new historical horizon. The abstract sentiments of Croce's 'absolute historicism' always lie in wait ready to propose a pact between a speculative conservatism and the resigned reception of the 'passive revolution' that the present ushers in. In this manner, the identification of historiography with politics, and ideology with philosophy, is, as Antonio Gramsci pointed out in his sustained criticisms of Croce, forever avoided. The repressed logic of representation is lost in the disciplinary fog of self-regulating protocols that recognise only the abstract authority of a bloodless 'scientificity' whose idealism sustains the positivist illusions of cultural and historical analysis.

Returning to Vico, and drawing energies out of the past, perhaps something else could emerge at this point. The philology of revolutions and reaction that

25 Antonio Gramsci, *Quaderni del Carcere* (Turin: Einaudi, 1975).

26 Gigliola Pagano de Divitiis, *Mercanti Inglesi nell'Italia del Seicento* (Venice: Marsilio, 1991).

swept across Europe and the New World in the closing decades of the eighteenth and the opening decades of the nineteenth centuries suggests that the 'destiny' of Naples needs continually to be charted on an altogether larger, yet always incomplete, map. As a Mediterranean, European and world city, its time, its historical tempo and temper, is not merely of its own making. It speaks, and is spoken, in multiple languages that are never simply autochthonous. Historically constructed and culturally construed, the city awaits further interpretations. It remains open to other forms of telling, and is destined to accommodate a historical sense whose tragic import and greatness lies precisely in the inability to either fully arrest or control the compass of meaning.

Progress

In 1672, faced with a serious grain shortage in Sicily, the city of Messina armed three ships to intercede and capture merchant vessels carrying grain through the Straits of Messina from Puglia to Naples. In a few months Naples, Campania and Calabria were reduced to the same state as Sicily. To combat the situation Naples hired two expensive Dutch war ships to escort the grain vessels from Puglia.

In *La Questione Meridionale* (1926), the Sardinian intellectual Antonio Gramsci offered a lucid analysis of the structural impoverishment of southern Italy in terms of existing economic, political and cultural forces. He spoke of stagnation characterised by the mass of peasantry in the economic and political clutches of large, often absentee, land owners. He spoke also of southern intellectuals supplying the administrative personnel of the Italian state, both locally and nationally, and of the role of such intellectuals (he was referring in particular to Benedetto Croce) in reproducing the status quo. Ten years later, incarcerated in a Fascist prison, he was to observe:

> The poverty of the Mezzogiorno was historically incomprehensible for the popular masses of the North; they could not comprehend that national unity was not achieved on the basis of equality, but as the result of the hegemony of the North on the Mezzogiorno and the territorial relationship of the city to the countryside; the North was an 'octopus' that enriched itself at the cost of the South, its industrial and economic progress was in a direct relationship to the impoverishment of southern industry and agriculture.[25]

Much of what Gramsci had to say then continues to echo within the existing political economy of the south and in its one-time capital city, Naples. Yet the 'sources' of this malaise perhaps lie not only in local economic and cultural peculiarities, but also in a deep-seated inheritance that today would be considered part and parcel of the processes of 'globalisation'.

Naples, unlike Genoa and Venice, was never a major port and commercial centre in the manner of its northern cousins. Up to the end of the sixteenth century, Venice and Genoa were 'world ports', central to a trading system that stretched from Beijing to Lima. The port of Naples served mainly for the importation of foodstuffs from Sicily and Puglia to feed its metropolitan population and immediate hinterland. In 1615 Naples was buying pepper from Livorno that had arrived from London. By then it was no longer the Mediterranean that sold spices to England and northern Europe, but spices arriving from London and Amsterdam that were now sold to the Mediterranean in the ports of Livorno, Naples and Istanbul.

By the mid-seventeenth century the cities of northern Italy had lost control of their commercial traffic; this was increasingly managed from London through the English merchant community established in the free port of Livorno. By the end of the seventeenth century virtually all of the sea-borne commercial traffic of the Kingdom of Naples was transported on English merchant ships. In the second half of the century the hegemony of English commerce in the Mediterranean, reinforced by the regular presence of the Royal Navy, supervised the structural undoing of the relationship between a commercial and industrial northern Italy and its complementary relationship to the agricultural south. Both the north, with its own commerce, cloth and silk industries subordinated to the needs of London and the emerging English textile industry, and the agricultural south were equally transformed into sources for primary materials for the markets and merchandising of northern Europe and the Atlantic seaboard. By 1680 the conditions of the 'Southern Question' – economic underdevelopment, social backwardness and cultural isolation from northern Italy – had been established, not so much via the Spanish domination of the Kingdom of Naples, or north Italian 'progress' where capital once invested in sea-going ventures was now conserved in the security of land and revenue, as by English mercantile hegemony in the Mediterranean.[26]

Of course, the brutal clarity of such a picture needs also to be seeded with local conditions and contradictions. Against the stereotype of an agrarian south subordinated to an industrial north, it is worthwhile recalling that the first Italian railway line was opened in 1839, running from Naples to Nocera, followed four years later by the Naples–Caserta line. It is not by chance that the building that now houses the national Railway Museum, where from 1842 onwards engines and railway stock were both built and repaired, is located at Pietrarsa on the outskirts of Naples. In 1861 the Pietrarsa works were also the site of the first spontaneous workers' assembly in Italy, resulting in seven deaths and twenty wounded when troops were called in to break it up. The 'industrialised' north, heavily financed by southern resources redistributed after 1860 through a newly centralised state, only really acquired shape after national unification when the hegemony of northern politics as much as 'economic' factors played a major role in configuring its development.

The more immediate woes of postwar Naples are invariably sought in the Allied occupation of the city, and the subsequent flourishing of the black market, contraband and organised crime. But these phenomena populated wartime landscapes all over Europe: from London to Berlin. More suggestive, as has already been noted, is the US-sponsored deployment of organised crime and compromised political and juridical hierarchies in order to ensure local order. This was indeed one of the more disquieting symptoms of a cynical postwar settlement. Similarly, the decision to establish both the south European headquarters of NATO, as well as that of the United States Sixth Fleet, in Naples was the most visible confirmation of United States hegemony in the postwar world of Italy, western Europe and the 'free' world. So, Naples found itself directly inserted in the national settlement Washington imposed and sustained via the hegemony of the Christian Democrat Party, the conservatism of the Catholic Church, and the strategic wartime revival and deployment of organised crime. Pre-existing modalities of power, whether drawn from the camorra or from the local oligarchy such as Achille Lauro (one-time Fascist functionary, as well as future mayor and overseer of the corrupt 'hands on the city' of the postwar boom), were reinstalled, just as the national state apparatuses returned to work largely unaltered from the experience of Fascism.

It was as though Fascism was a historical accident, an unfortunate interlude, in an altogether deeper and more democratic narrative. The illusions we live by, however, have a cost, sometimes an extremely high one. To blithely reduce twenty years of Fascist government composed in racial laws, authoritarian populism, savage colonialism, war crimes, and the suspension of parliamentary democracy, to a temporary aberration is also to avoid confronting the sources of its popularity and the possibility of its return. Unlike Germany, Italy experienced no Nuremberg Trials, and, apart from some summary executions by the partisans in the dying months of the war, no official war crimes were recognised, either at home or in the once-occupied territories of the Balkans, north and east Africa. A new constitution was installed, but the state bureaucracy, its personnel and institutions remain unaltered; there was apparently no need for radical revision.

The old order remained fundamentally intact, the prewar hierarchy, now seemingly purged of its Fascist parvenus, returned. Treated as an historical exception, the cultural and historical sense of Fascism, together with the disturbing testimony of Italy's longer-standing colonial empire (all those planes, concentration camps, aerial bombing and gas attacks on civilian targets in Ethiopia and Libya), was evacuated, abandoned to the dead landscape of the past; now a closed chapter. Yet the invention of Fascism as a political and cultural settlement did not fall out of the sky; and if initially it was violently asserted, it was also popularly sanctified and sustained. For Fascism was also the moment of a publicly orchestrated modernity. One only has to look at the architecture in Piazza Matteotti around Naples' main post office. Once the eye overcomes the blunt, neo-classical imperial rhetoric of the police headquarters and local government buildings, there is the remarkable curvilinear post office with its illuminated digital clock offering the time in Roman numerals, complete with the inscription announcing its completion in the 'XIV year of the Fascist Era'. The Piazza is surrounded by the then contemporary residential blocks topped off by the same interrupted apex that Philip Johnson was to stick on top of the AT&T Building in New York fifty years later. All of this has something to do with the nature of democracy; not so much with its institutional rhetoric as with its presence, or its absence, in everyday life. It has also to do with the cultural attraction of secular authoritarianism, with rhetorical representations of 'progress', and with a deeply embedded idealism intent on rendering its will explicit. Has contemporary Italian culture really come to terms with all this? Has modernity?

In a confessional culture, any crime, no matter how horrific, can ultimately be forgiven. No one is everlastingly damned. The transgression is not contested but absorbed. Forgiveness is further reinforced and extended through the pervasive creed of the family. With the weakness and sometimes absence of state institutions, the family becomes a primordial cultural and economic unit (and it is but a short step to extend this understanding to wider family networks and the 'clan' in both its legal and illegal variants). This encourages the emergence of parallel structures – both voluntary and illegitimate – that supplant public forms of solidarity. In this context, the counter-institutions of favours, corruption and crime – from street life to political patronage – become constitutive components of public life. To understand such phenomena is to acknowledge their structural formation; they are not simply 'exceptions', a few rotten apples in the barrel, but rather symptoms of a series of historical and cultural modalities. This is not merely a moral question; for those who do not accept the logic inevitably pay in economic and political terms, and sometimes directly with their lives; it is, above all, a profoundly historical issue with everyday consequences that sometimes stretch to include the political undoing of the legitimacy of democracy itself. To be cunning and cheat is not only to outwit another; it might also mean to cheat on oneself and reduce the fragile circumstances of liberty for everyone.

The problem of the mafia, organised crime, institutionalised corruption and the systematic abuse of power is the problem of the state and its particular historical and cultural formation. It is also important to recall here that, despite all the media drama surrounding the Sicilian mafia and the Neapolitan camorra, in the 1990s the real centre of corruption and the criminal exercise of political power was Milan. Yet once again, however dramatically focused such questions have been in Italy's recent political past and present, and no matter how easy it is to touch such 'corruption' in one's daily life, is this merely an Italian question? In considering the Machiavellian promotion of power and personal interests by whatever means, we should perhaps also be willing to turn the gaze elsewhere and consider the pervasive corruption of the lexicon of 'democracy' and 'freedom' in the increasingly media-directed rhetoric throughout the western world.

Mediterranean … Subterranean

May 2002 and I find myself on the second floor of the National Archaeological Museum gazing at the maps, the objects and the photographs of Kirghisistan; nomadic cultures from the Asiatic steppes, where history was made on horseback. On the floors beneath me, lining the corridors, filling up the rooms, are the artistic triumphs of Rome: huge-limbed statues and exquisite mosaics that decorated the urban lives of Pompeii and Herculaneum before it was all abruptly stifled by volcanic gas, ashes, boiling mud and lava. Here, in the suggestive sparseness of the exhibition devoted to the dwellers of the grasslands of central Asia, there are only the traces of what has been deposited by a few, privileged members of a steppe society in their burial mounds. The daily life of the nomad passed like the wind, leaving barely a trace. Only the millennium tracks of anonymous pastoral movement and seasonal migration add contemporary testimony to the chronicled passages of peoples arriving from the East. Downstairs the accumulation of an imperial domus that stretched outwards to incorporate the world, while here among the jewels and the ceremonial masks the only fixed point that is acknowledged when travelling beneath an endless sky is death. Yet, if, as Bruce Chatwin argued, nomadism is the crank handle of history, there lies in this intriguing proximity all the seeds of our time.

In 1287, Rabban Sauma, a Nestorian monk sent to Europe by the Mongols, witnessed from a rooftop a sea battle between the Neapolitans and the Aragonese.[27] Sauma had been sent by Ilkan Arghun, then Mongolian ruler of Iran, Iraq, Afghanistan and southern Russia. Arghun was the grandson of Hülegü, who in the 1250s conquered Persia, the Arab Middle East and destroyed the sect of the Assassins in their mountain fortress the 'Eagle's Nest' at Alamüt near the Caspian Sea. Hülegü, in turn, was brother to Qubilai Khan, and both were grandsons of Chingiz Khan. Sauma's account was written in Persian, but it has come down to us in an abridged Syriac translation. From the Mongolian empire to a Mediterranean city: orbits of influence and the unexpected overlapping of worlds that here seem strangely more immediate in their fluidity than those subsequently imposed via the rigid frontiers of a subsequent Western modernity.

Such unexpected subterranean links provide another cartography in which the sense of the city is no longer restricted to the strict environs of a single culture and place. Deposited in its language, in its fluctuating and indefinite space, are a multitude of traces that haunt

---

27 David Morgan, *The Mongols* (Oxford: Blackwell, 1999), 188.

28 Walter Benjamin, 'The Work of Art in the Age of Mechanical Reproduction', in *Illuminations*, trans. Harry Zohn (London: Fontana, 1973), 242–3.

29 Neal Ascherson, *Black Sea: The Birthplace of Civilisation and Barbarism* (New York: Vintage, 1996).

the official narrative with other stories, further openings and interrogations. We could leave the museum and go underground, either to take the subway to the central railway station and then the light rail to Herculaneum and Pompeii, or else dally underground in the subway stations themselves. The latter are themselves the unlikely locus of unexpected encounters. Their obvious functionality has been overlaid and transformed by modern art.

Descending the steps of the Museo station designed by Gae Aulenti, and passing the photographs by Mimmo Iodice, Fabio Donato, Antonio Biasiucci, Raffaele Mariniello and Luciano D'Alessandro that evoke the multiple memories of the city, I take a one-stop ride to Piazza Dante. Riding the escalator up to street level (the station is also by Gae Aulenti) I pass the conceptual art works of Joseph Kosuth, Jannis Kounellis, Michangelo Pistoletto, Nicola De Maria and Carlo Alfano. The sternness of Kounellis' *arte povera* – an untitled giant steel wall embossed with shoes and other objects clamped down and crushed beneath girders – contrasts with the twenty-metre coloured mosaic by Nicola De Maria entitled: 'A universe without bombs, kingdom of flowers, seven red angels (in memory of Francesco De Maria)'. Other stations offer other works: Sol Le Witt and Sandro Chia at Materdei; the sculptures of Mimmo Paladino, Augusto Perez, Perino e Vele, Lello Esposito and Raffaella Nappo at Salvator Rosa; the light box of Betty Bee and the massive metallic panels of Umberto Manzo at Cilea. The stations themselves are frequently also architectural/artistic works in their own right. The public that passes through these spaces each day is no doubt 'an absent-minded' examiner (Walter Benjamin), but if the movement of art and the art of movement here becomes temporarily indistinguishable it also gives rise to a metropolitan event that is irreducible to either transport or aesthetics.[28]

If it is Christmas, I could continue to stroll in this open-air gallery by wandering down Via Toledo from Piazza Dante to Piazza Plebiscito. On the way I would pass on my left side the permanent thirty-metre-high 'windmill' by Kounellis in the small square by the Feltrinelli bookshop, and then at Piazza Plebiscito find an arresting example of contemporary art. Between December 2002 and January 2003, Piazza Plebiscito hosted a Rebecca Horn installation composed of numerous skulls emerging from the paving stones, at night a trapeze of overhead neon illuminated these ghostly visitors. The Neapolitan cult of the dead, a paganism that has been sustained in the Catholic catacombs of the Fontanella where traditionally one adopted and polished one of the thousands of skulls, together with the mortal insistence of baroque aesthetics, are conjoined and displayed in a modernist art installation: the city returns to itself in order to go elsewhere.

Since the early 1990s, every Christmas Piazza Plebiscito has witnessed an installation by a noted contemporary artist: Paladino, Kounellis, Kapoor, Horn, Serra. Like the skulls emerging out of the ground, the presence of art in public space has provoked debate, dissent and discussion where previously there only reigned a public silence. Probably not since the baroque period and the artistic exhibitionism encouraged by the Counter-Reformation and its struggle to reclaim public space and private consent has art become such a civic presence and concern in the life of the city. It has rendered altogether more explicit the subterranean impulses behind the *Terrie Motes* exhibition of international artists (Polanski, Buys, Gilbert and George, Kiefer, Haring, Mapplethorpe, Paladin, Rauschenberg, Richter, Stefano, Tomboy, Warhol, among others) put together by the curator Lucio Amelio in the wake of the earthquake of November 1980 that shook Naples and the Campania area. In these times, where contemporary art is increasingly accredited solely through being evaluated in the international art market, this public sponsorship, even if it may frequently only confirm such recognition, draws such works out of the secluded spaces of the art gallery, the collector's living room and the specialist review. In the return to a public space, such art escapes its increasingly exclusive location in the commercial art circuit. As an object, or better as an event and an experience to be 'consumed' in non-financial terms, the work comes to accommodate desires and directions that are both stem from, and exceed, what Walter Benjamin once referred to as a 'market-orientated originality'.

Migrating modernities

'All human populations are in some sense immigrants. All hostility between different cultures in one place has an aspect of the classic immigrant grudge against the next boatload approaching the shore. To defend one's home and fields and ancestral graves against invasion seems a right. But to claim unique possession – to compound the fact of settlement with the aspect of a landscape into an abstract of eternal and immutable ownership – is a joke.'
Neal Ascherson, *Black Sea*[29]

Naples is a port city. Historically, like every major port, it has witnessed the arrival of diverse peoples and cultures. Some took up residence in the city, others passed through; all have left their traces: from the Arabs, Normans, Angevins, Genoans, Pisans and Catalans of the Middle Ages, through the Spanish and French to the Anglo-American invasion of 1943 and the contemporary harbour chock-a-block with cruise ships. Until recently set off from the city by a barrier, in recent years the port has been opened up to become the visual and physical extension of Piazza Municipio. Standing in the square in front of the town hall, the eye is pulled across to the harbour, its ships and traffic, to the twin white towers of the passenger terminal of 1936, before coming to rest on the peak of Vesuvius. The square, dominated on the land side by the gardens and building of the town hall, flanked to the west by the massive moated Angevin castle, and to the east by the imposing nineteenth-century building that once housed the Hotel de Londres, is now complemented by the open flank of the sea. The pedestrian and mechanical traffic that previously paralleled the hidden harbour, the sea and the horizon, is now intersected by this axis.

This symbolic complication underlines the fundamental, if often repressed, history of the port in the social composition of the city, its hinterland and southern Italy in general. Movement in and out of the port stretches over two millennium, and it is a movement that has not escaped the dramatic urgency that characterises modern migration. Just before crossing the road to enter the port itself there is a more modern high-rise building. Its red-brick style betrays construction in the 1950s, no doubt to replace buildings destroyed by Allied and German bombing. The building is topped by advertising hoardings announcing the offices of the Italian Slav and Ukrainian associations. Such a skyline acknowledgement of migration from the steppes of southern Russian and eastern Europe (often qualified women now being employed in domestic service) is, of course, only the most obvious signal of an altogether vaster movement. In fact, the largest transplanted community in Naples today is composed of migrants from Sri Lanka – overwhelmingly men who desperately seek in their free time to practise their cricket in the town's squares on summer nights until the police arrive to declare the game over.

30 Alessandro Dal Lago, *Lo straniero e il nemico.* (Genova: Costa & Nolan, 1998), 12.

31 Giorgio Agamben, *Homo Sacer: Sovereign Power and Bare Life* (Stanford, CA: Stanford University Press, 1998).

The arrival of the immigrant announces an historical and cultural caesura that is invariably resisted, rarely considered in its complex resonances with local realities and therefore never fully elaborated in a fresh cultural and political perspective. Most obviously, present migrancy – whether 'illegal' or not – invites the comparison and compassion evoked by the earlier migration of millions of Italians overseas. Both moments reveal a wider, ultimately worldly, context that invites us to consider the earlier migration of the poor and the desperate in the vivid light of contemporary migration from the Third World.

The unknown character and alterity of the stranger, the distrust of the 'homeless', the undocumented and the migrant, evokes the potential disturbance of a 'deviancy' that overflows local coordinates of belonging as well as the policed perimeters of a 'national' home and people. The foreigner is, above all, considered a potential enemy; his or her presence represents the simultaneous threat to, and reinforcement of, the present state through introducing a 'them' against which 'we' measure ourselves. The modern migrant draws the unrecognised into the field of vision. The arrival of the stranger poses the paradoxical political formation of the state when national rights are constituted explicitly on the negation of the rights of others; to be included, others have to be excluded. In the passage from the violent authoritarianism of the seemingly exceptional state of Nazism and the concentration camp to the 'normal' insistence on the preservation of national and local identities there emerges a harrowing proximity that many of us would prefer to ignore. Faced with immigration, the state of emergency – with its controls, permits, camps and deportations – reveals itself to be permanent. As the Italian sociologist Alessandro Dal Lago justly points out, nation states do not recognise the universal rights of mankind, only those of its citizens.[30] In the daily surveillance of frontiers, documents and identities, the state remains deaf to appeals to human rights. Such rights are explicitly denied in the name of national laws, and implicitly negated through defence of the imagined bio-political unity of a homogeneous 'people' and its citizenship. Those excluded are consigned to the incidental and indifferent category of what Giorgio Agamben calls 'bare life'.[31] All citizens are human, but not all humans are citizens.

The migrant, as the persistent reminder of altogether more unruly 'globalisation' than that proposed in official rhetoric, suggests far more than a political interrogation of the paranoid nature of the modern state. The very sense of 'our' culture and history, and the institutional tendency to elaborate such concepts through principles of exclusion and ethnic exclusivity, is increasingly challenged by a configuration that surpasses existing explanations. The modern phenomenon of mass migration is a perpetual reminder that the liberal rhetoric of the free movement of goods, capital and bodies has very real cultural, historical and political consequences; consequences that certainly exceed such idealised settlements as the 'melting pot' or 'multiculturalism'. The physical presence of the migrant stubbornly insists that the world in its extreme diversity and complexity is indeed global, unified, one. In this sense, the migrant undoes our 'self'. The uninvited guest exposes our (arbitrary) rules of conduct and, in insisting on staying, drags into the light the ignored premises upon which such rules depend for their authority. No longer external, but internal, the foreigner, the stranger, the immigrant, like the space between our words – silent but essential for meaning – becomes integral, central, to another conception of the world we all inhabit.

Inherited terms of reference – the state, the nation, the law, the people – are now revealed to be without stable or permanent foundation. Hence the arbitrary violence that their questioning unleashes; a structural brutality that irrupts into our world in the steps of the migrant. Fearful reactions, fuelled by the resentment of being forced to face one's own troubled history in a perspective that can no longer exclude the stranger, the foreigner, can rapidly lead to popular hysteria and the apocalyptical announcements of an immigration 'emergency'. The fear of being 'flooded' and 'invaded' – even though the actual numbers of illegal immigrants in Italy is rather low by European standards – suffocates wider reasoning in a provincial rage. Such fearful anger invariably falls back on the murderous defence of rigid localisms, and everywhere is endorsed by the exclusionary logic of the modern state. In this situation the migrant is already 'framed' prior to his or her arrival, positioned in a public discourse whose reasons and conclusions powerfully constrain his movement and her possibilities. This is not merely about the marshalling of existing stereotypes, although that reservoir of 'common sense' certainly participates in the subsequent identification and legitimating of the 'problem'. It is rather in the performative realisation of the question through the politically sensitised power of media coverage (which includes both popular outbursts and expert opinion), in the orchestration of public and political debate, which constructs the immigrant as a 'problem'. But this 'emergency' is not constituted by immigration – itself the product and generator of 'our' modernity – but by xenophobia; for it is 'we' who feel ourselves the 'victims' and who are in many ways the real problem.

This excursus serves to remind us of the extensive sweep of mass migration, both in terms of the numbers and the diversity of cultures, histories and 'homes', involved along the whole arc of modernity: from chained, black slaves boarding European ships in the Gulf of Guinea to those driven by poverty and hope drowning today in the Mediterranean. With this in mind, the port of Naples, and the city itself, proposes a site of both past and present migrant passages that continue to intercede and interrogate the present.

In front of Piazza Municipio and dominating the port is the white, twin-towered, modernist passenger terminal. It was completed in 1936, in the heyday of Fascism. It would be tempting to treat this building as material witness to the massive migration that saw millions of Italian men, women and children depart for another life in the Americas from the 1870s onwards. But that would be a myth. Restrictive legislation in the United States (the draconian Quota Acts of 1921 and 1924) fearful of 'aliens' diluting its 'white' Anglo stock, together with Fascist disapproval of the very idea of abandoning the 'homeland', had already closed the classical chapter in the history of Italian migration towards 'Merica'. The more immediate connotations of the gleaming passenger terminal are to be found along the palm-lined avenues leading westwards out of the city to the Mostra d'Oltremare (Overseas Exhibition Centre): the architectural signature of a barely acknowledged imperial past that led to the proclamation of the Empire in 1936.

Here our gaze is drawn into the folds of the deeply repressed history of an Italian imperial and colonial past, and the official attempts to conquer 'a place in the sun' from the 1880s onwards: Eritrea, Ethiopia, Somalia, Libya (and then Rhodes, Albania, Yugoslavia and Greece). Although structurally negated, this history has inevitably had a significant impact on the formation of Italian modernity. This, of course, is the case throughout the West; although it exists in a profoundly repressed register, modernity is in many ways *the* colonial moment. The sculptured decorations on the front of the passenger terminal evoke the global reach of navigation stretching out from the Neapolitan seafront to embrace the world: Rome, Athens, Cairo, east Africa, New York, Calcutta and Rio de Janeiro; once connected by the imperial

32 Piero Bevilacqua, 'Società rurale e emigrazione', in *Storia dell'Emigrazione Italiana*, eds. Piero Bevilacqua, Andreina De Clementi and Emilio Franzina (Rome: Donzelli, 2001).

33 Ernesto De Martino, *La fine del mondo. Contribuito all'analisi delle apocalissi culturali* (Turin: Einaudi, 2002).

34 Paul Gilroy, *Postcolonial Melancholia* (New York: Columbia University Press, 2005).

galleys of the Roman empire, today by the modern ocean-going steamship and the airplane. It is but a short step from colonial 'reason' to the elaboration of the modern metropolis. In both cases the territory is catalogued, defined and dominated in order to be possessed by 'progress'. The 1936 proclamation of the Empire was the final chapter in a persistent series of colonising expeditions in Africa and the Mediterranean. It was only in the postwar period that a new, but altogether more minor, boom towards both North and South America and Australia would take place, involving mainly skilled and intellectual labour, and increasingly travelling by jet plane rather than steam ship.

Migration is deeply entwined in the making of modern Italy, touching every corner of the peninsula. Money earned abroad was sent home, and eventually more than twelve million migrants also returned to their villages of origin. The radical uprooting from a local, rural culture, and dramatic relocation to an urban environment constructed in another language, was neither necessarily permanent nor always endurable. Peasants from southern Italy often had their first sustained experience of the city in New York or Buenos Aires, rather than in Naples, Rome or Milan. In an age before mass communications and mass literacy, the eventual journey for those crowded into unsafe and unsanitary ships was altogether further than the actual physical distance of Naples from New York might suggest.

This, again, is a classical, almost stereotypical passage, frequently explored in the New World male bonding and mean streets of Martin Scorsese's films; but there was also a significant migration from rural-to-rural society, as in the case of Brazil and Argentina. After 1900, the major source of Italian emigration shifted to the south and Naples become the principal port of departure. 1913 was the peak year of transatlantic migration, with more than 200,000 migrants departing through the port. In the city itself, the poor peasants, with their bundles and cardboard suitcases would already be considered 'foreigners' by the Neapolitans themselves. Prior to boarding they would have to run the hostile gauntlet of unsavoury hostels, unscrupulous shipping agents, and a savvy street population of hawkers, crooks and urchins ready to feed on their disorientation while they waited, horded up on the quays, exposed to the elements, for the ship's arrival.

Italian emigration was only part of a far wider wave – Irish, English, German, Scottish, Spanish, Polish, Greek, Russian, Norwegian, Swedish – of European emigration, particularly towards the Americas, that characterised the second half of the nineteenth century and the opening decades of the twentieth. In fact, the number of those emigrating from Britain and Italy in the same period was roughly the same, but whereas the former overwhelmingly emigrated to a shared linguistic and cultural community, whether in North America or the 'white' colonies of the British Empire (Australia, New Zealand, South Africa), the Italians moved to a decidedly 'foreign' environment destined to encourage nostalgia for 'home' and national community building abroad.

Emigration from Italy was provoked by a generalised European agricultural crisis that included plant diseases and, above all, the fall in prices provoked by cheap wheat being rapidly imported from the prairies of North and South America, Australia and southern Russian. Added to this were the more immediate difficulties induced by the hereditary division of property, fiscal pressure, poor soil and the growing demand for cash exchange. It all added to an increasingly unstable rural world, further undermined by the decline in cottage industries now unable to compete with cheaper factory production. This, in turn, led to changed perceptions of everyday life and its eventual possibilities. The rural world was never fully autonomous, and now, more than ever, it experienced the ingression of external forces and possibilities, increasingly represented by questions of capital and cash, together with the largely uncontrolled velocity introduced by mechanisation and modern transport.[32]

The unwinding of an earlier rural society produced an emerging interchange with a far wider world that did not necessarily speak Italian or acknowledge Europe as its homeland, or Catholicism as its religion. When such emigration was also accompanied by a subsequent return in significant numbers to the region of origin then, and only probably then, did regional peasants become 'Italians'. In the postwar period such complex cultural itineraries were further intensified and concentrated in migration to northern Europe and the massive 'internal' migration to the northern industrial belt of Milan and Turin that characterised the economic 'boom', of the late 1950s and early 1960s; swelling major urban centres, it involved more than nine million Italians. Peasants from Lucana, working in the Alfa Romeo factory, dreaming of their lost village life and clinging to familial ties in the midst of urban indifference: this is the turbulent setting so dramatically evoked in Luchino Visconti's *Rocco and His Brothers* (1960).

By 1960 it also becomes possible to register the closing of European emigration – between 1945 and 1960 some six million British, Dutch, German and Italians emigrated towards the Americas and Australia – and the simultaneous growth of immigration from the 'Third World' towards the northern hemisphere; initially towards the 'Mother Country' of a dying colonialism, and then more simply towards the overdeveloped world. Three decades later, Italy, once a country of emigration, was becoming a country of immigration. In the subsequent decade, two shared histories come together to shadow and interrogate each other as the fate of yesterday's migrating poor – *la povera gente* – is increasingly overtaken by outbursts of xenophobia and an increasingly rigid immigration legislation. The sea, yesterday the Atlantic, today the Mediterranean, continues to give up its dead. Yet they are still far too few who are willing to listen to the ghosts that testify to the links in a migrant chain that stretches from Africa 500 years ago to the beaches of southern Italy today, girding together the hidden, yet essential, history of modern migration. The denial of a memory evoked by the interrogative presence of the migrant is also the failure to consider one's own past, and its place in the constitution of the present. According to the great Italian anthropologist Ernesto De Martino, emigration was considered as the critical equivalent of death amongst the southern peasantry.[33] Such a death and departure into another life has perhaps yet to be mourned in a manner – that is worked through and elaborated – that clears a space in the present for the living.[34] This latter possibility would transform mere negation, an absolute loss, into the potential acquisition of a further sense in which your home is no longer necessarily constructed on the denial of a home for the other.

Since the beginning of the 1990s, public discourse in Italy has increasingly been concerned with the 'immigration problem'. The tone is usually alarmist, if not apocalyptical, and has now acquired much political presence in the organisation of right-wing political consensus. The dramatic arrival of 'illegal' immigrants – often rescued from overcrowded and sinking hulks, not to speak of the hundreds, probably thousands who have anonymously drowned – is something that is publicly denounced while privately absorbed in order to meet the growing requirements of the work force: from child and old people minders through domestic service to agricultural labour and skilled factory work. It will be these very same workers, once officially 'recognised', whose taxes will fund the pension schemes and health

35 Hannah Arendt, *The Origins of Totalitarianism* (London: Harcourt Brace Jovanovich, 1973).

36 Benjamin, 'Theses on the Philosophy of History' (see note 28), 255–66.

services of an increasingly ageing native population. In the wake of radical morphological changes in urban culture brought about by immigration from the Third World, there has also been discussion, usually in less bitter accents, of the development of a multicultural society, of the hybridisation of cultural styles and languages and an emerging métissage world. This latter phenomenon, however, even when it is not viewed through a fearful lens, is invariably treated as something of recent origin, and certainly of no major importance in the historical formation of modern Italy. As opposed to the United States, Britain or France, Italy officially represents itself as having never participated directly in the imperial sacking of the world, although it was clearly supportive of the racist slavery, colonial greed and authoritarian imperialism practised by others. The spectres of this particular history that every so often returns to disrupt the urban scenes of Los Angeles, London or Paris are not considered to be a part of the national narrative.

Or, rather, that is the story that continues to circulate, both in the popular medium of common sense as well as in the institutional versions of the native culture. Yet Italy is also part of occidental modernity; its famed espresso coffee, its ubiquitous tomatoes, not to speak of the richness of its baroque architecture (and Naples is a *summa* of all three), are the explicit fruits of its participation in the colonial epoch. More obviously, there were the imperial projects pursued in eastern and North Africa, first by the liberal state and then under Fascism. The palms that line so many roads and parks are not 'native'; they symbolise the 'overseas' dream that was eventually shattered with the defeat of Fascism. As Hannah Arendt noted, the modern, metropolitan interior was composed through imperial exploitation elsewhere.[35] Every time one drinks coffee (or tea) there is the unconscious confirmation of five centuries of global 'progress' inaugurated by an Italian navigator setting foot in the New World. Similarly, yesterday's emigrant who left Naples aboard a ship bound for Buenos Aires and today's immigrant who sets out from Sri Lanka to be abandoned on a beach in Puglia are separated in time but unified in a shared history.

This colonial and immigrant past is, of course, the site of a collective refusal to remember. In the public imaginary, colonialism, imperialism, the mass European migration of yesterday and the global Third World migration of today continue to evoke only a series of marginal and discrete narratives. Yesterday's colonialism and mass emigration remain in quarantine, locked up in the sepia tones of a fading past; they are rarely permitted to bear directly on a sense of the national culture, its 'problems' and the quotidian structures of its everyday life. It is easier and more comfortable to forget: after all, this is the limitless lesson of modernity continually intent on ushering in tomorrow; that our electricity, our richness and power are also someone else's darkness, poverty and powerlessness barely has time to register in the onward rush of 'progress'. Yet the 'modernity' that a language, a literature, a culture, a history reveals can never be considered simply autonomous or autochthonous. In this sense we are always already global citizens, and live in conditions where no culture, whether national or local, can ever pretend to separate its sense and formation from the surrounding world. The traffic between cultures and histories, however much it may be resisted and denied, is the very basis of our modernity. It is such a worldly location, frequently buried within a 'colonial unconscious', that today provides the critical key to remembering and retelling the histories that our culture and our very selves have repressed.

Interesting, you might say, but what has this really got to do with Italy, the Mediterranean, and Naples in particular? Very simply it is to suggest that a culture, a history, a sense of one's self, that ignores the complex and disquieting making of modernity has chosen a path that is destined to remain imprisoned in the thickets of provincialism and the deathly verdicts of a moribund historicism. Of course, each and every culture seeks to impose a homogeneous vision of its past. Neapolitan culture is no exception; it, too, as we saw in the monumental presence of '1799', continues to propose the self-assurance of its own historicised myths, even those myths that evoke disaster, defeat and the ultimate stasis of death.

Each and every culture seeks to impose a consensual and hegemonic vision of its past. Even if delineated in the melancholy tones of defeat, such a framing of the past permits a rapid and rational comprehension of the contemporary state of affair and, subsequently, of proposed 'solutions'. Formal education and the mass media here combine in multiple ways to 'discipline' national and local understandings of one's past and present, and in this sense all histories and literatures tend inevitably towards a static sense of self-confirmation. Here, as a sombre reminder, it is worthwhile recalling Walter Benjamin's decisive phrase: 'There is no document of civilisation which is not at the same time a document of barbarism.'[36] The problem, of course, is that even if this disciplined repression of the past were to be recognised, cultural closure would continue to be popularly enforced in the name of national unity and cultural autonomy. The very idea of welcoming the interrogations that emerge from a repressed complexity, and to propose a polyphonic sense of the creolised cultures, literatures and languages that pass under the presumed homogeneity of modernity, remains *unrecognisable* in the existing framing of the world. Each and every culture would have to let go, unlearn itself and become a little less narcissistic as it rethought its formation in the wider, worldly and altogether more fragile constellation of a multilateral modernity.

And yet, walking the streets around Piazza Garibaldi near the central railway station, that other modernity is encountered in every step I take, in every voice I hear, in every street sign I observe. In Via Bologna, the shops' owners are Arab or African, there are also some Chinese outlets. Arab fast food – kebabs and falafels – is readily available. It is all very reminiscent of the Barbès district of Paris. But if the first language one hears here is also French, it is a French that arrives via the colonial routes of North and West Africa. The mix is not merely metropolitan – all occidental cities have their 'ethnic' communities – but now reaches into the furthest recesses of the shops themselves in a multinational collage in which local taste and foreign costume juggle for our attention in a display that wavers between ethnic kitsch and marketable exotica: Chinese foodstuffs and Italian pasta side by side on the same shelf; Native American dream weaver amulets, Hindu deities and leather goods from North Africa; counterfeited logo sports clothing; pirate software; 'Oriental' scarves; CDs and videocassettes, mainly from Egypt. Further down the street there is a sign in English indicating one of the city's many 'Phone Centers' offering cheap connections to the rest of the world: India 23 c, Ghana 20 c, Morocco 30 c, Ukraine 20 c, Senegal 20 c … In its imitations, its popular prices, its cosmopolitanism, this, too, is modernity.

This text was originally published in Iain Chambers, *Mediterranean Crossings: The Politics of an Interrupted Modernity* (Durham, NC: Duke University Press, 2008).

. Vele

Tobias Zielony

Vela Azzurra, 2010.
Credit: Tobias Zielony

Structure, 2010. Credit: Tobias Zielony

Mini-bike, 2010. Credit: Tobias Zielony

Pearl, 2010.
Credit: Tobias Zielony

Vela Rossa, 2010.
Credit: Tobias Zielony

Stairs, 2010.
Credit: Tobias Zielony

Corridor, 2010. Credit: Tobias Zielony

Sail, 2010. Credit: Tobias Zielony

Sail, 2010.
Credit: Tobias Zielony

Beam, 2010.
Credit: Tobias Zielony

The porous quarter: An experiment in combination

Marlene Lötsch

[1] Sophie Wolfrum and Alban Janson, *Die Stadt als Architektur* (Birkhäuser, 2019).

[2] Walter Benjamin and Asja Lacis, 'Naples', in Rexroth von Tillman, ed., *Gesammelte Schriften, Band IV* (Suhrkamp Verlag, 1991) (trans. provided by publisher).

The work takes as its starting point the concept of the porous city as classified and described as an urbanist principle by Sophie Wolfrum and Alban Janson in *The City as Architecture*.[1]

Based on the metaphor of porosity from Walter Benjamin and Asja Lacis in the essay *Naples* (1925), the urban space is presented here as a place of physical and social ambivalences:

'The architecture is as porous as its rock. Buildings and action merge into one another in courtyards, arcades and staircases. In everything, the room for development is preserved, enabling it to become the setting for new, unforeseen constellations. One avoids the definitive, the marked. No situation appears as it is, conceived for ever, no shape asserts its "this way and no other". This is how architecture, this most flush piece of communal rhythm, comes about here.'[2]

How can a (new) neighbourhood be conceived so that it can generate the qualities of a porous city and at the same time those of the expanded city in the urban space?

Such a newly conceived territory can only emerge in the space between the grown city and the periphery, because that is where both worlds meet and are thus connected with each other.

Ideal:

A neighbourhood with different densities of buildings and residents that alternate and balance each other out. If a pixel has a very high density of residents, its surroundings should be filled with a structure with a lower density of residents.

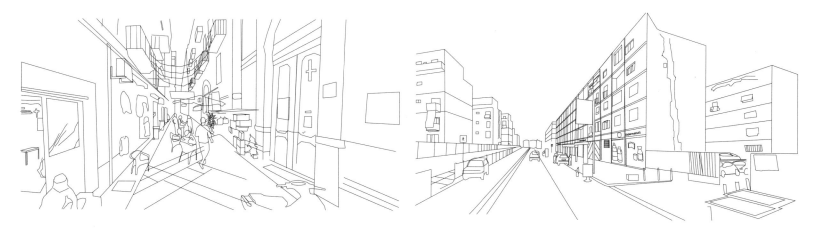

The porous street

Periphery

Project by Marlene Lötsch.
Design studio: *Grand Tour Italy* by Michael Obrist and Antonietta Putzu.
Summer semester 2019 at TU Wien.

First attempt:
Combining the pixel elements

Pixel Rione Cesare Battisti: Loosely built-up with wide spacing areas, nevertheless extremely high population density

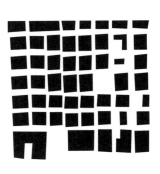

Pixel Quartieri Spagnoli: Extremely narrow, small street grid, high population density

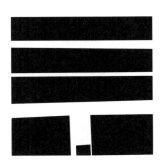

Pixel Centro Antico: Very high degree of urbanisation, high density of events and experiences

Pixel Vele di Scampia: Low building density per km² due to high building heights, high inhabitant density

First attempt:
Copy and combination
+ strong mixture
+ megastructure forms entrance to quarter
- difficult to link with other neighbourhoods

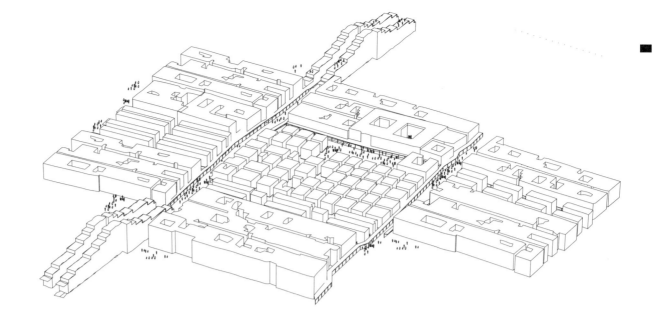

Second attempt:
Fill in, bring in public functions
+ Megastructure as link
+ interconnectable functions
- large scale
- small-scale structure only in the core

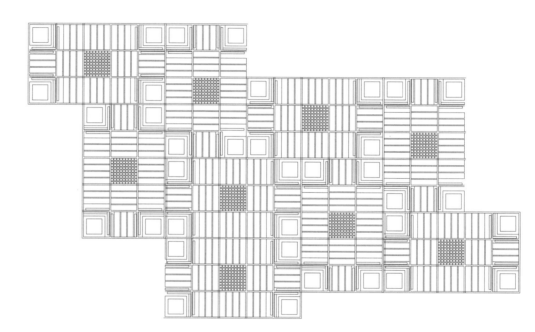

Third attempt:
Square fractal
+ all neighbourhoods with core or edge location to create spatial density along streets
- Megastructure can be merged
- large scale
- appears arbitrary

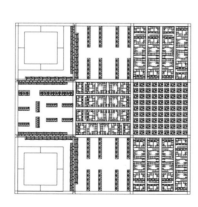
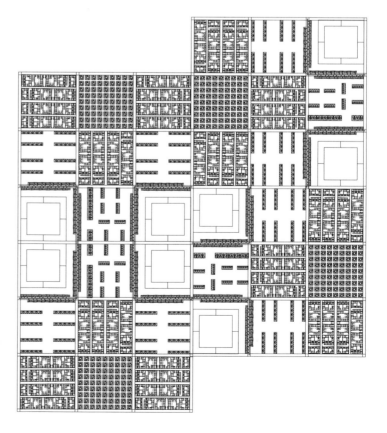

Fourth attempt:
Rectangular fractal
+ open edge zones with
  increasing density
+ megastructure spans road
+ different clashes
- scale too large
- public facility separated

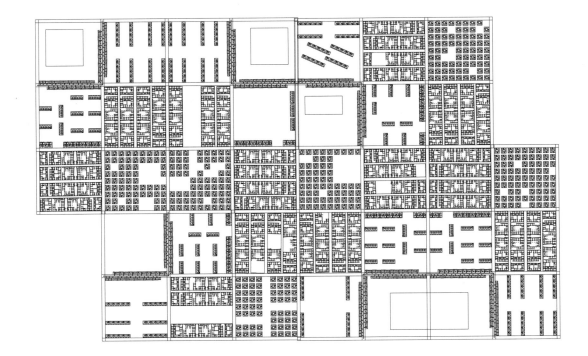

Fifth attempt:
Pixel
+ strong mixing
+ linear megastructure
+ exciting sequences
- Fractals result in random
  but purely formalistic
  structure

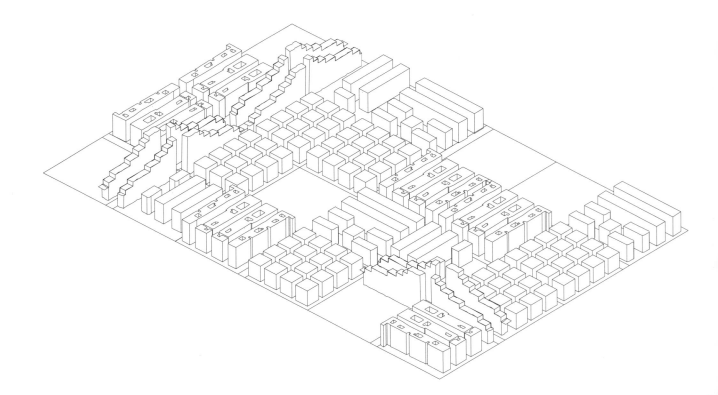

The porous district recombined

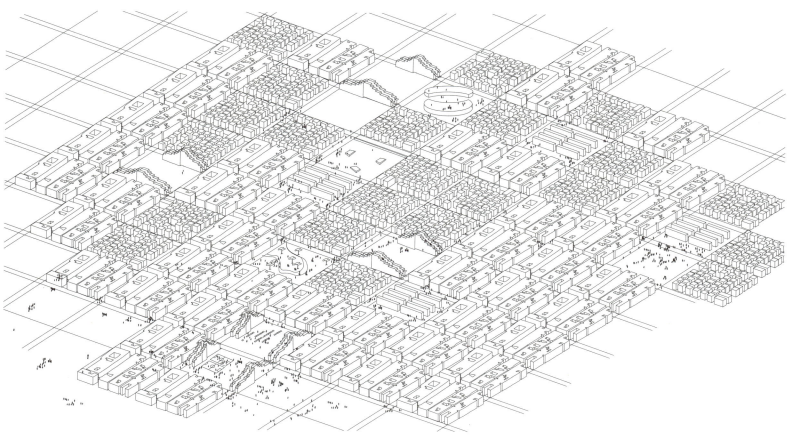

Axonometry of the porous district recombined

Great wall strategy.

Safety barrier strategy.

Strategies of prevention

Katrin Kirschner

Buildings without planning permission (*case abusive*) are not uncommon in Italy. With the construction of an illegal building, one saves both the tedious legal journey through the procedures of public administrations as well as a lot of money, since certain safety and building regulations do not have to be observed. Potentially lucrative but also questionable landscape spots serve as building sites; these may offer a beautiful view but harbour (hydro)geological hazard potential. For these cases, *condono* (clemency), the granting of subsequent building permission, is not an option. This is also the case in the *zona rossa* (red zone) around Mount Vesuvius in Naples, which will almost certainly be affected if the volcano erupts.

In that specific situation, how can a prevention and evacuation strategy be developed that goes beyond the officially known parameters?

In this work by Katrin Kirschner, these visions are presented in the form of vedutas following the typical historical representation of Naples, with Vesuvius in the background acting as a memento mori. The first part shows strategies for averting the damage of a volcanic eruption. In the second part, water is conceived as the last safe place and living strategies are devised away from the danger zone.

Project by Katrin Kirschner.
Design studio: *Grand Tour Italy* by Michael Obrist and Antonietta Putzu.
Summer semester 2019 at TU Wien.

Beach extension strategy: the illegal buildings often spread right up to the coast. Instead of demolition, it seems easier to expand the beach by 150 metres.

Emergency cruise ship strategy: short-term solution for shelter.

Rinascita Vele di Scampia 2.0 strategy: a new island of protection.

Islands

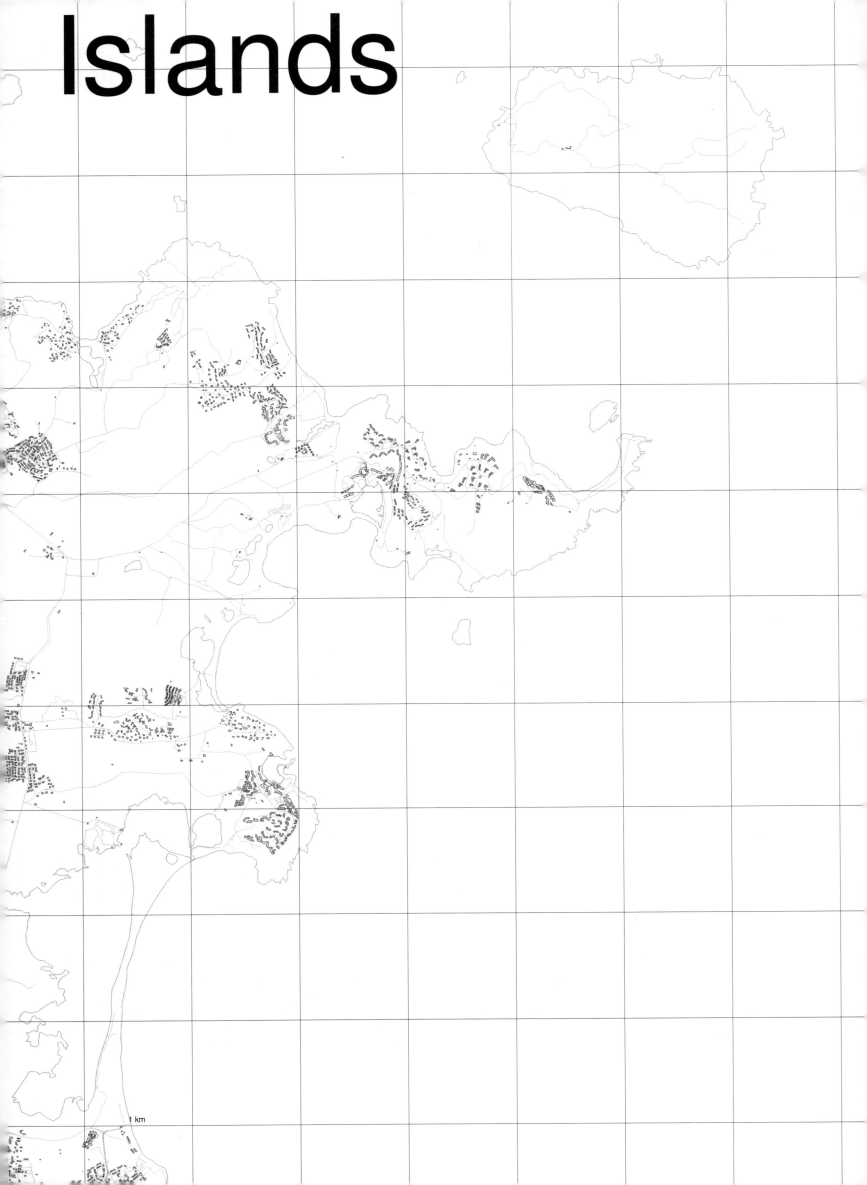

1 km

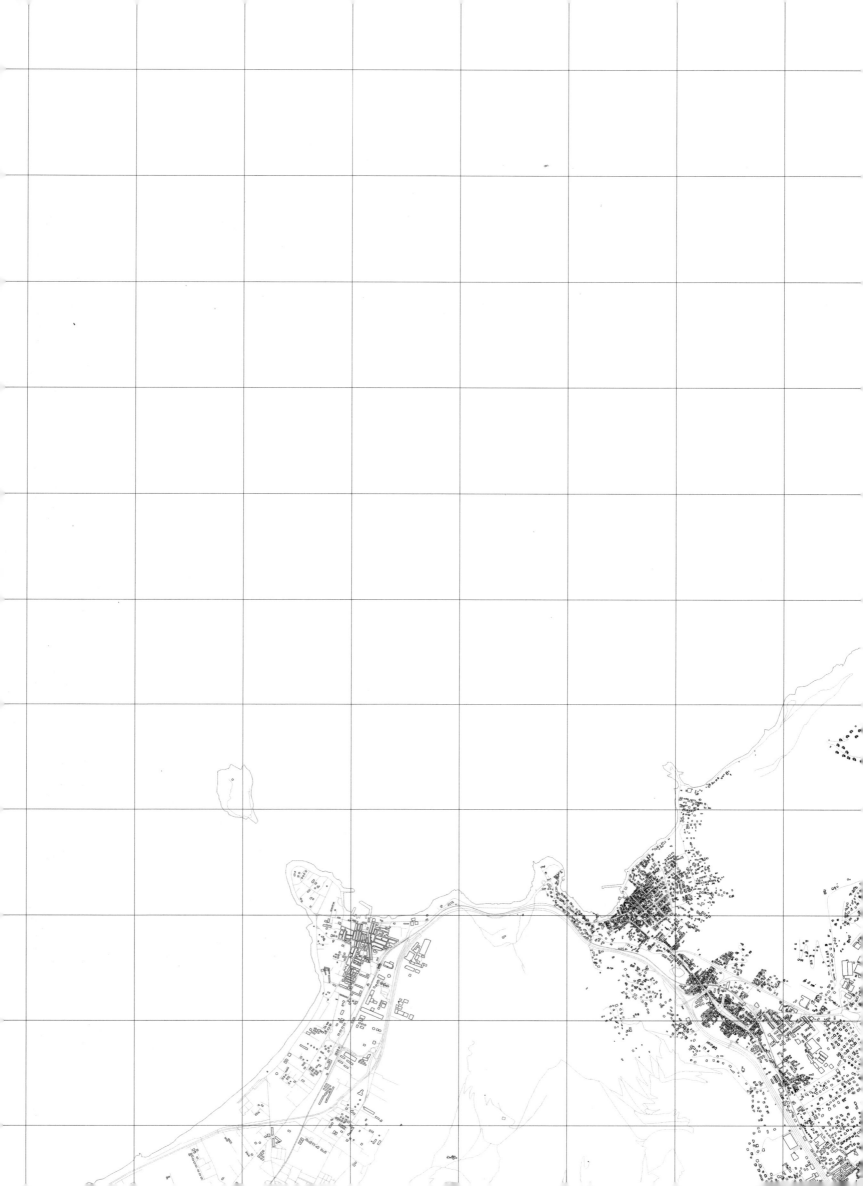

Housestories: Power

Berlusconi's Villa Certosa on Sardinia.

Scale: 1: 3000, aerial photo from 2012. Data: Italian Ministry for Environment, Land and Sea Protection

Emperor Tiberius' Villa Jovis on Capri.

Scale: 1: 3000, aerial photo from 2012. Data: Italian Ministry for Environment, Land and Sea Protection

. The Incompiuto manifesto

Alterazioni Video
Fosbury Architecture

Incompiuto Siciliano has been the key to interpreting public sector architecture in Italy since the Second World War. Its sheer scale, territorial extent and architectural oddness have made *Incompiuto Siciliano* essential to an understanding of Italy's history over the last forty years. The smugness of many Sicilian town councils has generated an architectural style that conveys the many-faceted nature of the culture that fostered it.

Unfinished projects are the ruins of modernity, monuments born of laissez-faire creative enthusiasm. In the years when positive economic sentiment and growth unexpectedly gave Italians financial peace of mind, imagination and exuberance were the driving forces behind a reconfiguration of the land. Landmarks in their own way, unfinished public buildings radiated out from Sicily to the rest of the peninsula, creating an unfinished Italy.

This work was originally published in Alterazioni Video/Fosbury Architecture, *Incompiuto: La nascita di uno Stile/The Birth of a Style* (Milan: Humboldt Books, 2018).

University residence, Oristano, Sardinia.

I. The Incompiuto Has Been the Leading Architectural Style in Italy Since the Second World War.
A revolution of the gaze that alters the perception of incomplete public works from negative to positive.

II. The Incompiuto Is Based on Its Own Ethics and Aesthetics.
In over forty years, the number of works on the Italian territory and their state of incompletion has given rise to an ideological programme independent of the wishes of planners.

III. The Incompiuto Resolves the Tension Between Form and Purpose. Its Lack of Purpose Becomes a Work of Art.
Works of public architecture bereft of function and utility become monuments open to the imagination.

IV. Unfinished Works Are Contemporary Ruins Generated by the Creative Enthusiasm of Liberalism.
Products of a compressed time, their postulate is the partial execution of the original project. They do not fall into ruin, but rather they rise into ruin.

V. The Incompiuto Redefines the Italian Landscape.
The incomplete public works celebrate the conquest of the territory by modern man. A bare-faced, determined and visceral colonisation that reflects an incomplete Italy.

VI. Nature Dialogues With the Works of the Incompiuto, Taking Back Control of Places.
Spontaneous vegetation colonises the surfaces, redefining the shapes. In these ruins, nature does away with history and transforms architecture into a secondary form of nature.

VII. Reinforced Concrete Provides the Very Building Blocks of the Incompiuto.
Matter in its purest state, the backbone of modernity, the lifeblood of economic development.

VIII. The Incompiuto Gathers Together Places of Contemplation and Thought.
Contemplating in these ruins means observing the world through the gaze of the imagination and experiencing time itself.

IX. The Incompiuto Is Both a Symbol of Political Power and of Artistic Sensitivity.
The metaphor of a complex and articulated social organism that is celebrated through the call for tender.

Dam, Torpè, Sardinia.

Road, Cagliari, Sardinia.

Museum, Quartucciu, Sardinia.

Viaduct, Mussomeli, Sicily.

Viaduct, Mussomeli, Sicily.

Viaduct, Cammarata, Sicily.

Theatre, Gibellina, Sicily.

Incompiuto: Nostalgia or harbinger?

Marc Augé

What a curious experience to revisit those fragments of landscapes that even a few years ago already bore the fractured, incomplete and interrogative character of memory. To somehow express the quirkiness of this initial situation, during the filming of *Per troppo amore* – the film shot by Alterazioni Video in Giarre in 2012 – there had been talk of turning me into an extraterrestrial, disguised as a dog so as not to startle any humans. While recently looking at videos and photographs from that time – how rapidly six or seven years pass these days! – I have the sensation of reliving those experiences in a more authentic fashion. It is as though reliving a memory conveys the true substance of the places where I once travelled, shifting them back in time.

I'm perpetuating this experience by evoking the much more distant memory of the Mayan citadel in Tikal, Guatemala, which reminded me of unfinished public structures of Giarre in Sicily. Confronted with ruins, we usually face a desert that simply alludes to what the site was before it was a desert: quite often we don't have the vaguest notion what those ruins meant in the eyes of those for whom the site was not a ruin.

Our ignorance is thus twofold: it at once touches upon the ruin's context in the past and the basis for its present charm. I previously indicated that, as far as charm was concerned, it no doubt had to do with the palpable presence of time, of a form of 'pure' time that enkindled the brutal coexistence of elaborate architectural forms and wild nature. I've never forgotten the impression I felt at Tikal of this perception of time, at once sharp and as though it had been slowed down by the action of an invisible film camera. Over the passing years, this sensation has even been amplified, to the point of entirely subjugating the place of memory.

At the unfinished polo stadium in Giarre, we were initially struck by the apparent suddenness of the halt in the works. Even though this stoppage, far from being the consequence of a natural disaster, was due to political and economic negligence, it conferred a particular beauty to all the abortive enterprises in the capital city of this apparent scandal: the beauty of projects of which ruins were the harbingers, the beauty of that which could have been, the beauty of a moment when everything was still possible, the beauty of the original gesture and the primary impulse that had been brusquely interrupted. Nature had seized these anticipated ruins, so to speak, in order to dissolve them into the beauty of the surrounding landscape by modestly carpeting them here and there with a vegetative veil. Virtuality, the unknown of what might have been feasible, came to replace history, the unknown of the past. And, as the passage of time erases the differences, I now feel as if I also experienced a sort of 'pure time' at Giarre.

In the Incompiuto Siciliano, however, what the designers originally envisaged is often perceptible; not only is it obvious in Giarre, 'capital of the Incompiuto', but also in Gibellina, in Catania, as well as in many other localities: a school, a stadium, an Olympic swimming pool, even a cathedral; an architectural series conceived as innovative, powerful, and imposing, offering the aesthetic framework of a refashioned social life. We could, of course, lampoon the inability of the then decision-makers and policy-makers to ultimately deliver on any one of their grand ambitions. We could also, however, examine all these sketches one by one, some of which were not that far from implementation. Finally, we can imagine the ensemble they would have formed, had they been realised: the premises for radiant cities in which everyone, perhaps, would have found their niche.

We will then tell ourselves that these ambitious projects – just like the 'great narratives' of the nineteenth century evoked by the French philosopher Jean-François Lyotard – emerged too early in a world unprepared to embrace them; they failed the test of history. This explains the ambivalent feelings of hope, nostalgia and melancholy they inspire in those who, on discovering them today, question themselves, as they do the writings of Saint-Simon, Fourier and Karl Marx, whether these projects still herald something of a potential future or merely represent the grandiose vestiges of an abandoned dream.

Paris, 2018.
This work was originally published in Alterazioni Video/Fosbury Architecture, *Incompiuto: La nascita di uno Stile/The Birth of a Style* (Milan: Humboldt Books, 2018).

Unfettering reveries: The Incompiuto Siciliano

Robert Storr

Ruins are, in many respects, an invitation to dream. If they are not, they're not much of anything. You can pick which dream you want to have or you can pick which invitation you want. In the eighteenth and nineteenth centuries, romantic artists picked the classical past and visited the sites of Roman or Greek ruins. And that was the beginning of their dream. Consider, in France, the paintings by Hubert Robert or those by Nicolas Poussin where ancient archaic relics lie about on the ground: that is the start of a *rêverie*. In our case, we're standing in a place where what lies about on the ground are spray cans, and these spray cans are responsible for the graffiti on the building behind me. There are different kinds of dreams – sometimes you dream in the present or about the recent past. But they are dreams, nonetheless. And if you think that most ruins are built out of dreams and out of imperial lies of one kind or another, or grandiose hypotheses about how the future should look – futures that never arrive – then you have something very different. For example, all the way through the twentieth century, people invented the new city, the utopia of the golden dream of their age. All around Europe and in the rest of the world, incomplete statements of this nature abound. Examples can be found in the then Soviet Union, in South America, as well as in the United States, for instance. In the 1960s, this tendency was widespread. In the United States a number of artists got particularly involved in this dream, during the beginning of what we now call a postmodern era. Chief among them are Tony Smith and Robert Smithson.

One night in 1951, Smith took an unsanctioned car ride on the unfinished New Jersey Turnpike. Experiencing the site of that enormous highway where construction was suspended was to have a lasting impact on him. By his own account years later, it was a revealing experience that contributed to freeing him from many of his views about art. A native of New Jersey, between 1953 and 1955 Smith lived in Munich with his wife, an opera singer, and there he saw bits and pieces of the wounds of the Nazi era. Subsequently, he resettled in Nuremberg where stood the stadium in which Hitler had held the Nazi party rallies. Smith developed a sort of taste for that forbidden fruit which was the grandiosity of Fascist architecture. In May 1955, he returned to live in New Jersey, which most people think of as a place to go through and not to go to, and that earlier experience of a suspended highway contributed to letting new ideas germinate in his work in sculpture.

Smithson was interested in ruins as well. He went to Yucatán with his wife, the artist Nancy Holt, and found an old, decrepit motel, Hotel Palanque – a two-storey concrete-block motel that someone stopped building halfway – and he explored it as though it were an ancient ruin of the Aztec or Inca civilisations. Visits to industrial sites and abandoned wastelands in New Jersey also impacted his art. In Passaic, New Jersey, where he was from, he explored such sites and called them the monuments of Passaic, New Jersey. (In 1967 he published a tongue-in-cheek guide to such highlights, titled *A Tour of the Monuments of Passaic, New Jersey*.)

Everywhere you go, you will find in modernity – for modernity is still going on, even though post-modernity has declared something else – leftovers of previous iterations of an ideal that somehow, for lack of leadership or lack of funds, got dropped at a certain point, abandoned. I find these to be particularly interesting places to dream. Because they don't embody the classical dream. Instead, they encapsulate a dream of perfection that never was: something totally inaccessible. It is as if you were invited to dream of a human imperfection that you know all too well from yourself and everyone you have met in your existence. One encounters this dimension also by looking at buildings which have experienced all kinds of destructions of modern times. But there it is touched with actual tragedy, whereas in incomplete buildings there is no such tragedy; there is no apocalypse being evoked, no pain and suffering embodied in them. What you experience is the incompleteness of something – a building, a monument that somebody thought up and couldn't arrive at. Such places make us feel not triumphant but imperfect. Because all monuments of this type are out of scale to the human beings that inhabit them; all of them put us in our place. This is an important function of such ruins. Finding one's scale in relation to something that is out of scale is a positive benefit of the exploration.

Furthermore, these ruins are akin to detective stories. I'm a great reader of detective stories and at the heart of every detective story is a mystery. As Alfred Hitchcock taught us, the mystery is often a complete you-know-nothing. Hitchcock called it 'the MacGuffin': a plot element capturing the viewers' attention and driving a work of fiction by including something that is entirely unexplained. An absurd hypothesis. We read a detective story to find out the answer to an absurd question which has an absurd answer, but we enjoy the experience in the process. Good detective storywriters are not the creators of good plots, but the creators of a good MacGuffin, which is to say the creators of good fictions that have no reason for being other than their effectiveness. Good detective stories are like benign lies. We live in a society where there is nothing but lies, and the big lies that we are being told we are asked only to accept and to sort of endure, whereas benign lies are something you can enjoy and something you can believe in because you know they can't possibly be true.

There is nothing lost by finding pleasure in these ruins. There is a good deal to be gained from them because they are exceptional: they are unlike anything else that we see around us, partly because they are things we know, but stripped naked. In French they say *désincarné* to describe the result of the process of taking a body and stripping away all its muscles. This ruin/monument is the *désincarné* of an ideal of some kind. Think of how in classical statuary sculptures render an ideal body. As opposed to that tradition, the *désincarné* is all the bits and pieces from an anatomical point of view minus the beauty of the surface. And these ruins are somehow a *désincarné* of architecture.

Considering architectural modernism in general, it is revealing to look at how in some cases, in certain places, the notion of the grand modernist masterpiece meets the ruin. Some of such buildings are in a different state from their original modernist intention. For example, I remember going to Ahmedabad, in India, where I saw two buildings, designed by Le Corbusier and Louis Kahn, respectively. Le Corbusier's building, the Mill Owners' Association Building (1951), is tacky and falling apart. So much so that if you see it in relation to his Carpenter Center for the Visual Arts in Cambridge, Massachusetts (1963), which is another version of the same idea, architecturally you can sort of savour the contrast between the example of a perfectly maintained building – the Carpenter Center – and the Le Corbusier ruin in India. In Ahmedabad, you experience a ruin, a new ruin, or an architecture on its way to being a ruin. In the same city, Kahn built a great university building – the Indian Institute of Management (1962) – but, since it is made of brick, it is constantly wearing down in that climate. So, you see these wonderful ruins of a brick wall that has been subject to the wearing and tearing of the wind, of the heat and the rains. The time that I was there they were repairing the wall. They built these enormous scaffoldings of bamboo. It was interesting to see these formally strong but structurally weak walls by Khan being repaired by men standing on formally weak but structurally strong scaffolds that belonged to a centuries-old tradition. Meanwhile, there was a twentieth-century building being brought back to life little by little, but only in order for it to fall apart again.

A case in point is also the city of Djenné in Mali, located in the interior part of the country where two great rivers meet. Every year, the rainy season washes this city away, very nearly. It is entirely built of adobe. The adobe buildings, which are ancient, have a mud coat on the outside that lends them their distinctive shape. The adjoining mosque is the largest mosque of its kind anywhere in the world. The whole city is built in the same way. After the rainy season, they have to do exactly what I was describing taking place in Ahmedabad. They have to rebuild the city right. To do so, they fill the streets with huge piles of mud mixed with cow manure, mixed with oil, and they build a big pool of plaster. Then they climb the buildings on very rickety structures and they add coats and coats of adobe until, by the end of the process, you have a brand-new building on top of something which is ancient. This is in a way a variation of an idea which is also present in Japan, where they don't preserve ruins. They actually rebuild them from scratch. You have temples in Japan where what you see is an ancient design, but the wood – all of it – is brand-spanking-new or every number of years it is brand-spanking-new. So, the romance of the ruins, the 'ruin lust' – a term that comes from the English writer Rose Macaulay and her beautiful 1953 book *Pleasure of Ruins* – is a very Western thing. It bespeaks of our romance with history, the idea that being of another time is somehow more interesting than being of our time. Under this impulse, one tends to worship that which is old and decrepit rather than that which is new and beautiful. In Japan or in Africa, the idea is that the forms and the function of the building are beautiful, and that the building itself is only as old as it happens to be according to whatever is done to make it better.

In many respects, I am speaking from a position of very ambivalent feelings about all of this, because while I am drawn to ruins, I think that the worship of ruins in Western art has often led to the rather worrisome, disoriented fetishisation of the past. So, if you can, then enjoy twentieth-century ruins. They are not so far from the present and you can find pleasure in them as incomplete versions of the future rather than as ideals of the past. That is a very different orientation, historically and poetically. Many of today's ruins would have been in fact horrific: think of those from Nazi Germany or from the Soviet system. And yet the pull of such ruins remains. For instance, with his installations, the artist Ilya Kabakov has been making ruins of the future and ruins of the recent past. An architect of Soviet mental spaces, he employs ruins as his main stock-in-trade, so to speak, as an artistic metaphor. I find a great deal of attraction to those environmental works.

Furthermore, in Cuba there are many buildings that were realised during the 1960s. As generations and generations were confronted with the embargo, those architectures have worn down: they present incomplete walls, moisture seepages and so on. One looks at them and sees, first of all, in many cases, a very beautiful modern building, and secondly a building that has a kind of poignancy to it because it was realised out of extreme poverty and out of an ambition to create an early modern state in a very poor and oppressed country. A country oppressed by its patron, the then Soviet Union, and by its leadership, the Castro regime. But one has to try to understand the humanity of how that came to be. Because Castro's failure was not a foregone conclusion. The hostility of the United States was a big reason for it and the opportunism of the Russians is another big reason for it. So, if you think about all of these aspects together, these ruins are, again, not the golden age that you missed but the thing that just never happened and then did happen in its way.

No country is richer in ruins and therefore richer in dreams than Italy. It has everything: classical Greece, classical Rome, the baroque era, the modern era, and what you'd call the postmodern era. A particular kind of ruin developed in the 1950s, 1960s and 1970s and on into the 1980s and 1990s, up to the present: the incomplete ruin. Not a building or monument that was torn apart; rather, one that was never completely finished. This kind of architecture creates a different type of ruin because the additions and subtractions from the whole are arbitrary in ways that are completely unpredictable. It is almost as if a surrealist-like builder had suddenly started and suddenly stopped for reasons you will never divine. Thus, you may encounter staircases that lead to nowhere and posts that support nothing. Every kind of anomaly of architecture occurs. The pleasure of looking at these ruins is the pleasure of figuring out how they got where they did and why they stopped as they did. It is a style which is international, in a way, but it is peculiarly Italian, in fact peculiarly Sicilian since this is the region where it began.

Understanding the way things generally work in Italy – think of the number of governmental changes and of the number of regional, municipal and national divisions – it is not hard to know that in these situations nobody was actually in charge, but somebody was in charge for some part of it and then somebody else was in charge for some other part of it, and then everybody walked away from it at a certain point. Yet the fact that a building is a failure because nobody finished it doesn't mean that it is an example of failure in design. In many cases, these are municipal and government buildings, big public projects. They generally have interesting elegant structures. And they employ technologies of the late-twentieth and twenty-first centuries in ways which are quite remarkable. Their beauty resides precisely in their being incomplete. In them, you can see the bare bones of style in ways that set the experience of them apart from that of a finished building in use. If you look at the way a singular pillar stands out in space – a mysterious marker that paradoxically calls to mind memories of ancient steles – or you consider the way a railroad platform can be viewed as a perspective problem, and the way a gap in a bridge can be viewed as a sketch of a bridge that isn't in fact built, then you will find that you can perceive what the architect was thinking even though the thought was not completed by the structural construction workers. All of these unfinished buildings are mind games and visual games. Yet they really do exist. You can study them closely; you can draw them the way one used to draw ruins; the way artists used to draw ruins. But in their presence, we are faced with conceptual play, based on the perceptual reality.

Many find it difficult to appreciate the beauty of modern and contemporary architecture because their materials don't connote the same things that those they associate with classical building connote. In many ways, it has to do with the anthropomorphisation of the making of these buildings. Reinforced concrete is the predominant material of these unfinished monuments. It is poured by the tonne, and it is active and alive in itself but it has no handwork in it to speak of – except perhaps if we think of those who make the framing. Many find this absence of the hand somehow alienating. Why should it be? Concrete is one of the primary materials used by modernist architects. It has its own tactile expressiveness and a remarkable ability to take any shape. Its use in this particular manner is entirely human; it is intentional. For example, there are some great naval buildings that show you how beautiful concrete can be when finely crafted.

But even when it is not level and when it is a vernacular, steady building device, concrete affords all kinds of opportunities for visual incident, lending articulateness to a surface. In these buildings, the concrete is not well mixed and applied and, as a result, the surface is very rough. In these cases, concrete does not hold up as well as it should and that is the beginning of the ruin. But, at the same time, all of those incidents and particularities make that failure of materials, paradoxically, a particular detail to look at. That being said, concrete is a liquid that turns solid and therefore, in a sense, what you see is the embodiment of a metamorphosis in front of your eyes, suspended in its final form. I enjoy this type of ruin a great deal, and in some ways even better than I like the old ruins because those teach you loss, evoking an unapproachable Golden Age, whereas this contemporary type of ruin is approachable. Its scale is impressive. Its surfaces, even if so rough, are impressive. The humanity of it is manifest, including its foolishness. So that is to be considered as a philosophical object. Marcel Duchamp, basically, talked about thought objects and most architecture, whether good or bad, fully realised or left incomplete, is a thought object. To be able to meander among thought objects of this kind is to be alone with other people and just find your way. There is always a little sense that maybe this is a kind of haunted house, as well, so that when you come alone you might be slightly at risk. There might be somebody hiding in there. There might be a danger, a Minotaur in the cave. So, is there a Minotaur in this cave? Probably not, but you never know.

New York, 2018.
This work was originally published in Alterazioni Video/Fosbury Architecture, *Incompiuto: La nascita di uno Stile/The Birth of a Style* (Milan: Humboldt Books, 2018).

Housestories: Passion

La Cupola of Antonioni and Vitti, by Dante Bini, Costa Paradiso, Sardinia. Credit: Bruno Melis

In the late 1960s, architect and inventor Dante Bini designed La Cupola in the then-secluded Costa Paradiso on the northern coast of Sardinia. The futuristic summerhouse was commissioned by Michelangelo Antonioni and his partner at the time, actress Monica Vitti. This poetic symbol of a lovers' nest – described as one of the best buildings of the last hundred years by Rem Koolhaas – is now in a state of neglect and abandonment. Sara Nieddu, the founder of De Rebus Sardois, started an online petition for its preservation as an architectural and cultural landmark.

La Cupola of Antonioni and Vitti, by Dante Bini, Costa Paradiso, Sardinia. Credit: Bruno Melis

La Cupola of Antonioni and Vitti, by Dante Bini, Costa Paradiso, Sardinia. Credit: Elisabetta Carboni

La Cupola of Antonioni and Vitti, by Dante Bini, Costa Paradiso, Sardinia. Credit: Elisabetta Carboni

Towards an entity of decolonisation

Sandi Hilal
Emilio Distretti
Alessandro Petti

In 1940 the fascist regime established the 'Entity of Colonization of Sicilian Latifundia / Ente di Colonizzazione del Latifondo Siciliano', following the model of the 'Entity of Colonization of Libya' and the colonial architecture in Eritrea and Ethiopia, and what had already been experimented with in the plans of integral reclamation and 'internal colonisation' of the Pontine Marshes around Rome. Using different forms of violence and oppression, genocidal forms against colonised peoples, and social engineering and class violence on the Italian front, fascism had identified in these 'territories' an abstract, uniform and homogeneous geographical space to 'modernise' and 'repopulate', as it was considered 'empty', 'underdeveloped' and 'backward'. For this purpose, Sicily had become, in the eyes of fascism, the last front of modernisation, whose rural world, as opposed to the city, was considered a 'virgin' land to be occupied.

Before the world conflict prevented it, fascism inaugurated eight Sicilian villages by 1943, while others remained unfinished. Following the principles of modernist aesthetics and plans of fascist colonial architecture, the villages were built around the void of the square, the 'civic centre' of the state institutions aimed at 'civilising' the countryside considered empty and lifeless: the Church, the Post Office, the School, Casa del Fascio, the Entity of Colonization are just some of the institutions designated to forge the cultural, political and spiritual education of the 'new fascist colonist'. Thus, the new founding villages would 'connect' the various parts of the new Italian Empire to each other.

To celebrate this fictitious unity, many of the Sicilian villages, including Borgo ~~Bonsignore~~, Borgo ~~Fazio~~ and Borgo ~~Giuliano~~, took the name of fascist martyrs and soldiers and settlers who died in Ethiopia during the colonial war of occupation. Simultaneously, fascism had continued the 'internal colonisation' as an instrument and strategy of oppressing internal dissent. If, on the one hand, the villages were conceived as an instrument and space for the agricultural transformation of the Sicilian countryside in an extensive, extractive and capitalist key, the forced migration plans to the south served the regime to prevent revolts in the northern countryside, break the ties between the agricultural workers with anti-fascist movements and transform labourers into small landowners.

Today most of these villages have fallen into disrepair. The depopulation and migrations of the Sicilian countryside after the war, over time, have meant that the buildings that housed the fascist institutions fell into neglect, or in some cases were transformed by residents into homes. Today these villages are the materialisation of a suspension, not the definitive elimination of a historical and political trajectory. Despite the fall of fascism and the end of historical colonialism, Italy's de-fascistisation and decolonisation remain unfortunately unfinished processes. To date, the lack of a critical review process has meant that the cultural and political apparatus of colonialism and fascism has survived: among these, institutional racism and a widespread feeling of the presumed superiority of European civilisation, the consequent dehumanisation of populations from the (post-)colonial world, the surviving of monuments and streets that celebrate fascist and colonial ideology and history, and the lack of an education in critical knowledge of the past within the Italian educational system.

In Italy, as demonstrated by the Sicilian villages, this long-lasting political and cultural impasse is very visible through the normalisation or neglect of fascist architecture. As has been debated by postcolonial critics and literature in recent years, and loudly contested in 2020 on the wave of global uprisings against the presence of symbols celebrating imperial and colonial violence in urban spaces of the Northern Hemisphere, in Italy it is very common to find colonial/fascist buildings (as well as monuments, plaques, memorials and toponymy) which, rather than being removed, dismantled or destroyed, have been left intact. Since the end of the Second World War, fascist architecture (and urban projects) has been reused or developed by republican governments to give a home to the new Italian liberal democratic institutions. The relics of fascism and colonialism have been progressively normalised within urban landscapes, escaping the critical gaze of anti-fascist culture and politics.

To date, with the 'return' of fascism on a global scale and the increasing arrival in recent decades of migrants from the former colonial world, the need to reopen the processes of decolonisation and de-fascistisation has become more urgent than ever. And with them, new questions on 'what to do' with the fascist colonial architectural 'heritage'. Is it possible to imagine reuse without running the risk of eternally perpetuating this same ideology and against the danger of self-absolution and nostalgia?

DAAR (Decolonizing Architecture Art Research) has presented an art installation for the 2020 *Quadriennale d'Arte 2020* – FUORI at Palazzo delle Esposizioni in Rome, home to the first international exhibition of colonial art (1931). It proposes to rethink the villages built by fascism in Sicily starting from the appointment of Asmara as a world heritage site. In the summer of 2021 they organised the Difficult Heritage summer school, in Borgo ~~Rizza~~, Municipality of Carlentini (Siracusa), one of the rural settlements built by fascism.

Shortened version of a text by DAAR, online at https://www.decolonizing.ps/site/difficult-heritage-borgo-rizza/

Difficult Heritage summer school, in Borgo Rizza. Credit: Alessandro Petti

Difficult Heritage summer school, in Borgo Rizza. Credit: Sara Pellegrini

La Maddalena: Atlas of an occupation

Eterotopia

Elena Sofia Congiu
Matteo De Francesco
Carlotta Franco
Samanta Sinistri
Giuditta Trani
Mara Usai

Navigation around the islands: view from La Maddalena island. Credit: Alexandra Kononchenko

La Maddalena (*A Madalena* in Gallurese, *Sa Madalena* in Sardinian) is an Italian town of 10,846 inhabitants in the province of Sassari (the northernmost in Sardinia) on the archipelago of La Maddalena that is formed by various islands and islets, including the homonymous island of La Maddalena, Caprera, Santo Stefano, Spargi, Budelli, Santa Maria and Razzoli. The town of La Maddalena, which began to develop around 1770, lies to the south of the main island and faces the town of Palau.[1]

Municipality, archipelago, island, town – it's difficult to say what the true face of La Maddalena is, or how its name should really be pronounced. Should we define it as a landscape, an inhabited centre, or rather a tale to be told?

La Maddalena is first of all a territory, which brings together and embraces all these secret yet manifest identities.

In our tale La Maddalena is a sort of Vitangelo Moscarda,[2] a Pirandellian character who doesn't need to be defined by name but who, appearing from time to time in different guises, claims the right to be a complex combination of things: a territory, a stratification of places and events, inhabitants, things and environments.

It is a complex ecosystem, among many in Italy as in countless other places. The Eterotopia territorial laboratory workshop tried to reveal many of these aspects: La Maddalena is a hyperobject[3] to be interrogated, in much the same way as the Chimborazo volcano studied by Alexander von Humboldt.[4]

Any attempt to outline its multifaceted characters must take into consideration a tangled history of conquests and curious events, intertwined against a unique and sumptuous natural backdrop enclosed by the perimeter of an island cosmology.

History of an occupation

The history of the archipelago develops in fits and starts, alternating moments of success which have allowed its wealth of resources to emerge, and moments of decline, characterised by exploitation, poor governance or simply underestimation of the area's potential.

From the first informal settlements that indicate a rather later occupation of La Maddalena territory when compared to the major neighbouring islands of Sardinia and Corsica, the history of the archipelago unfolds through an irregular succession of occupations by different groups. These range from shepherds to migrants, hermits to exiles, and from military forces to foreign workers up to the tourists who fill its beaches every summer. All these occupying groups have contributed to writing the history of the territory and designing its morphological and social structure which today is both heterogeneous and complex. From the Savoyard-Piedmontese army to NATO, each of these waves of invaders represented moments of conflict but also of fruitful collaboration, which then often failed in a violent and dramatic way.

La Maddalena's strategically central position in the Mediterranean has condemned it to be considered a military objective since 1767, when the Sardinian-Piedmontese decided to occupy it and make it a support base for the ships of the Royal Sardinian Navy. These could then take to the waters of northern Sardinia in greater safety against smugglers, Barbary pirates and also the ever-feared revenge by the French.

Over the next two centuries, several outposts were built that made it possible to exploit the strategic power of the archipelago and which evolved together with military technologies. La Maddalena still bears witness to its military history, from the more traditional passive military fortifications to 'entrenched camps' and to the hugely powerful and cleverly camouflaged gun batteries designed to loose salvoes over the water. In more recent times, the NATO settlement in the archipelago (concentrated mainly on the island of Santo Stefano, with its 35 hectares entirely controlled by the United States Navy), was the most important strategic military centre in the Mediterranean, partly for the US Navy and also for the 60% of the Italian military easements in the area.

The presence of the marines based in La Maddalena in 1975 not only led to the installation of a large-scale military base but also supported the island's economy, creating structures and infrastructures, changing the numbers and the structure of the island's society. The sudden abandonment of the island by the Americans in 2008 left a void in La Maddalena's social, economic and architectural elements.[5]

In the aftermath of this traumatic event, the Italian Protezione Civile (civil defence force) replaced the foreign military presence with the creation of a complex intended to host the G8 conference in the same year. What was supposed to be a gesture intended to increase the fortunes of the archipelago turned out to be yet another failure, with the sudden decision to move the event to L'Aquila following the catastrophic Abruzzo earthquake. Even the yacht club intended to take over from the G8 event at the former Moneta military Arsenal was never built.

A rather more subtle colonisation has been under way for thirty years: tourism is devouring what is most precious to the archipelago. While its beaches, urban centres and crystal-clear waters are trivialised into postcard images, natural resources are threatened by the huge anthropogenic load on the territory.[6]

The French *Village magique* (Club Med) was a forerunner of this phenomenon, although at the time it was viewed by the inhabitants of La Maddalena with curiosity and economic interest. Today, the beach on the island of Budelli, a symbol of the exceptional natural wealth of La Maddalena, is closed to the public after tonnes of pink sand were systematically removed by barbarian hordes of foreigners on holiday.

Other colonisers

Although throughout the island's history the despotic occupation of the territory has been the centre of political and media attention, numerous other stories can be told from different points of view.

Since ancient times La Maddalena has represented much more than a defenceless territory to be conquered: when the Romans discovered the oceanic trade routes and decided to challenge the Strait of Bonifacio, they found themselves facing a fearsome number of obstacles. The violent winds, the rocks and the pirates immediately became part of the threatening atmosphere created by La Maddalena intended to intimidate adventurers. The area's underwater canyons are still home to numerous wrecks, silent witnesses to lost ships and routes.[7]

The Taphros Strait[8] (the 'pit' that so often swallowed up passing ships) was feared, challenged and courted by navigators in search of overseas riches. Echoes of this contrary but beautiful natural phenomenon can still be heard in Guido Piovene's imaginative narrative.

> With its deserted roads going towards Santa Teresa, between La Maddalena and Olbia and on the coasts facing Corsica, Gallura is strewn with boulders, almost bombarded over the millennia by meteors. There are many and of such strange shapes that when you are lost in the middle of them, they seem to come alive and move, as if you were witnessing an immense migration of petrified peoples. Many have been dug away by erosion, similar to gigantic

---

1 *La Maddalena*, wikipedia.it, online at www.it.wikipedia.org/wiki/La_Maddalena

2 Main character of *Uno, nessuno, centomila*, by Luigi Pirandello. 'La vita non conclude. E non sa di nomi, la vita. Quest'albero, respiro tremulo di foglie nuove. Sono quest'albero. Albero, nuvola, domani libro o vento: il libro che leggo, il vento che bevo. Tutto fuori, vagabondo,' ['Life does not end. And it knows no names, life. This tree, trembling breath of new leaves. I am this tree. Tree, cloud, tomorrow book or wind: the book I read, the wind I drink. All outside, vagabond.' Trans. Ed.] in Luigi Pirandello, *Uno, nessuno, centomila* (Turin: Einaudi, 2014).

3 Timothy Morton, *Hyperobjects: Philosophy and Ecology after the End of the World* (Minneapolis: University of Minnesota Press, 2013).

4 Elena Sofia Congiu, Matteo De Francesco, Carlotta Franco, Samanta Sinistri, Giuditta Trani, and Mara Usai, eds., *La Maddalena: Atlas of an Occupation* (Matera: Quodlibet, 2022).

5 Costantino Cossu, 'Progetti NATO per La Maddalena', in *il manifesto* (23 August 2016).

6 'Humans must learn to care for fatal substances that will outlast them and their descendants beyond any meaningful limit of self-interest. What we need is an ethics of the other, an ethics based on the proximity of the stranger,' Morton, *Hyperobjects* (see note 3), 124.

7 Alessandro Porqueddu, 'Appunti sulla storia della navigazione nelle Bocche di Bonifacio,' in *Almanacco Maddalenino VII* (La Maddalena: Paolo Sorba Editore, 2016), online at: www.lamaddalena.info/appunti-storia-della-navigazione-nelle-bocche-bonifacio.

8 Pliny the Elder, in his *Naturalis Historia*, tells of an inevitable crossing point between Sardinia and Corsica, and between the western Mediterranean and the Tyrrhenian Sea (the so-called Fretum Gallicum). The Strait of Bonifacio was a dangerous shortcut: the history tells us that the Romans had been trading with their colonies since the third century BCE; following the introduction of new extensive farming techniques and large slave-run Latifundia, the surplus production had driven them to transport wine and sauces made from long-keeping fish to the oceanic routes, as can be seen in the finds from the wrecks of Secca Corsara and Spargiottello.

broken and emptied eggshells. Others […] reproduce animal forms with an extraordinary similarity. The ridges that emerge from this chaos are a few hundred metres high, but apparently impervious. Saying that they are jagged or serrated does not do them justice. In reality, those crests terminate with a barbaric frieze of towers, square or round boulders, animals or idolatrous figures. One thinks of a Hindu temple or, if you like, of those castles that children make on the beaches by the sea, adorned with dripping sand. More than mountains, they are rocks that have emerged from a sudden drying up of the water and still recall the bottom of a cave, with whimsical stalagmites and anthropomorphic figures which suddenly extend as far as the eye could see. When a fire is lit this primeval landscape is enveloped in fragrant fumes. Its appearance is terrifying. Yet I have seen even here how relative human judgment is. An inhabitant of Nuoro, accustomed to even harsher landscapes, described Gallura as graceful.[9]

Thus, the image of the archipelago is itself a representation of an interior and natural conflict that becomes symbolic through its forms.

Standing out from their surroundings and establishing a strong identity is one of the islands' characteristics. They are apparently unspoilt thanks to their isolation, and much prized by geographers and scientists engaged in the study of the taxonomies of species. Alongside the unrepeatable endemic plant associations (the *Artemisia Densiflora* and *Juniperus phoenicea* are unique to the archipelago), the names of many other species belie their original exoticism: *Pinus canariensis*, the *Arenaria balearica* and *Pancratium illyricum* all refer to distant imported pasts. Plant colonisation, whether the reforestation of the pine forests in Caprera or the holm oak and olive groves on La Maddalena, is a phenomenon caused both by man and by the wind and tides which, by transporting seeds from distant lands, contribute to the shaping of the territory.

These pioneer plants are witnesses to a further story of heroic transformation and conservation of the Maddalena landscape. The action of these colonisers challenges the adverse conditions of an arid and rocky soil by placing their roots on the rocks without going deep. Their presence thus allows sand and earth to settle on them and prevent atmospheric agents from taking them away. As the earth accumulates, other plants can settle and create more complex formations.

Yet it is underwater that the most spectacular miracle of the emerged lands of this archipelago takes place: when crushed and transported by coastal drift and bottom currents, the calcareous shells of *Miniacina miniacea*, a foraminiferous protozoan that inhabits the rhizomes of the *Posidonia oceanica*, create the roseate panorama of Budelli beach, an earthly paradise that teaches us that interspecies alliances can create unparalleled works of art.

The history of contamination and cross-pollination in the archipelago has therefore only been caused by man in a very limited way. It turns out the entire territory of La Maddalena is an open system of continuous colonisation, an island that has been relentlessly sculpted and rebuilt.[10]

The history of La Maddalena is thus built on the most diverse ancestries which have alternated, evolved and put down layers. Even the town of La Maddalena, called 'Little Paris' since the first half of the last century, has differentiated itself from the rest of Sardinia, standing out for its openness and cutting-edge social dynamics. This inclination to include the most diverse of characters has allowed it to welcome and embrace unexpected situations and unique episodes.

It was in 1856 when Garibaldi bought the northern half of the island of Caprera, which was as much as his brother's inheritance allowed him. He who had journeyed through oceanic solitudes, earning the title of 'The Hero of Two Worlds,' had chosen the island within the island to fulfil his dream of a community in harmony with the territory. There, around his Casa Bianca, an expression of his love for overseas, he gave life to the ideals of a man who had dedicated his existence to freedom.

This work was originally published in Eterotopia, *La Maddalena: Atlante di un'occupazione/Atlas of an Occupation* (Matera: Quodlibet, 2022).

---

[9] Guido Piovene, 'Viaggio in Italia. Da Sassari a Nuoro, 4/6/1956', on *Radio Uno* (1956), online at: www.teche.rai.it/1956/06/viaggio-in-italia-da-sassari-a-nuoro

[10] 'Perhaps as sensual molecular curiosity and definitely as insatiable hunger, irresistible attraction toward enfolding each other is the vital motor of living and dying on earth. Critters interpenetrate one another, loop around and through one another, eat each another, get indigestion, and partially digest and partially assimilate one another, and thereby establish sympoietic arrangements that are otherwise known as cells, organisms, and ecological assemblages,' Donna Haraway, *Staying With the Trouble: Making Kin in the Chthulucene* (Durham, NC: Duke University Press, 2016), 58.

The lichens are colonisers of the granite in La Maddalena.
Credit: Diana Ferro

Garibaldi's house, Caprera.
Credit: Joonas Parviainen

The centre of the town of La Maddalena. Credit: Ivo Pisanti.

Punta Rossa battery in Caprera. Credit: Ivo Pisanti

The Mediterranean maquis in La Maddalena. Credit: Alexandra Kononchenko

Pioneer plants, Cava Francese. Credit: Carlotta Franco

(ab)Normal is a creative agency engaged in the multidisciplinary exploration of areas within design, architecture, scenography and graphic design. (ab)Normal has been published in magazines such as *Domus* and *Abitare* and has contributed works to various cultural events related to design and architecture, such as the Oslo Triennale (OAT2019), the Ljubljana Biennale (BIO26), the Swiss Architecture Museum (S AM), the Triennale of Milan and Haus der Architektur in Graz (HDA). (ab)Normal was founded in 2018 by Marcello Carpino, Mattia Inselvini, Davide Masserini and Luigi Savio.

Ursula Aichner (*1996) is a student of architecture who has worked at the Research Unit of Housing and Design at TU Wien, as well as several architectural offices. Her work focuses on the relationship between landscape and the built environment.

Alterazioni Video is an artists' collective made up of Paololuca Barbieri Marchi, Alberto Caffarelli, Matteo Erenbourg, Andrea Masu and Giacomo Porfiri that was founded in Milan in 2004 and is based in New York, Berlin and Milan. Their work has been displayed in museums and at international art institutions, including the 52nd Venice Art Biennale, Manifesta 7, the Fondazione Sandretto Re Rebaudengo in Turin and the Hamburger Bahnhof Museum of Berlin. They are known for *Incompiuto Siciliano*, a project reinterpreting the Italian landscape and its unfinished architecture, displayed at the 12th Venice Architecture Biennale and at the MAXXI Museum of Rome.

Florencia Andreola is an independent researcher with a PhD in the history of architecture (University of Bologna). She is interested in sociology, politics and the various disciplines that hybridise research on architecture and the city. She is co-founder with Azzurra Muzzonigro of the Sex & the City association, which investigates the city from a gender perspective. She and Muzzonigro are the authors of *Milan Gender Atlas/Milano Atlante di genere* (LetteraVentidue, 2021).

Franco Arminio (*1960) is an Italian poet, writer and director who was born in Bisaccia. A self-described '*paesologo*' (writer and researcher of villages), he has described the small towns of Italy, in particular those in the south, with extreme realism. He has published many books and has written for local and national newspapers. He is also an animator of civil battles and has made several documentaries. An inspiration and focus for many actions against the depopulation of the inner areas of Italy, he conceived and runs the Casa della paesologia in Bisaccia and the La luna e i calanchi festival in Aliano.

Marc Augé (*1935) is a French ethnologist and anthropologist. He was director of the École des Hautes Études en Sciences Sociales (EHESS) in Paris and has published numerous books, including his best-known work, *Non-Places: An Introduction to Supermodernity* (Verso, 2009).

Michael Baick is a writer and editor who has collaborated with CRA–Carlo Ratti Associati since 2020. He grew up in western Massachusetts and earned his bachelor's degree from Harvard College in 2022, where he studied history and literature with a minor in economics.

Marco Baravalle is a researcher, activist and curator. He is a member of Sale Docks, a collective and self-managed space for visual arts activism in Venice. He is part of the IRI (Institute of Radical Imagination) and a research fellow at the Istituto Universitario di Architettura di Venezia (IUAV). He is the author of *L'autunno caldo del curatore. Arte, neoliberismo, pandemia* (Marsilio, 2021) and co-editor of *Art for UBI (Manifesto)* (Bruno, 2022).

Lorenza Baroncelli is an Italian architect who is currently artistic coordinator and chief curator for architecture, urban regeneration and cities at the Milan Triennale. She has been a council member for urban regeneration and international projects for the city of Mantua, associate for special projects at the Serpentine Galleries in London, as well as consultant for urban and cultural strategies to Edi Rama, Prime Minister of Albania. She was scientific director of the Swiss Pavilion, curated by Hans Ulrich Obrist, at the Venice Biennale 2014 and scientific director of *15 Rooms*, the exhibition curated by Klaus Biesenbach and Obrist at the Long Museum in Shanghai.

Daniele Belleri is a partner in charge at CRA–Carlo Ratti Associati design and innovation office, where he is responsible for all editorial and curatorial projects. Having started his career as a Milan-based journalist contributing to *Domus*, Reuters and *Wired*, he taught at the Strelka Institute for Media, Architecture and Design in Moscow, was an executive curator at the 8th Bi-City Biennale of Urbanism/Architecture in Shenzhen, and ran the Urban Vision for Manifesta 14 Prishtina.

Alessandro Benetti (*1987) is a licensed architect and a PhD candidate in history of architecture at Université Rennes 2 and the Politecnico di Milano. He has contributed to collective publications about modern and contemporary architecture for such publishers as Hoepli, Quodlibet and Skira. He is a regular contributor to *Domus* and is editor of the magazine *Urbano*. Since 2021 he has been a member of the board of directors of ANCSA, the Italian National Association for Historic Artistic Centres.

Stefano Boeri (*1956), born in Milan, is an architect and designer of the Bosco Verticale, who teaches urban planning at the Politecnico di Milano and directs the Future City Lab at Tongji University in Shanghai. Since February 2018 he has been the president of the Fondazione La Triennale di Milano. He has edited the international magazines *Domus* and *Abitare*. He is founder of the studio Stefano Boeri Architetti, with offices in Milan and Shanghai. His publications include *USE: Uncertain States of Europe* (2009), *Biomilano: Glossary of Ideas for a Biodiversity-Based Metropolis* (2011), *L'anticittà* (2011), *Doing More With Less* (2012), *A Vertical Forest: Instructions Booklet for the Prototype of a Forest City* (2015) and *La città scritta* (2016).

Shumi Bose is a teacher, curator and editor based in London. She is a senior lecturer in architecture at Central Saint Martins and a visiting lecturer at the Architectural Association. She is also an associate at the African Futures Laboratory and founder of Holdspace, a discussion platform for architecture outside the academic sphere. She has worked as a curator of exhibitions at the Royal Institute of British Architects and at the Venice Biennale of Architecture.

Emanuele Braga (*1975) is an artist, theorist and activist whose work focuses on the relationship between art, economics and new technologies. He has co-founded and developed several projects, including the Balletto Civile dance company and the Institute of Radical Imagination (IRI), a transnational research centre questioning post-capitalist alternatives, and is a member of the MACAO new centre for art and culture in Milan, and Landscape Choreography. He has been professor of big data at the faculty of social sciences department at the University of Milan.

Massimo Bricocoli is the head of the Department of Architecture and Urban Studies at the Politecnico di Milano, where he is full professor in urban planning and policies and teaches housing and neighbourhoods as well as urban ethnography. His research focuses on urban regeneration policies, housing policies and projects, social change patterns, migration and the restructuring of local welfare policies, and qualitative and ethnographical approaches to urban research.

Leonardo Caffo is professor of aesthetics of fashion, media and design and semiotics of art at NABA in Milan. He also teaches aesthetics at IULM, also in Milan. He previously taught theoretical philosophy at the Politecnico di Torino. He has curated dozens of exhibitions, and worked directly on artist installations and designs for museums and galleries, including the research series on the concept of huts, *Cab-in-Out*. He has written novels and diaries on the border between literature and philosophy, including *Il cane e il filosofo* (Mondadori, 2020), *Essere Giovani* (Ponte alle Grazie, 2021) and *La montagna di fuoco. Etna la madre* (Ponte alle Grazie, 2022). His forthcoming novel, published by Fandango publishing house, is called *Due sogni*. His works are translated and commented on in numerous languages.

Simone Capra is a founding partner at STARTT: Studio of Architecture and Territorial Transformations, based in Rome. He graduated with honours in architecture from the University of Roma Tre. He received his PhD in architecture from the IUAV University Institute, Villard D'Honnecourt International Doctoral School. At STARTT he is responsible for research projects and competitions design. Since 2016 he has been an adviser for landscape architecture at the American Academy of Rome. Since 2015 he has taught architectural urban design at Iowa State University, Rome Program (College of Design, Department of Architecture).

Francesco Careri co-founded in 1995 the practice of Stalker, an artistic and nomadic research group exploring actions, research and exhibitions. Since 2005 he has been associate professor of urban and architectural design at Roma Tre University, where he is co-director of the environmental humanities master's programme, and where he runs the civic arts course, a peripatetic laboratory grounded in walking explorations of emerging phenomena. His main publications include *Constant's New Babylon, una Città Nomade* (Testo & Immagine, 2001), *Walkscapes: Walking as an Aesthetic Practice* (Editorial Gustavo Gili, 2002), *Pasear, detenerse* (Gustavo Gili, 2016), *Stalker/Campus Rom* with Lorenzo Romito (Altrimedia, 2017), *Nomadismo Architettura Ospitalità* (Bordeaux Edizioni, Roma, 2020) and *C.I.R.C.O. Un immaginario di città ospitale* with Laboratorio CIRCO (Bordeaux Edizioni, Roma, 2021).

Chiara Carpenter lives and works in Milan. She is an editor at Humboldt Books and was part of its founding group, and was project manager of *San Rocco* magazine.

Iain Chambers has taught cultural, postcolonial and Mediterranean studies at the University of Naples, 'L'Orientale', for many years. Among his publications are *Migrancy Culture Identity* (1994), *Mediterranean Crossings* (2008), *Postcolonial Interruptions, Unauthorised Modernities* (2017), *Mediterraneo Blues* (2020) and, with Marta Cariello, 'At history's edge: the Mediterranean question', *New Formations*, 106 (2022). He participated in *documenta fifteen* (2022) as a member of the collective Jimmie Durham & A Stick in the Forest by the Side of the Road.

Mattia Chinellato (*1994) is an architect who lives and works in New York. He graduated from IUAV and the Politecnico di Milano. His work investigates different scales of research from scenography to international urban planning (focusing on Italy, Slovenia and Australia). He has worked with Architecten De Vylder Vinck Taillieu and OFFICE Kersten Geers David Van Severen in Belgium. He is currently collaborating with SO – IL in Brooklyn as a designer.

Pippo Ciorra is an architect, critic and professor at SAAD (University of Camerino) as well as the director of the PhD programme 'Villard d'Honnecourt' at IUAV. The author of books and essays, he was part of the curatorial team for the 1991 Architecture Venice Biennale and juror for the 2016 edition. He has curated exhibitions in Italy and abroad. Since 2009, he has been Senior Curator of MAXXI Architettura in Rome and co-director of Premio Italiano d'Architettura. His main research fields are late-twentieth-century Italian architecture, museums and exhibitions, urban and architectural theory and its social and political implications.

Davide Curatola Soprana (*1982) is an Italian photographer and architect who graduated from La Sapienza in Rome after attending courses in Seville and Madrid and studying at the R. Rossellini Institute of Cinematography. In 2015 he moved to Madrid to start documentary photography research, focused on the visual study of landscape, city and territory.

Since 2018 he has exhibited at the 16th Venice Architecture Biennale, the Seoul Biennale of Architecture and Urbanism and the Oslo Triennale in 2022. He received the photography prize at the 15th Spanish Biennial of Architecture and Urbanism. In 2022 he started research for a master's in architecture and landscape representation on the relationship between infrastructure, nature and depopulation. He currently works on photography as a participatory art.

Gianluca D'Incà Levis (*1969) is founder and curator of Dolomiti Contemporanee (DC), a residency project in the Dolomites, and is the director of the Nuovo Spazio di Casso in the Vajont area. Within DC, he launched the projects Progettoborca, the cultural enhancement of an abandoned village, and the international art contest Two Calls for Vajont (2014). Since 2010, he has launched a series of reflections and curatorial projects that link contemporary art and the recovery of industrial or civil disused sites and mountains. At its core is the idea of producing innovative images that critically and proactively engage with the natural environment while rejecting stereotypical readings.

Giorgio de Finis is an anthropologist, artist and independent curator. He was the creator of the MAAM Museo dell'Altro e dell'Altrove di Metropoliz_città meticcia, and in 2018–19 was director of the MACRO Asilo, the experimental project that rethought the Museum of Contemporary Art in Rome. He is currently working as artistic director at a new museum format (RIF Museo delle periferie) dedicated to the suburbs and urban studies.

Antonio De Rossi, architect and PhD, is full professor of architectural and urban design and editor of the international magazine *ArchAlp* at the Politecnico di Torino. He currently coordinates Politecnico di Torino's Masterplan and related architectural projects. Between 2005 and 2014, he was director of the Urban Center Metropolitano di Torino. He has several architectural realisations and regeneration projects in the Alpine region to his credit, for which he has won prizes and awards. He is the editor of the collective book *Riabitare l'Italia* (Donzelli, 2018) and won the Mario Rigoni Stern prize with the two volumes of *La costruzione delle Alpi* (Donzelli, 2014 and 2016).

Irene Di Noto is an activist and campaign researcher with BPM (Blocchi Precari Metropolitani, Metropolitan Precarious Blocks). She holds master's degrees in political science (L'Orientale, Naples) and in communication (La Sapienza, Rome). She works in the field of communication and as a children's educator in a school and on the street. Her publications include *R/home diritto all'abitare dovere capitale* (Bordeaux Edizioni, 2018), 'Quale decoro?' published in *Maam Museo dell'Altro e dell'Altrove di Metropoliz_citta meticcia* (Bordeaux Edizioni, 2017) and 'Roma: l'ospitalità occupata' in *L'utopia dell'asilo. Il diritto di asilo in Italia nel 2005* (Ega Editore, 2006).

Emilio Distretti is a researcher, writer and educator. He is research tutor at the School of Architecture at the Royal College of Art in London and a postdoctoral fellow at the University of Basel. He engages with critical research methodologies and pedagogy, centred around the entanglements between repair, reparations and decolonisation in the Mediterranean basin and in the Horn of Africa. His work has featured in journals, books and magazines, including *Cabinet*, *e-flux*, the *Journal of Architecture*, *Future Anterior* and *Antipode*.

Andrea Di Tommaso (*1994) obtained his bachelor's degree in architecture at TU Wien. He has worked at renowned architecture firms in Vienna and Zurich, including feld72 and pool Architekten. He is currently completing his studies at the Politecnico di Milano. His interests range from handcrafted design to sustainable development.

esterni, a cultural enterprise working to transform the value of places, was founded in 1995 by Lorenzo Castellini, Nicolò Bini, Carlo Gabardini, Giacomo Faina and Beniamino Saibene. It now has more than a hundred employees/collaborators.

Eterotopia is a territorial research and practice group founded in 2017 by a heterogeneous group of Italian architects. Eterotopia investigates the contemporary condition of the Italian territory and its complexity, interweaving manifest and imaginative conditions, sustaining the dignity of what defines the immaterial heritage of territories. Eterotopia's work has been exhibited at the Venice Biennale and at the Urban Center of the Milan Triennale. In 2022 Eterotopia published *La Maddalena: Atlas of an Occupation* (Quodlibet, 2022). Eterotopia is currently collaborating with the Municipality of Ascrea (RI) on a territorial enhancement project, winner of the Lazio Region's call for proposals, '*Un paese ci vuole*'.

Caroline Faber is an architect and researcher whose work focuses on the critical analysis of socio-spatial impacts of capitalist spatial production. She graduated from TU Wien and is currently doing her PhD at the University of Luxembourg, examining historical and contemporary transformation processes of rural areas with a focus on Luxembourg and the Greater Region. Her interests include urban development issues such as the socio-ecological transition, housing provision and the question of land.

Silvia Federici is a feminist activist, writer and teacher. In 1972 she was one of the co-founders of the International Feminist Collective. In the 1990s, after a period of teaching and research in Nigeria, she was active in the anti-globalisation movement and the anti-death penalty movement in the United States. From 1987 to 2005 she taught international studies, women's studies and political philosophy courses at Hofstra University in Hempstead, NY. She has written books and essays on philosophy and feminist theory, women's history, education and culture, and more recently the worldwide struggle against capitalist globalisation and for a feminist reconstruction of the commons.

Martin Feiersinger (*1961) studied architecture at the University of Applied Arts in Vienna and at Rice University in Houston. In 1989, he established his architecture practice in Vienna.

Werner Feiersinger (*1966) studied art at the University of Applied Arts in Vienna and at the Jan van Eyck Academie in Maastricht. He is a sculptor and photographer now based in Vienna.

The Feiersinger brothers are the authors of *Italomodern*, a two-volume work on postwar architecture in northern Italy, published by Park Books in Zurich.

feld72 operates at the interface of architecture, applied urbanism and art. The 35-member team, centred around partners Anne Catherine Fleith, Michael Obrist, Mario Paintner, Richard Scheich and Peter Zoderer, has realised numerous projects of various sizes in national and international contexts, ranging from master plans for buildings, urban studies, spatial and exhibition designs to urban strategies and large-scale interventions in public spaces. The award-winning works (including several Austrian State Prizes and the Gold Medal of Italian Architecture) are characterised by a socially responsible, innovative and sustainable approach to topics of architecture and urbanism. The work of feld72 has been shown in major exhibitions for architecture and urbanism worldwide, including the Venice Biennale of 2016, 2011, 2010, 2008, 2004, International Architecture Biennial São Paulo 2007 and Architecture Biennale Rotterdam 2003.

Giulia Fiocca is an architect, independent researcher, activist and lecturer in public art with Lorenzo Romito at NABA, Rome and in the Stalker unit at the master's in environmental humanities programme at Roma Tre University (2016–). Since 2006 she has dealt with urban and social transformations related to marginal communities, abandoned spaces and self-organisation practices with Stalker in Rome. She was co-founder of PrimaveraRomana (2009–13), SUN, Scuola di Urbanesimo Nomade (2017–) and NoWorking (2016–).

Forensic Oceanography was founded by Charles Heller and Lorenzo Pezzani in 2011 as a collaborative project based at Goldsmiths, University of London, that has developed innovative methodologies to document the conditions that lead to migrants' deaths at sea. In 2021, they established the Geneva-based research and investigation agency, Border Forensics, which extends their work beyond the Mediterranean.

Fosbury Architecture is a collective founded in 2013 by Giacomo Ardesio, Alessandro Bonizzoni, Nicola Campri, Veronica Caprino and Claudia Mainardi. FA is a spatial practice interpreting architecture as a tool that mediates between collective and individual needs; expectations and resources; sustainability and pragmatism; environment and human beings. FA is curator of the Italian Pavilion at the Architecture Biennale 2023. The collective edited, with Alterazioni Video, the publication *Incompiuto, La Nascita di uno Stile* (Humboldt Books, 2018) and was awarded an honourable mention in the Compasso d'Oro awards 2020.

Sarah Gainsforth (*1980) is an independent researcher and freelance writer. Her work focuses on urban planning, housing, social inequalities, gentrification and tourism. She writes for Italian media, including *L'Essenziale* and *Internazionale*, among others. She is the author of *Airbnb Città Merce, Storie di resistenza alla gentrificazione digitale* (DeriveApprodi, 2019), a Premio Napoli 2020 finalist; *Oltre il turismo, Esiste un turismo sostenibile?* (Eris Edizioni, 2020); *Abitare Stanca, La casa: una storia politica* (effequ, 2022); and *Cameriera* (Einaudi, 2022).

Roswitha Goy completed her studies at TU Wien in 2020 with her diploma thesis 'The Davos Phenomenon: In the Field of Tension between Urbanity and Rurality'. With her research work, she examined the extent to which rural Alpine spaces take on urban characteristics, based on the highest city in Europe. In 2021 she presented her findings to the people of Davos at the forum Bau+Kultur. She is currently working for Nickl und Partner Architekten in Munich, an internationally active office primarily specialising in health and research buildings.

Julian Graf (*1996) studied architecture at TU Wien and Aalborg Universitet in Denmark, and is currently working on his diploma at the Department of Building Theory by Design at TU Wien. During his studies he worked in architecture offices in Salzburg and Vienna, such as Fally + Partner and Delugan-Meissl Associated Architects. He won second place in the international Healthy Homes design competition and presented his project at the CLIMA Conference 2022 in Rotterdam.

Alessandro Guida is an architect, photographer and filmmaker working between Italy and the Netherlands. At the core of his research are the transformations of contemporary landscapes. In 2016 he co-founded the collective Urban Reports with other photographers and researchers. In 2021, in collaboration with Viviana Rubbo, he created paesaggisensibili, an independent observatory on landscape changes. Alongside his research he is also a lecturer at different universities and organises workshops.

Charles Heller is a researcher and filmmaker whose work has a long-standing focus on the politics of migration and of aesthetics within and at the borders of Europe. He is the director of the Border Forensics research and investigation agency, and research associate at the Graduate Institute, Geneva. He is a board member of the Mobility & Politics book series and of the Migreurop network.

Sandi Hilal is an architect, artist and educator. She has developed a research and project-based artistic practice that is both theoretically ambitious and practically engaged in the struggle for justice and equality. She is currently the co-director of DAAR (Decolonizing Architecture Art Research), an architectural and art collective that she co-founded in 2007 with Alessandro Petti and Eyal Weizman, in Beit Sahour, Palestine, as well as Lise Meitner visiting professor at Lund University's Department of Architecture and the Built Environment. In 2012, with Petti, she founded Campus in Camps, an experimental educational programme in the Dheisheh refugee camp in Bethlehem. Their latest publications include *Refugee Heritage* (Art and Theory, Stockholm, 2021), a book-dossier that challenges dominant definitions of heritage and mainstream narratives, proposing exile instead as a radical perspective that can take us beyond the limitations of the nation-state.

Gustav Hofer was born in 1976 in Sarnthein, South Tyrol, Italy. After his studies in communication science at the University of Vienna and cinema at Middlesex University in London, he moved to Rome. He works as a freelance journalist and independent filmmaker, including for the French-German broadcaster Arte and the German TV Deutsche Welle as a correspondent from Italy. With his partner in life and work for twenty-three years, Luca Ragazzi, he has directed four feature film: *Suddenly Last Winter* (2008), *Italy Love it or Leave it* (2011), *What Is Left?* (2014) and *DicKtatorship* (2019). The titles were invited to more than 200 film festivals around the world, including the Berlinale, HotDocs Toronto, Rio De Janeiro, SXSW, Thessaloniki, EIDF Seoul, winning jury prizes, audience awards and special mentions. All the films are distributed internationally and are available on many VOD platforms.

Andrés Jaque founded the Office for Political Innovation, an international architectural practice based in New York and Madrid, in 2003. He has brought a transectional approach to architectural design, practising architecture as the intervention on complex composites of relationships. He is a professor at and the dean of Columbia University Graduate School of Architecture, Planning and Preservation. He has also been director of the Advanced Architectural Design Program at GSAPP, and visiting professor at Princeton University and the Cooper Union. In 2018 he co-curated Manifesta 12 in Palermo and he is the chief curator of the 13th Shanghai Biennale, 'Bodies of Water'.

Katrin Kirschner (*1995), originally from southern Germany, received her bachelor of architecture degree at the University of Arts in Linz in 2017 and completed her master of science at TU Wien in 2021. After working for several studios in Austria and Germany, she is currently based in Basel, Switzerland, where she is part of a young studio that works in different scales and fields of architecture and interior design.

Michael Klein (*1980) works at the Research Unit of Housing and Design, TU Wien, on the intersections between architecture, the arts, history and urbanism, with a specific focus on housing, domesticity and everyday life and how it has been shaped through discursive formations and material forces. He is a member of the editorial board of *dérive*, the journal for urban research, and a board member of the Austrian Society for Architecture (ÖGFA). Books include *The Design of Scarcity* (Strelka Press, 2014), *Modelling Vienna – Real*

Fictions in Social Housing (Turia+Kant, 2015) and *Building Critique, Architecture and its Discontents* (Spector Books, 2020). Together with Sasha Pirker, he made the film *60 Elephants – Episodes of a Theory* on the work of Yona Friedman.

Isabel Köhler (*1991) is a budding architect who currently lives and works between Munich and Vienna. She will complete her diploma in 2023 (at TU Wien) and is training additionally in the field of UX/UI. Particularly interested in the 'hows and whys', she follows a research-based approach to design, operating within a framework of design research, critique and storytelling. Research interests include the relationship between design and identity and the psychological value of aesthetic practices.

Wilfried Kuehn is an architect, curator and writer based in Berlin and Vienna. Together with Simona Malvezzi and Johannes Kuehn, in 2001 he founded the architectural practice Kuehn Malvezzi, which is known for its realisations of cultural spaces and museum venues. He is the author of articles reflecting the idea of architecture as a form of curatorial design, such as 'Model and Event' (2009), 'Kontextkonstruktion' (2010) and 'Reconstruction or Re-enactment' (2021). He co-curated the exhibition *Wohnungsfrage* at Berlin's HKW and the transdisciplinary show *Carlo Mollino – Maniera Moderna* at Haus der Kunst Munich. Since 2018 he has been a professor and head of the Department of Spatial Design at TU Wien.

Giovanni Laino (*1957) is a social planner and full professor of planning at the Department of Architecture, University of Naples Federico II. He is the author of 'The Building Where I Live: A Social Mapping of the City' in *Bulletin de correspondance hellénique* and 'The Neapolitan Urban Kaleidoscope' in *Post-Metropolitan Territories: Looking for a New Urbanity* (Routledge, edited by A. Balducci, V. Fedeli and F. Curci).

Leroy S.P.Q.R'DAM teaches art at a high school in Rome. As an architect and artist, he has helped to transform vacant buildings into squats, among them the Metropoliz and 4 Stelle Hotel.

Armin Linke is a photographer and filmmaker who combines a range of contemporary image-processing technologies to blur the border between fiction and reality. His oeuvre of photographs and films function as tools to provoke awareness of the different design strategies. In a collective approach with other artists, as well as with curators, designers, architects, historians, philosophers and scientists, the narratives of his work expand on the level of multiple discourses. His works have been exhibited internationally. His installation *Alpi* won the special prize at the 2004 Venice Biennale of Architecture and *Image Capital* was awarded the Kubus. Sparda Art Prize in 2019.

Alice Lomonaco has a PhD in sociology and social research, and is currently junior assistant professor at the Department of Sociology and Business Law, University of Bologna. She has been a research fellow (2020–23) and is a member of the Horizon2020 Welcoming Spaces project. Her research investigates the processes of territorial and social marginalisation and the interaction between socio-territorial regeneration and the reception system. Her interests include: housing inequalities; housing policies and foreign population; national and international migration; territorial inequalities, with a focus on shrinking areas, inner areas; territorial regeneration; inclusion and foreign population; processes of ageing.

Marlene Lötsch studied architecture in Vienna and Gothenburg. Her work focuses on public space and common infrastructures. With a systematic approach, she investigates inscribed knowledge of the urban fabric and translates identified qualities to meet new social, ecological and spatial requirements. As a member of the Sudden Workshop collective, she took part in the design of the Austrian Pavilion at the Venice Biennale 2020/21. She currently works at Mostlikely Architecture.

Angelo Lunati (*1973) studied architecture at the Politecnico di Milano, FAUP Porto and received his PhD at ETH Zurich with a dissertation on modern architecture in Milan. In 2011 he founded Onsitestudio together with Giancarlo Floridi. Their built work includes the Pirelli Learning Centre, BASE Cultural Centre and other urban buildings in Milan, receiving numerous honours and awards. He has taught as a guest professor at TU Wien (2021–22) and IUAV (2014–21) and, since 2010, he has been unit professor at the Politecnico di Milano.

Roberta Marcaccio (*1984) is an educator, editor and research and communication consultant. Her research on historical and emerging modes of practice informed the book *Architects After Architecture* (2020) and further work is currently being supported by a Graham Foundation grant and a research publication fellowship awarded by the Architectural Association. Her writing has featured in *AA Files*, *Blueprint* and in the books *Real Estates* (2014) and *Erasmus Effect* (2014). Most recently she co-edited an issue of *Architectural Design* titled 'The Business of Research' (2019).

Julia Maretzki (*1995) is a German architect. She studied architecture in Vienna and Hanover and currently works in an office in Hamburg on projects at the interfaces of housing. She explores a tactile understanding of space in the form of theoretical contributions for various publications (including '*Die Insel als Raum: Positionen, Perspektiven und Näherungen*', Metatektur, 2022). She is particularly enthusiastic about the connection between architecture that communicates strongly through visual stimuli in contrast with fragile human existence.

Diego Martínez (*1988) is an architect based in Vienna. He was born in Mexico and grew up in Berlin. He studied architecture at the BTU Cottbus-Senftenberg, the Universidad Nacional de Colombia Medellín and the University of Art and Design Linz. His master's thesis at TU Wien addresses large-scale architecture in Rome. Using hand drawings, sketches and collages as tools for research and design, he is interested in the implications of architectural practice, the built environment and its impact on social realities in cities.

Laura Mascino, architect and PhD, has taught urban design at the Politecnico di Milano. She currently works at the Istituzione Veneziana, where she deals with social housing and welfare. On regeneration issues, she recently led the projects for *Terraferma: Parco agricolo del Veneziano* for DD Social in Venice Dorsoduro, and for *Crocevia Piave* in Mestre. She has won several national and international competitions, and has realised architectural projects in Italy, Great Britain and Japan. She is part of the promoting group of Riabitare l'Italia.

Michael Meier & Christoph Franz work as an artist duo in Zurich. Places and their social, historical and political background are the starting point of their artistic practice. In careful, research-based processes, the artists appropriate these places and refer to them with conceptual works. Their thematic focus is on the city both as a concrete field of interaction and as a space for thought, dealing with the processes of change in our built environment. They use specific approaches to negotiate the sediments of the urban, question its development and set it in motion.

Martina Motta (*1987) is a researcher, architect and activist. Currently she is a PhD candidate in history of architecture at the Politecnico di Torino. Since 2014, she has developed research projects for La Biennale di Venezia, OMA – Office for Metropolitan Architecture, Manifesta12, MAAT – Lisbon Museum of Art, Architecture and Technology and Oslo Architecture Triennale, among others. She is a member of LabiSAlp (Laboratorio di Storia delle Alpi at Università della Svizzera italiana). She also part of SISAm (Società Italiana Storia Ambientale).

Valerio Muscella is a freelance photographer based in Rome. He is interested in issues of social movements, human rights and forced migration in Europe and the Middle East. Together with Paolo Palermo, he captured life in the 4 Stelle Hotel in the web documentary of the same name between 2013 and 2015.

Azzurra Muzzonigro, PhD in urban studies at the Roma Tre University, is an architect, curator and independent urban researcher. She teaches urban design in various universities including the Politecnico di Milano and Domus Academy. She is co-founder of Sex & the City association, which investigates the city from a gender perspective. She and Florencia Andreola are the authors of *Milan Gender Atlas/Milano Atlante di genere* (LetteraVentidue, 2021).

Umberto Napolitano (*1975) was born in Naples where he studied architecture at the Università Federico II, and then at the Ecole Nationale Supérieure d'Architecture de Paris La Villette. Founder of LAN (Local Architecture Network) with Benoit Jallon in 2002, he also conducts theoretical work through research projects, exhibitions and conferences all around the world. He was a professor at the Columbia University GSAPP of New York and at the AA (Architecture Association) School of Architecture in London, and currently teaches at TU Wien. He has been a member of the French Academy of Architecture since 2016 and was appointed Chevalier de l'Ordre des Arts et des Lettres in 2018.

Maik Novotny (*1972) studied architecture and urban planning in Stuttgart and Delft. He is based in Vienna as the architecture critic for the newspaper *Der Standard* and the weekly *Falter*, regularly contributes to numerous Austrian and German architecture magazines and has co-edited books and publications. He teaches at TU Wien and was one of the inaugural fellows of the Harvard GSD Richard Rogers Fellowship in London. Since 2022, he has been the chairman of the ÖGFA (Austrian Society of Architecture).

Marek Nowicki (*1991) was born in rural Upper Austria. He is currently working on his master's thesis at TU Wien, which addresses past, present and future conditions of social housing in Vienna. He has worked in offices such as Sandbichler Architekten and feld72, and since 2019 at Expanded Design founded by Andreas Rumpfhuber. He also has held a position as a tutor at the Urban Design Institute. As a co-founder of cmd-kollektiv, he engages in small-scale projects and competitions, as well as collaborating with a varying number of partners.

Michael Obrist (*1972), born in Bolzano, is an architect and partner at feld72 architects in Vienna (with Anne Catherine Fleith, Mario Paintner, Richard Scheich and Peter Zoderer). Since 2018, he has been full university professor and head of the Research Unit of Housing and Design at the Faculty for Architecture and Planning at TU Wien. He has also undertaken various guest professorships (Politecnico di Milano, Kunstuniversität Linz, International Summer Academy of Fine Arts Salzburg, Architectural Association Visiting School Slovenia, etc.) and was guest editor (with Christina Lenart and Bernadette Krejs) of *ARCH+ 244* magazine's issue 'Vienna – The End of Housing (as a Typology)'. He is editor of *The Last Grand Tour* (with Antonietta Putzu).

Manuel Orazi (*1974), born in Macerata, is a historian of architecture and of cities, and a visiting professor at Accademia di architettura di Mendrisio. He published, with Yona Friedman, *The Dilution of Architecture* (Park Books, Zurich, 2015) and edited *Rem Koolhaas, Études sur (ce qui s'appelle autrefois) la ville Paris* (Payot, 2017). In 2021 he curated the exhibition and catalogue *Carlo Aymonino: Loyalty to Betrayal* (Electa) at the Milan Triennale. He is currently researching the Adriatic region together with Marco Vanucci of London South Bank University.

Alessandro Penso, born in Italy, studied clinical psychology at Sapienza University of Rome. He went on to study photojournalism with a scholarship at the Roman School of Photography and Cinema. He is deeply committed to social issues and in recent years has focused on the issue of immigration in the Mediterranean. He works regularly with Italian and international publications and organisations, including *The International Herald Tribune*, *Time*, *The Washington Post*, *Businessweek*, *The Guardian*, BBC, Human Rights Watch, *L'Espresso*, *D di Repubblica* and *Vanity Fair Italy*. His images have been widely exhibited at photography festivals in Europe, and he regularly conducts workshops and professional seminars.

Ippolito Pestellini Laparelli is an architect and curator whose work encompasses technology, politics, design and environmental practices. Formerly a partner at OMA, he founded the interdisciplinary agency 2050+ in Milan to deploy space as a medium rather than a goal. He teaches Data Matter at the Royal College of Arts in London, a research and design studio exploring the entangled relationship between data and the material world. His work has been shown internationally at various institutions, festivals and exhibitions.

Gianni Pettena (*1940) is an architect, architecture critic, historian and university professor. He was part of the original nucleus of Italian 'Radical Architecture' and still carries out experimental activities aimed at eliminating disciplinary boundaries and revisiting design languages through projects, furniture, installations, exhibitions, theoretical writing, essays and texts. Unlike other 'radicals', he prefers to use the tools and languages of the visual arts rather than the traditional ones of architecture design.

Alessandro Petti is a professor of architecture and social justice at the Royal Institute of Art in Stockholm and co-director of DAAR (Decolonizing Architecture Art Residency), an architectural studio and residency programme centred around the relation of politics and architecture. In 2012, with Sandi Hilal, he founded Campus in Camps, an experimental educational programme in the Dheisheh refugee camp in Bethlehem. Their latest publications include *Permanent Temporariness* (Art and Theory, Stockholm, 2019), a book-catalogue that is the product of fifteen years of research and experimentation within and against the condition of permanent temporariness.

Zara Pfeifer (*1984) is an artist based in Vienna and Berlin whose work is concerned with the social phenomena of large-scale infrastructure. Her documentation of the modernist housing project Alterlaa (*Du, meine konkrete Utopie*, 2013–17) and her series on truck drivers (*Good Street!*, 2018–22) involved extended periods of immersion in the day-to-day life of her subjects. She has worked with institutions including the MAK Center in Los Angeles and the Austrian Cultural Forum in Berlin. She studied architecture at the Academy of Fine Arts Vienna and photography at the Friedl Kubelka School for Artistic Photography in Vienna. She holds lecturing positions at TU Wien and TU Berlin.

Fit Phuong (*1992) has worked as an architectural designer in construction planning for several firms in Austria, and contributed in competitions, alongside doing her bachelor degree at TU Wien. Her master's thesis focuses on the implementation of civil guidelines and civil law in the architectural practice.

Andreas Pichler (*1967), born in Bolzano, studied in Berlin and Bologna and works as a documentary director, writer and producer in Italy, Germany and Austria. Most of his documentaries are European co-productions and have been screened at numerous international festivals. Among other awards, he won the German Grimme award, the French-German journalist award, and *The Venice Syndrome* won Best City Film at Open City Docs, London.

Antonietta Putzu studied architecture at the Academy of Fine Arts Vienna and is currently a researcher at TU Wien (Research Unit of Housing and Design). In her teaching and PhD thesis she focuses on the production and discourse of architecture and design in Italy's second postwar period and its juxtaposition to the concurrent mass migration that characterises this decade. She is editor of *The Last Grand Tour* (with Michael Obrist).

Luca Ragazzi (*1971) was born in Rome and graduated in literature and philosophy from the city's La Sapienza university. He works as a journalist, film critic, photographer, casting director and independent filmmaker. With his partner in life and work for twenty-three years, Gustav Hofer, he has directed four feature film (see above).

Carlo Ratti is a scientist, designer and public intellectual working on cities and the built environment. One of the top ten most cited scholars in the field of urbanism, he teaches at MIT in Boston, where he directs the Senseable City Lab. He is a founding partner of the international design and innovation office CRA-Carlo Ratti Associati (New York City and Turin).

Theresa Reiter completed her master's degree in architecture at TU Wien in 2021. In her thesis 'The Temporary Habitat: A Home Between Retreat and Participation', she dealt with the question of what 'home' means to people, focusing on the idea of reducing the private space as a refuge for the individual and a maximisation of collective spaces to create a renewed togetherness of people. Since August 2021 she has worked for the technology and art office ARCHITEKTUR.dlx in Dortmund.

Lorenzo Romito is professor of space and design strategies at KU Linz, a lecturer, with Giulia Fiocca, of public art at NABA Rome and of the Stalker module at the master's in environmental humanities programme at Roma Tre University (2016–23). He was awarded the Prix de Rome Architecte at the French Academy, Villa Medici, Rome (2000–01) and was a co-founder of Stalker (1995–), Osservatorio Nomade (2002–09), PrimaveraRomana (2009–13), Biennale Urbana (2014–), NoWorking (2016–) and SUN, Scuola di Urbanesimo Nomade (2017–).

Viviana Rubbo is an architect and independent researcher. As project coordinator of no-profit international think-tanks (International Urban Development Association: INTA; The International Federation for Housing and Planning: IFHP; INTI: The International New Town Institute) she organised labs and action-led knowledge exchanges on urban dynamics in Europe, Asia and Latin America. In 2016 she was awarded the METREX Bernd Steinacher Fellowship on metropolitan governance models in Europe. In 2016 she co-founded Urban Reports, and in 2021, in tandem with photographer Alessandro Guida, she created paesaggisensibili, an independent observatory on landscape changes.

Carina Sacher works at the intersection of architecture and urban research in the field of housing, focusing in particular on issues of social inequality. She studied architecture at TU Wien with an Erasmus year at the École Nationale Supérieure d'Architecture de Versailles. She has practised in various architectural offices in Vienna and Paris, most recently at Lacaton & Vassal. After three years as assistant in Anne Lacaton's studio at ETH Zurich she has taught at the Alpen-Adria-Universität Klagenfurt (WS19/20) and currently at the Research Unit of Housing and Design at TU Wien.

Beniamino Saibene (*1974) has been dealing with public spaces and public goods in Europe since 1995. Among the projects he has been involved in are the Milano Film Festival (artistic director then president), Cascina Cuccagna (founder), Base.Milano (founder), esta es una plaza (founder), Public Design Festival (artistic director) and Affari Pubblici (founder). In 1995 he was a co-founder of esterni (see above).

Carolina Sartori (*1994), born in Venice, is an architect and photographer currently based in New York. She graduated in architecture from IUAV and the Politecnico di Milano. Her visual research explores the crossroads between natural and urban contexts through the investigation of spatial conditions. Her latest work, *Echoes* (2022), was exhibited at Superattico in Milan. In 2016 she contributed to the academic publication *Lampedusa. La Cattedrale di Salomon* (Vol II). As an architect, she has collaborated with Renato Rizzi, SANAA and OMA.

Isabella Sassi Farìas studied architecture at IUAV and for one year at FAUP in Porto, where she soon developed an interest in photography, studying with Guido Guidi and Lewis Baltz. Since 2005, she has shown her photographic and video work in collective exhibitions including in Lille, Barcelona, Treviso, Rubiera and Como, at the Triennale di Milano and in the 16th Venice Architecture Biennale. She currently works in the educational field as an art history teacher and combines this with professional activity as an architectural and landscape photographer.

Luigi Savio is an architect and artist, and founder of (ab)Normal. After studying at the Politecnico di Milano, he collaborated with baukuh in Milan (2016) and OMA/Rem Koolhaas in Rotterdam (2016–17), where he worked mainly within the AMO research unit. He collaborated with Studio Folder of Milan, in particular for the exhibition design of the XXII Triennale of Design *Broken Nature*, curated by Paola Antonelli, and the installation 'The Color of the Air' in the exhibition *Disegnare Il Futuro* at the Royal Museums of Turin. His works have been published in magazines such as *Domus* and *Abitare*, and he has contributed to various cultural events related to design and architecture, such as the Oslo Triennale (OAT2019), the Ljubljana Biennale (BIO26), the Museum Swiss Architecture (S AM), Triennale di Milano and Haus der Architektur in Graz (HDA).

Sophie Schaffer (*1997) graduated in architecture from TU Wien, the Politecnico di Milano and Università Federico II in Naples. She has ongoing research on domestic perspectives emerging from digitalisation with a critical reflection on architecture, society and the representation of the self. She has worked with architecture offices such as (ab)Normal (IT), Parasite 2.0 (IT), Breathe Earth Collective (AT) and Querkraft (AT). Her work had an honourable mention at the Pfann-Ohmann Award (2021), and she was winner of the first prize at the LAP (2019, Vienna). She has exhibited at Milan Design Week, Spazio Maiocchi (IT) and Vienna Design Week (2020) and participated in architecture biennales, including Tallinn (2022) and Venice (2021), with an installation for the open workshop, as well as at the AA visiting school, 'The Possibility of an Island' (IT, 2021).

Lotte Schreiber is a filmmaker, artist and film curator, based in Vienna, who works mainly on experimental and documentary films. Her works have been awarded prizes at international film festivals and presented in exhibitions, including Kunsthaus Graz, NSK State Pavilion 57th Biennale di Venezia. In 2019 she received the Con-Tempus Prize for Contemporary Visual Arts, in 2015 the Diagonale Prize for Innovative Cinema and in 2011 the Outstanding Artist Award for Avantgarde Film from the Austrian Federal Government.

Paul Sebesta (*1994) is an independent photographer with a focus on architecture and urban environments, as well as a student of architecture and study assistant at the Research Unit of Housing and Design at TU Wien. His works, which range across the field of visual culture and architectural image production, have featured in international publications and exhibitions.

Alexandra Seibel is an author and film critic working for the daily newspaper *Kurier*. She followed film studies at New York University and is an editorial member of the film magazine *kolik.film*. She lives and works in Vienna. She has had numerous publications, including *Visions of Vienna: Narrating the City in 1920s and 1930s Cinema* (Amsterdam University Press, 2017), 'Beauty of the Peripheral: On the Films of Tizza Covi and Rainer Frimmel' in Isabella Reicher's (ed.) *Eine eigene Geschichte. Frauen Film Österreich seit 1999* (Sonderzahl, Vienna, 2020).

Sex & the City is a social promotion association (APS), founded in 2022 by Florencia Andreola and Azzurra Muzzonigro, which observes cities from a gender point of view through specific projects, public meetings and research projects. In 2021 LetteraVentidue published their research developed for Milano Urban Center on the city of Milan, *Milano Atlante di genere/Milan Gender Atlas*, a mapping of the condition of the city with regard to the daily life of women and gender minorities.

Giovanna Silva (*1980) lives and works in Milan. Her photographic books have been published by Mousse, Hatje Cantz and Nero, among others. Her work has been shown at the 10th and 14th Venice architectural biennales, MACRO in Rome, Fondazione Bevilacqua La Masa in Venice, the Triennale in Milan, the American Academy in Rome, FRAC Orléans, c/o Berlin, the Biennale de Rabat 2019 and the Italian Cultural Institute in New York. She is the founder and editor-in-chief of Humboldt Books and the co-founder of *San Rocco* magazine. She teaches photography at NABA Milan, IUAV's master in photography programme and ISIA Urbino.

Giorgio Dietmar Sokoll graduated in architecture from the University of Roma Tre with the thesis *Riace, Urban Regeneration and Reception* for which he conducted field research. From 2012–17 he collaborated in teaching architectural and urban design courses at the University of Roma Tre and the Politecnico di Milano. Over the years he has worked as an architect and urban planner for competitions, private and public works. His research interests are oriented towards the perceptual and social qualities of inhabited space.

Lukas Spreitzer works on the visualisation of architecture, space, politics and society, including architecture studies (since 2013) and assistance at TU Wien (2017–21), and as a graphic designer and illustrator (since 2018). The shown contribution *Triptychon*, a work on Aldo Rossi's narration and visualisation techniques, was nominated for the Pfann-Ohmann Award 2019. Other works include 'A New Style' (2021, in progress), 'Gemeindebau-Matrix' (2021, ARCH+), 'Vienna Map' (2022) and 'The Secret Journey' (2022, DVB-Verlag). Since 2022, he has been part of the collective Studio Walls.

Stalker is a collective of architects and researchers connected to the Roma Tre University who came together in the mid-1990s. In 2002, Stalker founded the research network Osservatorio Nomade (ON), which consists of architects, artists, activists and researchers working experimentally and engaging in actions to create self-organised spaces and situations. Stalker have developed a specific methodology of urban research, using participative tools to construct a 'collective imaginary' for a place. In particular they have developed the method of collective walking to 'actuate territories', which for them is a process of bringing space into being.

Robert Storr is an artist, critic and curator. He received a BA from Swarthmore College in 1972 and an MFA from the School of the Art Institute of Chicago in 1978. He is dean of the Yale School of Art. Among other positions, he was curator of the Department of Painting and Sculpture at New York's Museum of Modern Art and director of the 2007 Venice Biennale.

Pier Paolo Tamburelli (*1976) is one of the founding partners of baukuh, which completed the House of Memory in Milan (2015), the entrance pavilion of the Poretti Brewery in Induno (2019) and is currently designing the new police headquarters in Tirana and the new European library in Milan. He has taught at the Berlage Institute Rotterdam, and at TUM Munich, FAUP Porto, Harvard GSD, UIC Chicago and the Politecnico di Milano. He currently holds the chair of design theory at TU Wien. He was one of the founders and editors of the architectural magazine *San Rocco*. In 2022 he published *On Bramante* for MIT Press.

Alexandra Torggler (*1997) is an architecture student at TU Wien. She has worked with architecture offices such as Querkraft (AT) and Parasite 2.0 (IT), with whom she realised a project during the AA visiting school 'The Possibility of an Island' (IT, 2021). This was exhibited at Milan Design Week and in Spazio Maiocchi (IT, 2021). 'I am here to learn' received an honourable mention at the Pfann-Ohmann Award. She is currently researching the sustainable aspects of the building material, clay. The work will be exhibited at the Clay Building Conference located at AzW (AT, 2023).

Marco Vanucci (*1977) is an architect, design director of Opensystems Architecture and a lecturer at London South Bank University. He has taught at the AA, KTH Stockholm and Cardiff University. He co-founded, with Manuel Orazi, Adriatica, a think tank to study the evolution of urbanisation along the Adriatic coast. He has co-authored articles on the Adriatic for *Log*, *Il Foglio* and *Domus*. He has published articles and essays on the origin of parametric (UCL's *Prospectives* journal, 2022) and associative design methods (*Drawing Matter*, 2021) and he is currently working on the relationship between architecture and AI, taking part in exhibitions (UTSOA) and writing papers and a chapter for an upcoming book to be published by Wiley.

Lowie Vermeersch (*1974) is a Flemish automotive and mobility designer. He started his career at Pininfarina, where he became design director in 2007, and was responsible for iconic designs such as the Ferrari 458 and FF. In 2011 he founded Granstudio, a transdisciplinary mobility design and research studio. Granstudio now has a team of sixty-five, based in Turin, and is active in the full mobility ecosystem. Their work ranges from designs such as the Dallara Stradale and the solar car Lightyear One to the definition of mobility plans and strategies at city-scale. Vermeersch is also coordinator of the Masters in Mobility design unit at IED Torino.

Paola Viganò, an architect and urbanist, is professor in urban design at EPFL (Lausanne) and at IUAV. She was awarded an honorary doctorate from UCL in 2016, the Grand Prix de l'Urbanisme in 2013, and received the Flemish Culture Award for Architecture in 2017 and the Golden Medal at the Milan Triennale in 2018. In 1990 she founded Studio with Bernardo Secchi, working on projects and visions in Europe.

Since 2015 StudioPaolaViganò has won several international competitions and works mainly on public spaces and on urban and landscape projects. Recent publications include *The Horizontal Metropolis: A Radical Project*, edited with C. Cavalieri (2019).

Gerald Weber (*1965) studied history, geography, philosophy and film studies in Vienna and Barcelona. He was a founding member of 'Projektor: Discussion Forum Film and New Media' and co-organiser of the international symposium 'film-[SUBJECT]theory' (1996). Since 1997 he has been a permanent employee of sixpackfilm, which operates the sales and distribution of Austrian documentary, short and experimental films. Within the framework of sixpackfilm, he has overseen the realisation of a large number of film-mediating events and presentations of Austrian and international film and video art at home and abroad. In addition, he undertakes occasional lectures, moderation of film talks and freelance curatorial and journalistic activities.

Cyrille Weiner (*1976) is a photographer who trained at the Ecole nationale supérieure Louis-Lumière. His work has been published by numerous international magazines (*M Le Monde, Foam, British Journal of Photography, Art Press* …) and exhibited at MAC Lyon, the Rencontres d'Arles, the galerie laurent mueller in Paris and at the Villa Noailles in Hyères. He was the laureate of the Prix Lucien Hervé and Rudolf Hervé in 2012 and the author of *Presque île* (2009) and *Twice* (2015). His work recurrently poses the question of space, and how individuals appropriate their living spaces, distanced from directives coming from 'on high'. Progressively leaving the documentary register, he proposes a universe crossed by fiction, one that he establishes with exhibitions, editorial projects and installations.

Alberto Winterle graduated in architecture from IUAV and registered with the Ordine degli Architetti of the province of Trento. He is co-owner with Lorenzo Weber of the studio weber+winterle architetti in Trento, founded in 1998. From 2011 to 2015 he was president of the Ordine degli Architetti PPC of Trento. Since 2015 he has been director of *Turris Babel*, the magazine of the South Tyrol Architecture Foundation. From 2016 to 2021 he was president of the Associazione Architetti Arco Alpino.

Veronika Wladyga is studying architecture in Vienna, currently working at the Research Unit of Housing and Design at TU Wien. She has worked on publications (*ARCH+ 244*), exhibitions (*archdiploma*, 2019) and in student representation (2015–19). She is a member of the feminist collective claiming*spaces, including organisation and participation in both of its international conferences (2019 and 2021). Her diploma thesis focuses on historical and current housing policy and accessibility in Vienna.

Tobias Zielony is known for his photographic depiction of juvenile minorities in suburban areas – a subject he started out with during his studies in Newport, Wales. For his first book project, *Behind the Block* (2004), he extended his research to four European cities to observe adolescents in public spaces, often at night. Themes and social realities touched on by his research include structural change, migration and drug abuse, as well as sex work. His critical approach to documentarism manifests in a specific aesthetic and relationship with fiction. People are often portrayed in a casual fashion that is sensitive to the visual language, gestures and poses they use to set their stage.

Cino Zucchi (*1955), born in Milan, earned a BSAD at the Massachusetts Institute of Technology and a *laurea in architettura* at the Politecnico di Milano, where he is currently chair professor of architectural and urban design. He has taught in many international design workshops and has been John T. Dunlop visiting professor in housing and urbanisation at the Graduate School of Design of Harvard University. He is the author of several articles and books on architectural history and theory, and participated in various editions of the Milano Triennale and the Venice Biennale of Architecture: the installation 'Copycat' won an honourable mention in the 2012 edition, and he was the curator of the Italian Pavilion in the 2014 edition. He has been the president of the jury of the Mies van der Rohe Award 2015, and he is member of the international research team ARE_Living on housing innovation.

Imprint

For the Research Unit of Housing and Design, Institute of Architecture and Design, Faculty of Architecture and Planning, TU Wien:
Editors: Michael Obrist, Antonietta Putzu
Editorial staff: Veronika Wladyga

Translations: Christopher Huw Evans, Pamela Johnston
Copy editing and proofreading: Colette Forder
Graphic design concept: Bueronardin
Graphic design and setting: Veronika Wladyga
Digital image processing: Mario Rott
Printing and binding: Gugler GmbH

With great appreciation to all the contributors and facilitators who kindly shared their work, time and knowledge and made this multi-faceted book possible.

Special thanks to Veronika Wladyga for her continuous commitment which made the implementation of the publication from spreadsheet to this book a reality.

With thanks to, in alphabetical order:
Dana Faridani-Rad, Sinah Hackenberg, Michael Klein, Hannah Luca Kögler, Christina Lenart, Kathrin Lugbauer, Julia Nuler, Christian Nuhsbaumer, Cäcilia Putschek, Leon Scheufler, Paul Sebesta, Lorenzo Vicari, Natascha Weiss, Lisi Zeininger, Costanza Zeni, Margherita & Noemi Zoderer, Peter Zoderer; and to the academic staff of the Research Unit of Housing and Design as well as the students who contributed to this publication.

Maps in this publication were created by Veronika Wladyga using data provided by Geofabrik GmbH under a Creative Commons licence.
© for the maps: Geofabrik GmbH and OpenStreetMap Contributors

All rights reserved; no part of this publication may be reproduced, stored in a retrieval system or transmitted in any form or by any means, electronic, mechanical, photocopying, recording, or otherwise, without the prior written consent of the publisher.

Despite best efforts, we have not been able to identify the holders of copyright and printing rights for all the illustrations. Copyright holders not mentioned in the credits are asked to substantiate their claims, and recompense will be made according to standard practice.

© 2023 Michael Obrist, Antonietta Putzu and Park Books AG, Zurich
© for the texts: the authors
© for the images: see image credits

Park Books
Niederdorfstrasse 54
8001 Zurich
Switzerland
www.park-books.com

Park Books is being supported by the Federal Office of Culture with a general subsidy for the years 2021–2024.

Cover photo: © Carolina Sartori
ISBN 978-3-03860-323-8

WOHNBAU UND ENTWERFEN
ARCHITEKTUR UND ENTWERFEN
TU WIEN

TECHNISCHE UNIVERSITÄT WIEN